SALEM HEALTH

Psychology & Behavioral Health

SALEM HEALTH

Psychology & Behavioral Health

Volume 4
Parenting and behavioral addictions – Sleep

Editor

Paul Moglia, PhD
South Nassau Communities Hospital
Oceanside, NY

SALEM PRESS
A Division of EBSCO Information Services, Inc.
IPSWICH, MASSACHUSETTS

GREY HOUSE PUBLISHING

Some of the updated and revised essays in this work originally appeared in *Magill's Encyclopedia of Social Science: Psychology*, edited by Nancy A. Piotrowski, PhD (2003) and *Magill's Survey of Social Science: Psychology*, edited by Frank N. Magill (1993).

Publisher's Cataloging-In-Publication Data
(Prepared by The Donohue Group, Inc.)

Psychology & behavioral health / editor, Paul Moglia, PhD. – Fourth edition.

   5 volumes : illustrations ; cm. -- (Salem health)

   At head of title: Salem health.
   Previously published as: Psychology & mental health.
   Includes bibliographical references and index.
   Contents: Volume 1. Ability tests-Community psychology -- volume 2. Comorbidity-Health psychology -- volume 3. Hearing-Parental alienation syndrome -- volume 4. Parenting styles-Sleep -- volume 5. Sleep apnea-Philip Zimbardo; Appendixes; Indexes.
   ISBN: 978-1-61925-543-2 (5-volume set)
   ISBN: 978-1-61925-810-5 (vol.1)
   ISBN: 978-1-61925-811-2 (vol.2)
   ISBN: 978-1-61925-812-9 (vol.3)
   ISBN: 978-1-61925-813-6 (vol.4)
   ISBN: 978-1-61925-814-3 (vol.5)

   1. Psychology, Applied--Encyclopedias. 2. Mental health--Encyclopedias. 3. Mental illness--Encyclopedias. 4. Medicine and psychology--Encyclopedias. I. Moglia, Paul. II. Title: Psychology and behavioral health III. Title: Salem health IV. Series: Salem health (Pasadena, Calif.)

BF636 .P86 2015
150.3

FIRST PRINTING
PRINTED IN THE UNITED STATES OF AMERICA

COMPLETE LIST OF CONTENTS

VOLUME 1

VOLUME 2

VOLUME 3

VOLUME 4

VOLUME 5

Parenting and behavioral addictions

TYPE OF PSYCHOLOGY: Addiction; Clinical; Counseling; Developmental; Family; Health; Psychopathology; Psychotherapy; School; Social

Parents and primary caregivers of children and adolescents have critically important roles in the development, identification, and treatment of behavioral addictions such as gambling, shopping, eating, and video gaming. Parental roles may contribute to or counter the emergence of behavioral addictions. In nearly all cases, parental supportive confrontation is necessary for these addictions to be identified and treated.

KEY CONCEPTS:
- Behavioral addiction
- Endorphins
- Genetic heritability
- Parental supportive confrontation

CAUSATIVE PARENTING

Parents have three potential mechanisms by which they influence the development of behavioral addictions in their children though none of these directly cause behavioral addictions.

The first and most fundamental way parents influence children in this regard is through genetic heritability. Addiction is promoted through a neuronal reward system in which the pleasure areas of the brain are stimulated and the behavior which brought the pleasurable experience to the individual is identified and repeated. A well-known example is the "endorphin rush" runners or cyclists experience. At some point during the exercise, the physical expenditure of energy triggers a release of brain chemicals (neurotransmitters), most notably endorphin, which the athletes experience as pleasurable. While this pleasurable response to vigorous exercise is almost universal and can be brought about by any number of strenuous physical activities, individual sensitivity is primarily genetically inherited from one's biological parents. If it takes a lot of exercise before parents experience the pleasure of endorphin release, it is likely that their children will require a similar amount in order to experience the endorphin release. How much activity one has to engage in to bring on the pleasurable experience, how intense (and thus addictive) that experience is, and how long that experience lasts, are all largely determined by what was true for one's parents. Parents pass down a tendency toward or a tendency away from pleasurable addiction; they do not pass down specific behavioral addictions like pornography or kleptomania.

The second mechanism through which parents influence the development of behavioral addiction is through imitative behavioral and social learning. Parents who are addicted to exercise, gambling, social networking, or shopping, for instance, are modeling behaviors that can be viewed within the family context as "normal." Most behavioral addictions are merely the extremes of normally encountered and readily observed behaviors all individuals exhibit. When parents are addicted to any of these behaviors, children are exposed to the unspoken sense that the behaviors are not "that bad" because the parents provide the behaviors with a legitimacy that they would otherwise not have. Most children will not come to see a spotlessly clean and highly organized home as normal unless they are raised in an environment where compulsive cleaning and incessant organizing were the environmental norm.

The third and most common mechanism for parents to influence and sustain behavioral addictions in their children is enabling. The cycle begins with children engaging in a commonly accepted behavior such as video gaming. There is also a good chance that children have participated with their parents in that activity. Because the threshold between normal, daily activity and driven addiction is more soft and nuanced than hard and sharply defined, it usually takes a substantial period of time to go from family entertainment to individual addiction. The behavior crosses the threshold into addiction when: (1) it directly or indirectly harms the child; (2) interferes with other health- and growth-promoting activities (e.g., school work, socializing with friends, participating in family functions); and (3) becomes the major focus or prime motivation for how the child allocates his or her time. Addicted children, like their adult counterparts, are on a quest to satiate urges and avoid anxiety they will feel when those urges are not met. The addict's focus is on how soon he or she will be able to satisfy the next, looming urge. But even with these three conditions as a guideline, it still can be difficult to distinguish passion and dedication from compulsion and absorption. When does "two-a-days" football practice become an exercise addiction? It is usually hard to tell until the addiction is well established and at this point parents are at risk of promoting the addiction by sustaining the lifestyle their children have, knowingly or not. The very behavior that is troubling to parents and harmful to their children ends up being enabled because of parents' uncertainty, unreliability, and hesitation about how they should respond to their child and his or her problem. Parents have ultimate authority and influence over their children's lives. They provide life's biological essentials, food, clothing, shelter, and security. They also provide life's social essentials: identity, belonging, and support for a social life outside the home through financial and material means.

Helping children is generally a quite natural predisposition in parents. This predisposition becomes problematic when children begin to manipulate parents and other family members to fulfill their addictive cravings. When parents minimize or deny that their children's behavior, such as excessive shopping or compulsive eating is a problem, they essentially condone their engagement in these behaviors without recognizing that they have a problem.

Without consciously realizing it, children study parental behavior and learn from it. Parents' behavior cues children about what is allowable, what will be confronted, what will be ignored, what will or will not be tolerated. By parents' failing to name the behavior and its impact on children and family as "a problem," they subconsciously influence how children see the addictive behavior.

In the emotionally challenging spot of wanting to love and support children without overly challenging them, sometimes parents take responsibility for the actions and behaviors of their children. This allows the child to shrug all of their responsibility for the consequences of their behavior. This feeds the addiction because the child never faces any consequence and is never forced to look at the harmful outcomes of their behavior. These parents feel the guilt and shame that the child has to feel if they are to stop the addicted behavior. If parents feel the difficult emotions, the children do not have to. Parents' own guilt and sense of helplessness, children's overdeveloped sense of justice and need to make their own choices renders parental influence inept and quite likely enabling. The line between parental behaviors that can help stop addiction and parental behaviors that can foster addiction can be quite thin.

Children with behavioral addictions often display an alarming lack of concern for those they hurt and disarming narcissistic self-concern. In the jargon of the addiction treatment world, this becomes an example of "It's not the person but the addiction speaking." Parents cannot recognize the once loving and thoughtful children

they raised. At this stage, these children have learned to manipulate their parents to get what they need to feed their addiction. Parents' attempts to control children's access environments and people promoting addiction are vigorously opposed or cleverly bypassed. Children lie, steal, and mislead to overcome the obstacles parents have put in the way. The home environment becomes hostile, discordant, and conflict-ridden. It no longer feels like home and parents wonder what they have done wrong for the family they are raising to live with so much bitterness. To establish a form of stability, calm, and peace, parents second guess how they should act around their addicted children, what should they say or not say, what feelings should they share or keep to themselves. Family life feels sterile and unnatural; the relationship between parents and the addicted children feels strained, forced, uncomfortable and unfamiliar. In an environment of indecision, addicted children can assume the mantle that all is fine, at least until parents' express concern or confrontation. Children then often respond in the extreme. Pleading, promises, punishment, coercion, and reward have lost their effectiveness. Punishment and coercion are no longer effective tools. Even if both sides do not want a discordant climate, they will lack the language and direction to make sustainable changes for the better. However, in any family that is understood to function as a "system," it takes only one member to move the rest of the family in a healthier direction. Knowing where to get help is critical.

CURATIVE PARENTING

At the most basic level, parents must acknowledge how their response has made the addiction worse and treating it more difficult. Going against better judgment, not standing their ground, punishing, bribing, co-dependently watching and reacting to their troubled child have all made the family system less functional, trustworthy, and effective. Parents' owning their contribution to sustaining an addiction they never wanted their children to have becomes the first step toward treating the family system. Parents can rarely directly control their children's harmful behavior. Parents can always control their response to those behaviors. They can begin to end their dysfunctional responses.

Parents must educate themselves about addiction itself and the specific behavioral addiction that has been plaguing their families' and children's lives. This will include but not be limited to parents demonstrating their own healthier behaviors all of which will have the common theme that they will do whatever they can to help their children, but will do nothing that supports the addicted behavior. Parents' recognizing their limited ability to influence their children's decisions and their significant ability to impact their children's worlds shows the way for parents' focus and energy. Parents did not create the addiction, they cannot actually control it, nor can they cure it. Parents who educate themselves in what are healthy actions, rather than reactions, can begin the critical balancing of challenge, consequence, and support their addicted children need.

Progress is likely to be uneven. Parents can make great strides in recovery while the children seem to regress, or the reverse can occur. Key to this stage of recovery is accepting that it is a long term, even life-time commitment to practicing healthy behaviors. But, as long as one side incorporates even some positive behavioral changes, the entire family system will improve and the relationship between children and parents begin to mend. What became a troubled and inimical environment starts to become stable, nurturing and safe.

While these behavioral modifications are critical first steps toward a healthier, addiction-free life, they are not usually enough. Most parents and families cannot educate themselves on more advanced treatments for behavioral addiction. Routinely, parents' and children's recoveries will involve multidimensional treatment, often from a specially-trained clinician and group support. Families are encouraged to pursue treatment with a clinician along with outside support groups. There are many issues that surround addictions of all kinds so more than one form of help is often needed. One of the most important steps a parent can take is seeking out a specialist in addiction issues. Although it seems the problem lies with this child alone, addiction is a family disease and its effects can be devastating and long lasting. Sometimes drastic measures such as rehab or treatment facilities need to be taken. Behavioral addiction is more psychological than anything so psychological help and treatment is often necessary. These behaviors cannot just be stopped and recovery involves everyone in the addict's life, just as the addiction involved everyone.

Just as their children are seeking professional help and support groups, parents can do the same. There are clinicians trained specifically in dealing with addictions in the family and they can provide great tools for dealing with the addict's recovery. There are also self-help groups such as Al-Anon or CODA that parents can seek out that can provide additional support.

Addiction is a chronic disease that often does not go away after one attempt at treatment. It is necessary to address long-term behavioral changes when pursuing treatment. Only with a proper long-term recovery program can the child and the parents live a joyous and addiction free life. It is vital that parents and the child work separately at fixing their behaviors first. Then they will be able to work into a stable home environment where they control their behaviors instead of the addict's behavior controlling them.

The best place to start is with a counselor who is trained to work with addicts and their parents. The counselor will be able to set up a proper treatment plan and refer the patients to the right resources in order to change their lives.

BIBLIOGRAPHY

American Academy of Child & Adolescent Psychiatry, *Facts for Families*. American Academy of Child & Adolescent Psychiatry, Washington, DC, 2011. The Academy publishes this series, free for single print copies and able to be downloaded, as informational and response guides for parents and families facing a variety of real-world issues within families including behavioral addictions.

Bradshaw, John. *On the Family: A New Way of Creating Solid Self-Esteem.* Deerfield Beach, FL: Health Communications Inc., 1996. Based on his popular and still available public television series, Bradshaw remains one of the best introductions to understanding families are systems with dynamic, reactive energies. He explains in clear, insightful language the family's role in supporting on-going problematic and addictive behaviors in an individual family member.

Carnes, Patrick. *Don't Call It Love: Recovery from Sexual Addiction.* Bantam Books, New York, NY, 1991. Doctor Carnes discusses 11 behavioral types as well as presenting a three-year program of recovery that involves partners and children within a family-addiction context. Argues, somewhat controversially, that partners of sex addicts are their mirror images and have played enabling roles. Provides a program for recovery and family and partner healing.

Hayes, Steven and Levin, Michael. *Mindfulness and Acceptance for Addictive Behaviors: Applying Contextual CBT to Substance Abuse and Behavioral Addictions.* New Harbinger Books, Oakland, CA, 2010. First author, Dr. Steven Hayes is a pioneer in the application of mindfulness in treatment of substance abuse and addictions in general. This highly readable work is focused on helping the read apply this approach to any of a variety of behavioral addictions.

Mitchell, John. *How to Understand and Overcome Addiction Issues (Behavioral Issues).* Mitchellpublishing101@yahoo.com, 2010. Kindle edition available from Amazon Digital Services. A prolific self-help writer, Mitchell describes warning signs, family and individual denial, and practical advice about how behavioral addictions can be successfully managed.

National Institute on Drug Addiction, *NIDA Notes, The National Institute of Drug Abuse,* Washington, DC, 2011. The Notes is the Institute's major vehicle for relaying research findings to the field in a timely manner. It covers the areas of treatment and prevention research, epidemiology, neuroscience, behavioral research, health services research, and AIDS. The publication reports on advances in the drug abuse field, identifies resources, promotes an exchange of information, and seeks to improve communication among clinicians, researchers, administrators, and policymakers. The Institute publishes Notes bimonthly and it is free to the public and geared to the lay audience.

Sheppard, Kay, *From the First Bite: A Complete Guide to the Recovery from Food Addiction.* Health Communications, Inc., Deerfield Beach, CA, 2000. Warmly written for the person struggling with compulsive overeating, provides dietary guides that the whole family can participate in. Persuasively makes the case that food must be treated the way chemical addiction is treated.

WEB SITES OF INTEREST

Addiction and Recovery
http://www.netplaces.com/addiction-recovery
National Institute on Drug Abuse
http://www.nida.nih.gov
Substance Abuse and Mental Health Services Administration
http://www.samhsa.gov

Eugenia F. Moglia and Paul Moglia

SEE ALSO: Addiction; Childrearing; Family; Family dynamics.

Parenting styles

TYPE OF PSYCHOLOGY: Developmental psychology

Parenting styles have a significant impact on the development of children in terms of competence and independence. Numerous studies have identified differences in parenting styles according to how parents combine various aspects of responsiveness and demandingness. The most commonly identified styles of parenting are authoritarian, permissive, authoritative, and uninvolved.

KEY CONCEPTS
- Authoritarian style of parenting
- Authoritative style of parenting
- Demandingness
- Independence
- Induction
- Parenting style
- Permissive style of parenting
- Responsiveness
- Social responsibility
- Uninvolved style of parenting

INTRODUCTION

The research on parenting styles has examined patterns of child-rearing behavior exhibited by parents and corresponding behavior and personality characteristics found in their children. Parenting style can be categorized by two components: responsiveness, a parent's response to the child's needs and wishes, and demandingness or behavioral control, a parent's approach to discipline and the level of demands placed on the child. Numerous researchers have found that parenting style influences the development of children.

Although parenting styles have been described in a variety of terms by different authors, the most commonly identified styles of parenting were labeled by developmental psychologist Diana Baumrind during the early 1960s. Through extensive observation, interviews, and psychological testing, she identified three different approaches to child rearing and discipline as authoritarian, permissive, and authoritative. According to Baumrind, parenting style is the pattern of normal variations in parents' attempts to control and socialize their children. It represents the overall approach to child rearing rather than situation-specific practices by parents.

Each of the three parenting styles identified by Baumrind has been described in terms of high or low levels of emotional support and high or low levels of control or demandingness. Following Baumrind's early research, a fourth style labeled as uninvolved or neglectful is often included.

SPECIFIC STYLES OF PARENTING

The authoritarian style of parenting is a combination of low levels of emotional support and high levels of control. Authoritarian parents have a rigid set of absolute standards for child behavior that are strictly enforced through physical punishment. They expect instant and unquestioning obedience from their children. Respect for authority, work, and tradition is very important to authoritarian parents, and challenges to the parents' authority or questioning of rules is simply not tolerated. These parents exert restrictive control over their children's self-expression and independent behavior.

Parents with a permissive (or indulgent) style provide emotional support but exercise little control over their children. These parents are nonpunitive and make very little attempt to discipline their children or otherwise control their behavior. They place very few demands on their children for household chores and allow the children to make their own decisions about basic family policies such as television viewing and bedtime. Permissive parents are very responsive to their children and are accepting of their children's impulses, desires, and activities. Rather than purposefully directing, shaping, or altering their children's behaviors or decisions, they prefer to see themselves as resources that their children may consult if they wish.

The third style of parenting is referred to by Baumrind as authoritative. Authoritative (or democratic) parents set clear standards for mature and responsible behavior and expect their children to meet these standards. They firmly enforce rules but do not unduly restrict their children's activities or self-expression. In fact, authoritative parents recognize their children's individual rights, interests, and unique style and encourage them to think for themselves. These parents encourage verbal give-and-take regarding family rules, will listen to reasonable requests from their children, and are open to some degree of negotiation. When disciplining their children, authoritative parents rely on induction rather than coercion. Induction refers to the use of reasoning to explain and enforce parental expectations.

The uninvolved or neglectful style is a fourth possible parenting approach used by a significant minority. Some view this style as an extension of permissive parenting, but it lacks the high degree of involvement and represents instead a low level of both emotional support and control. Parents who are uninvolved tend to minimize the time and energy devoted to parenting. They know very little about their children's activities, show little interest in their children's experiences, and rarely talk to their children or consider their opinions when making decisions.

DIMENSIONS OF PARENTING BEHAVIOR

The prototypical styles of child rearing can be clearly distinguished from one another on the basis of two dimensions of parenting behavior: demandingness and responsiveness. Demandingness can be defined as the degree to which parents use control to demand that their children meet their high expectations with regard to mature, responsible behavior. Parental responsiveness refers to the degree of warmth, acceptance, and noncoerciveness evident in the parents' interactions with their children. The authoritarian parenting style has been described as high in demandingness and low in responsiveness. In contrast, the permissive parenting style is thought to be low in demandingness and high in responsiveness. The authoritative parenting style is high in the dimensions of both demandingness and responsiveness. The least effective parenting style, the uninvolved, is low in both demandingness and responsiveness. Parents with this style combine the emotional aloofness of authoritarian parenting with the disciplinary parenting of permissive parenting.

A further distinction can be made between the aspects of demandingness emphasized by authoritarian and authoritative parents. The demandingness displayed by authoritative parents is high in the use of firm control with their children; that is, they firmly and consistently enforce rules but do not extensively or intrusively direct their children's activities. On the other hand, authoritarian parents, also high in demandingness, tend to rely more on restrictive control, which involves the extensive use of rules that cover most aspects of their children's lives and severely restrict their autonomy to develop skills on their own.

CONSEQUENCES FOR CHILD DEVELOPMENT

In her research on child-rearing practices, Baumrind not only identified patterns of parenting styles but also identified characteristics of children reared by these parents. She found that parents' approaches to child rearing have important implications in terms of the degree of autonomy and responsible social behavior exhibited by children. The children of authoritative parents, in comparison to other peers, were found to be more self-reliant, self-controlled, content, and explorative. They were also energetic, friendly, curious, cooperative; they got along well with peers, and they exhibited high self-esteem. Furthermore, these children exhibited more mature moral judgments than their peers and were better able to control their own aggressive impulses and channel them into more appropriate, prosocial behaviors.

In contrast, authoritarian parenting is associated with children who are unhappy, socially withdrawn, distrustful, and moody. In addition, they tend to lack spontaneity and be overly dependent on adults for directions and decision making. Finally, these children are more likely to be rejected by their peers and suffer from low self-esteem. Parents who rely on a permissive style of child rearing tend to have children who are immature, lacking in impulse control, less exploratory, more dependent, and aggressive.

Children with uninvolved parents, labeled by some researchers as "disengaged" parents, may experience the most negative consequences. Although researched less than the other three styles, parents with this style are rarely there for their children in terms of either discipline or support. The largest differences in competence in general are found between children with unengaged parents and their peers with more involved parents. Children with disengaged parents are frequently absent from school, earn lower grades, and are less motivated to perform well in the classroom. When these children become adolescents, they tend to overconform to the pressures of the peer group because there is very little pressure at home to conform to parents' values and expectations. Those adolescents who have parents low in both demandingness and responsiveness (indifferent parents) are more likely to become engaged in delinquent behavior, as well as in early experimentation with drugs, alcohol, and sex.

Baumrind's original goal in her research was to identify the specific aspects of child-rearing practices that are instrumental in producing optimal competence in children. She described competence as a combination of social responsibility and independence. A socially responsible child is friendly and altruistic toward peers and cooperative with adults. In contrast, a socially irresponsible child would behave in a hostile and selfish fashion toward other children and be resistive with adults. Independence in a child is characterized by assertiveness,

leadership, and confident, purposeful activity. Children low in independence are described as suggestible, submissive followers engaged in disorganized and aimless activity. Children who were high in both social responsibility and independence were considered to be optimally competent. Competent children are mostly likely to be able to resolve social conflicts in a way that is both effective and fair as well as being sensitive and compassionate to the needs of others.

During the last half of the 1990s, many researchers published their studies on the relationship between parenting style and adolescent development. Originally, studies were conducted with preschool and elementary school children, but equal attention was not given to later development. The results from studies with adolescents have consistently shown the superiority of authoritative parenting over the other styles.

GENDER DIFFERENCES

Not surprisingly, when the factor of children's competence was examined and matched with parenting style, Baumrind found that children from authoritative homes were much more competent than their peers. In particular, she found that girls with authoritative parents were more likely to exhibit assertive, purposeful, and achievement-oriented behavior. Boys from authoritative homes were more likely to be friendly and cooperative in comparison to other boys their age. Lower levels of competence were observed in children coming from authoritarian and permissive households. Boys with authoritarian parents were low in social responsibility and tended to be hostile and resistive, whereas girls tended to be lower in independence and assertiveness. Permissive parenting was associated with low levels of social assertiveness in girls and low achievement orientation in both sexes.

It is clear from this research that parenting styles affect boys and girls in different ways. Differences in parenting styles appear to have a stronger impact on the development of social responsibility in boys than in girls, most likely because there is normally less variability between girls on this attribute. According to the literature on gender roles, cooperation and compassion toward others is an attribute most frequently associated with females, regardless of how they were reared. Similarly, child-rearing practices have a consistent and stronger impact on the development of independence and social assertiveness in girls than in boys. The characteristics of dominance, assertiveness, and leadership associated with the attribute of independence are more often found in males, regardless of their upbringing. In a sense, what authoritative parenting appears to do is strengthen the otherwise less developed component of competence in each sex and lead to a more balanced combination of both social responsibility and independence. Sandra Bem, a leading researcher in the area of sex roles, has used the term androgynous to refer to individuals who are high in positive characteristics typically associated with both males and females. There is much research to indicate that androgynous individuals are more likely to be competent and psychologically well adjusted in adulthood.

BIBLIOGRAPHY

Abela, Angela, and Janet Walker, eds. *Contemporary Issues in Family Studies*. Malden: Wiley, 2014. Print.

Asmussen, Kirsten. *The Evidence-Based Parenting Practitioner's Handbook*. New York: Routledge, 2011. Print.

Baumrind, Diana. "Rearing Competent Children." *Child Development Today and Tomorrow*. Ed. William Damon. San Francisco: Jossey-Bass, 1991. Print.

Cline, Foster W., and Jim Fay. *Parenting with Love and Logic*. Colorado Springs: Pinon, 2006. Print.

Darling, Nancy, and Lawrence Steinberg. "Parenting Style as Context: An Integrative Model." *Psychological Bulletin* 113 (1993): 487–96. Print.

Huxley, Ron. *Love and Limits: Achieving a Balance in Parenting*. New York: Singular, 1999. Print.

Peterson, Gary W., Suzanne K. Steinmetz, and Stephan M. Wilson, eds. *Parent-Youth Relations: Cultural and Cross-Cultural Perspectives*. New York: Routledge, 2012. Print.

Pruett, Kyle D. *Fatherneed: Why Father Care Is as Essential as Mother Care for Your Child*. New York: Free, 2001. Print.

Smith, Charles A., ed. *The Encyclopedia of Parenting Theory and Research*. Westport: Greenwood, 1999. Print.

Steinberg, Lawrence. *Beyond the Classroom: Why School Reform Has Failed and What Parents Need to Do*. New York: Simon, 1997. Print.

Steinberg, Lawrence, Nancy Darling, and Anne C. Fletcher. "Authoritative Parenting and Adolescent Adjustment: An Ecological Journey." *Examining Lives in Context: Perspectives on the Ecology of Human Development*. Ed. Phillis Moen, Glen H. Elder Jr., and Kurt Luscher. Washington: American Psychological Association, 1995. Print.

Strauss, Murray. *Beating the Devil Out of Them: Corporal Punishment in American Families*. New Brunswick: Transaction, 2001. Print.

Sunderland, Margot. *The Science of Parenting*. London: Dorling, 2006. Print.

Teyber, Edward. *Helping Children Cope with Divorce*. San Francisco: Jossey, 2001. Print.

Stephanie Stein; updated by Lillian J. Breckenridge

SEE ALSO: Attachment and bonding in infancy and childhood; Behavioral family therapy; Birth order and personality; Child abuse; Family systems theory; Father-child relationship; Juvenile delinquency; Mother-child relationship; Self-esteem; Strategic family therapy.

Parkinson's disease

TYPE OF PSYCHOLOGY: Psychopathology

Parkinson's disease is a chronic, progressive, neurodegenerative disorder of the nervous system that usually has its onset in middle age. Characteristic symptoms include tremor, rigidity, and slowness of movement. Although the exact causes are not known, both genetic and environmental factors are implicated.

KEY CONCEPTS
- Akinesia
- Bradykinesia
- Dementia
- Depression
- Dopamine
- Levodopa
- Rigidity
- Substantia nigra
- Transplantation of dopamine neurons
- Tremor

INTRODUCTION

Parkinson's disease is one of the most common neurological disorders, affecting one person in every thousand. James Parkinson, in 1817, aptly described some of the classic symptoms in his book *An Essay on the Shaking Palsy*. Parkinson reported the patients as having a chronic and progressive disorder of the nervous system that had a late-age onset with the first mild symptoms not appearing until middle age. He also noted a tremor or shaking which typically appeared in the hand on one side and later spread to the other side. The disease progressed for a variable number of years, eventually leading to invalidism and death. A significant contribution was his ability to recognize the disorder as a disease distinct from previously described diseases.

Although Parkinson's disease is thought of as a disease with its onset in middle age, there is a considerable variation in the age of onset, and there are other forms of the disease in addition to the classical form. The average age of onset is somewhere in the sixties. About 15 percent of patients develop symptoms between the ages of twenty-one and forty years. An extremely rare form of the disease, juvenile Parkinsonism, begins before the age of twenty-one. In addition to the severe neuromuscular symptoms, dementia may occur in some patients. In addition to tremors, other major symptoms are muscle stiffness or rigidity and bradykinesia or slow movement and even a difficulty in starting movement. Akinesia, an impairment of voluntary activity of a muscle, also occurs. A number of other symptoms may appear as a consequence of the major symptoms, such as difficulties with speech, bowel and bladder problems, and a vacant, masklike facial expression. There are striking variations among patients in the number and severity of the symptoms and the timing of the progression.

CLINICAL FEATURES

The disease that subsequently became known as Parkinson's disease was called "shaking palsy" by Parkinson. The shaking refers to the tremor which, although it is thought by many people to be invariably associated with Parkinson's disease, may be completely absent or present to a minor degree in some patients. Four symptoms which are present in many patients are a progressive tremor, bradykinesia and even akinesia, muscular rigidity, and loss of postural reflexes. There still is no specific test that can be used to diagnose Parkinson's disease. No biochemical, electrophysiologic, or radiologic test has been found to be completely reliable. As a result, misdiagnosis and underdiagnosis have been common with the disease. The situation is complicated further as a number of other diseases and conditions share some of the same symptoms, including Wilson's disease, familial Alzheimer's disease, Huntington's disease, and encephalitis, as well as responses to certain drugs. Symptoms of Parkinson's disease may also develop consequent to trauma to the brain.

A slight tremor in the hands may indicate the first symptoms of Parkinson's disease, and the tremor may or may not also be found in the legs, jaws, and neck. An interesting symptom that may appear in later stages of the disease is seborrhea or acne. Intellectual functioning usually remains normal, but approximately 20 percent of the patients may experience dementia and have a progressive loss of intellectual abilities and impairment of memory. It is not yet clear how the dementia of Parkinson's disease is related to the dementia associated with Alzheimer's disease. Depression also may occur in patients, with approximately one-third of them having depression at any one time. The depression may be directly related to the disease or it may be a reaction to some of the medication.

It has been convenient to divide the progression of symptoms of Parkinson's disease into five stages, according to the severity of the symptoms and the degree of disability associated with them. Stage 1 is marked by mild symptoms. In this stage, the symptom that brings the patient to a physician is likely to be a mild tremor usually limited to one hand or arm. The tremor usually is reduced or disappears during activity, but it may increase during periods of emotional stress. During this early stage of the disease, mild akinesia of the affected side and mild rigidity may be evident. Overall, many of these changes are subtle enough that the patient is not aware of them or, at least does not complain of them. Usually, symptoms are confined to one side, but as the disease progresses, it becomes bilateral in most patients in one or two years. In Stage 2, there now is bilateral involvement. Postural changes lead to the patient having a stooped posture and a shuffling walk with little extension of the legs. All body movements become slower and slower (bradykinesia). The difficulty and slowness of movements may cause patients to curtail many of their normal activities and, in many cases, may lead to depression. Stage 3 is characterized by an increase in the postural changes and movements, leading to retropulsion, a tendency to walk backward, and propulsion, a tendency when walking forward to walk faster and faster with shorter and shorter steps. As the disease progresses, movements occur more and more slowly, and there are fewer total movements. By Stage 4, symptoms have come so severe that they lead to significant disability, and the patient usually needs constant supervision. The course of the disease leads to Stage 5, a period of complete invalidism in which the patient is confined to a chair or bed. Interestingly, the tremor that is so characteristic of the initial onset of Parkinson's disease tends to lessen considerably during the later stages of the disorder. In addition to the dementia associated with aging, patients with

Parkinson's disease show an increased risk of dementia, occurring six to seven times more frequently compared to age-matched controls.

CAUSES

The most striking pathological change noted in Parkinson's disease is a loss of nerve cells in a region of the brain known as the substantia nigra, a layer of deeply pigmented gray matter located in the midbrain. The region contains nerve cells that produce dopamine, a neurotransmitter associated with the control of movement. The levels of dopamine are normally in balance with another neurotransmitter, acetylcholine. In Parkinson's disease, the loss of dopamine-producing cells causes a decrease in the levels of dopamine, with a consequent imbalance with acetylcholine. This leads to the symptoms of Parkinson's disease.

The factors that lead to an upset of the dopaminergic system in the disease are complex. The disease is found throughout the world and occurs in nearly equal frequency in males and females, with slightly more males being affected than females. Parkinson's disease is found in all ethnic groups, although there are some striking ethnic differences. The disease is relatively high among whites and relatively low among African blacks and Asians. Ethnic differences may reflect genetic and environmental differences. It is of interest to note that American blacks have a higher incidence than African blacks, indicating a likely role of local environmental factors.

The role of genetics in Parkinson's disease has been difficult to establish. A family history of Parkinson's disease appears to be a strong indicator of an increased risk of the disease. As part of its comprehensive genetic profiling of its entire population, the country of Iceland has gathered an immense amount of data on genetic diseases, including Parkinson's disease. In the study of late-onset Parkinson's disease, the risk ratio increased with increase in degree of relatedness, giving from 2.7 for nephews and nieces of patients to 3.2 for children of patients to 6.7 for brothers and sisters of patients. Much research remains to be done to determine whether single genes are playing a major causative role or whether the disorder is multifactorial, involving genetic and environmental factors.

TREATMENT

Once it became known that dopamine was depleted in patients with Parkinson's disease, a rationale opened for a potential treatment. Levodopa was the first drug to be used to treat Parkinson's disease successfully and is still the most effective treatment available. Dopamine can pass from the blood into the brain, and the drug increases the synthesis of dopamine. The drug does not cure the disease, but it is used in the attempt to control the symptoms. Although the effectiveness of levodopa may diminish somewhat after several years, most patients continue to benefit from its use. It is necessary to monitor patients closely to maintain proper dose levels as well as to register the appearance of new symptoms, side effects, and other complications.

A number of other drugs, alone or in combination, are being used or being tested. Drugs that enhance the action of dopamine are dopaminergic medications. Such drugs may increase dopamine release or may inhibit the breakdown of dopamine. Other drugs are known as anticholinergic medications, and these drugs inhibit the action of acetylcholine.

Surgery has also been used to treat symptoms of Parkinson's disease, but results have been somewhat mixed. Surgical techniques include thalamotomy, a procedure producing a lesion in the thalamus gland for relief of severe unilateral tremor, and pallidotomy, the removal of part of the globus palledus region of the brain, which is used to treat severe rigidity and akinesia. More recently, transplantation of dopamine neurons from human embryos directly into the brain of a patient with Parkinson's disease has been utilized. More trials are required, but results seem to indicate some improvement in symptoms including bradykinesia and rigidity. The use of human tissue has raised many ethical issues, since the tissue is taken from aborted human fetuses. Attempts to use tissues from cultured cells are in progress. It should be stressed that none of the treatments involving medication or surgery produced a complete reversal of the symptoms of Parkinson's disease.

BIBLIOGRAPHY

Cram, David L. *Understanding Parkinson's Disease: A Self-Help Guide.* Omaha, Nebr.: Addicus Books, 1999. A physician himself, Cram provides a well-written account of the symptoms and progression of the disease from his personal perspective and also discusses present and future treatments.

Garie, Gretchen, and Michael J. Church. *Living Well with Parkinson's Disease: What Your Doctor Doesn't Tell You . . . That You Need to Know.* New York: Collins, 2007. The authors both suffer from Parkinson's, so this resource offers practical tips for living with the disease. It covers such topics as treatment options, emotional challenges, and dealing with relationships.

Jahanshahi, Marian, and C. David Marsden. *Parkinson's Disease: A Self-Help Guide*. New York: Demos Medical Publishing, 2000. This book is an excellent self-help guide. In addition to chapters on the basic medical facts about Parkinson's disease, there are chapters dealing with living and coping with the disease from the personal and family point of view.

Kondrack, Morton. *Saving Milly: Love, Politics, and Parkinson's Disease*. New York: Public Affairs, 2002. The author provides a moving memoir of his life with his wife, Milly, and the development and impact of Parkinson's disease.

Lanad, Anthony E., and Andres M. Lozano. "Parkinson's Disease: The First of Two Parts." *The New England Journal of Medicine* 339, no. 15 (1998): 1044-1052. A comprehensive review of Parkinson's disease that information on diagnosis and clinical features, pathology, epidemiology, genetics, and list of ninety-three references.

_____. "Parkinson's Disease: Second of Two Parts." *The New England Journal of Medicine* 339, no. 16 (1998): 1130-1143. The second part of a two-part review on Parkinson's disease. The article covers the pathophysiology and various types of treatment and includes a list of 199 references.

Weiner, William J., Lisa M. Shulman, and Anthony E. Land. *Parkinson's Disease: A Complete Guide for Patients and Families*. 2d ed. Baltimore: Johns Hopkins University Press, 2007. This book does an excellent job not only of giving current information on the features and management of Parkinson's disease but also of providing valuable information on how families and patients can deal with the practical and emotional aspects.

Donald J. Nash

SEE ALSO: Alzheimer's disease; Brain damage; Brain structure; Coping: Chronic illness; Nervous system; Neuropsychology

Passive aggression

DATE: 1945 forward
TYPE OF PSYCHOLOGY: Emotion; Personality; Psychopathology; Stress

Passive aggression is a covert expression of anger, hostility, or displeasure, often directed against a figure of authority. Sustained use of passive aggression across social situations may be classified as passive-aggressive (negativistic) personality disorder. Characteristics of passive aggression make it difficult to detect and study.

KEY CONCEPTS
- Anger
- Defense mechanisms
- Defiant behavior
- Interpersonal relationships
- Negativistic personality disorder
- Personality disorders
- Resistance
- Self-expression
- Self-protection

INTRODUCTION

Passive aggression is the hidden expression of anger and is found in all types of social settings. A common example is an employee who silently rebels against a controlling boss by completing work late or even going so far as to undermine the boss. Another example is a student who shows resistance to the demands of a teacher by not performing to expectation. Specific behaviors attributed to passive aggression include procrastination, feigned deafness or lack of comprehension, forgetfulness, defiance, poor performance, stubbornness, and moodiness. The passive expression of anger may be conscious or unconscious and is often meant to frustrate and irritate the intended victim. In extreme cases, the passive behavior may lead to failed achievement or loss of employment.

HISTORY

The term originated after World War II, when it was first used to describe insubordination among soldiers. The behavior is often linked to passive-aggressive (negativistic) personality disorder, which is defined by the American Psychiatric Association's *Diagnostic and Statistical Manual of Mental Disorders (DSM)* as "a pervasive pattern of negativistic attitudes and passive resistance to demands for adequate performance in social and occupational situations that begins by early adulthood and that occurs in a variety of contexts." The categorization and inclusion of the term in the association's manual began in 1952 and has remained a subject of debate among researchers.

The debate on the classification of passive aggression as a personality disorder exists, in part, because the small amount of existing research indicates that it is a difficult behavior to detect, and instruments that have been developed to aid in detection or diagnosis have not been found to be reliable or valid, including the criterion established in the American Psychiatric Association's manual. Martin Kantor notes in his book on passive aggression that some researchers argue that it is not a disorder in need of treatment but simply a type of normal behavior. The existing literature on passive aggression documents a need for more research and study to better understand this behavior and its inclusion as a personality disorder.

CAUSES

The exact cause of passive aggression is not known; however, some theories have been put forward. There is some agreement in the literature that the behavior is often elicited as a defense mechanism. Other theories speculate that passive aggression is a learned response to stressful situations; that it may be due to the genetic makeup of an individual; that it is the result of inconsistent parenting; that it is a normal part of adolescent development; or that it is exhibited by individuals with an extreme fear of expressing their anger, as documented by Joseph T. McCann. In some cases, passive aggression may even be viewed as a socially acceptable form of self-expression and self-protection. In his research, Norman Epstein found that passive aggression may be a socially acceptable tool for expressing anger without causing strife in interpersonal relationships. Mark A. Fine, James C. Overholser, and Karen Berkoff, in reviewing research data on passive-aggressive personality disorder, suggest that passive aggression can vary from mild to extreme, appears to be common in all populations, and may depend on specific social situations.

BIBLIOGRAPHY

Epstein, Norman. "Social Consequences of Assertion, Aggression, Passive Aggression, and Submission: Situational and Dispositional Determinants." *Behavior Therapy* 11.5 (1980): 662–69. Print.

Fine, Mark A., James C. Overholser, and Karen Berkoff. "Diagnostic Validity of the Passive-Aggressive Personality Disorder: Suggestions for Reform." *American Journal of Psychotherapy* 46.3 (1992): 470–83. Print.

Hopwood, Christopher J. "A Comparison of Passive-Aggressive and Negativistic Personality Disorders." *Journal of Personality Assessment* 94.3 (2012): 296–303. Print.

Kantor, Martin. *Passive-Aggression: A Guide for the Therapist, the Patient, and the Victim.* Westport: Praeger, 2002. Print.

Long Jody E., Nicholas J. Long, and Signe Whitson. *The Angry Smile: The Psychology of Passive-Aggressive Behavior in Families, Schools, and Workplaces.* 2nd ed. Austin: Pro-Ed, 2009. Print.

McCann, Joseph T. "Passive-Aggressive Personality Disorder: A Review." *Journal of Personality Disorders* 2.2 (1988): 170–79. Print.

Perry, J. Christopher, and Raymond B. Flannery. "Passive-Aggressive Personality Disorder: Treatment Implications of a Clinical Typology." *Journal of Nervous and Mental Disease* 170.3 (1982): 164–73. Print.

Wetzler, Scott. "Sugarcoated Hostility." *Newsweek* 120.15 (1992): 14. Print.

Whitson, Signe. "The Passive Aggressive Conflict Cycle." *Reclaiming Children and Youth* 22.3 (2013): 24–27. Print.

Pattern recognition

TYPE OF PSYCHOLOGY: Cognition

Making sense of the visual world is a difficult job, but it is one that human beings perform very well. Every three-year-old has pattern-recognition capabilities far beyond those of the most sophisticated computer. The information processing that the human visual system uses to accomplish this feat has many features in common with logical problem solving.

KEY CONCEPTS
- Convergence
- Fixation
- Fovea
- Retina
- Template

INTRODUCTION

How are objects recognized? This simple question encapsulates a difficult problem for the human visual system: taking a pattern of light from the world and finding in it surfaces, objects, other people, dangers, and pleasures. A paradox of the pattern-recognition process is that it all seems so easy: a person simply looks, and all the complexities of the world seem to jump out. One school of psychologists, typified by James Jerome Gibson, emphasizes direct perception, which to Gibson means that the first thing of which a person is aware in the perceptual process is objects themselves. All the intermediate stages, including the retinal image and numerous levels of physiological processing in the brain, simply do not matter to psychology.

That is how things appear, but there is considerable information processing between the light that strikes the eye and the recognition of a table or a friend. After the light is converted into electrical signals by the retina at the back of the eye, millions of nerve cells process the visual information. At the later stages of processing, many of the strategies used by the visual system are similar to the logical processes that one uses consciously in solving problems. Because the visual system performs these processes unconsciously, its operation has been called "unconscious inference." This term was coined by Hermann von Helmholtz in the mid-nineteenth century to refer to the logical processes that occur in vision.

Perspective illusions provide an example of this unconscious processing. An image of a small bar can be placed on a photograph of railroad tracks that converge in the distance. The bar will appear small if it is over the near part of the tracks, but larger if it is over the more distant tracks. On the photograph, one's visual inference process fails, because it is using a scheme that ordinarily works very well in the real world: near objects must produce a larger image on the retina to have the same real-world size as more distant objects. The human visual system puts distance and retinal size together so effectively that one normally experiences object constancy—the perception that objects at different distances are the same size even though they project as different sizes on the retina.

DISTANCE AND PATTERN

One part of pattern recognition involves the distance of the pattern. Perception of distance is a good example of the unconscious inference that occurs in vision, because so many different sources of information go into a distance estimate. One source, based on binocular vision, is particularly useful because it can provide an estimate of absolute range. If one fixates an object with both eyes, the convergence of the eyes tells the brain how far away the object is. This is called the "stereoscopic cue," and it depends on coordination of the two eyes.

Other distance cues are effective even in a single eye. One is superposition: if one object partly covers another,

the covered object must be more distant. This cue gives only relative distance, not absolute distance, as does the stereoscopic cue. Superposition works at any distance, however, while stereoscopic vision is useful only for objects within a few meters of the head. Another cue works only at very long distances—very distant objects, such as mountains, will look blue and hazy, while closer objects are sharp.

Still another source of distance information is motion. When one moves one's head, nearby objects will sweep by faster than more distant ones. If the brain knows the distance to any one point of this sweeping texture (such as the distance to the pavement beneath one's feet), it can calculate the distances to all other objects. These calculations would be difficult to do consciously even if one knew the mathematics required, but the brain performs the operations almost instantly.

Add to these distance cues other information such as familiar distance (one knows how far away the other side of one's living room is without measuring it), and one has a large palette of information sources that can provide information about the distance of an object. These cues are put together and weighted according to their reliability, and the brain produces a composite distance estimate. A similar process occurs in recognizing objects. The visual image, sound and touch information, and one's knowledge of the situation all combine to identify objects, even if they are at unfamiliar angles or if they cannot be seen clearly. It is the combination of many information sources, including memory, that makes the process quick and reliable.

A powerful theory of pattern recognition by psychologist Irving Biederman holds that people analyze objects into components that he calls "geons." These can be simple shapes, such as cylinders and cones, or patterns of edges. Each object has a characteristic set of geons, often not more than two or three, that defines it.

PATTERN AND COGNITION

Pattern recognition stands at the center of human activity—it is essential for all aspects of mental life. In appreciating art, one is recognizing patterns, but the process also extends to the most mundane activities, such as recognizing coins when making change. The traditional way to study mental processes is to make a task requiring those processes more difficult until a subject can no longer perform it. In finding where and how the processes fail, psychologists can learn about their structures.

One way psychologists break down pattern recognition is to degrade images until they can no longer be seen. A classic experiment by Jerome Bruner presents a good example. Bruner presented out-of-focus slides to groups of students, asking them to identify the objects in the slides as soon as they could. At first no one could name the objects, but as they became sharper and the visual information improved, the task became easier. The first guesses about the identities of the objects, however, were frequently wrong. Then Bruner played a trick on his subjects. Half of them saw the slides beginning in a very unfocused state, and many made wrong guesses about the objects presented. When most subjects had a guess but were still uncertain, the other half of the subjects were allowed to see the same slides for the first time. As the pictures came into focus, the second group was able to identify the objects sooner than the first, who had seen the unfocused images longer. The reason was that the first group had a lot of incorrect assumptions about the pictures, and these assumptions hindered their ability to change their minds as new information became available. The experiment shows the value of the information that one brings to a perceptual situation.

Another set of experiments, by Biederman, showed the key role of context and situation in identifying objects. A common object such as a sofa could be easily identified in a familiar setting such as a living room, but the same object in an unexpected setting, such as in a street scene, was very difficult to find. Subjects took several seconds to find the sofa in the street, even though they found it immediately in the living room. The sofa was identical in the two pictures—only the context was changed.

These examples show a contrast between two different types of information used to identify patterns. One begins with signals from the senses, called "bottom-up" information. It originates at the eyes, ears, and skin and is processed before arriving at the visual cortex. There the bottom-up information meets attention, motivation, and memory, the "top-down" sources of information. It is the meeting of top-down and bottom-up information that defines perception.

Another application of pattern recognition is in clinical medicine, where some patients experience brain damage that interferes with their pattern-recognition abilities. The damage is usually from strokes (interruptions of the blood supply to part of the brain), surgery, or accidents. Damage in different parts of the brain interferes with different aspects of the pattern-recognition process. It is clear that an injury that interrupts the nerve fibers linking the eye and the brain, for example, would interrupt pattern recognition by causing blindness. More interesting cases leave visual thresholds intact while disturbing recognition. Patients with this kind of damage have no difficulty in knowing that an object is present, or in avoiding it if it comes toward them, but do not know what it is.

One such case, described by Oliver Sacks in his book *The Man Who Mistook His Wife for a Hat and Other Clinical Tales* (1987), concerns a professor of music who remained productive and valued as a teacher although he had difficulty in recognizing things using vision alone. He would fail to recognize his students, for example, until he heard their voices. Then everything would snap into place and the lessons could begin. The professor suffered from visual agnosia, the inability to recognize objects. Milder forms of agnosia involve symptoms such as the difficulty in telling one person from another by looking at their faces or the inability to identify particular things in similar categories, such as the identities of flowers. These patients cannot be cured, but knowledge of the many sources of information in pattern recognition can help them cope with their handicaps. They can be taught to take more advantage of other information sources, such as sounds and context.

PATTERN AND PERCEPTION

Interest in pattern recognition is as old as the ancient Greeks, but little progress was made in explaining its mechanisms until well into the nineteenth century. During that century, mostly in Germany, methods were invented to investigate perception. Visual illusions, such as the railroad-track illusion described above, revealed some of the shortcuts that the visual system used to interpret scenes. These illusions are examples of the technique of stressing perception until it breaks down and learning about the process from the behavior of the system when it fails. The railroad-track illusion shows that vision uses perspective, among other things, to judge distance. Even when perspective cannot work, as in viewing a photograph or a drawing on a flat sheet, the system tries to use it anyway.

Perception is more than bringing a pattern into the brain. A pattern without a meaning is of no practical use. Perception, then, is the attaching of meaning to a pattern, a link of top-down with bottom-up information. At the core, it is a matching process. This has been described as template matching, like putting a stencil over a pattern. If the stencil (the template or concept in the head) matches the pattern (the signal from the eyes), then the world contains what was in the stencil and the pattern is recognized.

One real-world example of the importance of such template matching comes from neuroscience research on autism spectrum disorder (ASD). Studies conducted by neuroscientist Marcel Just and others suggest that while those with ASD can recognize patterns such as human faces, their brains have difficulty synchronizing the various parts of the brain that would give them meaning, such as their emotional content or familiarity.

There are many theories of perceptual recognition, but they all boil down to some form of template matching. Some machines, such as dollar-changing machines, also recognize patterns in this way. They look for exactly the required pattern—no variation is allowed. If the dollar bill is dirty or upside down, it is rejected. The system works well at rejecting counterfeit bills, but it is not flexible enough to do the sort of recognition in many contexts that humans do. Simple templates do not work very well when the pattern varies, as in identifying both "e" and "e" as the same letter. A template that matched the first letter would not recognize the second and would interpret the two patterns as having different meanings.

One solution to the matching problem is to match not the geometric pattern itself but some transformation of it. The pattern in the head would then have the same transformation. The letter "e," for example, could be recognized by its features, as "closed pattern above a curved tail running from upper left to lower right." This pair of features would identify both "e" and "e," without picking other letters falsely. Some modern computer-based pattern-recognition machines use features in this way. The future of pattern-recognition research will be directed toward identifying the features that nature uses to recognize patterns and toward designing machines that use effective features. The human use of context and probability in recognition will also be built into more powerful recognition systems.

BIBLIOGRAPHY

Biederman, Irving. "Perceiving Real World Scenes." *Science* 7 July 1972: 77–80. Print.

Bridgeman, Bruce. *The Biology of Behavior and Mind.* New York: Wiley, 1988. Print.

Gregory, R. L. *Eye and Brain: The Psychology of Seeing.* 5th ed. Princeton: Princeton UP, 1998. Print.

Hamilton, Jon. "What's Different about the Brains of People with Autism?." *Morning Edition.* NPR, 4 June 2012. Web. 2 July 2014.

Root-Bernstein, Michele, and Robert Root-Bernstein. "What's the Pattern?." *Psychology Today.* Sussex, 31 Mar. 2011. Web. 2 July 2014.

Sacks, Oliver. *The Man Who Mistook His Wife for a Hat and Other Clinical Tales.* London: Picador, 2011. Print.

Snowden, Robert, Peter Thompson, and Tom Troscianko. *Basic Vision: An Introduction to Visual Perception.* Rev. ed. New York: Oxford UP, 2012. Print.

Solso, Robert L., Otto H. Maclin, and M. Kimberly Maclin. *Cognitive Psychology.* 8th ed. Boston: Pearson, 2008. Print.

Weisberg, Robert W., and Lauretta Reeves. *Cognition: From Memory to Creativity.* Hoboken: Wiley, 2013. Print.

Bruce Bridgeman

SEE ALSO: Attention; Facial feedback; Logic and reasoning; Pattern vision; Sensation and perception; Visual system; Vision: Brightness and contrast; Vision: Color.

Pattern vision

TYPE OF PSYCHOLOGY: Sensation and perception

Human pattern vision and machine pattern vision have many properties in common. After extracting lines and other elements from a visual scene, pattern vision devices extract depth using many kinds of cues, and identify objects by interactions with memory. The knowledge can be applied in such settings as virtual reality.

KEY CONCEPTS
- Algorithm
- Fovea
- Receptive field
- Retina
- Virtual reality

INTRODUCTION

The human visual system is designed to see patterns. In fact, the system uses light only as a medium for detecting patterns; the actual intensities of light in various parts of the visual field are discarded at the first stage of visual processing, and only relative intensities remain. The fate of these patterns of intensities in the visual brain is the concern of pattern vision.

Vision relies on two kinds of information: patterns of intensity and patterns of color. Intensity patterns are resolved into objects in a number of steps. The steps can be conceived either in terms of the responses of single neurons at various levels of the visual pathways or as a series of rules, or algorithms, governing the transformations that visual information undergoes. The process begins in the retinas of the two eyes, where each receptor cell is exposed to a tiny sample of the visual world, a small spot of sensitivity. The receptor cells pass their messages to other cells at higher levels, and the visual image is reorganized, or recoded, at each step.

VISION PROCESSING

From the point of view of pattern vision, a particularly significant step occurs when the signals enter the visual cortex, after several stages of processing. Each neuron in the cortex is excited by signals from many receptors lying in a straight line, so that the neuron responds best to a line in the visual field. The line is a receptive field, an area of the world to which the neuron responds. The line must have a particular location and orientation. The neuron responds best, in fact, to a group of parallel lines at a particular spacing. This helps to improve the reliability of the system. Other neurons at the same time respond to lines at other locations, orientations, and spacings.

From this set of line-shaped receptive fields, the visual system constructs an internal model of the visual world. First, the outlines of objects can be recognized from patterns of lines. Next, particular patterns of lines are assigned particular meanings. For example, sometimes two lines will meet at a T junction. In this case, the visual system generally assumes that the crossbar of the T is in front of the upright part, because the crossbar interrupts a line. From an image that contains many such lines and intersections, the visual system reconstructs the surfaces and objects of the world.

MOTION AND SHADING

Often, however, this is not enough. There may remain ambiguities, unanswered questions about what objects are present in the world. The visual system has several additional methods by which to interpret the image. One of them is motion, which is usually present in the visual field. If there is no motion of objects in the world, there is often motion of the observer, so that objects move past the observer at different rates. The visual system can take any group of lines that is moving in the same way and conclude that they represent a single object moving relative to other parts of the visual world.

Objects can also reveal their shapes by their motion. A circular image, for example, might be either a disk or a sphere. A rotating sphere, however, will not change its shape, while a flipping disk will appear round, then elliptical, then flat as it tumbles. Other objects have characteristic changes in appearance as they rotate, providing the visual system with information about their structure. How the system decodes this information is the shape-from-motion problem.

The shading of objects also reveals something about their structure. A surface that is facing a source of illumination will be brighter than a surface at another angle. A rounded object will have continuous changes in shading. This is the shape-from-shading problem, and solving it gives still more information about the structure of the visual world. In this way, the visual system combines information from many cues, or sources of input from the image, and normally the brain does a remarkably good job of interpreting the visual world quickly and accurately.

Color gives still more information about visual patterns, helping the system to distinguish surfaces and textures. It is handled by separate visual mechanisms and cannot resolve as much detail as the form-processing mechanism.

MACHINE VISION

One reason it is important to know how pattern vision works is that an understanding of visual processing is necessary to enable machines to interact effectively with the visual environment. As humans interact more with patterns generated in graphics-oriented computers and in art, it becomes important to understand what goes on in the human mind when patterns are processed. One necessity for building robots to do many tasks is to give them the ability to recognize objects in their surroundings. Generally, the robots are computer-based and use television cameras for visual input; interpretation of the image comes next. This has proved to be more difficult than anticipated; even the first step in the process, abstracting lines and edges from the world, remains imperfect in existing systems. One of the efforts in the area of artificial pattern recognition, then, has been to investigate the pattern-recognition mechanisms of humans and animals and to try to build similar mechanisms into the machines. Every three-year-old has far better pattern-recognition capabilities than the most sophisticated machines.

One of the problems facing machine vision is that, although the identifying of lines, edges, and patterns might work well in the laboratory, the process is less successful in the real world. Humans have a remarkable ability to recognize patterns even in "noisy" environments, despite shadows, occlusions, changes in perspective, and other sources of variation. The emerging discipline of artificial intelligence is concerned with such problems.

VIRTUAL REALITY

Another application of visual pattern recognition is in the area of virtual reality, the effort to design displays that create in a computer user the illusion that one is actually in a different environment. Usually, the observer wears goggles that present images to the two eyes, reproducing everything that the observer would see in another environment. When the user's head turns, the environment presented in the goggles rotates in the opposite way, just as it would in the real world. The system might present an undersea or space environment, for example, and can even include an artificial image of the observer's own hand calculated from the position of an electronically equipped glove worn by the user. Here the difficulty is in deciding what the display should offer to the user; it is impractical to reproduce an entire visual world in all its richness and detail. The designer of a virtual-reality system must select the patterns that will be presented and must know what information is essential to pattern vision and what can be left out. Again, knowledge of what information the human visual system will extract from the scene is essential to guide decisions about what to present.

An example of how research in pattern vision can influence the design of virtual-reality systems is in the amount of detail that must be presented to the observer. The fovea of the eye, at the center of vision, sees much finer detail than the rest of the retina, and the farther from the fovea one goes, the less detail can be resolved. Engineers take advantage of this property of human vision by designing systems that present rich detail near objects of interest and less detail elsewhere. It is easier to update the information in this kind of display than to recalculate a finely detailed image for the whole visual field. Similarly, color information need not be presented in great detail over the entire visual field.

Other economies in design can be used in virtual-reality systems as well as in other computer displays. One such shortcut takes advantage of more subtle properties of visual pattern processing. The shading cues that are used to give an object the appearance of depth need not be accurate ones. The visual system is not sensitive to some kinds of distortions in shading and will accept an object as appropriately shaded even if the mathematics that generate the computer's shading are simplified and distorted.

Another example of a simplification that engineers can make is in the presentation of motion. Humans are not very sensitive to differences in rates of acceleration, so these differences need not be presented accurately. In summary, the human visual system uses shortcuts in interpreting the visual image, and artificial systems can use similar shortcuts in constructing the image.

THEORETICAL DEVELOPMENTS

The beginnings of research on pattern vision can be traced to the work of René Descartes in the seventeenth century. Descartes dissected a cow's eye and found that a small upside-down image of the world was projected on the back of the eye. All the information that comes from vision passes through a similar stage in human eyes as well. For more than two centuries, however, little progress was made in deciphering what happened to visual information after it left the retina. Anatomists learned where in the brain the visual fibers led, but they could not find out what was happening there.

One of the advances that has made work on pattern vision possible is the realization that vision must be studied at many levels of analysis. One level is neurophysiology, the understanding of what goes on in the nerve cells and in the fibers that connect them. Another level is the algorithm, the set of internal rules for coding and interpreting visual information. Researchers at this level ask what steps the visual system must take to interpret a pattern. The steps themselves are taken care of at the neurophysiological level. A third level is behavior: Researchers investigate the capabilities of pattern vision in the intact human. At this more global level, one studies visual pattern processing as a whole rather than dissecting its pieces. It is relating one level to another that advances understanding. At the behavior level, it is observed that people are capable of recognizing patterns from lines alone, as in cartoons. At the algorithmic level, it is found that extracting lines from an image is a useful step in interpreting the image. At the neurophysiological level, it is found that some neurons are sensitive to lines in the visual world.

Modern theories of pattern vision all share several ideas. First, information is transformed in small steps, not all at once, from the image to its meaning. The early steps are largely independent of the use to be made of the visual pattern. Later steps involve interactions with memory and with the use to be made of the visual information. At these later stages, even single nerve cells code information from a wide region of the visual field, as these cells have the job of integrating images from large areas. At the algorithmic level, the brain engages a number of assumptions about the structure of the visual world and the objects in it to interpret a scene quickly and reliably. The visual field is represented over and over in the brain as information passes to more specialized regions that emphasize movement, pattern recognition, visual-motor interactions, and other uses that the brain makes of visual inputs.

Another common idea in pattern vision is that the image is analyzed in several different ways at once. Depth, for example, might be sought in stereoscopic vision (small differences in the images arriving at the two eyes), in superpositions (using the T junctions described above, among other methods), in shading, and in other clues. If one method does not come up with a meaningful interpretation, another one will. In this way, a reliable pattern vision system can be created from unreliable components.

BIBLIOGRAPHY

Bridgeman, Bruce. *The Biology of Behavior and Mind.* New York: Wiley, 1988. Print.

Daw, Nigel. *Visual Development.* 3rd ed. New York: Springer, 2013. Print.

Del Viva, Maria M., Giovanni Punzi, and Daniele Benedetti. "Information and Perception of Meaningful Patterns." *PLoS One* 8.7 (2013): 1–9. Print.

Gregory, R. L. *Eye and Brain: The Psychology of Seeing.* 5th ed. Princeton: Princeton UP, 1998. Print.

Hubel, David H., and Torsten N. Wiesel. *Brain and Visual Perception: The Story of a Twenty-Five-Year Collaboration.* New York: Oxford UP, 2004. Print.

Humphreys, G. W., and M. J. Riddoch. *To See but Not to See: A Case Study of Visual Agnosia.* London: Erlbaum, 1995. Print.

Solso, Robert L. *Cognitive Psychology.* 8th ed. Boston: Pearson, 2008. Print.

Strasburger, Hans, Ingo Rentschler, and Martin Juttner. "Peripheral Vision and Pattern Recognition: A Review." *Journal of Vision* 11.5 (2011): 1–82. Print.

Tovée, Martin J. *An Introduction to the Visual System.* New York: Cambridge UP, 2008. Print.

Waltz, David L. "Artificial Intelligence." *Scientific American* 247 (October, 1982): 118–33. Print.

Bruce Bridgeman

SEE ALSO: Brain structure; Facial feedback; Logic and reasoning; Pattern recognition; Virtual reality; Vision: Brightness and contrast; Vision: Color; Visual system.

Pavlov, Ivan Petrovich

BORN: September 27, 1849
DIED: February 17, 1936
BIRTHPLACE: Ryazan, Russia
PLACE OF DEATH: Leningrad, U.S.S.R. (now St. Petersburg, Russia)
IDENTITY: Russian physiologist and psychologist
TYPE OF PSYCHOLOGY: Biological bases of behavior; Cognition; Learning

Pavlov developed the concept of the conditioned response, which indicated that living organisms could continuously adapt their behavior to changing circumstances.

Ivan Petrovich Pavlov was born in the central Russian city of Ryazan. As the son of a parish priest, he was assured of access to education and, after graduating from the local church school and briefly attending Ryazan Seminary, studied natural sciences at St. Petersburg University.

Pavlov was a promising student and, under the influence of professor I. F. Tsion, developed a strong interest in physiology. After graduation from St. Petersburg University in 1875, he continued his physiological studies at the Military Medical Academy, working with Sergei. P. Botkin and K. N. Ustimovich. In 1879, he received an M.D. degree and, three years later, completed a doctoral dissertation on the nerves found in the heart.

From 1884 to 1886, Pavlov lived in Germany, studying the physiology of invertebrates. In 1890, he was appointed professor in the department of pharmacology and director of the physiology section of the Institute of Experimental Medicine in St. Petersburg. It was there that he established a reputation as an exacting researcher. In 1904, he won the Nobel Prize in Physiology or Medicine by focusing on the difficult problem of digestion, which involved the interplay of the circulation of the blood, the activities of the nervous system, and the workings of enzymes.

The conditioned reflex (CR) was Pavlov's most important discovery. Through a number of carefully controlled experiments, he demonstrated the conditions under which dogs came to associate the appearance of food with signals such as ringing bells, thereby converting a normally unconditioned response such as salivation to a conditioned one. This breakthrough, described in *Dvadtsatiletnii opyt obektivnogo izucheniia vysshei nervnoi deiatelnosti zhivotnykh* (1923; *Conditioned Reflexes*, 1927), showed how living creatures could learn to respond physiologically to nonphysiologically-based signals. The ramifications of this discovery occupied him for the rest of his scientific career.

The implications of the conditioned reflex were enormous. Its extension to a whole chain of associations (called higher-order conditioning) reinforced materialistic philosophies such as Marxism, supported the idea that nurture was more important than nature, and buttressed behaviorist psychology. Its central concept, that living beings could continuously adapt their behavior to a changing environment, challenged both biological and psychological theories of determinism.

Because of the political significance of Pavlov's theory, the Soviet regime provided him with financial support. He also received strong international recognition; most notably, he was awarded France's Order of the Legion of Honor. His death on February 17, 1936, was widely mourned by Russians and non-Russians alike.

BIBLIOGRAPHY

Babkin, B. P. *Pavlov: A Biography.* Chicago: University of Chicago Press, 1974. Written by a former colleague, this resource provides useful information on Pavlov's life and personality.

Gray, Jeffrey Alan. *Ivan Pavlov.* New York: Viking Press, 1980. Grey offers an excellent summary of Pavlov's achievements and examines his place in the behaviorist tradition.

Johnson, George. *The Ten Most Beautiful Experiments.* New York: Vintage, 2009. Among the ten experiments written about in this readable resource is the one performed by Pavlov on his dogs, which was the genesis of his theories on conditioning.

Todes, Daniel. *Ivan Pavlov: Exploring the Animal Machine.* New York: Oxford University Press, 2000. Aimed at young adults, Todes's work reviews Pavlov's

accomplishments, emphasizing the thought processes involved in his investigations.

Michael J. Fontenot

SEE ALSO: Behaviorism; Conditioning; Pavlovian conditioning; Reflexes.

Pavlovian conditioning

DATE: 1890's forward
TYPE OF PSYCHOLOGY: Learning

Pavlovian conditioning is a basic process of learning that relates especially to reflexes and emotional behavior. Interest in this form of learning has been long-standing and continues to the present day. Pavlovian principles apply to a very wide range of organisms, situations, and events.

KEY CONCEPTS
- Conditioned emotional reaction (CER)
- Conditioned response (CR)
- Conditioned stimulus (CS)
- Discrimination
- Extinction
- Flooding
- Second-signal system
- Spontaneous recovery
- Stimulus generalization
- Systematic desensitization
- Unconditioned response (UR)
- Unconditioned stimulus (US)

INTRODUCTION

Pavlovian conditioning, also known as respondent conditioning and classical conditioning (to distinguish it from instrumental or operant conditioning), is an elementary learning process and has been of major interest to psychologists ever since the Russian physiologist Ivan Petrovich Pavlov discovered that a dog could learn to salivate to a neutral stimulus after the stimulus was paired repeatedly with food.

Pavlov's early career focused on the study of heart circulation and digestion in animals (usually dogs), for which he received the Nobel Prize in Physiology or Medicine in 1904. However, by that time Pavlov had already turned his attention to experiments on conditioned reflexes, from which flowed a new psychological nomenclature.

CONDITIONING

The core of Pavlovian conditioning is the pairing (association) of stimuli to elicit responses. Food (meat powder) placed in a dog's mouth naturally produces salivation. Pavlov called the food an unconditioned stimulus (US) and salivation, elicited by the food, the unconditioned response (UR). When a neutral stimulus—for example, a tone that does not naturally elicit salivation—is repeatedly followed by food, the tone alone eventually evokes salivation. Pavlov labeled the tone a conditioned stimulus (CS) and the response (salivation) elicited by it the conditioned response (CR).

Pavlov's formulation can be summarized as follows:

Before conditioning:
> Food (US) elicits Salivation (UR)

Conditioning procedure:
> Neutral Stimulus (Tone) plus Food (US) elicits Salivation (UR)

After conditioning:
> Tone (CS) elicits Salivation (CR)

Pavlov believed that conditioned responses were identical to unconditioned responses. That is usually not the case. For example, conditioned responses may be less pronounced (weaker) or a bit more lethargic than unconditioned responses.

Several phenomena turn up in studies of Pavlovian conditioning. Extinction, generalization, and discrimination are among the most important. Extinction refers to the procedure as well as to the elimination of a CR. If the CS is repeatedly presented without the US, extinction occurs: The dog stops salivating to the tone. During the course of extinction, the CR may return from time to time until it is finally extinguished. Pavlov called the occasional return of the CR "spontaneous recovery."

Stimulus generalization refers to responding not only to a particular CS but also to similar but different stimuli. Further, the magnitude (amount of salivation) of a generalized response tends to decline as stimuli become less and less like the CS. For example, a dog trained to salivate to a 5,000-cycle-per-second (cps) tone is likely to salivate also to 5,300 cps and 4,700 cps tones without specific training to do so (stimulus generalization). Responses tend to weaken in an orderly way as tones become more and more unlike the CS—that is, as the tones move away from the CS in both directions, say, to 4,400 cps from 4,100 cps, and 5,600 cps to 5,900 cps, the flow of salivation becomes less and less.

Stimulus generalization in effect extends the number of stimuli that elicit a conditioned response. Discrimination procedures restrict that number by conditioning a subject not to generalize across stimuli. The procedure involves two processes: acquisition and extinction. The CS is paired repeatedly with the US (acquisition) while the US is withheld as generalized stimuli are presented repeatedly (extinction). If the dog now salivates to the CS and not to the generalized stimuli, the dog has learned to discriminate or to act discriminatively. Pavlov reported that some dogs displayed a general breakdown in behavior patterns (experimental neurosis) when called on to make discriminations that were too difficult for them. Pavlov's work on what he called the second-signal system implies that conditioning principles are relevant to human as well as to animal learning. Once, say, a tone is established as a CS in first-order conditioning, the tone can be paired with a neutral stimulus to establish a second-order CS. Thus, in the absence of food, a light might precede the tone (CS) several times until the light itself begins to function as a CS. Second-order conditioning appears to follow many of the same rules as first-order conditioning.

Pavlov's work has clearly provided one way to study the learning process in great detail. It has also provided the kind of data and theory that have affected research in other areas of learning, such as instrumental conditioning and, subsequently, cognitive science and neuroscience.

RANGE OF PAVLOVIAN CONDITIONING

Pavlovian phenomena have been demonstrated with different kinds of organisms and a wide variety of stimuli and responses far beyond those studied by Pavlov. Stimuli that precede such unconditioned stimuli as sudden loud noises (leading to rapid heart rate), a puff of air delivered to the eye (evoking blinking), or a large temperature increase (eliciting sweating) may become conditioned stimuli capable of eliciting conditioned responses on their own. The idea of second-order (higher-order) conditioning is profoundly important because it suggests how rewards such as words of praise and money are established apart from primary (biologically necessary) rewards, such as food and water. It also may in part explain the power of films, plays, novels, and advertisements to evoke strong emotion in the absence of direct experience with primary (unconditioned) stimuli. Studies concerned with conditioned emotional reactions (CER), especially fear and anxiety in people—a subject much more complex than simple reflexes—have been of special interest to researchers and therapists for many years.

ADDITIONAL RESEARCH FINDINGS

Studies of conditioning essentially look at how various unconditioned and conditioned stimuli influence responses under different arrangements of time and space. Following are a few general findings.

Pavlovian conditioning tends to be readily established when stimuli or responses or both are strong rather than weak. For example, in response to a near-drowning experience, some people promptly learn to fear such conditioned stimuli as the sight of water, boats, palm trees, bathing suits, and so on. In such cases, relevant stimuli and responses (panic) are presumably quite strong.

Conditioned stimuli are most likely to elicit conditioned responses when unconditioned and conditioned stimuli are paired consistently. If a mother always hums when she rocks her infant daughter to sleep, humming is likely to become a potent and reliable CS, which soothes and comforts her daughter. This outcome is less likely if mother hums only occasionally.

When several stimuli precede a US, the one most often paired with the US will likely emerge as the strongest CS. If, for example, both parents threaten to punish their young son, but only father always carries out the threats, father's threats are more likely than mother's to evoke apprehension in the child.

For some responses, such as eye blinking, conditioned stimuli tend to be strongest when they precede the US by about one-half second. The optimal interval for other responses varies from seconds to fractions of seconds: A neighbor's dog barks immediately before little Sophie falls from her swing, bumping her nose very hard. She cries. If the dog's bark subsequently makes Sophie feel uneasy, the bark is functioning as a CS. This outcome becomes less and less likely as the bark and fall increasingly separate in time.

Conditioned responses are usually not established if a US and CS occur together (simultaneous conditioning)—the potency of the UC overshadows the potential CS—or when a neutral stimulus follows the US (backward conditioning).

SOME PRACTICAL APPLICATIONS

In a widely cited study reported in 1920, American researchers John B. Watson and Rosalie Rayner conditioned a phobic reaction in an eleven-month-old infant named Albert. The researchers discovered that Albert feared loud noises but seemed unafraid of a number of other things, including small animals.

Watson and Rayner subsequently placed a white rat in Albert's crib. When Albert reached for it, the researchers struck a piece of resonant metal with a hammer, making a "loud sound." After a few such presentations, presenting the rat alone elicited crying and various avoidance reactions. Albert also showed signs of fear to similar things, such as a rabbit, a furry object, and fluffy clumps of cotton (stimulus generalization). Thus, Watson and Rayner provided early experimental evidence that Pavlovian principles are involved in the acquisition of human emotional reactions.

While this study induced a phobic reaction in the subject, systematic desensitization is a procedure designed to eliminate phobias and anxieties. The procedure was largely developed and named by South African-born therapist Joseph Wolpe. Noting that it is very difficult to have pleasant and anxious feelings simultaneously, Wolpe fashioned a systematic technique to teach clients to engage in behavior (relaxation) that competes with anxiety.

Therapy typically begins with an interview designed to identify specific sources of the client's fears. The therapist helps the client assemble a list of items that elicit fear. Items associated with the least amount of fear are positioned at the bottom of the list; most feared items are placed near the top. For example, if a client has a strong fear of dogs, the therapist and client would develop a list of scenes that make the client fearful. Situations may vary from hearing the word "dog" to seeing pictures of dogs, being in the vicinity of a dog, hearing a dog bark, being close to dogs, and patting a dog.

The client is next taught to relax by tensing and releasing various groups of muscles—shoulders, face, arms, neck, and so on. This phase of treatment ends when the client has learned to fully relax on his or her own in a matter of minutes.

The client and therapist now move on to the next phase of therapy. While remaining fully relaxed, the client is asked to imagine being in the first situation at the bottom of the list. The image is held for several seconds. The client then relaxes for about twenty seconds before imagining the same situation again for several seconds. When the client is able to imagine an item and remain fully relaxed, the therapist presents a slightly more fearful situation to imagine. This procedure continues until an image causes distress, at which time the session ends. The next session begins with relaxation, followed by the client slowly moving up the list. As before, the client stops at the point of distress. Therapy is successful when the client can imagine all the items on the list while remaining fully relaxed. The technique is less helpful when clients have difficulty identifying fearful situations or calling up vivid images.

In the hands of a skillful therapist, systematic desensitization is an effective technique for reducing a wide variety of fears. Its Pavlovian features involve pairing imagined fearful scenes with relaxation. When relaxation successfully competes with fear, it becomes a new CR to the imagined scenes. As relaxation becomes sufficiently strong as a CR, anxiety is replaced by calmness in the face of earlier aversive stimuli.

Extinction offers a more direct route to the reduction of fear than systematic desensitization. The technique called flooding makes use of extinction. Flooding exposes the client to fear-arousing stimuli for a prolonged period of time. Suppose a child is afraid of snakes. Although fear is likely to increase initially, flooding would require the child to confront the snake directly and continuously—to be "flooded" by various stimuli associated with the snake—until the conditioned stimuli lose their power to elicit fear. Some therapists think that the application of this technique is probably best left to professionals.

SOME EVERYDAY EXAMPLES

Pavlovian principles may be plausibly applied to daily life, as the following examples illustrate.

Couples sometimes refer to a certain tune as "our song." A plausible interpretation is that Pavlovian conditioning has been at work. The favored tune may have been popular and repeated often at the time of the couple's courtship and marriage. The tune has since become a CS that evokes a variety of pleasant feelings associated with initial love.

A babysitter notes that giving a young child a blue blanket in the absence of his mother markedly reduces his irritability. Most likely the blanket has been sufficiently associated with the soothing actions of his mother (US) and now functions as a calming stimulus (CS).

An adolescent steadfastly avoids the location where he was seriously injured in an automobile accident. He says that just thinking about the highway makes him nervous. The location doubtless contains a number of conditioned aversive stimuli that now trigger unpleasant feelings (CR) and avoidance.

After a bitter divorce, a woman finds that the sight of household items (CS) associated with her former husband is terribly upsetting (CR). She has reduced her resentment by getting rid of the offending items.

A wife often places flower arrangements in her husband's den. The flowers (CS) now bring him a measure of comfort (CR) when she is away on trips.

RESPONDENT CONDITIONING AND REINFORCEMENT

Pavlovian behaviors are principally elicited by antecedent events (just as low temperatures elicit shivering), while many behaviors are strengthened (in reinforcement) or weakened (in punishment) by what follows behavior. In Pavlovian conditioning, two stimuli are presented, one following another, regardless of what a subject does. What follows behavior is usually not important in this form of conditioning. In studying the role of reinforcement on behavior (instrumental or operant conditioning), the consequences that follow a person's actions often determine what the person is likely to do under similar circumstances in the future. What follows behavior is important in this type of conditioning.

The topic of reinforcement is introduced here because Pavlovian conditioning and reinforcement are intricately related in that any Pavlovian conditioning is likely to contain elements of instrumental conditioning, and vice versa. For example, if someone has a near-drowning experience and now avoids bodies of water, it is plausible to say that conditioned stimuli associated with the experience evoke unsettling feelings. The person reduces the unpleasant feelings by avoiding bodies of water. In this example, negative feelings are conditioned according to Pavlovian principles. The avoidance reaction is maintained by (negative) reinforcement and involves instrumental learning. Virtually all the previous examples can be analyzed similarly.

BIBLIOGRAPHY

Baldwin, John D., and Janice I. Baldwin. *Behavior Principles in Everyday Life*. 4th ed. Upper Saddle River, N.J.: Prentice Hall, 2001. Print.

Hergenhahn, B. R. *An Introduction to the History of Psychology*. 6th ed. Belmont: Wadsworth/Cengage Learning, 2009. Print.

Levis, Donald J. *Foundations of Behavioral Therapy*. New Brunswick: Transaction, 2010. Print.

"Pavlovian Test Finds Sleeping Consciousness." *New Scientist* 26 Sept. 2009: 18. Print.

Ramnerö, Jonas, and Niklas Törneke. *ABCs of Human Behavior: Behavioral Principles for the Practicing Clinician*. Oakland: New Harbinger, 2008. Print.

Redish, A. David. *The Mind Within the Brain*. Oxford: Oxford UP, 2013. Print.

Rescorla, Robert A. "Pavlovian Conditioning: It's Not What You Think It Is." *American Psychologist* 43.3 (May 1988): 151–60. Print

Watson, J. B., and R. Rayner. "Conditioned Emotional Reactions." *Journal of Experimental Psychology* 3 (1920): 1–14. Print.

Wolpe, Joseph. *The Practice of Behavior Therapy*. 4th ed. Boston: Allyn, 2008. Print.

Frank J. Sparzo

SEE ALSO: Aversion therapy; Behaviorism; Conditioning; Habituation and sensitization; Implosion; Learned helplessness; Learning; Little Albert study; Operant conditioning therapies; Pavlov, Ivan Petrovich; Phobias; Reflexes; Systematic desensitization.

Peabody individual achievement test (PIAT)

DATE: 1970 forward

TYPE OF PSYCHOLOGY: Intelligence and intelligence testing

The Peabody Individual Achievement Test is a widely used, individually administered achievement test for children and adolescents from kindergarten through high school. It provides overall age-equivalent and grade-equivalent scores and subtest scores. It is used in many educational and assessment settings.

KEY CONCEPTS
- Achievement
- Basal level
- Ceiling level
- Educational testing

INTRODUCTION

The Peabody Individual Achievement Test is a widely used, individually administered achievement test. Developed in 1970 by Lloyd M. Dunn and Frederick C. Markwardt, it was revised in 1989 by Markwardt. The original version, often called the PIAT, and the revision, often called the PIAT-R, are for children aged five through eighteen. In 1997, the test's normative scores were updated to reflect changes in average level of performance, resulting in the PIAT-R/NU, which is for children aged five through twenty-two. The PIAT measures widely expected educational outcomes, not specific to any particular curriculum.

The PIAT measures achievement in five areas: general information, reading recognition, reading comprehension, mathematics, and spelling. The revision added one more area, written expression. For the general information portion, the examiner reads questions aloud, and the child answers aloud. For reading recognition, the child reads aloud. For reading comprehension, the child reads a sentence silently and then chooses a picture that best illustrates the sentence. For mathematics, the child answers multiple-choice questions on topics ranging from recognizing numbers to solving geometry and trigonometry problems. For spelling, the child chooses the correct spelling of the word that the examiner speaks. For written expression, depending on the child's level, the child either copies and writes words or writes a story in response to a picture.

The items are arranged in increasing order of difficulty. For each child, the examiner starts with some sample items and then obtains basal and ceiling levels. The basal level is the point where the child correctly answers five items in a row. The ceiling level is the point where the child misses five items out of seven. The number of items answered correctly between the basal and ceiling levels determines the child's score. The child's score is matched with scores of children of the same chronological age. The PIAT provides an overall score, percentile ranks, and age-equivalent, grade-equivalent, and standard scores for the overall score and for each portion.

An adult, who is typically an educator or a psychologist or someone working under supervision, administers the PIAT to one child at a time. No formal training is required, but the adult must be able to follow the instructions precisely. Typically, testing occurs in a private, quiet, well-lit room and takes about an hour to complete. The items are not timed, except for written expression. Although it is typically given in one session, the child may take a break or come back for a second session if needed.

USES AND LIMITATIONS

The PIAT has several uses. PIAT scores can be useful whenever someone needs an assessment of scholastic achievement or insight into the individual's specific strengths and weaknesses. For the child, this information might be useful in designing a program, providing guidance and counseling, making admissions and placement decisions, and grouping students. In terms of research, the PIAT can be used for evaluation of an educational program. Also, because the test assesses individuals from preschool to post-high school, the PIAT can be used in longitudinal studies on achievement and human development. It could also be used for basic research questions, such as showing how two achievement areas are related or determining the relationship between academic achievement and other traits.

As is true of any test, the PIAT has limitations. One potential limitation is that sometimes people forget that it is a score that the individual made on one specific test on one specific day. They mistakenly believe that the score defines them. Children or adolescents who are ill, distracted, or having an off day for other reasons may perform well below their typical level. Another potential limitation is that the PIAT is limited to English-speaking children in the United States. Children who have other backgrounds would typically be at a disadvantage. Also, the PIAT must be administered in a standardized way. An examiner who deviates from the instructions might quickly inflate or deflate the child's score.

BIBLIOGRAPHY

Andrade, Heidi. "Assessing Learning." *Education Digest* 78.3 (2012): 46–53. Print.

Costenbader, Virginia K., and John W. Adams. "A Review of the Psychometric and Administrative Features of the PIAT-R: Implications for the Practitioner." *Journal of School Psychology* 29 (Fall 1991): 219–28. Print.

Flanagan, Dawn P., Patti L. Harrison. *Contemporary Intellectual Assessment: Theories, Tests, and Issues.* New York: Guilford, 2012. Print.

Grimley, Liam K. "Academic Assessment of ADHD Children." *Handbook of Hyperactivity in Children.* Ed. Johnny L. Matson. Needham Heights: Allyn, 1993. Print.

Kasomo, Daniel W. *Measurement and Evaluation in Humanities and Education: Teaching, Evaluation, Assessment and Testing.* Saarbrucken: Lambert Academic, 2010.

Luther, James B. "Review of the Peabody Individual Achievement Test—Revised." *Journal of School Psychology* 30 (Spring 1992): 31–39. Print.

Sattler, Jerome M. *Assessment of Children.* 5th ed. San Diego: Author, 2008. Print.

Smith, Douglas K. *Essentials of Individual Achievement Assessment.* New York: Wiley, 2008. Print.

Lillian M. Range

SEE ALSO: Ability tests; Assessment; Career and personnel testing; Career Occupational Preference System (COPS); College entrance examinations; Creativity: Assessment; General Aptitude Test Battery (GATB); Human resource training and development; Intelligence tests; Interest inventories; Kuder Occupational Interest Survey (KOIS); Race and intelligence; Scientific methods; Stanford-Binet test; Strong Interest Inventory (SII); Survey research: Questionnaires and interviews; Testing: Historical perspectives; Wechsler Intelligence Scale for Children-Third Edition (WISC-III).

Peak experiences

TYPE OF PSYCHOLOGY: Cognitive/emotional; Cross-cultural; Developmental; Religion; Psychology

Abraham Maslow called the mystical experiences of awe and absorption regularly described by self-actualized people "peak experiences." Subsequent research has found that the quality of peak experiences may vary by age and culture. Recently, Mihaly Csikszentmihalyi has described the related concept of the experience of "flow," that can occur when one is fully engaged in an activity.

KEY CONCEPTS:
- B-needs
- Flow
- Humanistic psychology
- Self-actualization

INTRODUCTION

In the 1970s, Abraham Maslow developed a humanistic theory of personality and motivation to describe people's positive potential, in contrast to many other psychological theories that focused on people's struggles and failings. Peak experience is a term coined by Maslow to describe a characteristic experience of people who were, in his view, self-actualized -- fulfilling their human potential. These people reported experiences of wonder, awe and ecstasy, in which their sense of individuality became absorbed in the world. The descriptions were of a decidedly spiritual, although not necessarily religious, nature. Maslow investigated these experiences through studying the lives of people who he felt were self-actualized, and through interviewing everyday people on their emotionally positive experiences.

In more recent times, Mihaly Csikszentmihalyi has researched a similar concept which he terms "flow." Like peak experiences, flow is a state of absorption that arises when one is engaged in activities that challenge one to use the full extent of his or her skills. The result can be a state of positive emotion in which the person "becomes one" with the activity. While peak experiences and flow are not equivalent concepts, they have considerable overlap and are regularly investigated in conjunction with each other.

THE NATURE AND EFFECT OF PEAK EXPERIENCES

To understand the nature of peak experiences, Maslow asked people to describe the most emotionally powerful experience in their lives. He found that people often described such experiences in mystical or spiritual terms. People described feeling intense happiness and integrated with the world. In *Religion, Values and Peak Experience*, Maslow describes peak experiences as "Feelings of limitless horizons opening up to the vision, the feeling of being simultaneously more powerful and also more helpless than one ever was before, the feeling of ecstasy and wonder and awe, the loss of placement in time and space with, finally, the conviction that something extremely important and valuable had happened, so that the subject was to some extent transformed and strengthened even in his daily life by such experiences."

Not all peak experiences are as intense as described above, but often people feel changed by them. In the interviews Maslow conducted people reported trying to repeat such experiences, and feeling more compassionate to others and more accepting and comfortable in the world than they had felt prior to the experience.

PEAK EXPERIENCES IN THE CONTEXT OF MASLOW'S THEORY OF MOTIVATION

Maslow's humanistic theory of personality and motivation sought to describe the positive potential of people. Maslow described people as having B-needs and D-needs. These are hierarchically arranged, often pictured as a pyramid, with the D-needs, D is an abbreviation for deficiency, forming the large pyramidal base. D-needs include physiological needs such as for food and sleep, safety needs such as security, love and belonging needs such as friendship, and esteem needs such as confidence and the respect of others. Once these needs are fulfilled

to a reasonable level, one can develop B-needs. B is an abbreviation for being. These are the needs associated with self-actualization and living to one's full potential. B-needs include justice, morality, and clear, realistic perception.

Maslow came to his description of self-actualization by examining the lives of historical figures such as Abraham Lincoln, Albert Einstein and Eleanor Roosevelt, as well as friends and acquaintances that he felt were examples of self-actualized or fully functioning people. He looked for commonalities among these people to describe the nature of self actualization. Maslow concluded that self-actualized people have a number of characteristics in common, including self-acceptance, realism, autonomy, spontaneity, democratic attitudes, and a need for solitude and privacy.

Maslow found that the people he described as self-actualized described peak experiences much more frequently than people who were not self-actualized, although he noted that almost all people experienced at least some peak experiences in their lifetimes. In interviews he did find some people, who he called "non-peakers," who claimed to never have had a peak experience. These people, he said, were overly cognitive, non-emotional, and overly controlled.

Maslow was not the only humanistic psychologist to describe the nature of self-actualization. Carl Rogers also used this term to describe what he saw as the innate tendency of the person to fulfill all his or her potentials. Rogers' focus was on how, in therapeutic relationships, this innate tendency could be fostered in the service of healing, while Maslow did not describe a therapeutic process. Maslow and Rogers described the self-actualized person in similar terms, but Rogers did not include peak experiences in his description. Perhaps most importantly, Rogers argued that all individuals strive for self-actualization, although under harsh circumstances this tendency for actualization can be thwarted. Maslow, in contrast, believed very few people, perhaps as little as two per cent of the population, attained self-actualization.

PERSONAL, CULTURAL, AND ENVIRONMENTAL VARIABLES RELATED TO PEAK EXPERIENCES

Maslow's investigations led him to conclude that peak experiences may vary with age. The college-age students he interviewed were more likely to describe emotionally intense experiences than were older individuals. Older individuals were more likely to describe their most positive experiences in terms of serenity rather than intense ecstasy. Maslow termed these "plateau experiences," in contrast with peak experiences. He found that these sorts of serene experiences were more consistent than were intense peak experiences, which could be relatively rare. In the later part of Maslow's life, he began to investigate how the practice of meditation might help one achieve and sustain plateau experiences.

The situations that evoke peak experiences vary from person to person, and perhaps from culture to culture. In general, however, being in nature, hearing or performing music, or being with loved ones are commonly cited as situations in which peak experiences are more likely to be experienced. These situations seem to encourage the emotional openness that may be a prerequisite for a peak experience. For some people, ingesting hallucinogenic drugs may also induce peak experiences.

Peak experiences may also vary by culture. Maslow himself did not study cultural differences, but psychologist Gayle Privette has researched them. Privette found that cultures might vary in the way they describe their most significant experiences. Chinese people, for example describe themselves experiencing more serenity than vivid joy in terms of their peak experiences. Portuguese students reported peak experiences related to developmental milestones more than did Chinese students. Much cross-cultural investigation remains to be done.

RESEARCH ON PEAK EXPERIENCES

By their nature, peak experiences are not likely to be subject to controlled experimentation in laboratory settings. Rather, interviews, questionnaires, and narrative analyses have formed the body of research on this topic. Maslow examined historical or archival records of people he felt were self-actualized, and conducted interviews with those he had access to. He also interviewed college students on their peak experiences. His mode of investigation has been criticized for being too open-ended and unsystematic. Such methods can provide a rich description, but may lack generality.

Other researchers have developed scales to measure peak experiences in order to conduct more systematic research with larger numbers of participants. Gayle Privette developed the Experience Questionnaire to study the nature of peak experiences, and examined the experiences of a variety of individuals with this questionnaire. From this research, three characteristics were found to signify peak experiences: One of these three characteristics was labeled Fulfillment. This referred to

the intrinsically rewarding nature of peak experiences. A second characteristic Privette called Significance, referring to the fact that participants considered the peak experiences to be important. The final characteristic was labeled Spirituality and referred to the absorption of the self into the experience.

Eugene Mathes and collaborators also examined peak experiences as measured by questionnaires called the Peak Scale and the Absorption Scale. College studentswho completed these scales were found to describe Peak Experiences as primarily mystical events, not simply moments of happiness.

RELATED CONCEPTS: FLOW, AND PEAK PERFORMANCE

The concept of "flow," described and researched by Mihaly Csikszentmihalyi, has several characteristics in common with peak experiences, and sometimes the terms are used interchangeably. However, although they share some qualities, flow and peak experiences do not seem to be identical experiences. Flow refers to the state of pleasurable absorption that can occur when one is engaged in an activity that challenges but does not exceed one's level of skill. Flow experiences generally occur when a task has clear goals and feedback. Like Peak Experiences in general, one's sense of self may not be distinct in flow experiences, they are emotionally positive, and one may lose a sense of time during both. Csikszentmihalyi has described meditative states as experiences of flow, but most theorizing and research on flow concerns activities such as sports and creative endeavors. Sometimes the term "Peak Performance" is used to describe the quality of the outcomes that may occur as a result of activities performed in flow.

Psychologist Gayle Privette has clarified the theoretical distinctions described above, and found support for them in the descriptions of experiences of college students. As mentioned above, peak experiences were distinguished by their fulfillment, significance and spirituality. Peak Performance was characterized by the intensity of the focus of the transaction of the self with the environment. Flow was characterized by a sense of play.

BIBLIOGRAPHY

Csikszentmihalyi, M. (1990). *Flow: The Psychology of Optimal Experience*. New York: Harper & Row. A very readable description of the concept of flow, and related research.

Maslow, A. (1968). *Toward A Psychology of Being* (2d ed.). New York: Van Nostrand. Maslow describes the self-actualized person, with several chapters on characteristics of Peak Experiences.

Maslow, A. (1970). *Religions, Values, and Peak-experiences,*. New York: Viking Press. Essays on aspects of Humanistic Theory as described by Maslow. The full text is available free online at several sites, including: http://www.nostrajewellery.org/files/Abraham-H.-Maslow-Religions,-Values-and-Peak-Experiences.pdf.

Privette, G. (2001). "Defining Moments of Self-actualization". In *The Handbook of Humanistic Psychology: Leading Edges In Theory, Research, and Practice*. Thousand Oaks, Calif.: Sage Publications. Privette describes modern research on Maslow's theory, with an emphasis on Peak Experiences.

Susan E. Beers

SEE ALSO: Abraham Maslow; Cognition; Consciousness; Euphoria; Experiences; Pleasure.

Penis envy

TYPE OF PSYCHOLOGY: Developmental psychology; Personality; Psychopathology; Psychotherapy; Social psychology

Penis envy was a concept formulated by Sigmund Freud based on his theory that girls experienced deep envy of boys for their possessing a penis and suffered emotionally from this lack. The theory was the basis of his biological frame of reference. Later analysts included the social environment in their concept of personality development and saw social and cultural conditions as more important in female personality development.

KEY CONCEPTS
- Castration
- Culture
- Masculine protest
- Masochism
- Psychoanalytic treatment
- Psychosexual development

INTRODUCTION

Sigmund Freud , the Austrian founder of psychoanalysis, formulated a theory of psychosexual development. The energy that drove this development was called libido, sexualized energy. This theory was biologically oriented and rested on the assumption that the goal of female development was to achieve what the male possessed, namely a penis. Freud believed that discovering the absence of a penis caused profound emotional injury and became the basis for future personality development in the female.

FREUD'S BIOLOGICAL THEORY

In 1905, in "Three Essays on the Theory of Sexuality," Freud stated that girls notice that boys have penises and, as a result, experience intense feelings of envy and wish to be boys. Later he added that both boys and girls develop a sexual theory in which both originally had a penis, and boys assume that girls originally possessed a penis but lost it through castration. This fear in boys of meeting the same fate leads to the resolution of the Oedipus complex, with the boy relinquishing his sexual feelings toward his mother and identifying with his father. Males then adopt a low opinion of females due to their lack of penises.

This envy that girls experience is supposed to profoundly influence their future personality development in several ways. Overcome by powerful feelings of envy, they feel unfairly treated. According to Freud, anatomy is destiny, in that girls want to possess the male sex organ. First they seize on the idea that the clitoris can serve as a penis substitute. Eventually, they are forced to concede that the clitoris is not an adequate substitute and experience a profound trauma as a result. One of the possible outcomes of this trauma is the development of the masculine protest. Girls may assume masculine personality characteristics or, as adults, may withdraw from sexual experience entirely to avoid powerful feelings of inadequacy.

When girls discover that all females lack a penis, hostility develops toward the mother, who is seen as having deprived them of this sex organ. They then wish for their father to give them either a penis or a baby, which serves as a penis substitute. The discovery of this wish was considered critical by Freud, who viewed it as a sign that bedrock had been reached in psychoanalytic treatment and that termination was at hand.

Another example of the importance that Freud placed on penis envy was his postulating a direct connection between masochism (the sexual pleasure derived from pain) and female personality development. In his attempt to demonstrate this connection, he selected penis envy as the first experience leading to this conclusion.

POST-FREUDIAN ELABORATION

Erik H. Erikson, a pupil of Freud's who emigrated to the United States, combined ego psychology with what he called life-span theory. In this theory, drives or instincts are significant, but the emphasis is on interaction with the significant people in one's own environment. Erikson accepted Freud's formulation that girls experience trauma at discovering their lack of a penis, but he differed from Freud in that he emphasized not abnormal behavior but rather the healthy, adaptive processes in the ego of the girl. He shifted away from the trauma of loss to the healthy ego resources that lead to a woman having a positive view of herself. Anatomy was important to Erikson because it provides a framework for male and female experience, but group membership, history, and individual personality all contribute to female personality development. He felt that while male and female ego processes have much in common, the differences in male and female experience and development should be identified and studied.

Karen Horney, a German-born psychoanalyst who emigrated to the United States, felt that this model was too restrictive and needed to expand to include the role of culture in personality development. She recognized that it was entirely possible that girls experience some feelings of envy due to their lack of a penis. However, she also noticed in her clinical practice that boys also experience envy in relation to girls. She found that boys envied girls' breasts and their ability to produce children when adult.

Horney stated that, in classical psychoanalysis, the libidinal development of women was evaluated from a male perspective, and she questioned whether, since observations are gender influenced, these formulations could be accurate. She emphasized that basing female development on male standards was at best incomplete, since female development includes events not found in male development, such as pregnancy and childbirth.

Horney stated that some penis envy may be entirely normal. Having the opportunity to contact his genitals through urination, the boy may find it easier to satisfy his sexual curiosity; the fact that the boy routinely contacts his genitals may make it more acceptable to take the steps toward masturbation. However, she felt that these feelings of envy in women would ordinarily not lead to feelings of inferiority or the development of the masculine protest. She found that Freud's formulation of the masculine protest was based on his study of neurotic women.

Horney stated that conditions other than penis envy would be necessary for a female to reject her gender. One such condition was if the father rejected his daughter's femaleness. Another condition was if the mother projected such a negative image of the female role that the girl did not wish to identify with that image.

Horney emphasized that culture plays a significant role in female personality development. She felt that girls are often subtly and sometimes harshly made to feel inferior and that due to the masculine nature of the culture, girls may be excluded from occupations and other opportunities, which would contribute to feelings of inferiority. She pointed out that in a culture that demeans women sexually, makes it unacceptable for women to be assertive, and makes it difficult for women to be economically independent, it would be easier for women to feel inferior, not because of a lack of a penis, but because of the prevailing attitudes that culture holds toward women.

BIBLIOGRAPHY

Balsam, Rosemary. "Freud, Females, Childbirth, and Dissidence: Margarete Hilferding, Karen Horney, and Otto Rank." *Psychoanalytic Review* 100.5 (2013): 695–716. Print.

Bayne, Emma. "Womb Envy: The Cause of Misogyny and Even Male Achievement?" *Women's Studies International Forum* 34.2 (2011): 151–60. Print.

Blanton, Smiley. *Diary of My Analysis with Sigmund Freud.* New York: Hawthorn, 1972. Print.

Erikson, Erik H. *Childhood and Society.* Rev. ed. New York: Norton, 1995. Print.

Freud, Sigmund. *The Standard Edition of the Complete Psychological Works of Sigmund Freud.* Ed. James Strachey. 24 vols. London: Hogarth, 1953–74. Print.

Horney, Karen. *Feminine Psychology.* 1967. New York: Norton, 1993. Print.

Monte, Christopher. *Beneath the Mask: An Introduction to Theories of Personality.* 8th ed. Hoboken: Wiley, 2009. Print.

Starr, Karen E., and Lewis Aron. "Women on the Couch: Genital Stimulation and the Birth of Psychoanalysis." *Psychoanalytic Dialogues* 21.4 (2011): 373–92. Print.

Leonard Feinberg

SEE ALSO: Children's mental health; Ego, superego, and id; Freud, Sigmund; Freudian psychology; Gender differences; Oedipus complex; Personality theory; Psychoanalytic psychology; Psychoanalytic psychology and personality: Sigmund

Freud; Psychosexual development; Women's psychology: Karen Horney; Women's psychology: Sigmund Freud; Women's mental health.

Person-centered therapy (PCT)

TYPE OF PSYCHOLOGY: Psychotherapy

Person-centered therapy is based on a philosophy that emphasizes an inherent human tendency for growth and self-actualization. Psychologist Carl R. Rogers developed and described person-centered therapy as a "way of being."

KEY CONCEPTS
- Congruence
- Empathy
- Genuineness
- Self
- Self-actualization
- Unconditional positive regard

INTRODUCTION

Psychologist Carl R. Rogers was the leading figure in the development of phenomenological therapy, and his name has been used synonymously ("Rogerian" therapy) with person-centered therapy (or client-centered therapy). Phenomenological theory is a method of exploration that emphasizes all aspects of human experience. In particular, it highlights the importance of an individual's creative power, in addition to genetics and environment. Moreover, this theory focuses primarily on a person's subjective experience (opinions, viewpoints, and understandings) and defines therapy on the basis of a good human-to-human relationship.

Rogers remained primarily concerned with the conditions for personal growth rather than with the development of personality theory; he focused on personality functioning rather than on personality structures. He did, however, offer formal conceptions of personality. The central concepts and key formulations of person-centered therapy were published in Rogers's *Counseling and Psychotherapy: Newer Concepts in Practice* (1942), *On Becoming a Person* (1961), and his landmark book, *Client-Centered Therapy* (1951). Rogers presented nineteen propositions about personality development. These propositions included the following concepts: Each individual exists in a continually changing world in which he or she is the center. Individuals react to the world as they experience and perceive it; thus, "reality" is defined

by the person's phenomenal field. Behavior is basically the goal-directed attempt of the organism to satisfy its needs as experienced in the phenomenal field. Each individual has a unique perspective—his or her own private world—and to comprehend a person, one must assume a frame of reference from the person's perspective. Emotion facilitates goal-directed behavior. The structure of the self is formed as a result of evaluative interactions with others; the self is an organized, fluid, yet consistent pattern of perceptions about oneself.

The phenomenal field refers to everything experienced by an individual at any given time. The term "internal frame of reference" refers to the process by which therapists attempt to perceive clients' experiences and "reality" as closely as they can. An individual's reality is essentially that which the person perceives. Moreover, it is the person's subjective experience and perceptions that shape the person's understanding of reality and guide behavior. Events are significant for an individual if the individual experiences them as meaningful. In treatment, therapists strive to understand clients by understanding their views of themselves and the environment in which they live.

IMPORTANCE OF SELF

A central concept within phenomenological theory is the "self" (a structure derived from experiences involving one's own body or resulting from one's own actions). The self (or self-concept), then, is a self-picture or self-awareness. It is a changing process that incorporates the individual's meaning when he or she refers to the characteristics of "I" or "me" in isolation or in relationships with others. The concept of self is also considered to be an organized, consistent, and learned attribute composed of thoughts about self. Rogers views the need for positive regard to be universal. The self-concept depends, in large part, on the "conditions of worth" that a child has learned through interactions with significant others. According to Rogers, the child's need to maintain the love of parents inevitably results in conflict with his or her own needs and desires. For example, as young children assert greater autonomy, a growing awareness of individuality and uniqueness follows. Quite often, the young child demonstrates a negativistic pattern wherein conflicts become more common as the child's needs are in conflict with parent desires.

Maladjustment occurs when there is a lack of consistency between one's concept of self and one's sensory and visceral experiences. If the self-concept is based on many conditions of worth and includes components of failure, imperfection, and weakness, then a lack of positive self-regard will be evident. When such incongruence occurs, individuals are viewed as being vulnerable to psychological problems. Of particular importance is self-esteem (feelings about self), which is often negative or problematic in clients. Poor self-esteem occurs when the phenomenal self is threatened. A threat for one person is not necessarily a threat for another. A person will experience threat whenever he or she perceives that the phenomenal self is in danger. For example, if a well-adjusted athlete misses the final shot at the buzzer in a close basketball game, he or she will not blame the referees or claim physical illness, but instead will examine this experience and perhaps revise his or her self-concept.

SELF-DIRECTION, SELF-ACTUALIZATION, AND CONGRUENCE

Other key principles that underlie person-centered theory involve the processes of self-direction and self-actualization. According to Rogers, humans have an innate tendency to maintain and enhance the self. In fact, all needs can be summarized as the urge to enhance the phenomenal self. Although the process of self-actualization may become disrupted by a variety of social, interpersonal, and cultural factors (determined in large part by the actions of parents, teachers, and peers), Rogers states that the positive growth tendency will ultimately prevail. This actualizing tendency is what produces the forward movement of life, the primary force on which therapists rely heavily in therapy with clients. Self-actualization refers to the concept that unhampered individuals strive to actualize, enhance, and reach their full potential. Via self-actualization, a person becomes a fully functioning individual. The qualities of a fully functioning person include being open to experience all feelings while being afraid of none; demonstrating creativity and individual expression; living in the present without preoccupation with past or future; being free to make choices and act on those choices spontaneously; trusting oneself and human nature; having an internal source of evaluation; demonstrating balance and realistic expressions of anger, aggression, and affection; exhibiting congruence between one's feelings and experience; and showing a willingness to continue to grow.

Congruence is the term used by Rogers and others to imply the correspondence between awareness and experience. If a client is able to communicate an awareness of feelings that he or she is currently experiencing, the behavior is said to be congruent or integrated. On the other hand, if an individual attempts to communicate a feeling (love, for example) to another person while experiencing incongruence (hostility toward that person), the recipient of that individual's expression of feelings may experience an awareness of miscommunication.

EVOLUTION OF STUDY

Person-centered theory and therapy have evolved since the 1940s. When Rogers published *Counseling and Psychotherapy,* the predominant view among mental health professionals was that the therapist should act as an expert who directs the course of treatment. Rogers, however, described counseling as a relationship in which warmth, responsiveness, and freedom from coercion and pressure (including pressure from the therapist) are essential. Such an approach to treatment emphasized the client's ability to take positive steps toward personal growth. This phase, from 1940 to 1950, has been called Rogers's nondirective period. The second phase, reflective psychotherapy, spanned the years from 1950 to 1957. During this period, Rogers changed the name of his approach to "client-centered counseling" and emphasized the importance of reflecting (paraphrasing, summarizing, and clarifying) the client's underlying feelings.

The third phase, experiential psychotherapy, has been described as lasting from 1957 to 1970. During this phase, Rogers focused on the conditions that would be necessary and sufficient for change to occur. Results of his studies demonstrated that the most successful clients were those who experienced the highest degree of accurate empathy, and that client ratings, rather than therapist ratings, of the quality of the therapeutic relationship were most closely associated with eventual success or failure. Also evident during this phase of development was Rogers's deemphasis of psychotherapy techniques, such as reflection. Instead, he focused more on the importance of basic therapist attitudes. By so doing, he encouraged a wider range of therapist behaviors to establish the essential relationship components of empathy, positive regard, and congruence. Therapists were encouraged to attend to their own experiences in the session and express their immediate feelings in the therapy relationship.

In 1974, Rogers changed the name of his approach to person-centered therapy. Rogers believed that person-centered therapy more appropriately described the human values that his approach incorporates. Since the 1970s, an additional phase of person-centered therapy, incorporating a more eclectic approach to treatment, has evolved. Specifically, person-centered therapists frequently employ strategies that focus on thoughts, feelings, and values from other schools of psychotherapy within the framework of a productive, accepting relationship. Person-centered approaches have been successfully incorporated into teaching and educational curricula, marriage programs, and international conflict-resolution situations.

THERAPEUTIC RELATIONSHIPS

Person-centered therapy aims to increase the congruence, or matching, between self-concept and organismic experience. As Rogers described it, psychotherapy serves to "free up" the already existing capacity in a potentially competent individual, rather than consisting of the expert manipulation of techniques designed to change personality. The primary mechanism for reintegration of self and experience is the interpersonal relationship between therapist and client. In fact, the therapeutic relationship is viewed as being of primary importance in promoting healing and growth. Thus, it is this relationship in and of itself that produces growth in the client. Rogers argues that the process of therapy is synonymous with the experiential relationship between client and therapist; change occurs primarily as a result of the interaction between them.

As described by N. J. Raskin and Rogers in 1989, the most fundamental concept in person-centered therapy is trust—that is, trust in clients' tendency to grow toward actualization and trust in clients' ability to achieve their goals and run their lives. Similarly, it is important that the therapist be seen as a person in the relationship (not as a role), and that the therapist be appreciated and regarded with trust. Rogers stated that clients enter treatment in a state of incongruence, often resulting in vulnerability and anxiety. For treatment to be effective, he identified three necessary and sufficient ingredients for constructive change: The counselor experiences empathic understanding of the client's internal frame of reference, the counselor experiences unconditional positive regard for the client, and the counselor acts congruently with his or her own experience, becoming genuinely integrated into the relationship with the client. It is also essential to the therapy process that the counselor succeed in communicating unconditional positive regard, genuineness, and empathic understanding to the client.

Of particular importance is empathy. Empathy reflects an attitude of interest in the client's thoughts, feelings, and experiences. Moreover, Rogers describes empathy as "a way of being" that is powerfully curative because of its nonevaluative and accepting quality. In fact, the process of conveying accurate empathic understanding has been described as the most important aspect of the therapeutic endeavor. Therapists who convey this form of sensitivity to the needs, feelings, and circumstances of the client can in essence climb inside the client's subjective experience and attempt to understand the world as he or she does. Empathy facilitates a process through which clients assume a caring attitude toward themselves. Moreover, empathy allows clients to gain a greater understanding of their own organismic experiencing, which in turn facilitates positive self-regard and a more accurate self-concept.

In perhaps all of their previous relationships, clients have learned that acceptance is conditional on acting in an acceptable manner. For example, parents typically accept children if they do as they are told. In therapy, however, Rogers argued that no conditions of worth should be present. Acceptance of the client as a fallible yet essentially trustworthy individual is given without ulterior motives, hidden causes, or subtle disclaimers. The primary challenge of the therapist's unconditional positive regard comes with clients whose behavior and attitude run strongly counter to the therapist's beliefs. A sex offender, an abusive parent, or a lazy client can test a therapist's level of tolerance and acceptance. Rogers's position is that every individual is worthy of unconditional positive regard.

Genuineness refers to the characteristic of being congruent—the experience of therapists who appropriately express the behavior, feelings, and attitudes that the client stimulates in them. For example, a person does not laugh when sad or angry. Similarly, acting congruently with one's own emotional experience does not mean hiding behind a mask of calm when a client makes upsetting statements. Rogers believed that, in the long run, clients would respond best to a "real person" who is dedicated to the client's welfare and acts in an honest and congruent manner.

SEVEN STEPS OF THERAPY

In person-centered treatment, sessions are usually scheduled once or twice a week. Additional sessions and telephone calls are typically discouraged to avoid dependency on the therapist that will stifle personal growth. Rogers has described the general process of therapy as involving a series of seven steps. Step one is an initial unwillingness to reveal self and an avoidance of feelings; close relationships may be perceived as threatening or dangerous. In step two, feelings are described briefly, but the person is still distant from his or her own personal experience and externalizes issues; the person begins to show recognition that conflicts and difficulties exist. In step three, describing past feelings becomes unacceptable; there is more self-disclosure and expression, and the client begins to question the validity of his or her constructs and beliefs.

Step four involves the description of personal feelings as owned by the self and a limited recognition that previously denied feelings may exist; there is an increasing expression of self-responsibility. Step five involves the free expression and acceptance of one's feelings, an awareness of previously denied feelings, a recognition of conflicts between intellectual and emotional processes, and a desire to be who one really is. In step six, there is an acceptance of feelings without the need for denial and a willingness to risk being oneself in relationships with others. In step seven, the person is comfortable with his or her self, is aware of new feelings and experiences, and experiences minimal incongruence.

INFLUENCES

As Rogers began his career during the late 1930s, psychoanalysis was the primary approach to psychotherapy and the dominant model in personality theory. Though Rogers was subjected to traditional psychoanalytic influences, his perspective was nearly the exact opposite of Sigmund Freud's theory; Rogers tended to reject the notion of unconscious processes. Instead, he was strongly influenced by the therapeutic approach of psychoanalyst Otto Rank (and his followers at the University of Pennsylvania School of Social Work), the relationship therapy of social worker Jessie Taft, and the feeling-focused approach of social worker Elizabeth Davis. Rank believed that clients benefit from the opportunity to express themselves in session, exhibit creativity in treatment, and even dominate the therapist. Taft emphasized that there are key components to the therapeutic relationship (including a permissive therapeutic environment and a positive working relationship between the therapist and client) that are more important than psychoanalytic explanations of the client's problems. Davis focused almost exclusively on the feelings being expressed in treatment by her clients. From his association with Davis, Rogers developed the therapy component referred to as reflection of feelings. Rogers believed strongly that no individual has the right to run another person's life. Thus, his therapeutic approach was generally permissive and accepting, and he generally refused to give advice to clients.

CONTRIBUTIONS TO PSYCHOLOGY

Person-centered approaches have made major contributions to therapy, theory, and empirical research. In fact, Rogers was responsible for the first systematic investigations of the therapeutic process. He was the first to employ recordings of therapy sessions to study the interactive process and to investigate its effectiveness. Although the use of such recordings is now commonplace in most training programs, Rogers's willingness to open his approach to such scrutiny was unusual for its time.

Person-centered therapy has generated numerous research contributions. A 1971 review of research on "necessary and sufficient" conditions concluded that counselors who are accurately empathic, genuine, and nonpossessively warm tend to be effective with a broad spectrum of clients regardless of the counselors' training or theoretical orientation. The authors also concluded that clients receiving low levels of such conditions in treatment showed deterioration. Many researchers have questioned the "necessary and sufficient" argument proposed by Rogers, however; they suggest that the therapeutic conditions specified by Rogers are neither necessary nor sufficient, although such therapeutic approaches are facilitative.

Although Rogers's approach was developed primarily for counseling clients, the person-centered approach has found many other applications. Person-centered approaches are frequently used in human relations training, including paraprofessional counselors, YWCA-YMCA volunteers, crisis center volunteers, Peace Corps and VISTA workers, and charitable organization workers. Small group therapy programs and personal growth groups also make frequent use of person-centered approaches.

BIBLIOGRAPHY

Bazzano, Manu. "One More Step: From Person-Centered to Eco-Centered Therapy." *Person-Centered & Experiential Psychotherapies* 12.4 (2013): 344–54. Print.

Joseph, Stephen, and David Murphy. "Person-Centered Approach, Positive Psychology, and Relational Helping: Building Bridges." *Journ. of Humanistic Psychology* 53.1 (2013): 26–51. Print.

Kirschenbaum, Howard. *Life and Work of Carl Rogers*. Alexandria: American Counseling Association, 2009. Print.

Prouty, Gary. *Theoretical Evolutions in Person-Centered/ Existential Therapy*. Westport: Praeger, 1994. Print.

Raskin, N. J., and Carl R. Rogers. "Person-Centered Therapy." *Current Psychotherapies*. Ed. Raymond J. Corsini and Danny Wedding. 4th ed. Itasca: Peacock, 1989. Print.

Rogers, Carl R. *Client-Centered Therapy*. 1951. Reprint. Boston: Houghton, 1965. Print.

Rogers, Carl R. *Counseling and Psychotherapy: Newer Concepts in Practice*. 1942. Reprint. Boston: Houghton, 1960. Print.

Rogers, Carl R. *On Becoming a Person*. Boston: Houghton, 1995. Print.

Rogers, Carl R. *A Way of Being*. Boston: Houghton, 1995. Print.

Smyth, David. *Person-Centered Therapy with Children and Young People: A Child-Centered Approach*. London: Sage, 2013. Print.

Thorne, Brian. *Carl Rogers*. 2d ed. Thousand Oaks: Sage, 2003. Print.

Thorne, Brian, and Elke Lambers, eds. *Person-Centered Therapy: A European Perspective*. Thousand Oaks: Sage, 1998. Print.

Gregory L. Wilson

SEE ALSO: Abnormality: Psychological models; Allport, Gordon; Existential psychology; Gestalt therapy; Humanistic psychology; Humanistic trait models: Gordon Allport; Psychotherapy: Effectiveness; Psychotherapy: Goals and techniques; Rogers, Carl R.; Self-actualization.

Personal constructs
George A. Kelly

TYPE OF PSYCHOLOGY: Personality

Personal construct theory examines the way each person thinks about the world; it attempts to provide avenues for understanding and making use of one's subjective experiences. It demonstrates how cognitions change when one incorrectly predicts the future on the basis of those cognitions.

KEY CONCEPTS
- Construct
- Constructive alternativism
- Dichotomy
- Fixed role therapy
- Fundamental postulate
- Role
- Role Construct Repertory Test

INTRODUCTION

Personal construct theory maintains that all people are motivated to reduce uncertainty in their lives. In this manner, each person is like a scientist who is attempting to solve complex problems. Instead of dealing with complex equations in chemistry and physics, however, people are attempting to unravel the complexities of their own lives and the relationships that they have developed. Just as scientists are constantly making changes in their theories and research claims based on the availability of new evidence, people change the way they look at their subjective worlds on the basis of new evidence. That evidence appears in the form of new interactions with significant others in people's lives, such as spouses, children, parents, and bosses. When new evidence is made available, people will alter their thought patterns to reduce uncertainty in the future. This view forms the basis of George Kelly's principle of constructive alternativism—the view that people are entitled to their own views of the world and that they will make use of those views to reduce uncertainty in the future.

Kelly became involved in personal constructs theory late in his career. Ironically, Kelly's early experiences as a psychologist did not even involve the study of personality. It was only in 1955, twelve years before his death, that he published *The Psychology of Personal Constructs: A Theory of Personality*. In this work, he defined and discussed the concept of a construct. For Kelly, a construct is a thought that a person has for the purpose of attempting to interpret events; these interpretations may prove to be accurate or inaccurate. In those situations in which a construct leads to an incorrect prediction of an event, the person is likely to change the construct. All of Kelly's constructs are dichotomous in nature. That is, they are made of pairs of polar opposites that cannot be simultaneously correct when referring to the same person. For example, one cannot view one's boss as both intelligent and unintelligent at the same time. Similarly, one's boyfriend or girlfriend cannot be seen as cruel and kind at the same moment.

FUNDAMENTAL POSTULATE AND COROLLARIES

Kelly claimed that constructs operate according to a fundamental postulate. This postulate maintains that each person directs thoughts and cognitions in a way that permits the most accurate prediction of future events. If a woman has a personal construct which states that her boyfriend is a thoughtful person, and he sends her flowers while she is in bed with the flu, her construct would be regarded as an accurate one. If, however, that same boyfriend used her illness as an opportunity to date other women and ignored her illness in the process, it would be necessary to adjust her construction system because it does not accurately predict her boyfriend's behavior. This process of changing one's construction system to predict future events more accurately is an ongoing one designed to decrease uncertainty in the future.

Although the fundamental postulate is critical to Kelly's attempts to predict and explain behavior, it is not sufficient to cover all aspects of a person's behavior and the choices that are made which cause that behavior. To address this additional detail, Kelly provided a series of eleven corollaries to his fundamental postulate. These corollaries are supporting statements that provide a detailed analysis of thoughts and behaviors that cannot be directly derived from the fundamental postulate.

The construction corollary maintains that people continue to learn as they are presented with similar events in life. For example, if a man's mother has given him a birthday present for the last thirty years, his prediction that he will receive another present from her on his next birthday makes sense. Similarly, if a person has watched a particular television program such as *Nightline* at 11:30 p.m. on weekdays for the past several years, that individual can reasonably predict that it will again be on television at the same time tonight.

Another important corollary to Kelly's fundamental postulate is the dichotomy corollary. This states that all constructs consist of pairs of opposites. That is, a college course may be either interesting or uninteresting, but it cannot be both at the same time. One important aspect of the dichotomy corollary is that each construct must include three members or items, with two of the members having the same characteristic and the third member having the opposite characteristic. For example, breathing and not breathing would not be a legitimate construct in evaluating three friends. Because all of them breathe, the proposed construct would not tell how the three individuals are different as well as alike. Therefore, it would not reduce uncertainty in the future.

A third corollary to Kelly's system that is particularly important is the range corollary. This maintains that a construct is only relevant in dealing with a finite number of events. The events for which a construct is deemed applicable is called its range of convenience. Terms such as "happy" and "sad" would not be within the range of convenience in depicting the characteristics of a tree or a book, while they might be critical in evaluating one's relatives.

Varying degrees of applicability can be found within a series of constructs. For example, the construct "kind versus cruel" would be more relevant in evaluating a relative or girlfriend than it would be in considering the qualities of an elevator operator one occasionally encounters. Kelly's fundamental postulate and supporting corollaries provide considerable information. The theory also provides some interesting applications in terms of personality assessment and therapeutic intervention.

USE WITH CAREER GOALS

Kelly's personal construct theory has been used to explain, predict, and attempt to modify behavior in a wide range of circumstances. One interesting application involves the use of personal constructs in formulating career goals. A high school student, for example, may establish a goal of becoming a successful surgeon in the future. The nature of her constructs can then be examined to determine whether her constructs (as they relate to her own characteristics) are likely to lead to a medical career. She currently views herself as unintelligent rather than intelligent, dedicated to immediate gratification rather than delayed gratification, and lazy rather than hardworking. If she is eventually to become a successful physician, she must reject those constructs and develop a new construction system that is consistent with her career goals. The application of Kelly's theory to career choice is important. Although no one expects first-grade children to examine their own characteristics realistically in considering career options, much more is required of high school and college students. It is not sufficient for people to state that they want to pursue a given career: The nature of their constructs must be evaluated to determine if they are consistent with their career goals. In those circumstances in which inconsistencies exist, either the constructs or the career goals must change.

ROLE CONSTRUCT REPERTORY TEST

One of the most interesting applications of Kelly's personal construct theory involves the development of an assessment device, the Role Construct Repertory Test.

This test defines a role as a set of behaviors that are performed by a person in response to the construction systems and behaviors of others. The test itself determines the nature of a person's system of constructs as it is related to the significant others in that person's life. The test can be used as a means of evaluating progress during psychotherapy or as a vehicle for detecting changes in interpersonal relationships.

The test involves the creation of a grid in which significant others in the life of the person are listed. Examples would be self, mother, spouse, boss, friend, and successful person. The client then considers these individuals in groups of three provided by the therapist. The client comes up with a word that typifies two of these individuals and a second word that is the opposite of the first word but typifies the third person. This procedure is followed for a group of twenty sorts, or sets of comparisons. This enables the therapist to determine the behaviors and thoughts of the client concerning the significant others in her life.

One of the determinations that can be made involves the flexibility of the client in dealing with others. That is, in listing those individuals on the grid who possess certain positive characteristics, the therapist would examine whether the same individuals on the grid are given credit for all the positive characteristics listed while a second group is always viewed negatively. This would indicate a lack of flexibility in the client and might offer an area for needed change in the future.

FIXED ROLE THERAPY

As an application of Kelly's theory, the Role Construct Repertory Test is an initial step in the therapeutic process. An interesting follow-up provided by Kelly is fixed role therapy. This technique begins by asking the client to develop an in-depth description of himself or herself, written in the third person. This is called a self-characterization sketch. The third-person style is used to produce greater objectivity than would be achieved with first-person narratives. This gives the therapist a clear look at the client from the client's own perspective. The therapist then establishes a role for the client that is directly opposite many of the characteristics in the self-characterization sketch. The client is asked to act out that new role for a period of time. The role would include positive characteristics not found in the self-characterization sketch. The ultimate goal of the technique is to have the client maintain many of those new positive characteristics on a long-term basis.

In evaluating applications of Kelly's work, the emphasis must be placed on the importance of knowing one's own construction system and, when appropriate, taking steps to change that system. Although this may be handled through formal techniques such as fixed role therapy, many therapists make use of Kelly's emphasis on cognitive change without strictly employing his terminology. To this extent, the influence of Kelly's work should increase in the future.

KELLY'S CAREER

Kelly did not begin his career with the intention of developing personal construct theory. In fact, his initial training was not even in the field of personality psychology. Kelly's original specialty in graduate school was physiological psychology, and his dissertation was concerned with the areas of speech and reading disabilities. Having received his degree around the time of the Great Depression, however, Kelly came to the conclusion that the principles and concepts contained within his areas of specialization offered little solace to those who were emotionally and financially devastated in the aftermath of the Depression. He turned to clinical psychology, with an initial emphasis on the psychoanalytic approach. He noted that concepts such as the id and the libido seemed of no use in dealing with victims of the Depression.

Kelly's initial academic position was at Fort Hays State College in Kansas. While at Fort Hays, he developed a series of traveling psychological clinics designed to treat the emotional and behavioral problems of students. This experience was crucial in the eventual formulation of personal construct theory. Kelly tried numerous forms of treatment with the students and determined that the optimal technique varied across cases. This led him to conclude that any clinical technique that is successful should be retained, while techniques that result in repeated treatment failure should be discarded. This flexibility, reflected in his later theoretical claims regarding constructive alternativism and his fundamental postulate, has made Kelly unique among personality theorists. Kelly's willingness to respect subjective reality as determined by each human being is reflective of his unwillingness to commit himself totally to any one theoretical perspective. Although Kelly was influenced by many theorists, he clearly traveled his own path in the development of his psychology of personal constructs.

BIBLIOGRAPHY

Bannister, Donald, and Fay Fransella. *Inquiring Man: The Theory of Personal Constructs.* 3d ed. New York: Routledge, 1993. Print.

Bannister, Donald, and J. M. M. Mair, eds. *The Evaluation of Personal Constructs.* New York: Academic, 1976. Print.

Burnham, Simon. *Let's Talk: Using Personal Construct Psychology to Support Children and Young People.* Los Angeles: Sage, 2008. Print.

Butt, Trevor. George Kelly: *The Psychology of Personal Constructs.* New York: Macmillan, 2008. Print.

Caputi, Peter, Linda L. Viney, Beverly M. Walker, and Nadia Crittenden. *Personal Construct Methodology.* Malden: Wiley, 2012. Print.

Cortina, Jose M., and Ronald S. Landis. Modern *Research Methods for the Study of Behavior in Organizations.* New York: Routledge, 2013. Print.

Duck, Steve, and David T. McMahan. *The Basics of Communication: A Relational Perspective.* Thousand Oaks: Sage, 2009. Print.

Kelly, George Alexander. *Clinical Psychology and Personality: The Selected Papers of George Kelly.* Ed. Brendan Maher. New York: Wiley, 1979. Print.

Kelly, George Alexander. *The Psychology of Personal Constructs: A Theory of Personality.* New York: Norton, 1955. Print.

Neimeyer, Robert A. *The Development of Personal Construct Psychology.* Lincoln: U of Nebraska P, 1985. Print.

Lawrence A. Fehr

SEE ALSO: Abnormality: Psychological models; Cognitive psychology; Cognitive social learning: Walter Mischel; Cognitive therapy; Kelly, George A.; Mischel, Walter; Personality theory; Social perception.

Personality disorders

TYPE OF PSYCHOLOGY: Psychopathology

The personality disorders are a cluster of psychological disorders characterized by inflexible and longstanding patterns of relating to others and the environment that create significant impairment in functioning.

KEY CONCEPTS
- Antisocial personality disorder
- Avoidant personality disorder
- Borderline personality disorder
- Dependent personality disorder
- Histrionic personality disorder
- Narcissistic personality disorder
- Paranoid personality disorder
- Personality
- Obsessive-compulsive disorder
- Schizoid personality disorder
- Schizotypal personality disorder

INTRODUCTION

Personality is a term used to describe long-standing patterns of thinking, behaving, and feeling. A group of traits that are consistently displayed are considered to be part of a person's personality. A person's mood, for example, is considered to be a more fleeting expression of one's overall personality. Personality comprises traits, attitudes, behaviors, and coping styles that develop throughout childhood and adolescence. Personality can be thought of as a relatively consistent style of relating to others and the environment, developing as a result of genetic and environmental influences. Psychologists have developed several theories to explain personality development. Austrian psychoanalyst Sigmund Freud believed that personality development originates in early childhood. Freud proposed that personality emerges as a result of unconscious conflicts between unacceptable aggressive and hedonistic instincts and societal mores. According to Freudian psychology, unresolved unconscious conflicts from childhood later influence personality development. In contrast to Freud's psychoanalytic theories about personality, other researchers focused on specific traits as the building blocks of personality development. Many classification systems have been developed in an attempt to organize and categorize personality traits and styles. The Big Five system proposes that five basic trait dimensions underlie personality structure: extroversion versus introversion, agreeableness versus disagreeableness, conscientiousness versus impulsiveness, emotional stability versus neuroticism, and openness to experience versus rigidity. Personality disorders may reflect extreme variants of these basic personality dimensions.

The personality disorders are a group of psychological disorders characterized by inflexible and maladaptive patterns of relating to others that result in impairments in day-to-day functioning. The personality disorders are reflected by personality traits that are significantly extreme or exaggerated, making it difficult to establish functional relationships with others. According to the *Diagnostic and Statistical Manual of Mental Disorders* (DSM-5) of the American Psychiatric Association, the personality disorders are defined by an enduring pattern of inner experience and behavior that is consistently dysfunctional and creates impairment in functioning. Symptoms of personality disorders are usually evident by early adulthood, coinciding with the developmental period when personality patterns have become established in most people. The DSM-5 identifies the following major personality disorders: paranoid personality disorder, schizoid personality disorder, schizotypal personality disorder, borderline personality disorder, antisocial personality disorder, narcissistic personality disorder, histrionic personality disorder, avoidant personality disorder, dependent personality disorder, and obsessive-compulsive personality disorder. The personality disorders are broken down into three groups, or clusters, based on similar symptomatology.

CLUSTER A

The personality disorders in Cluster A consist of paranoid personality disorder, schizoid personality disorder, and schizotypal personality disorder. The behavior of people with a cluster A personality disorder is described as odd or eccentric.

Paranoid personality disorder is characterized by a pervasive distrust of others, chronic suspicion about others' motives, and paranoid thinking. Others often avoid individuals with paranoid personality disorder, which reinforces their mistrust of others. The suspicion is chronic and creates a difficulty in establishing and maintaining interpersonal relationships. Paranoid personality disorder is more prevalent in males than females.

Schizoid personality disorder (SPD) is characterized by a pervasive and long-lasting indifference toward others. The term "schizoid" was initially chosen to refer to the preliminary symptoms or latent symptoms of schizophrenia; whether there is a genuine relationship between schizoid personality disorder and schizophrenia is uncertain, however. A person with SPD has little or no interest in interacting with others and is viewed as a loner. People with SPD have little interest in sexual or emotional intimacy and tend to display a limited range of emotions. These individuals often are dull and lack a sense of humor. They may be unable to experience normal pleasures and may be indifferent to praise or criticism. They

are perceived by others as being aloof or apathetic and may appear disheveled or unkempt. It is more often diagnosed in men than in women, but whether this represents a true gender difference is debatable.

Schizotypal personality disorder is characterized by peculiar patterns of behaving and thinking. People with this disorder may express superstitious beliefs or may engage in fantasy-based thinking. Although their thought processes might be unusual, their beliefs are not considered to be of delusional proportions. Because the symptoms of cluster A personality disorders resemble symptoms of schizophrenia, researchers believe these disorders may be genetically related to schizophrenia.

CLUSTER B

The personality disorders of cluster B are borderline personality disorder, antisocial personality disorder, narcissistic personality disorder, and histrionic personality disorder. The cluster B personality disorders are described as dramatic, erratic, and emotional. The behavior of people with such a disorder creates significant impairment in establishing and maintaining interpersonal relationships.

Borderline personality disorder (BPD) is the most prevalent personality disorder. It is characterized by a long-standing and inflexible pattern of emotional instability and unstable personal relationships. Individuals with BPD have an intense fear of abandonment and tend to form intense and unstable relationships with others. They tend to fluctuate between having positive and negative feelings about significant people in their lives. This behavior is referred to as "splitting" and may contribute to the emotional instability displayed by these people. People with BPD often engage in self-destructive behavior, such as self-mutilation, suicidal acts, or drug abuse. Those with BPD report chronic feelings of emptiness. A 2011 literature review by Randy and Lori Sansone indicates that while women have historically been diagnosed with BPD more often, this has often been the result of confusion with other, coexisting psychiatric conditions in men, and that the prevalence of BPD is in fact equal in both sexes.

Antisocial personality disorder (ASPD) is exemplified by an enduring pattern of behavior that disregards and violates the rights of others. The term "antisocial" refers to behaviors that are antisociety. ASPD is often preceded by conduct disorder in the early adolescent stages of development. Many people with ASPD often appear initially to be charming and intelligent, yet they are also manipulative and grandiose. They lack a moral code that would disallow unacceptable or hurtful behaviors. Therefore, an individual with ASPD is likely to engage in criminal acts, manipulative behavior, and the exploitation of others.

Freud coined the term "narcissistic personality disorder" in reference to the Greek myth of Narcissus, who fell in love with his own reflection in a pool of water, preventing him from forming relationships with others. The essential feature of narcissistic personality disorder (NPD) is an exaggerated sense of self-importance. This disorder is characterized by a need to be the center of attention and a preoccupation with fantasies of one's success or power. A person with NPD has difficulty understanding the feelings of others and constantly demands attention. These grandiose behaviors typically mask feelings of insecurity.

Symptoms of histrionic personality disorder (HPD) include excessive emotionality and attention-seeking behavior. A person with HPD is overly dramatic and emotional and is inappropriately seductive to gain the attention of others. Although HPD has traditionally been diagnosed as a disorder of women, clinical researchers have typically reported only a slight female predominance or, in some cases, approximately equal prevalence in both sexes.

CLUSTER C

Cluster C disorders include avoidant personality disorder, dependent personality disorder, and obsessive-compulsive personality disorder. The behavior of people with a cluster C personality disorder is described as anxious or fearful.

People with avoidant personality disorder (AvPD) display a pervasive pattern of social discomfort and a fear of being disliked by others. Because of these feelings, a person with this disorder avoids social interactions with others. People with AvPD are extremely shy and have great difficulty establishing interpersonal relationships. They want to be liked by others, but their social discomfort and insecurities prevent them from engaging in interpersonal relationships with others.

Dependent personality disorder is characterized by a chronic pattern of dependent and needy behavior, with an intense fear of being alone. People with this disorder attempt to please other people to avoid potential abandonment. They may say certain things just to be liked by others. They have difficulty making their own decisions

and are submissive with others. Individuals with this disorder have difficulty separating from others.

Obsessive-compulsive personality disorder is characterized by an inflexible and enduring need for control and order. People who suffer from obsessive-compulsive personality disorder are so preoccupied with order and organization that they may lose sight of the main objective of an activity. People with this disorder are usually excessively work-oriented and have little patience for leisure time. They are intolerant of indecisiveness or emotionality in others and favor intellect over affect. People with this disorder are perceived as difficult to get along with and unwilling to be a team player. Obsessive-compulsive personality disorder is different from obsessive-compulsive disorder (OCD), which is categorized as an anxiety disorder and involves obsessive thoughts and compulsive behaviors.

DIAGNOSIS

A number of issues have created debate related to the difficulty in and reliability of the diagnosis of personality disorders. The distinction between "normal" personality characteristics and a personality disorder is not necessarily clear in the clinical definition of a personality disorder. The DSM notes that when personality traits are inflexible and create significant distress or impairment in functioning they constitute a personality disorder. New to the fifth edition, the DSM includes two approaches to diagnosis: the convention method based on existing models of personality disorders and an alternative, hybrid model that identifies the individual's specific trait impairments and their severity. Some argue that there is considerable room for debate about the point at which a trait is considered to create impairment.

The personality disorders have been the subject of criticism by researchers because of the difficulty in diagnosing them reliably. Individuals with a personality disorder often display symptoms of other personality disorders. For example, researchers have debated about the distinction between schizoid personality disorder and avoidant personality disorder, as both disorders are characterized by an extreme in social isolation. Individuals with personality disorders are more likely than the general population to suffer from other psychological disorders, such as depression, bulimia, or substance abuse. This overlap of symptoms may lead to difficulty with diagnostic reliability. The personality disorders occur so frequently with other types of psychological disorders that it is challenging to sort through symptoms to determine what is evidence of each disorder. It is difficult to estimate the prevalence of personality disorders in the United States, as individuals with these disorders do not recognize that they are dysfunctional and are therefore less likely to seek treatment for their disorder. A 2007 study by M. F. Lenzenweger et al. estimated that 9.1 percent of the US adult population had a personality disorder in the preceding twelve-month period and that only 39 percent of those were receiving treatment.

Researchers have explored the problem of gender bias in the diagnosis of personality disorders. It is believed that some of the symptoms of certain personality disorders are more characteristic of one gender than the other. For example, the aggression and hostility associated with antisocial personality disorder may be traits associated more frequently with the average male population, thus affecting the diagnosis among men compared with women. This supposed gender bias is theorized to be related to the greater prevalence of borderline personality disorder and histrionic personality disorder among women compared with men. Perhaps some of the diagnostic symptoms of this disorder, such as emotionality or fears of abandonment, are simply behaviors more characteristic of the female population than the male population.

CAUSES

Various theories have been developed to explain the etiology of personality disorders. The biological perspective examines the roles of genetics and brain functioning in the development of personality disorders. Evidence suggests that the cluster A disorders (paranoid, schizoid, and schizotypal personality disorders) are more prevalent among first-degree relatives of individuals suffering from schizophrenia, suggesting a possible genetic commonality among those disorders.

The underlying symptoms of borderline personality disorder (impulsivity and emotionality) are inherited. Much research confirms that borderline patients are more likely to report a childhood family history that included sexual abuse, domestic violence, and the early loss (either through death or abandonment) of a parental figure. It is believed that this history may be related to the later development of borderline personality disorder. According to developmental theorist Erik H. Erikson, a sense of basic trust during childhood is an essential component of normal personality development. Erikson stated that a basic sense of trust or mistrust in the self and the world develops in the first year of life.

The experience of being abandoned by a parent, then, would foster a sense of mistrust in the world and would affect personality development. In the 1950s, University of Wisconsin psychologist Harry Harlow explored the effects of attachment on later personality development. Harlow concluded that rhesus monkeys who were separated from their mothers shortly after birth displayed abnormal behaviors later in life, such as unusual fear or aggression, difficulty engaging in mating behaviors, and difficulty with parenting their offspring. Maternally deprived animals, therefore, were more likely to display dysfunction, as is seen in individuals with disorders associated with maternal deprivation, such as borderline and antisocial personality disorders.

Genetic factors may be influential in the development of ASPD, as children of biological parents who engage in criminal behavior are more likely to engage in criminal behavior themselves. Learning theorists propose that antisocial behaviors may be learned by mimicking parents with similar behaviors. Individuals with ASPD have displayed an abnormally low arousal level, which might enable them to ignore physiological cues that indicate danger or punishment. Research has also suggested that the unusually low level of arousal may cause the individual with ASPD to engage in behaviors that increase physiological arousal, or create a "rush."

TREATMENT

Treatment of a personality disorder is difficult because of certain key issues related to these disorders. People with personality disorders tend to lack insight about their dysfunctional ways of interacting with others. Because they do not see themselves as having a problem, they are unlikely to pursue treatment. When a person with a personality disorder does seek treatment, it is usually for some secondary issue, such as alcoholism or depression. People suffering from personality disorders tend to end therapy prematurely because of their perception that their behavior is not the source of problems. One of the central features of the personality disorders is an impaired ability to maintain relationships with others; therefore, developing a relationship with a therapist is difficult. When the opportunity for treatment does arise, treatment approaches differ depending on the unique characteristics of each of the personality disorders.

The treatment of BPD has received much research attention. American psychologist Marsha M. Linehan is credited with the development of dialectical behavioral therapy (DBT), a treatment approach for borderline personality disorder that integrates cognitive, behavioral, and Zen principles to help the patient to develop essential coping skills. One of the basic tenets of DBT is that individuals with borderline personality disorder may react abnormally to a normal stimulus (such as an interaction with another person) because of negative or traumatic past experiences (such as sexual abuse). Such individuals may quickly display an increase in emotion and may take a longer period of time to reduce their emotional arousal. Treatment focuses on decreasing self-destructive behaviors and helping individuals to regulate their emotions.

People with ASPD who participate in treatment usually are made to do so by the legal system. Efficacy of treatment interventions for the person with ASPD is often measured in terms of the number of crimes committed by the person after treatment, rather than by any significant change in personality characteristics. Treating any substance abuse issues is an integral component of treatment of ASPD. Some believe that prevention is the most important part of managing antisocial behavior.

Researchers have found that low levels of antipsychotic medications are effective in alleviating some symptoms of schizotypal personality disorder. Several studies suggest that antipsychotic medications such as haloperidol may decrease symptoms of depression and impulsivity in the schizotypal individual. People with NPD are more apt than those with other personality disorders to seek out treatment, using the therapist's office as yet another stage to be the center of attention.

BIBLIOGRAPHY

Claridge, Gordon. *Origins of Mental Illness*. 2nd ed. Cambridge: Malor, 1996. Print.

Dobbert, Duane L. *Understanding Personality Disorders: An Introduction*. Lanham: Rowman, 2010. Print.

Dumont, Frank. *A History of Personality Psychology: Theory, Science, and Research from Hellenism to the Twenty-First Century*. Cambridge: Cambridge UP, 2010. Print.

Erikson, Erik H. *Identity: Youth and Crisis*. New York: Norton, 1994. Print.

Linehan, Marsha M. *Cognitive-Behavioral Treatment of Borderline Personality Disorder*. New York: Guilford, 1993. Print.

Livesley, W. John, Marsha L. Schroeder, Douglas N. Jackson, and Kerry L. Jang. "Categorical Distinctions in the Study of Personality Disorder—Implications for Classification." *Journal of Abnormal Psychology* 103.1 (1994): 6–17. Print.

Maxmen, Jerrold S., Mark Kilgus, and Nicholas G. Ward. *Essential Psychopathology and Its Treatment*. 3rd ed. New York: Norton, 2009. Print.

Nathan, Peter E., Jack M. Gorman, and Neil J. Salkind. *Treating Mental Disorders: A Guide to What Works*. New York: Oxford UP, 2000. Print.

Paris, Joel. "A Diathesis-Stress Model of Personality Disorders." *Psychiatric Annals* 29.12 (1999): 692–97. Print.

"Personality Disorders." *Mayo Clinic*. Mayo Foundation for Medical Education and Research, 31 Jan. 2014. Web. 2 July 2014.

Sarkar, Jaydip, and Gwen Adshead. *Clinical Topics in Personality Disorder*. London: Royal College of Psychiatrists, 2012. Print.

Sellborn, Martin. "Personality Disorders in the DSM-5 and Beyond." *Gavel*. APA Division 18: Psychologists in Public Service, July 2013. Web. 19 Feb. 2014.

Widiger, Thomas A. *The Oxford Handbook of Personality Disorders*. Oxford: Oxford UP, 2012. Print.

Widiger, Thomas A., and Paul T. Costa. "Personality and Personality Disorders." *Journal of Abnormal Psychology* 103.1 (1994): 78–91. Print.

Janine T. Ogden

SEE ALSO: Antisocial personality disorder; Borderline personality disorder; Conduct disorder; Histrionic personality disorder; Narcissistic personality disorder; Obsessive-compulsive disorder; Paranoia; Schizoid personality disorder; Schizophrenia: Background, types, and symptoms; Schizotypal personality disorder.

Personality interviewing strategies

TYPE OF PSYCHOLOGY: Personality

Various approaches to interviewing are used to determine a person's personality; interviewing is valuable to assess both healthy and unhealthy personalities.

KEY CONCEPTS
- Objectivity
- Reliability
- Resistance
- Theoretical orientation
- Validity

INTRODUCTION

The assessment of personality is an activity that occurs frequently and can be very important. On an informal level, people make decisions about someone's personality based on their experiences with that person. If they have had positive experiences, they might say the person has a "nice personality." Although these informal assessments have significant implications for friendships among people, more formal personality assessments may have a far-reaching impact on a person's life. Formal personality assessments are commonly used in making employment decisions and decisions about the status of people's mental health. Interview strategies used to assess personality usually are seen as either structured or unstructured. Interview questions are influenced by the theoretical orientation of the interviewer.

Fred Kerlinger's discussion of the use of interviews in *Foundations of Behavioral Research* (1986) goes beyond using interviews to assess personality. In personality research, the interview is used to obtain information about the person's thoughts, beliefs, behavior, and feelings to determine how they combine into what is called personality, as well as how they are influenced by or influence other life events. From the research perspective, the personality interview is an in-depth study of all facets of a person's psychological and behavioral makeup.

STRUCTURED AND UNSTRUCTURED INTERVIEWS

Personality interviews may be placed on a continuum from highly structured at one extreme to highly unstructured at the other. In actuality, few interviews occupy extreme positions. Most interviews are designed to elicit as much useful information as possible from the person being interviewed. Therefore, there is a propensity to prefer one style over the other, although there is no rigid adherence to this tendency. Both structured and unstructured (or standardized and unstandardized) interviews are used in psychology to assess a number of things, including personality. As an approach to assessment, personality interview strategies must conform to expectations of reliability (the quality of delivering the same basic results after each of several interview sessions), validity (the quality of assessing the content that the interviewer intends to assess), and objectivity (the quality of being free of bias or prejudice).

Structured interviews are designed to obtain specific information about the person being interviewed. In the most highly structured type of interview, a list of questions is presented in its entirety to every person completing the interview. The questions are always presented in the same way and in the same order. The interviewer is not allowed the flexibility to pursue topics of interest; however, the structured interview is actually conducted with somewhat more flexibility in most applied settings. The interviewer is given a list of topics about which information is desired. In gathering the information, the interviewer is free to vary the order of the topics and is able to request elaboration of specific points as needed. This flexibility increases the likelihood that the desired information will be obtained, because the interviewer can vary the order of the interview to put the interviewee at ease while still covering all topics. Structured interviews are sometimes called "standardized interviews" because the interview topics and procedures are established in advance. Another name for the structured interview is the "directive interview" because the interviewee is directed into areas that interest the interviewer.

Unlike structured interviews, unstructured interviews, also called "nondirective" or "unstandardized" interviews, place control of the interview with the interviewee. Instead of asking "How many people are in your family?," for example, interviewers using unstructured approaches use open-ended questions such as "Tell me about your family." By using the open-ended question, the interviewer has the opportunity to learn more about the person's family than with the structured interview. The unstructured interview may produce considerable information yet does not ensure that all topics are covered, as in the structured interview.

Regardless of the type of interview used, the interviewer is charged with observing and interpreting interviewee behavior. Changes in body posture, eye contact, and length of time between question and response are all suggestive of different emotional reactions to the interview. It is up to the interviewer to determine the accuracy of what is being reported by looking for patterns of consistency and inconsistency in the person's behavior. Some determination must be made about whether the person is trying to minimize certain facets of his or her personality to save face or, conversely, is exaggerating facets for their inherent shock value. It is important for the interviewer to test various hypotheses about why the interviewee answers in a certain way if an accurate assessment of personality is to take place.

OBSTACLES

A number of common obstacles must be overcome in an interview. One of these is resistance, or the interviewee's reluctance to talk about certain topics, perhaps because the topics are too painful or embarrassing. Resistance may be overcome by allowing the interviewee time to become more comfortable with the interviewer and time to broach the difficult topics in his or her own way. Other complications of the interview are interruptions from other people, distracting settings, and the interviewer's emotional reactions to the person being interviewed.

Another approach to personality interviewing is the use of a computer-administered interview. When a computer is used to administer the interview, a branching program is used. Answering "yes" or "no" to a question may lead to additional questions on that topic or to entirely new topics. Some people have found that computerized interviewing leads to more complete answers. This may be especially true when the subject matter is intimate and potentially embarrassing.

USE IN CLINICAL SETTINGS

Typically, personality interviews are used in clinical settings or to make employment decisions; they are usually used in conjunction with formal psychological testing. Occasionally, they are used for research purposes; however, the training necessary to develop a skilled interviewer and the expense involved in the interview process usually limit the settings in which they are used to those where they are particularly significant.

In clinical settings, interviews are used for two reasons. First, they are used to gather information about the client or patient's life and about the reason the person is seeking services. Second, the interview is the vehicle for intervention in most forms of psychotherapy. Gary Groth-Marnat discusses the role of the interview within the larger context of psychological assessment in his *Handbook of Psychological Assessment* (2003). In clinical settings, the interview is used to gather intake information (the intake interview) and to establish the person's current emotional and cognitive state (the mental status examination). The intake interview is sometimes known as the initial interview, and it is the first significant contact with the interviewee. The purpose of the intake interview is to determine why the person has sought psychological services. This involves determining the person's symptoms or chief complaint.

Once this information is obtained, the interviewer tries to learn more about the person's life. In addition to asking about specific areas of one's life—for example, educational experience and relationship history—the interviewer begins to assess the personality of the interviewee. The personality assessment requires careful observation and integration of both verbal and nonverbal behavior. The interviewer must be aware of how the person reacts to different questions or topics. Some people will always try to please the interviewer, while others may appear nervous, sad, or angry at different times during the interview. Integrating all this information helps the interviewer understand the personality and circumstances of the person being interviewed.

MENTAL STATUS EXAMINATION

The mental status examination is an extension and elaboration of information necessary to understand the personality of the interviewee. Although some of the information included in the mental status examination is acquired through direct questioning, much of it is learned through careful listening and observation of the person during the intake interview. Kaplan and Sadock's *Comprehensive Textbook of Psychiatry* (2009) provides a detailed description of the mental status examination. Typically, this examination includes information in the following areas: physical appearance and how the person is dressed; attitude toward the interviewer and others; any unusual motor behavior or movements; oddities of speech and language, including accents, speech impediments, and unusual words; disturbances in thought content and process such as delusional beliefs or difficulties expressing thoughts; perceptual problems in the form of hallucinations or illusions; changes in cognition, which may include memory impairments and other intellectual changes; disturbances in orientation and sensorium, which refers to the person's knowledge of who and where he or she is, as well as to a determination of the level of alertness; the current affective or emotional state; and the degree of insight into the person's current circumstances.

Each aspect of the mental status examination contributes information that helps in the understanding of a person's personality. Information obtained through this part of the interview is also valuable in the diagnosis of psychological disorders. Certain deviations from the norm that may be revealed by the mental status examination are associated with disorders such as anxiety, depression, schizophrenia, and personality disorders. Thus, the intake interview and the mental status examination used together provide the foundation for understanding a person's personality and psychological disorders.

USE IN EMPLOYMENT SETTINGS

Personality interviewing is also an integral part of employment interviews. One important area in which personality interviews are used to help make employment decisions is in the selection of law-enforcement officers. The goals of the interview are twofold. First, it is used to identify those candidates who, because of their personality, are likely to make good or effective police officers. These are people with good coping skills, well-developed intellectual abilities, and good observational abilities. Second, the personality interview is used to identify candidates who are likely to make poor law-enforcement officers. In the area of law enforcement, it is crucial to consider liability issues and the protection of the public in making hiring decisions. Personality interviews provide information that can help to improve the quality of the hiring decisions and ultimately the quality of law-enforcement agencies.

Personality interviewing is also used in other employment settings. The interview is a significant part of the application process; used either informally or formally, it yields important information about the applicant's motivation and suitability for the position. Information from the interview helps an employer decide whether the applicant's personality will mesh or clash with coworkers, will convey the appropriate image for the position, or will satisfy other considerations salient to the job. As in clinical settings, the use of the personality interview in employment decisions is frequently combined with formal psychological testing. In both employment and clinical uses, it is important to note areas of similarity and difference between the interview and the testing.

ROLE IN THERAPEUTIC PROCESS

The use of interviewing, in various guises, has been central to psychological investigations of personality as well as to psychotherapeutic approaches to helping patients or clients. Sigmund Freud called one of the central aspects of psychoanalytic interviewing "free association"—a highly unstructured effort to obtain information that is as uncensored as possible. The interviewee is told to talk about whatever comes to mind without concern for its relevance or appropriateness. Following this uncensored revelation by the interviewee, the interviewer eventually makes interpretations about personality and unconscious conflicts. Although personality interviewing and free association remain hallmarks of psychoanalysis, the interview has also been important to others in psychology and psychotherapy.

Carl R. Rogers, the founder of person-centered therapy (or nondirective therapy), considered the interview critical to the therapeutic process. He and his followers believed that, without controlling the direction of the interview, they could learn more about the person that would be useful in resolving the person's problems. Rogerian psychologists are firm believers in the nondirective approach because it allows the client to discover, independent of someone else's opinion, the solution to the problem.

Behavioral psychologists, as exemplified by Kenneth P. Morganstern, place their emphasis on a person's observable behavior. Personality is not defined as something a person has but rather as the perceptions of other people based on the person's behavior. Thus, personality interviewing from a behavioral perspective focuses heavily on observations of the person's behavior in different situations. Many behavioral psychologists believe that a person's personality is modifiable if his or her prior learning experiences can be identified and if it is possible to ensure that specifiable consequences can follow behaviors that the client is trying to change.

Many psychologists, including Groth-Marnat, believe that computers are likely to be used more frequently to administer interviews. Assessment interviews will be more important in determining accountability for treatment decisions and therefore are likely to become more structured. As interviews become increasingly structured, it is also likely that they will represent an integration of different theoretical positions rather than the parallel interview styles that have been developing among psychologists adhering to different theories.

BIBLIOGRAPHY

Cormer, Sherry, Paula S. Nurius, and Cynthia J. Osborn. *Interviewing and Change Strategies for Helpers*. 7th ed. Belmont: Brooks/Cole, 2013. Print.

Groth-Marnat, Gary. *Handbook of Psychological Assessment*. 5th ed. New York: Wiley, 2009. Print.

Kerlinger, Fred N., and Howard B. Lee. *Foundations of Behavioral Research*. 4th ed. Belmont: Wadsworth, 2000. Print.

Kirschenbaum, Howard. *The Life and Work of Carl Rogers*. Alexandria: Amer. Counseling Assn., 2009. Print.

Morrison, James. *The First Interview*. 4th ed. New York: Guilford, 2014. Print.

Pheister, Maria. "Psychiatric Interviewing: What to Do, What Not to Do." *International Handbook of Psychiatry: A Concise Guide for Medical Students, Residents, and Medical Practitioners*. Ed. Laura Weiss Roberts, Joseph B. Layde, and Richard Balon. Hackensack: World Scientific, 2013. 78–101. Print.

Sadock, Benjamin J., Virginia Sadock, and Pedro Ruiz, eds. Kaplan and Sadock's *Comprehensive Textbook of Psychiatry*. 9th ed. Philadelphia: Lippincott, 2009. Print.

James T. Trent

SEE ALSO: Assessment; Behavioral assessment; Career and personnel testing; Case study methodologies; Clinical interviewing, testing, and observation; Diagnosis; Freud, Sigmund; Person-centered therapy; Psychoanalysis; Rogers, Carl R.; Survey research: Questionnaires and interviews.

Personality
Psychophysiological measures

TYPE OF PSYCHOLOGY: Personality

Psychophysiological studies comparing individuals with different personality traits have sought to determine the physical characteristics of particular behavioral characteristics. Such research can provide information that helps clarify the importance of various personality types with regard to risk of psychological and physical disorders.

KEY CONCEPTS
- Anxiety sensitivity
- Locus of control
- Personality
- Psychophysiology
- Type A behavior pattern

INTRODUCTION
A broad definition of personality typically includes the dimensions of stability, determinism, and uniqueness. That is, personality changes little over time, is determined by internal processes and external factors, and reflects an individual's distinctive qualities. Personality also can be thought of as unique, relatively stable patterns of behavior, multiply determined over the course of an individual's life. There are many theories for understanding the development of these patterns of behavior.

Twin studies have provided evidence that biological factors help to shape personality; such studies support Hans Eysenck's theory that personality is inherited. The psychodynamic perspective holds that personality is determined primarily by early childhood experiences. Some of the most influential contributions to this perspective came from Sigmund Freud. He argued that unconscious forces govern behavior and that childhood experiences strongly shape adult personality via coping strategies people use to deal with sexual urges. B. F. Skinner, founder of modern behavioral psychology, assumed that personality (or behavior) is determined solely by environmental factors. More specifically, he believed that consequences of behavior are instrumental in the development of unique, relatively stable patterns of behavior in individuals. According to Albert Bandura's social learning theory, models have a great impact on personality development. That is, patterns of behavior in individuals are influenced by their observations of others. Finally, the humanistic perspective of Carl R. Rogers suggests that personality is largely determined by the individual's unique perception of reality in comparison to his or her self-concept.

PERSONALITY ASSESSMENT
Assessment of personality can be accomplished from three domains: subjective experience, behavior, and physiology. Traditional means for assessing personality have included objective and projective paper-and-pencil or interview measurements that tap the domain of subjective experience. Behavioral assessment techniques such as direct observation of behavior, self-monitoring (having the individual record occurrences of his or her own behavior), self-report questionnaires, role-play scenarios, and behavioral avoidance tests (systematic, controlled determination of how close an individual can approach a feared object or situation) tap the domains of subjective experience and objective behavior. These techniques have been used in clinical settings to aid in the diagnosis and treatment of deviant or abnormal behavior patterns.

Although psychophysiological measurement of personality has not gained popular use in clinical settings, it complements the techniques mentioned above and contributes to understanding the nature and development of psychological and physical disorders. Just as patterns of responding on traditional personality tests can indicate the possibility of aberrant behavior, so too can tests of physiological patterns. Typical measures taken during this type of assessment include heart rate, blood pressure, muscle tension (measured via electromyography), brain-wave activity (measured via electroencephalography), skin temperature, and palmar sweat gland or electrodermal activity. These measures of physiological activity are sensitive to "emotional" responses to various stimuli and have been instrumental in clarifying the nature of certain psychological and physical conditions. One of the fundamental assumptions of psychophysiology is that the responses of the body can help reveal the mechanisms underlying human behavior and personality.

Physiological responsivity can be assessed in a number of different ways. Two primary methodologies are used in the study of the relations between personality and physiology. The first method simply looks at resting or baseline differences of various physiological measures across individuals who either possess or do not possess the personality characteristic of interest. The second method also assesses individuals with or without the characteristic of interest but does this under specific stimulus or situational conditions rather than during rest. This is often referred to as measuring reactivity to the stimulus or situational condition. Resting physiological measures are referred to as tonic activity (activity evident in the absence of any known stimulus event). It is postulated that tonic activity is relatively enduring and stable within the individual while at rest, although it can be influenced by external factors. It is both of interest in its own right and important in determining the magnitude of response to a stimulus. On the other hand, phasic activity is a discrete response to a specific stimulus. This type of activity is suspected to be influenced to a much greater extent by external factors and tends to be less stable than tonic activity. Both types of activity, tonic and phasic, are important in the study of personality and physiology.

Standard laboratory procedures are typically employed to investigate tonic activity and phasic responses to environmental stimuli. For example, a typical assessment incorporating both methodologies might include the following phases: a five-minute baseline to collect resting physiological measures, a five-minute presentation of a task or other stimulus suspected to differentiate individuals in each group based on their physiological response or change from baseline, and a five-minute recovery to assess the nature and rate of physiological recovery from the task or stimulus condition. Investigations focusing on the last phase attempt to understand variations in

recovery as a response pattern in certain individuals. For example, highly anxious individuals tend to take much longer to recover physiologically from stimulus presentations that influence heart rate and electrodermal activity than individuals who report low levels of anxiety.

Studies of physiological habituation—the decline or disappearance of response to a discrete stimulus—also have been used to investigate personality differences. Physiological responses to a standard tone, for example, eventually disappear with repeated presentations of the tone. The rate at which they disappear varies across individuals; the disappearance generally takes longer in individuals who tend to be anxious. Thus, individuals who tend to have anxious traits may be more physiologically responsive, recover from the response less rapidly, and habituate to repeated stimulation more slowly than those who tend to be less anxious. Such physiological differences may be an important characteristic that determines anxious behavior or results from subjective feelings of anxiousness.

RELATIONSHIP TO PHYSIOLOGY AND HEALTH

Research has demonstrated that there is considerable variability across individuals in their physiological response patterns, both at rest and in response to various situational stimuli or laboratory manipulations. Evidence indicates that part of this variability across individuals may in some cases be attributable to certain personality traits or characteristic patterns of behavior. Furthermore, research suggests that these personality traits may also be related to the development of psychological or physical disorders. Although the causal links are not well understood, a growing body of research points to relations among personality, physiological measures, and psychopathology/health.

Examples of these relationships are evident in the field of psychopathology, or the study of abnormal behavior. Eysenck proposed that the general characteristics of introversion and extroversion lead individuals to interact very differently with their environment. Some psychophysiological studies support this notion and suggest that the behaviors characteristic of these traits may be driven by physiological differences. Anxiety sensitivity and locus of control are two personality traits that some suggest are related to the development of anxiety disorders and depression, respectively. To varying degrees, anxiety disorders and depression have been investigated in the psychophysiology laboratory and have been found to differentiate individuals with high and low levels of the personality trait, based on their physiological responses.

Introversion describes the tendency to minimize interaction with the environment; extroversion is characterized by the opposite behaviors, or the tendency to interact more with the environment. Eysenck proposed that such traits reflect physiological differences that are genetically determined and reflected in the individual's physiology. Introverted individuals are thought to be chronically physiologically hyperaroused and thus to seek to minimize their arousal by minimizing external stimulation. Extroverted individuals are believed to be chronically physiologically underaroused and to seek a more optimal level of arousal through increased environmental stimulation. It should be easy to confirm or disprove such a theory with psychophysiological studies of resting physiological activity in introverts and extroverts. Electroencephalograph (EEG) studies have produced contradictory evidence about the validity of Eysenck's theory, however; problems in EEG methodology, experimental design, and measurement of the traits themselves have led to considerable confusion about whether the traits actually do have a physiological basis.

ANXIETY SENSITIVITY

Anxiety sensitivity describes the tendency for individuals to fear sensations they associate with anxiety because of beliefs that anxiety may result in harmful consequences. Research in the development and assessment of this construct was pioneered by Steven Reiss and his associates in the late 1980s. They developed a sixteen-item questionnaire, the Anxiety Sensitivity Index (ASI), to measure anxiety sensitivity and found it to be both reliable and valid. Anxiety sensitivity has been most closely related to panic disorder, an anxiety disorder characterized by frequent, incapacitating episodes of extreme fear or discomfort. In fact, as a group, individuals with panic disorder score higher on the ASI than individuals with any other anxiety disorder. Furthermore, some researchers have demonstrated that individuals scoring high on the ASI are five times more likely to develop an anxiety disorder after a three-year follow-up.

Research investigating responses to arithmetic, caffeine, and hyperventilation challenges in the laboratory has demonstrated that individual differences in anxiety sensitivity levels are probably more closely related to the subjective experience of anxiousness than to actual physiological changes. Individuals high and low on anxiety sensitivity, however, have exhibited differential heart-rate reactivity to a mental arithmetic stressor. That is, individuals high on anxiety sensitivity show a greater acceleration in heart rate than individuals low on anxiety sensitivity when engaging in an arithmetic challenge. Individuals scoring high on the ASI also more accurately perceive changes in their physiology when compared with their low-scoring counterparts. Such heightened reactivity and sensitivity to physiological change may partially explain how anxiety sensitivity influences the development of anxiety disorders. Individuals high in anxiety sensitivity may be more reactive to environmental threat; therefore, their increased sensitivity may have a physiological basis. They also may be more likely to detect changes in their physiology, which they are then more likely to attribute to threat or danger.

On a more general note, cardiovascular and electrodermal measures can differentiate between anxiety patients and other people at rest. The differences become greater under conditions of stimulation. Delayed habituation rates in anxiety patients are also part of the pattern of physiological overarousal typically seen in individuals with heightened anxiety. Indeed, heightened physiological arousal is one of the hallmark characteristics of anxiety.

LOCUS OF CONTROL

Locus of control, made popular by Julian Rotter in the 1960s, refers to individuals' perceptions of whether they have control over what happens to them across situations. This personality construct has been related to the development of depression. Specifically, it is believed that individuals who attribute failures to internal factors (self-blame) and successes to external factors (to other people or to luck) are more susceptible to developing feelings of helplessness, often followed by despair and depression. Locus of control also is hypothesized to have implications in the management of chronic health-related problems.

In oversimplified categorizations, individuals are labeled to have an internal or external locus of control. External individuals, who believe they have little control over what happens to them, are said to be more reactive to threat, more emotionally labile, more hostile, and lower in self-esteem and self-control. Psychophysiological assessment studies have revealed heart-rate acceleration and longer electrodermal habituation for externals in response to the presentation of tones under passive conditions. When faced with no-control conditions in stress situations such as inescapable shock, internals show elevated physiological arousal, while findings for externals are mixed. Thus, the locus of control has varying effects on physiology, depending on the circumstances. Such effects may play a role in psychological disorders such as depression and anxiety. Heightened physiological reactivity may also inhibit recovery from acute illness or affect the course of chronic health problems such as hypertension.

In addition to the relevance of personality to physiological reactivity and psychopathology, research has demonstrated that certain personality types may be risk factors or serve protective functions with regard to physical health. Type A behavior pattern and hardiness are two examples. The Type A behavior pattern is characterized by competitiveness, time urgency, and hostility. It has been identified as a potential risk factor for the development of coronary heart disease. Psychophysiological studies have suggested that, under certain laboratory conditions, males who exhibit the Type A pattern are more cardiovascularly responsive. This reactivity is the proposed mechanism by which Type A behavior affects the heart. More recent research has suggested that not all components of the Type A pattern are significantly associated with heightened cardiovascular reactivity. Hostility seems to be the most critical factor in determining heightened reactivity. Males who respond to stress with hostility tend to show greater heart-rate and blood-pressure increases than individuals low in hostility. Some research suggests that hostility is also a risk factor for heart disease in women.

In contrast to hostility, hardiness is proposed to buffer the effects of stress on physiology. Hardy individuals respond to stressors as challenges and believe that they have control over the impact of stressors. They also feel commitment to their life, including work and family. Psychophysiological studies have supported the buffering effect of hardiness. Individuals who are more hardy tend to be less physiologically responsive to stressors and to recover from stressors more rapidly. Again, the construct of hardiness seems to be more relevant for males, partially because males have been studied more often.

These studies show that various personality types can be distinguished to varying degrees by psychophysiological measurement. The implications of such findings include possible physiological contributions to the development of various psychological problems, and personality contributions to the development or course of physical disease. Many of those who study psychophysiology

hope that it will lead to new biofeedback-based treatments for various psychological issues.

EVOLUTION OF RESEARCH

Although the sophisticated techniques and instruments that have enabled psychologists to study physiological events were not developed until the twentieth century, the notion that physiology and psychology (body and mind) are linked dates back as far as ancient Greece. Hippocrates, for example, described four bodily humors or fluids thought to influence various psychological states such as melancholy and mania. Although the link between mind and body has received varying degrees of emphasis in scientific thinking across the centuries, it regained prominence in the mid-1900s with the development of the field of psychosomatic medicine along with the widespread influence of Sigmund Freud's theories of personality.

Psychosomatic medicine embraced the notion that personality and physiology are intertwined. Psychosomatic theorists believed that certain diseases, such as diabetes, asthma, and hypertension, were associated with particular personality characteristics. They suggested that personality influenced the development of specific diseases. Although much of this theorizing has been disproved, these theorists did return the focus to investigating the interactive nature of a person's psychological and physiological makeup.

Psychophysiologists acknowledge the influence of personality characteristics on physiology and vice versa, and they are working to characterize these relationships. They hope that future work will better measure particular personality constructs and will clarify the interaction of gender with personality and physiology. Psychophysiologists also must be concerned with the external validity of the data they obtain in the laboratory. It has not been satisfactorily demonstrated that physiological responses measured in a given individual in the laboratory are at all related to that individual's response in the natural environment. Thus, to establish fully the usefulness of laboratory findings, psychophysiologists must also study individuals in their natural environments. Recent technological advances will enable ongoing physiological measurement, which should achieve this goal and further establish the relations among personality, physiology, and behavior.

BIBLIOGRAPHY

Cacioppo, John T., Louis G. Tassinary, and Gary G. Berntson, eds. *Handbook of Psychophysiology.* 3d ed. New York: Cambridge UP, 2007. Print.

Edmonds, W. Alex, and Gershon Tenenbaum. *Case Studies in Applied Psychophysiology: Neurofeedback and Biofeedback Treatments for Advances in Human Performance.* Chichester: Wiley, 2012. Print.

Eysenck, Hans. *The Biological Basis of Personality.* New Brunswick: Transaction, 2006. Print.

Potter, Robert F., and Paul David Bolls. *Psychophysiological Measurement and Meaning: Cognitive and Emotional Processing of Media.* New York: Routledge, 2012. Print.

Schmidt, Louis A., and Sidney J. Segalowitz. *Developmental Psychophysiology: Theory, Systems, and Methods.* Cambridge: Cambridge UP, 2008. Print.

Stern, Robert Morris, William J. Ray, and Karen S. Quigley. *Psychophysiological Recording.* 2d ed. New York: Oxford UP, 2001. Print.

Surwillo, Walter W. *Psychophysiology for Clinical Psychologists.* Norwood: Ablex, 1990. Print.

Weiten, Wayne, Margaret A. Lloyd, and R. L. Lashley. "Theories of Personality." *Psychology Applied to Modern Life: Adjustment at the Turn of the Century.* 9th ed. Belmont: Wadsworth, 2008. Print.

Virginia L. Goetsch and Lois Veltum

SEE ALSO: Clinical interviewing, testing, and observation; Emotions; Genetics and mental health; Nervous system; Neuropsychology; Projection.

Personality rating scales

TYPE OF PSYCHOLOGY: Personality

Personality rating scales are used to describe personality trait systems through the measurement of psychological individual difference dimensions, or traits along which people can be ordered, although not all represent explicit theories. They can include rating oneself (self-rating) or rating by a peer (observer rating). Their utility in research and applied settings has been demonstrated, and their use has become commonplace and widespread.

KEY CONCEPTS
- Bandwidth
- Extroversion
- Factor analysis
- Factor level
- Introversion
- Neuroticism
- Personality traits
- Prediction
- Primary, secondary, and superfactors
- Psychometrics
- Psychoticism
- Rating scales
- Taxonomy

INTRODUCTION

Personality rating scales represent one approach that is used by psychologists and others to measure scientifically dimensions of personality for purposes of summarizing, predicting, and explaining human behavior. In recent history, there has been considerable research on and application of the use of personality rating scales, typically to measure psychological individual difference dimensions or traits along which people can be ordered, such as extroversion or neuroticism. Traits are consistent patterns in the way individuals behave, feel, and think.

Trait psychology can be considered the theoretical underpinnings for measurements of personality, including personality rating scales. However, the use of rating scales does not provide a sufficient explanation of personality, and there is more to personality than traits. Personality traits must be inferred through measurement, since they are hypothetical constructs that cannot be observed directly, although some trait psychologists, such as Hans Eysenck and Gordon Allport, view traits as "neuropsychic entities." Support for this view has been provided by neuroscience findings that have suggested a genetic link to the major dimensions of personality traits; however, those findings are still preliminary, with half of the variance, at the most, being attributed to genes, and the environment or the interaction of traits with the environment accounting for the rest. Research into polygenetic influence on personality traits is emerging in light of several null replications of earlier single-gene studies.

Strictly speaking, a personality rating scale is a subset of items that all describe the same personality characteristic, variable, or trait along a continuum, with multiple categories that are assigned a number and can therefore yield a score. For example, in assessing the extent to which the item "cautiousness" describes a person, Likert scales may be used, such as "very much like the person"; "somewhat like the person"; "uncertain"; "somewhat unlike the person"; "not at all like the person." The rater makes an evaluative judgment by choosing which category along the continuum most accurately depicts the person who is being rated (the ratee). Like physical and mental attributes, traits vary in the population in a continuous and normal distribution (bell-shaped), with most falling within the middle range and fewer lying within the extremes.

Because traits are pervasive across situations, scores on trait measures should be relatively consistent across time, and ratings on scale items measuring the same underlying trait should be in agreement, as should ratings on items assessing different aspects of the same trait, such as test retest and internal consistency reliability, respectively; both represent criteria for scientific soundness of scales set forth by psychometricians.

Personality can be described by rating oneself (self-ratings). Also, persons can be described based on the impressions that they make on others who observe them. Thus, informants rate another person based on their observations and perceptions of the individual that they are assessing. These are referred to as "observer ratings" and can be made by a peer, supervisor, teacher, or counselor. Research has also shown consistency between the different methods of assessing personality, providing support for the scale's reliability validity (that is, that the scale is measuring the construct that it is intended to measure, an additional criterion set forth by psychometricians to evaluate the scientific soundness of personality assessment measures).

Lewis Aiken noted in 1997 that personality rating scales are included in inventories and may be a part of questionnaires. Both inventories and questionnaires are sometimes commercially labeled as "scales." Regardless of what form they take and how they are labeled, personality rating scales are widely used in both research and applied settings. Various subdisciplines of psychology—such as personality, social, developmental, educational, school, industrial, clinical, and forensic psychology—rely extensively on rating scales for the scientific assessment of personality for research purposes. They may be used in applied settings, such as medical and health care, to assess behavioral risk factors; mental health treatment, to measure psychopathology; colleges, to assist with vocational guidance; business and industry, to aid in personnel selection; the armed services, to aid in selection of those who are the most fit; and criminal justice, in the area of profiling.

ORIGIN, DEVELOPMENT, AND HISTORY

The foundation for the family of paper-and-pencil methods (of which personality rating scales are members) to obtain scientific information about people, products, or events evolved out of work in a variety of disciplines. Pierre-Simon Laplace and Carl Friedrich Gauss conducted seminal research on probability theory—the bell-shaped, normal distribution now termed "Gaussian distribution"—in the early eighteenth century, which made it possible to infer logically the characteristics of populations (whether physical, mental, or personality traits) from the analysis of sample data. Adolphe Quetelet extended Laplace's and Gauss's work to biological and social data, which marked the beginnings of vital statistics, that is, data pertaining to human life. Gustav Fechner's work in the nineteenth century in the area of psychophysics (subjective mental events) and the mathematical measurement of physical stimuli that gave rise to them produced Fechner's law, that sensation increases with the logarithmic value of the stimulus. Sir Francis Galton worked in the 1880s with Karl Pearson in the area of statistical methods and also contributed pioneering methodologies in the area of individual differences. The Woodworth Personal Data Sheet, the first formal, self-report, multi-item scale personality inventory that assessed psychoneurotic tendencies, was constructed by R. S. Woodworth in 1918 for purposes of weeding out unfit military personnel in World War I. Other early personality measures constructed in the first half of the twentieth century include the attitude inventories of L. L. Thurstone and his colleagues, the Strong's Vocational Interest Blank for Men, the Vernon and Allport Study of Values, the Bernreuter Personality Inventory, and the Minnesota Multiphasic Personality Inventory.

CURRENT STATUS AND APPLICATIONS

Since 1960, a number of scales have been created to measure traits and to organize them into a coherent structure or taxonomy. This effort was significantly advanced by the successful use of factor analysis in the development of a taxonomy of mental abilities and the use of high-speed computers in psychological research. This increased the efficiency and precision of factor analysis in grouping correlated items into factored scales that purportedly map the personality sphere.

Some have regarded trait systems as the theoretical model and scales and inventories as their application, although not all scales and inventories represent explicit theories. Raymond B. Cattell used an empirical approach in which he defined the "personality sphere" with words in the language that are used by observers to describe behavior. Others, such as J. Paul Guilford and Hans Eysenck, have been influenced by existing theory (Carl Jung's psychological types) and their own factoring of existing items and scales in addition to the research of others. On the other hand, Andrew Comrey and Douglas Jackson have been less concerned with covering the total domain of personality. Instead, psychometric soundness has been the priority in their development of explicit procedures for item selection, scale construction, and validation in defining sets of primary trait scales that best define those areas of the domain that had been well researched.

These approaches have all yielded different numbers of factored scales: Cattell's has sixteen; Eysenck's, three; Guilford's, thirteen; and Comrey's, eight. A review and critical analysis by Saul Sells and Debra Murphy of the dimensions of personality represented by these factored scales pointed out considerable difference across systems, yet extensive overlap and common content. The differences are partially due to whether lower-order (narrower) or higher-order (more general) factors have been the focus, with Eysenck emphasizing the higher-order ones (that is, the superfactors of psychoticism, extroversion, and neuroticism) and Cattell, Guilford, and Comrey focusing on lower-order or primary factors. Some psychologists hold that separate scales based on the lower-order primary factors have greater richness and predict better than those with two scores that compress all of the information. Further, the utility of the levels may depend on the situation; for instance, for Eysenck's psychophysiological experiments, the higher-order factors may be better and the primaries may be more suitable in the fields of clinical and personnel.

In attempts to resolve the discrepancies, there have been several investigations of congruences among the personality factor-trait systems, including one by Sells, Robert G. Demaree, and D. P. Will (the most ambitious project ever attempted in personality questionnaire research at that time) in which they administered Cattell's and Guilford's items to a sample of 2,500 individuals and factored them in the same analysis. The findings yielded eighteen factors, with five being common to both the Cattell and Guilford systems (emotional stability, social extroversion, conscientiousness, relaxed composure versus suspicious excitability, and general activity). With the inclusion of agreeableness, all but one (openness to experience) of the five broad bipolar dimensions that P.

T. Costa Jr. and R. R. McCrae have deemed the Big Five were reflected in their results.

The Big Five are posited as accounting for most of the personality-attributable variation in human behavior, although at least thirteen other non-Big Five factors (six attributable to Guilford, five attributable to Cattell, and two attributable to neither) were extracted in the Sells, Demaree, and Will analysis. The two factors attributable to neither contained items that were similar in content but were dissimilar in terms of the source factors from which they were drawn. Expansion of the Big Five to include traits that are represented by combinations of pairs of factors has been suggested by some.

The research of Jackson and colleagues has yielded results that suggest that there are many dimensions of behavior beyond the Big Five and, further, that the narrower facets, thought to be subsumed under the broader Big Five factors, may provide more accurate behavioral prediction than the Big Five alone.

Further, the review by Sells and Murphy found that "two factors with labels similar to those emphasized by Eysenck, neuroticism and extroversion-introversion, were addressed across all five of the systems (Cattell, Eysenck, Jackson, Comrey, and Sells, Demaree, and Wills), although not exactly in the same manner or in the same terms." They additionally point out that factor level can be "an artifact of the composition of the variables in the matrix" and that bandwidth of the various factors produced may be more important—that is, the extent to which the factors are very broad (made up of dissimilar items) or very narrow (made up of tautological items) may be more important than factor level in understanding the relationships among these factors.

In the light of the fact that personality factors and their measures are human constructs, research to determine the predictive validity of scales that already exist and those that are developed continues to be critical in assessing their theoretical and practical utility. Furthermore, debates on whether broad bandwidth factors or narrower band components have more predictive and explanatory power can best be served by examining each one's specific situational utility within a hierarchical framework of the domain that encourages choice of assessment level.

BIBLIOGRAPHY

Arroyo, Daniela, and Elias Delgadillo. *Encyclopedia of Personality Research*. Hauppauge: Nova Science, 2012. Print.

Butcher, James, and Julia Perry. *Personality Assessment in Treatment Planning: Use of the MMPI-2 and BTPI.* New York: Oxford UP, 2008. Print.

Ewen, Robert B. "The Trait Perspective." *An Introduction to Theories of Personality.* New York: Psychology, 2010. 239–86. Print.Fiske, Susan T., and Patrick E. Shrout. Personality Research, Methods, and Theory.. New York: Taylor, 2014. Print.

Jackson, Marc-Antoine, and Evan F. Morris. *Psychology of Personality.* Hauppauge: Nova Science, 2012. Print.

John, Oliver P., Laura P. Naumann, and Christopher J. Soto. "Paradigm Shift to the Integrative Big Five Factor Taxonomy: History, Measurement, and Conceptual Issues." *Handbook of Personality Theory and Research.* Ed. John, Richard W. Robins, and Lawrence A. Pervin. 3rd ed. New York: Guilford, 2008. 114–58. Print.

Kraus, Michael W. "Do Genes Influence Personality?" *Psychology Today.* Sussex, 11 July 2013. Web. 1 July 2014.

Paunonen, S. V., and M. C. Ashton. "Big Five Factors and Facets and the Prediction of Behavior." *Journal of Personality and Social Psychology* 81. 3 (2001): 524–39. Print.

Paunonen, S. V., and D. N. Jackson. "What Is Beyond the Big Five? Plenty!" *Journal of Personality* 68 (2000): 821–35. Print.

Pope, Kenneth S., James Neal Butcher, and Joyce Seelen. *The MMPI, MMPI-2, and MMP1-A in Court: A Practical Guide for Expert Witnesses and Attorneys.* 3rd ed. Washington: Amer. Psychological Assn., 2006. Print.

Saucier, G., and L. R. Goldberg. "Evidence for the Big Five in Analyses of Familiar English Personality Adjectives." *European Journal of Personality* 10 (1996): 61–77. Print.

Sells, S. B., and Debra Murphy. "Factor Theories of Personality." *Personality and the Behavior Disorders.* Ed. N. S. Endler and J. M. Hunt. New York: Wiley, 1984. Print.

Debra L. Murphy

SEE ALSO: Beck Depression Inventory (BDI); Behavioral assessment; California Psychological Inventory (CPI); Children's Depression Inventory (CDI); Clinical interviewing, testing, and observation; Diagnosis; Minnesota Multiphasic Personality Inventory (MMPI); Personality: Psychophysiological measures; Personality interviewing strategies; Personality theory; State-Trait Anxiety Inventory (STAI); Thematic Apperception Test (TAT).

Personality theory

TYPE OF PSYCHOLOGY: Personality

Personality theories seek to describe and explain the characteristics of thought, feeling, and behavior that differ among individuals and the coherence of these characteristics within a single individual. Personality theories describe approaches to human nature and provide the foundation for psychological therapies.

KEY CONCEPTS
- Attribution theory
- Humanistic theory
- Personality trait
- Psychoanalytic theory
- Social learning theory

INTRODUCTION

Psychologists who study personality are interested in explaining both the coherence of an individual's behavior, attitudes, and emotions, and how that individual may change over time. To paraphrase Clyde Kluckhohn, personality theorists seek to describe and explain how each individual is unique, how groups of people meaningfully differ from one another, and how all people share some common attributes. In developing answers to these questions, theorists use widely varying definitions of personality that may differ greatly from the way the term "personality" is used in everyday language. Indeed, if there is a single overriding basic issue in personality theory, it is What is personality?

PERSONALITY AND ESSENCE

Theorists agree that people have an internal "essence" that determines who they are and that guides their behavior, but the nature of that essence differs from theory to theory. Psychoanalytic theories such as Sigmund Freud's see the essence of personality as arising from conflict among internal psychic processes. In Freudian psychology, the conflict is viewed as occurring among the urges for instinctual gratification (called the id), the urges for perfection (the superego), and the demands of reality (the ego). Humanistic theories such as those of Carl R. Rogers and Abraham Maslow also see people as often engaged in conflict. For these theorists, however, the conflicts are between an internal self that is striving for positive expression and the constraints of a restrictive external social world. In general, humanistic psychology has a much more optimistic outlook on human nature than does psychoanalytic psychology.

Still other theorists are more neutral with respect to human nature. George Kelly's cognitive personality theory, for example, views people as scientists, developing and testing hypotheses to understand themselves better and to predict events in their world. Social learning theorists such as Walter Mischel, Albert Bandura, and Julian Rotter see people as developing expectations and behavioral tendencies based on their histories of rewards and punishments and on their observations of others.

To some extent, the question of "essence" is also the question of motivation. Psychoanalytic theorists view people as trying to achieve a balance between instinctual urges and the demands of reality. In contrast, humanistic theorists view people as motivated toward personal growth rather than homeostatic balance. Social learning theory views people as motivated to avoid punishments and obtain rewards.

Related to the question of the "essence" of personality is the notion of whether part or all of the personality can be hidden from the person him- or herself. Psychoanalytic theorists believe that the driving forces of the personality are in the unconscious and thus are not directly accessible to the person except under exceptional circumstances such as those that arise in therapy. Humanists are much more optimistic about the possibility of people coming to know their inner selves. According to Rogers, parts of the self that were once hidden can, when the individual receives acceptance from others, become expressed and incorporated into self-awareness. Social learning theories do not place much weight on hidden personality dynamics. From the social learning perspective, people are viewed as unable to verbalize easily some of their expectations, but no special unconscious processes are hypothesized.

Noimetic psychology, promulgated by Eric R. Maisel, combines some of these elements: unlike the psychoanalytic and social learning theories, it posits that each person is born with an original personality, but as in psychoanalysis and humanism, this personality is unknowable. Rather, the individual's "formed personality" is a product or version of that unknowable personality plus experience, and it is the individual's "available personality" that enables changes in personality.

PERSONALITY CHANGE
Theories also differ in the degree to which a person's personality is seen as changing over time. Most personality

theories address the development of personality in childhood and the possibility for change in adulthood. Psychoanalytic theorists believe that the most basic personality characteristics are established by the age of five or six, although there are some minor further developments in adolescence. While the person may change in adulthood in the course of psychotherapy and become better able to cope with the conflicts and traumas experienced during the early years, major personality transformations are not expected. Again, humanists are more optimistic than psychoanalytic theorists about personality change, although humanists, too, see the childhood years as important. For example, Rogers suggests that during childhood the parents may communicate their approval of some of the child's feelings and their disapproval of others, leaving the child with a distorted self-concept. Yet, from the humanistic point of view, the person's true inner self will constantly strive for expression. Thus, positive personality change is always seen as possible. Social learning theorists also see personality as changeable. Behaviors learned in childhood may later be changed by direct training, by altering the environment, or by revising one's expectations.

A final issue is the relationship between personality and behavior. For social learning theorists, behaviors and related expectations are personality. A person's behaviors are taken as a sample of a full behavioral repertoire that forms who the person is. Both psychoanalytic and humanistic theorists view behavior as a symptom or sign of underlying, internal personality dynamics rather than a sample of the personality itself. According to this viewpoint, a person's behaviors reflect personality only when interpreted in the light of the underlying traits they reveal. Diverse behaviors may thus be related to a single internal characteristic.

PERSONALITY MEASURES
The study of personality is a scientific discipline, with roots in empirical research; a philosophical discipline, seeking to understand the nature of people; and the foundation for the applied discipline of psychological therapy. While these three aspects of personality often support and enrich one another, there are also tensions as the field accommodates specialists in each of these three areas.

The approach that focuses on personality as a scientific discipline has produced an array of methods to measure personality characteristics. They range from projective tests, such as having people tell stories inspired by ambiguous pictures, to more standardized paper-and-pencil personality tests in which people respond on bi-polar numerical or multiple-choice scales to questions about their attitudes or behaviors. Methodologically, personality testing is quite sophisticated; however, people's scores on personality tests often are rather poor predictors of behavior. The poor record of behavioral prediction based on personality traits, coupled with evidence that suggests that behavior does not have the cross-situational consistency that one might expect, has led Mischel and many other personality specialists to question the utility of most traditional personality theories. Social learning approaches, which emphasize the power of the situation in determining a person's behavior, tend to fare better in these analyses.

PREDICTING BEHAVIOR

Yet research has found circumstances under which people's behavior can be predicted from knowledge of their underlying personality characteristics. If one classifies personality characteristics and behaviors at a very general level, combining observations and predicting a group of behaviors, prediction improves. For example, predictions would be more accurate if several measures of a person's conscientiousness were combined, and then used to predict an overall level of conscientious behavior in a variety of situations, than if one measured conscientiousness with a single scale and then attempted to predict behavior in one specific situation. Prediction on the basis of personality traits also improves when the situations in which one seeks to predict behaviors allow for individual variation as opposed to being highly constrained by social norms. Five basic personality traits often emerge in investigations: extroversion, agreeableness, conscientiousness, emotional stability, and culture (high scores on culture reflect characteristics such as intelligence and refinement). Some researchers view these trait terms as accurately describing consistent personality differences among people, while others view them as reflecting the "eye of the beholder" more than the core of personality.

Ultimately, people's personality traits and situations interact to produce behavior. Situations may often determine behavior, but people choose to place themselves in specific situations that elicit their traits. A child with a predisposition to aggression may provoke others and thus set the stage for the expression of aggression; one who is highly sociable may seek out others in cooperative situations. The relation between personality and behavior is very complex, and it is difficult to describe fully using standard research methods.

Research is highly unlikely to answer philosophical questions concerning human nature; however, considering people from the different points of view offered by various theories can be an enriching experience in itself. For example, a Freudian perspective on a former US president, Lyndon B. Johnson, might see his leadership during the Vietnam conflict as guided by aggressive instincts or even sublimated sexual instincts. On the other hand, a humanist might look at Johnson's presidency and find his decisions to be guided by the need for self-fulfillment, perhaps citing his vision of himself as the leader of the Great Society as an example of self-actualization. Social learning theorists would view Johnson's actions as president as determined by the rewards, punishments, and observational learning of his personal learning history, including growing up relatively poor in Texas and accruing power and respect during his years in the US Senate, as well as by the reinforcements and punishments Johnson perceived to be available in the situations in which he found himself during his presidency. In the final analysis, none of these interpretations could be shown to be blatantly false or absolutely true. Historians, biographers, and others might find each to be an enriching viewpoint from which to consider this complex individual.

THERAPY

Multiple points of view also characterize the therapies derived from theories of personality. Most therapists take an eclectic approach, sampling from the ideas of various theories to tailor their treatment to a specific client. Each therapist, however, also may have her or his own biases, based on a particular theoretical orientation. For example, a client who often feels anxious and seeks help from a psychoanalytic therapist may find that the therapist encourages the client to explore memories of childhood experiences to discover the unconscious roots of the anxiety. Slips of the tongue, dreams, and difficulty remembering or accepting therapeutic interpretations would be viewed as important clues to unconscious processes. The same client seeking treatment from a humanistic therapist would have a different experience. There, the emphasis would be on current experiences, with the therapist providing a warm and supportive atmosphere for the client to explore feelings. A behavioral therapist, from the social learning orientation, would help the client pinpoint situations in which anxiety occurs and teach the client alternative responses to those situations. Again, no one form of therapy is superior for all clients. Successes or failures in therapy depend on the combination of client, therapist, and mode of treatment.

THEORIES AND EXPERIMENTATION

While people have long speculated on the causes and types of individual differences in personality, the theory of Freud was the first and most influential psychological personality theory. All subsequent theories have directly or indirectly addressed the central concerns of motivation, development, and personality organization first proposed by Freud. Psychoanalytic theorists such as Carl Jung and Alfred Adler, while trained by Freud, disagreed with Freud's emphasis on sexual instincts and developed their own theories, emphasizing different motivations. Similarly, Karen Horney, Erich Fromm, and others developed theories placing greater emphasis on the ego and its interaction with society than did Freud's.

Psychoanalytic theory has had somewhat less of an influence in the United States than it did in Europe. Personality psychology in the United States is relatively more research-oriented, practical, and optimistic. In the United States, Gordon Allport developed one of the first trait approaches to personality. The humanistic theories of Carl R. Rogers and Abraham Maslow, the social learning theories of Bandura and Rotter, and the cognitive theory of Kelly flourished in the 1950s and 1960s and continue to have their advocates. Modern personality psychologists, however, are much more likely to confine themselves to personality measurement and research than to propose broad theories of personality.

Many have questioned personality's status as a scientific subdiscipline of psychology. In 1968, Mischel's *Personality and Assessment*, arguing that the consistency and behavior-prediction assumptions inherent in all personality theories are unsupported by the evidence, was published. At the same time, attribution theories in social psychology were suggesting that personality traits are largely in the "eye of the beholder" rather than in the person being observed. For example, Edward Jones and Richard Nisbett argued that people are more inclined to see others as possessing personality traits than they are to attribute traits to themselves. The continued existence of personality as a subdiscipline of scientific psychology was debated.

The result has been a refined approach to measurement and personality analysis. Current research on personality does not boldly assert the influence of internal personality characteristics on behavior. Rather, attention is paid to careful assessment of personality and to the complex interactions of persons and situations. For example, research on loneliness has found that people who describe themselves as lonely often lack social skills and avoid interactions with others, thus perpetuating their feelings of loneliness. All personality characteristics, including loneliness, are most meaningfully seen as the product of a complex interrelationship between the person and the environment.

BIBLIOGRAPHY

Arroyo, Daniela, and Elias Delgadillo. *Encyclopedia of Personality Research*. Hauppauge: Nova Science, 2012. Print.

Ewen, Robert B. *An Introduction to Theories of Personality*. New York: Psychology, 2010. 239–86. Print.

Fiske, Susan T., and Patrick E. Shrout. *Personality Research, Methods, and Theory*. New York: Taylor, 2014. Print.

Hall, Calvin S., Gardner Lindzey, and John B. Campbell. *Theories of Personality*. 4th ed. New York: Wiley, 1998. Print.

Hampden-Turner, Charles. *Maps of the Mind*. New York: Macmillan, 1982. Print.

Jackson, Marc-Antoine, and Evan F. Morris. *Psychology of Personality*. Hauppauge: Nova Science, 2012. Print.

Maisel, Eric R. "What Is Your Original Personality?." *Psychology Today*. Sussex, 27 Nov. 2011. Web. 1 July 2014.

Mischel, Walter. *Introduction to Personality: Toward an Integrative Science of the Person*. 8th ed. Hoboken: Wiley, 2008. Print.

Mischel, Walter. *Personality and Assessment*. 1968. Reprint. Hillsdale: Analytic, 1996. Print.

Pervin, Lawrence A., Richard W. Robins, and Oliver P. John, eds. *Handbook of Personality: Theory and Research*. 3rd ed. New York: Guilford, 2008. Print.

Storr, Anthony. *Churchill's Black Dog, Kafka's Mice, and Other Phenomena of the Human Mind*. New York: Ballantine, 1990. Print.

Susan E. Beers

SEE ALSO: Allport, Gordon; Analytical psychology: Carl Jung; Bandura, Albert; Behavioral assessment; Cognitive social learning: Walter Mischel; Freud, Sigmund; Humanistic trait models: Gordon Allport; Jung, Carl; Maslow, Abraham;

Psychoanalytic psychology; Psychoanalytic psychology and personality: Sigmund Freud; Psychosexual development; Selfactualization; Social learning: Albert Bandura.

Personology theory
Henry A. Murray

TYPE OF PSYCHOLOGY: Personality

Henry A. Murray's study of personality, or personology, as he preferred to call it, highlights the uniqueness of the individual and the interaction between individual needs and environmental constraints. His theory precipitated the in-depth study of human needs and provided an instrument for assessing human personality.

KEY CONCEPTS
- Alpha press
- Beta press
- Need
- Need for achievement
- Press
- Thematic apperception test (TAT)

INTRODUCTION

Henry A. Murray was born into a wealthy family in New York City in 1893. His early life was unremarkable, and unlike numerous other personality theorists, he experienced no major traumas that obviously influenced his theory. He was not trained in psychology (in fact, he greatly disliked psychology classes); rather, he was trained as a biologist and later received his PhD in biochemistry from the University of Cambridge. His interest in psychology and personality processes was ignited during a three-week stay with Carl Jung, the eminent Swiss psychoanalyst. This meeting led to a change in career aspirations, whereupon Murray was brought to Harvard University to engage in personality research and establish the Harvard Psychological Clinic.

Murray's biomedical training is reflected in his belief that personality processes are dependent on brain functioning. He did not believe that personality actually existed; he believed that descriptions of personality were shorthand methods of describing various aspects of individuals and their behaviors. He thought that personality helped explain and predict an individual's actions, drives, needs, goals, and plans. He stated that his system of personality, "personology," was a tentative theory, as

psychologists did not yet know enough to capture completely the essence of each individual.

As opposed to personality theorists who developed their ideas in the clinic, working with emotionally disturbed individuals, Murray believed that the best way to investigate personality was to study normal individuals in their natural environments. While at Harvard, he undertook an intensive study of fifty-one male undergraduates during a six-month period. The undergraduates were examined by a council of twenty-eight specialists of various training and expertise so they might fully understand the personality of the students.

From these studies, Murray developed his ideas about human needs. He believed that these needs helped individuals focus their attention on certain events and guided their behaviors to meet those needs. There are primary needs that originate from internal bodily processes (for example, air, water, food, and sex) and secondary needs that are concerned with mental and emotional satisfaction (for example, achievement, dominance, understanding, and affiliation). He proposed a hierarchy of needs, a concept later elaborated on by Abraham Maslow, in which more basic needs such as food must be met before others can be addressed. Murray originally proposed a list of twenty basic human needs, although this list was later revised and expanded by his students and followers.

"PRESS" CONCEPT

Although Murray's elaboration and description of human needs was one of his major contributions to psychology, his focus on the situational context for behavior foreshadowed psychology's future emphasis on environmental events. He proposed the concept of "press," or forces provided by situations or events in the environment. These forces may help or hinder individuals in reaching their goals. For example, a student may have a need for achievement that would result in her attending college and receiving a degree. Environmental events such as poverty, however, may hinder her progress or pressure her away from these goals and necessitate that she take a job to support her family. In this situation, Murray also distinguished between "alpha press," or actual pressure resulting from environmental situations, and "beta press," or subjective pressure that results from individual interpretation of the events. In the example of going to college given above, alpha press might be the college board scores or the money necessary to go to certain colleges. These are real, and they involve little interpretation. Beta press might be the interpretation that if the student does not get into a certain college, she will be viewed as an embarrassment and a failure. This type of pressure comes from an internal evaluation of environmental events.

USE OF THE TAT

A final major contribution of Murray's personology theory comes from the device he used to determine individual needs and more generally measure personality. Along with Christiana Morgan, Murray developed the Thematic Apperception Test (TAT), which continues to be a widely used instrument for assessing human personality. The TAT consists of a set of ambiguous black-and-white pictures for which an individual is instructed to make up a story. The test subject is asked to tell what led up to the event in the picture, what is happening in the picture, including how the characters are thinking and feeling, and what will happen to the characters in the future. Murray's idea was that test subjects will project their needs into the picture, much as individuals who are on a diet will notice food in most situations that they encounter. It is similar to the children's game of identifying the shapes of clouds. Children may identify clouds with children's themes of dragons, monsters, or dinosaurs. Adolescents may view these same clouds as other boys and girls, cars, or sports figures. Murray hypothesized that certain themes would emerge from individuals' responses to the figures and that themes and expectations for the future would become evident. Mental health professionals continue to use the TAT for this purpose.

ACHIEVEMENT NEED

Murray's theoretical focus was to catalog all possible human needs. This led to a wide range of understanding; however, it was left to later researchers to add depth to the understanding of needs. One of the best researched of the secondary needs is the need for achievement. This need of individuals to overcome obstacles and accomplish what often are very difficult tasks has been investigated in detail by David McClelland and his colleague John Atkinson. They developed a system for scoring individuals' responses to TAT cards to abstract achievement-oriented themes. They observed that individuals who had a high need for achievement completed more tasks under competitive conditions, were more productive in their jobs, and tended to get better grades. They used this information and measuring system to develop a training program for industry that has been shown to increase employees'

need for achievement and job productivity. Their system was found to be working even two years after the program was begun. Interesting questions remain, however; for example, at what level does the need for achievement become unproductive? At some point it will lead to unrealistic expectations, unnecessary stress, and related health problems. One of the fascinating things about the McClelland and Atkinson method of assessing an individual's need for achievement is that it is not restricted to measuring responses from TAT cards. Their scoring system can be used with any written material; therefore, it can be adapted to a vast amount of literary, historical, and biographical information. McClelland conjectured that he could predict the economic growth and decline of a country from the number of achievement themes evident in its children's stories. He looked at the economic conditions of twenty-three countries from 1929 to 1950 and scored its children's stories from the prior decade (1920–29). While it is apparent that children's stories are not the only factor related to economic well-being, McClelland did discover that those countries with a higher number of achievement themes in the children's stories experienced the most economic growth.

GENDER DIFFERENCES IN ACHIEVEMENT

Another example of the importance of Murray's pioneering work on the need for achievement comes from research on how this need is demonstrated differently by men and women. It has been evident for many years that the expression of achievement has been more acceptable for men than for women. It has only been in recent years that the issues surrounding the achievement of women have been investigated. It is clear that these issues, in general, have been experienced much differently by women from the way they have been experienced by men. The paths for understanding and expressing ideas of achievement for men and women clearly differ very early in life. A series of studies supports the idea that women with a high need for achievement come from relatively stressful and difficult home lives, whereas men with a similar level of achievement strivings come from supportive, nonstressful homes. Additionally, girls tend to evidence their needs for achievement because of a desire for adult approval, while boys do not demonstrate this motivation.

One of the more interesting as well as distressing findings regarding sex differences in the need for achievement comes from the research of Matina Horner. She found that women experience considerable conflict and distress when faced with their need to achieve, whereas men do not experience a similar state. She proposed that the "smart girl" faced the prospect of considerable loss of social status and peer rejection as a result of her strivings to achieve. This may result in the behavior of acting "dumb" to prosper socially. Horner elaborated on Sigmund Freud's original idea that women actually may fear success because of its social consequences.

In a famous study by Horner, she had men and women write a story after being given an opening line. The women were to write a story about a woman who found herself at the top of her medical school class after the first semester. The men had the same story, except that it was a man who was at the top of the class. Far more women wrote stories of the unappealing and sometimes tragic consequences for the smart woman in class. They wrote about possible rejections and losses of friends and indicated that she would have a poorer chance of getting married. Many of the women came up with situations related to removing the student from the conflict situation, such as dropping out of medical school or settling for becoming a nurse. Finally, some of the students even indicated that she might receive bodily harm as a result of her stellar performance.

The conflicting messages of society regarding achievement for women are clearly shown by this study. It is apparent that women face considerable struggles in their attempts to compete and achieve equally with men. The factors that will alleviate this internal distress and aid women in the full expression of their abilities await further investigation. It was Murray's pioneering study of human needs that laid the groundwork for these types of investigation, which have the potential to inspire long-overdue social changes.

THEORETICAL CONTRIBUTIONS

Murray's theory of personology was a unique contribution to the early years of personality theorizing. His system differed from those before it (for example, Freud's psychoanalytic theory) in that it was not developed in a clinic as a result of working with clients. Murray studied normal individuals in great detail and gained knowledge from experts in a number of disciplines. This gave personality theory a certain degree of academic respectability it had not had previously acquired. Murray was also a highly influential teacher, with many students who in turn made significant contributions to psychology.

Murray's description of "needs" was a major contribution to the psychological study of motivation. His

research spurred many investigations of individual human needs. Additionally, his complementary emphasis on environmental events (that is, "press") was later to become a major shift in American psychology. The behavioral school of psychology, with its leaders John B. Watson and B. F. Skinner, was to become the dominant force for many years. Their focus on the manipulation of environmental events(for example, rewards and punishments) was to have a major influence on education, therapy, and child-rearing. The subjective interpretation of environmental events (that is, "beta press") also was a precursor to a major shift in theory. The cognitive school of psychology now focuses on these mental rearrangements of events and makes predictions based on individuals' expectations and fears. Murray's emphasis on the fact that the idiosyncratic perception of an event is not always the same as what actually happened is the foundation for this approach.

Finally, Murray's development of the TAT (with Christiana Morgan) was an early and influential contribution to the area of personality assessment. It and similar tests, such as the Rorschach inkblot test and the incomplete sentences blank, are frequently used for gathering personality information in the clinic. Even the weaknesses of the TAT (for example, different investigators may score it very differently) led to the development of more objective personality tests with standardized questions and scoring. Murray's influence, both in the classroom and in the clinic, was substantial.

BIBLIOGRAPHY

Anderson, James W. "Henry A. Murray's Early Career: A Psychobiographical Exploration." *Journal of Personality* 56.1 (1988): 139–71. Print.

Boring, Edwin G., and Gardner Lindzey, eds. *A History of Psychology in Autobiography.* Vol. 5. New York: Appleton, 1967. Print.

Carver, Charles S., and Michael F. Scheier. *Perspectives on Personality.* 7th ed. Harlow: Pearson, 2014. Print.

Engler, Barbara. *Personality Theories.* 9th ed. New York: Houghton, 2009. Print.

Feist, Jess, Gregory J. Feist, and Tomi-Ann Roberts. *Theories of Personality.* 8th ed. New York: McGraw, 2013. Print.

Friedman, Howard S., and Miriam W. Schustack. *Personality: Classic Theories and Modern Research.* 5th ed. Boston: Allyn, 2012. Print.

Hall, Calvin S., and Gardner Lindzey. *Introduction to Theories of Personality.* 3d ed. New York: Wiley, 1985.

Print.

Maddi, Salvatore, and Paul Costa. *Humanism in Personology: Allport, Maslow, and Murray.* New Brunswick: Aldine Transaction, 2008. Print.

Schultz, Duane, and Sydney Schultz. *Theories of Personality.* 9th ed. Stamford: Cengage, 2009. Print.

Smith, M. B., and J. W. Anderson. "Henry A. Murray (1893–1988)." *American Psychologist* 44 (1989): 1153–54. Print.

Brett L. Beck

SEE ALSO: Achievement motivation; Affiliation motive; Aggression; Behavioral assessment; Gender differences; Hierarchy of needs; Maslow, Abraham; Murray, Henry A.; Personality interviewing strategies; Personality theory; Projection; Psychoanalytic psychology; Work motivation.

Pervasive developmental disorders

TYPE OF PSYCHOLOGY: Developmental psychology

Characterized by delays in the development of socialization and communication skills, autism spectrum disorder (ASD) is a diagnosis encompassing the previous diagnostic categories of autistic disorder, Asperger's disorder, childhood disintegrative disorder, and pervasive developmental disorder-not otherwise specified. Children with ASD vary widely in language development, intelligence, and behavior. Some children do not learn to speak, others speak in limited phrases, and some have relatively normal language development.

KEY CONCEPTS

- Autism
- Asperger syndrome
- Rett syndrome
- Childhood disintegrative disorder (CDD)
- Pervasive developmental disorder, not otherwise specified (PDD-NOS)

INTRODUCTION

Defined by a marked impairment in socialization, communication, and sometimes sensory integration, autism spectrum disorder (ASD) is a diagnosis introduced in the fifth edition of the *Diagnostic and Statistical Manual of Mental Disorders* (DSM-5). It encompasses the previously separate diagnostic categories of autistic disorder, Asperger's disorder, childhood disintegrative disorder, and pervasive developmental disorder-not otherwise specified. Clinicians had long had difficulty distinguishing among these categories, and there was insufficient research to support maintaining them as separate diagnoses.

Autism spectrum disorders are thought to have a biological basis. One of the strongest associations is with genetics. ASD generally has a familial linkage and researchers have begun to identify combinations of genes responsible for the conditions. Pre- and perinatal disruptions have also been implicated in causing ASD. Research suggests that being born very prematurely, being exposed to viral infections in utero, and experiencing oxygen deprivation during the birth process can increase the likelihood of developing ASD. The notion that ASD is caused by vaccinations has been refuted by research.

ASD is usually diagnosed in children around three or four years of age. Some children with autism show signs of developmental issues throughout their infant and toddler years, while others develop in the expected manner at first, but then slow or even regress. Symptoms typically include deficits in using and understanding language and difficulty relating to people and events. Symptoms also include unusual play with toys and other objects and difficulty with changes in routine or surroundings. In some cases, children exhibit repetitive body movements or behavior patterns. Unusual responses to sensory information, such as loud noises and lights, are also common. The condition typically remains with the individual throughout his or her life, although the course of the disorder can improve with early behavioral intervention. For individuals with ASD, an applied behavioral intervention strategy known as discrete trials has been successful in improving functioning. Individuals with high-functioning autism can often lead successful lives, although the impairments in socialization and communication continue throughout their lives. Children with ASD can have intelligence test scores that range from profoundly retarded to gifted. Although rarely seen, autistic savants can display extraordinary talents in select areas such as painting, counting, and memory. These individuals, however, often display intelligence quotients (IQs) in the mental retardation range. Raymond Babbitt, the main character from the film *Rain Man* (1988), is a good example of an individual with autistic savant skills. Raymond was able to count cards and remember events when provided with a specific date but was otherwise incapable of caring for himself or even providing correct change to purchase a candy bar.

DIAGNOSIS

Individuals with ASD tend to show symptoms in two distinct areas. The first is deficits in communication and social abilities. People with ASD may have difficulty reading tone or body language, tending to take everything said at face value. They may not initiate conversations and may have difficulty sustaining a conversation once started. Often, they avoid eye contact and are uncomfortable with physical contact. They may also struggle to understand how other people feel or the reasons for their feelings. As a result, people with this disorder often have difficulty forming and maintaining interpersonal relationships.

The second category of characteristic symptoms is restrictive repetitive behaviors, interests, and activities, or RRBs. A person with ASD may have an extremely strong interest in one narrow subject and might talk about it constantly even if those to whom he or she is talking do not show any interest in it. Some autistic people may repeat a single word or phrase over and over or make repetitive nonverbal noises. They may also display repetitive physical behaviors, such as rocking back and forth or flapping their hands. Finally, they may be especially sensitive to sensory input of various kinds. The ways in which this sensitivity manifests vary among individuals, but some examples include being upset by loud noises, being bothered by particular clothing textures, and being a picky eater.

Severity of symptoms is classified according to a series of levels: Level 1, or requiring support; Level 2, or requiring substantial support; and Level 3, or requiring very substantial support. Individuals with mild, or Level 1, symptoms are usually able to attend school alongside neurotypical children their age, hold down jobs, and generally care for themselves. Meanwhile, those with more severe, or Level 3, symptoms may be unable to speak or perform basic self-care tasks and as such may require care throughout their lives. The two groups of symptoms are classified separately, so someone might have, for example, Level 2 difficulties with social behaviors but Level 1 RRBs.

PREVALENCE

As of 2007, the prevalence of ASD was estimated to be six cases per one thousand people. These rates have been found to be consistent across cultures and ethnic groups. However, they vary greatly by gender; on average, women and girls make up roughly one in four diagnoses of ASD, according to a 2009 study. ASD has, therefore, traditionally been considered to appear more frequently in males than in females, but more recently it has been proposed that females with ASD are underdiagnosed because they display different symptoms from males. ASD is often comorbid with other disorders, including epilepsy, intellectual disabilities, learning disabilities, and sensory processing disorder.

CONTROVERSY

The combination of the various disorders formerly categorized as pervasive developmental disorders into a single diagnosis in the DSM-5 has attracted criticism. Some of this criticism comes from people formerly diagnosed with Asperger's syndrome (a form of ASD without language development or cognitive delays), who feel that being considered autistic will increase the stigma against them. Another concern that has been raised is that the new criteria for ASD will make it more difficult to diagnose people whose symptoms are on the milder end of the spectrum.

CONCLUSION

Children with pervasive developmental disorders display impairments in communication and socialization, and often display stereotyped behaviors such as hand flapping, rocking, and intense interest in objects. The course of an autism spectrum disorder does not remit, although early intervention can improve social and communicative functioning. Individuals with severe versions of the disorder often require lifelong care. Higher-functioning individuals can often function independently and lead vocationally productive lives. Treatments for individuals with ASD usually involve behavioral therapy augmented by selected psychotropic medication. The cause of ASD is thought to be genetic, although researchers have not yet uncovered a definitive cause.

BIBLIOGRAPHY

Freitag, Christine M., et al. "Genetics of Autistic Disorders: Review and Clinical Implications." *European Child and Adolescent Psychiatry* 19.3 (2010): 169–78. Print.

Gardener, Hannah, Donna Spiegelman, and Stephen L. Buka. "Perinatal and Neonatal Risk Factors for Autism: A Comprehensive Meta-Analysis." *Obstetrical and Gynecological Survey* 66.12 (2011) 749–51. Print.

Godlee, Fiona, Jane Smith, and Harvey Marcovitch. "Wakefield's Article Linking MMR Vaccine and Autism Was Fraudulent." *BMJ*. BMJ, 6 Jan. 2011.

Web. 3 June 2014.

Hallahan, D. P., and J. M. Kauffman. *Exceptional Learners*. 11th ed. New York: Allyn, 2007. Print.

Huerta, Marisela, and Catherine Lord. "Diagnostic Evaluation of Autism Spectrum Disorders." *Pediatric Clinics of North America* 59.1 (2012): 103–11. Print.

Judd, Sandra J., ed. *Autism and Pervasive Developmental Disorders Sourcebook*. Detroit: Omnigraphics, 2007. Print.

Martin, R. P., and S. C. Dombrowski. *Prenatal Exposures: Psychological and Educational Consequences for Children*. New York: Springer, 2008. Print.

Myles, Brenda Smith, et al., eds. *Autism Spectrum Disorders: A Handbook for Parents and Professionals*. Westport: Praeger, 2007. Print.

Paxton, Katherine, and Irene A. Estay. *Counseling People on the Autism Spectrum: A Practical Manual*. Philadelphia: Jessica Kingsley, 2007. Print.

Tsakanikos, Elias, Lisa Underwood, Eugenia Kravariti, Nick Bouras, and Jane McCarthy. "Gender Differences in Co-Morbid Psychopathology and Clinical Management in Adults with Autism Spectrum Disorders." *Research in Autism Spectrum Disorders* 5.2 (2011): 803–08. Print.

Stefan C. Dombrowski

SEE ALSO: Asperger syndrome; Autism; Developmental disabilities; Genetics and mental health; Intelligence; Mental retardation.

Philosophy and psychology

TYPE OF PSYCHOLOGY: Cognition; Consciousness; Origin and definition of psychology

Psychology as a discipline has its origins in philosophy from which it differentiated on the basis of a commitment to the empirical method and psychology's resulting claim to scientific status. However, philosophy and psychology continue to address many of the same questions, albeit from different points of view, and the work of each discipline continues to illuminate that of the other.

KEY CONCEPTS
- Epistemology
- Free will versus determinism
- Intentionality
- Metaphysics
- Mind-body problem
- Ontology
- Phenomenology
- Philosophy of science

INTRODUCTION

The relationship between philosophy and psychology is complex. Psychology has its origins in philosophy, and until the mid-twentieth century, psychology was part of the philosophy department at universities. Psychology is often held to have split off from philosophy in 1879, with the founding of Wilhelm Wundt's experimental psychology laboratory in Leipzig, Germany. To recognize the split is to define psychology as an empirical science, as many have done. However, psychology and philosophy address many of the same questions, questions that have puzzled people since time immemorial and that have been addressed not only by psychology and philosophy but also by religion, anthropology, political science, and other social sciences and humanistic disciplines. Not all those questions can be or have been addressed empirically, and the empirical work of psychology has raised many philosophical questions in its own right. The concerns addressed by both disciplines include questions of metaphysics (including ontology), epistemology, and moral philosophy (ethics), although the distinctions between these areas often blur, and other topics have also been addressed by both disciplines (such as phenomenology and hermeneutics).

PHILOSOPHICAL ORIGINS OF PSYCHOLOGY

Many trace the origin of psychology to the ancient Greek philosophers, particularly Socrates, Plato, and Aristotle. Certainly, topics such as the ones favored by the philosophers were being addressed long before psychology developed a disciplinary identity. Throughout the Middle Ages, philosophers and theologians such as Peter Abelard, Thomas Aquinas, Saint Bonaventure, and William Ockham explored the realm of human knowing, thinking, feeling, and sensing, although without the extensive empirical investigation of these states that came to characterize the psychological method. From the time of the Renaissance, philosophers such as René Descartes, Thomas Hobbes, John Locke, George Berkeley, David Hume, James Mill, John Stuart Mill, and Immanuel Kant debated the topics that have come to be central to the discipline of psychology.

METAPHYSICS

Metaphysics is the branch of philosophy that addresses questions regarding the nature of reality and the sorts of things that exist in the world. In modern philosophical usage, this branch includes questions of ontology, including the philosophy of mind. Both psychology and philosophy are concerned with the philosophy of mind. The philosophy of mind traces its origins to the ancient Greek philosophers, as well as Franz Brentano, William James, and John Dewey, among others. The philosophy of mind has primarily been concerned with three questions: the meaning of intentionality, the mind-body problem, and the problem of free will versus determinism.

Philosophers have asked what it means to have intentionality. Some have asserted that mental states, such as wishing, believing, and thinking, are necessarily about something, which is termed the "intentional object" of the mental state. (For example, I think that it is almost time for dinner; I wish that my homework were done; I believe I can succeed.) However, this raises the question of whether intentions "cause" actions, in a strict philosophical sense. This line of thought has been pursued by the philosophers Ludwig Wittgenstein, Donald Davidson, and Derek Parfit.

The philosophy of mind also looks at the relationship between the mind and the body (the mind-body problem) and asks: If all mental acts arise from physical states, what claims are left for the realm of the purely mental, rather than physical? The mind-body problem is related directly to questions regarding idealism versus materialism (whether the world is reducible to ideas or to the material world) and indirectly to questions of free will versus determinism. It is also related to questions of dualism versus monism (for example, the question of whether there are two sorts of things in the world or one). Under dualism, if the brain and mind (or body and mind) are wholly separable, questions arise concerning how the two are linked and how something that has no physical properties might be related to, communicate with, or affect something that has exclusively physical properties. These types of questions have been addressed by research in cognitive neuroscience by scientists such as Paul Churchland and Patricia Churchland and by philosophers such as Davidson and Thomas Nagel. However, if mind and brain are assumed to be the same (monism), other questions arise. For example, if mental states are wholly determined by physical changes in the brain, in what sense is it possible to claim that human beings have free will?

Free will versus determinism is the third question addressed by the philosophy of mind. Although this issue is not completely separate from religious questions treated by philosophers and theologists, the question has taken a different form in psychology. Psychologists as varied as the American behaviorist B. F. Skinner and the Viennese psychoanalyst Sigmund Freud have held that human behavior is determined, either by conscious or unconscious forces, while the early American psychologist William James and the American founder of person-centered therapy Carl R. Rogers, as well as other humanistic and existential psychologists, have held that humans have free will. However, if humans have free will and therefore can make choices that are independent of antecedent conditions, the question arises of whether psychology is a science in the sense of being a discipline that can make reliable predictions that can be tested and produce results that can be replicated by others.

EPISTEMOLOGY

Epistemology is the branch of philosophy devoted to the question of how people know what they know. This includes questions regarding the nature, scope, and possibility of any knowledge, and psychological knowledge. Both psychology and philosophy have wrestled with such epistemological questions as the nature of consciousness, the possibility of intersubjectivity (how people know others' minds), and how people know their own minds.

The nature of consciousness has been a central question of both psychology and philosophy. This topic has been explored phenomenologically, including by Freud, and also through an attempt to identify the neural correlates of consciousness, a method pursued by cognitive neuroscientists as well as the philosopher John Searle. Questions regarding consciousness have become increasingly intriguing with the discovery of functional magnetic resonance imaging (fMRI), which permits correlation of the structures of the brain with the functions that they are performing in real time. Included in the study of consciousness are questions regarding sensation and perception, which raise philosophical problems, including whether the sensation of the object is separate from the perception of it, the knowledge of it, or both.

The problem of other minds, or intersubjectivity, has been of concern in both psychology and philosophy. It has taken many forms, including questions regarding how people know that others have minds and how they can have knowledge of others' mental states. Philosophers

Daniel Dennett and Davidson in particular have addressed this question. In psychology, this question is central to both clinical practice and research methodology, insofar as both depend on understanding the minds of those whom psychologists are studying and treating.

The question of how well people can know others' minds leads directly to a third question, namely, how people can know their own minds and whether introspection is possible and by what means. Philosophers have asked how people can be sure about the contents of their own minds and on what authority they issue claims about their self-knowledge. They also ask what the relationship is between people's claims of self-knowledge and the language they use to express them, as well as how to validate what people say about themselves. These questions have been pursued by the philosophers Wittgenstein and Davidson and the cognitive scientist Jerry Fodor. Such questions have clear implications for introspective (talk) psychotherapies, which rely heavily on first-person assertions by clients regarding their mental states.

PHILOSOPHY OF SCIENCE

The philosophy of science is primarily concerned with the question of whether and to what extent the claims made by empirical psychology can be justified; that is, whether psychology is in fact a science like chemistry and physics. This critique has its origin in the work of the philosopher of science Thomas Kuhn, who pointed out that sciences move forward through a process of paradigm shifts, in which previously inchoate data or anomalous data become organized by a new explanatory rubric that better accounts for them than the previous theory did. By such standards, many have concluded that psychology is a preparadigmatic science. The work of philosophers Karl Popper and Paul Feyerabend is related to this topic.

Psychoanalysis in particular has been concerned with questions of whether its findings are best judged by scientific criteria (a correspondence theory of truth) or by hermeneutic or aesthetic criteria (coherence or parsimony). This debate has gained force because the status of psychoanalysis as a medical, and therefore presumably scientific, treatment rests on data obtained through the methods of free association and recollection, which raise unique philosophical problems. This debate has often taken the form of whether psychoanalysis is a hermeneutic pursuit, with the philosopher of science Adolf Grunbaum and the American psychoanalysts Donald

Spence, Arnold Modell, and Roy Shafer weighing in on the matter.

MORAL PHILOSOPHY

Moral philosophy is the branch of philosophy that concerns ethics. Although ethics has been a major topic in philosophy, psychology's concern with ethics has been largely restricted to questions regarding the treatment of human and animal subjects in experiments and patients in clinical practice. Less attention has been devoted to broader questions of the place of values in human life, and such work has rarely drawn on the related work in moral philosophy.

PHENOMENOLOGY

Phenomenology is a branch of philosophy that studies people's conscious experiences of the world. Its premise is that reality is based on how objects and events are perceived or understood by the human consciousness and not on anything independent of human consciousness. Its philosophical origins are to be found in the works of Martin Heidegger, Edmund Husserl, Maurice Merleau-Ponty, Paul Ricoeur, and other twentieth century European philosophers. Its concern with first-person subjective mental states made phenomenology a natural fit for the emerging discipline of psychology, and existential and humanistic psychology in particular have conducted research to test phenemonological assertions as a guide to effective treatment. The work of the American person-centered psychologists Carl R. Rogers and Eugene Gendlin and the existential Swiss psychiatrists Ludwig Binswanger and Medard Boss have been influential among clinicians interested in phenomenology. The Society for Theoretical and Philosophical Psychology has served as one intellectual home for those interested in such topics.

BIBLIOGRAPHY

Honderich, Ted, ed. *The Oxford Guide to Philosophy.* New York: Oxford University Press, 2005. Print.

Leahey, Thomas. *A History of Psychology: Main Currents in Psychological Thought.* 7th ed. Englewood Cliffs, N.J.: Prentice Hall, 2007. Print.

MacLeod, Robert B. *The Persistent Problems of Psychology.* Pittsburgh: Duquesne University Press, 1975. Print.

McLaughlin, Brian P., et al. *The Oxford Handbook of Philosophy of Mind.* New York: Oxford UP, 2011. Print.

Messer, Stanley, Louis Sass, and Robert Woolfolk, eds. *Hermeneutics and Psychological Theory: Interpretive Perspectives on Personality, Psychotherapy, and Psychopathology.* New Brunswick, N.J.: Rutgers University Press, 1990. Print.

Presbey, Gail, Karsten Struhl, and Richard Olsen. *The Philosophical Quest: A Cross-Cultural Reader.* 2d ed. New York: McGraw-Hill, 2000. Print.

Schellekens, Elisabeth, and Peter Goldie. *The Aesthetic Mind: Philosophy and Psychology.* New York: Oxford UP, 2014. Print.Sneddon, Andrew. Like Minded: Externalism and Moral Psychology. Cambridge: MIT P, 2011. Print.

Elizabeth W. Davies

SEE ALSO: Dewey, John; Experimentation: Ethics and subject rights; Experimentation: Independent, dependent, and control variables; Freud, Sigmund; James, William; Psychoanalytic psychology; Psychology: Definition; Psychology: History; Rogers, Carl R.

Phobias

TYPE OF PSYCHOLOGY: Psychopathology

Phobias are exaggerated, unjustified fears of everyday objects or situations, such as fear of certain types of animals or fears of doing things in front of other people. Though many people experience irrational fears or phobias, few seek treatment; as a result, they suffer emotional pain and may find their lives limited by their phobias.

KEY CONCEPTS

- Conditioned response (CR)
- Conditioned stimulus (CS)
- Instrumental conditioning
- Pavlovian conditioning
- Unconditioned response (UR)
- Unconditioned stimulus (US)

INTRODUCTION

Phobias are a type of anxiety disorder characterized by a persistent, exaggerated, irrational fear of certain objects or situations and by efforts to avoid the object or situation. In many cases, the distress and the avoidance efforts significantly interfere with an individual's daily life. Phobias are common in the general population; approximately one person in ten suffers from mild phobias, and severe, disabling phobias are found in one person in five hundred.

The three major types of phobias are agoraphobia (a fear of situations in which escape is perceived to be difficult or assistance unavailable), social phobias, and specific (or "simple") phobias. In social phobias, being observed by others may elicit anxiety and the desire to avoid such situations. The person fears doing something that will lead to embarrassment or humiliation, such as being unable to speak or showing nervousness through trembling hands or other signs. Persons with specific phobias avoid a certain type of object or situation or suffer extreme anxiety when in the presence of these objects or situations. Some examples of common specific phobias are acrophobia, fear of heights; arachnophobia, fear of spiders; claustrophobia, fear of being in small, enclosed spaces; pathophobia, fear of diseases and germs; and xenophobia, fear of strangers.

In the presence of the feared object or situation, the severely phobic person's experience and reaction differ dramatically from the average person's. Physiologically, changes in the body cause an increase in heart rate and blood pressure, tensing of muscles, and feelings of fear. In many cases, a panic attack may develop, characterized by muscular trembling and shaking, rapid, shallow breathing, and feelings of unbearable anxiety and dizziness. Behaviorally, the person will stop or redirect whatever activity in which he or she is engaged, then try to escape from or avoid the phobic object or situation. Cognitively, a phobic person at a distance from the object or situation can recognize it as posing little actual danger; on approaching it, however, fear rises, and the estimation of risk increases.

THEORETICAL EXPLANATIONS

The many theories that attempt to explain how phobias develop can be grouped under three general headings: those that stress unconscious emotional conflicts, those that explain phobias based on the principles of learning, and those that consider biological factors. For Sigmund Freud, phobias represented the external manifestation of unconscious internal emotional conflicts that had their origin in early childhood. These conflicts typically involved the inhibition of primitive sexual feelings.

Learning-theory explanations of phobias are based on Pavlovian conditioning, instrumental conditioning, and social learning theory. According to a Pavlovian conditioning model, phobias result when a neutral stimulus—a dog, for example—is paired with an unconditioned stimulus (US), for example, a painful bite to the leg. After this event, the sight of the dog has become a conditioned stimulus (CS) that elicits a conditioned response (CR), fear; thus, a dog phobia has been learned. Instrumental conditioning (the modification of behavior as a result of its consequences) has been combined with Pavlovian conditioning in the two-factor model of phobias.

After the establishment of the phobia by Pavlovian conditioning, as above, a person will attempt to escape from or avoid the phobic object or situation whenever it is encountered. When this is successful, the fear subsides. The reduction in fear is a desirable consequence that increases the likelihood of escape/avoidance behavior in the future (that is, the escape/avoidance behavior is reinforced). The two-factor model thus accounts for both the development and the maintenance of phobias. Social learning theory suggests that human learning is based primarily on the observation and imitation of others; thus, fears and phobias would be acquired by observing others who show fearful behavior toward certain objects or situations. This occurs primarily during childhood, when children learn many behaviors and attitudes by modeling those of others.

Two theories suggest that inherited biological factors contribute to the development of phobias. The preparedness theory suggests that those stimuli that are most easily conditioned are objects or situations that may have posed a particular threat to humans' early ancestors, such as spiders, heights, small spaces, thunder, and strangers. Thus, people are genetically prepared to acquire fear of them quickly. Similarly, people vary in susceptibility to phobias, and this is also thought to be based at least partly on an inherited predisposition. A phobia-prone person may be physiologically highly arousable; thus, many more events would reach a threshold of fear necessary for conditioning.

Stressful life situations, including extreme conflict or frustration, may also predispose a person to develop a phobia or exacerbate an existing phobia. Further, a sense of powerlessness or lack of control over one's situation may increase susceptibility; this may partly explain why phobias are more common in women, as these feelings are reported more often by women than by men. Once initiated, phobias tend to persist and even worsen over time, and the fear may spread to other, similar objects or situations. Even phobias that have been successfully treated may recur if the person is exposed to the original US, or even to another US that produces extreme anxiety. Thus, many factors—unconscious, learned, and

biological—may be involved in the onset and the maintenance of phobias. As every person is unique in terms of biology and life experience, each phobia is also unique and represents a particular interaction of the factors above and possibly other, unknown factors.

CASE STUDIES AND THERAPY TECHNIQUES

The following two case studies of phobias illustrate their onset, their development, and the various treatment approaches typically used. These studies are fictionalized composites of the experiences of actual clients.

Ellen P. entered an anxiety disorders clinic requesting large amounts of tranquilizers. She revealed that she wanted them to enable her to fly on airplanes; if she could not fly, she would probably lose her job as a sales representative for her company. Ellen described an eight-year history of a fear of flying during which she had simply avoided all airplane flights and had driven a car or taken a train to distant sales appointments. She would sometimes drive through the night, keep her appointments during the day, then again drive through the night back to the home office. As these trips occurred more often, she became increasingly exhausted, and her work performance began to decline noticeably.

A review of major childhood and adolescent experiences revealed only that Ellen was a chronic worrier. She also reported flying comfortably on many occasions prior to the onset of her phobia, but remembered her last flight in vivid detail. She was flying to meet her husband for a honeymoon cruise, but the plane was far behind schedule because of poor weather. She began to worry that she would miss the boat and that her honeymoon, and possibly her marriage, would be ruined. The plane then encountered some minor turbulence, and brief images of a crash raced through Ellen's mind. She rapidly became increasingly anxious, tense, and uncomfortable. She grasped her seat cushion; her heart seemed to be pounding in her throat; she felt dizzy and was beginning to perspire. Hoping no one would notice her distress, she closed her eyes, pretending to sleep for the remainder of the flight. After returning from the cruise, she convinced her husband to cancel their plane reservations, and thus began her eight years of avoiding flying.

Ellen's psychologist began exposure therapy for her phobia. First she was trained to relax deeply. Then she was gradually exposed to her feared stimuli, progressing from visiting an airport to sitting on a taxiing plane to weekly flights of increasing length in a small plane. After ten weeks of therapy and practice at home and the airport, Ellen was able to fly on a commercial airliner. Two years after the conclusion of therapy, Ellen met her psychologist by chance and informed her that she now had her own pilot's license.

In the second case, Steve R. was a high school junior who was referred by his father because of his refusal to attend school. Steve was described as a loner who avoided other people and suffered fears of storms, cats, and now, apparently, school. He was of above-average intelligence and was pressured by his father to excel academically and attend a prestigious college. Steve's mother was described as being shy like Steve. Steve was her only child, and she doted on him, claiming she knew what it felt like to be in his situation.

When interviewed, Steve sat rigidly in his chair, spoke in clipped sentences, and offered answers only to direct questions. Questioning revealed that Steve's refusal to attend school was based on a fear of ridicule by his classmates. He would not eat or do any written work in front of them for fear he was being watched and would do something clumsy, thus embarrassing himself. He never volunteered answers to teachers' questions, but in one class, the teacher had begun to call on Steve regularly for the correct answer whenever other students had missed the question. Steve would sit in a near-panic state, fearing he would be called on. After two weeks of this, he refused to return to school.

Steve was diagnosed as having a severe social phobia. His therapy included a contract with his teachers in which it was agreed that he would not be called on in class until therapy had made it possible for him to answer with only moderate anxiety. In return, he was expected to attend all his classes. To help make this transition, a psychiatrist prescribed an antianxiety drug to help reduce the panic symptoms. A psychologist began relaxation training for use in exposure therapy, which would include Steve volunteering answers in class and seeking social interactions with his peers. Steve finished high school, though he left the state university at the end of his first semester because of a worsening of his phobias. His therapy was resumed, and he graduated from a local community college, though his phobias continued to recur during stressful periods in his life. These cases illustrate many of the concepts related to the study of phobias. In both cases, it is possible that a high emotional reactivity predisposed the person to a phobia. In Ellen's case, the onset of the phobia was sudden and appeared to be the result of Pavlovian conditioning, whereas in Steve's case, the phobia likely developed over time and involved

social learning: modeling of his mother's behavior. Steve's phobia may also have been inadvertently reinforced by his mother's attention; thus, instrumental conditioning may have been involved as well. Ellen's phobia could be seen to involve a sense of lack of control, combined with a possibly inherited predisposition to fear enclosed spaces. Steve's phobia illustrated both a spreading of the phobia and a recurrence of the phobia under stress.

HISTORICAL VARIATIONS IN PERSPECTIVES

As comprehensive psychological theories of human behavior began to emerge in the early 1900s, each was faced with the challenge of explaining the distinct symptoms, but apparently irrational nature, of phobias. For example, in 1909, Sigmund Freud published his account of the case of "Little Hans," a young boy with a horse phobia. Freud hypothesized that Hans had an unconscious fear of his father that was transferred to a more appropriate object: the horse. Freud's treatment of phobias involved analyzing the unconscious conflicts (through psychoanalysis) and giving patients insight into the "true" nature of their fears.

An alternative explanation of phobias based on the principles of Pavlovian conditioning was proposed by John B. Watson and Rosalie Rayner in 1920. They conditioned a fear of a white rat in an infant nicknamed "Little Albert" by pairing presentation of the rat with a frightening noise (an unconditioned stimulus). After a few such trials, simply presenting the rat (now a conditioned stimulus) produced fear and crying (the conditioned response).

EXPERIMENTAL MODELS

As B. F. Skinner's laboratory discoveries of the principles of instrumental conditioning began to be applied to humans in the 1940s and 1950s, experimental models of phobias in animals were developed. In the 1950s, Joseph Wolpe created phobia-like responses in cats by shocking them in experimental cages. He was later able to decrease their fear by feeding them in the cages where they had previously been shocked. Based on this counterconditioning model, Wolpe developed the therapy procedure of systematic desensitization, which paired mental images of the feared stimulus with bodily relaxation.

Social learning theory as advanced by Albert Bandura in the 1960s was also applied to phobias. Bandura conducted experiments showing that someone might develop a phobia by observing another person behaving fearfully. It was later demonstrated that some phobias could be treated by having the patient observe and imitate a nonfearful model.

Cognitive approaches to phobias were also developed in the 1970s and 1980s by therapists such as Albert Ellis and Aaron T. Beck. These theories focus on the role of disturbing thoughts in creating bodily arousal and associated fear. Therapy then consists of altering these thought patterns.

APPLICATIONS TO PSYCHOLOGY

Phobias can thus be seen as providing a testing ground for the major theories of psychology. Whether the theorist adopts a psychodynamic, learning/behavioral, or cognitive perspective, some account of the development and treatment of phobias must be made. No one theory has been shown to be completely adequate, so research continues in each area. The study of phobias also illustrates the importance to psychology of animal research in helping psychologists to understand and treat human problems. For example, Susan Mineka has used monkeys to demonstrate the relative importance of social learning versus biology in the development of phobias. Future research will also likely consider the interactions among the various models of phobias and the conditions that might predict which models would be most effective in explaining and treating specific cases of phobias. As the models mature and are integrated into a comprehensive theory of phobias, this knowledge can then be applied to the prevention of phobias.

BIBLIOGRAPHY

Axelby, Clayton P., ed. *Social Phobia: Etiology, Diagnosis, and Treatment*. New York: Nova Science, 2009. Print.

Beck, Aaron T., and Gary Emery. *Anxiety Disorders and Phobias: A Cognitive Perspective*. Reprint. Cambridge: Basic, 2005. Print.

Bourne, Edmund. *The Anxiety and Phobia Workbook*. 5th ed. Oakland: New Harbinger, 2010. Print.

Buchanan, Heather, and Neil Coulson. *Phobias*. Basingstoke: Palgrave, 2012. Print.

Doctor, Ronald M., Ada P. Kahn, and Christine Adamec. *The Encyclopedia of Phobias, Fears, and Anxieties*. 3rd ed. New York: Facts on File, 2008. Print.

Gold, Mark S. *The Good News about Panic, Anxiety, and Phobias*. New York: Bantam, 1990. Print.

Marks, Issac Meyer. *Fears, Phobias, and Rituals*. New York: Oxford UP, 1987. Print.

Mineka, Susan. "Animal Models of Anxiety-Based Disorders: Their Usefulness and Limitations." *Anxiety*

and the Anxiety Disorders. Ed. A. Hussain Tuma and Jack Maser. Hillsdale: Erlbaum, 1985. Print.

"Phobias." *MedLine Plus*. US Nat'l. Lib. of Medicine, 9 May 2014. Web. 25 June 2014.

Wilson, R. Reid. *Breaking the Panic Cycle: Self-Help for People with Phobias*. Rockville: Anxiety Disorders Association of America, 1987. Print.

David S. McDougal

SEE ALSO: Agoraphobia and panic disorders; Anxiety disorders; Conditioning; Learning; Nervous system; Observational learning and modeling therapy; Operant conditioning therapies; Panic attacks; Pavlovian conditioning; Reflexes; Systematic desensitization.

Physical development
Environment versus genetics

TYPE OF PSYCHOLOGY: Developmental psychology

Physical development includes a child's physical characteristics, motor development, growth, and brain and nervous system development; the dramatic changes that occur in these areas during the early years of life result from the combined influences of a child's genetic makeup and environmental factors.

KEY CONCEPTS
- Chromosome
- Critical period
- Dominant gene
- Gene
- Genotype
- Phenotype
- Polygenic trait
- Recessive gene
- Sex chromosomes
- Sex-linked trait

INTRODUCTION

Physical development generally refers to a child's physical characteristics (such as eye or hair color), growth (changes in height, weight, and bodily proportions), motor development (increasing control over movement, as in the progression from sitting up to standing to walking), and brain and nervous system development (an increase in the size and complexity of the brain and an increase in the efficiency of message transfers). Dramatic changes take place in these four areas during the early years of life because of the combined influence of a child's genetic makeup and the environment.

Genes provide a master plan, or blueprint, for development. Genes are chemical bases that form small sections of thread-like structures called chromosomes. Each chromosome is made of thousands of genes, and every cell in the human body has twenty-three pairs of chromosomes. Encoded in the genes are those traits common to the human race (such as the ability to walk upright) as well as those traits that make each child unique (such as the rate of maturation). Genes direct the form and sequence of development, including setting limits on a child's potential and predisposing him or her toward either a normal or an abnormal course of development.

GENETIC TRAITS
Parents pass traits along to their offspring in chromosomes. During the process of fertilization, the twenty-three chromosomes in the mother's ovum unite with the twenty-three chromosomes in the father's sperm. The resulting baby's traits depend on which genes from the mother are matched with which genes from the father. In some cases, certain genes are dominant or recessive. For example, the gene for brown eyes is dominant over the gene for blue eyes, which is recessive. If a child inherits the dominant gene for brown eyes from one parent and the recessive gene for blue eyes from the other parent, the child will have brown eyes. A child must receive the recessive gene for blue eyes from both parents to have blue eyes. In other cases, certain traits appear to be a mixture. These polygenic traits are the result of the combined influence of many genes; skin color is one example of a polygenic trait. Traits may also be sex linked, which means that the genes for certain traits (color blindness, for example) are carried in the sex chromosomes. Sex chromosomes constitute the twenty-third pair of chromosomes and function to determine a person's sex. (Women have two X chromosomes, whereas men have one X and one Y chromosome.)

ENVIRONMENTAL INFLUENCE
Whereas genes provide a blueprint for development, the environment may modify the extent to which the blueprint is followed by influencing the direction and speed of a child's physical development and the expression of certain traits. Environmental influences are those that exist outside the person; they generally include a person's physical and sociocultural surroundings. The physi-

cal environment includes such aspects of a child's immediate environment as the exposure of a fetus to drugs taken by its mother or the exposure of a young child to such environmental hazards as lead or mercury. The sociocultural environment refers to the influence that the people in a child's life may have on his or her development. For example, the parent-child relationship and the parents' ethnic backgrounds have been found to influence a child's physical development.

GENOTYPE AND PHENOTYPE RELATIONSHIP
Although some genotypes (a person's genetic makeup) are expressed directly in a person's phenotype (observable traits and behavior), as in the case of eye color or blood type, most phenotypes are the result of an interaction between genes and the environment. Some researchers, in fact, have stated that development is the expression of a person's genotype in the context of that individual's environment. For example, children may inherit a genetic tendency toward obesity or toward being athletic. Whether children become obese, however, may depend on the eating behaviors of their family; similarly, whether children develop their full athletic potential may depend on the children's nutritional status, opportunities available to participate in athletic activities, and the amount of parental support and encouragement received.

Genetic and environmental factors affect many aspects of physical development, ranging from common physical traits and everyday bodily functions to diseases and disorders. Children's physical features (such as hair and eye color), blood type, amount of body fat, body build, metabolism, weight, health, activity level, sensitivity, blood pressure, timing and rate of maturation, hormonal regulation, sequence of motor development, and hand preference are all examples of genetically based traits. Dominant gene traits include brown eyes, brown hair, curly hair, thick lips, and normal color vision, whereas blue eyes and blond hair are examples of recessive gene traits. Height and weight are two types of polygenic traits; color blindness is an example of a sex-linked trait.

GENETIC CAUSE OF DISORDERS
Defective (or absent) genes can cause genetic disorders and diseases that are acquired through these same inheritance patterns. Achondroplasia (a type of dwarfism that is apparent at birth) and Huntington's chorea (a genetic disease that affects the central nervous system

and causes progressive neural degeneration), for example, are dominant gene disorders. Sickle-cell anemia (a painful blood disorder that often leads to heart or kidney failure), congenital deafness, phenylketonuria (PKU, the lack of an enzyme to complete the metabolism of milk protein), cystic fibrosis (a metabolic error leading to sticky fluid in the lungs that clogs the airways), and galactosemia (defective milk sugar metabolism) are all recessive gene disorders. Many disorders are polygenic; among them are cleft palate and cleft lips, childhood diabetes, spina bifida, hip dislocation, and allergies. Color blindness, hemophilia (the inability of the blood to coagulate), and fragile X syndrome (a leading cause of intellectual disability among newborns) are all sex-linked disorders.

Developmental disorders may also result from faulty chromosome distribution. Down syndrome, for example, results when a child has three instead of the normal two number 21 chromosomes. Children with Down syndrome have distinct physical features and are moderately to severely intellectually disabled. Errors of sex-chromosome distribution can also occur—female children may lack a second X chromosome, or male children may have an extra X or Y chromosome. These sex-chromosome disorders generally result in infertility, some type of intellectual disability, or both.

ENVIRONMENTAL CAUSES OF DISORDERS

Some of the physical, social, and historical influences of the environment begin exerting their effects on a child's development even before birth. Diseases of the mother during pregnancy, such as syphilis, German measles, herpes, gonorrhea, and acquired immunodeficiency syndrome (AIDS), may have consequences for the fetus ranging from blindness, deafness, and brain damage to death. Also, drugs ingested by the mother during pregnancy (including alcohol and the nicotine in cigarettes) may affect the unborn child in mild or severe ways. Maternal emotional stress, inadequate medical care, incompatible blood types between the mother and the fetus, exposure to high levels of radiation, and malnutrition all have the potential for adversely affecting the developing fetus.

The impact of some of these environmental influences on development (especially drugs, disease, and malnutrition) depends in part on the timing and the dosage involved. Critical periods are specific times in development when developing organs, structures, or abilities are most vulnerable to environmental influences.

During prenatal development, the first three months of pregnancy is a critical period because all the basic structures (the eyes, ears, brain, heart, and limbs) and organ systems of the fetus are being formed. Shortly after birth, there is another critical period for brain development, as the brain is developing rapidly. Serious damage to the fetus or infant can result if it is exposed to harmful environmental influences during this time, because the parts of the body that are developing the most rapidly are the most vulnerable. If exposed to the same influences later, the child would most likely suffer less serious consequences.

After a child is born, health, medical care, nutrition, and disease continue to influence physical development. Exposure to environmental hazards such as lead or toxic mercury levels can also cause deformities, intellectual disability, and poor muscular development and control.

ROLE OF PRACTICE

Normal development not only requires the absence of genetic and environmental difficulties; it also requires practice. In studies of children, normal experience or practice has been found to be necessary for normal motor development. In addition, studies using animals have found that normal, everyday visual experience is necessary for the development of normal vision and that enriched or deprived sensory environments can affect brain development (for example, the weight of the cortex and the number of interconnections between the brain cells). In some instances, experience has also been found to speed up development. Philip Zelazo and his colleagues reported in the early 1970s that practice of the walking reflex early in life led to earlier walking in infants; other studies suggest that such practice can be harmful. Some studies have reported that infants who have experience sitting in someone's lap are able to sit alone earlier. Although some skills may be influenced by practice, physical and neural maturation limit what can be achieved.

SOCIOCULTURAL FACTORS

Sociocultural factors, such as family interaction patterns and ethnicity, affect development in a number of ways. Studies have found, for example, that parental attentiveness and encouragement are important factors influencing whether infants take an interest in and explore their environments. Studies of maternal deprivation have found that mothers who are emotionally neglectful, nonnurturant, cold, and unaffectionate toward their children can predispose their children toward a condition called psychosocial dwarfism. This condition is characterized by growth retardation and abnormally low levels of growth hormone in spite of the fact that these children have received proper food, have been given adequate medical care, and do not have an illness or physical defect. (Researchers believe that emotional deprivation affects normal hormonal functioning in the body, thereby inhibiting growth.) Physical development may also vary across cultures and ethnic backgrounds—the rate of maturation of African infants, for example, is such that they tend to reach motor milestones such as sitting and walking before European or American infants.

HISTORIC DEVELOPMENT OF STUDY

The question of the respective contributions of genes and the environment to development reflects a centuries-old debate by philosophers, psychologists, and others concerning human nature: whether inborn differences or the environment contributes more to human development.

Throughout most of the twentieth century, the predominant view in American psychology emphasized the role of the environment as the predominant influence on human development and behavior. At least part of the reason for this may be attributable to a lack of technology available for in-depth investigation and measurement of human biological processes. Advances in science and technology, however, have allowed better research that has greatly increased knowledge about such processes as brain development and its role in normal and abnormal development and behavior; the role of hormones in development, including the regulation of growth, maturation, sex differences, and other developmental processes and behaviors; and the identification of specific genes and their respective functions in normal and abnormal development. Significant advances in knowledge will continue to be made in these areas.

Whereas the genes versus environment debate has historically focused on the relative contribution of each to development, that view has been abandoned in favor of a focus on how genes and the environment interact. This is partly a result of the fact that most developmental psychologists accept that both factors are necessary for development. Robert Plomin's work in the late 1970s and Sandra Scarr's work in the early 1980s address this focus by suggesting that a person's genetic makeup may influence the kinds of environments that he or she experiences. For example, a child who is athletically inclined

may spend more time in athletics than in other kinds of activities, receive more attention and encouragement from coaches (compared with those not so gifted), associate frequently with sports-minded people, and (through increased athletic activity) further develop and refine his or her talents. This emphasis on how genes and the environment interact will continue to be a major focus of research in the field of developmental psychology.

IMPLICATIONS FOR PSYCHOLOGY

The examination of the determinants of physical development is important for a number of reasons. First, it sheds light on the causes (and consequences) of normal and abnormal growth patterns, motor development, and brain and nervous-system development. Second, it may provide insight into some of the causes of normal and abnormal psychological development and behavior because of the relationship between physical development and behavior. Third, it helps explain individual variations in development. Finally, this area of study asserts that human development is not based solely on either the environment or genetics, but rather is caused by the mutual influence of genes and the environment.

BIBLIOGRAPHY

Bateson, Patrick, and Paul Martin. *Design for a Life: How Behavior and Personality Develop*. New York: Simon, 2000. Print.

Beenstock, Michael. *Heredity, Family, and Inequality: A Critique of Social Sciences*. Cambridge: MITP, 2012. Digital file.Burga, A., and B. Lehner. "Beyond Genotype to Phenotype: Why the Phenotype of an Individual Cannot Always Be Predicted from Their Genome Sequence and the Environment That They Experience." FEBS Journal 279.20 (2012): 3765–75. Print.

Coll, Cynthia T. Garcia, Elaine L. Bearer, and Richard M. Lerner, eds. *Nature and Nurture: The Complex Interplay of Genetic and Environmental Influences on Human Behavior and Development*. New York: Psychology, 2013. Print.

Gagneur, Julien, et al. "Genotype-Environment Interactions Reveal Causal Pathways That Mediate Genetic Effects on Phenotype." *PLoS Genetics* 9.9 (2013): 1–10. Print.

Moore, David Scott. *The Dependent Gene: The Fallacy of Nature/Nurture*. New York: Times Books, 2002. Print.

Parens, Erik, Audrey R. Chapman, and Nancy Press, eds. *Wrestling with Behavioral Genetics: Science, Ethics, and Public Conversation*. Baltimore: Johns Hopkins UP, 2009. Print.

Thies, Kathleen M., and John F. Travers. *Growth and Development Through the Lifespan*. 2nd ed. Sudbury: Jones, 2009. Print.

Laura Kamptner

SEE ALSO: Development; Developmental psychology; Environmental factors and mental health; Evolutionary psychology; Gender differences; Genetics and mental health; Motor development; Prenatal physical development; Reflexes in newborns.

Piaget, Jean

BORN: August 9, 1896, in Neuchâtel, Switzerland
DIED: September 16, 1980, in Geneva, Switzerland
IDENTITY: Swiss child psychologist
TYPE OF PSYCHOLOGY: Cognition; Developmental psychology; Learning

Piaget's ideas have had a profound influence on American educators, which is ironic in light of the fact that, though he wrote extensively on growth and development, he rarely addressed himself to the topic of schooling.

Jean Piaget was the son of a professor of medieval literature and acquired his father's taste for hard intellectual work at an early age. He was awarded a Ph.D. in natural history from the University of Neuchâtel in 1918. Wishing to further his studies, Piaget traveled to Paris and spent two years at the Sorbonne, where he began working with early forms of intelligence tests.Intelligence tests Piaget discovered that children could not perform many of the logical tasks that adults find to be commonplace. Why, he asked himself, is this the case? This question led him into his life's work: studying how children develop logical patterns of thought.

Piaget held a number of important posts during his long, scholarly career. In 1921, at the age of twenty-five, he was appointed as director of studies at the Jean-Jacques Rousseau Institute in Geneva, where he served for the next fifty-four years. He also held faculty positions at the Universities of Geneva and Lausanne. Piaget published many books and articles on child growth and development. Among his better-known works are *Le Langage et le Pensée chez l'Enfant* (1923; *The Language and Thought of the Child*, 1926), *La Construction du Réel chez l'Enfant* (1937; *The Construction of Reality in the Child*, 1954), and *L'Équilibration des Structures Cognitives: Problème Central du Développement* (1975; *The Development of Thought: Equilibration of Cognitive Structures*, 1977).

In 1955, Piaget founded the International Center for Genetic Epistemology at the University of Geneva. The theory of knowledge, he believed, should be grounded in the biological sciences. Learning is the process by which the human organism establishes a working balance with the environment. Piaget called this balance equilibration, which is achieved in two ways: assimilation, where new information is absorbed into an already existing intellectual structure; and accommodation, where the intellectual structure is modified by new experiences.

Piaget is best known for his division of children's cognitive growth into four stages: sensorimotor stage (birth to age two), preoperational stage (ages two to seven), concrete operational stage (ages seven to eleven), and formal operational stage (age eleven through adulthood). All children pass through these four stages. There are no skips, jumps, or gaps along the way. Children before the age of two years learn by manipulating objects. Preoperational children have acquired language, but they cannot grasp the idea of reversibility in number sets. Concrete operational children can solve reversibility problems in concrete situations. Formal operational children are able to manipulate concepts similar to those found in abstract mathematics.

BIBLIOGRAPHY

Ginsburg, Herbert P., and Sylvia Opper. *Piaget's Theory of Intellectual Development*. 3d ed. Englewood Cliffs, N.J.: Prentice-Hall, 1988. A concise guide to Piaget's theories and his influence on modern educational practices.

Kohler, Richard. *Jean Piaget*. New York: Continuum, 2008. Penetrating account of Piaget and his work, including references to his life, his educational philosophy, and the impact of his work in the twenty-first century.

Vidal, Fernando. *Piaget Before Piaget*. Cambridge, Mass.: Harvard University Press, 1994. A thorough though somewhat heavy-going biography.

Stanley D. Ivie

SEE ALSO: Cognitive development: Jean Piaget; Cognitive psychology; Concept formation; Thought: Inferential.

Pinel, Philippe

BORN: April 20, 1745
DIED: October 25, 1826
BIRTHPLACE: Jonquieres, France
PLACE OF DEATH: Paris, France
IDENTITY: French physician and founder of scientific psychiatry
TYPE OF PSYCHOLOGY: Psychopathology; Psychotherapy

Pinel, a pioneer in the humane treatment of "the insane," brought the study, care, and cure of the mentally ill into the field of medicine.

Philippe Pinel was born in a small village in southwestern France. His mother came from a family of physicians, and his father was a surgeon who practiced in St.-Paul-Cap-de-Joux, where Philippe grew up. After a time at the Collège de Lavaur, he received a humanistic education from the Fathers of the Christian Doctrine at their Collège de l'Esquille in Toulouse, receiving the degree of master of arts in mathematics. Having decided on a religious career, he enrolled in the faculty of theology at the University of Toulouse in 1767, but, opting for the family profession, he later switched into the faculty of medicine, and he received his MD in 1773.

In 1774, he traveled to Montpellier, where, for four years, he studied at France's most famous medical school. Supporting himself by giving private lessons, he frequented hospitals, where he built trusting relationships with patients and began making detailed records of the histories and courses of their illnesses.

Pinel went to Paris in 1778. There, for fifteen years, he made a living by teaching mathematics, editing a medical newspaper, and translating medical works into French. In 1793, he became "physician of the infirmaries" at Bicetre, a Parisian asylum with over four thousand male inmates. The severely insane, believed to be demoniacally possessed, had been kept chained in dark dungeons for years, but Pinel, insisting that they be treated as patients, not outcasts, unchained these unfortunates and housed them in sunny rooms. Then, through warm baths and occupational therapy, he was able to mitigate their mental illness and return many, now cured, to the world.

His successes at Bicetre led to his becoming, in 1795, chief physician of the Hospice de la Salpétrière, where he assumed responsibility for eight thousand women suffering from various chronic illnesses. Salpétrière was the scene of his research for the rest of his life. Though Pinel's fame derives from his compassionate treatment of the mentally ill, his greatest contributions to medical science were his falsification of such traditional ideas as personal wickedness causing insanity and his championing of a new therapeutic approach that he called moral treatment. This involved improving his patients' diet, hygiene, and physical surroundings while helping them to "balance their passions" through exercise, small-group living, and purposeful work.

Pinel published the results of his experiments in several books, the most important of which was his Traité Médico-philosophique sur *l'Aliénation Mentale ou la Manie* (1801; *A Treatise on Insanity*, 1806). His writings contributed to making the mentally ill part of medicine, and his ideas constituted the foundations of modern psychiatry. He died at Salpétrière in 1826, and he was buried in Père Lachaise cemetery, the final resting place for many of France's luminaries.

BIBLIOGRAPHY

Ackerknecht, Erwin H. *Medicine at the Paris Hospital, 1794-1848*. Baltimore: Johns Hopkins UP, 1967. Print.

Eghigian, Greg. "The Early Psychiatrist: A Piercing Eye and Commanding Presence." *Psychiatric Times* 29.3 (2012): 9. OmniFile Full Text Mega (H.W. Wilson). Web. 24 June 2014.

Grange, Kathleen M. "Pinel and Eighteenth-Century Psychiatry." *Bulletin of the History of Medicine* 35.5 (1961): 442–53. Print.

Poirier, J., et al. "Figures and Institutions of the Neurological Sciences in Paris from 1800 to 1950. Part IV: Psychiatry and Psychology." *Revue Neurologique* (Paris) 168.5 (n.d.): 389–402. Biological Abstracts. Web. 24 June 2014.

Riese, Walther. *The Legacy of Philippe Pinel: An Inquiry into His Thought on Mental Alienation*. New York: Springer, 1969. Print.

Woods, Evelyn A., and Eric T. Carlson. "The Psychiatry of Philippe Pinel." *Bulletin of the History of Medicine* 35.1 (1961): 14–25. Print.

Robert J. Paradowski

SEE ALSO: Mental illness: Historical concepts; Psychotherapy: Historical approaches.

Pituitary gland

TYPE OF PSYCHOLOGY: Biological bases of behavior

Located at the base of the brain, the pituitary gland is central to the endocrine system; the production and regulation of hormones that play a role in certain behaviors are the primary functions of the pituitary.

KEY CONCEPTS
- Adrenal gland
- Anterior pituitary
- Endocrine system
- Hormone
- Hypothalamus
- Posterior pituitary

INTRODUCTION

Hormonesare loosely defined as chemical substances that are produced in certain parts of the body and then carried elsewhere by the bloodstream to perform their function. They include three general chemical types: short chains of amino acids, or proteins; derivatives of amino acids; and steroids. Many behaviors are regulated by hormones. Arguably, the most obvious behaviors are those associated with reproduction. For example, steroids secreted by the sex organs, or gonads, regulate both paternal and maternal behavior: aggression (testosterone), attraction for the opposite sex (pheromonea), uterine contraction (oxytocin), and so on.

The system that regulates hormone production is the neuroendocrine system, a series of ductless glands that secrete these chemicals directly into the blood. The pituitary gland is the central organ of the endocrine system. Slightly larger than a centimeter in diameter, it is located at the base of the brain in a bony cavity called the sella turcica. The gland is involved in the secretion of some ten different hormones.

The pituitary is formed from two distinct structures, the adenohypophysis (in the anterior portion of the gland) and the neurohypophysis, which forms the posterior lobe of the pituitary. Not only do the two portions function independently, but they also form independently during embryonic development. The adenohypophysis originates from the outer layer of embryonic tissue, while the neurohypophysis is an outgrowth of the developing forebrain. Not surprisingly, the neurohypophysis receives neurosecretions directly from the hypothalamus region of the brain. Therefore, one might not consider the posterior pituitary to be a gland at all, but rather a neural outgrowth of the brain.

NEUROSECRETIONS AND THE HYPOTHALAMUS

Sets of secretions from the anterior pituitary play various roles in the body. The first set, which includes hormones such as adrenocorticotropic hormone (ACTH), thyroid-stimulating hormone (TSH), follicle-stimulating hormone (FSH), and luteinizing hormone (LH), regulate secretions from the adrenal gland, the thyroid, and the gonads. Two additional hormones from the anterior pituitary, prolactin and growth hormone (GH), have a variety of effects on breast tissue and bone growth, respectively.

Regulation of hormone secretion by the anterior pituitary is primarily the function of the hypothalamus. The hypothalamus is connected through a portal circuit, a connection involving two capillaries from the brain that merge to form the vein that feeds directly into the adenohypophysis. Neural secretions from the hypothalamus either stimulate or inhibit the appropriate cells in the adenohypophysis, allowing for a finely tuned method of regulation. For example, if a person's fingers touch a hot stove, a sensory reflex allows the person to remove the hand quickly. At the same time, the anterior pituitary is "instructed" to secrete Adrenocorticotropic hormone-ACTH. The ACTH travels through the blood to the adrenals, which then secrete the appropriate steroids, which have an anti-inflammatory action. The rise in steroid level in the general circulation is monitored by the hypothalamus. At the appropriate level, a negative feedback results, in which ACTH secretion is stopped. The regulation of each hormone produced by the anterior pituitary is performed in an analogous manner.

As described above, the posterior pituitary is directly connected to the hypothalamus; it is not actually a gland. The neurons that make up the neurohypophysis originate in the hypothalamus. Extensions called axons then extend into, and become, the posterior pituitary. These neural structures are closely associated with a capillary network. The result is that neurosecretions produced in the hypothalamus pass through the posterior pituitary directly into the bloodstream.

There are two general types of neurosecretions in humans associated with the neurohypophysis: oxytocin and Vasopressinvasopressin. Oxytocin plays several roles in muscle contraction. For example, during childbirth, it causes the contraction of uterine muscle. Later, it becomes associated with the release of milk through the nipple. Vasopressin is the general name for a series of hormones that regulate blood pressure; it is often referred to as antidiuretic hormone (ADH). Regulation of these hormone levels is similar to that described for the adenohypophysis.

Despite the independent formation and function of the two lobes of the pituitary, regulation of each is carried out coordinately. For example, sucking at the nipple by an infant induces the release of oxytocin through the posterior pituitary. The same stimulus causes an inhibition of the follicle-stimulating hormone by the anterior pituitary. The result is that a nursing mother should be less fertile.

The neuroendocrine system is thus intimately involved with a variety of processes within the body. These include cell metabolism, development of organ systems such as the gonads, and certain kinds of behaviors. The role played by the pituitary is central to each of these processes, both in their induction and in their regulation. While the master gland in all these endeavors is ultimately the brain, it is through the pituitary gland that the appropriate messengers are sent throughout the body, controlling the function of most body tissues.

ROLE IN PHYSIOLOGY OF BEHAVIOR

Hormones of the endocrine system—in particular, those hormones associated with the pituitary gland—play a vital role in the physiology of behavior. This role may take several forms. For example, among the most obvious effects are those that result from systems that regulate body metabolism. Thyroid-stimulating hormone is produced within the anterior pituitary and is involved in regulating the secretion of thyroxin and trilodothyronine by the thyroid. Since thyroxin is particularly important in controlling the metabolic rate, overproduction of TSH may cause symptoms of nervousness, hyperactivity, and loss of sleep. On the other hand, lack of TSH production may result in hypothyroidism, an underactive thyroid. Individuals suffering from this condition are often mentally sluggish. It should be kept in mind, however, that an overactive or underactive thyroid may result from reasons other than inappropriate pituitary activity.

The activity of ACTH, the source of which is the anterior pituitary, is particularly illustrative of the multitude of effects associated with an individual hormone. The major activity of ACTH involves its effects on the adrenal glands. In response to ACTH production, the adrenal cortex (the outer region of the adrenal glands) begins production of a variety of steroid hormones. Several of these steroids, including cortisol, increase the rate of protein

and fat metabolism. As in the example presented earlier, cortisol may also act as an anti-inflammatory agent. The pharmaceutical hydrocortisone, used as an anti-inflammatory application to the skin, is based on the chemical formulation of cortisol.

The production of aldosterone by the adrenal cortex, again regulated by ACTH from the pituitary, promotes resorption of sodium from urine as it passes through the kidney. A variety of sex steroids produced within the adrenal cortex are also regulated through ACTH production. These include adrenal androgen, principally found in males but also produced in the female. Among older women, for example, higher than normal levels of adrenal androgen may result in the growth of facial hair. Thus, many sexual behaviors and characteristics indirectly come under the control of the anterior pituitary gland.

ACTH secretion exhibits a diurnal rhythm, with increasing production following the onset of sleep.Sleep The level continues to increase until the person awakens. ACTH secretion is also influenced by fever, surgery, or stress. In fact, many of the physiological responses to stress—elevation of glucose levels in the blood, elevation of blood pressure, and suppression of the immune response—result from increases in the output of ACTH.

Regulation of ACTH production is another example of the finely tuned negative feedback that the body uses to suppress pituitary activity. For example, when corticoid hormone levels in the blood rise, perhaps as the result of a stressful situation, they are monitored within the hypothalamus. At the appropriate time, such as during relaxation, ACTH production is turned off and adrenal activity slows down.

SEXUAL BEHAVIORS

Directly or indirectly, sexual behaviors are also the result of pituitary activity. Production of follicle-stimulating hormone (FSH), and luteinizing hormone (LH) influences the sex organs to produce sperm or eggs and a variety of sex hormones. Well-known mating and sexual behaviors among humans are therefore influenced by pituitary hormones. In the male, this results from testosterone activity—sexual aggressiveness being a prime example. Whether aggressiveness in general among human males is primarily attributable to hormonal action or to environmental conditioning is not completely clear. Among other primates, however, fighting behavior is definitely a result of testosterone production. Sex hormones also regulate maternal activity among a variety of mammals. The "nesting instinct" and huddling behaviors exhibited by primates, including some humans, are controlled in this manner.

Communication behaviors that result from gonadal hormone production are well known. Visual signals include changes in skin color among female chimpanzees at the time of ovulation and the production of fat pads on the shoulders of male squirrel monkeys during mating season. Production of pheromones, chemicals that exhibit distinct odors, is also used to exhibit sexual receptivity. A male dog may be aware of any receptive female within a radius of hundreds of meters. The use of perfumes or musk is based, in part, on the belief that analogous odors may also influence human activity.

OXYTOCIN

The release of Oxytocinoxytocin by the posterior pituitary is also influenced by a variety of sexual and maternal behaviors. As described above, oxytocin is actually a neuropeptide, a short chain of amino acids that are released into the posterior pituitary from neural axons that originate in the hypothalamus. Oxytocin causes contraction of smooth muscle. During sexual intercourse, release of oxytocin may result in the uterine contraction known as "tenting." This process may draw sperm into the uterus, increasing the likelihood of fertilization. In addition, the smooth muscle contraction in the male that occurs during ejaculation may be caused, in part, by the effects of oxytocin. The contraction of the uterus during labor and delivery is also caused by the effects of oxytocin. Finally, both oxytocin and prolactin, produced within the anterior pituitary, are activated by stimulation associated with suckling and result in milk production and letdown.

The pituitary gland is a principal component of the endocrine system. Hormones that originate within the anterior pituitary act on a variety of tissues and organs. The posterior pituitary, in turn, serves primarily as a "way station" for neuropeptides produced in the hypothalamus. In this manner, numerous physiological activities and behaviors are regulated by this set of glands.

HISTORY OF STUDY

Knowledge of pituitary function, like that of most tissues and organs in the body, evolved over the period of a millennium. Aristotle (in the fourth century b.c.e.) believed that the pituitary, as an extension of the brain, played a role in regulation of body temperature. He believed that the body humor known as phlegm (Latin pituita) passed through the gland into the nasal cavity. (Hence

a person's attitude, or humor, was related to the relative qualities of the four body fluids, or humours.) It was on this basis that Andreas Vesalius, the sixteenth century physician considered to be the founder of modern anatomy, named the gland "pituitary" in his classic work De humani corporis fabrica (1543; on the structure of the human body). This view continued to be held into the mid-nineteenth century.

The understanding of body functions is often associated with the correlation of behavioral or physiological changes with organ pathology. Such was the case with the pituitary gland. By 1850, it was recognized that pituitary tumors, particularly in children or young adults, often resulted in conditions such as gigantism, acromegaly, or sexual dysfunction. Furthermore, surgical removal of the gland, first in experimental animals and then in humans, resulted in numerous pathological changes. By the early twentieth century, it was clear that the pituitary played a key role in monitoring a variety of systems in the body.

MODERN RESEARCH AND UNDERSTANDING

As knowledge of pituitary hormones increases, the interaction of these molecules with target sites on other organs or glands can be better understood at the molecular level. At the very least, this can allow treatment or prevention of behavioral or physiological changes associated with abnormalities of the endocrine system. This can include, for example, an improvement in the effectiveness or safety of birth control techniques; a pill that would inhibit sperm production could be used by men.

Oxytocin and ADH, the hormones released through the neurohypophysis, are functionally neurotransmitters. This example illustrates the close structural and functional relationship between different systems—in this case, the endocrine and nervous systems. Clearly, hormonal control is complex and finely controlled. Precise mechanisms of control, however, remain to be worked out. For example, negative feedback was discussed earlier as a means by which adrenal hormones regulate their own secretion. The exact region in the brain that responds to elevated levels of adrenal hormones remains a source of controversy. A similar situation exists for other hormones. Presumably, regulation involves a specific series of neurons with specialized neurotransmitters. As the control mechanisms become better understood, modulation of behavior through proper drug treatment will become more of a reality. For example, use of the drug chlorpromazine results in an increase in prolactin production by the anterior pituitary. Further understanding of the integration of these systems will allow for additional applications in the future.

BIBLIOGRAPHY

Besedovsky, Hugo, George P. Chrousos, and Adriana Del Rey. *The Hypothalamus-Pituitary-Adrenal Axis.* Amsterdam: Elsevier Science, 2008. With a focus on the immune system, this text examines the relationship among the hypothalamus, the pituitary, and the adrenal gland and its role in regulation stress, digestion, mood. and sexuality.

Cotman, Carl W., and James L. McGaugh. *Behavioral Neuroscience.* New York: Academic Press, 1980. Originally developed as part of a course in neuroscience. The authors provide a broad overview of the topic without becoming bogged down in detail. Several chapters deal specifically with the endocrine system and associated clinical disorders.

Guillemin, Roger, and Roger Burgus. "The Hormones of the Hypothalamus." *Scientific American* 227 (November, 1972): 24-33. An excellent article that deals primarily with the regulation of the pituitary gland. The methods by which hormones of the neurohypophysis have been isolated and studied are highlighted. Particularly useful are the clear diagrams. Description of experimental approaches is minimized.

Holmes, Clarissa S., ed. *Psychoneuroendocrinology: Brain, Behavior, and Hormonal Interactions.* New York: Springer-Verlag, 1990. Presents a thorough discussion of the interdependence of hormonal and psychological factors. Includes discussion of endocrine disease on growth disorders, academic development, and social interactions in children. A section also discusses effects of replacement hormone treatment.

Holmes, R. L., and J. N. Ball. *The Pituitary Gland: A Comparative Account.* Cambridge, England: Cambridge University Press, 1974. A detailed text on the structure and function of the pituitary gland in a variety of vertebrates. Though not written for the casual reader, the text is profusely illustrated and contains an extensive bibliography.

Konner, Melvin. *The Tangled Wing: Biological Constraints on the Human Spirit.* Rev. ed. New York: Henry Holt, 2003. An informal discussion dealing with the biological basis for a variety of human behaviors and emotions, such as love, lust, and fear. Included are sections that discuss modifications of behavior and effects of differences in sex.

Swearingen, Brooke, and Beverly M. K. Biller, eds. *Diagnosis and Management of Pituitary Disorders.* Totowa, N.J.: Humana Press, 2008. With contributions for radiologists, ophthalmologists, pathologists, radiation oncologists, and neurologists, this comprehensive resource focuses on all the clinical aspects of the pituitary gland.

Wallace, Robert A., Gerald P. Sanders, and Robert J. Ferl. *Biology: The Science of Life.* 4th ed. New York: HarperCollins, 1996. A textbook of biology. Several chapters deal with the function of the pituitary gland and its effects on behavior. Extensive color illustrations and diagrams, and a text that is not overly detailed, allow easy comprehension of the subject.

Richard Adler

SEE ALSO: Adrenal gland; Endocrine system; Gonads; Hormones and behavior; Stress: Physiological responses; Thyroid gland.

Placebo effect

TYPE OF PSYCHOLOGY: Psychological methodologies

The perceived placebo effect is defined as the difference in response between the control subjects who receive a placebo as compared with the experimental subjects who receive the therapy being tested. This definition has been challenged, and the true placebo effect is defined as the difference in response between the control subjects treated with a placebo and the control subjects who are totally untreated.

KEY CONCEPTS
- Control group
- Double-blind study
- Experimenter bias
- Nocebo
- Single-blind study

INTRODUCTION

The term "placebo" is derived from a Latin term meaning "I shall please," but it has come to mean a false substance. A placebo is generally given to the control group in a scientific experiment while the independent variable (item being tested) is given to other experimental groups. The placebo effect is the response of the control group, any changes in behavior—usually measurable, observable, or reported improvements in behavior or health—brought about as a result of exposure to this false substance. Using a placebo controls for the expectations of the subjects, in that neither the experimental subjects nor the control subjects know what to expect. If the subjects do not know whether they are in the experimental or control group but the experimenter does, this is known as a single-blind study. If neither the subjects nor the experimenter knows which group is the experimental one and which is the control, this is known as a double-blind study. A double-blind study controls for both experimenter bias and subject expectations.

HISTORY

The placebo was first used in medicine in the late 1700's, when a placebo was considered any substance (false medicine) given to a patient to please or satisfy him or her, rather than to treat or cure the patient's symptoms. Through 1950, it was felt that the placebo could provide psychological comfort to the patient while doing no harm physiologically. In 1961, the term "nocebo" was coined to refer to the negative side effects that might be associated with the administration of a false substance.

By 1940, the placebo had also become a substance given to the control group in experiments to deal with subjects' expectations. In 1955, a seminal paper was written by Henry K. Beecher, Henry K. Beecher dealing with "the powerful placebo effect." In this paper, Beecher attempted to define and quantify the placebo effect on the basis of past research studies. Beecher used the term "placebo effect" to contrast with the effect that the independent variable had on the experimental group. Thus the placebo effect was defined as the effect felt by the control group as compared with the effect felt by the experimental subjects.

CHANGES

This commonly accepted definition was challenged by P. C. Getzsche in 1994. He contended that the placebo effect did not look at the difference between an experimental group exposed to an independent variable and a control group exposed to a placebo. Instead, he saw the placebo effect as the difference between the control group that was given a placebo, and a control group that had nothing done to it. Getzsche thus indicated that the placebo effect was the change in the subjects' response due to the administration of the false substance. This implies that the placebo effect actually refers to the difference between the response of the untreated control group versus the control group treated with a placebo, rather than the difference between the experimental group and the control group treated with a placebo. This distinction has now come to be referred to as the true placebo effect as compared with the perceived placebo effect.

BIBLIOGRAPHY

Beecher, H. K. "The Powerful Placebo." *Journal of the American Medical Association* 159 (1955): 1602-1606. This is the article in which Beecher introduced the potential importance of the placebo effect and shaped the field of experimental research for years to come by suggesting the use of double-blind studies.

DeCraen, A. J., T. J. Kaptchuk, J. G. Tijssen, and J. Kleijnen. "Placebos and Placebo Effects in Medicine: Historical Overview." *Journal of the Royal Society of Medicine* 92 (1999): 511-515. This article follows the course of the placebo effect in medicine over a forty-year period, looking at its significance over the years.

Ernst, E., and K. L. Resch. "Concept of True and Perceived Placebo Effects." *British Medical Journal* 311 (1995): 551-553. This article attempts to clarify the true nature of the placebo effect. It begins by defining the existence of a perceived placebo effect in a control group that is exposed to a placebo and contrasts this with a true placebo effect.

Evans, D. *Placebo Effect: Mind Over Matter in Modern Medicine.* New York: Oxford University Press, 2003. This 240-page book presents a history of the placebo effect. It goes on to evaluate scientific research dealing with the placebo effect, attempting to develop a logical explanation for how it works.

Getzsche, P. C. "Is There Logic in the Placebo?" *Lancet* 344 (1994): 925-926. In this article, the author proposed a different, somewhat controversial definition of the placebo effect.

Kienle, G. S., and H. Kiene. "The Powerful Placebo Effect: Fact or Fiction?" *Journal of Clinical Epidemiology* 50 (1997): 1311-1318. This article reviews the original 1955 research that identified the importance of the placebo effect and examines research involved with the placebo effect after that time.

Peters, D. *Understanding the Placebo Effect in Complementary Medicine: Theory, Practice, and Research.* Edinburgh, Scotland: Churchill Livingstone, 2001. This book explores the basis for the placebo effect in research and looks at the importance of the placebo effect as a tool used by practitioners of alternative medicine, while investigating potential uses in the future.

Robin Kamienny Montvilo

SEE ALSO: Drug therapies; Experimental psychology; Experimentation: Ethics and participant rights; Experimentation: Independent, dependent, and control variables; Psychopharmacology.

Play therapy

TYPE OF PSYCHOLOGY: Psychotherapy

Play therapy is a psychotherapeutic method designed to assist children in coping with emotional stress or trauma through play. Play therapy is conducted in a room specifically equipped for this purpose with toys and activity materials to aid the child in solving problems, to encourage the child to act out his or her feelings and concerns, and to enhance the child's mental health through the unconditional support of the therapist. It most commonly involves one child and one therapist, though it can be conducted with groups of children.

KEY CONCEPTS
- Communication
- Empathy
- Interpersonal matrix
- Limit setting
- Symbolism

INTRODUCTION

Children of all ages learn about their environment, express themselves, and develop relationships with others through their play activity. Play is an integral part of childhood, an activity that must be allowed to facilitate a child's development. In fact, play is seen as such an important aspect of a child's life that the United Nations made the right to play an inalienable right for children across the world. Some adults have labeled play a child's "work," and this may be an appropriate way of looking at children's play. Just as work fosters self-esteem for adults, so does play enhance the self-esteem of children. Just as adults learn to solve problems through their work, children learn to cope with and invent solutions to problems through their play.

GROWTH THROUGH PLAY

Through play, children grow and learn in a number of ways. First, play helps children grow emotionally; children learn to express their feelings, understand their feelings, and control their emotions through play by acting out a variety of situations and roles. They learn to share and cooperate with other children as well as language, they learn to think in symbols, and they learn that the same object can have different functions and that things can break and be repaired. They also act out rules and regulations in play with other children. They learn that some things hurt other people and should therefore not be done, and they realize that rules often serve a purpose of protection or safety. All these growth processes are extremely important by-products of play, but perhaps the most important aspect of play is that of communication, defined here as the sharing of information with other people, either through language or through other ways of interacting. Children tell about themselves and their lives through play. Even when they do not yet have language skills, they possess the ability to play.

ROLE OF THERAPIST AND SETTING

This aspect of communication through play is perhaps the most important element of play therapy. In play therapy, a therapist uses children's play to understand them and to help them solve problems, feel better about themselves, and express themselves better. Children often have difficulty telling adults what they feel and experience, what they need and want, and what they do not want and do not like. Often, they lack the language skills to do so, and sometimes they are too frightened to reveal themselves for fear of punishment or rejection.

In play therapy, however, the therapist is an adult who is empathic, sensitive, and—above all—accepting and nonthreatening. The child is made to feel comfortable in the room with this adult and quickly recognizes that this person, despite being quite old (at least from the child's perspective), understands the child and accepts his or her wishes and needs. Children learn to play in the presence of this therapist or with the therapist, and through this play, they communicate with the therapist. They reveal through their activity what they have experienced in life, how they feel, what they would like to do, and how they feel about themselves.

The toys and activities that play therapists use vary significantly, though therapists take great care to equip the room in which they work with the child in such a way as to allow maximum freedom and creativity on the child's part. Therapists generally have art supplies such as clay, crayons, and paints; toy kitchen appliances and utensils; baby items such as bottles and rattles; a variety of dolls and dollhouses; toy guns and soldiers; toy cars and boats; blocks and erector sets; and stuffed animals. All these materials share several important traits: They foster creativity, have many different uses, are safe to play with, and can easily be used by the child for communication. On the other hand, therapists rarely have things such as board games or themed toys (for example, television action heroes), because these toys have a definite use with certain rules and restrictions, are often used merely to re-create stories observed on television, or are not very handy for getting children to express themselves freely. Most of the time, the toys are kept in an office that is specifically designed for children, not a regular doctor's office. As such, the room generally has a child-size table and chairs but no adult-size desk. It usually has no other furniture but may have some large cushions that the child and therapist can sit on if they want to talk for a while. Often the room has a small, low sink for water play, and sometimes even a sandbox. Floor and wall coverings are constructed of easily cleaned materials so that spills are not a problem. The room is basically a large play area; children generally like the play therapy room because it is unlike any other room they have ever encountered and because it is equipped specifically with children in mind.

THERAPEUTIC PROCESS

There are many reasons a child may be seen in play therapy. For example, a referral may come from a teacher who is concerned about a drop in the child's academic performance; from day-care personnel who are concerned about the child's inability to relate to other children; from the child's pediatrician, who believes the child is depressed but cannot find a physical cause; or from parents who think the child is aggressive or withdrawn. Whatever the reason, therapy begins with an intake interview. The intake is a session during which the therapist meets not only with the child but also with the parents and siblings in an attempt to find out as much about the child as possible to gain an understanding of what is wrong.

Once the therapist knows what is happening with the child, recommendations for treatment are made. Sometimes the recommendation is for the entire family to be seen in family therapy. Sometimes the recommendation is for the parents to be seen. Sometimes the recommendation is for play therapy for the child.

Once a child enters play therapy, the child meets with the therapist once weekly for fifty or sixty minutes (sometimes, for very young children, sessions can be as short as thirty minutes) for several weeks or months. During the sessions, the child decides what to play with and how, and the therapist is there to understand the child, help the child solve problems, and facilitate growth and self-esteem. The therapist never recommends toys or activities to the child nor speculates aloud what the child's play might symbolize; instead, the child self-directs his or her play activity without guidance from the therapist. Often, while the child is being seen, the parents are also in some type of therapy session themselves. Children's problems often arise because of problems in the family, which is why it is rare that only the child is in treatment. Parents are often seen so that they can work on their relationship either with each other or with the whole family, or to learn parenting skills.

The first thing that happens in play therapy is that the therapist and the child get to know each other and develop a positive relationship. Once the child begins to trust the therapist, the child starts to reveal his or her needs, wishes, concerns, fears, and problems through play. The therapist observes and interacts with the child to help the individual work out problems, deal with strong feelings, accept needs, and learn to deal with often difficult family or environmental circumstances. All this work is done through the child's play in much the same way as children use play while growing up. In addition to using play activity, however, the therapist uses the trusting relationship with the child. Play therapy fosters open and voluntary communication, promotes creative problem-solving, and builds trust and mastery.

EXAMPLE OF THERAPY

The process of play therapy is best demonstrated by an example of an actual play therapy interaction between a child and therapist. A nine-year-old boy was referred by his teacher because he was depressed and frightened, had difficulty making friends, and was not able to trust people. In the intake interview, the therapist found out that the boy had been severely physically abused by his father and that he was abandoned by his birth mother at the age of two. His stepmother had brought three children of her own into the blended family and did not have much time for this child. In fact, it appeared as though he was left to his own devices most of the time. The family had a number of other problems but refused family therapy. Thus, the child was seen in play therapy. He had considerable difficulty trusting the therapist and showed this reluctance in his play. He would often start to play, then check with the therapist for approval, and then stop before he became too involved in any one activity. After six weeks, he realized that the therapist was there to help him, and he began to communicate about his family through play.

The following exchange is a good example of what happens in play therapy. One day, the boy picked up a large wooden truck and two small ones. He proceeded to smash the large truck into the small red one over and over. He took the other small truck and put it between the large one and the small red one, as if to protect the red truck from being hit by the large one. In the process, the small blue truck was hurt badly and had to retreat. The boy repeated this activity several times. The therapist picked up a toy truck of her own and drove between the large truck and both of the small trucks, indicating that she had a truck that was tough enough to stop the large truck from hurting the small ones. The child was visibly relieved and turned to another activity.

What had happened? Before the session, the therapist had received a call from the child's social worker, who told her that the night before, the boy's father was caught sexually abusing his four-year-old stepdaughter, who shared this boy's room. The boy had awakened and unsuccessfully tried to stop his father. He ran to a neighbor's house, and this woman called the police. The father was arrested but threatened to get revenge on both children before he was taken away. The boy had play-acted this entire scene with the toy trucks. The father was the large truck; the red truck, his sister; the blue one, himself. The relief sensed by the boy after the therapist intervened is understandable, as her truck communicated to the boy that he would be protected from his father.

EVOLUTION OF PLAY THERAPY

Children use their play in play therapy not only to communicate but also to solve problems and deal with overwhelming feelings. How this happens has been explained and described by many different therapists and theorists since play came to be viewed as an acceptable means of conducting therapy in the early 1930s, based on the work of Melanie Klein, Hug Hellmuth, and Anna Freud. These three psychologists developed theories and play therapy methods that were based on Sigmund Freud's earlier psychoanalytic theories. In this approach, free play was considered most important, and the therapist did not generally become engaged at all in the play.

The therapist merely reflected back to the child what was seen and occasionally interpreted to the child what the play may have meant.

In the 1940s, Virginia Axline developed her approach to play therapy, which was similar to Klein's and Freud's. Axline also believed in free play and did not play with the child. She interpreted and emphasized an environment that put no limits or rules on the child. She introduced the idea that children in play therapy need to experience unconditional acceptance, empathic concern, and a nondirective atmosphere. In other words, Axline's approach to play therapy was to sit and observe and not be involved with the child.

TYPES OF PLAY THERAPISTS

Since then, the lack of limit setting (imposing rules or regulations on another person and then enforcing them in a predictable way), as well as the lack of active involvement with children in play therapy, has been criticized by play therapists. Nowadays, play therapists are more likely to get involved in play and to respond to children through play activity (as in the example), as opposed to using language to communicate with them. There are two major groups of therapists who use play therapy. Traditional psychoanalytic or psychodynamic therapists who are followers of Klein or Axline make up one group; however, even within this group, there is much diversity with regard to how involved the therapist becomes with the child's play. The second group is composed of therapists who focus on the human interaction that takes place—that is, humanistic therapists.

Regardless of which group a play therapist belongs to, however, the primary ingredients that were proposed many years ago remain intact. Free play is still deemed important, and empathy is stressed in the relationship with the child. Many therapists believe that the interpersonal matrix—the environment and the relationship between two or more people who spend time together—that exists between the child and the therapist is critical to changes noted in the child. A national center for play therapy has been created at the University of North Texas, and the field is represented by the Association for Play Therapy, located in Fresno, California, which publishes three major quarterly periodicals: *The International Journal of Play Therapy*, *The Association for Play Therapy Newsletter*, and *Play Therapy*. Recent trends in the field include the incorporation of play therapy by elementary school counselors and early childhood educational entities; the incorporation of play therapy in family therapy, in the form of filial therapy, where parents are trained to use techniques with their children; and the application of play therapy theory to children with special needs or disabilities and children with limited language skills (such as children with severe autism). Overall, a primary focus remains on the symbolism (the use of indirect means to express inner needs or feelings; a way of sharing oneself without doing so directly or in words) and metaphor expressed by children through play.

BIBLIOGRAPHY

Axline, Virginia Mae. *Dibs: In Search of Self*. New York: Ballantine, 1990. Print..

Axline, Virginia Mae. *Play Therapy: The Inner Dynamics of Childhood*. Boston: Houghton, 1947. Print.

Davis, Eric S., and Jennifer K. Pereira. "Child-Centered Play Therapy: A Creative Approach to Culturally Competent Counseling." *Journal of Creativity in Mental Health* 9.2 (2014): 262–74. Print.

Dodds, J. B. A. *Child Psychotherapy Primer*. New York: Human Sciences, 1985. Print.

Gil, Eliana, and Athena A. Drewes. *Cultural Issues in Play Therapy*. New York: Guilford, 2005. Print.

Landreth, G. L. *Play Therapy: The Art of the Relationship*. 2nd ed. New York: Brunner-Routledge, 2002. Print.

Nemiroff, Marc A., and Jane Annunziata. *A Child's First Book About Play Therapy*. Washington: American Psychological Assoc., 1990. Print.

Pass, Stephanie. "The Mummy at the Door: Play Therapy and Surviving Loss." *Journal of Infant, Child & Adolescent Psychotherapy* 13.2 (2014): 142–53. Print.

Reddy, Linda A., Tara M. Files-Hall, and Charles E. Schaefer. *Empirically Based Play Interventions for Children*. Washington: American Psychological Assoc., 2005. Print.

Schaefer, Charles E., and S. E. Reid. *Game Play: Therapeutic Use of Childhood Games*. 2nd ed. New York: Wiley, 2001. Print.

Schaefer, Charles E., and Heidi Kaduson, eds. *Contemporary Play Therapy: Theory, Research, and Practice*. New York: Guilford, 2006. Print.

Schaefer, Charles E., and Kevin J. O'Connor, eds. *Handbook of Play Therapy*. 2 vols. Somerset: Wiley, 1983–1994. Print.

Swan, Karrie L., and Dee C. Ray. "Effects of Child-Centered Play Therapy on Irritability and Hyperactivity Behaviors of Children with Intellectual Disabilities." *Journal of Humanistic Counseling* 53.2 (2014): 120–33. Print.

Trice-Black, Shannon, Carrie Lynn Bailey, and Morgan E. Kiper Riechel. "Play Therapy in School Counseling." *Professional School Counseling* 16.5 (2013): 303–12. Print.

Christiane Brems

SEE ALSO: Attachment and bonding in infancy and childhood; Child abuse; Children's mental health; Family life: Children's issues; Freud, Anna; Music, dance, and theater therapy; Psychotherapy: Children; Psychotherapy: Goals and techniques; Separation and divorce: Children's issues; Strategic family therapy.

Pornography addiction

TYPE OF PSYCHOLOGY: Addiction; Biological bases of human behavior; Clinical; Counseling; Psychopathology; Psychotherapy; Social

Pornography addiction is the excessive viewing of pornographic or sexually explicit material that results in negative consequences (relational, social, professional, financial) and that interferes with daily life and healthy psychological functioning. There is debate among researchers and clinical practitioners about whether or not pornography addiction actually exists and if the language of drug addiction is appropriate in describing porn addiction. Increasingly, among researchers and clinicians, addiction to pornography is seen as a prevalent form of one of the behavioral addictions for which the language and orientation of addiction psychology and treatments is appropriate.

KEY TERMS
- Behavioral addiction
- Cybersex addiction
- Sexaholics Anonymous

INTRODUCTION

While pornography is not a medical diagnosis, psychologists and other behavioral health specialists believe that it is clinically and therapeutically useful to consider it as a variant of a possible hypersexual disorder. In many cases, pornography addiction may be better understood as overuse or problematic or compulsive use of sexually explicit materials without severe negative consequences, which often accompany other behavioral or drug addictions. Many psychologists who consider pornography addiction also consider pornography that is available online to be more problematic than traditional pornography because of accessibility, anonymously acquisition, and affordability.

Advocates of the diagnosis of pornography "addiction" argue that it is a behavioral addiction that activates the underlying neurological circuit involved in addictive drug use. Proponents also argue that the behavioral patterns are similar to those seen in drug addiction.

CAUSES

Given the nature of the human sex drive and the variety of psychological needs that sexual arousal and gratification serve, there is no one root cause for porn addition. Researcher Patrick Carnes has identified four core beliefs of persons struggling with sex or pornography addiction: they are essentially bad, unworthy persons; they are unlovable as they currently are; their needs will never be met if they depend upon others to meet them; and satisfaction of their sexual needs is the most important thing in their life.

Several researchers and therapists have proposed stages for this addiction, but these are not necessarily sequential and there is no general agreement on them. Reasons for excessive consumption of pornography appear to be rooted in a desire for sexual pleasure or sexual variety, an escape from stress, and a way to cope with negative emotions.

RISK FACTORS

Research indicates that adolescent and young adult men are the primary consumers of sexually explicit materials and are most likely to develop maladaptive patterns of pornography consumption. Other factors include early exposure to sexually explicit material, poor emotional attachment styles, and using pornography as a masturbatory aid. Generally, the maladaptive pattern of use and sexually acting-out is developed between adolescence and early adulthood; however, it can begin later in adulthood.

SYMPTOMS

Symptoms of pornography addiction are wide-ranging, but they generally follow those found for substance abuse (with appropriate modification). These symptoms include combinations of the following: recurrent viewing of pornographic material or images resulting in a failure to fulfill major role obligations at work, school, or home (such as repeated absences or poor work perfor-

mance, suspensions or expulsion from school, or neglect of children or household); recurrent viewing of pornographic material or images that results in legal (criminal) problems; and continued viewing of pornographic material despite having persistent or recurrent social or interpersonal problems (for example, domestic and family) caused or exacerbated by their effects. Adult sexual entertainment and play moves on a continuum of sexual behavior and involvement toward addiction when problematic symptoms appear. These include excessive personal (non-work-related) viewing of more than twenty hours per week, neglect or avoidance of previously rewarding personal relationships or interaction with peers, depression (either short- or long-term), underestimation of time spent viewing or searching for material, and pursuit of "highs" that have been experienced while online.

Generally, the pornography addict is unable to choose whether or not to perform the behavior (and is addictive or compulsive) and continues to view it in spite of clear, negative consequences (such as marital problems, financial problems, and sexual dysfunction). Also, the addict's thoughts center on the sexual content and the pornographic material (such as the next time it can be viewed, how to acquire it, anticipation of orgasm), which take up a significant amount of the person's cognitive and emotional energy.

SCREENING AND DIAGNOSIS

Several screening tools have been developed to study pornography addiction, none of which is considered the gold standard. Two screening tools of note are the Pornography Consumption Inventory (a fifteen-item, Likert-scale inventory with four subscales: sexual pleasure, emotional escape, sexual curiosity, and novelty) and the Men's Sexual Addiction Screening Test (a twenty-five-item screening tool used in clinical settings that is simple, quick, and easy to score).

Given that pornography addiction itself is not listed among the defined disorders in official medical literature, it is not actually a clinical diagnosis. Pornography addiction, however, remains a popular diagnosis and may fit under the diagnosis of hypersexual disorder or sexual disorder with paraphilia. These paraphilic and hypersexual diagnoses may be the result of an underlying organic pathology relating to a brain lesion (trauma or tumor), the side effect of medication, or a symptom of endocrine abnormality, as well as a learned behavior, so these diagnoses should be investigated early in treatment.

Differential diagnosis can be indicated by atypical symptomology, such as onset in middle-age or later, dramatic change from previously normal sexual habits or patterns, aggression, or seizure-like symptoms surrounding sexual arousal or behavior. Diagnosis of porn addiction as sexual paraphilia or hypersexuality should consider common addiction criteria such as tolerance, psychological or physiological withdrawal symptoms after extended periods of pornography viewing abstinence, progressive viewing of more explicit content, and a cycle of abstinence followed by relapse. A diagnosis of pornography or masturbatory compulsivity or hypersexuality also should be considered.

TREATMENT AND THERAPY

Individual psychotherapy and psychoeducation about the effects of pornography consumption are the most commonly used treatments. Interpersonal therapy and cognitive-behavior therapy are commonly employed to identify triggers and to treat comorbid psychological issues. In addition, support groups (such as Sexaholics Anonymous) and group therapy can be effective in treating this addiction, provided these therapeutic approaches consider matters of access, coping skills, relapse prevention, and recovery.

Online communities for recovery also exist, although computer access, availability, and the anonymous nature of the Internet can be problematic for recovery. To address these issues, therapists can employ filtering software to monitor use and prevent access to sexually explicit material. Pharmacotherapy for pornography addiction or a related diagnosis (such as an anxiety, mood, or hypersexual disorder) should also be considered, especially in severe cases.

PREVENTION

Given that the development of pornography addiction or viewing it compulsively is highly associated with sexually acting-out in response to the sexual arousal that viewing explicit material elicits, prevention is best achieved by avoiding the regular viewing of pornographic material. Refraining from viewing of sexually explicit materials as a regular part of sexual activity also is recommended.

BIBLIOGRAPHY

Carnes, Patrick, David Delmonico, and Joseph Moriarity, eds. (2007). *In the Shadows of the Net: Breaking Free from Compulsive Online Sexual Behavior*. 2nd ed. Center City, MN: Hazelden, Edited volume that covers core issues and recovery for both general readers and professionals. Highlights the role of the Internet in the delivery of pornographic material and in fostering pornography addiction.

Cooper, Al, ed. (2002). *Sex and the Internet: A Guidebook for Clinicians*. New York: Brunner. A landmark text for clinicians who are working with porn and cybersex addicts.

Maltz, Wendy, and Larry Maltz. (2008). *The Porn Trap*. New York: Collins. A comprehensive text written from a clinical perspective on the development and treatment of pornography addiction.

Mouras, H., et al. (2003). "Brain Processing of Visual Sexual Stimuli in Healthy Men: A Functional Magnetic Resonance Imaging Study." *Neuroimaging* 20: 855–69. Print. A brain-imaging study that reveals the neurological circuit activated when viewing pornography.

Reid, Rory C., et al. (2011). "Reliability, Validity, and Psychometric Development of the Pornography Consumption Inventory in a Sample of Hypersexual Men." *Journal of Sex and Marital Therapy* 37 (5): 359–85. Print. Examines the development of the pornography consumption inventory and the implications for how pornography addiction might be better understood, classified, and diagnosed.

Štulhofer, Aleksandar, Vesna Buško, and Ivan Landripet. (2010). "Pornography, Sexual Socialization, and Satisfaction among Young Men." *Archives of Sexual Behavior* 39 (1): 168–78. Print. An excellent article examining the effects of regular pornography viewing on the development of sexual attitudes.

WEBSITES OF INTEREST

Porn Addicts Anonymous
http://www.pornaddictsanonymous.org
Sexual Recovery Institute
http://www.sexualrecovery.com

William M. Struthers

SEE ALSO: Addiction; Behavioral addiction; Physical dependence; Sensitization; Sexuality.

Positive psychology

DATE: 1970s forward

TYPE OF PSYCHOLOGY: Origin and definition of psychology; Social psychology

Positive psychology is the field of study dealing with the human experiences and strengths that make life most worth living. This field encompasses the understanding and facilitation of valued qualities such as happiness and well-being, optimal experiences, good health, optimism, responsibility, and good citizenship that enable both individuals and the broader culture to thrive.

KEY CONCEPTS

- Flow
- Happiness
- Optimal experience
- Optimism
- Resilience
- Subjective well-being

INTRODUCTION

Positive psychology emerged as a defined field in the 1990s as a reaction against American psychology's better-known emphasis on psychopathology, or what might be called negative psychology, since about World War II. This is based in part on the founding of two major institutions at the end of the war. In 1946, the Veterans Administration (VA) was established, soon to become the largest single training site for and employer of psychologists. Thousands of clinical psychologists earned their living by diagnosing and treating the mental disorders of armed services veterans at VA hospitals. In 1947, the National Institute of Mental Health (NIMH) was founded. Academic psychologists soon discovered that NIMH looked favorably on funding grants that proposed research on pathology. The benefits of this "negative" focus became clear through the late 1990s as much was learned about helping those who suffered from mental illness. On the other hand, one consequence of this emphasis on fixing what was wrong with people was that psychologists neglected two additional missions of American psychology prior to World War II: the enhancement of fulfillment and productivity in normal people's lives and the nurture of exceptional human potential.

The widespread awareness of positive psychology among American psychologists probably dates to 1998. In that year, Martin E. P. Seligman, then president of the American Psychological Association and a professor at the University of Pennsylvania, determined that the theme of the national convention would be positive psychology. His vision was to revive and relaunch the scientific study of the best dimensions of human nature.

A basic definition of positive psychology is the study of average people and their virtues and strengths. Overall, the field focuses on topics dealing with the nature of effectively functioning people: what works well, what facilitates improvement, and what is right. Some of the well-researched areas in this field include subjective well-being, optimal experience and the related concept of flow, positive personal traits, good mental and physical health, resilience, and the nurture of excellence.

WELL-BEING, HAPPINESS, AND LIFE SATISFACTION

Subjective well-being may be understood as a combination of personal happiness and life satisfaction. David G. Myers, a social psychologist and professor at Hope College in Michigan, suggests two questions to frame this area. The first has to do with how happy people are in general, the second with the characteristics and circumstances of happy people. Myers reports global data on more than a million people in forty-five nations indicating that most people self-report that they are at least moderately happy. The average person rates himself or herself at 6.75 on a ten-point scale where 5 is neutral and 10 the highest extreme of well-being.

The second question deals with a number of variables: age, gender, wealth, relationships, religious faith, personality traits, and more. Despite a common belief that certain times of life (such as adolescence or old age), are less happy than others, there is no significant relationship between age and life satisfaction. Likewise, no difference can be found in self-reported happiness between men and women. Research on the relationship between wealth and happiness finds that with the exception that happiness is lower among the very poor, enduring personal happiness does not rise appreciably with increasing personal wealth or a stronger national economy.

By contrast, close, committed, and supportive relationships are strongly associated with both physical and psychological well-being. Looking at physical health, close attachments are associated with decreased rates of illness and premature death and increased survival rates for those with severe disease. Similarly, social support is associated with positive mental health measures, including greater self-reported happiness and improved coping with a variety of life stressors, including rape, divorce, and job loss.

Marriage, one form of a committed intimate relationship, has been repeatedly associated with greater happiness and life satisfaction as well as less depression and loneliness when compared to being divorced, separated, or never having been married. Likewise, more intrinsically motivated, religiously active persons report higher levels of life satisfaction and better coping with adversity, whether measured by level of spiritual commitment or religious attendance.

Finally, a number of studies identify four personality traits that characterize happy people. First, they like themselves and often even demonstrate a self-serving bias, indicating that they view themselves as more ethical, intelligent, healthy, and sociable than average. Second, they tend to be more extroverted, reflecting a genetic predisposition. Third, they experience a stronger sense of personal control over their lives. Fourth, they are optimistic. Contrary to popular notions, optimism has very little to do with "positive thinking" or repeating positive-self phrases. Optimism has much more to do with explanatory style or habitual ways of thinking about why good and bad things happen. Optimistic people are more likely to explain negative experiences in terms of external, temporary, specific causes ("I failed the test because I just did not have time to study this week—next week it will be different"). Positive experiences are likely to be understood in terms of internal, stable, global causes ("I received a high score on the exam because I'm smart").

FLOW AND OPTIMAL EXPERIENCE

Another important area in positive psychology has been the study of optimal human experiences. Mihaly Csikszentmihalyi, director of the Quality of Life Research Center at Claremont Graduate University in California, built his career on research examining the moments in time that people feel most happy. His first studies of optimal experience were based on interviews with several hundred experts in their fields—musicians, chess masters, mountain climbers, artists, surgeons—people who appeared to spend their time doing exactly what they wanted to do just for the joy of the experience. As he probed into their descriptions of what it felt like to engage in these highly valued activities, he began to conceptualize their optimal moments as times of "flow." Flow is a concept describing a state of deep enjoyment in which people are so engaged in a desired activity that nothing else seems to matter; it is a time of highly focused concentration resulting in the individual's complete absorption in his or her particular task. During these times of peak performance, people feel completely in control without exerting any particular effort. They forget themselves as they are immersed in the moment and often report that time seems to pass much more quickly than usual. The related phenomena of flow and optimal experience have generated such interest that researchers around the world collected more than eight thousand interviews and a quarter million questionnaires examining this state during the thirty years of research leading up to the year 2000.

Several conditions make the experience of flow most likely. First is clarity of goals. People who achieve flow (as when playing a musical instrument or engaging in an athletic event) generally know, moment by moment, what they need to do next. Ongoing momentary goals keep the action going. Another necessary condition is immediate feedback. To maintain focused concentration, it is essential to know how well one is doing. Finally, there must be an optimal balance between the level of challenge of the activity and one's level of skill. Optimal flow is usually reported when individuals are functioning above their mean or typical levels of both challenge and skill.

PSYCHOLOGICAL CONTRIBUTORS TO PHYSICAL HEALTH

An intriguing area of study in positive psychology has to do with psychological contributors to physical health. Psychologists have long posited that optimism, a sense of personal control, and the ability to give meaning to life are associated with mental health. Such qualities represent important reserves that provide resilience and a buffer to individuals in the midst of difficult life events. A subsequent line of research suggests that these sorts of qualities may provide benefits to physical health as well. For example, a series of such studies conducted at the University of California at Los Angeles deal with men with acquired immunodeficiency syndrome (AIDS) and human immunodeficiency virus (HIV) infection. Among other findings, it appears that a patient's ability to find meaning in this life-threatening illness is associated with a less rapid progression of the disease. In addition, those who remain optimistic, even unrealistically so, appear to gain health-protective benefits from their "positive illusions." Optimistic thinking is clearly linked to good physical health in other research as well, but two important prerequisites must also be in place. First, the optimistic thinking must lead people to active, sustained behaviors based on their optimism. Second, the active behaviors sustained by optimism must have some real association with health.

To summarize the general thrust of other research in this area, positive emotional states are believed to be associated with healthier functioning in the cardiovascular and immune systems, while negative emotional states are associated with unhealthy functioning in these systems (for example, the association between chronic anger and cardiovascular distress). Research targeting the interface of positive psychological states and physiological functioning represents an important and growing focus in the positive psychology movement.

BIBLIOGRAPHY

Argyle, Michael. *The Psychology of Happiness*. 2nd ed. Philadelphia: Routledge, 2001. Print.

Baumgardner, Steve, and Marie Crothers. *Positive Psychology*. Upper Saddle River: Prentice Hall, 2009. Print.

Biswas-Diener, Robert. *Positive Psychology as Social Change*. New York: Springer, 2011. Print.

Csikszentmihalyi, Mihaly. *Finding Flow*. New York: Basic, 1997. Print.

Diener, Ed, Eunkook M. Suk, Richard E. Lucas, and Heidi L. Smith. "Subjective Well-Being: Three Decades of Progress." *Psychological Bulletin* 125.2 (1999): 276–302. Print.

Fredrickson, Barbara L. "The Role of Positive Emotions in Positive Psychology." *American Psychologist* 56.3 (2001): 218–26. Print.

Gilham, Jane E., ed. *The Science of Optimism and Hope*. Philadelphia: Templeton Foundation, 2000. Print.

Heffernon, Kate, and Ilona Boniwell. *Positive Psychology: Theory, Research and Applications*. Maidenhead: McGraw, 2011. Print.

Lopez, Shane J. *The Encyclopedia of Positive Psychology*. Hoboken: Wiley-Blackwell, 2009. Print.

Lopez, Shane J., and C. R. Snyder. *The Oxford Handbook of Positive Psychology*. 2nd ed. New York: Oxford UP, 2011. Print.

Seligman, Martin E. P., Karen Reivich, Lisa Jaycox, and Jane Gillham. *The Optimistic Child*. Boston: Houghton, 2007. Print.

Seligman, Martin E. P., and Mihaly Csikszentmihalyi, eds. "Special Issue on Happiness, Excellence, and Optimal Human Functioning." *American Psychologist* 55.1 (2000). Print.

David W. Brokaw

SEE ALSO: Altruism, cooperation, and empathy; Attitude formation and change; Biofeedback and relaxation; Health psychology; Humanistic psychology; Meditation and relaxation; Psychology: History; Self-esteem; Seligman, Martin E. P.

Postpartum depression

TYPE OF PSYCHOLOGY: Psychopathology

Postpartum depression is a type of mood disorder that some women acquire in the days or weeks after giving birth. This disorder is characterized by feelings of sadness, fatigue, anxiety, and guilt. The treatment for postpartum depression includes therapy and, in some cases, antidepressant medications..

KEY CONCEPTS
- Estrogen
- Maternity blues
- Postpartum psychosis
- Progesterone

INTRODUCTION

Postpartum depression (PPD) has been a focus of research since 1970. Approximately 12 to 15 percent of mothers suffer from PPD. The disorder is defined as the onset of depression occurring within days or weeks after childbirth. Symptoms include sadness, frequent crying or tearfulness, loss of interest or pleasure in life, loss of appetite, loss of motivation, irritability, fatigue, anxiety, poor sleep, and feelings of hopelessness and guilt. PPD can arise days, weeks, or even months after childbirth. The most common onset is within a few days of delivery, perhaps due to the hormonal changes that the body experiences. Some women acquire PPD two to six weeks postpartum due to neuroendocrine changes and lifestyle changes that accompany caring for the infant. No one theory accounts for all cases of PPD, but almost all researchers in this area agree on the importance of biological and psychosocial factors in the development of PPD.

RELATED POSTPARTUM EMOTIONAL DISORDERS

In addition to PPD, there are other forms of psychiatric illness that can arise following childbirth. Maternity blues or "baby blues" affects 50 to 80 percent of mothers after delivery. The symptoms, which begin on the second or third day after childbirth, include anxiety, mood swings from joyfulness to tearfulness, irritability, and sleep difficulties, all of which typically remit within four weeks.

However, 25 percent of these women go on to suffer a more long-term and severe form of depression known as postpartum depression. A related disorder is postpartum psychosis, a serious psychiatric disorder that occurs two to four weeks postpartum and requires immediate professional attention. Symptoms of postpartum psychosis include hallucinations (such as hearing voices), delusions (bizarre false beliefs), and mania (hyperactivity, increased energy levels, rapid speech, and destructive impulsive behavior). A small number of women with postpartum psychosis experience obsessions having to do with harming themselves or their babies following delivery. In this instance, a differential diagnosis is important to assess the risk of harm to the mother and child.

WHO SUFFERS?

The strongest predictor of PPD is any form of depression during pregnancy, but any previous history of mood disorders elevates the risk of PPD. In addition, a lack of social support, mixed feelings about the pregnancy, an unplanned pregnancy, marital problems, or giving birth to a temperamentally difficult child all increase the chances of PPD. Furthermore, pregnant adolescents have a 30 percent chance of developing PPD. The majority of patients with PPD have a family history of mood or anxiety disorders. In general, stressful events that occur during pregnancy or delivery (such as illness during pregnancy, pregnancy complications, or a premature birth) increase the risk for developing postpartum depression. The risk of postpartum psychosis is higher for mothers who have bipolar disorder.

CAUSES OF PPD

Theories about the causes of PPD stress the importance of biological and psychological influences, although no single agreed-on theory has emerged. One biological theory of the cause of PPD is that hormonal changes in the woman's body after childbirth affect her mood. Three days after childbirth, the hormones estrogen and progesterone show a sharp drop from their previously high levels during pregnancy, and these changes may in-

Photo: iStock

duce chemical changes in the brain that play a role in causing depression.

Some psychosocial factors (such as ambivalence about the pregnancy or low social support) can serve to increase stress and undermine coping resources. The fact that a family history of mood disorders is predictive of PPD might suggest that certain women are biologically vulnerable, and the addition of negative psychosocial factors interacts with this vulnerability to produce PPD.

TREATMENT OPTIONS

There are several treatment options for PPD and its variations, and the treatment for PPD is similar to the treatment for any other forms of depression. Most women who suffer from postpartum "blues" are advised to seek social support from their spouses, family, friends, and doctors.

Other recommendations for new mothers experiencing the "baby blues" are to stay physically active, to take time to relax, and to pursue activities that are enjoyable to them. However, because 25 percent of women with maternal blues will develop PPD, physicians should advise and monitor those patients in case their symptoms become more severe or last longer than a few weeks. If the symptoms persist for an extended period of time, usually more than five weeks following delivery, women are generally encouraged to seek psychotherapy or counseling. Through therapy, patients can explore their thoughts and feelings, receive help for interpersonal problems, set realistic goals and expectations, and learn strategies for coping with stress. Oftentimes the therapy continues after the PPD is no longer present. With severe cases of postpartum depression, an antidepressant may be used to complement psychotherapy.

Nursing mothers should discuss the risks of taking an antidepressant while breastfeeding with their doctor. Postpartum psychosis requires immediate treatment. If the person with PPD experiences a psychotic reaction, then an antipsychotic medication is often warranted in addition to antidepressant drugs. Electroconvulsive therapy has also been recommended as an effective treatment for severe postpartum psychosis.

BIBLIOGRAPHY

"Depression During and After Pregnancy Fact Sheet." *WomensHealth.gov.* US Department of Health and Human Services, 16 July 2012. Web. 21 July 2014.

Dunnewold, Ann, and Diane G. Sanford. *Postpartum Survival Guide.* Oakland: New Harbinger, 1994. Print.

Kleiman, Karen. *Therapy and the Postpartum Woman: Notes on Healing Postpartum Depression for Clinicians and the Women Who Seek Their Help.* New York: Routledge, 2009. Print.

Kleiman, Karen R., and Valerie Davis Raskin. *This Isn't What I Expected: Overcoming Postpartum Depression.* 2nd ed. Philadelphia: De Capo, 2013. Print.

"Postpartum Depression." *Mayo Clinic.* Mayo Foundation for Medical Education and Research, 11 Sept. 2012. Web. 21 July 2014.

"Postpartum Depression." *The American College of Obstetricians and Gynecologists.* American College of Obstetricians and Gynecologists, Dec. 2013. Web. 21 July 2014.

Steiner, Meir, Kimberly A. Yonkers, and E. Eriksson, eds. *Mood Disorders in Women.* Malden: Blackwell Science, 2000. Print.

Twomey, Teresa M. *Understanding Postpartum Psychosis: A Temporary Madness.* Westport: Praeger, 2009. Print.

Lindsey L. Henninger and Laurence Grimm

SEE ALSO: Children's mental health; Depression; Endocrine system; Hallucinations; Hormones and behavior; Women's mental health.

Post-traumatic stress (PTS)

TYPE OF PSYCHOLOGY: Psychopathology

After an extreme psychological trauma, people tend to respond with stress symptoms that include reexperiencing the trauma through nightmares or unwanted thoughts, avoiding reminders of the traumatic event, loss of interest in daily life, and increased arousal; these symptoms can range from mild and temporary to severe, chronic, and psychologically disabling.

KEY CONCEPTS
- Flashback
- Hyperarousal
- Reexperience
- Traumatic event

INTRODUCTION

It is common knowledge that there are psychological aftereffects from experiencing an intense psychological trauma. This discussion of post-traumatic stress symptoms will be organized around post-traumatic stress disorder (PTSD), one of the diagnostic categories of anxiety disorders recognized by the American Psychiatric Association. It should be realized at the outset, however, that it is normal for people to experience at least some of these symptoms after suffering a psychological trauma. The first step in understanding PTSD is to know its symptoms.

The first criterion for PTSD is that one has suffered a trauma. The American Psychiatric Association's definition of PTSD states that the trauma must be something that "is outside the range of usual human experience and that would be markedly distressing to almost anyone." It is not so much the objective event as one's perception of it that determines the psychological response. For example, the death of one's parents is not "outside the range of usual human experience," but it can result in some of the symptoms described later. Some of the traumatic experiences deemed sufficient to cause PTSD include threat to one's own life or the life of a close relative or friend, sudden destruction of one's home or community, seeing another person violently injured or killed, or being the victim of a violent crime. Specific experiences that often cause PTSD include combat, natural or man-made disasters, automobile accidents, airplane crashes, rape, child abuse, and physical assault. In general, the more traumatic the event, the worse the post-traumatic symptoms. Symptoms of stress are often more severe when the trauma is sudden and unexpected. In addition, when the trauma is the result of intentional human action (for example, combat, rape, or assault), stress symptoms are worse than when the trauma is a natural disaster (flood or earthquake) or an accident (automobile crash). It has been found that combat veterans who commit or witness atrocities are more likely than their comrades to suffer later from PTSD.

The central symptom of post-traumatic stress disorder is that the person reexperiences the trauma. This can occur in a number of ways. The person can have unwanted, intrusive, and disturbing thoughts of the event or nightmares about the trauma. The most dramatic means of reexperiencing is through a flashback, in which the person acts, thinks, and feels as if he or she were reliving the event. Another way in which reexperiencing might be manifested is intense distress when confronted with situations that serve as reminders of the trauma. Vietnam veterans with combat-related PTSD will often become very upset at motion pictures about the war, hot and humid junglelike weather, or even the smell of Asian cooking. A person with PTSD often will attempt to avoid thoughts, feelings, activities, or events that serve as unwanted reminders of the trauma.

Another symptom that is common in people with PTSD is numbing of general responsiveness. This might include the loss of interest in hobbies or activities that were enjoyed before the trauma, losing the feeling of closeness to other people, an inability to experience strong emotions, or a lack of interest in the future. A final set of PTSD symptoms involves increased arousal. This can include irritability, angry outbursts, and problems with sleeping and concentrating. A person with PTSD may be oversensitive to the environment, always on the alert, and prone to startle at the slightest noise.

The paragraphs above summarize the symptoms that psychologists and psychiatrists use to diagnose PTSD; however, other features are often found in trauma survivors that are not part of the diagnosis. Anxiety and depression are common in people who have experienced a trauma. Guilt is common in people who have survived a trauma in which others have died. People will sometimes use alcohol or tranquilizers to cope with sleep problems, disturbing nightmares, or distressing, intrusive

recollections of a trauma, and they may then develop dependence on the drugs.

Post-traumatic stress disorder is relatively common in people who suffer serious trauma. In the late 1980's, the most extensive survey on PTSD ever done was undertaken on Vietnam combat veterans. It found that more than half of all those who served in the Vietnam theater of operations had experienced serious post-traumatic stress at some point in their lives after the war. This represents about 1.7 million veterans. Even more compelling was the fact that more than one-third of the veterans who saw heavy combat were still suffering from PTSD when the survey was done—about fifteen years after the fall of Saigon. Surveys of crime victims are also sobering. One study found that 75 percent of adult females had been the victim of a crime, and more than one in four of these victims developed PTSD after the crime. Crime victims were even more likely to develop PTSD if they were raped, were injured during the crime, or believed that their lives were in danger during the crime.

Symptoms of post-traumatic stress are common after a trauma, but they often decrease or disappear over time. A diagnosis of PTSD is not made unless the symptoms last for at least one month. Sometimes a person will have no symptoms until long after the event, when memories of the trauma are triggered by another negative life event. For example, a combat veteran might cope well with civilian life for many years until, after a divorce, he begins to have nightmares about his combat experiences.

FROM WAR TO EVERYDAY LIFE

Most of the theory and research regarding PTSD have been done on combat veterans, particularly veterans of the Vietnam War. One of the most exciting developments in this area, however, is that the theory and research are also being applied to victims of other sorts of trauma. This has a number of important implications. First, it helps extend the findings about PTSD beyond the combat-veteran population, which is mostly young and male. Second, information gathered from combat veterans can be used to assist in the assessment and treatment of anyone who has experienced a serious trauma. Because a large proportion of the general population experiences severe psychological trauma at some time, understanding PTSD is important to those providing mental health services.

An extended example will illustrate the application of theory and research findings on PTSD to a case of extreme psychological trauma. The case involves a woman who was attacked and raped at knifepoint one night while walking from her car to her apartment. Because of injuries suffered in the attack, she went to an emergency room for treatment. Knowledge about PTSD can help in understanding this woman's experience and could aid her in recovery.

First, research has shown that this woman's experience—involving rape, life threat, and physical injury—puts her at high risk for symptoms of post-traumatic stress. Risk is so great, in fact, that researchers have proposed that psychological counseling be recommended to all people who are the victims of this sort of episode. This suggestion is being implemented in many rape-recovery and crime-victim programs around the United States.

Knowing what symptoms are common following a traumatic event can help professionals counsel a victim about what to expect. This woman can expect feelings of anxiety and depression, nightmares and unwanted thoughts about the event, irritability, and difficulties in sleeping and concentrating. Telling a victim that these are normal responses and that there is a likelihood that the problems will lessen with time is often reassuring. Since research has shown that many people with these symptoms cope by using drugs and alcohol, it may also help to warn the victim about this possibility and caution that this is harmful in the long run.

One symptom of PTSD—psychological distress in situations that resemble the traumatic event—suggests why combat veterans who experience their trauma in a far-off land often fare better than those whose trauma occurs closer to home. Women who are raped in their home or neighborhood may begin to feel unsafe in previously secure places. Some cope by moving to a different house, a new neighborhood, or even a new city—often leaving valued jobs and friends. If an attack occurred after dark, a person may no longer feel safe going out after dark and may begin living a restricted social life. Frequently, women who are raped generalize their fear to all men and especially to sexual relations, seriously damaging their interpersonal relationships. Given the problems that these post-traumatic symptoms can cause in so many areas of one's life, it may not be surprising that one study found that nearly one in every five rape victims attempted suicide.

The main symptoms of post-traumatic stress are phobialike fear and avoidance of trauma-related situations, thoughts, and feelings, and the most effective treatment for PTSD is the same as for a phobia. Systematic desensitization and flooding, which involve confronting the thoughts and feelings surrounding the traumatic event, are the treatments that appear to be most effective. It may seem paradoxical that a disorder whose symptoms include unwanted thoughts and dreams of a traumatic event could be treated by purposefully thinking and talking about the event; however, Mardi Horowitz, one of the leading theorists in traumatic stress, believes that symptoms alternate between unwanted, intrusive thoughts of the event and efforts to avoid these thoughts. Because intrusive thoughts always provoke efforts at avoidance, the event is never fully integrated into memory; it therefore retains its power. Systematic desensitization and flooding, which involve repeatedly thinking about the event without avoidance, allow time for the event to become integrated into the person's life experiences so that the memory loses much of its pain.

Another effective way to reduce the impact of a traumatic event is through social support. Social support People who have a close network of friends and family appear to suffer less from symptoms of trauma. After a traumatic experience, people should be encouraged to maintain and even increase their supportive social contacts, rather than withdrawing from people, as often happens. Support groups of people who have had similar experiences, such as Vietnam veteran groups or child-abuse support groups, also provide needed social support. These groups have the added benefit of encouraging people to talk about their experiences, which provides another way to think about and integrate the traumatic event.

Psychotherapy can help trauma victims in many ways. One way is to help the patient explore and cope with the way the trauma changes one's view of the world. For example, the rape victim may come to believe that "the world is dangerous" or that "men can't be trusted." Therapy can help this person learn to take reasonable precautions without shutting herself off from the world and relationships. Finally, symptoms of overarousal are common with PTSD. A therapist can address these symptoms by teaching methods of deep relaxation and stress reduction. Sometimes mild tranquilizers are prescribed when trauma victims are acutely aroused or anxious.

HISTORY

The concept of post-traumatic stress is very old and is closely tied to the history of human warfare. The symptoms of PTSD have been known variously as soldier's heart, combat neurosis, and battle fatigue. Stephen Crane's novel *The Red Badge of Courage*, first published in 1895, describes post-traumatic symptoms in a Civil War soldier. It was the postwar experiences of the Vietnam combat veteran, however, studied and described by scholars such as Charles Figley, that brought great attention to issues of post-traumatic stress. It was not until 1980 that the American Psychiatric Association recognized post-traumatic stress disorder in its manual of psychiatric disorders. Since then there has been an explosion of published research and books on PTSD,

the creation of the Society for Traumatic Stress Studies in 1985, and the initiation of the quarterly *Journal of Traumatic Stress* in 1988. Since these developments, attention has also been directed toward post-traumatic symptoms in victims of natural disasters, violent crime, sexual and child abuse; Holocaust survivors; and many other populations. Surveys have found that more than 80 percent of college students have suffered at least one trauma potentially sufficient to cause PTSD, and many

---

DSM-IV-TR CRITERIA FOR POST-TRAUMATIC STRESS DISORDER (DSM CODE 309.81)

Person has been exposed to a traumatic event in which both of the following were present:
- person experienced, witnessed, or was confronted with event or events involving actual or threatened death or serious injury, or threat to physical integrity of self or others
- person's response involved intense fear, helplessness, or horror; in children, may be expressed instead by disorganized or agitated behavior

Traumatic event persistently reexperienced in one or more of the following ways:
- recurrent and intrusive distressing recollections of event, including images, thoughts, or perceptions; in young children, repetitive play may express themes or aspects of trauma
- recurrent distressing dreams of event; in children, frightening dreams without recognizable content may occur
- acting or feeling as if traumatic event were recurring (includes a sense of reliving the experience, illusions, hallucinations, and dissociative flashback episodes, including those occurring on awakening or when intoxicated); in young children, trauma-specific reenactment may occur
- intense psychological distress at exposure to internal or external cues that symbolize or resemble an aspect of traumatic event
- physiological reactivity on exposure to internal or external cues that symbolize or resemble an aspect of traumatic event

Persistent avoidance of stimuli associated with trauma and numbing of general responsiveness (not present before trauma), as indicated by three or more of the following:
- efforts to avoid thoughts, feelings, or conversations associated with trauma
- efforts to avoid activities, places, or people arousing recollections of trauma
- inability to recall an important aspect of trauma
- markedly diminished interest or participation in significant activities
- feeling of detachment or estrangement from others
- restricted range of affect (such as inability to have loving feelings)
- sense of a foreshortened future (such as not expecting to have career, marriage, children, or normal life span)

Persistent symptoms of increased arousal (not present before trauma), as indicated by two or more of the following:
- difficulty falling or staying asleep
- irritability or outbursts of anger
- difficulty concentrating
- hypervigilance
- exaggerated startle response

Duration of more than one month
Disturbance causes clinically significant distress or impairment in social, occupational, or other important areas of functioning
Specify Acute (duration less than three months) or Chronic (duration three months or more)
Specify if with Delayed Onset (onset at least six months after stressor)

people seeking psychological counseling have post-traumatic stress symptoms. Thus, it is fair to say that the attention garnered by Vietnam veteran readjustment problems and by the recognition of PTSD as a disorder by the American Psychiatric Association has prompted the examination of many important issues related to post-traumatic stress.

Because research in this area is relatively new, many important questions remain unanswered. One mystery is that two people can have exactly the same traumatic experience, yet one will have extreme post-traumatic stress and one will have no problems. Some factors are known to be important; for example, young children and the elderly are more likely to suffer from psychological symptoms after a trauma. Much research is needed, however, to determine what individual differences will predict who fares well and who fares poorly after a trauma.

A second area of future development is in the assessmentAssessmentpost-traumatic stress disorder of PTSD. For the most part, it is diagnosed through a self-report of trauma and post-traumatic symptoms. This creates difficulty, however, when the person reporting the symptoms stands to gain compensation for the trauma suffered. Interesting physiological and cognitive methods for assessing PTSD are being explored. For example, researchers have found that Vietnam veterans with PTSD show high levels of physiological arousal when they hear combat-related sounds or imagine their combat experiences. Finally, the future will see more bridges built between post-traumatic stress and the more general area of stress and coping.

BIBLIOGRAPHY

Crane, Stephen. *The Red Badge of Courage*. Reprint. New York: Pearson/Longman, 2008. This classic novel vividly portrays post-traumatic symptoms in Civil War soldiers, particularly in the main character, young Henry Fleming; first published in 1895, the book has been called the first modern war novel.

Figley, Charles R., ed. *Trauma and Its Wake: The Study and Treatment of Post-traumatic Stress Disorder*. New York: Brunner/Mazel, 1985. This book is one of the most often cited references in the field of PTSD and contains some of the most influential papers written on the subject. It is divided into sections on theory, research, and treatment; a second volume with the same title was published in 1986. It is part of the Brunner/Mazel Psychosocial Stress Series, the first volume of which was published in 1978; through 1990, this valuable series had published twenty-one volumes on many aspects of stress and trauma.

Figley, Charles R., and Seymour Leventman, eds. *Strangers at Home: Vietnam Veterans Since the War*. 1980. Reprint. New York: Brunner/Mazel, 1990. Containing chapters by psychologists, sociologists, political activists, historians, political scientists, and economists, this book presents a look at the experience of the Vietnam veteran from different perspectives. Many of the authors were Vietnam veterans themselves, so the book has a very personal, sometimes stirring view of its subject.

Grinker, Roy Richard, and John P. Spiegal. *Men Under Stress*. Philadelphia: Blakiston, 1945. Long before the term "post-traumatic stress disorder" was coined, this classic book described the stress response to combat in Air Force flyers. It is written in jargon-free language by men who had unusual access to the flight crews.

Horowitz, Mardi Jon. *Stress Response Syndromes*. New York: Jason Aronson, 1976. Horowitz is one of the leading psychodynamic theorists in the area of post-traumatic stress. In this readable book, he describes his theory and his approach to treatment.

Kulka, Richard A. *Trauma and the Vietnam War Generation*. New York: Brunner/Mazel, 1990. Presents the results of the federally funded National Vietnam Veterans Readjustment Study. In contrast to Strangers at Home, which is a subjective view of the Vietnam veteran's plight, this book is very factual. It contains dozens of tables and figures filled with statistics about the mental and physical health of Vietnam veterans. The same authors published The National Vietnam Veterans Readjustment Study: Tables of Findings and Technical Appendices in 1990. This companion volume contains hundreds of tables of detailed results from this comprehensive study.

Schiraldi, Glenn. *The Post-Traumatic Stress Disorder Sourcebook: A Guide to Healing, Recovery, and Growth*. New York: McGraw-Hill, 2009. Designed as a self-help program for those suffering from post-traumatic stress disorder, this book discusses emotional triggers, drug addiction, and successful treatments.

Smyth, Larry. *Overcoming Post-Traumatic Stress Disorder—Therapist Protocol: A Cognitive-Behavioral Exposure-Based Protocol for the Treatment of PTSD and the Other Anxiety Disorders*. Oakland, Calif.: New Harbinger, 2008. Written for the therapist, this book outlines a protocol that has worked successfully with those who are experiencing post-traumatic stress disorder. The sessions involve assessment, goal setting, developing coping skills, and assimilation.

Scott R. Vrana

SEE ALSO: Anxiety disorders; Aversion therapy; Coping: Social support; Disaster psychology; Fear; Implosion; Phobias; Stress: Behavioral and psychological responses; Social support and mental health; Support groups; Systematic desensitization; Women's mental health.

Power

TYPE OF PSYCHOLOGY: Motivation; Social psychology

Power in human affairs is the ability to bring about a change in one's situation. Its focus can be toward the self or another, and it can be deployed by a wide variety of means for a variety of ends.

KEY CONCEPTS
- Empowerment
- Influence
- Potentiality
- Social power
- Will

INTRODUCTION

Power, as the exertion of effort to effect a change, is one of the most significant and examined of all themes. However, the conceptualization of power is far from finished. It is clearly one of those curious phenomena whose breadth makes them easily recognizable even while their depth renders them very difficult to comprehend completely.

This scope poses a conceptual conundrum, as power is important to all three orders of existence: the physical, the vital, and the human. In the physical order, power refers to the causal impact of force—for example, the power of gravity on planetary motion. In this arena, power is ultimately the capacity to mechanistically transform matter or energy. In the biological domain, power is also a central notion to understanding the functioning of life. Examples include the power of the digestive system to transform protein into muscle, or the power of a virus to infect a host.

The concept of power in the human order shares this general notion of transformational ability, yet has distinctive features. In the human order, the transformation sought is something intended by the one wielding power. It is a goal—whether or not the results conform to what was sought. For the to-be-transformed person, the change has an intrinsic meaning. To understand this level, a concept of brute force is insufficient.

Relations between these levels can be very complicated. For example, the conviction that one's desires can bring about changes on the physical level (say, the belief that one can make it rain by wanting it to) is not power on the physical level, but the psychological experience of one's power. Conversely, the belief that one's thoughts are controlled by a radio transmitter in the ceiling, for example, reveals the person's experienced powerlessness— whether or not any such controlling physical power is actually operating. The relationship of experience with the biological level is even more complex. One's belief that one cannot do something (lift an object, overcome a disease) may render one less able to do so, whereas an optimistic sense of one's power can have the reverse impact. So, though the concept of power at the human order is not reducible to explanations from the domains of physical or vital power, it can be interrelated with them.

THE RANGE OF SOCIAL POWER

The concept of power at the human level is usually called social power, indicating its interpersonal context. As the famous sociologist Max Weber defined it, power in this sense is the ability to impose one's will on others. Yet even at this level of specificity, three dilemmas complicate matters. First, an array of disciplinary crosscurrents need clarification, since each of the social sciences includes its own specific sense of power. In the 1930s, philosopher Bertrand Russell presented social power as the meta-concept of all the social sciences. In addition to discovering this commonality, he reasoned that a complete analysis must distinguish among their different senses, for example: economic power (to accumulate and spend wealth), political power (to allocate the community's legal and financial capital), sociological power (the power of group norms—gender, age, race, and class), moral or religious power (the proverbial "higher power" to inspire or prohibit certain practices), and many others, as well as psychological power.

Second, a complete conceptualization of power must confront a variety of classification schemes that specify different historical types of social power. Three widely cited types are those set forth by historical sociologist Michael Mann, economist John Kenneth Galbraith, and futurologist Alvin Toffler. In the 1980s, Mann specified four types of interacting networks of power—economic, military, political, and ideological—and saw the past century as having been particularly dominated by ideology. In the 1980s, Galbraith analyzed the development of the Western world from feudalism through capitalism as the deployment of three successive types of power: condign (the power to coerce), compensating (the power to reward), and conditioned (the power to change belief). In the 1990s, Toffler identified three historical types of power—violence, wealth, and knowledge—each successively the dominant form for its era. For Toffler, the third wave (the present) is the information age, in which, aided by computers and communications technology, knowledge has become the dominant form of power.

Third, the long history of philosophical scholarship on the importance of power to human flourishing poses another dilemma for articulating the range of the concept. Beginning with the pre-Socratic Greeks and revived for the later generations by Friedrich Nietzsche, Henri Bergson, Martin Heidegger, and Paul Tillich, philosophy offers a tradition of conceiving of power existentially, as the very core of the person—the force of life—coextensive with a properly human life itself. In this understanding, having a sense of one's power to develop one's potential, to enact one's destiny, is the very hallmark of what makes a person human. Tillich's books on the subject (*The Courage to Be*, 1952, and *Love, Power and Justice: Ontological Analyses* and *Ethical Applications,* 1954) were particularly foundational to existential psychologists.

THE PSYCHOLOGY OF SOCIAL POWER

Although the large scope and many permutations of social power are exciting and evocative, its specifically psychological dimension remains to be understood. As the psychotherapist Rollo May showed, the effective use of other types of social power is dependent on one's emotions, motivations, perception, and thinking—that is, on the psychological dimension. How else to account, for example, for how a person with enormous wealth could experience his or her life as not worth living?

Social power is usually taken to be unidirectional: the power to get someone else to behave in a certain way, as Weber noted. However, a psychological analysis finds two bivalent directionalities to power, because the person one wants to behave in a certain way could also be oneself. The genius of Sigmund Freud, after all, was to reveal—through his psychoanalysis of everyday mistakes,

compulsions, obsessions, and anxieties—that power over one's own consciousness was far from assured or easy to attain. Therefore, in its psychological sense, power has two contexts: with regard to another or with regard to one's self. Psychoanalyst Ethel Person identified these two kinds of power as interpersonal (power over others) and personal (power as strength, self-confidence, efficacy). This latter kind she called authentic power, and described it as "the ability to live fully, with few regrets and fewer recriminations."

Psychological power over the self would seem to be the very condition for mental health, as the inability to remember what happened (repression) or the inability to stop thinking a certain thought (obsession) or to stop repetitively performing a certain action (compulsion) would seem to clearly indicate that lacking "self-power" is the hallmark of psychopathology. The anorexic, for example, who feels compelled to lose more weight though she weighs only eighty-five pounds, seems caught in a vortex over which she is powerless. However, themes of psychological power and powerlessness circle around each other very complexly. Perhaps controlling her weight so strictly is the only context in which the girl feels any power. Her psychology is indeed one of felt powerlessness, but the symptom may be a more subtle expression, rather than the cause, of that dilemma. A psychologically destructive experience of powerlessness, insignificance, and inferiority can ensue from a dynamic in a variety of unequal relationships (husband and wife, parent and child, boss and employee). For example, May showed the psychological cost to his African American patient of the impact of racism, and Joanna Macy extended this understanding to the whole society in her analysis of the sense of futility to prevent nuclear war that was widely felt during the 1980s.

A healthy sense of one's power with regard to oneself, or self-control—as a self-motivated autonomy—is considered a hallmark of psychological health. This capacity, usually called inner power or empowerment in self-help popular psychology literature, is the basis for many theories of psychological well-being. It was the cornerstone of the influential personality theory known as individual psychology, formulated by Alfred Adler. Likewise, May's classic analysis of love showed the prerequisite of a healthy capacity to will something to be. In this sense, psychology's analysis parallels Nietzsche's rendering of the will to power—not power over the world or others, but the power to be self-directed. This means a will to potential—to potentiate, to actualize, to realize (as in to make real) one's potential to be the person one can be. Such a project cannot be a mere theory but a lived, everyday reality. One finds the power to unfold one's potential in actual encounters. To do so, one must affirm one's own being. In that sense, power cannot be given to one person by another, it must be enacted.

The other direction of psychological power is power over another. Whereas power with regard to oneself is of primary importance to psychotherapists, this second type has attracted the most interest from areas beyond psychology, from boardrooms to ballrooms. From closing the deal to getting love, people have an abiding motivation to understand how to gain and deploy social power with regard to others. Dale Carnegie's *How to Win Friends and Influence People* (1936) launched a whole cottage industry that has only grown more sophisticated over time. This inquiry is so fascinating precisely because social power is not reducible to force, even in its most harsh form. The range of ways to influence another to do one's bidding extends across the entire spectrum from coercive to seductive.

Both Galbraith and Russell long ago specified three different means of influence: the power to threaten adverse consequences, the power to provide resources as rewards, and the power of persuasion. Expressed in an even older key, these three types of social power are the threat of the stick, the promise of the carrot, and the power to get the other to change his or her mind. No matter how primitive (pay the bill or go to jail) or sophisticated (deferred stock options) the inducements of sticks and carrots may be, these two uses of social power are no real mystery to psychology. Research regarding their use involves when and with whom to employ which one, and how to optimally arrange and administer the contingencies. However, the third type—the power to influence others to think differently to get them to behave differently—reveals how psychologically deep the use of social power can be. The range of persuasive techniques and applications is enormous: Impression management, perceptual shifting, and motivational speeches are all used in direct appeals with a psychological infrastructure, but these and other techniques also underlie much of the work in public relations, selling, negotiating, propaganda, leadership, inspiration, and mass advertising. All these involve using social power to get others to do, think, feel, want, see, or believe as desired.

An analysis of persuasive appeals by Robert Greene identified each technique with a maxim and a historical illustration. Examples include always say less than necessary; when asking for help, appeal to people's self-interest, never to their mercy or gratitude; do not build fortresses to protect yourself as isolation is dangerous; and preach the need for change but never reform too much at once. Such techniques were studied for their efficacy, regardless of the good or bad ends to which they were used. Con artists and corporate executives, after all, often use similar strategies.

Beyond the social power of changing the self and others toward one's own preferences, many other less well-known types of power have also been studied. Two particularly insightful typologies can represent such analyses: those by May, and George Kunz. May identified not only three types of social power over another (exploitative, manipulative, and competitive) but also two other types: nutrient, a power for the sake of the other, and integrative, a power to work with the other to accomplish something together. Kunz identified three types of power: behavioral, the power to exert effort to accomplish tasks; cognitive, the power that comes with knowing and understanding; and affective, the power to enjoy pleasure, to be satisfied, fulfilled, and happy.

SOURCES OF POWER

A final question concerns the sources of power. Beyond the deployment of techniques and practices, the question remains as to where they get their efficacy. This issue is complex and unsettled not only because of its controversial theme but also because the wide variety of sources makes any neat effort at classification extraordinarily difficult. For power in relation to one's self, everything from the way the young child's initial moves toward autonomy are met by the unconditional love of the parent to the existential courage to be in the face of one's aging can provide a wellspring. Clinical and personality psychologists such as Erik H. Erikson, R. D. Laing, D. W. Winnicott, Karen Horney, and Abraham Maslow have provided penetrating analyses of these developmental issues.

Among the many studies regarding the sources of power with regard to another, three much-cited classic studies and one later one provide useful illustration. The classic studies were by sociologist Steven Lukes, social psychologists John French and Bertram Raven, and Galbraith. Lukes examined power in institutional structures and saw that, beyond the power to make decisions and set agendas using the usual sources of influence and persuasion, lay a third source of power, less visible and measurable: the power of language, ideas, and values to shape preferences and even taken-for-granted norms. His work articulated this critical power and developed in parallel with similar studies by French philosopher Michel Foucault and Brazilian educator Paulo Freire.

A second classic analysis on the sources of power, still very widely cited, especially in organizational psychology, is the research by French and Raven in the 1950s to 1970s. They identified five sources of power. Positional or legitimate power, derived from the position of authority of the person, is the most evident and usually most important. Generally related to it are the second and third sources—reward power and coercive power—the also obvious abilities to deliver the respective carrots and sticks on which much social influence depends. Unlike these three, which have come to be called hard power, the other two are sources of soft power. They are expert or information power, the evident possession of credible and useful expertise, and referent power, the ability to attract and retain loyal followers, which can be used and misused by charismatic leaders, but more mundanely is a talent for social networking.

The third classic analysis is Galbraith's specification of the three sources as personality, property, and organization. As a source of power, personality means the power of an individual person—such as a king or leader—to effect change in the world. Galbraith sees this source as having been largely eclipsed by another—property—with the development of capitalism. However, that source, in turn, was eclipsed with the more recent development of another—organizations, the huge bureaucratic corporate and government structures that provide the source of so much of contemporary power, especially through their ability to shape and mold even one's desires and self-understanding.

Beyond these classic studies, a new generation of researchers are examining a different source of power, that of insight. For example, Gary Klein, author of *Sources of Power: How People Make Decisions* (1998) and *The Power of Intuition* (2004), analyzed the power involved in making effective choices and decisions. His research focuses on urgent situations in the real world, such as those faced by fighter jet pilots, nurses, and firefighters. His findings emphasize that the power to effectively deal with such situations involves a source beyond rational calculations; it draws from more intuitive abilities. Klein elaborates the sources of this power as arising from two major capacities: pattern recognition (seeing the big picture, having situational awareness) and mental simulation (seeing the past and the future). These, in turn,

are aided by one's facility with metaphor, analogy, storytelling, the ability to spot leverage points, as well as one's ability to improvise, make perceptual discriminations, read another's intent, and draw on the experience base of the group. This focus on intuition as the source of power is becoming more influential, especially as it is popularized by best-selling writers such as Malcolm Gladwell (*Blink: The Power of Thinking without Thinking*, 2007). Gladwell's well-written summaries of the research fascinate a wide audience with examples such as how marriage therapists can predict with almost unerring accuracy which marriages will survive after viewing only seconds of videotape of a couples' therapy session.

BIBLIOGRAPHY

Galbraith, John Kenneth. *The Anatomy of Power*. Boston: Houghton, 1983. Print.

Greene, Robert. *The Forty-Eight Laws of Power*. New York: Penguin, 1998. Print.

Greene, Robert. *Mastery*. New York: Viking, 2012. Print.

Guinote, Ana, and Theresa K. Vescio. *The Social Psychology of Power*. New York: Guilford, 2010. Print.

Klein, Gary A. *Sources of Power: How People Make Decisions*. Cambridge: MIT P, 1998. Print.

Kunz, George. *The Paradox of Power and Weakness*. Albany: State U of New York P, 1998. Print.

Lukes, Steven. *Power: A Radical View*. 2nd ed. New York: Macmillan, 2005. Print.

Mann, Michael. *The Sources of Social Power*. New York: Cambridge UP, 2012. Print.

May, Rollo. *Power and Innocence*. 1972. Reprint. New York: Norton, 1998. Print.

Person, Ethel. *Feeling Strong: The Achievement of Authentic Power*. New York: HarperCollins, 2002. Print.

Christopher M. Aanstoos

SEE ALSO: Adler, Alfred; Advertising; Erikson, Erik H.; Horney, Karen; Individual psychology: Alfred Adler; Maslow, Abraham; May, Rollo; Motivation; Punishment; Reinforcement.

Prejudice

TYPE OF PSYCHOLOGY: Social psychology

Prejudice, the expression of negative attitudes toward certain groups and members of groups, genders, races, and religions, is a worldwide concern. Among the effects of prejudice are discrimination, low self-esteem, demoralization, racial self-hatred, helplessness and lack of control, social ostracism, social avoidance, lack of opportunities, and political underrepresentation.

KEY CONCEPTS
- Attitudes
- Bias
- Discrimination
- In-group/out-group distinction
- Multicultural education
- Prejudice
- Realistic conflict theory
- Reverse discrimination

INTRODUCTION

Prejudice can be defined as a global view or attitude about a group of people; prejudicial views are characterized by their inflexibility, and they are usually considered to be negative and directed toward minority or out-groups. The effects of prejudice in American society, and throughout the world, are generally considered devastating, not only to the individuals who suffer injustice, humiliation, and violence as a result of discrimination based on prejudice but also to the integrity of society as a whole. Groups such as the Ku Klux Klan and other white supremacist groups attempt to promote segregation, prejudice, and discrimination, at least partly as a way of promoting a dominant status for the white race. Most people realize that this is both unconstitutional and unfair. Since people have no choice over the race, ethnicity, religion, or gender into which they are born, it is unjust to judge persons solely on the basis of biological givens such as skin color, hair color, facial structure, gender, or other such characteristics. Almost everyone has experienced some prejudice or discrimination and can understand its negative effects on self-esteem and self-image.

A classic book on prejudice that came from the field of social psychology is Gordon Allport's *The Nature of Prejudice*, published in 1954. His approach to prejudice is still considered contemporary because of his emphasis on cognitive factors such as categorization and normal cognitive bias. There are two broad categories of prejudice: personal prejudice and group prejudice. Allport's model involves in-group and out-group distinctions. In an extension of Allport's theory, Thomas Pettigrew proposed the ultimate attribution error in an article he published

in 1979. Pettigrew suggests that people tend to favor the actions of people in their in-group (those whom they perceive as being "like them") and attribute negative motives to the same actions by out-group members. If an in-group member observes a negative act by an out-group member, the in-group member is likely to attribute the action to genetics or some other concrete factor. On the other hand, if an in-group member observes a positive act by an out-group member, he or she may attribute the act to luck, an exception to the rule, high motivation and effort, or the particular situational context in which the behavior occurred.

A study published in 1947 by Kenneth Clark and Mamie Clark on color preference of dolls in preschool children showed that even very young children preferred the "white" dolls to those representing their respective race or skin color. In the 1970s, Jane Elliott conducted an experiment with elementary school children in which she instructed the brown-eyed children to sit in the back of the room and told them they could not use the drinking fountain. Blue-eyed children were given special privileges such as extra recess time and extra lunch helpings. The two groups of children were told not to interact with each other. Elliott belittled and berated the brown-eyed children, and their academic performance faltered. The favored blue-eyed group became even more belittling to the brown-eyed children than the teacher was. After several days, roles were reversed, and the negative effects of prejudice were repeated. Eventually all the children disliked one another, demonstrating the destructive effects of status inequalities based on something as superficial as eye color.

THEORIZING PREJUDICIAL INFLUENCES

Donn Byrne, a social psychologist, has written about theories on the conditions under which prejudice may develop. Byrne and others believe that periods of economic hardship and scarce resources characterized by lack of availability of food and jobs can contribute to the occurrence and intensity of various types of prejudice. In the field of social psychology, this premise is part of what is known as realistic conflict theory. Indeed, throughout history, in periods of resource scarcity and political unrest, the unfair effects of prejudice have flourished. From the mid-fifteenth and sixteenth centuries until the present, racial and religious prejudice leading to discrimination has resulted in violence against different ethnic and religious groups in what has been a worldwide phenomenon. From the United States to the various republics that, until 1992, made up the Soviet Union, and from Northern Ireland to South Africa, these problems have been significant. Efforts made by countries to achieve internal peace and stability have been difficult, at best, given climates of religious or ethnic intolerance and economic hardship.

Class status is one factor that has been found to have a profound effect on influencing prejudicial beliefs and expectations. In the 1940s, an epidemiological study of psychopathology, or mental illness, called the Midtown Study was initiated in Manhattan in New York City, and results were published in the 1960s. A number of stereotypes about lower-class patients that suggested they were incapable of achieving insight into their problems, unable to ask for psychological help, and unable to examine their motives or moods were disputed by this research. In fact, the research showed that lower-class patients did want to achieve psychodynamic understanding and insight into their problems. The research also showed that patients of lower socioeconomic status had less access to treatment facilities than their higher-class counterparts.

Racial and ethnic bias has been found to exist even among mental health professionals, a group of professionals who should, by definition, be objective and neutral in their work; however, very little research has been published in this area. Some investigators found no evidence of racial bias on diagnoses assigned by clinicians who were of different racial backgrounds. Others found that white, middle-class psychiatrists who recorded fewer symptoms for black patients as compared to white patients nevertheless concentrated on the more unusual or bizarre symptoms of the blacks. This practice resulted in the psychopathology of black patients appearing more severe than the psychopathology of white patients. Researchers and clinicians have noted that white patients have more often been given the label "neurotic" and black or Puerto Rican patients given the label "schizophrenic" for similar behaviors. Social psychologist Leonard Derogatis and others caution that race and social class designation are the most prominent indicators that affect psychological assessment and symptom presentation.

PREJUDICE AS AN "ISM"

Prejudice that has become widespread takes forms that are sometimes referred to as "isms": racism, classism, sexism, ageism, heterosexism, ableism, and so on. One of the most insidious forms of misunderstanding is the prejudicial attitudes held regarding the disabled,

of whom there were more than fifty-six million in the United States in 2010, according to a broad definition by the U.S. Census Bureau. In American society, those with emotional or learning disabilities (the invisible disabilities) often suffer the worst misunderstanding and discrimination caused by ignorance, perpetuation of myths, social ostracism, and avoidance of contact. It is known that nondisabled persons have demonstrated lack of empathy, avoidance of social interaction, lack of eye contact, and lack of respect for the disabled. Research has shown that even disabled persons hold negative attitudes toward other disabled persons if the others have a disability different from their own. In reality, those who are physically disabled have been found to have strong self-concepts and good social interaction skills and have often been more able to provide support to others than the other way around.

INVESTIGATING TECHNIQUES

Psychologists have developed various techniques for investigating and measuring social attitudes such as prejudice. Various scales exist for this purpose, from the Thurstone scale to the more frequently used Likert format. The Thurstone method of paired comparisons is thought to provide a method for the selection of items on an attitude test. In the Likert format, attitudes are measured according to approval rankings on positive and negative dimensions, with variations in between two opposite rankings as possible selection points. For example, the choices for the question "What do you think of homosexuals holding public office?" would be "strongly approve," "approve," "undecided," "disapprove," and "strongly disapprove." Respondents are asked to rank the intensity and direction of their attitudes by choosing one of the five available choices for a number of similar items. The semantic differential, another popular technique in social-attitude research, presents a concept or set of concepts, such as "Democrat," "God," or "Puerto Rican." The respondent is asked to rate the concept on a set of seven-point scales in which the endpoints are certain adjectives, such as "strong" and "weak," or "active" and "passive." The semantic differential has been criticized for difficulty with interpretations derived from it, but it remains popular for its ease of use. Public opinion surveys are also used to measure attitudes either for or against certain candidates, social issues, or legislation. These surveys, although useful, can be plagued with problems, such as interviewer bias, subject selection bias, and question bias, if not carefully designed.

EFFECTS

Many practical applications have developed from a knowledge of prejudice and its effects that go beyond surveys and attitude measurement instruments. Women, both Caucasians and minorities, who have been able to gain access to higher education and obtain advanced degrees have found that they are still paid less than men with the same credentials. Moreover, the phenomenon referred to as the glass ceiling suggests that there is only so far a woman can go in terms of advancement through corporate and institutional structures. It is true that very few top corporate positions or top government posts are filled by women. Some people believe that these few positions represent tokenism, or positive actions toward a few women to make it look as though the employer is playing fair. As a result of this glass ceiling, some women have filed discrimination suits and won. Others have taken a different path and have written extensively on the effect of gender bias on women. A 1991 book by Susan Faludi titled *Backlash: The Undeclared War against American Women* describes the insidious price that the author believes has been paid for the small progress made by women in American society.

Different people respond in different ways to the effects of prejudice. Active or effective responses are ones that empower people to confront and correct bias and injustice. In contrast, passive or ineffective responses may lead to a self-fulfilling prophecy, low self-esteem, and racial self-hatred in reaction to the negative stereotyping effects of prejudice. Minority group members' angry reactions to racial prejudice have been found ultimately to be a healthy response or a way to "fight back" against being oppressed. This anger, even rage, can evolve into what has been termed cultural paranoia, which is described as a defense mechanism that has allowed blacks and other minority groups to live in a society that is filled with racism. Martin Luther King, Jr., used this mechanism in a positive way to confront and to try to change racial oppression in American society.

SOCIAL AND EDUCATIONAL RESPONSES

Active, effective responses have been most notable in what might be called empowerment movements. Grassroots support groups formed for women's rights, civil rights, gay and lesbian rights, and patients' rights resulted in various institutions and organizations being formalized by these movements. These movements and their resulting institutions represent active responses to the effects of prejudice. In the late 1980s, for example, an advocacy group for AIDS victims called ACT UP (an acronym for AIDS Coalition to Unleash Power) was formed to take dramatic measures for calling national attention to the epidemic of AIDS.

In the educational arena, efforts have taken the form of the development of prejudice-reduction programs and workshops and an intensive effort to develop a multicultural curriculum at all levels of education. A multicultural approach to education stresses educational innovations that challenge the majority culture's views on historical and social issues and strives for inclusivity and fairness in noting the contributions of all cultures, genders, and races to society.

HISTORIC PREJUDICE

In the 1960s, with the inception of the civil rights movement, the social psychology research literature began to focus in earnest on the concepts of prejudice and discrimination. In the period of time from 1954 to 1964, conflict, organized protest, civil rights marches, demonstrations, riots and acts of violence, and social injustice brought the social problems to the forefront. Researchers were drawn to investigate the complex phenomena and mechanisms of prejudice and discrimination. In 1964, an expanded Civil Rights Act was passed; this made the research all the more urgent. It has been noted, however, that during this period the broader focus of research on culture and diversity was sacrificed.

The history of prejudice is a long one. The fifteenth and sixteenth centuries ushered in a particularly dark period of mass persecution of women who practiced self-healing methods and midwifery. During the medieval period, women had also been victims of religious persecution, including some who simply were homeless or had a "sharp tongue" as well as some who were probably mentally ill. All told, this period of religious persecution, led by religious male patriarchs of the time (mostly representatives of the church), resulted in hundreds of thousands of people being tortured and put to death. A key impulse underlying this massive prejudice and persecution was the Roman Catholic church's opposition to women's sexuality. Sexuality was seen to be insatiable in women, and lust in both genders was thought to be dangerous when not firmly controlled. This prejudice was so strong that everything from bad crops to miscarriages was blamed on women identified as witches.

The persecution and death of six million Jewish people by the Nazis is yet another—and probably the most frightening—example of the possible outcomes of extreme prejudice and discrimination. Indeed, any form of genocide is the ultimate end product of severe prejudice.

IMPACT OF SOCIAL MOVEMENTS

The women's movement (originating in the 1900s), the gay and lesbian liberation movement, the patients' rights movement, and the civil rights movement have all had major impacts on mitigating the effects of prejudice. As these organized political groups have gained more support, each has been instrumental in consciousness-raising; reducing prejudice, social inequity, and social injustice; and increasing political, educational, and economic opportunity for their members. Affirmative action programs continue, although they have met with criticism that they go beyond the goal of correcting inequity in hiring practices. Some people believe that these policies have led to a social phenomenon referred to as reverse discrimination (the idea that certain methods intended to reduce discrimination, such as hiring quotas, have backfired and actually lead to discrimination against members of a majority group who may be more qualified than others who are hired); however, others believe that certain groups, such as Latinos, African Americans, and Native Americans, have suffered long-term damaging effects from discrimination and therefore need the help of affirmative action programs. The language differences between English-speaking and Spanish-speaking children in the United States from a very early age begin to limit the educational and work opportunities for these children's futures. Bilingual education is one possible avenue to maximize educational opportunities and future economic opportunities.

SOCIAL CLASS AND CULTURAL DISTINCTIONS

Social class and cultural distinctions also continue to bring opportunity to some people while eliminating opportunity for those of lower socioeconomic status. Many black children and other minorities have been locked into a cycle of poverty and hopelessness that impairs educational progress and motivation at a very early age. Although some progress has been made with the funding opportunities for offspring of low-income families (such as Head Start programs), designed to pave the way for success in higher education, many programs are cut in times of economic hardship, when people need them the most. This perpetuates a cycle of poverty, with prejudice leading to economic hardship for affected groups. The term "feminization of poverty" has been used to describe the economic impact of low-wage, menial jobs on women in the United States, Puerto Rico, and other nations. Newspapers and television news frequently report acts inspired by prejudice, such as hate crimes against minorities. Violations of the civil rights of minorities still occur, leading to public outcries for examination and correction of the racial inequalities in American institutions and society. Much more progress is clearly needed in studying ways to reduce prejudice and its devastating effects.

BIBLIOGRAPHY

Allport, Gordon W. *The Nature of Prejudice.* 1954. Reprint. Cambridge: Perseus, 2003. Print.

Baron, Robert A., and Donn Byrne. *Social Psychology: Understanding Human Interaction.* 12th ed. Boston: Allyn, 2009. Print.

Brown, Rupert. *Prejudice: Its Social Psychology.* 2nd ed. Malden: Blackwell, 2010. Print.

Dixon, John, and Mark Levine. *Beyond Prejudice: Extending the Social Psychology of Conflict, Inequality and Social Change.* New York: Cambridge UP, 2012. Print.

Freeman, Howard E., and Norman R. Kurtz, eds. *America's Troubles: A Casebook on Social Conflict.* 2nd ed. Englewood Cliffs: Prentice, 1973. Print.

Jones, Melinda. *Social Psychology of Prejudice.* Upper Saddle River: Prentice, 2002. Print.

Lips, Hilary. *Sex and Gender: An Introduction.* 6th ed. Boston: McGraw, 2008. Print.

Morgan, Robin. *The Demon Lover: On the Sexuality of Terrorism.* New York: Pocket, 2001. Print.

Nelson, Todd D., ed. *Handbook of Prejudice, Stereotyping, and Discrimination.* New York: Psychology, 2009. Print.

Whitley, Bernard E., and Mary E. Kite. *The Psychology of Prejudice and Discrimination.* 2nd ed. Belmont: Wadsworth, 2010. Print.

Young-Bruehl, Elisabeth. *The Anatomy of Prejudices.* Cambridge: Harvard UP, 1998. Print.

Karen Wolford

SEE ALSO: African Americans and mental health; Ageism; Allport, Gordon; Asian Americans/Pacific Islanders and mental health; Attitude formation and change; Bullying; Gay, lesbian, bisexual, and transgender mental health; Groups; Latinos and mental health; Native Americans/Alaskan Natives and mental health; Prejudice reduction; Racism; Sexism; Social identity theory; Social schemata; Violence: Psychological causes and effects.

Prejudice and stereotyping

Type of Psychology: Cross-cultural; Clinical; Counseling; Social

Stereotyping is an immediate generalization regarding an individual or group which provides information about them. Prejudice refers to specifically negative judgments regarding a group of people.

Key concepts
- Covert/overt prejudice
- Empirical generalizations
- Generalizations
- Prejudice
- Stereotyping

INTRODUCTION

Stereotyping and prejudice are complex, and have caused widespread oppression and marginalization of many individuals and groups.

STEREOTYPE

A stereotype is an inflexible overgeneralization about a group of people. The common thought is that stereotypes are negative perspectives put on people by others, generally the dominant group. However, this is often not the case. Stereotypes have been referred to by scientists and researchers as empirical generalizations. These are ideas supported by some evidence and then applied to all situations or people. More often than not, there is truth behind stereotypes. A simple example of this is saying that all men love watching sports. Do a lot of men enjoy watching sports? Sure, they do. Does this mean that all men enjoy watching sports? No, that is not true. So the stereotype that all men love watching sports excludes the men that do not like sports and may indirectly imply that women do not like watching sports. This example represents a stereotype that may not hurt or offend anyone, but it is an overgeneralization of an experience that has some truth behind it.

BENEFITS OF STEREOTYPING

Although stereotypes have been assigned a negative connotation in our society, there are significant benefits to this process. Stereotyping is a way in which people are able to quickly assess and evaluate their situation. Stereotypes teach us how to interact with groups of people and how not to act. Because our brain does not have the ability to immediately process every piece of information at hand, we create groups, categories, and meaning associated with different people. There may be a stereotype that police officers are unapproachable. There may be truth behind this based on the duties of their jobs, again not meaning that this is true in all cases. However this stereotype may teach us that we do not approach police officers in a super casual manner or with any kind of suspicious behavior. The benefit of this stereotype is that it teaches us how to behave when interacting or approaching police officers. For example, it is usually not a good idea to rapidly approach a cop to pat him or her on the back or give a random hug. This stereotype is a quick way for brains to process how we should behave. Stereotyping has cognitive value as it helps to simplify our world. The problem arises when its limitations are not also incorporated into thought.

RISKS OF STEREOTYPING

There are also many disadvantages to stereotyping. As we quickly flip through our brain rolodex of information to pass judgment, we often overlook specifics and the importance of individuation. If we only follow our stereotypes of people and groups then we will miss out on getting to know individuals and broadening our perspective. Even if we believe that the stereotype highlights a positive trait about a group it can still be taken as offensive and frustrating such as all Asians are smart or all African Americans are great dancers. These stereotypes may sound like a positive thing; however they are overgeneralizations and it is impossible to assign the trait to every person in a group. This can be known as social categorization, thinking that all people in a group possess the same traits. Social categorization often stems from a privileged group creating meaning for the less privileged groups. When the dominant group in a society is able to define meaning for the underprivileged, this is often known as marginalization or oppression. Although there are some positive stereotypes, many are negative and hurtful.

Negative stereotypes often affect oppressed groups like racial minorities, women, low socioeconomic groups, overweight people, and people with homosexual orientation. Stereotypes can marginalize these groups and portray them as less than whom and what they are. For many years women have been considered not as smart or capable in the workplace as men. This hurtful stereotype materializes in real world disadvantages. Women are neither hired as often as men nor paid the same salary as men. Another negative stereotype is that racial minorities such as African Americans or Latinos may be more aggressive or violent than Caucasians. This racial stereotype has caused drastic differentials in arrest and incarceration rates for the same crimes.

Stereotypes can have a tremendous impact on oppressed groups. If police officers hold stereotypes that black men commit more crimes than white men, this will have a direct negative impact on the experiences and lives of black men. If women are told from a young age to aspire to homemaking or a non-education based job they may believe that they are not smart enough to pursue something different. Many women have been told by their families or communities to major in their M.R.S. degree in college. This stereotype that the value of women comes from being married is negative and hurtful.

These are examples of how stereotypes transfer from rapid judgments about others to having substantial influence on an entire group's position in society. There has been significant research focusing on racial stereotyping, asking people to assign personality traits and values to different racial groups. The findings have been catastrophic in the negative association of traits with minorities and positive traits assigned to the Caucasian dominant group. These stereotypes are so powerful that even people in the minority group have assigned negativity to their own group. One specifically powerful research experiment was done with very young children who were asked value questions about a black and white baby doll. Even the young black children choose the white doll when asked which one was prettier, smarter, or nicer. This example represents the sheer power negative stereotypes have in our society and how impactful they can be on the lives of entire groups.

PREJUDICE

The terms stereotyping and prejudice both involve prejudgments about others. Prejudice differs in that it is known as specifically negative thoughts and feelings toward a group whereas stereotyping by definition does not have to be a negative perspective. Prejudice takes another step where the negative judgments about a group of people often equate to oppressive and/or hurtful viewpoints and interactions. Prejudice can refer to internalized feelings about a group or can represent overt discrimination of a group. Similar to stereotyping, prejudice minimizes differences in groups and highlights the differences between them. For example, believing that

all Latinos behave, act, eat, and live in the same way exaggerates the differences between Latinos and Caucasians. Some of the most common prejudices include racism, sexism, classism, homophobia, ageism, and religious prejudice.

OVERT PREJUDICE

Prejudice can be displayed in both overt and covert ways. Overt prejudice is clearly expressed discrimination toward a person or group. This happens when people partake in direct protests, hate crimes, or decisions based on negative feelings about a whole group. Examples include protests against African Americans' right to vote and groups picketing a gay wedding. The prejudice in these situations is very clearly stated and communicated. The person who is on the receiving end of this prejudice generally is aware of the negative perspective others may have. This overt form of prejudice has led to widespread oppression such as abuse, violence, and marginalization of entire groups. Challenging overt prejudice often takes the form of public or political debates and social justice movements.

COVERT PREJUDICE

Covert prejudice refers to a form of discrimination that is not expressed in a straightforward manner. Instead of protests or fighting against equal rights, covert prejudice is a confusing and unclear manner of holding others down. Covert prejudice is more common in current society as overt prejudice was more acceptable when laws supported the discrimination. Covert prejudice is prevalent in modern day society and often the perpetrators are unaware of how their expressions or behaviors impact others. Covert prejudice may be a police officer pulling over an African American for speeding instead of the Caucasian driver who was also speeding. It could be a woman not being hired for a job or a gay couple being told that the hotel is full for the night. The victims in these actions may not have clear evidence that what they experienced was specifically prejudice, often leaving them feeling confused and hurt.

MANAGING STEREOTYPING AND PREJUDICE

Both stereotyping and prejudices have long histories. They also have some benefits such as the safety provided by the ability to classify people and situations and the information about how to behave around different groups. There are also many risks of stereotyping including prejudice itself. When we categorize all groups of people, we run the risk of overgeneralizing and missing out on learning about individuals.

When attempting to combat prejudice and negative stereotyping it is important to educate yourself regarding where such beliefs come from and challenging overgeneralizations. It is important to know that not all people in one group are the same and the difference between groups may not be as large as expected. The way to explore these ideas of sameness and differentness is to open up to new people, experiences, and opportunities. The chance of stereotyping and prejudice decreases when people step outside their comfort zone and increase interactions with people from other groups.

BIBLIOGRAPHY

Allport, G. W. (1954). *The Nature of Prejudice*. Reading, MA: Addison-Wesley. This seminal source provides the background and context of understanding prejudice and how it plays out for different groups.

Katz, D., & Braly, K. (1933). "Racial Stereotypes of One Hundred College Students". *Journal of Abnormal and Social Psychology*, 28, 280-290. This source specifically explores racial stereotypes and provides information on the views and stereotypes college students hold.

Fiske, S. T. (2000). "Interdependence Reduces Prejudice and Stereotyping". In S. Oskamp (Ed.), *Reducing Prejudice and Discrimination* (115-135). Mahwah, NJ: Erlbaum. This source explores differences between stereotypes and prejudice and ideas for reducing the negativity of prejudice.

McLeod, S. A. (2008). *Stereotypes*. Retrieved from http://www.simplypsychology.org/katz-braly.html This source provides information on stereotypes, including the benefits and risks.

Kimberly Ortiz

SEE ALSO: Conflict; Intergroup dynamics; Multiculturalism; Social behavior; Social psychology; Stereotypes.

Prejudice reduction

TYPE OF PSYCHOLOGY: Social psychology

Several approaches to the reduction of prejudice have been studied over the years. Intergroup contact, the introduction of a common enemy, the crossing of social categories, and the presentation of information in the media are all strategies that have been considered in the effort to reduce prejudice. Evidence regarding the effectiveness of these strategies is mixed, and research has been directed toward examining the specific mechanisms underlying prejudice reduction.

KEY CONCEPTS
- Belief congruence intervention
- Common-enemy strategy
- Cooperative team intervention
- Cross-categorization
- Intergroup contact
- Interpersonal contact
- Prejudice
- Subtyping

INTRODUCTION

Gordon Allport defined prejudice as an attitude toward the members of an out-group in which the evaluative tendencies are predominantly negative. It seems self-evident that the reduction and elimination of prejudice are among the most pressing real-world problems confronting psychology. Several different approaches to the reduction of prejudice have been examined.

Each of these approaches to prejudice reduction is derived from one or more of the suspected root causes of prejudice. Numerous explanations have been offered in attempts to account for prejudice. For example, some people believe that individuals develop negative attitudes toward other groups that are perceived as competing with their own group. Alternatively, it is possible that differences in familiarity with one's own group versus other groups can lead to differential perceptions and evaluations of the two groups. Prejudice might also develop as people grow up and learn from others about the features of different groups, especially if the features depict negative characteristics for certain groups. Finally, social thinking might inherently involve categorization processes that often lead people to divide the world into "us" and "them." The different strategies designed to reduce prejudice generally focus on one of these concerns and try to reduce that specific concern in the hope of reducing prejudice.

CONTACT HYPOTHESIS

One of the most obvious and most heavily researched techniques for reducing prejudice is exemplified by what is called the contact hypothesis: that association with persons from a disliked group will lead to a growth of liking and respect for that group. Scholarly considerations of this basic idea can be traced back at least to the 1940s; for example, it can be found in Robin Williams's 1947 book, *The Reduction of Intergroup Tensions*. It is the seminal work of Allport, however, that is generally credited with being the classic formulation of the contact hypothesis. *In The Nature of Prejudice* (1954), Allport developed a taxonomy of relevant factors necessary for contact to be successful in reducing prejudice. These factors emphasized the nature of the contact experience, and they included the frequency and duration of contact, the relative status of the two groups, and the social atmosphere of the contact experience. Extensive reviews of the research examining the contact hypothesis were published by Yehuda Amir in 1976 and Miles Hewstone and Rupert Brown in 1986. Some studies have demonstrated a reduction of prejudice toward the out-group, whereas other studies have shown contact actually to increase prejudice among members of the majority group along with causing a decrease in self-esteem and an increased sense of isolation among members of the minority group. Part of the difficulty may stem from the differences between intended contact and actual levels of contact. For example, Donald Taylor and his colleagues have argued that intergroup contact is often avoided. One study showed that black and white students in a desegregated school "resegregated" themselves into ethnic groups during classroom activities and recess. Thus, the general emphasis has shifted from "whether the contact hypothesis is valid" to "under what conditions, and in what domains, is the contact hypothesis valid."

A variant of the contact hypothesis in the context of desegregated schools is the cooperative team intervention. In this type of intervention, small groups of schoolchildren, including children of two ethnic groups, are assigned to complete a task in which they need to cooperate to succeed. Sometimes these small groups are later put into competition with other similar groups. Norman Miller and Gaye Davidson-Podgorny, in a study published in 1987, have shown that this type of cooperative team intervention is generally effective in reducing prejudice, at least in terms of attitudes toward out-group classmates.

BELIEF CONGRUENCE INTERVENTION

An alternative approach is known as the belief congruence intervention. According to this strategy, prejudice and intergroup hostility are driven by the assumption that members of the out-group hold beliefs that are different from those held by the in-group. Therefore, if it can be learned that members of the out-group are actually more similar to the in-group, then members of the out-group might be liked more and prejudice will be diminished. This approach is illustrated by Rachel Dubois's 1950 "neighborhood festival," in which members of different ethnic groups talked about nostalgic memories of childhood, holidays, and so on. The goal was for participants to recognize that group experiences, customs, and meanings are in fact remarkably alike and that different ethnic groups actually share membership in a broader commonality. While this intervention sounds very appealing, its success rests on a problematic assumption: the perceived differences between groups are illusory, and learning about intergroup similarities in beliefs will bring people to a more enlightened enjoyment of one another. If there are fundamental differences between the central beliefs of two groups (for example, as between Catholics and Protestants in Northern Ireland, or between Arabs and Jews in the Middle East), then the belief congruence approach is unlikely to be successful.

Finally, the role of the media in maintaining or reducing prejudice should be considered. Research has shown that ethnic minority groups are sometimes portrayed in negative ways in the news media and popular entertainment. While little research has examined the prejudice-reducing effects of the media, it is reasonable to speculate that more positive portrayals of ethnic minorities in the media might make a substantial contribution in the future to the reduction of prejudice. In line with this possibility, research by Fletcher Blanchard and his colleagues has found that exposure to the normative influence of other people expressing antiracist views can increase an individual's expression of antiracist views.

DESEGREGATION AND OTHER APPLICATIONS

There are several specific settings in which the contact hypothesis may be seen to operate. The most vivid example is desegregation in classroom settings. A considerable amount of research has examined this particular contact setting and, as indicated above, the results are mixed. As summarized by Janet Schofield in 1986, school desegregation in the United States may have had a less positive effect than one might have hoped because the problems that have characterized race relations in the United States have limited both the extent and the nature of intergroup contact in desegregated schools. Fortunately, there are several other contexts in which intergroup contact can be fostered. Unfortunately, the evidence regarding the effectiveness of these other contact interventions is also mixed. For example, in 1985 Amir and Rachel Ben-Ari reported that tourists visiting a foreign country did not evidence decreased prejudice toward the (out-group) members of that country. Similarly, in 1966 Otto Klineberg showed that the attitudes of foreign exchange students toward the local people were on the whole friendly on arrival, but became slightly less so on the average after a period of residence in that foreign country. Alternatively, in 1986 Ulrich Wagner and Uwe Macleit reported that increased contact with Gästarbeiter (guest workers, the majority of whom are Turkish) in the Federal Republic of Germany was associated with reduced prejudice toward these foreign workers.

As delineated by Hewstone and Brown, there is a large dilemma plaguing research on the contact hypothesis involving the nature of the contact itself. On one hand, the contact could be strictly interpersonal, where members of the two opposing groups interact with one another as individuals. This approach is emphasized in the work of Miller and Marilynn Brewer published in 1984. On the other hand, the contact could be strictly intergroup, where members of the two opposing groups interact with one another as group members. This approach is emphasized in the work of Hewstone and Brown. It is unclear which of these two types of contact is more effective. A related problem is the generalization of positive attitudes that might be stimulated by contact. The contact with specific individuals from another ethnic or national group might lead to more positive attitudes about those specific individuals, but this does not guarantee that those more positive attitudes will generalize to the rest of that ethnic or national group as a whole.

RECATEGORIZATION

This sets the stage for the fundamental paradox of the contact hypothesis. As discussed by Jennifer Crocker in 1984, information about a single exceptionally positive out-group member may engage a "subtyping" mechanism: the exceptionally positive member may be functionally subtyped into a separate category, leaving the overall out-group category intact. As illustrated in a discussion by John Pryor and Thomas Ostrom in 1987, the professor who holds the stereotype that "athletes are unintelligent" will create a separate subtype of "smart athletes" in response to meeting a smart athlete, rather than changing the overall stereotype for athletes. The general form of the paradox can be stated as follows: To have the potential to change the negative evaluation of

the out-group, the exceptional member of the out-group must be uniquely positive. If, however, the exceptional member of the out-group is uniquely positive, then he or she is likely to be subtyped into a class of his or her own, thereby leaving the overall negative evaluation of the out-group intact.

As the belief congruence approach shows, one concept of the reduction of prejudice is concerned with the idea that members of two groups can be led to redefine the boundaries between the groups. This idea is more directly illustrated in Willem Doise's research on cross-categorization. This refers to a situation in which one categorization that splits people into two groups (such as black-white) is crossed with a second categorization (such as liberal-conservative), so that people are split into four groups (white liberals, white conservatives, black liberals, and black conservatives). Doise has found that this cross-categorization reduces discrimination between the two original groups. Presumably, learning that some of "them" are really like "us" helps to mitigate the prejudice against "them."

An extreme version of a recategorization strategy is illustrated in an intervention that might be called the common-enemy strategy. This approach was illustrated in Muzafer Sherif and colleagues' 1961 "Robbers Cave" study. In this study, eleven-year-old boys in a summer-camp setting were divided into two groups. The two groups engaged in a series of competitions, which resulted in both verbal and physical signs of prejudice toward the other group. When the two groups were combined to compete against a team from another camp, however, the negative attitudes toward the (former) out-group diminished.

The basic assumption underlying the common-enemy strategy is that a common enemy should cause the two (initially conflicting) groups to set aside their differences to overcome the external threat represented by the "common enemy." While there is little research evidence that directly examines this strategy (Sherif's study is the notable exception), ample anecdotal evidence illustrates the all-too-often-employed strategy of drawing disparate and disagreeing members of a political unit together by casting them as a cohesive unit in the face of some threat posed by an external out-group.

There are two problems with this approach that should be recognized: First, the strategy is likely to be effective only in the short term. As discussed by Muzafer and Carolyn Sherif, the introduction of a common enemy in the Robbers Cave study did draw the two conflicting groups together in an effort to defeat the new opposing out-group. As soon as the opposing out-group left the scene, however, the old conflicts between the two original groups of campers reemerged. A similar affect was seen in the eruption of ethnic conflict in Eastern Europe after the fall of the Soviet Union. Second, this strategy does not really reduce overall levels of prejudice and conflict; it simply redirects it. In other words, although groups A and B are no longer in conflict, these two groups have now joined in conflict against group C. This intervention carries with it moral concerns about the justification for selecting group C as a target for prejudice in an effort to reduce the original prejudice that group A held toward group B.

SOCIAL PSYCHOLOGY

Understanding prejudice and developing strategies to reduce it have long been major concerns of social psychologists. Techniques used for studying prejudice, however, have changed over the years. Earlier research relied heavily on observing the outward behavior of one group's members toward another group's members and analyzing people's responses on surveys. The development of computers and other sophisticated experimental techniques has enabled researchers to probe more deeply into the specific cognitive workings that may result in prejudice. This has helped illuminate a number of intriguing features about prejudice.

For example, Patricia Devine, in a study published in 1989, showed that what distinguishes unprejudiced people from prejudiced people is not that unprejudiced people automatically respond in nonprejudiced, egalitarian ways. Rather, both prejudiced people and unprejudiced people may engage in automatic, learned responses of negative evaluation toward stereotyped out-groups. The unprejudiced people, however, are able to engage controlled cognitive processes that thwart the expression of these undesirable prejudiced responses. Viewed in this way, Devine suggests, prejudices may be likened to bad habits, and the replacement of prejudiced responses with nonprejudiced responses can be likened to the breaking of such habits.

The work by Devine illustrates a key ingredient in all efforts to reduce prejudice. The way people learn and process information about groups may inherently lead to differential perceptions and evaluations of these groups. Because of a need to simplify and organize information, these differential perceptions and evaluations may be incorporated into stereotypes, which may be negative for some groups. As discussed by Brian Mullen in 1991, for a technique for reducing prejudice to be successful, it must take this cognitive processing of information about different groups into consideration. There does not seem to be any magic solution to the problem of prejudice. It seems apparent, however, that people need to be aware at some level of the cognitive biases that can develop. Consistent with Devine's findings, becoming consciously aware of the biases in thinking about certain groups may be an important first step in the effort to reduce prejudice.

BIBLIOGRAPHY

Allport, Gordon W. *The Nature of Prejudice*. 1954. 25th anniversary ed. LaVergne: Basic, 2010. Print.

Chin, Jean Lau. *The Psychology of Prejudice and Discrimination*. Rev. and condensed ed. Santa Barbara: Praeger, 2010. Digital file.

Hewstone, Miles, and Rupert Brown, eds. *Contact and Conflict in Intergroup Encounters*. Oxford: Blackwell, 1986. Print.

Jones, James, M., et al. *The Psychology of Diversity: Beyond Prejudice and Racism*. Chichester: Wiley, 2014. Print.

Jones, James M. *Prejudice and Racism*. 2d ed. New York: McGraw, 1997. Print.

Miller, Norman, and Marilynn Brewer, eds. *Groups in Contact: The Psychology of Desegregation*. Orlando: Academic, 1984. Print.

Mullen, Brian. "Group Composition, Salience, and Cognitive Representations: The Phenomenology of Being in a Group." *Journal of Experimental Social Psychology* 27.4 (1991): 297–323. Print.

Oskamp, Stuart, ed. *Reducing Prejudice and Discrimination*. Hoboken: Taylor, 2013. Digital file.

Ponterotto, Joseph G., Shawn O. Utsey, and Paul B. Pedersen. *Preventing Prejudice: A Guide for Counselors, Educators, and Parents*. 2d ed. Thousand Oaks: Sage, 2006. Print.

Shields, David Light. "Deconstructing the Pyramid of Prejudice." *Phi Delta Kappan* 95.6 (2014): 20–24. Print.

Willis-Esqueda, Cynthia. *Motivational Aspects of Prejudice and Racism*. New York: Springer, 2008. Print.

Craig Johnson and Brian Mullen

SEE ALSO: Ageism; Cooperative learning; Intergroup relations; Prejudice; Racism; Sexism; Social identity theory.

Prenatal physical development

TYPE OF PSYCHOLOGY: Biological bases of behavior; Developmental psychology

Prenatal development usually progresses in a predictable fashion but can be disrupted by both environmental and genetic factors. Prenatal disruptions can create both physical and neurological abnormalities that range from fetal death, intellectual disability, and severe physical deformities to language deficits and attention disorders. Prenatal diagnostic tests may detect some of the more adverse outcomes.

KEY CONCEPTS
- Amniocentesis
- Amnion
- Chromosome
- Embryo period
- Fetal period
- Placenta
- Teratogen
- Zygote period

INTRODUCTION

Pregnancy encompasses the development of a single-celled fertilized egg into a trillion-celled baby. The many changes that transform the fertilized egg into a newborn infant over nine months of human pregnancy constitute prenatal development. Prenatal development comprises three stages (zygote, embryo, and fetus) and is also commonly categorized into three trimesters, each lasting three months. Although prenatal development typically follows a predictable course, development can be disrupted by both genetic and environmental factors. This disruption may result in a range of outcomes, from fetal death and severe abnormalities such as deformed or missing limbs, to minor abnormalities such as low birth weight and neurological dysfunction such as learning disabilities or attention-deficit hyperactivity disorder (ADHD).

The fourth century b.c.e. Greek philosopher Aristotle is regarded as the first in Western civilization to study prenatal development. In the years that followed, others superficially investigated the topic. However, it was not until the beginning of the twentieth century that researchers intensified their study of prenatal development. In the early 1900s, researchers were significantly influenced by the evolutionary theories of Charles Darwin and believed that all aspects of prenatal development were genetically determined.

Josef Warkany, a pioneering American scientist, engendered a shift in the thinking of the scientific community during the 1940s. Warkany documented that environmental factors, called teratogens, could adversely affect prenatal development and cause malformations at birth. About a decade later, the notion that environmental factors could harm prenatal development became mainstream after the 1950s thalidomide tragedy. Thalidomide was a drug given to pregnant women to combat symptoms of nausea. When taken in the first trimester of pregnancy, the drug produced severe physical deformities in infants, including missing arms and stunted limbs, and its use was subsequently banned. Following this tragedy and the resulting acceleration in understanding of the importance of intrauterine life, diagnostic tests have become routinely used to monitor the course of prenatal development.

STAGES OF PRENATAL DEVELOPMENT

Prenatal development begins when a sperm successfully fertilizes an egg (ovum) and usually lasts an average of thirty-eight weeks (nine months). The American College of Obstetrics and Gynecology has standardized the terminology used to describe the three stages of prenatal development. The first stage, the zygote (or germinal) stage, begins at fertilization and ends two weeks later, shortly after implantation of the zygote in the uterine wall. The second stage, the embryo stage (weeks three to eight), is the most vulnerable to teratogenic (environmental) insult. The fetal stage (weeks nine to thirty-eight) represents the final and longest stage of prenatal development.

THE ZYGOTE STAGE

Fertilization of an egg by a sperm creates a zygote. The two-week period of the zygote after conception ends with its implantation into the uterine wall. During these two weeks, the zygote grows rapidly and is carried by currents in one of the Fallopian tubes toward the uterus. The movement through the Fallopian tube usually takes five days. The zygote divides from a single cell into a mass of approximately one hundred cells. Approximately one week after fertilization, the zygote is ready to attach itself to the uterine wall. Many potential pregnancies terminate at this point as a result of implantation failure. Implantation takes approximately one week to complete, connects the zygote with the woman's blood supply, and triggers hormonal changes that prevent menstruation. At this stage, the implanted zygote is less than a millimeter in diameter but is beginning to differentiate into two structures: the germinal disc and the placenta. The germinal disc eventually develops into the baby, while the remaining cells transform into the placenta. The placenta is the structure through which nutrients and waste are exchanged between the mother and the developing child. Successful implantation and differentiation into the placenta and germinal disc mark the end of the period of the zygote.

THE EMBRYO STAGE

On successful implantation in the uterine wall, the zygote is called an embryo and pregnancy enters its second stage. The embryo stage typically begins three weeks after conception (fertilization) and lasts through the eighth week of pregnancy. At the beginning of the embryo stage, the embryo is only two millimeters long and less than an ounce in weight. The embryo is enclosed in a protective sac called the amnion, which is filled with amniotic fluid that cushions and maintains a constant temperature for the embryo. The embryo's cells form into three layers: The outer layer (ectoderm) becomes the hair, the outer layer of skin, and the nervous system; the middle layer (mesoderm) forms muscles, bones, and the circulatory system; and the inner layer (endoderm) forms the digestive system and lungs. At the beginning of this stage, the embryo looks more like a lizard than a human being, as a result of the shape of its body and head. By the end of the eighth week of pregnancy, the embryo manifests distinguishable human characteristics (eyes, arms, legs) and contains in rudimentary form all of its organs and body structures. Despite these significant changes, the embryo remains too small to be detected by the mother.

THE FETAL PERIOD

The longest and final phase of prenatal development is known as the fetal period. The fetal period represents a time when the finishing touches are put on the structures of the fetus. This period begins at nine weeks and ends with the birth of the baby. During this stage of pregnancy, the growth and development of the fetus is astounding. The fetus will increase in mass from less than one ounce at week nine, to eight ounces at four months, and to nearly eight pounds at birth. Around the start of the fetal period, the fetus begins to differentiate sex characteristics. At twelve weeks, the circulatory system becomes functional. At sixteen weeks, the mother can detect fetal movements known as quickening. By twenty weeks, a fine layer of hair (called lanugo) begins to grow over most of the fetus's body. Sucking and swallowing reflexes are present by twenty-four weeks of gestation. Brain specialization becomes particularly acute by about twenty-eight weeks. At thirty-two weeks of gestation (seven months), the fetus is viable outside the mother's womb. By this time, most systems function well enough that a fetus born at this age has a chance to survive. Despite the potential to survive, premature birth predisposes a baby to myriad additional developmental problems (health problems, learning disabilities, and cognitive deficits). By thirty-two weeks of prenatal development, the fetus has regular periods of physical activity, and the eyes and ears begin to function. By thirty-six weeks of gestation, the fetus experiences rapid weight gain, and development consists largely of an increase in weight and length. At approximately thirty-eight weeks of gestation, birth will occur. The average newborn baby weighs between seven and eight pounds.

DISRUPTIONS IN PRENATAL DEVELOPMENT

Although most of prenatal development progresses in a healthy and predictable fashion, numerous factors can disrupt the course of prenatal development. It is customary to divide the possible cause of these malformations into genetic factors (chromosomal abnormalities) and environmental factors (such as drugs or viral infections). There is often an interaction between environmental conditions and genetic factors such that the environment can either exacerbate or mitigate any potential adverse outcomes. The impact of both genetic and environmental factors may result in abnormalities that range from fetal death and severe structural defects to subtle neurological malformations that may not manifest themselves until several years after birth (as with learning disabilities or ADHD).

GENERAL RISK FACTORS

Parental age can have an impact on prenatal development. Women over the age of thirty-five are at greater risk of giving birth to children with birth defects such as Down syndrome and other chromosomal abnormalities. Recent research suggests that older men also have an increased risk of fathering children with birth defects as a result of the presence of damaged sperm that may fertilize the egg. Teenage girls are also at greater risk for giving birth to children with birth defects as a result of poor maternal health and inadequate prenatal care.

When prenatal nourishment and care are lacking, the baby is more likely to be born prematurely, have a lower birth weight, and be at greater risk for learning difficulties and a host of behavioral and emotional problems. Recent research has also implicated other factors during pregnancy as a general risk factor for psychological, behavioral, and educational outcomes.

GENETIC AND CHROMOSOMAL RISK FACTORS

Thousands of genetic and chromosomal anomalies can potentially disturb normal prenatal development. Although many of the causes of genetic and chromosomal abnormalities are unknown, some may be attributable to exposure to teratogens that damage the chromosomes during prenatal development. Research emerging out of the Human Genome Project is continuously documenting additional chromosomal abnormalities that may have an impact on prenatal development. A chromosome is a microscopic component of a cell that carries its genetic makeup. One of the most common chromosomal disorders is Down syndrome. Individuals with Down syndrome have slanted eyes; thick, fissured tongues; and a flat, broad face. They are often mentally disabled and have significant language impairments. Other chromosomal and genetic disorders include Turner syndrome, Klinefelter syndrome, fragile X syndrome, muscular dystrophy, and neural tube defects that result in spina bifida. Many of these conditions produce intellectual disability and physical anomalies such as brain damage, unusual appearance, and malformed limbs.

PRENATAL DIAGNOSTIC TESTS

Prenatal diagnosis of potential problems is possible using tests, such as amniocentesis, that can detect the presence of many chromosomal and genetic abnormalities. Amniocentesis involves the insertion of a hollow needle through the mother's abdomen into the amniotic sac and the withdrawal of fluid containing fetal cells. Amniocentesis can detect chromosomal abnormalities such as Down syndrome, but it is not usually performed until the fifteenth week of pregnancy. Chorionic villus sampling (CVS) provides the same information as amniocentesis, but at a much earlier gestational period (seven weeks). In CVS, fetal cells are obtained from the placenta by means of a tube inserted through the vagina. There is greater risk of infection and miscarriage with CVS. Fetoscopy is a surgical procedure involving the insertion of an instrument that permits actual viewing of the fetus and the obtaining of fetal tissue. This procedure is more precise than CVS and amniocentesis but carries a highter risk of miscarriage.

Ultrasound involves the use of sound waves that provide a computer-enhanced image of the fetus. It is a noninvasive, painless, and low-risk procedure that provides an actual image of fetal shape and movement. It is useful for detecting normal and abnormal fetal development and for determining fetal position and age. Preimplantation diagnosis is an experimental, highly technical genetic examination of cells before their implantation in the uterine wall. It typically follows in vitro fertilization and permits the detection of specific genetic disorders. In the future, it may be useful for correcting genetic disorders as well.

Through prenatal diagnostic tests, researchers are able to detect genetic weaknesses (and strengths) from the earliest moments of life. Researchers have also begun to experiment with ways of altering genetic messages, the results of which may lead to corrections of genetic abnormalities in the future.

ENVIRONMENTAL RISK FACTORS

A teratogen is an environmental agent such as alcohol, cocaine, or infectious organism that has an adverse impact on prenatal development following maternal exposure. The word has Greek origins and literally means "monster-forming." Certain stages of prenatal development are more vulnerable to teratogens than others. Exposure during the period of the zygote usually results in spontaneous abortion of the fertilized egg, while exposure during the embryo stage can lead to major defects in bodily structure and quite possibly death. Exposure during the fetal period usually produces minor structural defects, such as wide-set eyes, and neurological impairment, such as intellectual disability or learning problems. Some of the more commonly implicated teratogens include infectious agents such as cytomegalovirus, varicella virus, and human parvovirus B19, and drugs such as alcohol, cocaine, and nicotine.

The fetus is most vulnerable to the effects of teratogens during the first trimester. These effects are severe and may result in structural deformities and death.

Sarnoff Mednick and others at the University of Southern California reported on a more subtle form of prenatal disturbance following second trimester exposure. Mednick reported preliminary data that linked second trimester viral infections to later psychological outcomes such as depression and schizophrenia. Jose Cordero, former U.S. assistant surgeon general and director of the CDC's Center for Birth Defects and Disabilities, indicated greater need for awareness of a broader range of teratogens such as fever and infectious agents in relation to outcomes such as learning disabilities, mood disorders, and attention deficits. Stefan Dombrowski, a professor at Rider University in New Jersey, and Roy Martin, a professor at the University of Georgia, compiled the first book on the topic of prenatal exposures in relation to psychological, behavioral, and educational outcomes in children. These two researchers indicate that certain prenatal exposures including fever, influenza, stress, and air pollution may be associated with adverse psychological, behavioral, and educational outcomes. The hypothesis guiding this research is that a prenatal exposure disrupts the neurological development of the fetus and produces abnormal behavioral and psychological outcomes in offspring.

There are additional environmental agents that can potentially disrupt the normal course of prenatal development. Studies have investigated the impact of caffeine. Although the results are equivocal, exposure to moderate amounts of caffeine may result in lower birth weight and decreased fetal muscle tone. Excessive caffeine use during pregnancy should, therefore, be avoided. The impact of alcohol during pregnancy is well documented. Chronic alcohol use produces fetal alcohol syndrome and associated cognitive deficits and physical deficits such as heart problems, retarded growth, and misshapen faces. Maternal alcohol use during prenatal development is the most common cause of intellectual disability. Because even moderate daily alcohol use (two ounces of alcohol) has been associated with some of these outcomes, it is recommended that alcohol use during pregnancy be avoided. Nicotine exposure from cigarette smoking is another well-established teratogen. Research indicates that prenatal cigarette exposure increases the risk for low birth weight, cognitive deficits, learning problems, behavior problems, and even fetal death as a result of nicotine-induced placental and neurological defects.

Overall, the critical prenatal period for exposure to teratogens is during the first trimester of pregnancy. Within the first trimester, certain periods are even more sensitive to teratogens than others. For example, the first six weeks of pregnancy is a particularly sensitive period in the development of the central nervous system, while the eyes are vulnerable during weeks five through eight. It is commonly accepted that exposure to teratogens during the first eight weeks of pregnancy may induce major structural abnormalities. Exposure during the remainder of prenatal development, depending on the type of teratogen and intensity and duration of exposure, may lead to minor structural abnormalities (wide eyes, webbed hands) as well as cognitive, behavioral, and psychological difficulties. Although central nervous system development and brain growth are most vulnerable to disruptions during the first trimester of pregnancy, these structures continue to develop throughout the prenatal period. Thus, exposure to any environmental risk factor should be minimized if at all possible.

BIBLIOGRAPHY

Berk, Laura E. *Infants and Children: Prenatal through Middle Childhood*. 7th ed. Boston: Pearson, 2011. Print.

Cordero, J. F. "A New Look at Teratogens and Behavioral Outcomes: A Commentary." *Birth Defects Research Part A: Clinical and Molecular Teratology* 67 (2003): 900–902. Print.

Dombrowski, S. C., R. P. Martin, and M. O. Huttunen. "Association between Maternal Fever and Psychological/Behavioral Outcomes: A Hypothesis." *Birth Defects Research Part A: Clinical and Molecular Teratology* 67 (2003): 905–10. Print.

Marin-Padilla, Miguel. *The Human Brain: Prenatal Development and Structure*. New York: Springer, 2011. Print.

Martin, R. P., and S. C. Dombrowski. *Prenatal Exposures: Psychological and Educational Consequences for Children*. New York:. Springer, 2008. Print.

Moore, Keith L., T. V. N. Persaud, and Mark G. Torchia. *Before We Are Born: Essentials of Embryology and Birth Defects*. 8th ed. Philadelphia: Saunders/Elsevier, 2013. Print.

Paul, Annie Murphy. *Origins: How the Nine Months before Birth Shape the Rest of Our Lives*. New York: Free, 2011. Print.

Shepard, Thomas H., et al. "Update on New Developments in the Study of Human Teratogens." *Teratology* 65.4 (2002): 153–61. Print.

Warkany, Josef. Congenital Malformations. Chicago: Year Book, 1971. Print.

Watson, Jennifer B., Sarnoff A. Mednick, Matti O. Huttunen, and Xueyi Wang. "Prenatal Teratogens and the Development of Adult Mental Illness." *Development and Psychopathology* 11.3 (1999): 457–66. Print.

Stefan C. Dombrowski

SEE ALSO: Birth: Effects on physical development; Development; Developmental disabilities; Down syndrome; Imprinting; Mental retardation; Motor development; Nervous system; Pervasive developmental disorders; Reflexes in newborns.

Problem-solving stages

TYPE OF PSYCHOLOGY: Cognition

Problem-solving stages are the steps through which successful solutions to problems are obtained. Since problems are an inevitable and pervasive part of life, being successful at problem solving is an important asset.

KEY CONCEPTS
- Algorithms
- Evaluation
- Heuristics
- Implementation
- Potential solutions
- Problem

INTRODUCTION

Every person must solve problems every day. They solve problems as simple as deciding which television show to watch and as complex as deciding on a marriage partner. In either case, through effective thinking, a satisfactory answer can usually be found. Psychologists believe that there are a number of discrete stages in problem solving. Although they disagree over the exact number of stages required, as well as their exact descriptions and names, the following four stages are often described.

The first stage in problem solving is often called the information-gathering stage. During this stage, considerable information is collected, including the facts surrounding the problem, the goal or outcome desired, the major obstacles preventing a solution, and what information (knowledge) is needed to move toward the solution stage. One key factor in the information-gathering stage is the ability to separate relevant from irrelevant facts. Another key factor is assessing the problem accurately. A clear understanding of the problem is essential to problem solving.

In the second stage of problem solving, potential solutions are generated. Under normal situations, the more solutions generated, the better the chance of solving the problem, since a large number of potential solutions provide a wide choice of alternatives from which to draw.

One method used in generating solutions is called trial and error. Here the would-be problem solver tries one approach and then another and perhaps arrives, by chance, at a solution. Although time consuming, exhaustive procedures such as trial and error do eventually result in a solution. Psychologists call any method that guarantees a solution to a problem an algorithm.

Once one or more possible solutions have been generated, it is necessary to choose a specific course of action. The third stage of problem solving, the implementation stage, begins with making a decision. In some problem-solving situations, a number of solutions may be appropriate or suitable. Yet, in comparison, some solutions may be better than others. Some solutions may involve less time and may be easier or more efficient to implement.

The implementation stage involves carrying out the specific plan of action. For many people, this stage of problem solving is difficult. Especially with difficult or complex problems, people are often reluctant to follow through on courses of action. Commitment to follow through is, in many ways, the turning point of problem solving. Intentions and plans of action become meaningless unless there is the commitment to carry them out.

The fourth and final stage of problem solving, in this model, is the evaluation stage. Once the solution or plan of action has been implemented, the person needs to consider whether it has met the original goal (the intended outcome). If not, the person needs to consider other plans of action. In some situations the person may need to retrace his or her steps—beginning again with stage two, the potential solutions stage. Eventually, with perseverance and commitment, workable solutions are usually found.

Another stage worth consideration is incubation. Even though it is considered optional (occurring at some times and not others), incubation can be an important part of problem solving. Incubation refers to a period of time when the person stops thinking about the problem and focuses his or her attention on some other activity. During this time the solution may suddenly appear; it is often said to come "out of the blue."

Many people have experienced this sudden insight, and history is filled with reports of people who have made remarkable discoveries this way. Such reports point to the fact that it may be advisable to take time off from an unsolved problem. To continue to work ceaselessly on an unsolved problem may only create frustration.

TECHNIQUES FOR PROBLEM SOLVING

Heuristics are general strategies for problem solving that lessen the time and mental strain necessary for solving problems. Although much faster than algorithms—problem-solving methods that guarantee a solution—heuristics do not guarantee solutions. They work most of the time, but not always. A number of heuristic approaches exist. In hill climbing, the person moves continually closer to the final goal without ever going backward. In subgoal analysis, a problem is broken down into smaller, more manageable steps.

One often-used heuristic technique combines hill climbing and subgoals. Means-end analysis compares a person's current position with the desired end (the goal). The idea is to reduce the distance to the goal. By dividing the problem into a number of smaller, more manageable subproblems, a solution may be reached. Another heuristic strategy is called working backward. With this strategy, the search for a solution begins at the goal, or end point, and moves backward to the person's current position.

Brainstorming is another popular problem-solving technique. Here people are asked to consider all possible solutions while, at the same time, not considering (judging) their immediate value or worth. The advantage of brainstorming is that it increases the diversity of solutions and promotes creative problem solving. So far, in stage two, various methods have been mentioned to generate potential solutions. Yet in real life, problem solving often bogs down, and solutions to problems (especially difficult or complex problems) are hard to find. The importance of perseverance in problem solving cannot be overemphasized.

Another method used in problem solving is called information retrieval. Here the would-be problem solver simply retrieves information from memory that appears to have solved similar problems in the past; however, information retrieval is limited. Many problems do not fit neatly into patterns of the past. Moreover, memory is not always reliable or accurate.

TYPES OF PROBLEMS

In a review of problem-solving research published in 1978, J. G. Greeno classified problems into three basic types: problems that involve arrangement, problems that involve inducing structure, and problems that involve transformation.

Arrangement problems require the problem solver to arrange objects in a way that solves the problem. An example is arranging the letters t, g, l, h, and i to spell "light." Solving such problems often involves much trial and error.

The second type of problem requires a person to discover a pattern or structure that will relate elements of the problems to one another. For example, in solving the problem, "2 is to 4 as 5 is to ____," the problem solver discovers that 4 is twice as large as 2. Thus, the number needed to solve the problem may be twice as large as 5; that number is 10. Another possible solution is 7, because both the difference between 2 and 4 and that between 5 and 7 is 2.

The third type of problem is one of transformation. Transformation problems differ from the other two types by providing the goal rather than requiring solvers to produce it. Word problems that give the answer and require a person to find the means to the solution are one example.

EXAMPLES OF PROBLEM SOLVING

Typically, progress through problem-solving stages is done in a relatively short time. Other situations require more time. Days, weeks, or months may be needed. The following hypothetical examples show how the stages of problem solving can be applied to real-life situations.

Jim has a problem. A friend of his, Bob, recently returned from a year of studying in France. On meeting Jim, Bob was cold and distant; he was not like the person Jim once knew, who was jovial, warm, and happy. Moreover, Bob did not want to associate with Jim. Jim is surprised, hurt, and confused; he does not know what he should do.

First, Jim needs to gather all the information he can. This represents the first stage of problem solving. Jim talks with Bob's parents, other family members, and students who were with him in France. After collecting this information and separating the relevant facts from the irrelevant ones, Jim notes that his friend's disposition changed dramatically after his breakup with a girlfriend after a six-month relationship. Jim notes that the presenting problem (Bob being cold and distant) is, under close scrutiny, not the "real" problem. Bob's present behavior is only a symptom (a consequence) of the real problem, which centers on the breakup of the relationship.

Jim wishes to help his friend. He talks with Bob's family about what can be done. Together they produce three possible solutions. After comparing the solutions, they decide that the best solution would be for Bob to seek personal counseling. Together they encourage

Bob to make an appointment at the local mental health center. If Bob implements this plan of action, he may get the help he needs. If this does not work, the family and Jim will need to reevaluate the situation and try another plan of action.

Susan's assignment is to write a history paper; however, history has been a difficult subject for her in the past. She needs to do well on this paper to keep her grade-point average high. Susan needs to gather as much information as she can on her topic. She then needs to separate the relevant information from the more trivial or irrelevant. Next she needs to consider potential solutions to ensure a quality paper. She breaks down the paper-writing process into separate tasks (subgoals): preparing an outline, writing the first draft, editing, and rewriting. She executes the plan, doing one task at a time. After the final draft, she asks a classmate to read her paper and to make comments and suggestions. Finally, with a few modifications (revisions), Susan's paper is ready to be submitted.

Ellen is a high school senior. Her goal is to become a lawyer, but she is unsure of what steps she must take to accomplish this goal. Her first step is to gather all the information she can on how to become a lawyer. She begins by surveying the literature on lawyers in her public library. She also checks with her high school counselor. The counselor gives her some of the specifics: the number of years required for college and law school; the best courses to take as an undergraduate student; the admissions tests necessary for college and law school; the cost of college and law school (including sources of financial aid).

Her next two steps are to devise a plan of action and to implement this plan. She begins by taking a college entrance examination and applying to the college of her choice. After being accepted, she plans her course of studies, keeping in mind the educational requirements of law school. Early in the fall semester of her senior year, she takes the law school admission test and then applies to law school. If she is accepted to law school, her goal of becoming a lawyer is within reach. If she is not accepted, she needs to revise her plan of action or even her goal. She may need to apply to another law school, retake the law school admission test if her score was low, or consider other options: perhaps becoming a paralegal or law assistant or changing fields entirely.

Steve's car breaks down, and he has it towed to the garage. The mechanic on duty, whether he realizes it or not, applies various stages of problem solving. First of all,

he gathers information by asking Steve what happened. Steve states that he was driving down Main Street and suddenly the motor stopped. The mechanic thus focuses on things that can cause the motor to stop suddenly (the potential solutions stage). The most obvious is a problem with the electrical system. After checking various electrical components (the implementation stage), the mechanic notes that the ignition coil is dead. After replacing the coil, the mechanic attempts to start the car (the evaluation stage). The car starts.

EVOLUTION OF PROBLEM-SOLVING RESEARCH

Various writers have attempted to analyze the stages in problem solving. One of the first attempts was that of John Dewey in 1910. Dewey's five stages utilized the "scientific method" to solve problems systematically through the reasoning process. The five stages are becoming aware of the difficulty; identifying the problem; assembling and classifying data and formulating hypotheses; accepting or rejecting the tentative hypotheses; and formulating conclusions and evaluating them.

Another attempt to analyze the stages of problem solving was that of Graham Wallas in 1926. He proposed that problem solving consisted of the following four steps: preparation, incubation, illumination, and verification. Gyrgy Plya, in 1957, also considered problem solving as involving four stages: understanding the problem, devising a plan, carrying out the plan, and checking the results. In *The IDEAL Problem Solver* (1984), John Bransford and Barry Stein outline a method of problem solving based on the letters IDEAL: Identify the problem, define the problem, explore possible strategies, act on the strategies, and look at the effects of one's efforts.

One of the most famous scientific studies of the stages in problem solving was that of Karl Duncker in 1945. In his study, subjects were given a problem and asked to report aloud how their thinking processes were working. After examining the subjects' responses, Duncker found that problem solving did indeed involve a sequence of stages. Presently, computers are used to solve problems. One of the early attempts to use computers in this way was called the general problem solver (GPS), devised by Allen Newell, J. C. Shaw, and Herbert Simon. Historically, problem solving has not been an area of wide research or interest; however, with increasing interest in cognitive psychology and its emphasis on thinking processes, the study of problem solving seems to have a secure future. Considering the number and scope of the problems that face people from day to day, it seems reasonable to continue—and even expand—the study of problem solving.

BIBLIOGRAPHY

Andriole, Stephen J. *Handbook of Problem Solving.* Princeton: Petrocelli, 1983. Print.

Benjamin, Ludy T., J. Roy Hopkins, and Jack R. Nation. *Psychology.* 3rd ed. New York: Macmillan, 1994. Print.

Bransford, John, and Barry S. Stein. *The IDEAL Problem Solver.* 2nd ed. New York: Freeman, 2002. Print.

Coon, Dennis, and John O. Mitterer. *Psychology: A Journey.* Belmont: Wadsworth, 2014. Print.

Gerrig, Richard J. *Psychology and Life.* Boston: Pearson, 2013. Print.

Hayes, John R. *The Complete Problem Solver.* 2nd ed. Hillsdale: Lawrence Erlbaum, 1989. Print.

Huffman, Karen, et al. *Psychology in Action.* 10th ed. New York: Wiley, 2012. Print.

Kahane, Adam. *Solving Tough Problems: An Open Way of Talking, Listening, and Creating New Realities.* San Francisco: Berrett-Koehler, 2007. Print.

Puccio, Gerard J. *Creativity Rising: Creative Thinking and Creative Problem Solving in the Twenty-First Century.* Buffalo: ICSC, 2012. Print.

Robinson-Riegler, Gregory, and Bridget Robinson-Riegler. *Cognitive Psychology: Applying the Science of the Mind.* Boston: Allyn, 2012. Print.

Ted Eilders

SEE ALSO: Artificial intelligence; Computer models of cognition; Concept formation; Decision making; Dewey, John; Intervention; Logic and reasoning; Problem-solving strategies; Thought: Inferential.

Problem-solving strategies

TYPE OF PSYCHOLOGY: Cognition

Problem solving is one of the most basic tasks of life; psychologists have studied various obstacles to solving problems and have identified many of the strategies used in solving different types of problems.

KEY CONCEPTS
- Artificial intelligence
- Computer simulation
- Difference reduction
- Functional fixedness
- Means-ends analysis
- Mental set effect
- Problem solving by analogy
- Working backward

INTRODUCTION

Problem solving is a complex process that involves the use of cognitive skill, prior experiences and their memories, and general knowledge about how the world works. In other words, people use logical thinking and reasoning, memory, and common sense when trying to solve any problem. When psychologists study problem solving, the process is typically divided into three steps: forming a representation of the problem, using a strategy to plan an approach to the problem, and executing the strategy and checking the results. This basic sequence is repeated each time one encounters a problem. First, one must understand the nature of the problem. Second, one thinks of different ways that the problem could be solved, relying on one's reasoning skills, memory for similar problems, or common sense. Third, one attempts to solve the problem with whatever strategy was formed and, if unsuccessful, forms another strategy and tries again. For example, when a sports team plays a game, first the players study the other team, looking for strengths and weaknesses. Then a game plan is formed and executed. The process can fail at any step: The team members might not really understand their opponents, a bad game plan may be formed, or the implementation of the plan may fail. The inability to complete any step in the process results in an obstacle to solving the problem, whatever that may be.

An old story describes the problem-solving ability of a college student taking a physics examination. One question on the exam asked how a barometer could be used to measure the height of a building (a barometer is a device sensitive to changes in atmospheric pressure). The student responded that a string could be tied to the barometer, and, after the barometer was lowered from the roof of the building, the string could be measured. The professor found this solution unacceptable, since it did not rely on a principle from physics. The student's second solution was to drop the barometer from the roof, measure the time it took to hit the ground, and then calculate the height of the building using a formula involving gravity. Since this was not the solution for which the professor was looking, the student next suggested that the barometer be placed near the building on a sunny day and the height of the barometer as well as the length of the shadows from the barometer and building be measured. Then the student could develop two ratios and solve for the unknown quantity. While the professor was impressed, the student had not provided the desired solution, and the professor gave the student one more chance. If the student could think of one more method of using the barometer to discover the height of the building, the professor would give full credit. The student finally suggested that they find the owner of the building and say, "If you tell me how tall the building is, I will give you this barometer."

THREE TYPES OF STRATEGIES

Three different types of problem-solving strategies emerge when the issue is studied systematically: means-ends analysis, working backward, and problem solving by analogy. In means-ends analysis, the person examines and compares the solutions desired (sometimes called the goal state) with the methods (the means) available. When making this comparison of where one is to where one wants to be, subgoals are usually generated in such a way that when all the subgoals are completed, the problem is solved. For example, while the ultimate goal in planning a wedding is for two people to be married, there are also several subgoals to be considered, such as a marriage license, a minister, a place to be married, and what to wear. A person using means-ends analysis might develop subgoals to accomplish over time, keeping the ultimate goal in mind. This procedure of identifying the difference between the current state and the ultimate goal state and working to reduce the differences by using subgoals is called difference reduction, a particular form of means-ends analysis.

A second problem-solving strategy is to work backward. When one knows what the solution should be, often one can then work backward from the solution to fill in the means to the end. In solving a maze, for example, one may start working on the maze by beginning at the end line and working backward to the start line. After misplacing something, one often retraces one's steps, working backward to try to find the item. Another example is the person who wants to have a set amount of money left after paying all the bills. Working the problem in the forward direction (that is, paying the bills and seeing what is left over) may not result in the desired goal; starting with the goal first, however, can achieve the overall desired solution.

It should be noted that the working-backward strategy works only when the solution (or goal state) is known or believed to be known. When it is unknown, working backward cannot work. That is the case with a mechanic who is trying to fix a car when the exact cause of the malfunction is unknown. Although the desired solution is known (a working car), tracing the path backward does not work. In this type of situation, the mechanic is likely to try a means-ends strategy (for example, testing each major system of the car) or to use the next strategy, problem solving by analogy.

Solving problems by using analogies relies on the use of memories from prior problem-solving situations and the application of this information in solving a new problem. Often the initial representation of the problem may trigger memories for similar problems solved in the past. At other times, a person may actively search in memory for analogous or similar situations, then retrieve and apply such information.

The American educational system is largely based on the strategy of problem solving by analogy. Children are taught the facts, figures, and skills that are analogous to the facts, figures, and skills necessary in later life. Education is meant to be the prior experience, to be used in solving later problems. Homework is based on the idea of problem solving by analogy—providing early experiences that may be applicable to later problems (such as on a test).

FUNCTIONAL FIXEDNESS

The three general steps in the problem-solving process are problem representation, strategy formation, and execution of the strategy. Many obstacles in solving everyday problems are particularly sensitive to the role of problem representation. Two examples of common obstacles in problem solving are functional fixedness and mental set effects.

Functional fixedness is the idea that people often focus on the given function of an object while neglecting other potentially novel uses. Norman R. F. Maier in 1931 demonstrated functional fixedness in his now-classic two-string problem. In this problem, two strings hang from the ceiling of a room, too far apart for a person to reach both at once. Yet the strings are long enough to reach one another and be tied. The problem is to tie the strings together. The only objects available to the person are a chair, some paper, and a pair of pliers. Maier found that most people he tested exhibited functional fixedness (that is, they did not use the items in the room in novel ways to solve the problem). Those that did solve the problem realized they needed to attach a weight (the pliers) to one string and swing the string like a pendulum to tie the strings together, thus avoiding functional fixedness.

Another classic example of functional fixedness can be found in Karl Duncker's 1945 candle-and-box problem. In this problem, people are presented with a candle, a box of tacks, and a book of matches; the problem is to attach the candle to the wall so that the candle can burn in its upright, proper position. People who possess functional fixedness are unable to see the box holding the tacks as a candle holder, emptied and attached to the wall, with the candle attached to the top of the box. Whenever one uses a knife or a dime as a screwdriver, one is showing a lack of functional fixedness, that is, using an object in a manner for which it was not intended.

MENTAL SET EFFECTS

A second general obstacle in problem solving is called a mental set. A mental set is a conceptual block that prevents the appearance of an appropriate problem solution. Set effects most often occur because of sheer repetition of information (therefore, one does not search for alternative solutions) or because of a preconceived notion about the problem. One example of the mental set effect comes from Abraham Luchins's water-jug problem. In this problem, people were given three water jugs—A, B, and C—and the task was to manipulate the water in the jugs to obtain a desired quantity. For example, jug A holds 21 cups of water, jug B holds 127 cups, and jug C holds 3 cups; the desired amount is exactly 100 cups. The desired amount can be reached by filling B once, pouring once into jug A, then pouring twice into jug C. This answer can be expressed as "B − A − 2C" (or "127 − 21 − 3 − 3 = 100"). Luchins gave people a series of problems, all of which could be solved by this formula; however, he would occasionally include a problem that could also be solved by a simpler formula, such as A − C. People continued to use the more complex formula. Luchins thought that people get into a rut or mental set, and when the set yields positive results, they do not bother to exert effort to change (even when a simpler method exists).

NINE-DOT PROBLEM

A different example of the importance of problem representation is found with the nine-dot problem. In the nine-dot problem, three rows of three dots each must be connected by four straight lines, with the restriction that the pen or pencil cannot be lifted from the page. The natural box shape that the dots form presents an obstacle similar to mental set: People cannot solve the problem until they realize that the lines must go outside the perceived square before the problem can be solved.

IMPLICATIONS FOR PSYCHOLOGICAL STUDY

The formal study of problem solving is almost as old as the field of psychology itself. As early as 1898, Edward L. Thorndike studied the problem-solving ability of cats trying to escape from a puzzle box. This box was designed with levers, pulleys, and latches so that when the cat made a particular response inside, the door to the box would open and the cat could escape. Thorndike found that the cats could remember the escape sequence and that each time the cat was placed in the box, it escaped more quickly. He considered problem-solving ability as evidence of learning and called it the stamping in of behavior. Wolfgang Köhler in 1925 studied chimpanzees and found that they could experience a flash of insight (sometimes called the "aha!" phenomenon) in solving a problem, just as humans do. In the 1930s and 1940s, Edward C. Tolman studied the problem-solving abilities of rats in different types of mazes and found them to be very good at navigating a maze.

Problem solving is an exciting area in psychology because it is a basic, universal characteristic of all humans. Everyone faces a number of problems each day. To understand how people solve problems is, to a large degree, to understand basic human behavior, the goal of every psychologist. Problem-solving strategies and obstacles lie at the foundation of understanding humankind.

The future is bright for those interested in the study of problem solving. The increasing use of computer technology has advanced the field considerably. Computer simulations are used in an attempt to emulate (mimic) how humans solve problems. In this approach, the human is most important. In other words, computer simulations are valuable in helping to understand why people do the things they do. Artificial intelligence, on the other hand, uses computer technology to seek the best possible and most efficient solutions to problems—not necessarily mimicking the processes of humans. In the study of artificial intelligence, the problem is the most important aspect. Regardless of the specific area of study, the various strategies and obstacles observed by psychologists make intriguing work, and they lie at the very heart of what humans continually do: solve problems.

BIBLIOGRAPHY

Anderson, John R. *Cognitive Psychology and Its Implications*. 7th ed. New York: Worth, 2010. Print.

Eysenck, Michael W., and Mark T. Keane. *Cognitive Psychology: A Student's Handbook*. 6th ed. Hove: Psychology, 2010. Print.

Fogler, H. Scott, and Steven E. LeBlanc. *Strategies for Creative Problem Solving*. 3rd ed. Upper Saddle River: Prentice, 2014. Print.

Kalat, James W. *Introduction to Psychology*. 10th ed. Belmont: Wadsworth, 2013. Print.

Mayer, R. E. *Thinking, Problem Solving, Cognition*. 3rd ed. New York: Worth, 2007. Print.

R. Eric Landrum

SEE ALSO: Concept formation; Creativity and intelligence; Decision making; Group decision making; Learning; Logic and reasoning; Problem-solving stages; Thought: Inferential; Tolman, Edward C.

Procrastination

TYPE OF PSYCHOLOGY: Biological bases of human behavior; Clinical; Cognitive; Counseling; Educational; Psychopathology; Psychotherapy; Social

Procrastination means putting off and avoiding doing the things that need to be done by a certain time by doing other, less important or pleasurable things instead. The result is often waiting until the last minute. It invokes negative feelings, health issues, relationship difficulties, and a failure to obtain one's dreams. Procrastination comes at a great cost including robbing one of peace of mind and enjoying life. Further, exasperation and frustration often occurs with co-workers and significant others.

KEY CONCEPTS
- Eliminating procrastination tendencies in children
- Overcoming procrastination
- Procrastination
- Procrastinators vs non-procrastinators
- Rationalizations and justifications
- The individual cost to procrastinators
- Why students procrastinate

INTRODUCTION
Procrastination, for some people, can be persistent and tremendously disruptive to everyday life.

Procrastination is the practice or habit of completing low priority or unimportant tasks instead of high priority, important tasks that need to be done. It means doing pleasurable things in place of less pleasurable ones that need to be done. Such behavior results in putting off impending or priority tasks to a later time, sometimes to the last minute.

Procrastination does not mean doing nothing. It means the intentional delay of doing what needs to be done while doing preferred things instead. Such delays or mismanagement of time comes at a great cost to the procrastinator. Waiting until the last minute and working under self-imposed pressure can result in stress, anxiety, a sense of guilt, health problems, it can create unrelated crises, or result in harming social relationships with others for not reliably meeting responsibilities and commitments. For children, adolescents, and adults alike, procrastination can result in many unwanted, negative consequences.

Motives for procrastination are often incorrectly assigned to the procrastinator by others, resulting in a lack of support or understanding as to the cost of procrastination to the procrastinator. For some, procrastination is thought to be due to laziness, low willpower, low ambition, low ability, not being committed, being immature or manipulative. Most procrastinators would say that those "labels" are harmful and untrue.

Procrastination is more widespread in students than in the general population. One study found that increasing academic procrastination increases the frequency of academic misconduct such as copying from someone else's exam, using forbidden means in an exam, plagiarism, using fraudulent excuses, copying parts of other's homework, the fabrication or falsification of data, and other types of academic misconduct. The study argues that academic misconduct is seen as a means for coping with the negative consequences of procrastination.

Procrastination, in most cases, is not a sign of a serious problem and can be overcome and avoided. However, if procrastination becomes so chronic that it begins to have a serious impact on a person's daily life, the underlying causes may be rooted in a problematic lifestyle. For example, when one procrastinates in terms of paying one's bills, the person may be charged additional fees for late payments or their credit score may be impacted.

HOW DO PROCRASTINATORS DIFFER FROM NON-PROCRASTINATORS?

Non-procrastinators focus on the task that needs to be done when it needs to be done. They identify more with high self-esteem which is how they feel about themselves. Procrastinators delay what needs to be done until the last minute and are more concerned with social-esteem or a desire to have others like them.

RATIONALIZATIONS AND JUSTIFICATIONS FOR PROCRASTINATION

Rationalizations and justifications are defense mechanisms people use to diminish their uncomfortable feelings, stress and anxiety, feelings of inadequacy, and their depression or self-doubt when confronted with completing tasks on time. Ways in which we deceive ourselves with rationalizations and justifications for procrastinating include acting like we don't really know what needs to be done; not feeling in the mood to do it; needing time to think about the task; just not wanting to do it;

being in the habit of waiting until the last minute; or waiting for the right moment to get started. Believing such excuses can keep a person stuck in a negative cycle of procrastination.

Other maladaptive coping strategies include avoiding the locale or situation surrounding the task that needs to be done, immersing one's self in other behavior to prevent awareness of the task, trivializing the importance of the task, pretending or being in denial that one is procrastinating, or being highly satisfied with all the things one is achieving while avoiding the task that should be done by a certain deadline. The pseudo-benefit of procrastination is the illusion of perfection --- that when we start the task(s) we have avoided, we will start the project at the moment we say we will, we will be in the perfect mood, have perfect ideas, will produce perfect results, and complete it "right on time."

Simply put, procrastination is an inability to self-regulate one's behavior when faced with tasks to complete by a certain deadline. Procrastination then leads to last minute cramming or push to complete important tasks at a high cost to an individual.

THE COST OF PROCRASTINATION

Procrastination comes at a big cost to the procrastinator. It can result in the failure to complete dreams such as obtaining a college degree or developing one's talents as an athlete, musician, engineer, teacher, etc. Procrastination can cost someone their self-esteem, their happiness and leave someone unable to pursue their purpose in life. It can also cost one their health, their money, personal and professional success and even love.

WHY DO STUDENTS PROCRASTINATE?

William Knaus, a psychologist, estimated that 90% of college students procrastinate. Of that group, 25% are chronic procrastinators and often drop out of college.

Students who procrastinate often report that they keep putting off assignments, spend too much of their time with friends or at social activities, or just worry about assignments instead of completing them. They report having difficulty concentrating and wasting a lot of time when working on assignments in highly distracting, cluttered, noisy or unorganized places such as on their bed.

Not confronting one's fears about completing important tasks can lead to negative, untrue beliefs such as "I can't do this," "I don't have the skills to perform this task," or "I just don't do well on tests," or "I just can't concentrate long enough to learn all that is required for this exam." Some students are unrealistic and think studying comes easy for everyone else but is just too hard for them.

Students also report personal problems with their friends/roommate/girlfriend or boyfriend or with family members as well as financial difficulties as reasons for why they procrastinate. Some students report that they don't like an instructor or think an assignment is boring, therefore blaming the instructor for their procrastination. Unrealistic expectations and perfectionism can also be blamed for procrastination as when you think you MUST read everything ever written on a subject before beginning to write on a subject. Such unrealistic expectations can also result in a fear of failure when failing is defined by the student as anything but an "A" on an exam.

ELIMINATING PROCRASTINATION TENDENCIES IN CHILDREN

For children, putting off completing projects, homework, chores, etc., can be the start of a life long struggle with procrastination which can affect their level of achievement, self-confidence, their relationships with others, and their experiences at home, in school and elsewhere. Parents and teachers can help students eliminate procrastination tendencies and avoid procrastination by teaching a proactive approach to completing tasks on or before time regardless of distractions or negative feelings.

An activity for helping children eliminate or avoid procrastination is by teaching children, through positive practice, how to create and keep improving their own personal style as to how he or she will manage their time while completing tasks on time. The students could be taught what their best learning styles are and then can come up with creative ways to use those strengths to complete tasks in a happily productive way.

Students could be given unique and interesting projects to complete, that they will not complete, but will write down, draw, and explain to others how they will tackle the project. Using movie or book heroes as an example of how to complete tasks could be instructional and inspiring. Most importantly, each student would learn their very own personal, best way to learn and succeed at completing important things on time. Creating their own avatar could change for the better, their relationship to doing what they are supposed to be doing, when they are supposed to be doing it.

Parents and teachers could have the students make a list of the steps involved in what they are going to do, gauge the amount of time they will need, acquire all materials they might need, anticipate obstacles and how they will be handled. They could create a poster or checklist of the steps to be checked off when completed. Then students could be required to discuss their step-by-step process with two older students and two adults in addition to their parents with the understanding that they will keep adding to and getting better strategies as they practice completing tasks.

Such activities can teach students to set small achievable goals, set up breaks and rewards all along the way for both the completion of tasks and effort shown. After the students design how they will take on big or little tasks, they could be asked to close their eyes and imagine being so proud that he or she finished their project and had fun doing it. Listening and watching how others complete their projects and by practicing project completion, students can then learn how to apply their newly learned project completion skills in all areas of their life in happy and productive ways.

OVERCOMING PROCRASTINATION

One effective technique for making good progress on your work when paralyzed by procrastination is called the Pomodoro Technique. You will need a timer. First, choose a task. Set the timer for 25 minutes. Work until the timer rings. Take a five minute break. Set the timer again for 25 minutes and start again. Stop when the timer rings and take a five minute break. Each set of 25 minutes of on task behavior is called a pomodoro. After the completion of four pomodoros, take a longer break. Just walking outdoors is a great refresher. Then repeat. The length of time for each pomodoro can be increased depending on the difficulty of a subject.

Another strategy for getting started on a task requires you to quickly write out everything on your mind that is getting in the way of you concentrating. The list could include calls you need to make, errands to run, feelings you have about completing the task at hand, other tasks that need to be completed, movies you want to watch, people you want to see, things you want to order, etc. After completion of the list, look around and eliminate other distractions including wearing uncomfortable clothes, poor lighting, being thirsty, etc. Close everything that you don't need open on your computer and prevent interruptions whenever possible.

Begin by unpacking the task at hand. List what will need to be learned and or written. Remind yourself why you are doing the task such as to become a parole officer, physician, speech pathologist, special education teacher, forensic criminologist, etc. Assign what will be needed for each unpacked part of the task such as writing out things on index cards, designing large posters of information to stare at while watching television, or lying in bed, or printing off information from the internet to read.

Sometimes completing easy tasks first can help one build up focused attention for more difficult tasks.

Coach yourself in ways that empower you. Challenge yourself. Forgive yourself. Relax from time to time. Renew your energy by eating healthy, getting enough sleep, and taking breaks. Make learning fun by promising yourself desirable rewards for the completion of tasks such as catching up on sleep, taking a day off, spending time with friends, purchasing something you really like, seeing a movie, or time with friends, in person or via the Internet.

Notice if you keep doing something that doesn't work and quit doing it such as trying to study in a certain location or time of day. Keep track of what works for you and try new things when something doesn't work. Give yourself a study advantage by getting a tutor or finding out more about effective test taking tips and how to improve your memory.

Procrastination interferes with many great joys in life. Tackling it and overcoming it is one of the most valuable things a procrastinator could ever do to improve the quality of their life.

BIBLIOGRAPHY

Foster, Joanne. *Not Now, Maybe Later: Helping Children Overcome Procrastination*. Tucson, Arizona: Great potential Press, Inc., 2015 Joanne Foster has written extensively on gifted children and gifted education and has found that gifted children also procrastinate- but perhaps for very different reasons than the general population. Gifted children (and adults) may be bored with a task, or prefer another more exciting and stimulating task or interesting task.

Knaus, William. *Productive Energy!: 57 Ways To Embrace Change & Defeat Your Procrastination For Good: Procrastination Self Help*. New York: Createspace Publishing, 2014. Productive Procrastination – William Knaus is a psychologist who has written extensively on procrastination, and the underlying irrational beliefs that may cause it. Such irrational beliefs are based on the theory of Rational Emotive Therapy developed by Albert Ellis. Ellis and Knaus would indicate that the client's self-talk causes procrastination. The client or person may make such self-statements as "It's too hard, it's too difficult, it's terrible, awful, and horrible that I should have to perform such tasks- such as taking out the trash or some other noxious task. Knaus has written books to assist individuals in overcoming procrastination as well as helping individuals to better prioritize their time.

Ellis, A., & Knaus, W. J. (1977). *Overcoming Procrastination*. New York: Signet Books http://www.smartrecovery.org/resources/library/Articles_and_Essays/Most_Popular/procrastination.htm   This source will refer the reader to five books authored by Dr. William Knaus, one of the most prolific writers and scholars on the topic of procrastination

http://www.newyorker.com/magazine/2010/10/11/later

http://www.academia.edu/1456305/The_Evaluation_of_the_Major_Characteristics_and_Aspects_of_the_Procrastination_in_the_Framework_of_Psychological_Counseling_and_Guidance

June Shepherd and Michael Shaughnessy

SEE ALSO: Hyperactivity; Impulse control; Motivation; Personality traits; Self regulation.

Profiling

DATE: 1800s forward

TYPE OF PSYCHOLOGY: Motivation; Personality; Social psychology

Profiling is a psychological methodology that is used to collect information about known or unidentified individuals or groups to assess their psychological characteristics and how they relate to perpetuating a crime, participating in a behavior, or being victimized.

KEY CONCEPTS
- Behavioral patterns
- Forensic psychology
- Intuition
- Investigation
- Motivations
- Personality

INTRODUCTION

Profiling originated in the nineteenth century, when anthropologists hypothesized that criminals' psychological and physical traits could be correlated. Early efforts revealed that evaluating criminals' behavioral patterns during a police investigation aided in understanding their motivations and predicting future crimes they might commit and victims they might choose. Such techniques encouraged law-enforcement personnel reliant on traditional criminology methods to comprehend and pursue elusive, anonymous perpetrators.

Edgar Allan Poe's fictional detective C. August Dupin foreshadowed behavioral profiling in the 1841 short story "The Murders in the Rue Morgue." Factual profiling received public attention in the late 1880s in London, when police surgeon Thomas Bond profiled the serial killer Jack the Ripper by reconstructing crime scenes to study behaviors during the murders, such as covering victims' faces with a sheet and the repetition of wound patterns. Although Bond speculated about the age, demeanor, and appearance of Jack the Ripper, no suspects were ever convicted.

During World War II, the Office of Strategic Services (OSS), the predecessor of the Central Intelligence Agency (CIA), profiled Adolf Hitler's personality characteristics. Psychiatrist Walter Langer evaluated Hitler's behavior to help military authorities develop a strategy to interrogate Hitler if he were captured. Langer accurately speculated that Hitler would commit suicide instead of surrendering. In later conflicts, the US military utilized expert profiling of other enemy leaders such as Saddam Hussein and Osama bin Laden in an attempt to develop military plans to capture them and prevent terrorist actions they sponsored.

In the mid-twentieth century, psychiatrist James Brussels successfully profiled a serial bomber who terrorized New York City. Police were startled that profile details such as the bomber wearing a buttoned, double-breasted suit proved accurate when the criminal was apprehended.

MODERN PROFILING

The foundation of modern profiling is the realization that behavior reflects personality and that criminal actions satisfy the perpetrators' psychological or physical needs. Profilers attempt to think like both criminals and victims to comprehend why and how a crime occurred, and the role played in the crime by both perpetrators and victims. Behavioral scientists recognize that although every crime is unique, human behavior matches patterns.

Affiliated with law-enforcement officers who share evidence, profilers use scientific methods supplemented with their instincts about aberrant behavior to create a psychological profile for each murderer. The serial nature of crimes such as kidnapping, rape, molestation, and arson provide profilers with patterns to examine for behavioral consistencies and deviations. Isolated incidents, such as theft, carjacking, and vandalism, are not as successfully profiled.

Computer databases have proven less reliable than profilers' intuition about specific individuals because of the variability of factors among criminals. Profiling is constantly developing to meet law-enforcement needs. Cyberprofiling seeks to identify people who commit electronic crimes, such as hacking, based on behavior associated with that activity. Profilers choose techniques from several methods that they consider most useful.

THE FEDERAL BUREAU OF INVESTIGATION

In the 1960s, Howard Teten, a California police officer, became a US Federal Bureau of Investigation (FBI) special agent and collaborated with Pat Mullany, a specialist in abnormal psychology, to teach how crime-scene evidence revealed behavioral clues. Teten initiated a course on applied criminology at the FBI Academy in 1970. In the late twentieth century, the FBI's Behavioral Science Unit (BSU) professionalized profiling as a form of forensic psychology. After Teten retired in 1978, director

John Douglas and his colleague Robert Ressler emphasized organized (premeditated)/disorganized (impulsive) methodology to evaluate how criminals behaved at crime scenes.

From 1979 to 1983, BSU personnel interviewed prisoners concerning biographical information, their criminal actions, and choice of victims and sites. The BSU agents also collected court, police, and psychiatric records to compile a database useful for future profiling. The FBI's National Center for the Analysis of Violent Crime (NCAVC), established in 1984, helped law-enforcement efforts to detect similar criminal activity in various jurisdictions.

PROFILING "ANONYMOUS"

The FBI's Crime Classification Manual outlines how psychological profiles should be compiled and evaluated. Offender profiling focuses on the behavior of criminals and how they commit crimes, comparing these profiles with established personality types and mental disorders. Investigative profiling studies evidence from crime scenes.

Profiling is a powerful forensic tool to solve seemingly unsolvable cases. When suspects are unknown, profilers can find psychological clues in the choices the culprit made, such as selection and number of victims, crime site, weapons, and alteration of the crime scene by destroying items, displaying bodies, or taking souvenirs.

The first investigation stage involves profiling the victim and noting any associations with the assailant or what the victim might have symbolized to the attacker. Profilers hypothesize how the criminal behaved with the victim and the motivation for the crime, specifically whether it was a planned or an impulsive act and if it was based on anger and the need for power or because of a mental disorder or stimulant abuse. The assailant's behavior before and after the crime is also explored.

The use of weapons and restraints is evaluated and offers insight into the assailant's social skills, intellectual abilities, demographic description of race and age, and socioeconomic, marital, and employment status. Profilers speculate about the relationship the criminal has with family members and neighbors and any possible military service. Specific traits such as cowardice and feelings of inadequacy are identified in profiles.

In addition, profilers assess any messages left by the criminal for law-enforcement officers, media, or victims' family members. They integrate police and autopsy reports and interview survivors and witnesses to consider their perspectives about the assailant's personality. Profiles provide a psychological identity to guide law-enforcement personnel to find suspects who match specific behavioral patterns.

If they are aware of profiling, some criminals may purposefully alter their behavior to avoid apprehension, although some psychological traits are difficult to hide. Profilers look for any efforts at deception and focus on how offenders' signatures, which are behaviors not essential to the crime but which satisfy the offender, are present at crime scenes. If a suspect is captured, the profile is essential to the interrogation process.

INVESTIGATIVE PSYCHOLOGY

In 1985, Scotland Yard requested that David Canter help incorporate psychological concepts into investigation methods. Although dubious, Canter successfully utilized environmental psychology methods to identify John Duffy as the so-called Railway Rapist. Canter's work established investigative psychology (IP) in the United Kingdom. Like the FBI, Canter used statistical information concerning criminal offenders and offenses. His five-factor IP model focuses on how criminals and victims interact.

First, interpersonal coherence examines how criminals act with victims and is based on the assumption that they treat people similarly in both criminal and noncriminal interactions. This factor suggests that victims represent significant people to assailants, such as former spouses or parents, toward whom the criminal is expressing symbolic rage. Second, Canter states that the time and place of crimes is significant to determine facts about the criminal's lifestyle. Third, criminal characteristics are assessed, although Canter disagrees with the FBI, saying that organized and disorganized classifications of criminals are misleading because a criminal might display both behaviors.

Fourth, Canter says profilers should consider whether assailants have previously been criminally active, and, if so, what crimes they have committed and for what duration they have engaged in a criminal career. Such experiences might have resulted in skills or behaviors demonstrated during the crime that would reduce the number of possible suspects. The final factor is forensic awareness, which assesses whether culprits are knowledgeable enough of investigation procedures for gathering evidence to wear gloves or remove incriminating items from scenes. In addition, Canter's offender behavior model, the circle theory, describes a marauder model, in which

criminals operate from a base, and a commuter model, in which assailants travel to commit crimes.

BEHAVIORAL EVIDENCE ANALYSIS

Brent Turvey, a California forensic scientist, developed behavioral evidence analysis (BEA). Unlike other profiling methods, BEA reconstructs criminal events rather than psychologically interpreting an offender's behavior. By examining police, autopsy, and court records, Turvey recognizes how criminals can appear charming and gregarious but lie. His BEA profiling technique stresses that criminals frequently distort descriptions of their actions, which can influence reconstruction of their criminal behavior.

Four investigative steps occur in two phases. First, equivocal forensic analysis studies evidence to determine its most probable meaning. Second is victimology, in which the role of the victim is analyzed. The third step begins with crime scene characteristics, investigating why that location was chosen and its possible meanings to the criminal. Profilers decide if the site is a primary or secondary crime scene and if victims were moved. The final step focuses on offender characteristics, to assess the criminal's personality based on the previous three steps.

The investigative phase of BEA occurs when profilers develop a description of an unknown criminal type who is likely to have committed a known crime to provide investigators with leads. The trial phase evaluates evidence when a suspected culprit for a specific crime is known to assist investigators in conducting interrogations.

PUBLIC REACTION

Profiling success rates range from 50 to 85 percent. Profilers must objectively examine criminals' perceptions and how their behavior reveals their motivations without interjecting their moral values. Misrepresentations of profilers, often romanticizing them as being psychic, abound in films, television, fiction, and true-crime books. As a result, many law-enforcement officers ignore or dismiss profiling. Others rely on imprecise profiles. A 1993 profile of the Unabomber based on his victims, which suggested he was highly educated in science and held antitechnology views, was discarded in favor of a profile which said the Unabomber was a blue-collar aviation worker. As a result, the apprehension of mathematician Theodore Kaczynski was delayed because of the focus on invalid suspects.

Critics express concern that innocent people might be falsely arrested, convicted, and imprisoned based on profiles that they consider to be hunches rather than evidence. Such profiling opponents cite errors by leading profilers, including Douglas, who stresses that profiling can be fallible and should not replace a comprehensive investigation. Some people believe local investigators rather than FBI agents should profile suspects. Legal authorities note that, occasionally, organized offenders can leave a disorganized crime scene if they are committing crimes spurred by retaliation, drugs, or domestic violence. Such crime scenes might mislead profilers to describe incorrectly a perpetrator's behavior.

Many legal courts do not permit profiles to be submitted as evidence during trials because they do not prove an individual committed a specific crime, only that the person fits the profile of someone who could have been the perpetrator.

NONFORENSIC PSYCHOLOGICAL PROFILES

Noncriminal psychological profiling applications gauge personality characteristics compatible with professional, leisure, and consumer interests. Profiles can alert potential employers about possibly hazardous workers. They can also highlight employees who have the potential to be successful at various tasks. Psychological profiling can be incorporated into therapies to help patients understand their career and entertainment interests and modify their behavior.

Because of increased school violence, some schools are using psychological profiling to identify students who might pose safety risks. This intervention process is considered controversial because it relies on speculation and can unjustly accuse students, because no standard profile for violent students exists and children displaying identified behaviors exhibit them in varying degrees of intensity.

Some psychological profiling is unable to pinpoint assailants because of the diversity of people who exhibit shared psychological characteristics such as road rage. Racial profiling, often heightened after violent acts committed by members of a specific ethnic group, is controversial. Some argue that it is a necessary law enforcement practice while many contend that it infringes on civil rights and is an ineffective way to identify possible culprits.

BIBLIOGRAPHY

Ares, Gaston, and Paula Varela. *Novel Techniques in Sensory Characterization and Consumer Profiling.* Boca Raton: CRC, 2014. Digital file.Barrow, Lauren M., and Ron A. Rufo. Police and Profiling in the United States: Applying Theory to Criminal Investigations. Boca Raton: CRC, 2014. Digital file.Bloom, Richard W. Foundations of Psychological Profiling: Terrorism, Espionage, and Deception. Boca Raton: CRC, 2013. Digital file.

Canter, David V. *Criminal Shadows: Inside the Mind of the Serial Killer.* New York: Harper, 1995. Print.

Douglas, John E., with Mark Olshaker. *Mindhunter: Inside the FBI's Elite Serial Crime Unit.* London: Arrow, 2006. Print.

Holmes, Ronald M., and Stephen T. Holmes. *Profiling Violent Crimes: An Investigative Tool.* 4th ed. Los Angeles: Sage, 2009. Print.

Petherick, Wayne. *Profiling and Serial Crime: Theoretical and Practical Issues.* Burlington: Elsevier, 2013. Digital file.

Ressler, Robert K., and Tom Shachtman. *I Have Lived in the Monster.* New York: St. Martin's, 1998. Print.

Towl, Graham J., and David A. Crighton. *The Handbook of Psychology for Forensic Practitioners.* New York: Routledge, 2006. Print.

Turvey, Brent E., et al. *Criminal Profiling: An Introduction to Behavioral Evidence Analysis.* 4th ed. Oxford; Burlington: Academic, 2012. Print.

Wrightsman, Lawrence S. *Forensic Psychology.* 3d ed. Belmont: Wadsworth, 2009. Print.

Zonderman, Jon. *Beyond the Crime Lab: The New Science of Investigation.* Rev. ed. New York: Wiley, 1999. Print.

Elizabeth D. Schafer

SEE ALSO: Forensic psychology; Law and psychology; Personality theory; Violence: Psychological causes and effects.

Projection

TYPE OF PSYCHOLOGY: Personality

Projective personality traits are often assessed by tests that present ambiguous material to the person being tested; all behavior is included under the definition of personality, and responses to unstructured tests will reveal an individual's needs, wishes, and attitudes. It is assumed that the person will give responses that cannot or will not be given otherwise.

KEY CONCEPTS
- Defense mechanisms
- Projective method
- Psychopathology

INTRODUCTION

The concept of projection goes back to Sigmund Freud, who introduced this term to describe certain psychopathological processes. It was described as a defense mechanism that permits one to be "unaware of undesirable aspects of one's personality by attributing aggressive and/or sexual feelings to others or to the outside world." In that way, one can avoid being aware of those feelings in oneself. Projection is usually described as a defense mechanism whose purpose is to avoid feeling guilty or neurotically anxious. Freud's theory suggested that it was easier to tolerate punishment from the outside than to accept impulses inconsistent with one's self-concept and moral principles. Thus, it is simpler to accuse someone else of hating oneself than it is to admit hating the other person. Defense mechanisms are unconscious processes; one is not likely to admit consciously that one hates someone if one is neurotically anxious. In its extreme forms, Freud noted, distortion of reality can be of such major proportions that perception of the judgment of others takes the form of paranoia.

Freud later extended the use of the term "projection" to include times when there is no conflict. He believed that as one goes through life, memories of past events influence the way one sees the present. Early life experiences shape the future so that, for example, the kind of experiences one had with a brother when growing up influences how one sees "brothers" relate to their families. This leads to the basic assumption that all present responses to one's environment are based, as Albert Rabin put it, on personal needs, motivations, and unique tendencies. All of these are actually based on past experiences. Sheldon Korchin suggested that the weakening of the boundaries between self and others also occurs in empathy, which has been viewed as the opposite of projection. In empathy, one figuratively puts oneself in another person's shoes by accepting and experiencing the feelings of another person. Empathy, therefore, is an important part of establishing close and meaningful relationships with others and is an important aspect of personality.

Leopold Bellak saw projection as the term one uses to describe a greater degree of overall distortion. This is consistent with Freud's original use of the term. He differentiated this pathological and unconscious type of projection, which he called inverted projection, from simple projection. Simple projection occurs all the time and is not of great clinical significance.

For example, a woman wants to borrow her friend's hedge trimmer. As she walks down the block to her friend's house, she thinks about how she is going to ask for the hedge trimmer, since she knows that her friend is not overly enthusiastic about lending his garden tools. She begins to think that her friend might say that it took her a long time to return the trimmer the last time she borrowed it and perhaps that it needed maintenance after she used it. She answers this imagined comment by saying that it rained soon after she started and that she could not finish the job for three days.

She then imagines that her friend will say that she should have returned the trimmer and asked for it again later. She imagines answering that criticism by stating that she knew her friend had gone out of town and would not be back until later in the week. This imaginary conversation might continue until she arrives at her neighbor's house. Her neighbor is on the porch, and he greets her in a friendly manner. Nevertheless, she responds angrily by telling him that she would never want to borrow his old hedge trimmer anyway. Bellak would explain this incident by noting that the woman wants something from her neighbor but can recall his hesitancy to lend tools. He may turn her request down, which makes her angry. She then assumes that her friend is angry with her. Her response is to be angry with him because he is (theoretically) angry with her.

PROJECTIVE HYPOTHESIS AND TECHNIQUES

The projective hypothesis on which projective tests are based states that when one is confronted by an ambiguous stimulus, responses will reflect personal needs, wishes, and overall attitudes toward the outside world. This assumes that all of one's behavior, even the least significant aspects, is an expression of personality. As Anneliese Korner asserted, individuals who are presented with ambiguous material give responses that they cannot or will not give otherwise. The person who responds to projective techniques does not know what the presenter expects. The resistance to disclosing personal material (including wishes, fears, and aspirations) is diminished. In addition, Korner suggested that what is disclosed in response to projective techniques is not a chance event but is determined by previous life experiences.

Among the most widely known tests that use projective techniques are the Rorschach inkblot test and Henry A. Murray's Thematic Apperception Test (TAT). The Rorschach technique consists of ten standard inkblots to which a participant is asked to respond by telling the examiner what the blots look like. The TAT consists of twenty pictures designed to elicit stories that can give important clues to a person's life and personality. The set is sufficiently clear to permit one to tell stories without great difficulty, yet the pictures are ambiguous (unstructured) enough so that individuals will differ in the kinds of stories they will tell.

PROJECTION TESTS AND INTERPRETATIONS

John Exner raised the issue as to whether all responses to a projective technique such as the Rorschach test are necessarily aspects of projection. Is it true, he asked, that more ambiguous stimulus material produces more projection than does less ambiguous material? A simple example may be helpful. An individual might be shown a glass container with sand flowing from one portion of the glass to the other and asked to give this object a name. Most people will call it an egg timer. If, however, a thirty-five-year-old individual embellishes the description of the egg timer by stating that it represents the sands of time and is an indication that life is drawing to a close, that kind of response, in an individual of good health at that age, would seem to be an example of projection. Clearly, however, based on one response, it would be premature to build firm conclusions about this individual's attitudes toward life and death. Similarly, on the Rorschach test, one response descriptive of aggression may not be particularly diagnostic, but there is evidence that those who give higher frequencies of aggression responses show more aggressive verbal and nonverbal behaviors than those who do not.

Exner, in reporting on other studies, points out that Rorschach interpretations can also be useful with children. He noted that children change over time in their responses to the inkblots and that younger children change more than older children. Further, as children move into mid- and late adolescence, more overall stability is noted in the responses. Finally, he pointed out that perceptual accuracy stabilizes early.

A third study asked whether patients in a hospital setting who have experienced a major loss differ from patients who have not suffered such a loss. Mary Cerney defined three categories of major loss: death or serious injury to individuals close to the patient (including parents, close relatives, or friends); loss as a function of physical or sexual abuse such as incest, torture, or rape; and the observation of violence to other individuals. Cerney found differences in the responses between individual patients who had experienced such loss and patients who had not. She concluded that in this study, patients who had experienced early trauma had distinguishing Rorschach profiles. She further noted, however, that one needed further investigations to determine whether factors other than traumatic loss could contribute to this profile difference.

In a study designed to measure change in defense mechanisms following intensive psychotherapy, researchers compared two groups of individuals who were being treated in a small, long-term treatment facility with a psychoanalytic orientation. One group of patients was judged in advance to be composed of prime users of such defense mechanisms as repression and denial, while the other group was judged to comprise people who make much more use of projection. This categorization was based on a thorough evaluation six weeks after admission to the treatment center. After about fifteen months of intensive treatment, patients were evaluated again in a comprehensive manner. The use of defense mechanisms was established on the basis of responses to the TAT. Results indicated that all patients showed a reduction in the total use of defense mechanisms; this was associated with a reduction in psychiatric symptoms. Interestingly, the patients who made use of projection as a defense showed a greater decline in the use of that defense mechanism after treatment. Along with the decrease in psychiatric symptoms, both groups also showed, as one might expect, improved relationships with others from both a qualitative and a quantitative perspective.

APPLICATION TO PERSONALITY TRAITS

Freud also applied the concept of projection to everyday personality traits such as jealousy. He differentiated between normal jealousy, projected jealousy, and delusional jealousy. From a psychoanalytic view, he had little to say about normal jealousy; however, projected jealousy, he stated, came from two sources, either from actual unfaithfulness or from impulses toward unfaithfulness that have been pushed into one's unconscious. He speculated that married individuals are frequently tempted to be unfaithful. In view of that temptation, it is likely that one's conscience can be soothed by attributing unfaithfulness to one's partner. Jealousy arising from such a projection can be so strong as to take on the quality of a delusion. Many people are aware of individuals who incorrectly suspect their committed partner to be unfaithful. Freud would argue that these inaccurate expectations are unconscious fantasies of one's own infidelities and can be so analyzed in psychoanalytic therapy.

EVOLUTION OF RESEARCH

The term "projection" was introduced by Freud in 1894. Initially Freud viewed it as a defensive process, but by 1913 the concept was broadened to refer to a process that may occur even if there is no conflict. Exner believed that Freud's description of projection is most applicable in the context of projective tests. Exner also suggested that Freud's concept of projection fits in well with Murray's discussion of the TAT. Murray's broadened explanation of projection included the idea that the ambiguity of responding to a social situation (the test materials) provides clues to that individual's personality makeup and its expression through responses to projective methods. Projective method refers to any task that provides an open-ended response that may reveal aspects of one's personality; tasks or tests commonly include standard stimuli that are ambiguous in nature. Lawrence Frank further emphasized the connection between projective tests and the unique expression of an individual's personality by stating the projective hypothesis.

Applied psychology has been heavily involved with the study of intelligence and the development of tests to evaluate achievement, memory, motor skills, and other cognitive aspects of human functioning. The study of personality was more heavily focused on individual traits, such as extroversion versus introversion. Emphasis on test construction focused on group norms, and comparisons of individual scores on tests were based on their relationships to group data. According to Exner, early Rorschach research also attempted to focus on group norms. To some extent, the focus on determining the meaning of individual responses was probably a reaction to the more "scientific" behavioral and statistically based methods commonly used.

As Exner noted, initial work with the Rorschach inkblots emphasized attempts to quantify personality characteristics; there was relatively little interest in the actual content of the responses. As interest in psychoanalysis swept the country, clinical psychologists began to focus on individual responses to tests, in contrast to their prior emphasis on group comparisons. Projective tests were very controversial, however, and a dichotomy developed between projective tests and the so-called objective tests. The latter tests were ones that could be scored reliably and for which group norms existed. Concurrently, numerous scoring systems were developed for the Rorschach test as well as for other projective measures.

In the late 1970s, Exner developed a comprehensive scoring system for the Rorschach that incorporated many of the features of the existing systems and integrated them into one overall method. In addition, he collected normative data on children, adolescents, and adults that provide opportunities for group comparisons. His comprehensive system is now widely taught in colleges and universities and has provided a measure of unity to the Rorschach test, which is still the personality instrument most widely used by clinicians. The assessment of personality traits will probably continue to flourish, and there will probably be an increasing emphasis on both subjective and objective responses to assess personality. Furthermore, computerized scoring of responses is common for objective personality tests and is beginning to be used with projective personality measures; this is likely to influence the future of personality tests.

BIBLIOGRAPHY

Aiken, Lewis R. *Assessment of Adult Personality*. New York: Springer, 1997. Print.

Breakwell, Glynis, et al., eds. *Research Methods in Psychology*. 4th ed. Los Angeles: Sage, 2012. Print.

Campos, Rui C. "'It Might Be What I Am': Looking at the Use of Rorschach in Psychological Assessment." *SIS Journal of Projective Psychology and Mental Health* 18.1 (2011): 28–38. Print.

Cronbach, Lee J. *Essentials of Psychological Testing*. 5th ed. New York: Harper, 1990. Print.

Gacono, Carl B., and Barton Evans. *The Handbook of Forensic Rorschach Assessment*. New York: Routledge, 2008. Print.

Leiter, E. "The Role of Projective Testing." *Clinical and Experimental Psychiatry*. Ed. Scott Wetzler and Martin M. Katz. New York: Brunner/Mazel, 1989. Print.

Nathanson, S. "Denial, Projection, and the Empathic Wall." *Denial: A Clarification of Concepts and Research*. Ed. E. L. Edelstein, Donald L. Nathanson, and Andrew M. Stone. New York: Plenum, 1989. Print.

Schott, G. D. "Revisiting the Rorschach Ink-Blots: From Iconography and Psychology to Neuroscience." *Journal of Neurology, Neurosurgery and Psychiatry* 86.6 (2014): 699–706. Print.

Walsh, W. Bruce, and Nancy E. Betz. *Tests and Assessments*. 4th ed. Englewood Cliffs: Prentice, 2001. Print.

Norman Abeles

SEE ALSO: Abnormality: Psychological models; Clinical interviewing, testing, and observation; Defense mechanisms; Ego defense mechanisms; Murray, Henry A.; Personality interviewing strategies; Personology: Henry A. Murray; Psychoanalytic psychology and personality: Sigmund Freud; Rorschach inkblots; Thematic Apperception Test (TAT).

Psychoanalysis

DATE: 1880's forward

TYPE OF PSYCHOLOGY: Developmental psychology; Psychological methodologies; Psychotherapy

Psychoanalysis is a form of intensive psychotherapy to treat emotional suffering, based on the concept that people are often unaware of what determines their emotions and behavior. By talking freely, while in an intensive relationship with the psychoanalyst, a person is able to overcome worries that may have limited his or her choices in life. Psychoanalysis is also a comprehensive theory of the mind and a method for understanding everyday behavior.

KEY CONCEPTS
- Anxiety
- Certification
- Countertransference
- Depression
- Free association
- Inhibitions
- Psychoanalyst
- Psychoanalytic institutes
- Psychoanalytic psychotherapy
- Psychotherapy
- Symptoms
- Transference
- Unconscious

INTRODUCTION

Psychoanalysis began as a method for treating emotional suffering. Sigmund Freud, the founder of psychoanalysis, working at the beginning of the twentieth century, made many discoveries by studying patients with symptoms such as excessive anxiety (fear that is not realistic) or paralysis for which no physical cause could be found. He became the first psychoanalyst (often called analyst) when he developed the method of free association, Free association in which he encouraged his patients to say whatever came to mind about their symptoms and their lives. He found that by talking in this way, his patients discovered feelings and thoughts they had not known they had. When they became aware of these unconscious thoughts and feelings, their symptoms lessened or disappeared.

Psychoanalysis as a form of psychotherapy continues to be an effective method for treating certain forms of emotional suffering, such as anxieties and inhibitions (inner constraints) that interfere with success in school, work, or relationships. It is based on the understanding that each individual is unique, that the past shapes the present, and that factors outside people's awareness influence their thoughts, feelings, and actions. As a comprehensive treatment, it has the potential to change many areas of a person's functioning. Although modern psychoanalysis is different in many ways from what was practiced in Freud's era, talking and listening remain important. Psychoanalytic psychotherapy is a modified form of psychoanalysis, usually with less frequent meetings and more modest goals.

From the beginning, psychoanalysis was more than just a treatment. It was, and continues to be, a method for investigating the mind and a theory to explain both everyday adult behavior as well as child development. Many of Freud's insights, which seemed so revolutionary at the beginning of the twentieth century, are now widely accepted by various schools of psychological thought and form the basis for several theories of psychological motivation, most theories of child development, and all forms of psychodynamic psychotherapy. Some of Freud's ideas, such as his theories about women, turned out to be wrong and were revised by other psychoanalysts during the 1970's and 1980's. Other ideas, such as those about the nature of dreams, although rejected by some scientists during the 1980's and 1990's, were returned to by other scientists by the beginning of the twenty-first century. Psychoanalytic ideas and concepts are used in communities to solve problems such as bullying in schools and can be applied in many other fields of study.

In the early years of psychoanalysis, Freud trained most psychoanalysts. Later, different schools of psychoanalytic thought branched out from this original source. Groups of psychoanalysts joined together in organizations, and each organization developed its own standards for training psychoanalysts. There were no nationally accepted standards for psychoanalytic training in the United States until the beginning of the twenty-first century, when several of these groups joined together to establish the Accreditation Council of Psychoanalytic Education. This council agreed to core standards for psychoanalytic institutes (schools that train psychoanalysts). Psychoanalytic psychotherapy, while practiced by trained psychoanalysts, is also practiced by psychotherapists who are not trained as psychoanalysts.

PSYCHOANALYTIC TREATMENT

Psychoanalysis is a method for helping people with symptoms that result from emotional conflict. Common symptoms in the modern era include anxiety (fear that is not realistic), depression (excessive sadness that is not due to a current loss), frequent unhealthy choices in relationships, and trouble getting along well with peers or family members. For example, some people may feel continuously insecure and worried about doing well in school or work despite getting good grades or reviews. Other people may be attracted to sexual and emotional partners who treat them poorly. Others may experience loneliness and isolation because of fears about close relationships. Others may sabotage their success by always changing direction before reaching their goals. Children may have tantrums beyond the age when these are normal, or be afraid of going to sleep every night, or feel unhappy with their maleness or femaleness.

The same symptom can have several different causes, an etiology Freud termed overdetermination. For example, depression may be due to inner emotional constraints that prevent success, to biological vulnerability, or to upsetting events (such as the death of a loved one), or it may result from a combination of these. Therefore, most psychoanalysts believe in meeting with a person several times before deciding on the best treatment. Psychoanalysis is not for everyone who has a symptom. Sometimes psychoanalysis is not needed because the problems can be easily helped by other, less intensive forms of therapy. Sometimes biological problems or early childhood experiences leave a person too vulnerable to undertake the hard work of psychoanalysis. When psychoanalysis is not necessary, or not the best treatment for a particular person, a psychoanalyst may recommend psychoanalytic psychotherapy, a treatment that is based on the same principles as psychoanalysis but with less ambitious goals and, usually, less frequent sessions.

Psychoanalysis can treat specific emotional disorders, as described in the *Diagnostic and Statistical Manual of Mental Disorders: DSM-IV-TR* (rev. 4th ed., 2000), but can also help with multiple sets of problematic symptoms, behaviors, and personality traits (such as being too perfectionistic or rigid). Since psychoanalysis affects the whole person rather than just treating symptoms, it has the potential to promote personal growth and development. For adults, this can mean better relationships or marriages, jobs that feel more satisfying, or the ability to enjoy free time when this was difficult before. Children may do better in school after fears about competition and success diminish, or they may have more friends and get along better with parents after they begin to feel better about themselves.

Because psychoanalysis is a very individual treatment, the best way to determine whether it would be beneficial for an individual is through consulting an experienced psychoanalyst. In general, people who benefit from psychoanalysis have some emotional sturdiness. They tend to be capable of understanding themselves and learning how to help themselves. Usually, they have had important accomplishments in one or more areas of their lives before seeking psychoanalytic treatment. Often, they have tried other forms of treatment that may have been helpful but have not been sufficient to deal with all their difficulties. Sometimes they are people who work with others (therapists, rabbis, teachers) whose emotions have been interfering with their ability to do their jobs as well as possible. Whatever the problems, psychoanalysts understand them in the context of each individual's strengths, vulnerabilities, and life situation.

METHOD OF TREATMENT IN PSYCHOANALYSIS

A person who goes to a psychoanalyst for consultation usually meets with the analyst at least three times face-to-face before the analyst recommends psychoanalysis. Sometimes the patient and analyst meet for several weeks, months, or years in psychoanalytic psychotherapy; they decide on psychoanalysis if they identify problems that are unlikely to be solved by less intensive treatment.

Once they begin psychoanalysis, the analyst and patient usually meet four or five times per week for fifty-minute sessions, as this creates the intensive personal relationship that plays an important role in the therapeutic process. The frequent sessions do not mean that the patient is very sick; they are necessary to help the patient reach deeper levels of awareness. (People with the severest forms of mental illness, such as schizophrenia, are not usually treated with psychoanalysis.) Often the adult patient lies on a couch, as this may make it easier to speak freely. The couch is not essential, and some patients feel more comfortable sitting up.

By working together to diminish obstacles to free expression in the treatment sessions, the analyst and patient come to understand the patient's worries and learn how the patient's mind works. The patient learns about thoughts and feelings he or she has kept out of awareness or isolated from each other. Through the intensity that comes from frequent meetings with the analyst, the patient often experiences the analyst as if the analyst were a parent or other important person from the past. This is called transference. Eventually, the patient has a chance to see these feelings from a more mature point of view. Although the patient may experience intense emotions within the analytic sessions, the anxieties and behaviors that brought him or her to treatment gradually diminish and feel more under control. The patient feels freer and less restricted by worries and patterns that belong to the past.

For example, a patient may be very fearful of angry feelings and avoid telling the analyst about them, expecting punishment or rejection. As a result, the patient may turn the anger on himself or herself in a form of self-sabotage. Often this is the way the patient dealt with angry feelings toward significant people while growing up. Over time, as the patient and analyst understand this behavior, the patient feels freer to express angry feelings directly and eventually feels less need to sabotage or self-punish.

Gradually, in the course of the intensive analytic relationship, the patient learns more about his or her maladaptive ways of dealing with distressing thoughts and feelings that have developed during childhood. By understanding them in adulthood or (for a child) at a later age, the patient gains a different perspective and is able to react in a more adaptive way. Rigid personality traits that had been used to keep the childhood feelings at a distance are no longer necessary, and the patient is able to react to people and situations in a more flexible way.

During the course of the treatment, the analyst will often have strong feelings toward the patient, called countertransference. Well-trained analysts are required to undergo psychoanalysis themselves before treating patients. In their own analysis, they learn how to cope with their countertransference feelings in ways that will not hurt the patient. For example, they learn not to take the patient's expressions of anger personally but to help the patient express the emotion more fully and understand where it originates.

Children and adolescents can be treated with psychoanalysis or psychoanalytic psychotherapy by using methods suitable for their ages. Most children play with toys, draw, or explore the room, in addition to talking, during their sessions with the analyst, and these activities provide ways to explore inner thoughts and feelings. The analyst meets with the parents before the treatment starts and continues to do so regularly during the course of the child's therapy or analysis. Adolescents usually sit face-to-face or draw or write about their feelings and worries. Occasionally, older adolescents want to lie on the couch. Adolescents often prefer that the analyst not meet with the parents on a regular basis. Instead, the analyst and adolescent usually develop some way to keep the parents informed about what they might need to know about the treatment.

PSYCHOANALYTIC PSYCHOTHERAPY

Psychoanalytic psychotherapy is more varied than psychoanalysis. It may be very intensive, or it may be focused on a specific problem, such as a recent loss or trouble deciding about a job. In psychoanalytic psychotherapy, the patient and therapist usually sit face-to-face and approach the patient's problems, whatever they are, in a more interactive way. Most often, patient and therapist meet twice per week in fifty-minute sessions. Once per week is also common but not considered to be as helpful. More frequent meetings (three to five times per week) may be necessary if the patient is in crisis or has chronic problems that are not treatable with psychoanalysis.

Although psychoanalysts are well trained to practice psychoanalytic psychotherapy, this treatment is also practiced by psychotherapists who are not psychoanalysts. Some of these therapists have taken courses at psychoanalytic institutes.

MEDICATION AND CONFIDENTIALITY ISSUES

In the early days of psychoanalysis, analysts believed that treatment with medication would interfere with psychoanalysis. Most modern psychoanalysts believe that, although medicine can sometimes interfere, there are times when it can be used in a helpful way in combination with psychoanalytic psychotherapy or even with psychoanalysis.

"Confidentiality" is the term used to describe the privacy necessary for individuals to be able to speak freely about all their thoughts and feelings. Responsible psychoanalysts and psychotherapists agree to keep private everything about their patients, including the fact that the patient has come for treatment, unless the patient gives permission to release some specific information. One exception is when patients are at risk for hurting themselves or someone else. In *Jaffe v. Redmond* (1995), the U.S. Supreme Court confirmed that confidentiality is necessary for the patient to speak freely in psychotherapy.

TRAINING AND QUALIFICATIONS FOR PSYCHOANALYSTS

The International Psychoanalytic Association (IPA), formed during Freud's lifetime, is a worldwide organization of psychoanalysts that remained in place throughout the twentieth century. The American Psychoanalytic Association (APsaA) was founded in 1911 and grew to three thousand members during the course of the twentieth century. All its members also belonged to the IPA. Many schools for psychoanalysts, or psychoanalytic institutes, were accredited (examined and found to meet a set of standards) by APsaA over the years. APsaA also developed an examination called certification to test graduate psychoanalysts.

Because the first psychoanalysts in the United States believed that psychoanalysis would be more highly valued if connected with the medical profession, the APsaA initially accepted only psychiatrists (who are medical doctors) as members. Exceptions were made for professionals who applied to train as researchers. This contrasted with the practice in Europe, where many nonmedical psychoanalysts became members of the IPA. Nonmedical professionals, such as psychologists and social workers, who wanted to become psychoanalysts in the United States often trained in psychoanalytic institutes not recognized by the APsaA. Some were recognized by the IPA and later banded together under the name of the International Psychoanalytic Societies (IPS). Other institutes developed outside both organizations, sometimes creating their own standards for training. By the last quarter of the twentieth century, nonmedical mental health professionals (such as psychologists and social workers) were accepted as members of APsaA and grew in numbers, becoming a large proportion of the membership.

Because the title "psychoanalyst" was not protected by federal or state law in the twentieth century, anyone, even untrained, could call himself or herself a psychoanalyst in the United States. Many institutes developed in large cities, such as New York and Los Angeles, that were not connected with APsaA or IPS and admitted trainees with varying backgrounds and qualifications. Some of these defined psychoanalysis in their own way, so that arguments developed about the dividing line between psychoanalysis and psychoanalytic psychotherapy. The American Psychological Association eventually developed its own examination to qualify a psychologist as a psychoanalyst.

TRAINING IN THE TWENTY-FIRST CENTURY

Since, by the beginning of the twenty-first century, no laws were yet in place in the United States to define who could practice psychoanalysis, it remained difficult for the public to tell who was qualified. In the late 1990's, several national organizations of the core mental health disciplines came together in a coalition called the Consortium for Psychoanalysis. By the turn of the century, they had agreed on baseline standards that would be used to develop a national organization to accredit psychoanalytic institutes. These organizations were the American Psychoanalytic Association, the division of psychoanalysis of the American Psychological Association, the National Membership Committee on Psychoanalysis in Clinical Social Work, and the American Academy of Psychoanalysis.

Trained psychoanalysts in the twenty-first century who meet these standards already have a mental health degree, except in unusual cases, before becoming psychoanalysts. Once accepted for training at a psychoanalytic institute, these mental health professionals study many more years to become qualified psychoanalysts. They take courses and treat patients while supervised by experienced psychoanalysts. In addition, they are required to undergo psychoanalysis themselves to gain enough self-knowledge to keep their own problems from interfering with the treatment of patients.

PSYCHOANALYSIS AS A THEORY

All psychoanalytic theories are based on the idea that people are motivated by thoughts and feelings outside their awareness, that the past influences the present, and that each individual is unique. Because so much change and growth have occurred since Freud's era, psychoanalysis is no longer a single theory but encompasses many different theories. All psychoanalytic theories are theories of motivation (what makes people do what they do), theories of development (how people get to be the way they are), and theories of change (how psychoanalytic treatment works). Psychoanalytic theories are usually also theories of personality development (who people are) and personality disturbance.

Most theories emphasize the complexity of each person's symptoms and behavior and take into account many different influences. For example, the psychoanalytic theory called ego psychology describes development as a complex interaction of biology (inborn factors) and experience over time. Early childhood experiences are especially important because they influence the way a person's ability to cope with the world (ego functioning) develops. Each person adapts to the environment in a unique way that gradually becomes more consistent by the time the person grows to adulthood.

Psychoanalytic theories are comprehensive theories of mental functioning and disorder. For this reason, they originally formed the basis for the diagnosis and classification of mental disorders in the United States—DSM-I in 1952 and DSM-II in 1968. Many changes and developments took place in psychoanalytic theory during the second half of the twentieth century. The greatest change took place in theories about psychotic illness, female psychology, homosexuality, and the nature of the patient/analyst relationship. By the turn of the century, it was unusual to find, in real life, the silent analysts who were still sometimes created in films and cartoons.

Because of their complexity, psychoanalytic theories are more difficult to study and test than other theories. For example, Freud believed that dreams have meaning and are based on the fulfillment of unconscious wishes. Neuroscientists dismissed this theory for many years because it could not be demonstrated. Behavioral psychologists, who based their theories on observable behavior, did not consider thoughts and feelings outside a person's awareness to be important. Because of the emphasis on experimental testing and the increasing public expectation for quick cures during the last quarter of the twentieth century, psychoanalytic theories became less popular. The DSM-III, the third edition of the diagnostic manual for mental disorders which came out in 1980, was based on categories of symptoms and behaviors, without any reference to underlying theory. The categories of mental disturbance in DSM-III (and later, in 1994's DSM-IV) were described in a way that would be easy to test in controlled experiments. People, and particularly insurance companies, became more interested in medicines and short-term treatments for symptoms and were less willing to pay for treatments such as psychoanalysis that address the whole person.

Toward the end of the twentieth century and the beginning of the twenty-first, cognitive scientists (scientists who study the way people think) and neuroscientists (scientists who study the way the brain works) began to make discoveries that proved psychoanalytic theory to be correct in some important areas. For example, cognitive scientists proved that much of mental functioning goes on outside a person's awareness. Mark Solms, a neuroscientist, proved that dreams are formed in the part of the brain that deals with motivation and emotional meaning. Psychoanalysts began a dialogue with neuroscientists and cognitive scientists. Although some psychoanalysts thought psychoanalysis could not be studied experimentally in the same way as shorter-term therapies, others began to publicize studies demonstrating the effectiveness of psychoanalysis and psychoanalytic psychotherapy. Others began to develop further ways to study psychoanalytic theory and treatment.

PSYCHOANALYTIC THEORY APPLICATIONS

Psychoanalytic ideas have been applied in many fields of study. For example, psychoanalytic theories about loss and mourning have been used to help inner-city children cope with their reactions to losses in mourning groups. Psychoanalytic ideas about power and helplessness have been used in schools to decrease violence by changing the atmosphere in which bullies can thrive. Psychoanalytic ideas led to the concept of social and emotional learning whereby educators have demonstrated that intelligence is not just based on the ability to think but includes emotions and social abilities. Psychoanalytic ideas have been used in the study of literature to understand characters such as Hamlet and Othello. They have been used in the study of culture to understand terrorists and the cultures that support them. Psychoanalysts apply psychoanalytic theories in the help they offer to day care centers, businesses, diplomats, police officers, firefighters, rabbis, priests, and others.

BIBLIOGRAPHY

Brenner, Charles. *An Elementary Textbook of Psychoanalysis*. Rev. ed. New York: Anchor Press/Doubleday, 1994. This book introduces interested readers to the fundamentals of psychoanalysis, explaining core psychoanalytic concepts in clear language.

Gabbard, Glenn. *Psychodynamic Psychiatry in Clinical Practice, DSM-IV Edition*. 4th ed. Washington, D.C.: American Psychiatric Press, 2005. This is a textbook that approaches DSM-IV from a psychoanalytic point of view. It includes an introductory section describing psychodynamic principles and then sections describing Axis I and Axis II disorders from a psychodynamic perspective.

Gay, Peter. *Freud: A Life for Our Time*. 1988. Reprint. New York: W. W. Norton, 2006. This biography of Freud was written by his physician. It describes the history of psychoanalysis during Freud's lifetime.

Vaughan, Susan. *The Talking Cure: The Science Behind Psychotherapy*. New York: Henry Holt, 1998. This book is written for people who may want to visit a psychoanalyst or who want to learn about models of mind and brain that integrate psychoanalytic theories with other scientific theories. It includes several descriptions of what happens when patients visit psychoanalysts.

Wallerstein, R. S. *The Talking Cures: The Psychoanalyses and the Psychotherapies*. New Haven, Conn.: Yale University Press, 1995. This book provides a comprehensive history of psychoanalytic thought, including a detailed view of trends and developments in psychoanalysis from the 1940's onward. It describes conflicting and compatible psychoanalytic theories and the debate about the dividing line between psychoanalysis and psychotherapy.

Weiner, Irving B., and Robert F. Bornstein. *Principles of Psychotherapy: Promoting Evidence-Based Psychodynamic Practice*. 3d ed. Hoboken, N.J.: John Wiley & Sons, 2009. A comprehensive textbook that provides guidelines for delivering effective psychotherapy. Especially helpful are case examples that demonstrate the approach a therapist might take with a patient in certain situations.

Judith M. Chertoff

SEE ALSO: Adler, Alfred; American Psychiatric Association; American Psychological Association; Analytic psychology: Jacques Lacan; Analytical psychology: Carl Jung; Analytical psychotherapy; Brief therapy; Confidentiality; Ego psychology: Erik H. Erikson; Erikson, Erik H.; Freud, Sigmund; Freudian psychology; Fromm, Erich; Horney, Karen; Individual psychology: Alfred Adler; Jung, Carl; Jungian psychology; Psychoanalytic psychology; Psychoanalytic psychology and personality: Sigmund Freud; Psychotherapy: Historical approaches; Social psychological models: Erich Fromm; Social psychological models: Karen Horney; Women's psychology: Sigmund Freud.

Psychoanalytic psychology

TYPE OF PSYCHOLOGY: Origin and definition of psychology

Psychoanalytic and neoanalytic schools of thought provide explanations of human and neurotic behavior. Each of these models contributes to the understanding of personality development and psychological conflict by presenting unique theoretical conceptualizations, assessment techniques, research methodologies, and psychotherapeutic strategies for personality change.

KEY CONCEPTS
- Analytic psychology
- Dynamic cultural schools of psychoanalysis
- Individual psychology
- Neoanalytic psychology
- Psychoanalytic psychology
- Psychosocial theory

INTRODUCTION

One grand theory in psychology that dramatically revolutionized the way in which personality and its formation were viewed is psychoanalysis. Orthodox psychoanalysis and later versions of this model offer several unique perspectives of personality development, assessment, and change.

The genius of Sigmund Freud, the founder of psychoanalysis, is revealed in the magnitude of his achievements and the monumental scope of his works. Over the course of his lifetime, Freud developed a theory of personality and psychopathology (disorders of psychological functioning that include major as well as minor mental disorders and behavior disorders), a method for probing the realm of the unconscious, and a therapy for dealing with personality disorders. He posited that an individual is motivated by unconscious forces that are instinctual in nature. The two major instinctual forces are the life instincts, or eros, and the death instinct, or thanatos. Their source is biological tension whose aim is tension reduction through a variety of objects. Freud viewed personality as a closed system composed of three structures: the id, the ego, and the superego. The irrational id consists of the biological drives and libido, or psychic energy. It operates according to the pleasure principle, which seeks the immediate gratification of needs. The rational ego serves as the executive component of personality and the mediator among the demands of the id, the superego, and the environment. Governed by the reality principle, it seeks to postpone the gratification of needs. The superego, or moral arm of personality, consists of the conscience (internalized values) and the ego ideal (that which the person aspires to be).

According to Freud, the origins of personality are embedded in the first seven years of life. Personality develops through a sequence of psychosexual stages that each focus on an area of the body (erogenous zone) that gives pleasure to the individual; they are the oral, anal, phallic, latency, and genital stages. The frustration or overindulgence of needs contributes to a fixation, or arrest in development at a particular stage.

Freud also developed a therapy for treating individuals experiencing personality disturbances. Psychoanalysis has shown how physical disorders have psychological roots, how unbearable anxiety generates conflict, and how problems in adulthood result from early childhood experiences. In therapy, Freud surmounted his challenge to reveal the hidden nature of the unconscious by exposing the resistances and transferences of his patients. His method for probing a patient's unconscious thoughts, motives, and feelings was based on the use of many clinical techniques. Free association, dream interpretation, analyses of slips of the tongue, misplaced objects, and humor enabled him to discover the contents of an individual's unconscious mind and open the doors to a new and grand psychology of personality.

RESPONSES TO FREUDIAN THEORY

The theory of psychosocial development of Erik H. Eriksonoccupies a position between orthodox psychoanalysis and neoanalytic schools of thought. His theory builds on the basic concepts and tenets of Freudian psychology by illustrating the influential role of social and cultural forces in personality development. Erikson's observations of infants and investigations of the parent-child relationship in various societies contributed to his development of the model of the eight stages of human development. He proposed that personality unfolds over the entire life cycle according to a predetermined plan. As an individual moves through this series of stages, he or she encounters periods of vulnerability that require him or her to resolve crises of a social nature and develop new abilities and patterns of behavior. Erikson's eight psychosocial stages not only parallel Freud's psychosexual ones but also, more important, have contributed immensely to contemporary thought in developmental psychology.

Several other schools of thought arose in opposition to Freudian orthodoxy. Among the proponents of these new psychoanalytic models were Carl Jung, Alfred Adler, Karen Horney, and Harry Stack Sullivan. These theorists advocated revised versions of Freud's psychoanalytic model and became known as the neoanalysts.

JUNG'S APPROACH

Carl Jung's analytical psychology stresses the complex interaction of opposing forces within the total personality (psyche) and the manner in which these inner conflicts influence development. Personality is driven by general life process energy, called libido. It operates according to the principle of opposites, for example, a contrast between conscious and unconscious. An individual's behavior is seen as a means to some end, whose goal is to create a balance between these polar opposites through a process of self-realization. Personality is composed of several regions, including the ego (a unifying force at the center of consciousness), the personal unconscious (experiences blocked from consciousness), and the collective unconscious (inherited predispositions of ancestral experiences). The major focus of Jung's theory is the collective unconscious, with its archetypes (primordial thoughts and images), persona (public self), anima/animus (feminine and masculine components), shadow (repulsive side of the personality), and self (an archetype reflecting a person's striving for personality integration). Jung further proposed two psychological attitudes that the personality could use in relating to the world: introversion and extroversion. He also identified four functions of thought: sensing, thinking, feeling, and intuiting. Eight different personality types emerge when one combines these attitudes and functions. Like Freud, Jung proposed developmental stages: childhood, young adulthood, and middle age. Through the process of individuation, a person seeks to create an inner harmony that results in self-realization. In conjunction with dream analysis, Jung used painting therapy and a word-association test to disclose underlying conflicts in patients. Therapy helped patients to reconcile the conflicting sides of their personalities and experience self-realization.

ADLER'S APPROACH

The individual psychology of Alfred Adler illustrates the significance of social variables in personality development and the uniqueness of the individual. Adler proposed that an individual seeks to compensate for inborn feelings of inferiority by striving for superiority. It is lifestyle that helps a person achieve future goals, ideals, and superiority. Adler extended this theme of perfection to society by using the concept of social interest to depict the human tendency to create a productive society. He maintained that early childhood experiences play a crucial role in the development of a person's unique lifestyle. An individual lacking in social interest develops a mistaken lifestyle (for example, an inferiority complex). Physical inferiority as well as spoiling or pampering and neglecting children contributes to the development of faulty lifestyles. Adler examined dreams, birth order, and first memories to trace the origins of lifestyle and goals. These data were used in Adlerian psychotherapy to help the person create a new lifestyle oriented toward social interest.

HORNEY'S APPROACH

Karen Horney's social and cultural psychoanalysis considers the influence of social and cultural forces on the development and maintenance of neurosis. Her theory focuses on disturbed human relationships, especially between parents and children. She discussed several negative factors, such as parental indifference, erratic behavior, and unkept promises, which contributed to basic anxiety in children. This basic anxiety led to certain defenses or neurotic needs. Horney proposed ten neurotic needs that are used to reestablish safety. She further summarized these needs into three categories that depicted the individual's adjustment to others: moving toward people (compliant person), moving against people (aggressive person), and moving away from people (detached person). Horney believed that neurosis occurs when an individual lives according to his or her ideal rather than real self. She also wrote a number of articles on feminine psychology that stressed the importance of cultural rather than biological factors in personality formation. Like Freud, she used the techniques of transference, dream analysis, and free association in her psychotherapy; however, the goal of therapy was to help an individual overcome his or her idealized neurotic self and become more real as he or she experienced self-realization.

SULLIVAN'S APPROACH

Harry Stack Sullivan's interpersonal theory examines personality from the perspective of the interpersonal

relationships that have influenced it, especially the mother-infant relationship. Sullivan believed that this relationship contributed to an individual's development of a "good me," "bad me," or "not me" personification of self. He also proposed six stages of development: infancy, childhood, juvenile epoch, preadolescence, early adolescence, and late adolescence. These stages illustrate an individual's experiences and need for intimacy with significant others. Overall, his theory emphasizes the importance of interpersonal relations, the appraisals of others toward an individual, and the need to achieve interpersonal security and avoid anxiety.

USE OF CASE STUDIES

Psychoanalytic psychology and its later versions have been used to explain normal and abnormal personality development. Regardless of their perspectives, psychologists in all these schools have relied on the case study method to communicate their theoretical insights and discoveries.

The theoretical roots of orthodox psychoanalysis may be traced to the famous case of Anna O., a patient under the care of Josef Breuer, Freud's friend and colleague. Fascinated with the hysterical symptoms of this young girl and with Breuer's success in using catharsis (the talking cure) with her, Freud asked Breuer to collaborate on a work entitled *Studien über Hysterie* (1895; *Studies in Hysteria*, 1950) and discuss his findings. It was the world's first book on psychoanalysis, containing information on the unconscious, defenses, sexual cause of neurosis, resistance, and transference. Freud's own self-analysis and analyses of family members and other patients further contributed to the changing nature of his theory. Among his great case histories are "Dora" (hysteria), "Little Hans" (phobia), the "Rat Man" (obsessional neurosis), "Schreiber" (paranoia), and "Wolf Man" (infantile neurosis). His method of treatment, psychoanalysis, is also well documented in contemporary cases, such as the treatment for multiple personality described in the book *Sybil* (1974).

In his classic work *Childhood and Society* (1950), Erikson discussed the applicability of the clinical method of psychoanalysis and the case-history technique to normal development in children. His case analyses of the Sioux and Yurok Indians and his observations of children led to the creation of a psychosocial theory of development that emphasized the significant role played by one's culture. Moreover, Erikson's psychohistorical accounts, *Young Man Luther: A Study in Psychoanalysis and History* (1958) and *Gandhi's Truth on the Origins of Militant Nonviolence* (1969), illustrated the applications of clinical analyses to historical and biographical research so prominent today.

The founders of other psychoanalytic schools of thought have similarly shown that their theories can best be understood in the context of the therapeutic situations and in the writings of case histories. Harold Greenwald's *Great Cases in Psychoanalysis* (1959) is an excellent source of original case histories written by Freud, Jung, Adler, Horney, and Sullivan. Jung's case of "The Anxious Young Woman and the Retired Business Man" clarifies the differences and similarities between his theory and Freud's psychoanalytic model. In "The Drive for Superiority," Adler uses material from several cases to illustrate the themes of lifestyle, feelings of inferiority, and striving for superiority. Horney's case of "The Ever Tired Editor" portrays her use of the character analysis method; that is, she concentrates on the way in which a patient characteristically functions. Sullivan's case of "The Inefficient Wife" sheds some light on the manner in which professional advice may be given to another (student) practitioner. In retrospect, all these prominent theorists have exposed their independent schools of thought through case histories. Even today, this method continues to be used to explain human behavior and to enhance understanding of personality functioning.

EVOLUTION OF STUDY

Historically, the evolution of psychoanalytic psychology originated with Freud's clinical observations of the work conducted by the famous French neurologist Jean-Martin Charcot and his collaborations on the treatment of hysteria neurosis with Breuer. The publication of *Studies in Hysteria* marked the birth of psychoanalysis since it illustrated a theory of hysteria, a therapy of catharsis, and an analysis of unconscious motivation. Between 1900 and 1920, Freud made innumerable contributions to the field. His major clinical discoveries were contained in the publications *Die Traumdeutung* (1900; *The Interpretation of Dreams*, 1913) and *Drei Abhandlungen zur Sexualtheorie* (1905; *Three Contributions to the Sexual Theory*, 1910; also translated as *Three Essays on the Theory of Sexuality*, 1949) as well as in various papers on therapy, case histories, and applications to everyday life. During this time, Freud began his international correspondence with people such as Jung. He also invited a select group of individuals to his home for evening discussions; these meetings were known as the psychological Wednesday

society. Eventually, these meetings led to the establishment of the Vienna Psychoanalytical Society, with Adler as its president, and the First International Psychoanalytical Congress, with Jung as its president. In 1909, Freud, Jung, and others were invited by President G. Stanley Hall of Clark University to come to the United States to deliver a series of introductory lectures on psychoanalysis. This momentous occasion acknowledged Freud's achievements and gave him international recognition. In subsequent years, Freud reformulated his theory and demonstrated how psychoanalysis could be applied to larger social issues.

Trained in psychoanalysis by Freud's daughter Anna Freud, Erikson followed in Sigmund Freud's footsteps by supporting and extending his psychosexual theory of development with eight stages of psychosocial identity. Among the members of the original psychoanalytic group, Adler was the first to defect from the Freudian school, in 1911. Protesting Freud's theory of the Oedipus complex, Adler founded his own individual psychology. Two years later, in 1913, Jung parted company with Freud to establish analytical psychology; he objected to Freud's belief that all human behavior stems from sex. With Horney's publications *New Ways in Psychoanalysis* (1939) and *Our Inner Conflicts: A Constructive Theory of Neurosis* (1945), it became quite clear that her ideas only remotely resembled Freud's. Objecting to a number of Freud's major tenets, she attributed the development of neurosis and the psychology of being feminine to social, cultural, and interpersonal influences. Similarly, Sullivan extended psychoanalytic psychology to interpersonal phenomena, arguing that the foundations of human nature and development are not biological but rather cultural and social.

ACCOMPLISHMENTS AND INFLUENCE

The accomplishments of Freud and his followers are truly remarkable. The creative genius of each theorist spans a lifetime of effort and work. The magnitude of their achievements is shown in their efforts to provide new perspectives on personality development and psychopathology, theories of motivation, psychotherapeutic methods of treatment, and methods for describing the nature of human behavior. Clearly, these independent schools of thought have had a profound influence not only on the field of psychology but also on art, religion, anthropology, sociology, and literature. Undoubtedly, they will continue to serve as the cornerstone of personality theory and provide the foundation for new and challenging theories of tomorrow—theories that seek to discover the true nature of what it means to be human.

BIBLIOGRAPHY

Adler, Alfred. *Social Interest: A Challenge to Mankind.* New York: Capricorn, 1964. Print.

Erikson, Erik H. *Identity, Youth, and Crisis.* New York: Norton, 1994. Print.

Freud, Sigmund. *A General Introduction to Psychoanalysis.* New York: Norton, 1977. Print.

Gabbard, Glen O., Bonnie E. Litowitz, and Paul Williams. *Textbook of Psychoanalysis.* 2nd ed. Washington: American Psychiatric, 2012.

Greenwald, Harold, ed. *Great Cases in Psychoanalysis.* New York: Aronson, 1973. Print.

Horney, Karen. *The Neurotic Personality of Our Time.* New York: Routledge, 1999. Print.

Mitchell, Stephen A. *Freud and Beyond: A History of Modern Psychoanalytic Thought.* New York: Basic, 1996. Print.

Ricoeur, Paul. *On Psychoanalysis.* Malden: Polity, 2012. Print.

Safran, Jeremy D. *Psychoanalysis and Psychoanalytic Therapies.* Washington: APA, 2011. Print.

Sullivan, Harry Stack. *The Interpersonal Theory of Psychiatry.* New York: Routledge, 2001. Print.

Joan Bartczak Cannon

SEE ALSO: Adler, Alfred; Analytical psychology: Carl Jung; Case study methodologies; Defense mechanisms; Dreams; Ego defense mechanisms; Ego psychology: Erik H. Erikson; Erikson, Erik H.; Freudian psychology; Fromm, Erich; Hall, G. Stanley; Horney, Karen; Individual psychology: Alfred Adler; Jung, Carl; Jungian psychology; Psychoanalysis; Psychoanalytic psychology and personality: Sigmund Freud; Psychosexual development; Psychotherapy: Effectiveness; Social psychological models: Erich Fromm; Social psychological models: Karen Horney; Women's psychology: Karen Horney; Women's psychology: Sigmund Freud.

Psychoanalytic psychology and personality
Sigmund Freud

TYPE OF PSYCHOLOGY: Personality

Freud's theory of personality, emphasizing unconscious motivation, sexual instincts, and psychological conflict, is one of the most profound and unique contributions in psychology. Freud described both the normal and abnormal personality, and he proposed a therapy for the treatment of mental problems.

KEY CONCEPTS
- Anal stage
- Ego
- Genital stage
- Id
- Instincts
- Latency
- Oedipal conflict
- Oral stage
- Phallic stage
- Superego

INTRODUCTION

Sigmund Freud saw people as engaged in a personal struggle between their instinctual urges and the requirements of society. This conflict often takes place outside one's awareness, in the unconscious, and affects all aspects of people's lives. The instinctual energy that fuels the mind has its source in the unconscious. It is highly mobile, and, once engaged, it must achieve expression, however disguised the expression might be.

Freud likened the mind to an iceberg in that most of the mind is below the level of awareness—in the unconscious—as most of the mass of an iceberg is below the surface of the water. The id, the most primitive structure in the mind, is in the unconscious. The id is composed of the instincts (psychological representations of biological needs, they are the source of all psychological energy), including the sexual and other life instincts and the aggressive and other death instincts. For Freud, the sexual instincts were particularly important. They take a long time to develop, and society has a large investment in their regulation.

The instincts press for gratification, but the id itself cannot satisfy them, because it has no contact with reality. Therefore, the ego, which contacts the id in the unconscious but also is partly conscious, develops. The ego can perceive reality and direct behavior to satisfy the id's urges. To the extent that the ego can satisfy the id's instincts, it gains strength, which it can then use to energize its own processes, perceiving and thinking. It is important that the ego can also use its energy to restrict or delay the expression of the id. The ego uses psychological defense mechanisms to protect the individual from awareness of threatening events and to regulate the expression of the instincts. For example, a strong ego can use the defense mechanism of sublimation to direct some sexual energy into productive work rather than into sexual activity.

In the course of development, the superego develops from the ego. The ego attaches energy to the significant people in the child's world—the caregivers—and their values are then adopted as the child's own ideal and conscience. This process becomes particularly significant during the phallic stage, between the ages of four and six. At that time, the child becomes sexually attracted to the opposite-sex parent. In giving up that passion, the child adopts the characteristics of the same-sex parent; this process shapes the child's superego. The superego is mostly unconscious, and it strives for perfection. Throughout life, the id will strive for instinctual gratification, and the superego will strive for perfection. It is the task of the ego to mediate between the two, when necessary, and to chart a realistic life course.

IMPORTANCE OF CHILDHOOD YEARS

Freud considered the childhood years particularly significant, not only because during these years the ego and superego develop from energy captured from the id but also because during this time the sexual instincts manifest themselves in a variety of forms. The sexual instincts become focused on particular erogenous zones of the child's body in a set order. This produces a series of psychosexual stages, each characterized by instinctual urges, societal response, conflict, and resolution. During the course of this process, lasting personality traits and defenses develop. At first, the sexual energy is focused on the mouth. In this, the oral stage, conflicts may surround feeding. At approximately age two, the anal stage begins. The sexual instincts focus on the anus, and conflicts may occur around toilet training. The phallic stage, in which the child is attracted to the opposite-sex parent, follows. According to Freud, for boys this Oedipal conflict can be severe, as they fear castration from their father in retribution for their attraction to their mother. For girls, the conflict is somewhat less severe; in Freudian psychology, this less severe conflict means that in adulthood women will have less mature personalities than men. At approximately age six, the sexual instincts go into abeyance, and the child enters a period of latency. In adolescence, the sexual instincts again come to the fore, in the genital stage, and the adolescent has the task of integrating the

impulses from all the erogenous zones into mature genital sexuality.

Psychological problems occur when the psychosexual stages have left the instinctual urges strongly overgratified or undergratified, when the instincts are overly strong, when the superego is overly tyrannical, or when the ego has dealt with childhood traumas by severe repression of its experiences into the unconscious. Undergratification or overgratification of the instincts during childhood can result in fixations, or incomplete resolutions of childhood conflicts. For example, a person who is severely toilet trained can develop an "anal character," becoming excessively neat, miserly, or otherwise "holding things inside." If the id urges are too strong, they may overwhelm the ego, resulting in psychosis. An overly strong superego can lead to excessive guilt. If the ego represses childhood trauma, relegating it to the unconscious, that trauma will persist, outside awareness, in affecting a person's thoughts and behaviors.

Freud believed that no one could escape the conflicts inherent in the mind but that one could gain greater familiarity with one's unconscious and learn to direct instinctual energies in socially appropriate ways. This was the task of psychoanalysis, a form of therapy in which a client's unconscious conflicts are explored to allow the individual to develop better ways of coping.

IMPACT ON WESTERN SOCIETY

Freud's theory has had a dramatic impact on Western society, strongly influencing the ways people view themselves and their interactions with others. Terms such as "Freudian slip," "Oedipus complex," and "unconscious" are a part of everyday language. Emotions may be seen as "buried deep," and emotional expression may be called therapeutic. Assumptions about the unconscious influence both popular and professional conceptions of mental life.

The assumption that the expression of emotion is healthy and the repression of emotion is unhealthy may be traced to Freud. To some extent, this idea has received support from research which suggests that unresolved anger may contribute to physical health problems. Unfortunately, the release of anger in verbal or physical aggression may cause those aggressive behaviors to increase rather than to decrease. The vicarious experience of aggression via watching television or films may also teach aggression rather than reduce the urge to act aggressively.

ROLE OF DREAMS

Freud believed that dreams were one vehicle of unconscious expression. He viewed dreams as expressing the fulfillment of a wish, generally of a sexual nature. During sleep, the ego relaxes its restrictions on the id; instinctual wishes from the id, or repressed material from the unconscious, may be manifested in a dream. The bizarre sense of time and the confusing combinations of people and odd incidents in dreams reflect that the unconscious is without a sense of time, logic, or morality.

In dreams, the ego transforms material from the id to make it less threatening. Once one awakens, the ego further disguises the true meaning of the dream. Important points will be repressed and forgotten, and distortions will occur as the dream is remembered or told. For this reason, it is virtually impossible, according to Freud, to interpret one's own dreams accurately. A psychoanalyst interprets dreams by asking a patient to free associate—to say whatever comes to mind—about the dream content. In this fashion, the censoring of the ego may be relaxed, and the true meaning will be revealed to the therapist.

Revealing unconscious material is at the center of Freudian psychotherapy. Since Freud, many have viewed psychological problems as the result of childhood conflicts or traumas. Once the source is revealed, the patient is expected to improve. The nature of treatment is considerably more complicated than this might suggest, because the patient's ego may actively defend against acknowledging painful unconscious material. One of the few cases that Freud reported in detail was that of "Dora." Dora was referred to Freud because of a persistent cough that was assumed to be of psychological origin. According to Freud, such physical symptoms often are the result of childhood sexual conflict. Dora's cough and other psychosomatic complaints were found to be rooted in her sexual attraction to her father and to other men who were seen as resembling him—including a family friend and even Freud himself. Her attraction was accompanied by jealousy of her mother and the family friend's wife. The situation was complicated, because Dora's father was having an affair with the family friend's wife, to whom Dora was also attracted, and the family friend had expressed his attraction for Dora.

All this and more is revealed in two dreams of Dora that Freud analyzes in detail. The first is a dream of being awakened by her father, dressing quickly, and escaping a house that is on fire. The dream does its work by equating her father with the family friend, who once really was beside her bed as she awoke from a nap. This caused her to decide to "dress quickly" in the mornings, lest the friend come on her unclothed. Her unconscious attraction for the friend, however, is belied by the symbol of fire, which might be likened to consuming passion. In her second dream, Dora dreamed that her father was dead and that a man said, "Two and a half hours more." The dream symbolizes both Dora's turning away from her father as an object of her sexual interest and her intention (not evident to Freud at the time) of leaving therapy after two more sessions.

If Dora had not stopped therapy prematurely, Freud would have continued to bring his interpretation of her unconscious conflicts to the fore. In particular, he would have used her transference of childhood emotions to Freud himself as a vehicle for making the material revealed by her dreams, free associations, and behaviors evident to consciousness. The use of such transference is a key element of psychoanalysis. While this would not have completely resolved Dora's strong instinctual urges, it would have allowed her to come to terms with them in more mature ways, perhaps by choosing an appropriate marriage partner. Indeed, Freud reveals at the end of his report of this case that Dora married a young man she mentioned near the end of her time in therapy.

IMPACT AND CRITICISMS

Freud was a unique, seminal thinker. His personality theory was controversial from its inception; at the same time, however, it is such a powerful theory that, while many have criticized it, no subsequent personality theorist has been able to ignore the ideas Freud advanced. Psychoanalytic theory has also provided an interpretive framework for literary critics, historians, philosophers, and others.

Freud's theory was a product of his personal history, his training in science and medicine, and the Viennese culture in which he lived. Freud's early training was as a neurologist. As he turned from neurology to psychology, he continued to apply the skills of careful observation to this new discipline and to assume that the human mind followed natural laws that could be discovered. Viennese society at the time of Freud was one of restrictive social attitudes, particularly for women, and of covert practices that fell far short of public ideals. Thus it was relatively easy to see the psychological problems of the middle-class Viennese women who often were Freud's patients as being attributable to sexual conflicts.

Although Freud himself was dedicated to developing a science of mental life, his methods are open to criticism on scientific grounds. His theory is based on his experiences as a therapist and his self-analysis. His conclusions may therefore be restricted to the particular people or time his work encompassed. He did not seek to corroborate what his patients told him by checking with others outside the therapy room. Freud was not interested in the external "truth" of a report as much as its inner psychological meaning. He did not make details of his cases available to scrutiny, perhaps because of confidentiality. Although he wrote extensively about his theory, only five case histories were published. In all, these difficulties make the assessment of Freudian theory in terms of traditional scientific criteria problematic.

Freud's theory has had strong adherents as well as critics. Although theorists such as Alfred Adler and Carl Jung eventually broke with Freud, arguing against the primacy of the sexual instincts, his influence can be seen in their theories. Similarly, the important work of Erik H. Erikson describing human development through the life span has its roots in psychoanalytic theory. Many contemporary psychoanalytic theorists place a greater emphasis on the ego than did Freud, seeing it as commanding its own source of energy, independent of and equal to the id. Much contemporary literature and social criticism also possess a Freudian flavor.

BIBLIOGRAPHY

Cordón, Luis A. *Freud's World: An Encyclopedia of His Life and Times*. Santa Barbara: Greenwood, 2012. Print.

Ellis, Albert, Mike Abrams, and Lidia Dengelegi Abrams. *Personality Theories: Critical Perspectives*. Los Angeles: Sage, 2009. Print.

Fine, Reuben. *Freud: A Critical Re-evaluation of His Theories*. London: Routledge, 2014. Print.

Freud, Sigmund. *General Psychological Theory: Papers on Metapsychology*. New York: Touchstone, 2008. Print.

Freud, Sigmund. *An Outline of Psychoanalysis*. Trans. by James Strachey. New York: Norton, 1949. Print.

Gay, Peter. *Freud: A Life for Our Time*. 1988. Rpt. New York: Norton, 2006. Print.

Gay, Peter, ed. *The Freud Reader*. Rpt. New York: Penguin, 2007. Print.

Hall, Calvin S., and Gardner Lindzey. "Freud's Classical Psychoanalytical Theory." *Theories of Personality*. 4th ed. New York: Wiley, 1998. Print.

Jones, Ernest. *The Life and Work of Sigmund Freud*. New York: Basic, 1981. Print.

Kardiner, Abram. *My Analysis with Freud*. New York: Norton, 1977. Print.

Parker, Ian. *Psychology after the Unconscious: From Freud to Lacan*. New York: Routledge, 2014. Print.

Schimmel, Paul. *Sigmund Freud's Discovery of Psychoanalysis: Conquistador and Thinker*. New York: Routledge, 2014. Print.

Susan E. Beers

SEE ALSO: Abnormality: Psychological models; Defense mechanisms; Dreams; Ego defense mechanisms; Ego, superego, and id; Freud, Sigmund; Freudian psychology; Horney, Karen; Oedipus complex; Penis envy; Psychoanalysis; Psychoanalytic psychology; Psychosexual development; Psychotherapy: Children; Psychotherapy: Effectiveness; Psychotherapy: Goals and techniques; Psychotherapy: Historical approaches; Women's psychology: Sigmund Freud; Women's psychology: Karen Horney.

Psychobiology

TYPE OF PSYCHOLOGY: Biological bases of behavior; Cognition; Language; Learning; Memory; Sensation and perception

Psychobiology is the study of the relationship between the body and human experience, including sensation and perception, emotions, memory, language, movement, thinking, and learning..

KEY CONCEPTS
- Anterograde amnesia
- Broca's aphasia
- Hemi-inattention
- Neurons
- Neurotransmitters
- Prefrontal lobotomy
- Synapses
- Visual agnosia
- Wernicke's aphasia

INTRODUCTION

For centuries, philosophers and scientists have pondered the question of the relationship between the brain and the mind. In the 1600s, the French philosopher René Descartes proposed the dualistic theory, which is the belief that the mind and the body are different entities that work independently of each other but still interact. Descartes had problems, however, explaining how the invisible mind could influence a physical brain. He suggested that the mind and brain interact in the pineal gland, which is a small structure in the brain that releases the hormone melatonin.

Nearly all philosophers and neuroscientists today reject dualism. Their objection is that if the mind influences the brain, the mind must therefore be composed of matter or energy. The alternative description of the relationship between the brain and the mind is monism, which is the belief that the universe consists of only one kind of existence.

The identity position is a popular version of monism that most philosophers and scientists support. This view suggests that mental processes and brain processes are the same thing but are described in different terms. For example, if a man sees a speeding truck approaching him as he is crossing a street, fear might be his mental experience and running across the street to avoid the truck is his behavioral response. However, another description of the same experience could include how his brain records and interprets the threatening visual scene and then triggers other physical reactions, such as increases in heart rate and blood pressure and the release of stress hormones. These physical reactions then send a message back to the brain, which instructs the muscles to move, enabling the man to run.

With the help of brain imaging technology, such as magnetic resonance imaging (MRI) and positron emission tomography (PET), much more is known about how the brain and human experience relate to each other. An MRI is a method of imaging the living brain by using a magnetic field and a radio-frequency field to make certain atoms rotate in the same direction, then removing those fields and measuring the energy that the atoms release. The MRI allows neuroscientists to see the structure of the brain without damaging it. PET maps the activity of a living brain by recording the emission of radioactivity from injected chemicals. This allows neuroscientists to see what parts of the brain are active as the person is performing a particular task, such as solving math problems.

The human brain—composed of the hindbrain, the midbrain, and the forebrain—is an amazing structure. It is the only bodily organ with the ability to be aware of itself. This two- to three-pound gelatinous mass makes it possible for human beings to recognize and interpret sensory information, use complex systems of language, store and recall an infinite amount of factual information and a lifetime of experiences, create new ideas, and imagine the unseen.

HINDBRAIN AND MIDBRAIN

The hindbrain is the most primitive part of the brain and includes the medulla, the pons, the reticular formation, and the cerebellum. The medulla is just above the spinal cord and controls vital reflexes, such as breathing, heart rate, vomiting, salivation, coughing, and sneezing. The pons and the reticular formation (a set of pathways) mediate alertness and arousal, increasing and decreasing the brain's readiness to respond to stimuli. The cerebellum (from a Latin word meaning "little brain") is a large hindbrain structure that helps with balance and the coordination of motor movement. People who have a damaged cerebellum stagger when they walk and often lose their balance.

The midbrain in adult mammals is small and surrounded by the forebrain. In lower animals, such as birds, reptiles, and fish, it is larger and more prominent. The midbrain includes part of the reticular formation as well as other pathways and provides a route for important sensory information to reach the forebrain quickly.

FOREBRAIN

The forebrain consists of the limbic system, the thalamus, and the cerebral cortex. The limbic system includes several structures that mediate emotions and primary motivations, such as hunger, thirst, sex drive, and memory. These structures include the amygdala, the hypothalamus, and the hippocampus.

The amygdala plays an important role in the experience of fear and anxiety. Both fear and anxiety are "escape emotions," in that reacting to the emotion, for example by fleeing from a threatening stimulus such as a poisonous snake, causes the intensity of the emotion to diminish.

The hypothalamus is a pea-sized structure located near the base of the brain. It contains a number of distinct parts, some of which regulate the release of certain hormones. The hypothalamus also forms the biological basis of motivating behaviors that are crucial for survival, such as eating, drinking, temperature regulation, sexual behavior, and the fight-or-flight response.

The hippocampus (from a Latin word meaning "sea horse," so called because of its shape) is a large structure in the limbic system that is important in the creation of new memories. Memories are not stored in the hippocampus; rather, it is like a factory that creates new memories and then sends them to other areas of the brain for storage. A famous case study of a man known as HM illustrates the function of the hippocampus. HM had severe seizures that originated in the hippocampus and could not be controlled by medication. His hippocampus was surgically removed in a drastic attempt to eliminate his debilitating seizures. As a result, HM developed anterograde amnesia, which is the inability to form new memories. All the memories that had been stored in his brain before the surgery were unharmed. HM was essentially stuck in a perpetual present. He could read the same newspaper repeatedly and have no memory of ever reading it before. He could be introduced to a stranger and have a normal conversation, but when the person left the room and later returned, he would have no recollection of meeting the person or having the conversation.

The thalamus is also part of the forebrain. It looks like two small footballs in the center of the brain. The thalamus is a relay center for sensory information. Sensory receptors, such as those located in the retina or the eardrum, absorb physical stimuli from the environment, such as light or sound waves. The sensory systems send the information to the thalamus, which relays it on to the cerebral cortex for further processing. One exception is the olfactory system (the sense of smell), which has a direct connection to the cortex.

CEREBRAL CORTEX

The cerebral cortex ("cortex" being a Latin word meaning "bark" or "covering") is the outer part of the brain, which is most developed in humans. The cortex consists of two hemispheres, one on the left and one on the right. The corpus callosum connects the two hemispheres, allowing communication between them. Each hemisphere of the cortex is composed of four lobes: the occipital, parietal, temporal, and frontal lobes.

The occipital lobes, which are located in the back of the brain, process visual information. The receptor cells in the retina of the eye absorb light and then send the information along the optic nerve to the thalamus, which then relays it to the occipital lobes. Visual perception, which is the process of recognizing and interpreting sensory information, occurs in the occipital lobes. If certain parts of the occipital lobes are damaged, it may result in visual agnosia, which is the inability to interpret visual information. In his book *The Man Who Mistook His Wife for a Hat* (1985), neurologist Oliver Sacks describes a music teacher, Dr. P, who had a visual agnosia. Dr. P first noticed that something was amiss when he became unable to recognize his students. However, he could recognize them when they spoke, since his auditory perception was intact. Sacks describes an interview with Dr. P in which he showed him a glove and asked him to identify it. Dr. P examined the glove carefully and described it as some sort of container with five pouches that could be used to carry coins of different sizes. He was able to describe the different features of the object, indicating that he was not blind, but was unable to recognize the object as a glove.

The parietal lobes lie between the occipital lobes and the central sulcus, which is one of the deepest grooves in the surface of the cortex. The parietal lobes are important for processing tactile information (the sense of touch), as well as body position and location. The lobe of each hemisphere records and interprets tactile stimulation from the opposite side of the body. A quarter placed in a person's right hand will be recognized by the agency of the left parietal lobe, for instance. The parietal lobes also play an important role in proprioception, a sensory system that gives the brain information about the position and movement of the body without relying on vision.

People who experience damage to the right parietal lobe sometimes show a fascinating condition called hemi-inattention, or hemispatial neglect. When this occurs, the person is unable to attend to the left side of the body and the world. A person with hemi-inattention may shave or apply makeup to only the right side of the face. While dressing, he or she may put a shirt on the right arm but leave the left side of the shirt hanging behind the body. The person may eat from only the right side of the plate, not noticing the food on the left side. This condition is not due to visual problems or the loss of sensation on the left side of the body; rather, it is a deficit in the ability to direct attention to the left side of the body and the world.

The temporal lobes of the cortex are located on each side of the head, near the temples. They play an important role in recognizing and interpreting auditory information. Temporal lobes enable a person to identify familiar sounds, such as a police siren or a crying baby. Wernicke's area (named after Carl Wernicke, the neurologist who discovered its function), located in the left temporal lobe, mediates the ability to understand spoken language. When this area of the temporal lobe is damaged, the person may exhibit Wernicke's aphasia, a condition marked by poor language comprehension and difficulty remembering the names of objects.

The frontal lobes, located just behind the forehead, are specialized to control motor movements, spoken language, and higher-level thinking skills. The decision to scratch one's head or turn the page of a book is transmitted by the frontal lobes through the spinal cord to the muscles needed to perform the task. Like tactile sensation in the parietal lobes, each frontal lobe controls the opposite side of the body.

Broca's area (named after Paul Broca, the neurologist who discovered its function) is located in the frontal lobe, close to the motor area that controls facial and tongue movements. Most people who experience damage to this area in the left frontal lobe exhibit Broca's aphasia, which is an impairment of expressive language. People with Broca's aphasia may speak only in nouns and verbs, omitting other parts of speech such as prepositions, conjunctions, adjectives, adverbs, helping verbs, and word endings that indicate number or tense. They have particular trouble applying grammar rules for word order, although their pronunciation may be adequate. People with Broca's aphasia who communicate via sign language also show such difficulties, even though they are able to use their hands well in other ways.

The frontal lobes are also important in planning, initiating, and inhibiting behavior. They help people adapt to changes in the environment, including developing strategies to solve problems, monitoring the progress of such strategies, and being able to switch tactics when necessary.

In 1848, Phineas Gage, a railroad worker, suffered a severe accident in which an explosion caused an iron rod to pierce his cheek, slice through his frontal cortex, and emerge through the top of his head, where it lodged. Miraculously, Gage survived, but he experienced a dramatic personality change. He went from being a gentle, competent worker to being aggressive, emotionally volatile, and incapable of functioning normally. This case is considered the first known natural prefrontal lobotomy. The prefrontal lobotomy, in which the prefrontal cortex is surgically damaged or the connections between the prefrontal cortex and the rest of the cortex are cut, later became a drastic treatment for certain mental disorders.

In the United States, Walter Freeman and James Watts, professors of neurology and neurosurgery, published a report in 1942 titled "Psychosurgery in the Treatment of Mental Disorders and Intractable Pain." In the late 1940s and early 1950s, about forty thousand prefrontal lobotomies were performed in the United States. The therapeutic goal of such psychosurgeries was to make difficult, aggressive patients calmer without damaging their sensory or motor abilities. Freeman often employed crude methods in these surgical procedures, sometimes using electric drills or metal picks. He performed many of these operations in his office rather than in a hospital, often carrying his equipment, which he called his "lobotomobile," around with him. Prefrontal lobotomies were performed on a wide range of people thought to be mentally disordered, with common results including apathy, loss of the ability to plan and take initiative, generally blunted emotions, and the loss of facial expression. Patients also became unable to inhibit socially unacceptable behaviors and tended to act impulsively, without the ability to predict the consequences of their behavior. In the mid-1950s, when effective drug therapies became available to treat many mental disorders, the use of lobotomies declined drastically. Freeman eventually lost his privilege to practice in most hospitals, and other neuroscientists subsequently denounced his practices.

Damage to the frontal lobes due to stroke or other trauma often impairs a person's ability to initiate and organize behavior, as well as the ability to inhibit socially unacceptable behavior. After frontal lobe damage, a person who was once a model of social grace may become emotionally volatile, behaviorally explosive, and rude. Such people may use crude and profane language that they would never have uttered before the trauma.

LEARNING AND NEURONAL CONNECTIONS

Learning results in three different types of memory: semantic, procedural, and episodic. Semantic memories involve encoding and storing factual information, such as the name of one's first-grade teacher. Learning to type at a keyboard is an example of procedural memory, which itself is a form of implicit memory. When asked to recall the location of the "L" key, most people who know how to touch-type find themselves moving the third finger on their right hand. Recalling letters in the sequence in which they appear on a keyboard without using the fingers to mimic the required movement is a task that most people find quite difficult. This is because the memory is encoded and stored in the brain as a sequence of motor movements rather than as factual information. Memories of life experiences, or episodic memories, are represented in the brain as visual scenes that can be relived through imagination.

How is it that no matter how old a person becomes, there is always room in the brain to store new information and experiences? How can something as simple as learning a new word, which may take seconds to occur, form a memory in the brain that can potentially last a lifetime? The answer to these questions lies in the examination of the brain at the cellular level.

Neurons are specialized cells that have the ability to communicate with one another electrochemically. Most neurons do not physically touch each other but are separated by small gaps called synapses. When a neuron receives a message from another neuron, it triggers an electrical impulse, which travels from the receiving end of the neuron to the transmitting end. When the electrical impulse reaches the end of the neuron, it causes chemicals known as neurotransmitters to be released into the synaptic gap. The neurotransmitters then flood across this gap, triggering another electrical impulse in the next neuron, and the sequence continues. Since there are billions of neurons in the human brain and any one neuron can form synaptic connections with hundreds of other neurons, the potential for forming unique patterns of neuronal connections is virtually infinite. When learning a new word, a memory forms as a unique pattern of neuronal connections in the brain. Hearing the word only once and never recalling or using it again will likely result in the fading away of the new pattern of neuronal connections. However, recalling a word and using it repeatedly will likely cause its unique pattern of neuronal connections to become more durable, with the potential to last a lifetime. Thus, the neural representations of everything a person learns and remembers are unique patterns of neuronal connections in the brain.

BIBLIOGRAPHY

Breedlove, S. Marc, and Neil V. Watson. Biological *Psychology: An Introduction to Behavioral, Cognitive, and Clinical Neuroscience*. 7th ed. Sunderland: Sinauer, 2013. Print.

Calvin, William H., and George A. Ojemann. *Conversations with Neil's Brain: The Neural Nature of Thought and Language*. Reading: Addison, 1994. Print.

Czerner, Thomas B. *What Makes You Tick? The Brain in Plain English*. New York: Wiley, 2001. Print.

Kalat, James W. *Biological Psychology*. 11th ed. Belmont: Wadsworth, 2013. Print.

Kraly, F. Scott. *The Unwell Brain: Understanding the Psychobiology of Mental Health*. New York: Norton, 2009. Print.

Marshall, Louise H., and Horace W. Magoun. *Discoveries in the Human Brain: Neuroscience Prehistory, Brain Structure, and Function*. Totowa: Humana, 1998. Print.

Papathanasiou, Ilias, Patrick Coppens, and Constantin Potagas. *Aphasia and Related Neurogenic Communication Disorders*. Burlington: Jones, 2013. Print.

Pennington, Bruce F. *Explaining Abnormal Behavior: A Cognitive Neuroscience Perspective*. New York: Guilford, 2014. Print.

Pinel, John P. J. *Biopsychology*. 9th ed. Boston: Pearson, 2014. Print.

Sacks, Oliver. *The Man Who Mistook His Wife for a Hat and Other Clinical Tales*. New York: Summit, 1985. Print.

Cathy J. Bogart

SEE ALSO: Brain damage; Brain structure; Forgetting and forgetfulness; Kinesthetic memory; Lobotomy; Memory; Memory: Animal research; Memory: Empirical studies; Memory: Sensory; Memory storage; Thought: Study and measurement.

Psychologically healthy workplace

TYPE OF PSYCHOLOGY: Community; Consulting; Counseling; Clinical; Health; Occupational; Organizational; Social

Psychologically healthy workplaces today are run by companies with infrastructures designed to optimize the health and well-being of their employees while enhancing organizational outcomes. Together, such a focus results in healthier communities and happier, more satisfied employees who want to be stakeholders in their company.

KEY CONCEPTS
- A culture of support, respect, and fairness in the workplace
- Benefits of a PHW
- Components of a PHW
- Stakeholders
- Psychologically health workplaces (PHWs)

INTRODUCTION

In years past, an employee's physical safety at work was the primary focus and the definition of a healthy workplace. A psychologically healthy workplace (PHW) is no longer simply a workplace that avoids being unsafe, but one that optimizes health for all employees while maximizing organizational productivity. Today, most psychologically healthy workplace models include organizational policies and programs designed to enhance the well-being of employees (e.g., hope, resilience, optimism, self-efficacy) while enhancing organizational outcomes (e.g., reduced turnover, increased customer service, increased revenue). Together, the results are psychologically healthy social outcomes that benefit us all (e.g., healthier communities, reduced healthcare costs, increased community volunteering).

The concept of psychologically healthy workplaces is not new. More than two decades ago, Cooper and Cartwright argued that many financially healthy organizations were successful because they maintained and retained a workforce characterized by good physical, psychological, and mental health for their employees.

COMPONENTS OF A PSYCHOLOGICALLY HEALTHY WORKPLACE

In PHWs, the physical environment is constantly being analyzed and modified to impact employee well-being in a positive way by regulating noise, lighting, temperatures, the division of space among employees, and size of work areas. The environment is also modified to eliminate or drastically reduce the repetitive strain of work tasks that result in carpal tunnel syndrome, low back pain, neck pain, and tennis elbow. Methods used that have the potential to alleviate stress and enhance well-being include services such as easy parking, accessible fitness areas, cafeterias, and the use of ergonomic workstations.

In addition to the physical environment, the presence of health and safety initiatives makes a significant contribution to a healthy workplace. PHWs develop practices that help employees improve their physical and mental health, reduce health risks, and manage stress effectively. Free smoking cessation programs and other health initiatives including financial management and planning, improved nutrition, weight loss, and stress management are available to all workers and staff on any shift. Special incentives are sometimes offered to motivate employees seeking healthier lifestyles. Employees are given access to health facilities and health screenings and are provided adequate health insurance including mental health coverage. By offering an Employee Assistance Program, employees are able to seek professional assistance to help them address life problems such as alcoholism or bereavement.

Researchers have linked aspects of the psychosocial work environment and relationships at work to the health and well-being of employees and the success of organizations. Careful monitoring and quick adjustments are made in the PHWs regarding the high load and pace required for some employees and doing what they can to minimize the rotation of schedules, night work, and stressors specific to persons in high positions. Efforts are also made to promote an honest sense of job security and to develop the communications skills of persons with poor interpersonal relationships. Consideration is even given to persons whose job focus provides little stimulation and meaning.

Employee involvement refers to initiatives aimed at enhancing employees' involvement in decision-making, job autonomy, and empowerment which is known to increase job satisfaction and morale. Some examples of employee involvement include self-managed work teams, joint employee-management committees, employee suggestion forums, and continuous improvement teams. In some cases, it includes employee ownership. The result of an increase in employee involvement is increased commitment to the organization as well as to increased productivity. It also reduces turnover and absenteeism and enhances the quality of products and services.

PHWs develop programs and policies that facilitate work-life balance. At times, many employees find themselves caught in conflicts between work and their home life. Efforts to help employees improve work-life balance include eldercare benefits, flexible work arrangements which could include telecommuting or flextime, financial management, and assistance with childcare.

Providing opportunities for employee growth and development improves the quality of employees' work experience and helps them realize their full potential. Employees are able to gain knowledge, skills, and abilities that they can apply to new situations and, in many cases, help them manage stress. Opportunities that some organizations offer their employees include specific skill training, coaching and mentoring, career development and counseling services, and reimbursement for continuing education courses and college tuition reimbursement. Providing pathways to promotion and career enhancement is another way in which employee satisfaction and employee well-being are enhanced.

Employee recognition is a key factor to all psychologically healthy workplaces. Acknowledging employee efforts and making them feel valued and appreciated significantly increases employee satisfaction, morale, and self-esteem. The acknowledgements are awarded individually and collectively for their contribution to the organization. The recognition can be formal or informal,

Photo: iStock

monetary or non-monetary. Ways in which employees are recognized include ceremonies and awards, monetary compensation, performance-based bonuses, and pay increases. Some of the benefits of acknowledging employees are an increase in employee engagement and productivity, lower turnover, and the ability to retain top quality employees.

A key to the success of any workplace is the role of communication in the organization. In PHWs, employees are given ongoing opportunities to provide feedback to management and meet with managers. PHW strategies include developing policies that facilitate openness and transparency and having key organizational leaders lead by example by participating in psychologically healthy workplace activities that are visible to employees. Management clearly explain their availability and how to access them. In PHWs, employees have a "stake" in how their company runs and they are proud to be stakeholders.

PHWs invest time and resources in the development of a culture of support, respect, and fairness in the workplace. Such an environment encourages respectful relationships with and among employees, written policies on workplace respect, sensitivity or diversity training for managers, and the use of fair procedures to make workplace decisions. In PHWs, employees are treated and spoken to with dignity and respect.

BENEFITS OF A PSYCHOLOGICALLY HEALTHY WORKPLACE

Companies that do the work to meet general guidelines for psychologically healthy workplaces improve two important factors: they invest in employees' well-being and they increase productivity and profits. PHWs report that the quality of employee performance and quantity of organizational productivity stays significantly high and steadily improves. Customers report high satisfaction with how they are treated to by company personnel as well as with the quality of products. As a result, profits increase which benefits everyone including the "stakeholders."

Companies considered to be PHWs report an improved ability to attract and obtain top-quality employees. Potential employees learn that their potential employer invests in the well-being of their employees and they do what they can to reduce stress while increasing job satisfaction. Employees have genuine self-esteem related to their work performance and there is very little absenteeism and turnover. Turnover is a key factor in the stability of an organization and a crucial part of workplace success. Employees are seen as stakeholders and are treated respectfully, as the company's most important resource. Psychologically healthy workplaces support healthy and satisfied employees, reduce healthcare costs, and increase the overall well-being of their communities and, arguably, the world.

BIBLIOGRAPHY

Tjosvold, D. (1989). *Managing Conflict: The Key To Making Your Organization Work*. Minneapolis, MN: Team Media.

Kelly, J. E. (1982). *Scientific Management, Job Design and Work Performance*. New York, NY: Academic Press.

Goodman, P. S. (1986). Designing effective work groups. San Francisco, CA: Jossey Bass.

Peters, T., & Austin, N. (1985). *A Passion for Excellence*. New York, NY: Random House.

Crother, C. (2004). *Catch! A Fishmonger's Guide to Greatness*. San Francisco, CA: Berrett- Koehler.

Michael Shaughnessy and June Shepherd

SEE ALSO: Industrial and organizational psychology; Leadership; Occupational health; Stress; Work conditions.

Psychology and film

TYPE OF PSYCHOLOGY: Cultural; Social
DATE: 1895 forward

As Buster Keaton demonstrated in Sherlock Jr. *(1924) when he leaped into the movie he was projecting to become the protagonist of a film that represented the dream vision of his deepest imaginative aspirations, film can examine and express a version of "reality" that includes the full range of human behavior, as well as depicting the intricate interaction between practitioners of psychiatric therapy and the people they are assisting.*

KEY CONCEPTS
- Alternate reality
- Archetypal imagery
- Controversial therapies
- Empathetic identification
- Phobias
- Subconscious illumination

INTRODUCTION

Alfred Hitchcock, an innovator in many aspects of filmmaking, encapsulated the power of a cinematic rendering of a frightening psychopathology with his now-iconic title *Psycho* (1960), a film which presented a seemingly pleasant young man, Norman Bates, whose dissociative disorder drove him to a homicidal frenzy. Through the first half of the twentieth century, filmmakers had been wary of directly confronting cases of mental instability, although Hitchock had explored some of the effects of a war-time trauma in *Spellbound* (1945) in which Gregory Peck's psychiatrist was experiencing post-traumatic stress symptoms represented by hallucinations depicted through inventive images that Salvador Dali created for the film. Only a fraction of Dali's drawings were utilized due to the concerns of the studio which wanted to place the relationship between Peck and a fellow therapist played by Ingrid Bergman as the central focus of the film. The timidity of the major studios concerning controversial subjects meant that it remained for low-budget "B" pictures by innovative directors like Samuel Fuller's *Shock Corridor* (1963) to even consider manifestations of mental disorders. But since the earliest days of film production, the potential for this new medium to convey a sense of the psychological reality that had not been previously explored in a visual medium was apparent to its most discerning practitioners and commentators.

Hugo Münsterberg, an influential pioneer of industrial psychology, in his groundbreaking essay "The Means of the Photoplay" in 1916, recognized the power of the cinema to express a version of a character "overcoming reality" which, for him, meant going beyond the literal "reality" of his life as portrayed in the familiar realistic construction.

As he put it:

> The photoplay shows us a significant conflict of human actions in motion pictures which freed from the physical forms of space, time and causality, are adjusted to the free play of our mental experiences and which complete isolation from the practical world through the perfect unity of plot and pictorial experience.

Münsterberg's term, "the photoplay," was a summary of pictorial elements, which he asserted could adjust "the events to the forms of the inner world, namely attention, memory, imagination and emotion," the components of the subconscious which film could project with a force that equaled the realistic portrayals that were the standard for literature at the dawn of the Modernist era.

PSYCHOLOGICAL REALITY AND CINEMA VERITÉ

Rouben Mamoulian understood the capability for a cinematic rendering of this "inner world" in his depiction of the transition of Dr. Jekyll to Mr. Hyde in the 1931 film. As Frederick March undergoes the transformation, Mamoulian uses a subjective camera perspective to enable to viewer to see with tremendous force the world changing for Jekyll, in this case a full 360 degree panorama, as the camera swirls in a rapid circle of blurred images, the confusion and uncertainty of Jekyll's mind rushing beyond his capacity for comprehension. Employing one of the fundamental elements of cinematic structure, Mamoulian cuts between Jekyll's vision and shots of Jekyll's face illustrating his confusion, distress and wonder at what's taking place. This is a crucial aspect of film, the means to show both what a character is seeing and the character's reactions and responses to the phenomena that affects the response.

Mamoulian was more familiar with Sigmond Freud's theories than most of his American peers when he began directing films in the United States in 1929, and had been impressed by the adventurous explorations of psychic states in *The Cabinet of Dr. Caligari* (1919). Dr. Caligari has been described as the progenitor of the "sinister psychiatrist," and the film's use of distorted perspectives, harshly dramatic lighting and unsettling oblique and diagonal architecture drawn from the German Expressionist movement locates the viewer within the consciousness of all the characters to some degree. While Siegfried Kracauer's thesis in *From Caligari to Hitler* (1947) argues that the rise of Nazism can be traced from the phenomena depicted in the film, the film itself is regarded by scholars as a reflection of the massive social trauma occurring after WW I, and as the culmination of a trend (with Fritz Lang's ingenious creation of Dr. Mabuse) focusing on films fascinated by the interest in hypnosis linked to Freud's development of psychoanalytic therapy. George Méliès's *The Hypnotist at Work* (1897), D. W. Griffith's *The Criminal Hypnotist* (1909) and Maurice Tourneur's *Trilby* (1915) – an adaptation of the popular novel featuring the "evil hypnotist" Svengali – are typical examples of the films that predated Caligari, pioneering efforts to use the fundamental power of film to create a vision of a character's "reality" so convincing that the viewer was as startled as the audience at the Lumière brother's famous *The Arrival of a Train at La Ciotat* (1895), who, according to a popular myth, shrunk back in their seats in fear. Although the actual film does not have this effect, the legend is a testament to the striking power of the new medium.

MONSTERS, PSYCHOS AND SOCIOPATHS

The understandable appeal of the caring, competent therapist in contrast to the malevolent exploiter consumed with his or her own needs accounts for the mod-est success of films like, *The Three Faces of Eve* (1957), *David and Lisa* (1962), *Charly* (1968), *Ordinary People* (1980) and *Lars and the Real Girl* (2007) which featured compassionate professionals devoted to their patients to the extent that they were prepared to sacrifice their own well-being if they could assist some one else. Judd Hirsch's Dr. Berger in *Ordinary People* projects a warmth and humane concern that is convincing enough to substantiate the progress he makes with his patients, and even if the "cures" depicted in *Eve* were not based on actual evidence, or not supported by clinical data in *David and Lisa*, or not permanent as was the case with *Charly*, the hope for and evidence of some improvement was sufficient to satisfy the positive outcome of the narrative. Significantly, *Ordinary People* won the Oscar for Best Picture in the same year that Martin Scorsese's *Raging Bull* was released. The inner turmoil verging on pathology that energized Jake LaMotta in *Raging Bull* was expertly examined and revealed but the film was not nearly as immediately popular as *Ordinary People*. LaMotta's character was closer to the dangerous monster than the suffering innocent, which, even if it hasn't resulted in immediate acclaim from the industry, has often proved to be a more enduringly compelling subject, especially if the danger is overcome or thwarted or the monster has some discernible human qualities. King Kong, Frankenstein, Godzilla, and other archetypal expressions of a primal, threatening force have been the subject of some of the most memorable films, revealing an extreme psychic dimension beyond the bounds of familiar behavior.

Along these lines, but without the redeeming pathos of a creature burdened with powers defying immediate identification, films that dealt with the horrifying actions of Hannibal Lecter (*The Silence of the Lambs*, 1991), Nurse Ratched (*One Flew Over the Cuckoo's Nest* 1975), Anton Chigurh (*No Country for Old Men* 2007), Alex Forrest (*Fatal Attraction*, 1987), or some of the other unforgettable villains of the genre have an irresistible allure for many viewers. These films have been especially effective in portraying the loathsome results of their compulsions, and the rigid certainty with which they proceed is both gripping and repelling. While Norman Bates or Alex De Large (*A Clockwork Orange*, 1971) and Phyllis Dietrichson (*Double Indemnity*, 1946) are responsible for crimes as dreadful as those of the others ranked as "Top Villains" in the American Film Institute's list., their characters are delineated with wider and deeper invocation of traits evoking a degree of pity verging on empathy. By the conclusion of *A Clockwork Orange*, there is an urge among some viewers to restore Alex to his condition prior to treatment. This is due to the filmmaker's skill at taking the viewer into Alex's world, and at the high energy and exuberance that informs Malcolm McDowell's performance, while Tony Perkin's performance as Norman Bates has so much of the boyish charm that Perkins exuded that there is almost a sense of loss at his capture. Similarly, Barbara Stanwyck makes Dietrichson so vulnerable and needy that her evolving uncertainty and eventual awareness of her guilt tends to reduce the revulsion that would usually follow her murderous scheming. When the world of the film is apprehended almost entirely from the perspective of a particular character, the resistance of the viewer to some of his actions is ameliorated. For gangsters, who have a special place in American films due to an inclination to celebrate the outsider/underdog/rebel, this is an important feature, notably illustrated by Jimmy Cagney's indelible portrayal of Cody Jarrett in *White Heat* (1949), a clear case of a mentally disturbed individual whose behavior is hard to justify but whose distinctive, virile charm is also difficult to resist, just as Warren Beaty's Clyde Barrow in Arthur Penn's *Bonnie and Clyde* (1967) projects a charismatic outlaw appeal that overcomes his lethal impulses. Penn was prepared to confront the psycho-sexual motivation underscoring Barrow's mixture of traits in a way that films had generally avoided, and his radical take on the Billy the Kid legend with Paul Newman in *The Left-Handed Gun* (1958) was another version of an anti-hero calling for the viewer's sympathy and understanding.

CATEGORIES AND CLASSIFICATIONS

During the latter decades of the 20th century, as social trends expanded the field of films concerned with mental health issues, and subjects previously considered inappropriate for discussion such as the proliferation of addictive substances were brought under scrutiny, characters superficially classified as psychopathologic personalities were presented with much more insight. The demeaning stereotype of women as nurturing mothers (the domestic goddess) or destructive harridans (witches, harpies and whores) was countered with a much more sensitive and subtle exposition of psychological motivations. The so-called "woman's film" such as *The Women* (1939) which offered a gamut of "types" was joined by films like *Girl, Interrupted* (1995) concentrating on the specific psychic issues of a sympathetic character, and "classic" films dealing with alcoholic addiction like the *The Lost Weekend* (1945) proliferated into a subgenre

of films exploring the use of psychedelic agents like *Requiem For A Dream* (2000). As the concept of "normal" standards of behavior was challenged by an acknowledgment of the range of human particularity, films gradually began to recognize the legitimacy of transgender experience (*Boys Don't Cry,* 1999), the actual rate of occurrence of depression among people in contemporary society (*The Hours,* 2002; *American Beauty,* 1999), and the complexities of a brilliant and likeable person afflicted with mental disorders (*A Beautiful Mind,* 2001).

The captivating, complicated relationship between the therapist and the patient has been one of the essential themes of film from its earliest days, but what Münsterberg was probing in his study *The Film: A Psychological Study* went beyond remedy to examine how "the photoplay succeeds in overcoming reality." He meant the literal "reality" of literature in the Western World, and by 1916 James Joyce had already begun the composition of Ulysses, while according to Virginia Woolf as she turned toward the inner life of her characters, "…on or about December 1910 human character changed." Some of the most striking and memorable characters in the history of film have been illuminated by their comprehension of the world they inhabit, a stirring blend of an inner world in correspondence with their participation in the events of the narrative, which the viewer comes to know through the filmmaker's art. The vivid psychological "reality" of Cary Grant's Roger O. Thornhill in *Hitchcock's North By Northwest* (1958), his ingenuity and adaptability, is exhibited by the famous scene in the corn field south of Chicago; the inward confidence and poise of Steve McQueen's Hilts in *The Great Escape* (1959) is conveyed through his composure amidst violent action; the independence and intelligence of Katherine Hepburn's Amanda Bonner in *Adam's Rib* (1949) emerges in her defense of a woman accused of attempting to murder her husband; the determination and persistence of Jack Nicholson's McMurphy in *One Flew Over the Cuckoo's Nest* (1975) is palpable as he proclaims, "At least I tried!;" the incredible inner strength of Daniel-Day Lewis's Christy Brown in *My Left Foot* (1989) is revealed in an extraordinary feat of kinesthetic control; the courage and conflict of Meryl Streep's Sophie in *Sophie's Choice* (1982) is a part of a gallery of indelible performances that Streep has achieved. Each of these characters has a reality for the viewer perhaps more meaningful than many of their acquaintances, and the events of their lives in these films sometimes as resonant as the personal experiences of the viewers themselves.

BIBLIOGRAPHY

Packer, Sharon. *Cinema's Sinister Psychiatrists: From Caligari to Hannibal*. Jefferson, NC: McFarland & Company, 2012. Written with style and verve, an incisive examination of the practices at the core of a relationship which the film industry exploited with more interest in drama than an accurate or balanced rendition.

Robinson, Daniel. *Reel Psychiatry: Movie Portrayals of Psychiatric Conditions*. Port Huron, MI: Rapid Psycler Press, 2003. Many examples from a wide range of films analyzed for accuracy. Designed for mental health professionals, but accessible and informative for anyone interested in the subject. Not as good on the films themselves as their subjects.

Wedding, Danny; Boyd, Mary Ann; and Niemiec, Ryan. *Movies and Mental Illness; Using Films to Understand Psychopathology*. Cambridge, MA: Hogrefe Publishing, 2010. Comprehensive, informative and engaging, with many lists, appendices and other useful organizational features that provide an extensive grounding in the discipline.

Young, Skip Dine. *Psychology at the Movies*. West Sussex, UK: Wiley-Blackwell, 2012. A wide-ranging and sprightly consideration of the central themes and motifs of films that can be considered from the utilization of their psychological perspectives and approaches.

Leon Lewis

SEE ALSO: Consumer psychology; Entertainment; Film; Interdisciplinary studies; Media; Popular culture.

Psychology
Definition

TYPE OF PSYCHOLOGY: Origin and definition of psychology

Despite psychology's long history and major impact, attempts to define it lack a clear and unified sense. As a result, psychology has been defined in a variety of ways, each with its own particular advantages. Psychology has come to define itself as a science of mind and behavior, but these terms continue to carry the ambiguities of earlier controversies.

KEY CONCEPTS
- Behavior
- Cognition
- Consciousness
- Experience
- Intrinsic versus extrinsic
- Logos
- Psyche

INTRODUCTION

Psychology is recognized to be a hugely successful field. It is the largest social science in virtually any country in the world, as demonstrated by such indicators as the number of professionals, students, dollars invested, and publications, and its impact on society. Given this success, it is surprising that the simple question "What is psychology?" has yet to be clearly answered. Attempts to resolve this question have a long and frustrating history and have proceeded from a variety of starting points, each leading to its own particular search path. For example, the position that psychology is a word leads to searching for its definition through its etymological history. If psychology is taken to be the study of the psychological, then the nature of its subject matter becomes the key focus of the inquiry. Likewise, the assertion that psychology is what psychologists do leads to an examination of its practices and methods. Whereas the position that psychology is a discipline directs the search to examine its institutionalization. For a definition that has proven as elusive as psychology's, all these paths are worthy pursuits, each offering valuable insights toward that needed clarification.

A DEFINITION BY ETYMOLOGY

The word psychology can be broken down into two parts, "psych" and "ology," both of which are of Greek origin, though the Greeks did not combine them into one word. In Greek mythology, stories describe a young mortal woman named Psyche (a name that is usually translated as "soul"). The god Eros falls in love with her, and following a long series of separations and tribulations, they marry and give birth to an offspring, named Pleasure.

Exactly what the Greeks meant by "soul," however, is not clear. The Oxford English Dictionary traces the etymology of the Greek word psyche back to psukhe, originally Greek for "breath." Psychologist George Kunz, in *The Paradox of Power and Weakness* (1998), points out that it was most likely in that sense that Homer originally used this term to refer to life, or soul. Kunz's thesis is that psyche, as the soul, is generated by others breathing life into the self. He draws this insight from the French philosopher Emmanuel Levinas, author of *Autrement qu'être: Ou, Au-delà de l'essence* (1974; *Otherwise Than Being: Or, Beyond Essence*, 1998), whose thesis was that psyche as one's soul is the other in one's self, an intersubjective relationship and ground of ethical responsibility. In other words, for the original Greek root, psyche is not a thing one possesses, but rather a capacity for relatedness.

In Judaism, a similar parallel can be found. The Hebrew word for breath is ruah, which means the spirit of God that infuses creation. Likewise, there are fascinating parallels between Greek thought and that of India at the time. In old Sanskrit, the word for "breath" is prana, which is considered to be the vehicle of the mind because prana is taken to be that which makes the mind move, as described in Sogyal Rinpoche's *The Tibetan Book of Living and Dying* (1992). In both the older Vedic tradition and the later Buddhist practice, a form of mediation that centered on the breath became a key to enlightened understanding. Through meditation on the breath, one becomes aware of the interdependent interconnectedness of all.

The origin of the other part of the term "psychology," logos is perhaps the most central term in early Greek philosophy. It is usually translated simply as "the study of" or sometimes the more arcane "the wording of." This correlation with "wording" is both intriguing and misleading, both of which are exemplified by the translation of logos as "word" in the Gospel of John: "In the beginning was the Word." This connection comes from the derivation of logos from its antecedent, leigen, which meant something like "to speak." By Aristotle's time, this was its general sense. However, for the pre-Socratic philosophers, this term, and from it logos, meant not just putting something into words, but a laying forth, a gathering meaningfully together into wholeness. Martin Heidegger in *Early Greek Thinking* (1975) masterfully recovers this deeper sense of logos by returning to the early philosopher Heraclitus, who said, "According to the logos, all is one." Heraclitus also spoke of the logos of psyche, but acknowledged that one would not be able to discover the limits of psyche "so deep a logos does it have." Here also, the early Greek thinking emphasized this relational sense of the psychological. However, by the latter period of Greek thought, dominated by Aristotle, author of the major tritise *De anima* (*On the Soul*, 1812), the soul became a more material or biological concept and thus a more separate kind of entity.

During the medieval period, thinking about psyche as relation was lost altogether since the concept of the soul acquired a connotation of something fundamentally separate from this world. With this duality, no further talk of psyche ensued for a thousand years, until it was reawakened by the Renaissance humanists. In refocusing attention on it, they also provided the first use of the compound term "psychology" (usually in its Latin form psicologia) and formulated this word as the name of an intellectual discipline. The first to do so was the Croatian humanist scholar Marko Marulić in 1520, followed over the next several decades by the German Johannes Thomas Freig, the French Noël Taillepied, and the Germans Rudolf Göckel and Otto Casmann. This burst of interest in the concept of psychology rose with the tide of a humanistic vision. As an antidote to the medieval dualism, Renaissance thinkers proceeded with a "determined decompartmentalization," described in Richard Tarnas's *The Passion of the Western Mind: Understanding the Ideas That Have Shaped Our World View* (1991), seeking to again reconnect psyche and world, in a web of interrelationships.

DEFINING THE SUBJECT OF PSYCHOLOGY

Psychology can be defined by its subject matter: the study of the psychological, or, more precisely, the psychological dimension of human existence. Pointing to a dimension of existence as psychological distinguishes it from the more clearly defined physical and biological orders, and so the question of whether it is independent of them, reducible to their level, or integrates them into something more comprehensive becomes critical to the definition.

In the physical order, the relations between one feature and another are mechanistic; they are governed by cause and effect. For example, modern physical science began when Isaac Newton could specify the laws of planetary motion that accounted for the rotation of the planets around the sun. He could express this relationship entirely in mathematical laws because the mechanical force of gravity was entirely sufficient to account for this relationship: The sun does not keep its planets in orbit because of any desire to do so, nor do the planets remain in rotation out of preference or a sense of compulsion. The "laws" are about merely extrinsic relations because Newton was able to demonstrate that these were entirely sufficient to explain the phenomenon of planetary motion, and with them, he could predict where any planet would be at any time in the future.

In contrast to such causal, extrinsic relations, the experienced meanings characteristic of human relationships open a different dimension, one beyond the mechanism of cause and effect. For example, although such categories of intrinsic meaning as desire and preference have no place in a mechanistic analysis of extrinsic relations, they are crucial to any understanding of the relationships toward which human action is directed. For example, the question "Why does Jill cut herself?" asks for a quite different type of answer than "Why do planets rotate around stars?" The former seeks reasons, whereas the latter seeks causes. This distinction harkens back to a very old argument that has taken many different forms over the centuries. This form of it is credited to German philosopher and historian Wilhelm Dilthey, author of "Ideen über eine beschreibende und zergliedende Psychologie" (1894; "Ideas Concerning a Descriptive and Analytic Psychology," 1977).

During the last third of the nineteenth century, however, leaders in psychology persuaded the field to follow the prevailing model of extrinsic relations borrowed from the physical sciences, leading Wilhelm Dilthey to note that psychology had sought to become a science of the soul by leaving out the soul. Their model of science had been founded during the seventeenth century, especially by the French philosopher René Descartes and the English mathematician Isaac Newton. Neither of them, nor the other promoters of this new science, such as John Locke or Gottfried Leibniz, even mentioned the word psychology. In its place came talk of physiology and anatomy, as dissection and surgery become the new paradigm by which to understand the person. (Descartes even considered the pineal gland in the brain to be the seat of the soul.)

By the nineteenth century, the natural sciences were generally and even popularly seen as having delivered the goods via technological change, as the Industrial Revolution instantiated the scientific vision of the world as a storehouse of resources to exploit for productive gain. Giant steam engines, factories, steamships, railroads, and telegraphs yielded a great power and changed ways of life. So the natural sciences—physics, mechanics, chemistry, and biology—enjoyed a high-level reputation as arbiters of reality. However, the disciplines that focused on human affairs had lagged behind, because although they had imported a scientific conception of persons, their methodologies were still largely philosophical, in contrast to the experimental methodology of the natural sciences.

In 1879, Wilhelm Wundt, a German psychologist, sought to remedy this gap by establishing a psychological laboratory in which to conduct experiments, strictly along the lines of the experimental method used by the physical sciences. He studied sensation and called his work "physiological psychology." In doing so, he deliberately and with great fanfare sought to establish psychology as a true natural science. The rhetorical success of his endeavor resulted in the widespread adoption by the end of the nineteenth century of this view that psychology must follow the scientific method, and it emerged in its present self-definition as a science. Astute philosophers have noted that psychology's commitment to be a science preceded deep contact with its subject matter, thus causing it to lose touch with its origin and meaning—as in Ludwig Wittgenstein's *Philosophische Untersuchungen/ Philosophical Investigations* (1953), P. D. Ouspensky's *The Psychology of Man's Possible Evolution* (1950), and Edmund Husserl's *Die Krisis europäischen Wissenschaften und die transzendentale Phänomenologie: Ein Einleitung in die phänomenologische Philosophie* (1954; *The Crisis of European Sciences and Transcendental Phenomenology: An Introduction to Phenomenological Philosophy,* 1970).

With respect to the question of what particular contents it takes its subject to be, psychology since the nineteenth century has looked to the mind (also called consciousness), then looked to behavior, then to the mind again (this time also using the terms cognition and consciousness). Later definitions emphasize both behavior and mind. For example, psychology's own scientific and professional organization, the American Psychological Association, defines psychology as "the study of the mind and behavior." However, simply pointing to either "behavior" or "mind" is insufficient as a definition. First, behavior is unduly too broad a term, since all the social sciences study behavior. Sociology, criminal justice, anthropology, history, economics, political science, and the like all take behavior as a key. "Behavior" is not therefore synonymous with "the psychological"; rather, behavior somehow provides a portal to the psychological. However, what can be glimpsed of the psychological through that portal must still be defined.

Two very different ways of doing so are available in psychology, basically mirroring the distinction Dilthey had introduced. The former was crystallized by John B. Watson's *Behaviorism* (1925; rev. ed., 1930), founding a narrowly behavioristic approach to psychology with the argument that such reductionism was the only way psychology could achieve scientific status. He specifically eschewed the study of the soul, mind, or consciousness. Indeed, he ridiculed the notion there was any such thing and labeled it a "superstition" akin to witchcraft, to be driven from psychology. For him, behavior was nothing but a reflex, conditioned by reinforcement, but ultimately just as reflexive as those unconditioned reflexes that are genetically hardwired.

The other approach to behavior, developed in the nineteenth century contemporaneously with Wundt's experimental psychology, took it to be action, as described in Franz Brentano's *Psychologie vom empirischen Standpunkte* (1874; *Psychology from an Empirical Standpoint*, 1973). This view inspired two early twentieth-century developments: Husserl's formulation of phenomenological psychology, which took behavior as based on experience as it is lived, and the Gestalt psychology school of Kurt Koffka, Wolfgang Köhler, and Max Wertheimer, who read in relation to a meaningful world rather than meaningless stimuli. By the 1930s to 1940s, French theorists had synthesized phenomenology and Gestalt to provide a way to understand behavior as improvisational conduct directed to intrinsically meaningful features of the situation, as in Maurice Merleau-Ponty's *La Structure de comportement* (1942; *The Structure of Behavior,* 1963) and Aron Gurwitsch's *The Field of Consciousness* (1964).

Likewise, for the definition of psychology as "the mind" or "mental life," a similar pair of approaches—reductionistic and nonreductionistic—are pursued. In the former, characteristic of much of contemporary neuropsychology, the mind is reduced to an effect of brain function, whereas for the latter, the issues of mental life are taken on their own terms. This latter path itself has two very different approaches within it. The contemporary cognitive paradigm, while holding that cognition can be investigated independently of brain function, nevertheless generally assumes that an underlying neurophysiology will someday be determined. The other approach, typically more influenced by phenomenology, usually speaks of consciousness rather than cognition and makes no assumption that consciousness is reducible to brain function.

METHODS, PRACTICES, AND INSTITUTIONALIZATION

Psychology's self-understanding is greatly tied to its methodology, whether it be in its research or applications. Beginning first with the research side, psychology's quest to become a science in the same sense as the natural sciences has led it largely to follow the scientific method. This has meant a method built around the central assumption of positivism, namely the goal of measuring relationships between independent and dependent variables to test a hypothesis for its statistical significance. The ultimate method for such a test has been the experimental method, as it has allowed researchers to freely manipulate the presence of the independent variable on the dependent variable. Other methods, such as surveys, tend to also rely on the ability to measure operationally defined variables as the scientific legitimation of the methodology.

A true alternative to this natural-science-based methodology later was formed from Dilthey's proposed alternative, that a descriptively based method would be more appropriate to the quest to understand the intrinsic relations of the human order. Twentieth century psychologists, especially those in the humanistic tradition, began devising qualitative methods to access people's actual experience. Early on, these usually took the form of phenomenological investigations, as described in Amedeo Giorgi's *Phenomenology and Psychological Research* (1985). However, a wide range of qualitative methods have been developed, as seen in Constance T. Fischer's *Qualitative Research Methods for Psychologists* (2005) and Giorgi's *Descriptive Phenomenological Method in Psychology: A Modified Husserlian Approach* (2008).

On its applied side, psychology has been practiced largely in clinical and psychotherapeutic contexts, in which the methodological questions to be resolved concern those of treatment rather than research. Four major systems emerged: psychoanalytic, humanistic, behavioral, and cognitive. The former two are oriented to the explication of the lived meanings of the client, and the latter two more toward symptom reduction. Given the effect of health insurance coverage on the practice of psychology, it is not surprising that the latter two approaches came eventually to dominate clinical practice. They are merging in various ways to form a cognitive behavioral approach to therapy.

Beyond the clinical, applied psychologists also work in many other contexts, most of these being industrial, organizational, educational, engineering, military, community, health, and consulting settings. In these, methodological questions are less central, and it has not been in these contexts that definitional issues are typically worked out.

As an institution, psychology's two forms are "housed" in very different institutional settings. Science, devoted largely to research and teaching, is housed largely in academia and to a lesser extent in independent research foundations. Psychology's applied profession, dedicated largely to improving individual and organizational welfare, is housed largely in clinical and corporate settings. Ideally, these two wings complement, support, and nourish each other. All too often, however, they are out of touch with each other, exacerbating definitional differences.

Within the research side, the subfields of psychology include such major areas as developmental, social, personality, and neuropsychological. With finer resolution, topics include such processes as perception, learning motivation, emotion, thinking, imagination, and memory. These topics each contribute to defining the basic processes of psychological life. Within the clinical side, neighboring paradigms of medicine on one hand and counseling on the other likewise provide the gist for the definitional work of psychology.

NEW DIRECTIONS

The question remains as to why psychology has not been better able to resolve an issue as central as its own self-definition. Its definition is elusive because it is a particularly difficult question to answer. However, that difficulty is compounded by the divisive and fragmentary ways psychology has struggled within itself for a clarified definition, all too often with the result that self-limiting presuppositions have strait-jacketed the development of more comprehensive understandings.

There are some indications that psychology is becoming more open to wider integrations. Four trends are emerging, each offering a promising interdisciplinary cross-fertilization through which psychology is becoming more integral. These trends include psychology's collaborations with economics, ecology, holistic health, and spirituality.

BIBLIOGRAPHY

Arnold, William, ed. 1975 *Nebraska Symposium on Motivation*. Lincoln: U of Nebraska P, 1976. Print.

Burnham, John C. *After Freud Left: A Century of Psychoanalysis in America*. Chicago: U of Chicago P, 2014. Print.

Giorgi, Amedeo. *Descriptive Phenomenological Method in Psychology: A Modified Husslerian Approach*. Pittsburgh: Duquesne UP, 2008. Print.

Kimble, Gregory A. *Portraits of Pioneers in Psychology: Volume III*. New York: Psychology Press, 2014. Print.

Koch, Sigmund, and David Leary, eds. *A Century of Psychology as Science*. Washington: American Psychological Association, 1998. Print.

Levitin, Daniel J. *Foundations of Cognitive Psychology*. Upper Saddle River: Pearson, 2010. Print.

Levitin, Daniel J. *Foundations of Cognitive Psychology: Core Readings*. 2nd ed. Boston: Allyn & Bacon, 2012. Print.

Robinson, Daniel. *Consciousness and Mental Life*. New York: Columbia UP, 2008. Print.

Christopher M. Aanstoos

See Also: Behaviorism; Cognitive psychology; Consciousness; Experimental psychology; Psychology: Fields of specialization; Psychology: History.

Psychology
Fields of specialization

Type of psychology: Origin and definition of psychology

Psychology is both a theoretical and an applied science. Psychologists use observational and experimental methods to reach a greater understanding of the human mind and human behavior. They then use this knowledge in a variety of settings to help people in their daily lives.

Key Concepts
- Behaviorism
- Cognitive psychology
- Gestalt psychology
- Social psychology
- Structuralism

INTRODUCTION

Because the fields of specialization within psychology are so numerous, the science must first be examined as an entity unto itself. This involves defining psychology, exploring the reasons for its existence, reviewing its history, and surveying the diverse specialists who assist various populations. Although the semantics of defining psychology differ from text to text, the actual explanation remains constant: It is the science of human behavior as it relates to the functions of the mind. More specifically, it provides evidence for why people experience a gamut of emotions, think rationally or irrationally, and act either predictably or unpredictably.

The discipline's very existence justifies humankind's need to plumb the depths of its interior to search for the self, to process conflict, to solve problems, and to think critically as well as act pragmatically. Its challenge is to assist people in understanding themselves. Humans have a natural curiosity; it moves them to try to determine their relationship to the world in which they live. With this comes the inclination to observe and compare the ideas, behavior patterns, and abilities of other people. These analyses and comparisons, which people cannot help but make, involve the self as well as others. People may be either overly harsh or selectively blind when examining themselves; both these situations can be a handicap and both can be helped by psychology.

At times, people's anxiety levels may peak uncontrollably. Through the science of the mind, people seek to temper their agitation by becoming familiar with and acknowledging vague fears and uncomfortable feelings. Thus, they learn about the source of their tension. From this, experts learn how behavior originates. They assist people in learning to cope with change; people discover how to make adequate adjustments in daily living. The fast pace that humans in industrialized society keep requires them, more than ever before, to have a working knowledge of people—their thought processes and behavior patterns. From all of this, experts are able to arrive at reasonable predictions and logical conclusions about humankind's future behavior.

HISTORY AND SYSTEMS OF PSYCHOLOGY

Psychology did not become accepted as a formal discipline until the late nineteenth century. Before then, even back to antiquity, questions were directed to philosophers, the wise men of the time. Though they were versed in reasoning, logic, and scholarship, only a few of these thinkers could deal with the complexities of the human mind. Their answers were profound and lengthy, but these scholars frequently left their audiences bewildered and without the solutions they sought. Some of these logicians used the Socratic method of reasoning; they often frustrated those who questioned them and expected realistic replies. Inquires were redirected to questioners, whose burden it was to arrive at their own solutions.

Gustav Fechner, a nineteenth century philosopher and physicist, postulated that the scientific method should be applied to the study of mental processes. It was his contention that experimentation and mathematical procedures should be used to study the human mind. From the mid-nineteenth century onward, many disciplines contributed to what was to become the science of psychology. Wilhelm Wundt and Edward Titchener were the

leaders of the structuralist school, which identified the elements and principles of consciousness.

Other early giants of the field included William James and John Dewey. They inaugurated the study of functionalism, which taught that psychological knowledge should be applied to practical knowledge in fields such as education, business law, and daily living. A champion of behaviorism, John B. Watson, advocated that the study of psychology should concentrate on observable behavior; he urged that objective methods be adopted. The Gestalt movement was originated by Max Wertheimer. In concert with Kurt Koffka and Wolfgang Köhler, Wertheimer embraced the premise that the whole may be different from its parts studied in isolation.

Psychoanalysis was developed by Sigmund Freud. He studied the unconscious using techniques of free association, hypnosis, and body language. The neobehaviorist model, in contrast, defended the behaviorist position that complicated phenomena such as mental and emotional activities cannot be observed. Love, stress, empathy, trust, and personality cannot be observed in and of themselves. Their effects, however, are readily apparent.

Carl R. Rogers and Abraham Maslow pioneered the area known as humanism in the 1950s and 1960s. Areas of interest to humanistic psychologists are self-actualization, creativity, transcendence, the search for meaning, and social change. Its goals are to expand and to enrich human lives through service to others and an increased understanding of the complexity of people, as individuals, in groups, organizations, and communities.

In the mid-twentieth century, with the development of cognitive psychology, mental processes such as attention, memory, and reasoning became the focus of direct study. This approach to understanding human thought analyzes cognitive processes into a sequence of ordered stages; each stage reflects an important step in the processing of information. In the 1980s and 1990s, the fields of cognitive science and cognitive neuroscience emerged. Psychologists began working with computer scientists, linguists, neurobiologists, and others to develop detailed models of brain and mind relationships.

MAJOR FIELDS IN PSYCHOLOGY

Psychology is both a theoretical and an applied science with more than a dozen major fields. The American Psychological Association has more than fifty divisions, representing psychologists working in settings as diverse as community mental health clinics and large corporations, and with interests ranging from adult development and aging to the study of peace, conflict, and violence. Academic and research psychologists use observational and experimental methods to reach a greater understanding of the human mind and human behavior. Psychologists in the clinical specialties then use this knowledge to help people in their daily lives.

For example, children who are abused or neglected, or who experience difficulties as a result of being members of dysfunctional families, require the services of child psychologists, who evaluate, diagnose, and treat youngsters; this usually occurs in a clinical setting. Thus, child psychologists are considered clinical practitioners. More than one-half of the doctoral degrees awarded in 1999 were in either clinical or counseling psychology. In 2006 the National Science Foundation reported that, of all psychology doctoral degrees awarded between 1996 and 2005 in the United States, 37 percent were for clinical psychology and 14 percent were for counseling psychology.

Many psychologists also work in the area of education. Educational psychologists develop and analyze materials and strategies for effective educational curricula. School psychologists design instructive programs, consult with teachers, and assist students with problems.

Genetic psychologists study the activities of the human organism in relation to the hereditary and evolutionary factors involved; functions and origin play a central role. Physiological psychologists examine the biological bases of behavior. They are often interested in the biochemical reactions underlying memory and learning. Engineering psychologists design and evaluate equipment, training devices, and systems. The goal is to facilitate the relationship between people and their environment. Industrial and organizational (I-O) psychologists research and develop programs that promote on-the-job efficiency, effectiveness, challenge, and positive disposition. They study ability and personality factors, special training and experience, and work and environment variables, as well as organizational changes.

Personality psychologists tudy the many ways in which people differ from one another; they are instrumental in analyzing how those differences may be assessed and what their impact is. Criminal psychologists study the complexities of a perpetrator's thought process. They are keenly interested in a criminal's habits, idiosyncrasies, and possible motives. Developmental psychologists study changes in people as they age and mature. Their work may be protracted over the span of an individual's

life; their theories may be advanced several years after they were first conceived.

Social psychologists study how people influence one another. They may be interested, for example, in the concept of leaders and followers. Environmental psychologists monitor the physical and social effects of the environment on behavior. They are interested in how elements such as heat, noise, health, and activity affect the human condition. Their contributions are in the areas of urban planning, architecture, and transportation.

Consumer psychologists determine factors that influence consumer decisions, exploring such issues as the effect of advertising on purchasing decisions, brand loyalty, and the rejection or acceptance of new products. Experimental psychologists design and conduct basic and applied research in a variety of areas, including learning, sensation, attention and memory, language, motivation, and the physiological and neural bases of behavior. Comparative psychologists study the behavior, cognition, perception, and social relationships of diverse animal species. Their research can be descriptive as well as experimental and is conducted in the field or with animals in captivity.

TESTS AND MEASURES OF INDIVIDUAL DIFFERENCES

The scope of psychology's fields of specialization is great. The professionals who work in these areas strive to help people know, understand, and help themselves. To accomplish this, psychologists use numerous tests to help them ascertain specific information about an individual, a group of people, or a particular population. Ability tests measure multiple aptitudes, creativity, achievement, and intelligence levels. Psychologists may perform occupational and clinical assessments. Also included in the area of assessment are personality tests, which encompass self-report inventories, measures of interests, attitudes and values, projective techniques, and performance and situational evaluations.

An example of a multiple-aptitude test is the Differential Aptitude Test (DAT), first published in 1947, then revised in 1963, 1973, and 1991. Its primary purpose is to counsel students in grades eight through twelve in educational and vocational matters. Creativity tests have received much attention from researchers and practitioners alike. The Aptitudes Research Project (ARP) was developed by the University of Southern California. It is a structure-of-intellect (SI) model, which encompasses all intellectual functions. Though its initial platform was reasoning, creativity, and problem solving, its base was expanded to divergent production. Until the ARP, research resources in this area were very limited.

Achievement tests, which differ from aptitude tests, measure the effects of specific instruction or training. Some of the most respected tests are the California Achievement Tests, the Iowa Tests of Basic Skills, the Metropolitan Achievement Test, and the Stanford Achievement Test. Their significance lies in reporting what the individual can do at the time of test administration. Aptitude instruments, on the other hand, make recommendations about future skills. Intelligence tests measure forms of intelligence; however, the scores given by the Stanford-Binet test and the various Wechsler intelligence scales are only part of a big picture about any given human being and should be evaluated accordingly.

Personality tests measure the emotional, motivational, interpersonal, and attitudinal characteristics of an individual. The Kuder Interest Inventories list occupations according to a person's interest area. The Rorschach Inkblot Projective Technique investigates the personality as a whole. The Thematic Apperception Test (TAT) researches personality and attitude. The Myers-Briggs Type Indicator is a widely used measure of personality dispositions and interests based on Carl Jung's theory of types.

PSYCHOLOGY AND SOCIETY

Psychology as a formal discipline is still relatively new; of its many specializations, some have found their way to maturity, while others are still in their early stages. The development of diverse fields has been justified by the changing nature of social and psychological problems as well as by changing perceptions as to how best to approach those problems. For example, because more people live closer together than ever before, they must interact with one another to a greater degree; finding ways to deal with issues such as aggression, racism, and prejudice therefore becomes crucial. Several divisions of the American Psychological Association reflect the diverse groups that interest psychologists: the Society of Pediatric Psychology, the Society for the Psychological Study of Ethnic Minority Issues, and the Society for the Psychological Study of Lesbian, Gay, and Bisexual Issues.

Economic conditions require most parents to work—whether they are single parents or parents in a two-parent family—thus depriving children of time with their parents. This has created a need for daycare centers; the care and nurturing of young people is being transferred, to a significant degree, to external agents. Moreover, older children may be expected to assume adult responsibilities before they are ready. All these issues point to an increasing need for family counseling. Educational institutions demand achievement from students; this can daunt students who have emotional or family problems that interfere with their ability to learn. The availability of school counselors or psychologists can make a difference in whether such children succeed or fail. Businesses and organizations use psychologists and psychological testing to avoid hiring employees who would be ineffective or incompatible with the organization's approach and to maximize employee productivity on the job.

The specialized fields of psychology have played both a facilitative and a reflective role. Therapists and counselors, for example, have enabled individuals to look at what they have previously accomplished, to assess the present, and to come to terms with themselves and the realities of the future. The future of psychology itself will hold further developments both in the refining of specializations that already exist and in the development of new ones as inevitable societal changes require them.

BIBLIOGRAPHY

Butler, Gillian, and Freda McManus. *Psychology: A Very Short Introduction.* 2d ed. New York: Oxford UP, 2014. Print.

Colman, Andrew M. *What Is Psychology?* 3d ed. New York: Routledge, 2000. Print.

Helms, Jeffrey L., and Daniel T. Rogers. *Majoring in Psychology: Achieving Your Educational and Career Goals.* Malden: Wiley, 2010. Digital file.

Johnson, W. Brad, and Nadine Kaslow, eds. *The Oxford Handbook of Education and Training in Professional Psychology.* Oxford: Oxford UP, 2014. Digital file.

Koch, Sigmund, and David Leary, eds. *A Century of Psychology as Science.* Washington, DC: APA, 2009. Digital file.

Neimeyer, Greg J., et al. "The Diminishing Durability of Knowledge in Professional Psychology: A Second Look at Specializations." *Professional Psychology: Research and Practice* 45.2 (2014): 92–98. Print.

Passer, Michael W., and Ronald E. Smith. *Psychology: The Science of Mind and Behavior.* 4th ed. Boston: McGraw, 2009. Print.

Rieber, Robert W., and Kurt Salzinger, eds. *Psychology: Theoretical-Historical Perspectives.* 2d ed. Washington, DC: APA, 2009. Print.

Schreiber, Katherine. "Careers in Psychology." *Psychology Today* 47.2 (2014): 81–89. Print.

Simonton, Dean Keith. *Great Psychologists and Their Times: Scientific Insights into Psychology's History.* Washington, DC: APA, 2009. Digital file.

Denise S. St. Cyr;
updated by Allyson Washburn and Ursula Goldsmith

SEE ALSO: Behaviorism; Cognitive psychology; Community psychology; Consumer psychology; Developmental psychology; Disaster psychology; Educational psychology; Environmental psychology; Existential psychology; Experimental psychology; Forensic psychology; Humanistic psychology; Industrial and organizational psychology; Media psychology; Multicultural psychology; Neuropsychology; Psychoanalytic psychology; Psychology: Definition.

Psychology
History

TYPE OF PSYCHOLOGY: Origin and definition of psychology

Psychological inquiry and psychology as a field have a varied history going back thousands of years.

KEY CONCEPTS
- Behaviorism
- Clinical psychology
- Cognitive psychology
- Connectionism
- Empiricism
- Functionalism
- Introspection
- Positivism
- Psychoanalysis
- Rationalism
- Scientific method
- Self psychology
- Structuralism

INTRODUCTION

Psychology can be assessed from points of view that regard it as a folk, cultural, or religious process; as a philosophical approach; as a scientific method; as an academic discipline; or as a set of postmodern assumptions.

From the folk process point of view, peoples have formed their own cultures and religions from the beginning of human history. These different cultures and religions have unique values and norms within which the person is considered and evaluated. Out of these norms come the everyday beliefs and expectations that members of the group will hold about themselves, other people, and the world. Thus, in every culture there is an implicit theory of psychology. Since this process is always operative, it has always been a factor in how specific thinkers such as philosophers, scientists, and psychologists, as well as laypeople, have been able to think about the human person. The folk process remains an especially important factor in some areas of psychology, such as humanistic psychology

Philosophy began to emerge about the year 600 BCE. At that time, Thales, a Greek thinker, began to consider systematically the nature of the world. His view that the world's basic element is water demanded that the philosopher give up the folk process, or "common sense," and argue for a conclusion based on rational premises. This new way of thinking led to a much broader set of possibilities in the understanding of the world and the human being. In terms of psychology, philosophers would concentrate on topics such as the relationship between the mind and the body and the process of acquiring knowledge, especially about what is outside the body. In the last decade of the twentieth century, cognitive psychology was strongly influenced by philosophic thinking.

By the end of the Middle Ages and the beginning of the Renaissance, another way of thinking and solving problems began to emerge. As a result of dissatisfaction with both religious and philosophic answers to understanding the world and its place in the cosmos, as well as knowledge about the nature of the human being, a process of systematic and repeated observation and rigorous thinking began to emerge. This new process, which has been labeled a part of modern thinking, has become the scientific method, requiring another separation from the folk process. For instance, when the Polish astronomer Nicolaus Copernicus and the Italian mathematician and astronomer Galileo Galilei argued from their observations that the earth revolved around the sun rather than the opposite, "common-sense" view, they offended both religious authorities and philosophers, but they opened the door to a new way of solving problems and understanding the world and human beings. This new way was named science.

Thanks to both philosophy and science, by the middle to end of the nineteenth century various scholarly areas had emerged, each with a unique use of methodology and subject matter. One of these disciplines was psychology. In 1879, Wilhelm Wundt, a German philosopher and physiologist, set up what is generally considered the first laboratory in experimental psychology. From that point, psychology began to be recognized as a discipline by scholars in the Western world.

Through an interaction with disciplines such as anthropology and linguistics, which were thriving on relativistic assumptions, and a philosophy of language that limited meaning to the particular and situational case, a psychological point of view developed in the mid- to late twentieth century called social constructionism. Although promoted by those who identify with the discipline of psychology, social constructionism is at odds with the assumptions of the modern period, including many of those that go with science, and is, therefore, labeled postmodern. Such an approach seeks only to describe and interpret rather than to explain, as is the aim in science. Parallel developments such as deconstruction in the field of literary criticism were taking place at the same time.

THE PHILOSOPHERS

Over the years, philosophers asked questions about the world and how humans come to have knowledge of it, provided assumptions that would limit or promote certain kinds of explanations, and attempted to summarize the knowledge that was available to an educated person.

Those thinkers who considered the nature of reality and the world between the years ca. 624 to 370 BCE were called pre-Socratics. One of them, Heraclitus, opposed Thales's idea of water as the basic element with his idea that fire was the basic element, and therefore the world and everything in it was in a state of flux and constant change. Empedocles went a step further to propose that there were four basic elements: earth, air, fire, and water. This scheme, when applied by physicians such as the Greek Hippocrates and the Greco-Roman Galen led to the notion of the four humors and a prototheory of personality that has been influential for almost two thousand years.

From his understanding of the thinking of Socrates and Pythagoras, Plato constructed a systematic view of the human as a dualistic creature having a body that is material and a soul that is spiritual. This doctrine had significant consequences for religion, for philosophy, and for psychology. Plato also saw knowledge as acquired by the soul through the process of recollection of the form, which exists in an ideal and abstract state. Plato's student

Aristotle systematized the study of logic, promoted the use of observation as a means of acquiring knowledge, and presented a different view of the human as one whose senses were reliable sources of information and whose soul, while capable of reasoning, was the form that kept the body (and the person) in existence.

The philosophers who came during the medieval period generally split into two camps: those who followed Plato and those who followed Aristotle. Just prior to the medieval period, Saint Augustine, bishop of Hippo (now part of Algeria), had combined Neoplatonism, Christianity, and Stoicism (to the extent of believing that following the natural law was virtuous). The Neoaristotelian tradition was typified by Thomas Aquinas, an Italian Dominican priest, who integrated Aristotelian thought with Christianity and who promoted the use of reason in the obtaining of knowledge. Although not anticipated by Thomas, this Aquinas point of view would ease the way for what would become scientific thinking.

René Descartes, a French Renaissance philosopher, created a dualistic system called interactionism, where the soul, which was spiritual, interacted with the body, which was material. Both the notion of interaction and its site, the pineal gland, were so open to debate that the theory led to two different traditions: a rationalist tradition and an empiricist tradition. The rationalist tradition was led by German thinkers such as Gottfried Wilhelm Leibniz, who was also an inventor of the calculus; Immanuel Kant, who taught that the mind had an innate categorizing ability; and Johann Friedrich Herbart, who held that, if expressed in mathematical terms, psychology could become a science. All the rationalists opted for the notion of "an active mind," and Herbart's thinking was very influential for those, such as Wundt, who would view psychology as a scientific discipline. The empiricist tradition was stronger in France and England. Several decisive representatives of empiricism were Englishmen John Locke, David Hume, and John Stuart Mill. Empiricism postulated that all knowledge came through the senses and that the ideas that made up the mind were structured on the percepts of the senses. Eventually, in Mill's thinking, the ideas of the mind were held together through the laws of association.

Another tradition developed past the midpoint of this period was positivism. Positivism, as developed by Frenchman August Compte, argued that the only knowledge that one can be sure of is information that is publicly observable. This would strongly influence both the subject matter and the methodology of science in general and psychology in particular.

In the beginning of the twentieth century, Englishman Bertrand Russell introduced symbolic logic, and his student Ludwig Wittgenstein created a philosophy of language. Both of these developments were necessary precursors of the late twentieth century interest in the nature of mind, in which many disciplines came together to form cognitive science. Wittgenstein's work would open the door for social constructionism.

THE SCIENTISTS

The development of the scientific method was only one of the factors that was associated with the change from the Middle Ages to the Renaissance. Developments in anatomy, physiology, astronomy, and other fields from the middle of the sixteenth century to the beginning of the twentieth century have had a major impact on the understanding of science and have paved the way for psychology as a science. The work of Copernicus and Galileo, in freeing astronomy from folk and religious belief, was a start. In the field of anatomy Flemish scientist Andreas Vesalius published in 1543 the first accurate woodcuts showing the anatomy of the human body. This was a decisive break with the tradition of Galen. By 1628, Englishman William Harvey had described accurately the circulation of blood.

In the meantime, Englishman Francis Bacon, a contemporary of Galileo, offered a view of science that favored inductive reasoning on the basis of a series of observations. This was another break with the tradition of relying on the classical authorities. In 1687, the *Principia* was published by Englishman Isaac Newton, who laid the foundation for the calculus, enhanced the understanding of color and light, grasped the notion of universal gravitation, and produced laws (natural law) of planetary motion.

Soon Swiss mathematicians, members of the Bernoulli family and Leonhard Euler, were refining the differential and integral calculus that was invented independently of Newton by the philosopher Leibniz.

In 1751, a Scot, Robert Whytt, working on frogs, noted the importance of the spinal cord for reflex action. Localization of function in the nervous system was beginning.

By 1754, Swedish botanist Carolus Linnaeus had produced a system of classification for plants, animals, and minerals that made observation and discussion in science simpler.

German anatomist Franz Gall maintained that "faculties" of the brain were discernible by observing the contours of the skull: Phrenology was another step in localization but a false one that violated scientific axioms. It spread rapidly, especially in the United States, as a form of folk psychology and diagnosis.

In 1795, an assistant at the Royal Observatory in Greenwich, England, was found to be recording times of stellar transit consistently later than his supervisor. German astronomer Friedrich Wilhelm Bessel recognized that this was involuntary and might be calibrated as a personal equation. This recognition of reaction time foreshadowed many studies in the laboratories of psychology.

Italian physician and physicist Luigi Galvani in 1791 stimulated movement in a frog's leg with electricity, demonstrating that electrical stimulation had a role in neural research. Englishman Charles Bell, in 1811, and Frenchman François Magendi, in 1822, demonstrated differential functions of the dorsal (sensory) and ventral (motor) roots of the spinal cord. Again, localization of function was promoted. In 1824–1825, Pierre Flourens introduced the technique of ablation studies for brain tissue.

The field of physiology came together in the *Handbuch der Physiologie des Menschen für Vorlesungen* (1833–1840; *Manual of Physiology*), published by German Johannes Müller. Müller's law of specific nerve energies, which claimed that there was a specific pathway and type of signal for each kind of sensation, was a significant contribution.

German Ernst Weber expanded the study of touch and kinesthesis and created the Weber fraction and the two-point threshold. Gustav Theodor Fechner expanded Weber's work into Weber's Law and provided a rationale and methodology for early psychology with his development of psychophysical methods.

Frenchman Paul Broca made use of the clinical method of studying brain lesions. With this methodology, the language area was localized in the third frontal convolution of the cortex.

German Hermann von Helmholtz, a student of Müller who argued against his teacher's support for vitalism, applied the law of conservation of energy to living creatures, measured rate of nerve conduction, and wrote esteemed handbooks on the physics and physiology of vision and audition. An opposing theorist, German Ewald Hering, a nativist, created the opponent process theory of color vision.

In 1870, Germans Gustav Fritsch and Eduard Hitzig introduced electrical stimulation of the brain, which demonstrated the motor areas of the brain.

From the middle to the latter part of the nineteenth century, Englishman Francis Galton, a cousin of Charles Darwin who was also interested in evolution, promoted mental testing and the study of individual differences. He also stimulated the work of Englishman mathematician Karl Pearson, who invented the statistics to support such studies and much of psychology.

By 1902, an American, Shepard Ivory Franz, combined the ablation technique with training procedures to investigate the function of the frontal lobes in cats. His work led to the work of the great American neuropsychologist Karl Lashley, who led the quest to find the neural basis for memory in his 1950 work *In Search of the Engram*. Two of Lashley's students, Canadian Donald O. Hebb, with his work on cell assemblies and phase sequences, and American Roger Sperry, with his work on split-brain preparations in the 1960s, would do much to promote neuropsychology and prepare for cognitive science.

BEGINNING OF PSYCHOLOGY AS A DISCIPLINE

In 1879, Wilhelm Wundt, a student of Helmholtz, brought together his two disciplines of physiology and philosophy by creating a laboratory for experimental psychology at the University of Leipzig in Germany. His laboratory attracted many of the individuals who would become leaders in the new science of psychology. Among these were German Oswald Külpe, Englishman Edward Titchener, and American James McKeen Cattell.

Meanwhile, in the United States, William James, a scientist and philosopher who was familiar with European scholarly trends, published the defining American work on psychology, *The Principles of Psychology* (1890). This became the dominant text in the English-speaking world and attracted many more Americans to the study of psychology. Both Wundt and James were instrumental in separating psychology from other disciplines both in methodology and in subject matter. Both saw psychology as an introspective science that was to study adult human consciousness. Introspection required that the investigator focus on her or his own experience or awareness, that is, what the individual is thinking and feeling at any one moment.

THE SCHOOLS OF PSYCHOLOGY

There were very quickly a number of individuals who either agreed partly or disagreed wholly with Wundt and James. Some of these individuals argued their points persuasively and a number of schools or points of view coalesced around them during the last decade of the nineteenth century and the first several decades of the twentieth century.

Coming from the German rationalist tradition of philosophy, Wundt took as his goal the understanding of consciousness using the method of introspection. Wundt's point of view has become known as voluntarism Wundt stressed the role of will, choice, and purpose, all of which he saw present in attention and volition.

Wundt's student Titchener created a somewhat similar school of thought when, in 1892, he came to Cornell University in Ithaca, New York. Titchener also wanted to study consciousness using the introspective method. He differed from Wundt in that his preferred philosophy was English empiricism, and this led him to a different understanding of consciousness. His approach was to discover the elements of consciousness, and this approach was called structuralism. His successful program led to a strong interest in experimentation, especially on sensation and perception, in American psychology. He trained a large number of Americans in the almost four decades that he taught at Cornell.

American psychologists were not wholly devoted to either Wundt's or Titchener's approach to psychology even if they had received their PhDs with them. Instead, they often were motivated by their appreciation for the work of Charles Darwin, who had published his theory of evolution in his famous *On the Origin of Species by Means of Natural Selection* (1859). Darwin's writing had been popularized in the English-speaking world by the English writer and speaker Herbert Spencer, who promoted the idea of social Darwinism, that is, that processes of competition among groups of humans would weed out the unfit and thus help to perfect the human race. Following Spencer, many psychologists in the United States saw adaptation as a fundamental concern for their academic field. Among these was philosopher and psychologist John Dewey, whose 1896 article, "The Reflex Arc Concept in Psychology," was seen as the formal beginning of the school of functionalism.

One student of both Wundt and James who was very influential in early functionalism was American G. Stanley Hall, who founded the American Journal of Psychology in 1887 and who founded Clark University and its psychology department in 1888. He was a leading proponent for developmental psychology, the founder of the American Psychological Association (in 1892), and an untiring organizer.

Very influential in the promotion of applied psychology was a Prussian student of Wundt who had followed James in the laboratories of Harvard University, Hugo Münsterberg, who arrived at Harvard University in 1892.

Two major branches of the school of functionalism were associated with the University of Chicago and Columbia University. There were three leaders at the University of Chicago. Dewey served from 1894 to 1904, when he moved to Teacher's College at Columbia University. He was succeeded by James Rowland Angell, who served for twenty-five years and who was followed by his student, Harvey Carr, who specialized in the adaptive acts of learning and perception.

At Columbia University, the first significant leader was James McKeen Cattell, who accepted a professorship in 1891 and who stayed for twenty-six years. In addition, very influential was a student of Cattell, Robert S. Woodworth. Woodworth wrote extensively on many topics in psychology, including physiological psychology, the history of psychology, motivation, and experimental psychology. He wrote the significant *Experimental Psychology* in 1938. The third major influence at Columbia was the very productive Edward L. Thorndike. Thorndike was active at Columbia from 1899 until 1940. He wrote on animal learning, developing a theory called connectionism that accounted for learning in an animal or human on the basis of a strengthening of a connection between a stimulus and a response. Besides learning theory, Thorndike also wrote on verbal behavior, educational practices, intelligence testing, and the measurement of other types of psychological and sociological phenomena. As a school of thought, functionalism came to represent the interests of a great number of American psychologists who were involved in areas that called for practical intervention such as testing, clinical, social, and developmental psychology.

The reaction to Wundtian psychology took a different direction in Europe. Influenced by a group of teachers who adopted a more holistic view of human functioning, a system known as Gestalt psychology started in Germany in 1910. Among the teachers was Franz Clemens Brentano. Brentano, trained in Aristotelian philosophy, promoted an "act psychology," which stated that the study of the mind had to do with mental acts (such as willing or perceiving), not the study of consciousness divisible into elements. One of Brentano's students at the University of Vienna was Austrian Christian von Ehrenfels, who was himself licensed to teach at Vienna in 1888. Ehrenfels wrote a paper, "Über Gestaltqualitäten" (1890; "On Gestalt Qualities"), that would be the formative document in the thinking of all future Gestalt psychologists. This paper asserted that the significant aspect in any perception was the pattern created by the individual elements and not the individual elements themselves, as with the melody rather than the individual notes of the melody. Foremost among the Gestalt psychologists was Czech-born Max Wertheimer, who received his PhD in 1904 from the University of Würzbürg. In 1910, Wertheimer involved the two other founders of Gestalt psychology in a study of apparent movement that became known as the phi phenomenon. These two were German Kurt Koffka and Estonian Wolfgang Köhler. Both had just received their PhDs at the University of Berlin under the direction of German Carl Stumpf, who was himself a student of Brentano and whose lifework was devoted to the study of music, space perception, and audition. His work would lead to the phenomenological approach that was common to Gestalt psychology. In the 1930s, with the coming to power of National Socialism in Germany, the three main Gestalt psychologists—Wertheimer, Koffka, and Köhler—emigrated to the United States, where they found behaviorism's associationism and elementism as unacceptable as it was in both Wundtian psychology and psychoanalysis.

William McDougall was born in England, educated in England and at the University of Göttingen in Germany, and began his teaching at Oxford University in England. In 1920, he came to the United States, where he developed his brand of psychology called hormic psychology, from the Greek word horme, which means "urge." He called himself a behaviorist, but one who viewed behavior as instinctually directed and at the same time as purposeful. McDougall was widely admired but seemed out of step with the dominant behaviorism of his time. His views are much more congenial with the cognitive psychology of the late twentieth century.

Basing part of his rationale on the work of Russian reflexologist Ivan Petrovich Pavlov, who discovered the principles of conditioning while doing work on the digestive system of dogs, American John Broadus Watson promoted a radical behaviorism that rejected introspection as a method and suggested that the study of animal behavior was the equivalent of the study of human behavior.

His lectures at Columbia University, which were published in the *Psychological Review* in 1913 under the title "Psychology as the Behaviorist Views It," are seen as the beginning of behaviorism. They certainly separated behaviorism from both structuralism and functionalism.

In 1900, Mary W. Calkins, an American student of James, began her defense of a self psychology. Despite the functionalist interest in adaptation and the behaviorist rejection of introspection, Calkins would continue to assert that the self was an existential reality; that is, it was knowable in one's own awareness. After her death in 1930, the self came to be considered a conceptualization. Gordon Allport, an American who studied extensively in Europe, became the leading self psychologist for another thirty years. In Allport's later years, clinicians such as Carl R. Rogers, who developed client-centered therapy (later known as person-centered therapy), would keep the idea of self and its centrality alive in psychology until the cognitive revolution of the 1960s and 1970s allowed the self to become a popular integrating construct again.

Austrian physician Sigmund Freud published *Studien über Hysterie* (1895; *Studies in Hysteria*, 1950) and began the school of therapy known as psychoanalysis. Psychoanalysis soon became a general theory of personality. Freud's possessiveness about the theory led to the ouster from his inner circle of two theorists who would go on to create their own approaches to psychoanalysis. The first was Austrian Alfred Adler in 1911. Adler's point of view would become known as individual psychology. The second, in 1913, was Swiss Carl Jung, who questioned the sexual basis of the motivating energy proposed by Freud. Jung's point of view has become known as analytical psychology. By the 1930s, Freud's classic psychology of the unconscious had shifted to a greater appreciation of the conscious. Thus, Freud's daughter, Anna Freud, following the interests of her father, published *Das Ich und die Abwehrmechanismen* (1936; *The Ego and the Mechanisms of Defense*, 1937). Classic psychoanalysis had changed into ego psychology. The best-known representative of the new ego psychology was the child analyst and writer Erik H. Erikson. Erikson, who was born in Germany and who had been analyzed by Anna, came to the United States in 1933. His *Childhood and Society* (1950) made connections to and enriched developmental psychology, especially in terms of his reworking of Freud's five developmental stages into the "eight ages of man."

APPLIED PSYCHOLOGY

Frenchman Alfred Binet published the first individual test of intelligence in 1905. Lewis Madison Terman, an American student of G. Stanley Hall, published his revision of Binet's test, called the Stanford Binet, in the United States in 1912. An industry was born. The test was reissued in 1916, 1937, 1960, 1986, and 2003. Group tests of intelligence were developed for the military during both World War I and World War II. The needs of the military also promoted another applied psychology: clinical psychology. In World War II, short-term psychotherapy was found to be useful in returning combatants to active service. Many academic psychologists were pressed into training programs to become psychotherapists. By the time the war ended, a number of psychologists viewed themselves as clinicians and returned to redirect graduate programs in psychology toward clinical psychology. By the late 1940s testing, diagnosis, and clinical practice were well established.

NEOBEHAVIORISM

In 1924, a group of philosophers in Vienna, Austria, known as the Vienna Circle, revised and refined positivism into logical positivism, and in 1927, Percy Williams Bridgman, an American physicist, proposed operationism, in which every theoretical construct would be defined by the operations that were used to measure it. These developments allowed experimenters to deal positivistically with abstract variables and led to a more sophisticated behaviorism labeled neobehaviorism. Americans Edward C. Tolman, Clark L. Hull, and B. F. Skinner were notable representatives of neobehaviorism, which specialized in the study of learning and motivation, mostly with nonhuman species. Skinner differed from the others in that he favored induction and description as the basis for his studies. Neobehaviorism was superseded by changes that brought about the cognitive revolution in the 1960s and 1970s. Its heritage remains in psychology in the area of methodology.

In addition, by the 1950s, a rift that had begun in the days of Titchener between those who saw themselves as pure scientific psychologists as opposed to those who practiced an applied psychology was reconceptualized as a conflict between the academic psychologists who maintained a behavioristic approach and the clinicians who were heavily influenced by psychoanalysis and were beginning to appreciate Rogers's person-centered approach. This struggle was exacerbated by the growing number of practitioners, who began to outnumber the academic psychologists. One result of this disciplinary conflict was the foundation of a separate organization for the academics, the American Psychological Society, formed in 1988.

THE 1960S AND 1970S

The emergence of the computer both as a tool and as a model of the human mind had a major effect on psychology. Neuroscience, philosophy, anthropology, linguistics, artificial intelligence, and psychology came together in the 1960s to form the basis for a new discipline: cognitive science. The new technology and the opportunity to work with people and ideas from other disciplines freed psychology to reinvestigate questions of mental functioning and consciousness.

In 1954, American Abraham Maslow published the influential *Motivation and Personality,* which began humanistic psychology, a movement seen by Maslow as an antidote to the dehumanizing assumptions of both behaviorism and psychoanalysis. By 1961, there was the *Journal of Humanistic Psychology* and, by 1962, the American Association of Humanistic Psychologists. Rogers, with his person-centered therapy, added to the attractiveness of the movement for American psychologists. Its emphasis on admitting the whole person to psychology gained more general acceptance and, together with the cognitive revolution, promoted a more humanistic and cognitively oriented general psychology.

THE 1980S AND 1990S

Developmental psychology, building on the work of Swiss Jean Piaget from the 1920s through the 1960s, and cognitive psychology, stimulated by the early 1960s work of Americans George A. Miller and Jerome Bruner, began once again to study consciousness and its development, but this time from infancy through adulthood. A student of Miller, German-born Ulric Neisser built on this and his earlier work, *Cognitive Psychology* (1967), to bring to the 1980s and 1990s an integrative approach to consciousness, concept formation, perception, and selfhood. In general, the period was one of eclecticism and was labeled neofunctionalism by one historian.

SOCIAL CONSTRUCTIONISM

Another trend that impacted psychology was postmodern thought. Although present in philosophy and anthropology through the twentieth century, it became obvious in psychology only in the 1970s, where it was known as social constructionism. Since the 1970s, it has made its

presence obvious in the subfield called cultural psychology and in social psychology. When applied to personality development, the concept of narrative as an inborn mechanism has become a focus for those who wish to describe the process of self-development.

THE 2000S AND 2010S

Notable milestones in genetics and neuroscience during the 2000s and 2010s provided the basis for ongoing research into human development and pathology. In April 2003, the Human Genome Project reported that it had produced a finished version of the human genome sequence, with 99 percent of genome sequenced, an accuracy rate of less than one error per ten thousand nucleotide base pairs, and less than four hundred sequence gaps. In 2013, the Obama administration announced the formation of Brain Research through Advancing Innovative Neurotechnologies, also called the BRAIN Initiative or Brain Activity Map Project. The initiative's goal is to map every neuron in the human brain over a ten-year period. In April 2014, the first installment of the National Institute of Mental Health–funded BrainSpan Atlas of the Developing Human Brain project, produced by Seattle's Allen Institute for Brain Science, was reported online by Nature. The project intends to profile gene activity over the course of the brain's development and thereby help researchers understand the genesis of brain-based disorders such as schizophrenia and autism.

BIBLIOGRAPHY

Allen Institute for Brain Science. *BrainSpan Atlas of the Developing Human Brain.* Allen Inst. for Brain Science, 2004–2014. Web. 27 June 2014.

Brett, George Sidney. *A History of Psychology.* London: Routledge, 2014. Digital file.

Gardner, Howard. *The Mind's New Science: A History of the Cognitive Revolution.* New York: Basic, 1998. Print.

Hergenhahn, B. R. *An Introduction to the History of Psychology.* 6th ed. Belmont: Wadsworth, 2009. Print.

Hilgard, Ernest Ropiequet. *Psychology in America: A Historical Survey.* New York: Harcourt, 1987. Print.

Hunt, Morton. *The Story of Psychology.* 2d ed. New York: Doubleday, 2007. Print.

Koch, Sigmund, and David Leary, eds. *A Century of Psychology as Science.* Washington, DC: American Psychological Association, 1992. Print.

Russell, Bertrand. *A History of Western Philosophy.* New York: Simon, 1945. Print.

Stevenson, Leslie, and David L. Haberman. *Ten Theories of Human Nature.* 5th ed. New York: Oxford UP, 2009. Print.

Stroebe, Wolfgang, and Arie W. Kruglanski. *Handbook of the History of Social Psychology.* New York: Psychology, 2012. Digital file.

Everett J. Delahanty, Jr.

SEE ALSO: Adler, Alfred; Allport, Gordon; Analytical psychotherapy; Behaviorism; Binet, Alfred; Cognitive psychology; Dewey, John; Ego psychology: Erik H. Erikson; Freud, Sigmund; Freudian psychology; Gestalt therapy; Hall, G. Stanley; Humanistic psychology; James, William; Jung, Carl; Jungian psychology; Maslow, Abraham; Mental illness: Historical concepts; Pavlov, Ivan Petrovich; Philosophy and psychology; Piaget, Jean; Positive psychology; Psychoanalytic psychology; Psychology: Definition; Psychology: Fields of specialization; Rogers, Carl R.; Skinner, B. F.; Structuralism and functionalism; Thorndike, Edward L.; Watson, John B.

Psycho-oncology

TYPE OF PSYCHOLOGY: Behavioral medicine; Biological bases of human behavior; Clinical; Counseling; Family; Health; Social

Originally, psycho-oncology was a subspecialty area of oncology that investigated, assessed, and treated the social and psychological aspects of having cancer. Currently, psycho-oncology also includes the study and amelioration of pain stemming from cancer and its treatments, subjective emotional responses to receiving and carrying the diagnosis (anxiety, depression, degree of hope/hopelessness, delirium), application of patients' effective coping, functional status and quality of patients' lives, role of spiritual and philosophical beliefs, managing stress on care-givers and professional staffs, and the interactions between psychological and emotional factors on immune systems

KEY TERMS:
- Behavioral medicine
- Health psychology
- Oncology
- Psychoimmunology

Historically, receiving a cancer diagnosis was receiving a terminal diagnosis. In a humanely motivated effort to protect patients from complete loss of hope and push-

ing them into states of despair, not revealing the diagnosis to patients was routinely done though families were generally told. Earlier work conducted at Memorial Sloan-Kettering Cancer Center in New York and the Massachusetts General Hospital in Boston on patients' psychological reactions to having and being treated for cancer supported the emerging idea in the mid 1970's that it was generally more harmful to patients to keep their diagnosis a secret. Early services in psycho-oncology were manifest in promoting truth-telling to patients, encouraging patients with similar diagnoses to meet for emotional support and disseminate treatment information, educating professionals about the quality of life considerations and the values in comfort care over curative intervention among grave prognostic cases. These growing changes in the environment of cancer treatment were concurrent with improvements in actual cancer treatments themselves and growing survival rates. Today, psycho-oncology professionals provide multiple services under the umbrella of engaging the psychological and psychosocial aspects of having cancer.

APPLICATIONS AND FUNCTIONS

Psycho-oncology researchers have developed many instruments that assess a wide-range of patients' reactions to cancer including pain, anxiety, depression, and delirium. These instruments assist with the evaluating the efficacy of interventions made and provide quantitative parameters through which on-going research in psycho-oncological methods can be tracked and understood. Pre-existing psychological "tests" or instruments were not normed on populations that were this medically ill and routinely over-reported patients' experiences. There now exist scales derived from patient responses to sets of questions that are tumor-site specific. Psycho-oncology's contribution to outcomes research (whether a new treatment, drug, procedure is effective, worth the costs and risks, etc.) has moved it beyond whether the intervention increases survival, but whether the survival is worth having—does sustaining this life allow the patient to enjoy a quality of life. Oncological treatments now have to have more impact on their effectiveness at reduction of tumor growth, but also promote sufficient functional status for them to be considered efficacious and beneficial. Quality-adjusted life years is a widely cited statistic combing survivability (how much longer does this treatment add to patients' lives) with measures of patients' quality of life. Mortality rate statistics are inadequate by themselves.

Psycho-oncology practitioners who serve on consultation-liaison services commonly treat adjustment disorders that arise in cancer patients. In effect, they treat not the disease, but the disturbed state of mind and emotion that understandably arise in the face of coping with cancer. They treat not cancer, but patients' reactions to having cancer.

Health psychologists study how patients cope with illness and comply with treatment plans. This has become a standard component of what psycho-oncologists work to facilitate in their patients: adaptive patterns of feeling, thinking, and behaving in facing cancer and its treatments and informed compliance with treatment plan options. Psycho-oncology practitioners unite understanding patients' subjective experiences without judgment or reprimand, respect for patients' rights to react in the way they do, and compassionate positive regard for their emotional suffering with the focused treatment of the cancer itself.

Practitioners of psycho-oncology also focus on preventive and behavioral health measures, helping patients effect lifestyle, nutritional, and habit changes to reduce risk of developing cancer. Reducing sun exposure, high fat, high calorie intake, eliminating tobacco use, and achieving and maintaining healthy levels of exercise meaningfully reduce cancer risk.

TRAINING AND CERTIFICATION

Because psycho-oncology is a clinical and research application of professional training, there is not a universally-accepted academic credential through training programs exist at most major cancer treatment centers. Professional organizations promoting the work of psycho-oncology include the American Society of Psychosocial and Behavioral Oncology, the British Psychosocial Oncology Group, and the International Psycho-oncology Society. Their membership consists of oncologists, psychiatrists, and allied health professionals.

Those practicing or researching psycho-oncology come from several professional disciplines who apply their training to the psychological and psychosocial treatment of cancer patients and their families: Residency-trained physician oncologists, residency-trained physician psychiatrists, clinical health psychologists, nurse practitioners, medical social workers, and pastoral counselors. (This last group is not routinely required to possess a state license.) Professionals follow the individual requirements of their disciplines regarding obtaining licenses to practice their specialty independently,

obtaining privileges to treat patients from the institutions where they practice, obtaining specialty board certification (where applicable), and maintain (renew) board certification.

Specific training in psycho-oncology usually occurs as an elective track or certificate program at the major cancer treatment centers for the professionals in training there. Psycho-oncology is not typically a requirement of curricula in oncology, psychiatry, health psychology, or social work. Thus, people who engage in its practice are generally those who have actively sought out training, reflecting high degrees of interest and commitment.

The National Comprehensive Cancer Network (NCCN) is an organization representing nearly all of the major comprehensive cancer care centers in North America. They have produced standards for psychosocial cancer care and clinical practice guidelines for those involved in providing psycho-oncology services, including non-licensed professionals like pastoral counselors. Institutional regulatory and oversight bodies like the Joint Commission of Accreditation of Heathcare Organizations (JCAHO), the American Osteopathic Association (AOA), and governmental departments of health have not yet fully incorporated these guidelines or psycho-oncological care itself as standard criteria for providing treatment to cancer patients.

Reimbursement for and revenue generation by psycho-oncology interventions is meager relative to other cancer treatment modalities (e.g., surgery, radiation oncology, chemotherapy). When institutions reassess fiscal priorities, psycho-oncology services and programs are often among the first to be discontinued.

PATIENT-CENTERED MEDICAL CARE

Psycho-oncology's contribution to cancer treatment includes the provision of comfort and palliative care so that patients who are terminally ill do not suffer needlessly as a result of aggressive or invasive treatments that prolong time at the cost of reducing functional ability. Helping patients and their loved ones deal with life-threatening disease means that psycho-oncologically oriented treatments encourage inclusion of patients' spiritual beliefs, religious practices, and search to find meaning when dying is the process and death inevitable.

The high emotional demands on dealing with life and death, the uncertainty of treatments, the cancer-causing physical and emotional pain profoundly affect health care professionals and caregivers. Psycho-oncology interventions include protocols and strategies to avoid provider burnout and depression.

Psycho-oncology's broad reach runs from the cancer team and patient family to the patients' cellular immune response, relevant for cancers that are immunogenic (stemming from a virus as opposed to cancers that are chemically medicated as in cigarette smoking causing lung cancer). Physical and psychological stressors are associated with dysregulation of immune response compromising the natural killer response of cells. Psycho-oncology has revealed both real and statistical associations between psychological and behavioral factors and the initiation and/or progression of these types of cancers.

BIBLIOGRAPHY

Barraclough, Jennifer. (1999). *Cancer and Emotion: A Practical Guide to Psycho-oncology.* New York: Wiley. Accessible to both lay and professional readers, this remains an excellent introduction and review to the role that emotions play in developing and treating various cancers.

Bearison, David J. & Mulhern, Raymond K. (eds.), (1999). *Pediatric Psychooncology: Psychological Perspectives on Children With Cancer.* New York: Oxford. Chapters written by experts in the field, this provides in depth discussion of selected topics of keen interest to those working or living with children who have cancer.

Holland, Jimmie C., et al (eds.). (1998). *Psycho-oncology.* New York: Oxford. Academically-oriented text book that serves as both introduction to psycho-oncology and discussion of its advancement into integrative care. A work ahead of its time.

Lewis, Clare E., Barraclough, Jennifer, & O'Brien, Rosalind. (2002) *The Psychoimmunology of Cancer.* New York: Oxford. Ground-breaking work presenting applied research findings which strongly argue for the ameliorative role on including psychological and emotional factors in cancer treatments and the deleterious effects of not doing so.

ONLINE RESOURCES, ORGANIZATIONS AND PROFESSIONAL SOCIETIES

While more suited for the professional psychologist who wishes to be additionally educated and trained in psycho-oncology, each also has educational resources for patients and their families.

American Society of Clinical Oncology
1900 Duke Street, Suite 200
Alexandria, VA 22314
703-299-7130
www.asco.org

International Psycho-Oncology Society
c/o Custom Management Group
2365 Hunters Way
Charlottesville, VA 22911
434-293-5350
www.ipos.org

National Comprehensive Cancer Network
500 Old York Road, Suite 250
Jenkintown, PA 19046
215-690-0300
www.nccn.org.

Multilingual Core Curriculum in Psycho-Oncology
On-line Lecture Series
www.ipos-society.org
National Breast Cancer Coalition
800-622-2838
www.natlbcc.org

Paul Moglia

SEE ALSO: Cancer; Health; Interdisciplinary studies; Lifestyle; Oncology; Pharmacology.

Psychopathology

TYPE OF PSYCHOLOGY: Psychopathology

As a field of study, psychopathology has as its focus the descriptions and causes of abnormal behavior and psychological and emotional problems. Approaches to psychopathology differ with respect to the assumed causes of psychological problems. Many clinicians integrate different models to understand the basis of a client's problems and combine different treatments to maximize effectiveness.

KEY CONCEPTS
- Behavior therapy
- Biological approach
- Biopsychosocial approach
- Cognitive approach
- Cognitive therapy

- Culture and psychopathology
- Learning approach
- Mental illness
- Somatic therapy

INTRODUCTION

Psychopathology refers to psychological dysfunctions that either create distress for the person or interfere with day-to-day functioning in relationships, work, or leisure. Psychological disorders, abnormal behavior, mental illness, and behavior and emotional disorders are terms often used in place of psychopathology.

As a topic of interest, psychopathology does not have an identifiable historical beginning. From the writings of ancient Egyptians, Hebrews, and Greeks, it is clear that ancient societies believed that abnormal behavior had its roots in supernatural phenomena, such as the vengeance of God or evil spirits. Although modern science opposes this view, in the twenty-first century, many people who hold fundamentalist religious beliefs or live in isolated societies still maintain that abnormal behavior is the result of possession by spirits.

The Greek physician Hippocrates rejected the theory of demonic possession. He believed that psychological disorders had many natural causes, including heredity, head trauma, brain disease, and even family stress. While he was wrong about the specific details, it is remarkable how accurately he identified broad categories of factors that do influence the development of psychopathology. The Roman physician Galen adopted Hippocrates's ideas and expanded on them. His school of thought held that diseases, including psychological disorders, were due to an imbalance of four bodily fluids, which he called humors: blood, black bile, yellow bile, and phlegm. Too much black bile, called melancholer, was believed to cause depression. Galen's beliefs have been discredited, but many of the terms he used have lived on. For instance, a specific subtype of depression is named after Galen's melancholer: major depressive disorder with melancholic features.

A major figure in the history of psychopathology is the German psychiatrist Emil Kraepelin. He claimed that mental illnesses, like physical illnesses, could be classified into distinct disorders, each having its own biological causes. Each disorder could be recognized by a cluster of symptoms, called a syndrome. The way in which Kraepelin classified mental disorders continues to exert a strong influence on approaches to categorizing mental illnesses. The official classification system in the United States is the *Diagnostic and Statistical Manual of Mental Disorders: DSM-5* (5th ed., 2013). Many features of this manual can be traced directly to the writings of Kraepelin in the early years of the twentieth century.

EXAMPLES OF PSYCHOPATHOLOGY

There is a very broad range of psychological disorders. The DSM-5 lists more than two hundred psychological disorders that differ in symptoms and the degree to which they affect a person's ability to function.

It is normal for someone to feel anxious on occasion. Generalized anxiety disorder is diagnosed when a person engages in excessive worry about all sorts of things and feels anxious and tense much of the time. Most people who have this disorder function quite well. They can do well at work, have good relationships, and be good parents. It is the fact that they suffer so much from their anxiety that leads to a diagnosis. In contrast, schizophrenia can be completely debilitating. Many people with schizophrenia cannot hold a job, are hospitalized frequently, have difficulty in relationships, and are incapable of good parenting. Common symptoms of schizophrenia include delusions (a system of false beliefs, such as the belief that there is a vast conspiracy among extraterrestrial aliens to control the government), hallucinations (seeing things that are not there or hearing voices that other people cannot hear), incoherence (talking in a way that no one can understand), and expressing emotions out of context (such as laughing when telling a sad story). The symptoms of schizophrenia make it difficult or impossible for the person to function normally, and the fact that symptoms interfere with functioning is more important than the distress that the person feels.

Many disorders are marked by both subjective distress and impaired functioning. One such disorder is obsessive-compulsive disorder (OCD). An obsession is a recurrent, usually unpleasant thought, image, or impulse that intrudes into a person's awareness. Some common examples are thinking that every bump hit in the road while driving could have been a person struck by the car, believing that one is contaminated with germs, or picturing oneself stabbing one's children. Obsessions cause a great deal of distress and typically lead to the development of compulsions. A compulsion is a repetitive act that is used by the person to stop the obsession and decrease the anxiety it causes. People who believe they have been contaminated may wash themselves for hours on end; those who believe that they have hit another person while driving may not be able to resist the urge to stop and look for someone injured. Behavioral compulsions can sometimes occupy so much time that the person cannot meet the demands of everyday life.

CAUSES OF PSYCHOPATHOLOGY

The most important goal of researchers in the field of psychopathology is to discover the causes, or etiology, of each disorder. If the causes for disorders were known, then psychologists could design effective treatments and perhaps even be able to prevent the development of many disorders. Unfortunately, theories of psychological disorders are in their infancy, and there are many more questions than there are answers. There is no general agreement among psychologists as to where to look for answers to the question of etiology. Consequently, some researchers stress the importance of biological causes, other researchers focus on psychological processes, and still others emphasize the crucial role of learning experiences in the development of behavior disorders. All these approaches are important, and each supplies a piece of the puzzle of psychopathology, but all approaches have their limitations.

The Learning Approach. Psychologists who work within this model of psychopathology believe that abnormal behavior is learned through past experiences. The same principles that are used to explain the development of normal behavior are used to explain the development of abnormal behavior. For example, a child can learn to be a conscientious student by observing role models who are conscientious in their work. Another child may learn to break the rules of society by watching a parent break the same rules. In each case, observational learning is at work, but the outcome is very different. Using another example of a learning principle, a person who is hungry and hears someone preparing food in the kitchen may begin to salivate because the sounds of food preparation have, in the past, preceded eating food, and food makes the person salivate. Those sounds from the kitchen are stimuli that have become conditioned so that the person learns to have the same reaction to the sounds as to food (salivation). This learning process is called classical or Pavlovian conditioning. Similarly, experiencing pain and having one's life threatened causes fear, so a person who is attacked and bitten by a dog might well develop a fear response to all dogs that is severe enough to lead to a diagnosis of a phobia. Just as the sounds in the kitchen elicit salivation, the sight of a dog can elicit an emotional response. The same underlying principle of classical conditioning can account for the development of normal

behavior as well as of a disorder. There are many other principles of learning besides observational learning and classical conditioning. Together, psychologists use them to account for forms of psychopathology more complex than those exemplified here. Nonetheless, there are many disorders in which a learning approach to etiology seems farfetched. For example, no one believes that intellectual disability, childhood autism, or schizophrenia can be explained by learning principles alone.

The Psychological Approach. This model, sometimes called the cognitive approach, holds that many forms of psychopathology are best understood by studying the mind. Some psychologists within this tradition believe that the most important aspect of the mind is the unconscious. The Austrian psychoanalyst Sigmund Freud believed that many forms of psychopathology are the result of intense conflicts of which the person is unaware but which, nevertheless, produce symptoms of disorders.

Many psychological disorders are associated with obvious problems in thinking. Schizophrenics, people with attention-deficit hyperactivity disorder (ADHD), and those who suffer from depression all show difficulties in concentration. Memory problems are central in people who develop amnesia in response to psychological trauma. People who are paranoid show abnormalities in the way they interpret the behavior of others. Indeed, it is difficult to find examples of psychopathology in which thinking is not disordered in some way, be it mild or severe. Within the cognitive approach, depression is one of the disorders that receives the most attention. People who are depressed often show problems in emotion (feeling sad), behavior (withdrawing from people), and thinking. The cognitive formulation assumes that thinking is central, specifically the way depressed people think about the world, themselves, and the future. Dysfunctional thinking is believed to give rise to the other aspects of depression. Most of the research in the field of psychopathology derives from the cognitive perspective. One of the major challenges to this approach is determining whether thinking patterns cause disorders or whether they are aspects of disorders that themselves are caused by nonpsychological factors. For example, depressed people have a pessimistic view of the future. Does pessimism figure into the cause of the depression, or might depression be caused by biological factors and pessimism is just one of the symptoms of depression?

The Biological Approach. The biological (biogenic) approach assumes that many forms of psychopathology are caused by abnormalities of the body, usually the brain. These abnormalities can be inherited or can happen for other reasons. What these "other reasons" are is unclear, but they may include birth complications, environmental toxins, or illness of the mother during pregnancy.

Schizophrenia is one disorder that receives much attention among those researchers who follow the biogenic approach. A great deal of research has been conducted on the importance of neurotransmitters. Nerve cells in the brain are not connected; there is a small space between them. A nerve impulse travels this space by the release of chemicals in one nerve cell, called neurotransmitters, which carry the impulse to the receptors of the next cell. There are a large number of neurotransmitters, and new ones are discovered periodically. Early research on the relationship between neurotransmitters and psychopathology tended to view the problem as "too much" or "too little" of the amount of neurotransmitters. It is now known that the situation is much more complicated. In schizophrenia, the neurotransmitter dopamine has received most of the attention, with many studies suggesting that excessive amounts of dopamine cause some of the symptoms of schizophrenia, and drugs that reduce the availability of dopamine to the cells are successful in alleviating some symptoms of the disorder. However, not all people with schizophrenia are helped by these drugs, and some people are helped by drugs that one would not expect if the main cause of schizophrenia were too much dopamine. Researchers are finding that the way in which dopamine and another neurotransmitter, serotonin, work together may lead to a better biological theory of schizophrenia than the excessive-dopamine hypothesis.

The biological approach is a highly technical field that relies heavily on advances in technologies for studying the brain. Powerful new tools for studying the brain are invented at a rapid pace. For example, researchers are now able to use neuroimaging techniques to watch how the brain responds and changes from second to second.

Heredity appears to be important in understanding who develops what kind of psychological disorder, but it is often unknown exactly what is inherited that causes the disorder. The fact that schizophrenia runs in families does not reveal what is being passed on from generation to generation. The fact that inheritance works at the level of gene transmission places hereditary research squarely within the biological approach.

One method for addressing the question of whether a disorder can be inherited is by studying twins. Some twins are identical; each twin has the same genes as the other. Other twins share only half of their genes; these are fraternal twins, who can be of opposite sexes. If one identical twin has schizophrenia and the disorder is entirely inherited, the other twin should also develop schizophrenia. Yet research has shown that among identical twins, if one twin is schizophrenic, the other twin has a 48 percent chance of having the same disorder, not a 100 percent chance. Among fraternal twins, if one is schizophrenic, there is a 17 percent chance that the other twin will have the disorder. If neither twin has schizophrenia and no one else in the immediate family has the disorder, there is only a 1 percent chance of developing this form of psychopathology.

Two important points can be made. First, genes matter in the transmission of schizophrenia. Second, the disorder is not entirely due to heredity. Researchers who focus on heredity have found that some other disorders seem to have a genetic component, but no mental illness has been found to be entirely due to heredity. Clearly, there are other factors operating, and the biological approach must be integrated with other approaches to gain a full picture of the etiology of psychopathology.

The Biopsychosocial Approach. As its name suggests, the biopsychosocial approach seeks to understand psychopathology by examining the interactive influences of biology, cognitive processes, and learning. This is the most popular model of psychopathology and, in its most basic form, is also referred to as the diathesis-stress model. A diathesis is a predisposing factor, and the diathesis may be biological or psychological. When discussing biological diatheses, most theories assume that the diathesis is present at birth. A problem with the regulation of neurotransmitters, which may lead to schizophrenia or depression, is one example. An example of a psychological diathesis is when a person's style of thinking predisposes him or her to a disorder. For instance, pessimism, minimizing good things that happen and maximizing negative events, and attributing failures to personal defects may predispose a person to depression. The stress aspect of the diathesis-stress model refers to the negative life experiences of the person. An early, chaotic family environment, child abuse, and being raised or living in a high-crime neighborhood are examples of stressful environments. From this perspective, a person who has a predisposition for a disorder in combination with certain potentially triggering life experiences will develop the disorder.

Because the biological, learning, and psychological approaches have all contributed to the understanding of psychopathology, it is no surprise that most psychologists want to combine the best of each approach—hence, the biopsychosocial model. Given the present state of knowledge, each model represents more of an assumption about how psychopathology develops rather than a single theory with widespread scientific support. Psychologists continue to debate the causes of virtually every psychological disorder.

CULTURE AND PSYCHOPATHOLOGY

The importance of understanding the cultural context of psychopathology cannot be overstated. To be sure, some disorders span cultures—depression, intellectual disabilities, and schizophrenia are examples—but a culture not only defines what should be considered abnormal behavior but also determines how psychopathology is expressed. "Cultural relativism" refers to the fact that abnormality is relative to its cultural context; the same behavior or set of beliefs can be viewed as abnormal in one culture and perfectly familiar and normal in another. When viewed from an American perspective, the remedies, rituals, and beliefs of a witch doctor may seem to reflect some disorder within the witch doctor rather than a valued and culturally sanctioned means of treatment within that culture. No doubt members of a tribal culture in South America would regard the behavior of North American adolescents on prom night as grossly abnormal.

Some disorders exist only in certain cultures. A disorder known as pibloktoq occurs in Eskimo communities. The symptoms include tearing off one's clothes, shouting obscenities, breaking furniture, and performing other irrational and dangerous acts. This brief period of excited behavior is often followed by the afflicted individual having a seizure, falling into a coma for twelve hours, and then awakening with no memory of his or her behavior.

Some disorders may be very similar across two cultures but contain a cultural twist. For instance, in the United States, the essential feature of social anxiety disorder is a fear of performance situations that could lead to embarrassment and disapproval. In Japan and Korea, the main concern of people with this disorder is the fear that one's blushing, eye contact, or body odor will be offensive to others.

There are numerous examples of culturally based psychopathologies, and the DSM-5 is notable for a more comprehensive treatment of the subject than that found in previous editions. Section 3 includes a chapter on

cultural formation, featuring the Cultural Formulation Interview (CFI), which addresses disorders in terms of "cultural definition of the problem," "cultural perceptions of cause, context, and support," "cultural factors affecting self-coping and past help seeking," and "cultural factors affecting current help seeking." In addition, the appendix includes a section titled "Glossary of Cultural Concepts of Distress." Moreover, throughout the manual, the descriptions of most disorders are accompanied by a brief statement on the role of ethnic and cultural factors that are relevant for the given disorder, which can help the clinician arrive at an accurate diagnosis.

TREATMENT

The major forms of treatment for psychological disorders can be grouped according to the most popular models of psychopathology. Thus, there exists behavior therapy (learning approach), cognitive therapy and psychoanalysis (psychological approach), and somatic treatment, such as the use of medications (biological approach). Consistent with the biopsychosocial model, many therapists practice cognitive behavior therapy (CBT) while their clients are taking medication for their disorders. These treatments, as well as the models from which they derive, represent common and popular viewpoints, but the list is not exhaustive; for instance, another model of disorders is family systems theory, the treatment for which is family therapy.

The link between models of psychopathology and treatment is not as strong as it appears. Therapists tend to adopt the treatment belief of "whatever works," despite the fact that all therapists would prefer to know why the person is suffering from a disorder and why a specific treatment is helpful. In addition, even if the therapist is sure that the problem is a consequence of learning, he or she might have the client take medication for symptom relief during therapy. In other words, psychologists who are aligned with a specific model of psychopathology will still employ an array of treatment techniques, some of which are more closely associated with other models.

Behavior Therapy. Based on learning theory, behavior therapy attempts to provide new learning experiences for the client. Problems that are fear based, such as phobias, will benefit from gradual exposure to the feared situation. If social anxiety is determined to be caused by a deficit in social skills, a behavior therapist can help the person learn new ways of relating to others. If the disorder is one of excess, as in substance abuse, the behavior therapist will provide training in self-control strategies.

The parents of children who show conduct disorders will be taught behavior modification techniques that they can use in the home.

Behavior therapy focuses on the client's present and future. Little time is spent discussing childhood experiences, except as they clearly and directly bear on the client's presenting problem. The therapist adopts a problem-solving approach, and sessions are focused on a learning-theory-based conceptualization of the client's problems and discussions of strategies for change. Homework assignments are common, which leads behavior therapists to believe that therapy takes place between sessions.

Cognitive Therapy. The basic tenet of cognitive therapy is that psychological problems stem from the way people view and think about the events that happen to them. Consequently, therapy focuses on helping clients change their viewpoints. For example, with a client who becomes depressed after the breakup of a relationship, the cognitive therapist will assess the meaning that the breakup has for the person. Perhaps he or she holds irrational beliefs such as "If my partner does not want me, no one will" or "I am a complete failure for losing this relationship." The assumption is that the client's extreme negative thinking is contributing to the depression. The therapist will challenge these beliefs and help the client substitute a more rational perspective, such as "Just because one person left me does not mean that the next person will" or "Even if I failed at this relationship, it does not mean that I am a failure in everything I do."

Cognitive therapy has some similarity to behavior therapy. There is a focus on the present, history taking is selective and related to the presenting problem, and homework assignments are routine. Indeed, because the two approaches share many things in common, many therapists use both forms of treatment and refer to themselves as cognitive behavioral therapists.

Somatic Therapy. Somatic therapy is the domain of physicians, specifically psychiatrists, because this form of treatment requires medical training. By far the most common example of somatic therapy is the use of psychotropic medications, medicine that will relieve psychological symptoms. Less common examples are electroconvulsive shock treatment, in which the client is tranquilized and administered a brief electric current to the brain to induce a convulsion, and brain surgery, such as leukotomy or lobotomy (rarely practiced).

The use of medications for psychological disorders has become enormously popular since 1970. Three main

reasons are that the biological approach to understanding psychopathology is becoming more prominent, new drugs are being released each year that have fewer side effects, and a great deal of research is being conducted to show that an ever-increasing number of disorders are helped by medication. The use of medication for psychological disorders is not viewed as a cure. Sometimes drugs are used to help a person through a difficult period. At other times they are an important adjunct to psychotherapy. Only in the most severe forms of psychopathology would a person be medicated for the rest of his or her life.

WHICH THERAPY IS BEST?
Researchers approach the question of which therapy is best in the context of specific disorders. No one therapy is recommended for every disorder. For instance, behavior therapy has proven to be highly successful with phobias, cognitive therapy shows good results with depression, and a trial of medication is essential for schizophrenia and bipolar disorder.

No matter what the presumed cause is of a specific disorder, a common practice is to provide medication for symptom relief, along with some form of psychotherapy to improve the person's condition over the long run.

BIBLIOGRAPHY
American Psychiatric Association. *Diagnostic and Statistical Manual of Mental Disorders: DSM-5.* 5th ed. Washington: APA, 2013. Print.
Barlow, David H., and V. Mark Durand. *Abnormal Psychology: An Integrative Approach.* 6th ed. Belmont: Wadsworth, 2012. Print.
Beauchaine, Theodore P., and Stephen P. Hinshaw, eds. *Child and Adolescent Psychopathology.* 2nd ed. Hoboken: Wiley, 2013. Print.
Blaney, Paul H., and Theodore Millon, eds. *Oxford Textbook of Psychopathology.* 2nd ed. New York: Oxford UP, 2009. Print.
Castonguay, Louis G., and Thomas F. Oltmanns, eds. *Psychopathology: From Science to Clinical Practice.* New York: Guilford, 2013. Print.
Craighead, W. Edward, David J. Miklowitz, and Linda W. Craighead, eds. *Psychopathology: History, Diagnosis, and Empirical Foundations.* 2nd ed. Hoboken: Wiley, 2013. Print.
Kanfer, Frederick H., and Arnold P. Goldstein, eds. *Helping People Change: A Textbook of Methods.* 4th ed. New York: Pergamon, 1991. Print.

Maddux, James F., and Barbara A. Winstead, eds. *Psychopathology: Foundations for a Contemporary Understanding*. 3rd ed. New York: Routledge, 2012. Print.

Laurence Grimm and Lindsey L. Henninger

SEE ALSO: Abnormality: Biomedical models; Abnormality: Psychological models; Behavior therapy; Brief therapy; Cognitive behavior therapy; Cognitive therapy; Couples therapy; Drug therapies; Environmental factors and mental health; Genetics and mental health; Gestalt therapy; Group therapy; Observational learning and modeling therapy; Personcentered therapy; Play therapy; Psychopharmacology; Psychotherapy: Children; Psychotherapy: Effectiveness; Psychotherapy: Goals and techniques; Psychotherapy: Historical approaches; Rational emotive therapy; Reality therapy; Shock therapy.

Psychopharmacology

TYPE OF PSYCHOLOGY: Biological bases of behavior; Psychopathology; Psychotherapy

Psychopharmacology is the study of drug effects in the brain and in psychological processes. A wide range of drugs have psychological effects, including those used to treat mental illnesses such as schizophrenia, depression, bipolar disorder, and anxiety, as well as drugs that are subject to compulsive abuse, such as stimulants, depressants, and hallucinogens. The best way to understand this broad range of drugs is to investigate their effects on the functioning of cells in the brain.

KEY CONCEPTS

- Antidepressants
- Antipsychotics
- Anxiolytics
- Drugs of abuse
- Mood stabilizers
- Pharmacodynamics
- Pharmacokinetics
- Psychotropics
- Tolerance
- Withdrawal

INTRODUCTION

Psychopharmacology is the scientific study of the effect of drugs on psychological processes. The field of psychopharmacology has two interrelated goals. The first is to understand the way that drugs interact in the brain and the effects that these interactions have on behavior, consciousness, cognition, emotion, and other psychological processes. The second goal is to use knowledge of the effects of drugs to improve human psychological welfare. In most cases, this involves studying drug effects in the hope of developing and improving drugs used to treat psychiatric disorders such as depression and schizophrenia. In other cases, drug effects may be studied in the hope of learning ways to prevent people from taking drugs in ways that cause harm to both individuals and society.

Although psychopharmacological research may involve any drug with the capacity to alter psychological experience (a psychotropic drug), most studies have focused on the examination of drugs that fall into two broad categories: those that are useful in the treatment of psychological disorders (therapeutic drugs) and those that have the capacity to produce compulsive patterns of use and abuse in the people who take them (drugs of abuse).

HISTORY

Though psychopharmacology is a relatively new scientific field, archaeological evidence indicates that human beings have been using drugs to manipulate their psychological experiences and to treat disease since prehistory. Many psychotropic substances are naturally occurring or produced by natural processes, and early people were often adept at exploiting and, in many cases, cultivating the plants from which they came. Many of these psychotropic substances, including opium, cocaine, alcohol, and peyote (a hallucinogen), were used both for their ability to influence individual experience and in social, cultural, and ceremonial contexts. In some cases, they were used medicinally to treat a variety of physical and psychological ailments.

The ancient Greeks used a variety of drugs to treat mental illness and had formed a specific theory of illness and health that guided their use. Hippocrates theorized that mental and physical illnesses were caused by an imbalance in one or more of the four bodily fluids (humors): blood, bile, choler, and phlegm. Specific drugs and other treatments were used to increase or decrease these humors in an effort to reestablish the balance. For example, symptoms thought to be caused by an excess of blood, such as mania, might be treated by bleeding the patient. Bleeding would, indeed, often slow the patient down, and this would be taken as evidence of the validity of the underlying theory. Though modern medicine requires a different level of proof of efficacy, the strategy of treating symptoms by using remedies that produce opposite or counteracting effects to the symptoms of interest remains a mainstay of pharmacological approaches to treating psychological disorders.

The modern psychiatric drug era got its start in the 1950s. During this decade, early examples of virtually all major classes of psychiatric drugs were discovered, in many cases by accident. In 1949, John Cade was conducting a series of experiments involving injecting uric acid into guinea pigs. When he added lithium in an effort to increase the water solubility of the solution, he noted that the animals were much calmer, so he tested the effects of lithium in people with mania. Lithium has become a commonly prescribed mood stabilizer, effective in the treatment of bipolar disorder. Though originally investigated as an antihistamine and surgical sedative, the first antipsychotic medication, chlorpromazine (Thorazine), was found to be useful in treating patients with schizophrenia in 1952. Iproniazid (Marsilid), an early antidepressant drug approved for use in 1958, was initially intended to treat tuberculosis. Meprobamate (Miltown, Equanil, Meprospan), an anxiolytic or anti-anxiety medication, became available about the same time.

These medications produced a revolution in the treatment of mental illness. Before the advent of modern medications, the available treatment options for patients with serious mental illnesses were rarely effective and in some cases were downright barbaric. Most patients with serious mental illness were confined in psychiatric hospitals and asylums. The new drugs dramatically reduced the number of institutionalized psychiatric patients and improved the quality of life of countless individuals. Nevertheless, none of these drugs were completely effective, and they all had a tendency to produce troubling side effects in a significant number of the people who took them.

In the decades that followed, many chemical modifications of these drugs were explored, occasionally creating minor improvements in effectiveness or reducing some of the side effects. By the late 1980s, a smaller breakthrough occurred with the successful reintroduction of clozapine (Clozaril), a new, atypical antipsychotic medication, and the development of fluoxetine (Prozac), an antidepressant. These drugs were somewhat novel in the way they acted in the brain. They offered distinct advantages in practice and stimulated new avenues for research. As understanding of the underlying causes of psychiatric disorders improves, researchers hope to develop safer and more effective medications for mental illness.

DRUG EFFECTS

Before any drug can alter psychological experience, it must reach target receptors in the brain, typically from some other part of the body. Pharmacokinetics refers to the study of drug movements throughout the body over time. The speed of drug onset and the duration of drug effect are important variables in determining the qualitative experience of taking the drug. For example, drugs of abuse that are absorbed and distributed quickly tend to produce stronger rewarding properties than those with more gradual onsets. For this reason, drug abusers may try to change the way that drugs are administered in an effort to speed their onset.

Psychopharmacologists also need to understand specifically what drugs do once they reach their targets in the brain. This topic is referred to as pharmacodynamics. Psychotropic drugs produce their effects by interacting with proteins in the membranes of individual neurons in the brain. These proteins normally interact with naturally occurring chemicals in the brain called neurotransmitters, which serve as chemical bridges across the spaces between neurons, called synapses, so that signals can be transmitted from one neuron to another. There are many different neurotransmitters, and for each of these, there may be a number of different specific receptor proteins. The various receptor proteins are not evenly distributed throughout the brain; different regions of the brain vary in terms of the density of different types of receptors for different neurotransmitters. Membrane proteins on both sides of the synapse are involved in the process of releasing, receiving, and recycling these chemical messengers, and psychotropic drugs can interact at any point along the way.

Psychotropic drugs can interact with these proteins in a host of different ways, thereby altering the activity of naturally occurring neurotransmitters in various regions of the brain. In general, drug effects are classified as either agonist or antagonist effects. Agonists are drugs that increase the natural activity of the neurotransmitter in some way. An agonist drug might mimic the effects of the neurotransmitter at the receptor itself, or it might stimulate the release of a neurotransmitter or prolong its effectiveness by preventing the neuron's normal process of eliminating the neurotransmitter once it is used. Because all these potential effects would ultimately enhance the function of the neurotransmitter, they would all be classified as agonist effects. In contrast, antagonist effects serve to reduce the functioning of the neurotransmitter. Sample antagonist effects include blocking receptor proteins or preventing the storage of neurotransmitters.

"Affinity" refers to the degree to which a drug interacts with membrane proteins. Drugs with high affinity interact strongly, readily, or for relatively long durations. Low-affinity drugs interact weakly, incompletely, or briefly. Thus, the effects of various drugs can be described in terms of how strongly they interact (affinity) and in what ways they interact (agonist or antagonist) with which specific receptors for which specific neurotransmitters. In principle, drugs can be designed to be quite specific, though in practice most drugs that are commonly used have multiple effects.

CLASSES OF PSYCHIATRIC MEDICATIONS

The main classes of psychiatric medications are antipsychotics, antidepressants, mood stabilizers, and anxiolytics.

Antipsychotics. Antipsychotics are used to treat symptoms of psychosis related to a range of conditions or disorders, including mania, delusional disorders, and psychotic depression. Most commonly, however, they are used in patients suffering from schizophrenia. There are many antipsychotic medications available, but they can be broadly classified into two groups: typical (first generation) and atypical (second generation). The typical antipsychotics, also called neuroleptics or major tranquilizers, are dopamine antagonists. They work primarily by blocking the D2 subclass of receptor proteins for the neurotransmitter dopamine. By blocking these receptors, typical antipsychotics reduce dopamine activity in specific circuits within the brain. The more strongly a typical antipsychotic binds or interacts with the D2 receptor, the more potent the drug. This, and other evidence, has suggested a dopamine hypothesis of schizophrenia—that is, that schizophrenia is caused by overactivity of dopamine circuits in the brain.

Though generally effective, the typical antipsychotics have important limitations. D2 receptors are concentrated in regions of the brain that are important to the regulation of movement, and blocking these receptors produces significant movement-related side effects. In addition, typical antipsychotics are effective in treating only the more overt, or positive, symptoms of schizophrenia, such as hallucinations; they do little to help

with the negative symptoms, such as emotional flatness and social withdrawal. These drugs also are simply not effective in some patients.

Since the 1990s, a flurry of antipsychotic development has occurred, based largely on the finding that a specific antipsychotic drug, clozapine, can be effective in treating psychosis without producing the movement-related side effects. Clozapine and similar drugs that were developed later are referred to as atypical agents because although they are relatively weak D2 receptor blockers, they were thought to be at least equal to the typical drugs in treating the positive symptoms of schizophrenia and better at treating the negative symptoms, with a low risk of movement-related side effects. However, further study has shown that this may not necessarily be the case, and some scientists have questioned whether the distinction between typical and atypical antipsychotics is truly a meaningful one.

Antidepressants. Antidepressants are a diverse class of drugs that are effective in the treatment of depression. Though different individuals may respond better or worse to any particular drug, overall the drugs are roughly equal in clinical effectiveness. They are not, however, equal in the side effects that they produce or in the effects that they have at the synapse. The oldest class of antidepressant drugs is the monoamine oxidase (MAO) inhibitors, or MAOIs. Monoamine oxidase is an enzyme that usually functions to degrade three different neurotransmitters: dopamine, serotonin, and norepinephrine. The MAO inhibitors attach to this enzyme and prevent it from doing its work. Therefore, these drugs are ultimately agonists for the three neurotransmitters. This mechanism of action, however, has an inconvenient and potentially dangerous side effect. Monoamine oxidase is used not only in the brain but also in the human digestive system to metabolize tyramine, a substance found in aged cheeses and meats, some nuts and beans, and assorted other foods. People prescribed MAOI antidepressants need to be quite careful about what foods they eat to avoid those high in tyramine. If they do not, serious and potentially dangerous elevations in blood pressure can occur.

A second category of antidepressant drug is the tricyclic antidepressants. The tricyclics are also agonists for the neurotransmitters serotonin and norepinephrine, but they accomplish this in a different way. In addition to being degraded by MAO inside the cell, these neurotransmitters are also reabsorbed by the neuron once they have been released. The process is called reuptake. By blocking reuptake, the tricyclics allow these neurotransmitters to stay in the synapse for a longer period of time, enabling them to repeatedly interact with receptor proteins in adjacent cells. Like the MAOIs, the tricyclics have numerous side effects, but the most troubling is the fact that these drugs can be very toxic, indeed lethal, in overdose.

The second wave of drug development was led by the antidepressant fluoxetine (Prozac)—an example of a third category of antidepressant referred to as selective serotonin reuptake inhibitors (SSRIs). Like the tricyclics, the SSRIs block reuptake. However, they are more specific to the neurotransmitter serotonin and have a much better safety profile than the other classes of antidepressants. The most troubling problems associated with the SSRIs are sexual side effects.

A fourth class of antidepressant is often simply referred to as atypicals. These drugs are quite varied in terms of their effects in the brain and do not fit neatly into any other category. Some drugs combine reuptake blocking with effects on postsynaptic receptors. Others are relatively specific to the neurotransmitter dopamine. Like the other antidepressants discussed, these drugs are roughly equal in effectiveness, although their side effects can differ considerably.

Mood Stabilizers. Mood stabilizers are used in the treatment of bipolar spectrum disorders (formerly known as manic-depressive illnesses). These disorders are characterized by emotional volatility; the individual has some combination of periods of mania, depression, or both interspersed with more normal functioning. Therefore, there are three treatment issues: the treatment of mania, the treatment of depression, and the stabilization of mood over time.

The most common substance used to stabilize mood is lithium. Lithium is typically considered to be an effective treatment for stabilizing mood across time as well as an effective, if slow, treatment for reducing mania. Its effectiveness as an antidepressant is less clear. The precise mechanism of action that makes lithium effective is unclear, as it has many effects in the brain. A number of medications, including anticonvulsants, antipsychotics, and antidepressants, have been proposed to treat bipolar disorder either in place of or in addition to lithium. Combination therapy (prescribing multiple drugs from different categories to treat the disorder) is a common practice in treating bipolar disorder.

Anxiolytics. Anxiolytic is another name for an anxiety-reducing drug, also known as a tranquilizer. Most of the typical or traditional anxiolytics are central nervous system depressants. These drugs operate by enhancing the effects of an inhibitory neurotransmitter called gamma-aminobutyric acid (GABA), which reduces the electrical activity of the brain. The most common anxiolytics, a class of drugs called the benzodiazepines, have a neuromodulatory effect at the GABA receptor. When these drugs interact with the receptor, naturally occurring GABA is more effective. The benzodiazepines are highly effective in treating symptoms of anxiety in the short term and are commonly used in treating anxiety associated with generalized anxiety disorder and panic attacks. They are less effective in dealing with some symptoms associated with other anxiety disorders, such as post-traumatic stress disorder and obsessive-compulsive disorders. An additional limitation is that the benzodiazepines, though generally safe to use as prescribed, can become a substance of abuse if taken inappropriately, for long periods of time, or in relatively high doses. In addition, when taken in high doses or with alcohol or other central nervous system depressants, these drugs can be quite dangerous.

Alternatives to the benzodiazepines include the novel antianxiety drug buspirone (BuSpar) and several of the antidepressant medications discussed earlier. These drugs have several important advantages over the benzodiazepines and one major drawback. They are not central nervous system depressants and therefore do not cause sedation or interact with alcohol or other central nervous system depressants. However, they are very slow to take effect in comparison to benzodiazepines. It typically takes a week before even the initial responses are observed and several weeks before the full clinical effect is reached.

DRUGS OF ABUSE AND SUBSTANCE DEPENDENCE
Although the majority of drugs used in the treatment of psychological disorders are not prone to abuse, a broad range of other drugs with differing therapeutic purposes and different synaptic functions are. In substance dependence, the effects that a drug produces change across time in two ways. First, tolerance and withdrawal may occur. In this case, more and more of the drug is required to achieve the same intoxicating effect (tolerance), and negative effects occur when the drug is removed (withdrawal). Second, substance dependence is characterized by loss of control over use of the substance; dependent individuals will use the drug in greater quantity or frequency than they intend and will be unable to curtail their use.

The synaptic changes associated with drug tolerance and drug withdrawal depend on the particular type of drug that has been used. In the case of the opiate drugs, for example, receptors in a region of the brain called the locus coeruleus decrease their responding when the drugs are taken. However, over time and over repeated administrations of the drug, this region of the brain will begin to adapt. The cells become less responsive to the opiate drugs by altering the sensitivity of those receptors with which the drugs interact. Therefore, more of the drug is needed to produce the original effect, and the system becomes dysregulated if the drug is abruptly removed. Synaptic changes of this nature occur with dependence involving other drugs as well, though the precise details of these changes differ from drug to drug. Although important in the treatment of drug addictions, changes associated with tolerance and withdrawal are not complete descriptions of the common denominator that links diverse substances as drugs of abuse.

A feature that all drugs of abuse share is that they are potent reinforcers—they feel good to humans (and animals). All rewards, whether natural or drug, activate dopamine release in a region of the brain called the nucleus acumbens. Direct electrical stimulation of pathways related to the nucleus acumbens will also serve as a powerful reinforcer, and this system is activated with drugs of abuse. Drugs as diverse as amphetamines, cocaine, alcohol, opiates, nicotine, phencyclidine (PCP), and marijuana all trigger the release of dopamine in this reward circuit. Similar to the changes seen with tolerance and withdrawal, the sensitivity of dopamine receptors in this circuit changes when repeatedly activated by drugs of abuse. In time, the sensitivity of the reward system is adjusted; stronger rewards—that is, more drugs—become necessary to activate the system.

BIBLIOGRAPHY

Advokat, Claire D., Joseph E. Comaty, and Robert M. Julien. *Julien's Primer of Drug Action: A Comprehensive Guide to the Actions, Uses, and Side Effects of Psychoactive Drugs.* 13th ed. New York: Worth, 2014. Print.

Ebmeier, K. P., C. Donaghey, and J. D. Steele. "Recent Developments and Current Controversies in Depression." *Lancet* 367.9505 (2006): 153–67. Print.

Hyman, S. E., and R. C. Malenka. "Addiction and the Brain: The Neurobiology of Compulsion and Its Persistence." *Nature Reviews: Neuroscience* 2.10 (2001): 695–703. Print.

Lieberman, Jeffrey A., et al. "Effectiveness of Antipsychotic Drugs in Patients with Chronic Schizophrenia." *New England Journal of Medicine* 353.12 (2005): 1209–23. Print.

López-Muñoz, F., et al. "Half a Century since the Clinical Introduction of Chlorpromazine and the Birth of Modern Psychopharmacology." *Progress in Neuro-Psychopharmacology & Biological Psychiatry* 28.1 (2004): 205–8. Print.

Maj, Mario. "The Effect of Lithium in Bipolar Disorder: A Review of Recent Research Evidence." *Bipolar Disorders* 5.3 (2003): 180–88. Print.

Marin, Humberto, and Javier I. Escobar. *Clinical Psychopharmacology: A Practical Approach.* Hackensack: World Sci., 2013. Print.

Meltzer, Herbert Y. "Mechanism of Action of Atypical Antipsychotic Drugs." *Neuropsychopharmacology: The Fifth Generation of Progress.* Ed. Kenneth L. Davis et al. Philadelphia: Lippincott, 2002. 819–31. Print.

Meyer, Jerrold S., and Linda F. Quenzer. *Psychopharmacology: Drugs, the Brain, and Behavior.* 2nd ed. Sunderland: Sinauer, 2013. Print.

Sobel, Stephen V. *Successful Psychopharmacology: Evidence-Based Treatment Solutions for Achieving Remission.* New York: Norton, 2012. Print.

Stahl, Stephen M. *Stahl's Essential Psychopharmacology: Neuroscientific Basis and Practical Applications.* 4th ed. New York: Cambridge UP, 2013. Print.

Tyrer, Peter, and Tim Kendall. "The Spurious Advance of Antipsychotic Drug Therapy." *Lancet* 373.9657 (2009): 4–5. Print.

Linda R. Tennison

SEE ALSO: Alcohol dependence and abuse; Antianxiety medications; Antidepressant medications; Antipsychotic medications; Anxiety disorders; Bipolar disorder; Depression; Drug therapies; Mood disorders; Mood stabilizer medications; Schizophrenia: Background, types, and symptoms; Substance use disorders.

Psychosexual development

TYPE OF PSYCHOLOGY: Personality

Psychosexual development proceeds along five distinct stages, named for the primary body parts from which individuals derive pleasure during a given period of their lives; they are the oral, anal, phallic, latency, and genital stages. According to Sigmund Freud, passing through these stages successfully is critical to the healthy development of human beings.

KEY CONCEPTS
- Developmental stages
- Ego
- Fixation
- Gratification
- Id
- Libido
- Psychopathology
- Regression
- Superego

INTRODUCTION

Psychosexual development is a major developmental theory, proposed by Sigmund Freud, which suggests that humans behave as they do because they are constantly seeking pleasure. During different periods, or stages, of life, the types of pleasure a person seeks will change. Each change in body location where the person finds pleasure represents one stage in psychosexual development. There are a total of five stages; four of them are named for the primary body part from which a person derives pleasure during a given time in life.

PSYCHOSEXUAL STAGES

The first stage is the oral stage, which begins at birth and ends around one and a half years of age. Pleasure is gained from activities of the mouth, such as sucking at a mother's nipple to obtain nourishment. The purpose of this behavior is to secure physical survival, as the infant depends on parents for food. The infant is entirely dependent, seeks immediate gratification of needs, and does not consider other people's needs or wishes or even recognize others as separate human beings. The selfish energy that drives the infant at this age is called libido and is attributed to the child's id, the pleasure-seeking part of a person.

The second stage is the anal stage, named for the child's preoccupation with feces and urine, as this is generally the time of toilet training. This stage begins at age one and a half and ends around age three. The child now sees herself or himself as separate from other people and begins to assert wishes. The child becomes more demanding and controlling and often refuses parents' wishes, but the child also learns to delay gratification and put up with frustration. For example, the child will learn to hold in a bowel movement until a time convenient for the caregiver, rather than eliminate it as soon as pressure is felt on the sphincter. Learning to be assertive and autonomous and learning to delay gratification are the two most important advances for the child that occur during this stage of development. They make up an important part of a child's ego, the part of the psyche that defines who a person is and what a person wants from life.

Between age three and age six, the child passes through the phallic stage of psychosexual development. The child now knows who she or he is and who her or his parents are, and the child begins to have a sense of rules and regulations. Behavior becomes more moral, and the opinions of others begin to gain importance. The child begins to love others and wants to be loved by them. To ensure that others will continue to love and cherish her or him, the child learns to suppress pleasure derived from the genitalia because of social pressures against behaviors such as masturbation. According to Freud, children at this age fall in love with their parent of the opposite sex and envy their same-sex parent. This pattern is called the Oedipus complex in boys and the Electra complex in girls. The Oedipus complex results in the fear that the boy may be hated by his father for loving his mother. To prevent being punished (the feared punishment being castration), the boy begins to identify with and behave like his father and slowly learns to distance himself from his mother. Through this process of modeling and imitating the father, the boy learns rules and becomes a moral being. In the Electra complex, he girl feels that, because she has no penis, she has already received the ultimate punishment of castration. To compensate for the resultant feelings of envy of the male's penis, she decides that pregnancy will be important one day, as this is something not obtainable by the male. The girl's desire to bear a child begins. As she knows that only women bear children, she begins to identify with and model after her mother and begins to distance herself from her father. The most important change in this stage of development is the child's acquisition of a superego, an internal sense of what is right and what is wrong that guides behavior and inhibits illegal or immoral acts.

The distancing from the same-sex parent in the phallic stage of development, which occurs around age five or age six, is seen as ushering in the latency stage. At this time, children withdraw from the opposite sex and no longer seek pleasure from their own bodies. Instead, they reorient their behavior toward skill acquisition and learning, as well as peer interaction. This makes them ready for school and play with their peer group. Not until approximately age thirteen will the desire for pleasure reawaken.

At around age thirteen, the adolescent enters the final stage of psychosexual development, the genital stage. At this time, the person has matured enough to be able to love others in an unselfish and altruistic manner and should be willing to put the welfare of others ahead of her or his own. Empathy and caring for humans begins, and the libido, which was selfishly directed in infancy, is now directed toward giving pleasure to others. The desire awakens to be intimately involved with a person of the opposite sex, according to Freud. This desire, however, is aim-inhibited, is complemented by feelings of affection, and does not find expression until the person has matured beyond adolescence. Mature sexuality develops as an activity that is pleasuring for both people involved, is the result of mature love, and serves procreation. Such maturity is the final goal of this stage of development.

DEVELOPMENT OF EGO AND SUPEREGO

The two most important outcomes of psychosexual development are the development of the ego and superego and the development of psychopathology (emotional or mental illnesses or problems of sufficient severity to warrant treatment by a psychologist or psychotherapist) if the stages are not successfully mastered. The anal and phallic stages are particularly critical in the development of the ego and superego. During the anal stage, ego development progresses rapidly as the child learns what he or she likes and what distinguishes him or her from other people. In the phallic stage, the development of the superego occurs as a result of the Oedipus and Electra complexes.

Only if the child accepts the rules of society—that is, falls out of love with the opposite-sex parent and identifies with the same-sex parent—is she or he able to feel free of fear of punishment. Thus, the child learns to live by rules and regulations out of fear of punishment. The internalized sense of rules is represented by the child's superego. The superego serves to counteract the selfish and pleasure-seeking actions of the id, which is present at birth and remains with all human beings throughout the life span. Often, the superego and id will come into conflict because a selfish desire expressed by the id is being opposed by the superego. The ego will then mediate between the two and will attempt to come up with a compromise solution. For example, a college student who has to study for an exam sometimes is overcome by

the desire to attend a party instead. This desire is driven by the id. The superego then admonishes the student to stay home and continue to study without any breaks. The ego may finally step in and mediate, and the student may decide to study for two more hours, take a break for pleasure for an hour, and return to study some more.

DEVELOPMENT OF PSYCHOPATHOLOGY

The development of psychopathology is closely related to psychosexual development. First, pathology is seen as a possible consequence of fixation—that is, the child's failure to resolve a given stage and advance beyond it. Second, psychopathology may be caused by regression—the return to an earlier stage of development because of conflicts or problems. Adults with oral pathology, those who either did not move beyond or regressed to the oral stage, are said to be dependent and afraid to be alone, or else very hostile, evidencing verbal biting sarcasm to prevent getting too close to people. People with anal pathology can be either very retentive (miserly, tense, orderly, and constricted) or expulsive (impulsive, disorganized, free-spending, and venting). Both types of pathology are severe and were considered by Freud to be not treatable through psychoanalysis. Only pathology arising from the phallic stage lends itself well to treatment. It is referred to as neurosis and implies that the person has significant conflicts between id wishes and superego restrictions that cannot be successfully mediated by the ego.

Neurotic pathology is seen as a result of a boy's failure to pass through the Oedipus complex or a girl's failure to pass through the Electra complex. In both cases, the child may fail to withdraw attachment to the same-sex parent or may fail to identify with the same-sex parent. Thus, healthy development is hampered and stopped. The child will live with the conflict of having a superego that is not completely developed and the awareness that the id's wish to possess the opposite-sex parent is inappropriate. The superego chastises the person yet is unable to stop the ego. Conflict is ever-present in the person, as the wishes of the id cannot be controlled by the incomplete superego but certainly can be recognized by the superego as inappropriate. This pathology sometimes leads the person to regress to earlier stages of development and develop an oral or anal personality. If there is no regression, only fixation at the phallic stage, the person will show traits of neurosis, such as being focused on gaining pleasure for the self in general, being centered on seduction, developing symptoms of hysteria, or developing physical complaints.

Pathology does not arise from the latency or genital stages, as progression to the latency stage implies successful resolution of the Oedipus and Electra complexes: The person has matured psychosexually beyond a point of development at which neurotic pathology develops. This is true because the child is considered to have developed all necessary structures of the self, or psyche, by the end of the phallic phase. The personality structure and characteristics evidenced by the child at that time are deemed lifelong traits and are not prone to significant future change.

Psychosexual development is critical from Freud's perspective primarily because it is responsible for the development of a healthy self-structure that consists of an id, an ego, and a superego. Further, it is the most important factor in the development of the psychopathology of human beings. Mastery or failure in the realm of psychosexual development has extremely important implications for a person's functioning and mental health.

HISTORIC CONTEXT

The Freudian stages through which psychosexual development progresses must be considered within the historical framework present at the time that Freud conceptualized them, that is, from the perspective of the late 1800s and early 1900s. The spirit of the times was much different from that of today, particularly with regard to how freely people were allowed to express themselves in general and with regard to sexuality in particular. It was a time in which morals and ethics forbade many normal human urges and resulted in people having to deny large parts or aspects of themselves.

This atmosphere of self-denial resulted in many different symptoms, especially among women, who were expected to follow even stricter codes of behavior than men were. For example, sometimes people were observed to have paralysis of a hand that could not be explained by any neurological damage. Freud was one of the first physicians to recognize that this paralysis had psychological rather than physical causes. He hypothesized that the strong moral restrictions placed on the individual were directly contrary to what the person wanted to do (perhaps masturbate, a definite transgression of permissible behavior). He believed that this person had a very strong id without a sufficiently strong superego to control it. The person's unconscious mind had to devise some other strategy to keep the id controlled—hence the paralysis of the hand. The idea that the individual has an unconscious was a crucial development in psychology and has

been maintained to date by many types of psychologists, though not by all. It is directly related to the theory of psychosexual development.

IMPACT ON PSYCHOLOGY

Psychosexual development was proposed by Freud strictly to explain why certain symptoms developed in individuals. His ideas had an extremely strong impact on the future of psychology, as they were complex and explained human behavior in an understandable manner (given the spirit of the times in which they were formulated). Many followers applied Freud's theories to the treatment of psychopathology, and the profession of psychoanalysis was born. Psychoanalysts specialized in the treatment of persons with neuroses; they did so through daily sessions that lasted fifty minutes. Treatment often continued for many years. Only through this approach, psychoanalysts believed, could they effect changes in a person's psychic structure—that is, in the person's ego and the relationship between the id and superego. The profession of psychoanalysis is still a prominent one, but many changes have been made. Few psychoanalysts today follow a strictly Freudian approach to the development of a person's psyche; new ways of understanding human development and behavior have been developed. Psychoanalysis and psychosexual development, however, remain important features of psychology's history. They were important milestones in the discipline of clinical psychology, the branch of psychology concerned with the treatment of mental illness.

BIBLIOGRAPHY

Freud, Sigmund. *Civilization and Its Discontents*. New York: Norton, 2005. Print.

Freud, Sigmund. *Dora: An Analysis of a Case of Hysteria*. New York: Simon, 1997. Print.

Freud, Sigmund. *A General Introduction to Psychoanalysis*. New York: Garden City, 1952. Print.

Freud, Sigmund. *Three Case Histories*. New York: Collier, 1963. Print.

Lauretis, Teresa de. *Freud's Drive: Psychoanalysis, Literature, and Film*. New York: Palgrave, 2008. Print.

Newman, Barbara, and Philip R. Newman. *Development through Life: A Psychosocial Approach*. 11th ed. Belmont: Wadsworth, 2012. Print.

Quindeau, Ilka. *Seduction and Desire: The Psychoanalytic Theory of Sexuality since Freud*. London: Karnac, 2013. Print.

Rychlak, Joseph F. "The Beginnings of Psychoanalysis: Sigmund Freud." *Introduction to Personality and Psychotherapy.* 2nd ed. Boston: Houghton, 1981. Print.

Christiane Brems

SEE ALSO: Abnormality: Psychological models; Analytical psychotherapy; Defense mechanisms; Dreams; Ego defense mechanisms; Freud, Sigmund; Freudian psychology; Gender differences; Gender identity formation; Horney, Karen; Oedipus complex; Penis envy; Psychoanalysis; Psychoanalytic psychology; Psychoanalytic psychology and personality: Sigmund Freud; Psychotherapy: Children; Social psychological models: Karen Horney.

Psychosomatic disorders

TYPE OF PSYCHOLOGY: Psychopathology

Psychosomatic disorders are physical disorders produced by psychological factors such as stress, mental states, or personality characteristics. A variety of psychological or psychotherapeutic interventions have been developed to alter the individual's ability to cope with stressful situations and to change the personality or behavior of the individual.

KEY CONCEPTS
- Behavior modification
- Biogenic
- Biopsychosocial
- Cognitive
- Locus of control
- Psychogenic
- Psychological factors affecting physical condition
- Psychosomatic disorders
- Self-efficacy
- Type A behavior pattern
- Stress

INTRODUCTION

The term "psychosomatic" was introduced by physician Flanders Dunbar in the early 1940's, shortly after Hans Selye presented the concept of stress. Psychosomatic disorders are physical disorders that are caused by, or exacerbated by, psychological factors. These psychological factors fall into three major groups: stress resulting from encounters with the environment, personality characteristics, and psychological states. It should be noted that

psychosomatic disorders are different from two other conditions with which they are often confused. Psychosomatic disorders are real—that is, they are actual physical illnesses that have underlying psychological causes or that are made worse by psychological factors. In somatoform disorders (such as hypochondriasis), by contrast, there is no physiological cause; another condition, malingering, is the faking of an illness.

Psychosomatic disorders can affect any of the organ systems of the body. Included among them are skin disorders, such as acne, hives, and rashes; musculoskeletal disorders, such as backaches, rheumatoid arthritis, and tension headaches; respiratory disorders, such as asthma and hiccups; and cardiovascular disorders, such as hypertension, heart attacks, strokes, and migraine headaches. Other disorders have also been related to psychological factors, including anemia, weakening of the immune system, ulcers, and constipation. Genitourinary disorders such as menstrual problems, vaginismus, male erectile disorder, and premature ejaculation are included among psychosomatic disorders, as are certain endocrine and neurological problems.

The relationship between the mind and the body has long been the subject of debate. Early societies saw a clear link between the mind and the body. Early Greek and Roman physicians believed that body fluids determined personality types and that people with certain personality types were prone to certain types of diseases. Beginning during the Renaissance, the dominant line of thought held that there was little or no connection between the mind and the body. Illness was seen as the result of organic, cellular pathology. Destruction of body tissue and invasion by "germs," rather than personality type, were seen as the causes of illness.

Sigmund Freud's hysteria work with patients suffering from conversion hysteria began to demonstrate both the importance of psychological factors in the production of physical symptoms of illness and the value of psychological therapy in changing the functioning of the body. Research conducted in the 1930's and 1940's suggested that personality factors play a role in the production of a variety of specific illnesses, including ulcers, hypertension, and asthma.

THE ROLE OF STRESS

Even though Freud demonstrated the role of psychological factors in illness, the medical field has remained focused on the biological roots of illness and has largely rejected or ignored the role of emotions and personality. Nevertheless, the ascending line of thought can be described as a biopsychosocial model of health, which begins with the basic assumption that health and illness result from an interplay of biological, psychological, and social factors. This view provides a conceptual framework for incorporating human elements into the scientific paradigm. A man who suffers a heart attack at age thirty-five is not conceptualized simply as a person who is experiencing the effects of cellular damage caused by purely biological processes that are best treated by surgery or the administration of drugs. The victim, instead, is viewed as a person who also has engaged in practices that adversely affected his health. In addition to drugs and surgery, therefore, treatment for this man might include changing his views on the relative value of work and family as well as emphasizing the importance of daily exercise and a healthful diet. If he smokes, he will be encouraged to quit smoking. He might receive training in stress management and relaxation techniques.

Few people would argue with the proposition that stress is a fact of life. Most have far more experience with stressors than they would willingly choose for themselves. Stress is one of the major causes of psychosomatic disorders. Stressors are often assumed to be external events, probably because stressful external events are so easily identified and recognized. Many stressors, however, come from within oneself. For example, individuals often set strict standards for themselves and, in failing to meet those standards, often make harsher personal judgments than anyone else would make. Especially since the late 1970's and early 1980's, cognitive psychologists have focused attention on the internal thinking processes, thoughts, values, beliefs, and expectations that lead people to put unnecessary pressure on themselves, which results in the subjective sense of stress.

Another contribution made by cognitive psychologists was the realization that a situation can be a stressor only if the individual interprets it as stressful. Any event that people perceive as something with which they can cope will be perceived as less stressful than an event that taxes or exceeds their resources, regardless of the objective seriousness of the two events. In other words, it is the cognitive appraisal of the event, coupled with one's cognitive appraisal of one's ability to deal with the event, rather than the objective reality of the event, that determines the degree to which a person subjectively experiences stress.

PERSONALITY TYPES

Continuing the tradition of the early Greek and Roman physicians, modern personality theorists have often noted that certain personality characteristics seem to be associated with a propensity to develop illness, or even specific illnesses. Other personality characteristics appear to reduce vulnerability to illness. One of the best-known examples of a case in which personality characteristics affect health is that of the Type A behavior pattern (or Type A personality). The person identified as a Type A personality typically displays a pattern of behaviors that include easily aroused hostility, excessive competitiveness, and

---

DSM-IV-TR CRITERIA FOR [SPECIFIED PSYCHOLOGICAL FACTOR] AFFECTING [GENERAL MEDICAL CONDITION] (DSM CODE 316)

General medical condition (coded on Axis III) present

Psychological factors adversely affect general medical condition in one of the following ways:
- factors have influenced the course of general medical condition as shown by close temporal association between psychological factors and the development or exacerbation of, or delayed recovery from, general medical condition
- factors interfere with treatment of general medical condition
- factors constitute additional health risks for individual
- stress-related physiological responses precipitate or exacerbate symptoms of general medical condition

Name based on nature of psychological factors (the most prominent, if more than one factor present):
- Mental Disorder Affecting [General Medical Condition]
- Psychological Symptoms Affecting [General Medical Condition]
- Personality Traits or Coping Style Affecting [General Medical Condition]
- Maladaptive Health Behaviors Affecting [General Medical Condition]
- Physiological Response Affecting [General Medical Condition]
- Other or Unspecified Psychological Factors Affecting [General Medical Condition]

a pronounced sense of time urgency. Research suggests that hostility is the most damaging of these behaviors. Type A personalities typically display hyperreactivity to stressful situations, with a corresponding slow return to the baseline of arousal. The hostile Type A personality is particularly prone to coronary heart disease. By contrast, the less driven Type B personality does not display the hostility, competitiveness, and time urgency of the Type A personality, and is about half as likely to develop coronary heart disease.

Studies conducted in the 1970's and 1980's led to the suggestion that there is a Type C, or cancer-prone, personality. Although the role of personality characteristics is heavily debated in terms of the development of cancer, personality various characteristics related to stress have been found to suppress the immune system, thereby making an individual more vulnerable to some cancers. Personality characteristics have therefore also been found to be somewhat influential in the course of the disease. It is well known that many natural and artificial substances produce cancer, but many researchers have also noted that people with certain personality characteristics are more likely to develop cancer, are more likely to develop fast-growing cancers, and are less likely to survive their cancers, whatever the cause. These personality characteristics include repression of strong negative emotions, acquiescence in the face of stressful life situations, inhibition, depression, and hopelessness. Encounters with uncontrollable stressful events appear to be particularly related to the development or course of cancer. In addition, some research suggests that not having strong social support systems may contribute to the development or affect the outcome of cancer.

Research has begun to focus on the possible interactions among risk factors for cancer. For example, depressed smokers are many more times likely to develop smoking-related cancers than are either nondepressed smokers or depressed nonsmokers. One theory suggests that the smoking provides exposure to the carcinogenic substance that initiates the cancer, and depression promotes its development.

It has been suggested that hardiness is a broad, positive personality variable that affects an individual's propensity for developing stress-related illness. Hardiness is made up of three more specific characteristics: commitment (becoming involved in things that are going on around oneself), challenge (accepting the need for change and seeing new opportunities for growth in what others see as problems), and control (believing that one's actions determine what happens in life and that one can have an effect on the environment). It has been hypothesized that people who possess these characteristics are less likely to develop stress-related disorders because they view stressful situations more favorably than do other people. Commitment and control seem to be more influential in promoting health. Locus of control is a related concept that has received much attention.

Researchers have also examined the link between resiliency and stress. Using animal models, researchers have found that mice that are resilient to stress maintain steady brain chemical levels when stressed, whereas those mice that are not resilient produce more of a specific protein. This same chemical has been found in elevated levels in the brains of depressed people. Further, the more experience an animal has with any stressor, the more likely that the animal will feel it has control over future stressors. When an animal experiences this sort of mastery, it is less likely to become depressed later on while encountering other stressors, so experience with stressors makes it more likely that an animal or a human will be able to deal with future stressors.

CONTROL AND HELPLESSNESS

Locus of control refers to the location where one believes control over life events originates. An external locus of control is outside oneself; an internal locus of control is within oneself. The individual who perceives that life events are the result of luck, or are determined by others, is assuming an external locus of control. The belief that one's efforts and actions control one's own destiny reflects an internal locus of control. Internalizers are thought to be more likely to assume responsibility for initiating necessary lifestyle changes, to employ more direct coping mechanisms when confronted with stressful situations, and to be more optimistic about the possibility of successfully instituting changes that are needed. This last characteristic is sometimes called self-efficacy. Self-efficacy refers to the belief that one is able to do what is needed and attain the intended effect.

The concept of learned helplessness, on the other hand, produces feelings of complete lack of control and a fatalistic acceptance of events. Martin E. P. Seligman began to investigate this phenomenon in 1964. He found that when people are faced with a situation that they cannot prevent or escape, they learn the attitude of helplessness. Seligman and colleagues later investigated the question of why some people do not adopt this attitude. They concluded that people who adopt a pessimistic explanatory style become helpless when adversity is encountered, but that an optimistic explanatory style prevents the development of learned helplessness.

Seligman has described the chain of events by which the pessimistic explanatory style may lead to illness. Beginning with unfortunate experiences such as a serious loss, defeat, or failure, the person with a pessimistic explanatory style becomes depressed. The depression causes leads to depletion of a neurotransmitter substance called catecholamine, and the body increases the secretion of endorphins—the body's own naturally produced form of morphine. When receptors in the immune system detect the increased presence of the endorphins, the immune system begins to turn itself down. Any disease agents that are encountered while the immune system is weakened have a much greater likelihood of overwhelming the remaining defenses of the immune system. This process is very similar to the situation faced by the individual who contracts the human immunodeficiency virus (HIV) and develops acquired immunodeficiency syndrome (AIDS). When the immune system of the person with AIDS is unable to function effectively, opportunistic infections against which the body could normally defend itself are able to take over. It is those opportunistic infections that kill, rather than the HIV itself.

INTERVENTIONS

It is important that a differential diagnosis be made between psychosomatic disorders and three other conditions listed in the *Diagnostic and Statistical Manual of Mental Disorders: DSM-IV-TR* (rev. 4th ed., 2000), which is the official classification system for mental disorders published by the American Psychiatric Association. Psychosomatic disorders, which are covered by the category Psychological Factors Affecting Physical Conditions, are not themselves considered mental disorders. Although the psychological factors that cause the physical illness are unhealthy or abnormal from a psychiatric or psychological perspective, the psychosomatic disorder is a real, physical illness or condition controlled by real, physical processes.

Somatoform disorders, on the other hand, are mental disorders that manifest themselves through real or imagined physical symptoms for which no physical cause exists. These symptoms are not intentionally produced by the client. Conversion disorder is one of the somatoform disorders that laypeople often confuse with psychosomatic disorders. Unlike the case with psychosomatic disorders, there is no organic or physiological pathology that

would account for the presence of the physical symptoms displayed by the person suffering from a conversion disorder. Hypochondriasis is the second somatoform disorder that is often confusing for laypeople. The person suffering from hypochondriasis fears or believes that he or she has the symptoms of a serious disease, but the imagined "symptoms" are actually normal sensations or body reactions that are misinterpreted as symptoms of disease.

Malingering is the third condition that is sometimes confused with psychosomatic disorders. The person who is malingering is faking illness and is reporting symptoms that either do not exist at all or are grossly exaggerated. The malingering is motivated by external goals or incentives.

By eliminating many of the diseases that used to be epidemic, especially those that killed people early in life, medical science has increased the average life expectancy of Americans by about thirty years since the beginning of the twentieth century. Eliminating the psychological factors that cause psychosomatic disorders holds promise for another increase in average life expectancy in the next few decades. Heart disease, cancer, and strokes are the top three killer diseases in the United States, and each has a powerful psychosomatic component. The reduction in human suffering and the economic benefits that can be gained by controlling nonfatal psychosomatic disorders are equally promising.

Cognitive and health psychologists have, particularly since the 1970's, tried to determine the degree to which cognitive psychotherapy interventions can boost immune system functioning in cancer patients. They have also used behavioral and cognitive therapy approaches to alter the attitudes and behaviors of people who are prone to heart disease and strokes with considerable success. They are likely to focus their efforts on two major fronts. The first will involve further attempts to identify the psychological factors that might increase people's propensity to develop psychosomatic disorders. The second will involve continuing efforts to develop and refine the therapeutic interventions intended to reduce the damage done by psychosomatic disorders, and possibly to prevent them entirely.

BIBLIOGRAPHY

Chopra, Deepak. *Creating Health.* Rev. ed. Boston: Mariner Books, 1995. Chopra is a proponent of meditation, an approach that many American psychologists do not necessarily feel comfortable advocating. Nevertheless, this book is written by a practicing physician for the layperson. He covers a wide variety of psychosomatic disorders, suggests a variety of healthy habits, and presents the viewpoint that "health is our natural state."

Levenson James L., ed. *Essentials of Psychosomatic Medicine*. Washington, D.C.: American Psychiatric Publishing, 2007. A collection of articles on psychosomatic medicine and its relation to heart, lung, renal, and gastrointestinal disease, as well as to cancer, chronic fatigue and other illnesses. It also looks at how psychological factors affect recovery from surgery and medical compliance.

Seligman, Martin E. P. *Learned Optimism*. Reprint. New York: Vintage Books, 2006. Chapter 2 provides an especially interesting account of how two young upstart graduate students can blow a hole in one of the most basic assumptions of a well-entrenched viewpoint and promote the development of a new way of looking at things. Chapter 10 describes how explanatory styles might affect health and the mechanism by which this is thought to occur. The last chapters focus on how to develop an optimistic orientation.

Taylor, Shelley E. *Health Psychology*. 7th ed. New York: McGraw-Hill, 2009. A moderately high-level college textbook that comprehensively covers the general field of health psychology. As could be expected, many research studies are presented, and not all of them corroborate one another.

Wedding, Danny, ed. *Behavior and Medicine*. 4th ed. St. Louis: Mosby Year Book, 2006. This large volume covers an extensive area of behavior and medicine, which includes stress and various behaviors that may affect physiological health. The articles cover such behavioral issues as substance abuse, stress management, pain, placebos, AIDS, cardiovascular risk, and adherence to medical regimens. It also covers other behavioral issues relating to love and work, as well as developmental issues from infancy to death, dying, and grief. The book is very readable, and includes illustrations, relevant poetry, bibliographies, summaries, and study questions at the end of each article.

John W. Nichols;
updated by Martha Oehmke Loustaunau, Ayn Embar-Seddon O'Reilly and Allan D. Pass

SEE ALSO: Cancer and mental health; Cognitive behavior therapy; Cognitive therapy; Emotions; Endocrine system; Factitious disorders; Health psychology; Hypochondriasis, conversion, and somatization; Learned helplessness; Meditation and relaxation; Pain; Pain management; Seligman, Martin E. P.; Stress: Physiological responses; Stress-related diseases.

Psychosurgery

DATE: 1930s forward
TYPE OF PSYCHOLOGY: Psychological methodologies

Psychosurgery is brain surgery where brain parts are disconnected or removed to eliminate psychiatric problems such as aggression, anxiety, and psychoses. It was used most from 1935 to 1965, until psychoactive drugs began to replace it. Psychosurgery is not carried out to relieve psychiatric symptoms due to structural brain disease such as brain tumors.

KEY CONCEPTS
- Electroconvulsive therapy
- Psychopharmaceuticals
- Psychosurgery techniques
- Somatic theory of insanity

INTRODUCTION

In the early twentieth century, the treatment of mental disease was limited to psychotherapy for neurotics and long-term care of psychotics in asylums. In the 1930's, these methods were supplemented by physical approaches using electroconvulsive therapy (ECT), or shock therapy, and brain operations. The operations, psychosurgery, were in vogue from the mid-1930s to the mid- to late 1960s. They became, and still are, hugely controversial, although their use had drastically declined by the last quarter of the twentieth century. Controversy arose because, for its first twenty-five years of existence, crude psychosurgery was too often carried out on inappropriate patients.

ECT developed after the 1935 discovery that schizophrenia could be treated by convulsions induced through camphor injection. Soon, convulsion production was accomplished by passage of electric current through the brain, as described in 1938 by Italian physicians Ugo Cerletti and Lucio Bini. ECT was most successful in alleviating depression and is still used for that purpose. In contrast, classic psychosurgery by bilateral prefrontal leukotomy (lobotomy) is no longer done because of its bad effects on the physical and mental health of many subjects. These effects included epilepsy and unwanted personality changes such as apathy, passivity, and low emotional responses. It should be remembered, however, that psychosurgery was first planned to quiet chronically tense, delusional, agitated, or violent psychotics.

HISTORY AND CONTEXT OF PSYCHOSURGERY

Psychosurgery is believed to have originated with the observation by early medical practitioners that severe head injuries could produce extreme changes in behavior patterns. In addition, physicians of the thirteenth to sixteenth centuries reported that sword and knife wounds that penetrated the skull could change normal behavior patterns. Regardless, from the mid-1930s to the mid-1960s, reputable physicians performed psychosurgery on both indigent patients in public institutions and on the wealthy at expensive private hospitals and universities.

Psychosurgery was imperfect and could cause adverse reactions, but it was performed because of the arguments advanced by powerful physician proponents of the method; the imperfect state of knowledge of the brain at the time; the enthusiasm of the popular press, which lauded the method; and many problems at overcrowded mental hospitals. The last reason is thought to have been the most compelling, as asylums for the incurably insane were hellish places. Patients were beaten and choked by attendants; incarcerated in dark, dank padded cells; and subjected to many other indignities. At the same time, little could be done to cure them.

LOBOTOMY

The two main figures in psychosurgery were António Egas Moniz, the Portuguese neurologist who invented lobotomy, and the well-known American neuropathologist and neuropsychiatrist Walter Freeman, who roamed the world persuading others to carry out the operations. The imperfect state of knowledge of the brain in relation to insanity was expressed in two theories of mental illness. A somatic (organic) theory of insanity proposed it to be of biological origin. In contrast, a functional theory supposed life experiences to cause the problems.

The somatic theory was shaped most by Emil Kraepelin, the foremost authority on psychiatry in the first half of the twentieth century. Kraepelin distinguished twenty types of mental disorder, including dementia praecox (schizophrenia) and manic-depressive (bipolar) disorder. Kraepelin and his colleagues viewed these diseases as genetically determined, and practitioners of psychiatry developed complex physical diagnostic schema that identified people with various types of psychoses. In contrast, Sigmund Freud was the main proponent of the functional theory. Attempts to help mental patients included ECT as well as surgical removal of tonsils, sex organs, and parts of the digestive system. All these methods had widely varied success rates that were often subjective and differed depending on which surgeon used them. By the 1930s, the most widely effective curative procedures were several types of ECT and lobotomy (psychosurgery).

The first lobotomy was carried out on November 12, 1935, at a hospital in Lisbon, Portugal. There, Pedro A. Lima, Egas Moniz's neurosurgeon collaborator, drilled two holes into the skull of a female mental patient and injected ethyl alcohol directly into the frontal lobes of her brain to destroy nerve cells. After several such operations, the tissue-killing procedure was altered to use an instrument called a leukotome. After its insertion into the brain, the knifelike instrument, designed by Egas Moniz, was rotated like an apple corer to destroy chosen lobe areas.

Egas Moniz—already a famous neurologist—named the procedure prefrontal leukotomy. He won a Nobel Prize in Physiology or Medicine in 1949 for his invention of the procedure. Within a year of his first leukotomy, psychosurgery (another term invented by Egas Moniz) spread through Europe. Justification for its wide use was the absence of any other effective somatic treatment and the emerging concept that the cerebral frontal lobes were the site of intellectual activity and mental problems. The selection of leukotomy target sites was based on two considerations: using the position in the frontal lobes where nerve fibers—not nerve cells—were most concentrated and avoiding damage to large blood vessels. Thus, Egas Moniz targeted the frontal lobe's centrum ovale, which contains few blood vessels.

After eight operations—50 percent performed on schizophrenics—Egas Moniz and Lima stated that their cure rates were good. Several other psychiatric physicians disagreed strongly. After twenty operations, it became fairly clear that psychosurgery worked best on patients suffering from anxiety and depression, while schizophrenics did not benefit very much. The main effect of the surgery was to calm patients and to make them docile. Retrospectively, it is believed that Egas Moniz's evidence for serious improvement in many cases was very sketchy. However, many psychiatric and neurological practitioners were impressed, and the stage was set for wide dissemination of psychosurgery.

LOBOTOMY PROCEDURES

The second great proponent of leukotomy—the physician who renamed it lobotomy and greatly modified the methodology used—was Freeman, professor of neuropathology at George Washington University Medical School in Washington, D.C. In 1936, he tested the procedure on preserved brains from the medical school morgue and repeated Egas Moniz's efforts. After six lobotomies, Freeman and his associate James W. Watts became optimistic that the method was useful to treat patients exhibiting apprehension, anxiety, insomnia, and nervous tension, while pointing out that it would be impossible to determine whether the procedure had effected the recovery or cure of mental problems until a five-year period had passed.

As Freeman and Watts continued to operate, they noticed problems, including relapses to the original abnormal state, a need for repeated surgery, a lack of ability on the part of patients to resume jobs requiring the use of reason, and death due to postsurgical hemorrhage. This led them to develop a more precise technique, using the landmarks on the skull to identify where to drill entry holes, cannulation to assure that lobe penetration depth was not dangerous to patients, and use of a knifelike spatula to make lobotomy cuts. The extent of surgery also varied, depending on whether the patient involved was suffering from an affective disorder or from schizophrenia. Their method, the "routine Freeman-Watts lobotomy procedure," became popular throughout the world.

Another method used for prefrontal lobotomy was designed by J. G. Lyerly in 1937. He opened the brain so that psychosurgeons could see exactly what was being done to the frontal lobes. This technique also became popular and was used throughout the United States. Near the same time, in Japan, Mizuho Nakata of Nigata Medical College began to remove from the brain parts of one or both frontal lobes. However, the Freeman-Watts method was most popular as the result of a "do-it-yourself manual" for psychosurgery that they published in 1942. Watts's book theorized that the brain pathways between cerebral frontal lobes and the thalamus regulate intensity of emotions in ideas, and acceptance of this theory led to better scientific justification of psychosurgery.

Another lobotomy procedure that was fairly widespread was Freeman's transorbital method, designed not only to correct shortcomings in his routine method but also as an attempt to aid many more schizophrenics. The simple, rapid, but frightening procedure drove a transorbital leukotome (similar in appearance to an ice pick, thus the popularity of the term "ice pick lobotomy" for the procedure) through the eye socket, above the eyeball, and into the frontal lobe. Subjects were rendered unconscious with ECT, and the procedure was done before they woke up. Use of this method gained many converts and, gruesome as it sounds, the method caused less brain damage than other psychosurgery procedures. It was widely used at state hospitals for the insane and was lauded by the press as making previously hopeless cases normal immediately.

Subsequently developed stereotaxic surgical techniques, such as stereotactic cingulatory, enabled psychosurgeons to create much smaller lesions by means of probes inserted into accurately located brain regions, followed by nerve destruction through the use of radioactive implants or by cryogenics. Currently, psychosurgery is claimed to be an effective treatment for patients with intractable depression, anxiety, or obsessional problems and a method that improves the behavior of very aggressive patients. Opponents say that these therapeutic effects can be attained by means of antipsychotic and antidepressant drugs. The consensus is that psychosurgery can play a small part in psychiatric treatment when long-term use of other treatments is unsuccessful and patients are tormented by mental problems.

MODE OF ACTION OF PSYCHOSURGERY

Collectively, the brain's limbic system is composed of the hippocampus, amygdala, hippocampal and cingulate gyri, limen insulae, and posterior orbital regions of cerebral frontal lobes. This system, its components linked by nerve pathways, controls emotional expression, seizure activity, and memory storage and recall. Moreover, cerebral lobe limbic system connections from the dorsal convexity of a frontal lobe comprise two pathways running to the cingulate gyrus and hippocampus and the hypothalamus and midbrain. The frontal lobe orbital surface also projects to the septal area of the hypothalamus. The limbic brain architecture therefore yields two neurotransport circuits in a frontolimbic-hypothalamic-midbrain axis. These are a medial frontal, cingulate, hippocampus circuit (MFCHC) and an orbital frontal, temporal, amygdala circuit (OFTAC), which control hypothalamic autonomic and endocrine action. The MFCHC and OFTAC connect in the septa, preoptic area, midbrain, and hypothalamus.

The original Egas Moniz lobotomy divided the frontolimbic structures, and its bad effects were due to the disabling impairment of frontal lobe function. Psychosurgery on the anterior cingulate gyrus and on the thalamofrontal bundle (bimedial leukotomy) divided different parts of the same main circuit. Orbital undercutting severs red nerve tracts running from the posterior orbital cortex to the limbic system. Although psychosurgery is currently an uncommon procedure, when it is performed, the methods used are lower medial quadrant leukotomy, making lesions just before the fourth ventricle; stereotactic-subcaudate-tractotomy, making lesions with rear halves in the subcaudate area; removal of the anterior two inches of the cingulate gyrus; and stereotactic limbic leukotomy, lesioning the lower medial frontal lobe quadrant. These operations cause varied endocrine and autonomic disconnections and are thus chosen to suit the mental condition being treated.

DIAGNOSIS AND TREATMENT

Diagnosis of a need for psychosurgery is based on observation of symptoms supporting abnormal psychological behavior. Examples are extremes of aggression, anxiety, obsession, or compulsiveness, as well as psychoses other than schizophrenia. The exclusion of schizophrenics, except for those having marked anxiety and tension, is based on data supporting poor responses by schizophrenics to lobotomy and other leukotomies. Surveys have shown that good surgical outcomes were obtained in only 18 percent of schizophrenics who underwent lobotomy, as compared with 50 percent of depressives.

Psychosurgery's unfavorable record between 1935 and 1965, and its postoperative irreversibility, speak to the need for careful study before suggesting such brain surgery. In addition, many members of the medical community believe that the choice of psychosurgery should be based on the long-term nature of symptoms untreatable by other means as well as a severe risk of suicide. In most countries, before psychosurgery is attempted, other methods must be exhausted, such as repeated ECT, prolonged psychoanalysis, and aggressive pharmaceutical treatments with antipsychotic drugs. Some sources suggest, as criteria for choosing psychosurgery, the persistence of symptoms for more than ten years of treatment under conditions where all possible nonsurgical methodology has been exhausted after its aggressive use. Others believe it inhumane to require a decade of illness before allowing the possibility of a cure.

Symptom severity is another hugely important criterion for psychosurgery. Examples of this are the complete inability to work at a job or carry out household chores, as well as long-term and severe endogenous depression. It is also suggested that patients who have strong psychological support from their families and stable environments are the best candidates. Careful assessment of patient symptoms, handicaps, and problems should always be carried out. Formal rating scales, personality assessment via school and work records, and information coming from close relatives or friends are also viewed as crucial.

In most of the world, the use of psychosurgery has declined sharply throughout the late twentieth and early twenty-first centuries and is limited to a very small number of patients not helped by existing chemotherapeutic or psychoanalytical methodology. Only a few countries, such as China and Russia, continue to perform psychosurgery regularly. A wide variety of new techniques have made psychosurgery capable of destroying smaller and smaller targets. In the twenty-first century, the focus of psychosurgery research has also begun to shift from the destruction of brain tissue to the stimulation of said tissue using implanted electrodes. As knowledge of the brain and its functioning increases, it appears possible that modern psychosurgery may yet prove to be useful where other methods fail.

BIBLIOGRAPHY

Dully, Howard, and Charles Fleming. *My Lobotomy.* New York: Three Rivers, 2008. Print.

El-Hai, Jack. *The Lobotomist: A Maverick Medical Genius and His Tragic Quest to Rid the World of Mental Illness.* Hoboken: Wiley, 2007.

Fulton, John F. *Frontal Lobotomy and Affective Behavior: A Neuropsychological Analysis.* New York: Norton, 1951. Print.

Illes, Judy, and B. J. Sahakian. *The Oxford Handbook of Neuroethics.* Oxford: Oxford UP, 2011. Print.

Lader, Malcolm H., and Reginald Herrington. *Biological Treatments in Psychiatry.* 2d ed. New York: Oxford UP, 1996. Print.

Raz, Mical. *The Lobotomy Letters: The Making of American Psychosurgery.* Rochester: U of Rochester P, 2013. Print.

Rodgers, Joann Ellison. *Psychosurgery: Damaging the Brain to Save the Mind.* New York: Harper, 1992. Print.

Sachdev, Perminder S., and Xiaohua Chen. "Neurosurgical Treatment of Mood Disorders: Traditional Psychosurgery and the Advent of Deep Brain Stimulation." *Current Opinion in Psychiatry* 22.1 (2009): 25–31. Print.

Turner, Eric A. *Surgery of the Mind.* Birmingham: Carmen, 1982. Print.

United States. Department of Health and Human Services. Public Health Service. *Stereotactic Cingulotomy as a Means of Psychosurgery.* By Ernes Feigenbaum. Rockville: n.p., 1985. Print.

Valenstein, Elliot S. *Great and Desperate Cures: The Rise and Decline of Psychosurgery and Other Radical Treatments for Mental Illness.* New York: Basic, 1986. Print.

Valenstein, Elliot S., ed. *The Psychosurgery Debate: Scientific, Legal, and Ethical Perspectives.* New York: Freeman, 1980. Print.

Sanford S. Singer

SEE ALSO: Anxiety disorders; Bipolar disorder; Brain structure; Depression; Lobotomy; Mental illness: Historical concepts; Psychotic disorders; Schizophrenia: Background, types, and symptoms; Schizophrenia: Theoretical explanations; Shock therapy.

Psychotherapy
Children

TYPE OF PSYCHOLOGY: Psychotherapy

Psychotherapy with children involves the use of psychological techniques in the treatment of children with behavioral, cognitive, or emotional disorders. The specific focus of treatment varies and may involve children only, parents only, or a combination of these individuals.

KEY CONCEPTS
- Behavior therapy
- Behavioral parent training
- Cognitive behavioral therapy
- Cognitive therapy
- Externalizing disorders
- Family therapy
- Internalizing disorders
- Interpretation
- Learning theory
- Play therapy
- Working through

INTRODUCTION

Various psychological techniques designed to treat children's behavioral, cognitive, or emotional problems are used in psychotherapy with children. The number of children with psychological disorders underscores the need for effective child psychotherapy: the Centers for Disease Control and Prevention (CDC) reported in 2013 that an estimated 13 to 20 percent of children in the United States experienced a mental disorder each year from 2005 to 2011, and that the prevalence of these conditions increased between 1994 and 2011. According to the National Institute of Mental Health, CDC data collected as part of the National Health and Nutrition Examination Survey between 2000 and 2004 also showed that only about half of the children ages eight to fifteen with mental disorders were treated for their disorder within the past year.

Children, like adults, may experience many different kinds of psychological disorders. For example, in the *Diagnostic and Statistical Manual of Mental Disorders* (DSM-IV-TR; rev. 4th ed., 2000), published by the American Psychiatric Association, nearly forty separate disorders that primarily affect children are listed. This number does not include many disorders, such as major depressive disorder, which primarily affect adults but may also affect children. In DSM-5 (5th ed., 2013), however, children's disorders no longer have a separate chapter. Instead, each diagnostic chapter is organized chronologically, with diagnoses primarily affecting children listed before those affecting adolescents and adults. In general terms, children's disorders can be divided into two major categories: externalizing and internalizing disorders.

EXTERNALIZING AND INTERNALIZING DISORDERS

Externalizing disorders are those in which children engage in activities that are physically disruptive or are harmful to themselves or others. An example of this type of disorder is conduct disorder. Conduct disorder is characterized by children's involvement in a continued pattern of behavior that demonstrates a fundamental disregard for the safety or property of others. In contrast to externalizing disorders, internalizing disorders create greater emotional distress for the children themselves than for others around them. An example of an internalizing disorder is generalized anxiety disorder, in which the child experiences persistent, unrealistic anxiety regarding numerous situations and events, such as peer acceptance or school grades.

TYPES OF TREATMENT

Psychoanalytic Therapy. In response to the prevalence and variety of childhood disorders, many different treatments have been developed to address children's psychological problems. Historically, the earliest interventions for addressing these problems were based on psychoanalytic theory, developed by Sigmund Freud. Psychoanalysis is a type of psychotherapy based on the idea that individuals' unconscious processes, derived from early childhood experiences, are responsible for the psychological problems they experience as adults. One of the first therapists to adapt Freud's psychoanalysis to the treatment of children was Anna Freud, his daughter.

Psychoanalysis had to be modified for the treatment of children because of its heavy reliance on individuals' verbalizing their unconscious thoughts and feelings. Anna Freud realized that children would not be able to verbalize regarding their experiences to the extent necessary for effective treatment. Therefore, beginning in the 1920s, she created play therapy, a system of psychotherapy in which children's responses during play provided information regarding their hidden thoughts and feelings. Although play therapy had its roots in Sigmund Freud's psychoanalysis, this type of therapy came to be associated with other systems of psychotherapy. For example, Virginia Axline demonstrates her version of play therapy in the 1964 book *Dibs: In Search of Self*; her approach is based on Carl R. Rogers's person-centered therapy.

Behavior Therapy. In addition, in the 1920s, Mary Cover Jones was applying the principles of behavior therapy developed by John B. Watson and others to the treatment of children's fears. Behavior therapy rests on the notion that all behavior, whether adaptive or maladaptive, is learned and thus can be unlearned. Jones's treatment involved reconditioning, a procedure in which the object of which the child is afraid is gradually associated with a pleasurable activity. By regularly associating the feared object with a pleasurable activity, Jones was able to eliminate children's fears.

Family Therapy. Although early child analysts and behaviorally oriented psychologists attributed many children's problems to difficulties within their family environments, these treatment providers' primary focus was on treating the children, not their parents. In the early 1940s, however, Nathan Ackerman, a psychiatrist trained in the psychoanalytic tradition, began to treat children in conjunction with their families. His justification for seeing all family members in treatment was that families, like individuals, possess hidden conflicts that prevent them from engaging in healthy psychological functioning. Therefore, the role of the family therapist was to uncover these family conflicts, thus creating the possibility that the conflicts could be addressed in more

adaptive ways. Once these family conflicts were properly handled, the causes of the child's psychological problems were removed. Ackerman's approach marked the beginning of the use of family therapy for the treatment of children's problems.

Parent Training. Another historical movement within child psychotherapy is behavioral parent training (BPT). BPT evolved from the recognition that parents are important in shaping their children's behavior and that they can be trained to eliminate many of their children's problems. Beginning in the late 1960s, researchers such as Gerald Patterson and Rex Forehand began to develop programs designed to target parents as the principal people responsible for change in their children's maladaptive behavior. In this system of psychotherapy, parents were taught ways to assess and to intervene to correct their children's misbehavior. The role of the child was de-emphasized to the point that the child might not even be seen by the therapist during the treatment process.

Cognitive and Cognitive Behavioral Therapies. In the 1970s, some psychologists, including Donald Meichenbaum, began to apply the principles of behavior therapy to not only overt but also covert behaviors (that is, thoughts). Thus, the cognitive tradition was begun. Cognitive therapies are based on the mediational model, a model based on the belief that cognitive activity affects behavior. The goal of cognitive therapy is to institute behavioral changes via modifications in thoughts, especially maladaptive ones. Many child therapies actually use both cognitive and behavioral approaches in combination: cognitive behavior therapy. The cognitive behavior approach can be conceptualized as a two-pronged approach addressing both thoughts and behaviors while emphasizing their reciprocal relationship (thought affects behavior and behavior affects thought).

TREATMENT FORMATS

It is estimated that more than two hundred different types of child psychotherapy exist; however, these specific types of therapy can be roughly divided into three larger categories of treatment based on the primary focus of their interventions. These three categories are children only, parents only, or children and parents combined.

Child-Only Format. Individual child psychotherapy, the first category of psychotherapy with children, focuses on the child alone because of the belief that the greatest amount of improvement can result when the child is given primary attention in treatment. An example of individual child treatment is psychodynamic play therapy. Originating from the work of Anna Freud, psychodynamic play therapy has as its basic goal providing the child with insight into the internal conflicts that have caused his or her psychological disorder. Once the child has gained sufficient insight, he or she is guided in handling these conflicts in more adaptive ways. Play therapy can be divided into three basic phases: initial, interpretative, and working-through phases.

In the initial phase of play therapy, the major goal is to establish a cooperative relationship between the child and the therapist. The attainment of this goal may require considerable time for several potential reasons. These reasons include a child's unwillingness to participate in therapy, lack of understanding regarding the therapy process, and lack of a previous trusting relationship with an adult. The participation in play activities provides an opportunity for the therapist to interact with the child in a relaxed and interesting manner. The specific kinds of play utilized differ from therapist to therapist but may include competitive games (such as checkers), imaginative games involving different figures (hand puppets, for example), or cooperative games (playing catch).

Once a sufficient level of cooperation is established, the therapist can begin to make interpretations to the child regarding the play. These interpretations consist of the therapist identifying themes in the content or style of a child's play that may relate to a psychological problem. For example, in playing with hand puppets, a child referred because of aggressive behavior may regularly enact stories in which a larger puppet "beats up" a smaller puppet. The child's therapist may interpret this story as meaning that the child is aggressive toward others because he or she feels inadequate.

Once the child gains insight into the internal conflict that has caused his or her problematic behavior, the child is guided by the therapist to develop a more adaptive way of handling this conflict. This final process of therapy is called working through. The working-through phase may be the most difficult part of treatment, because it involves the child abandoning a repetitive and maladaptive manner of handling a conflict in favor of a new approach. In comparison to most other psychotherapies, this treatment process is lengthy, ranging from months to years.

Parent-Only Format. The second category of child psychotherapy, parent training, focuses intervention on the parents, because they are viewed as potentially the most effective persons available to alleviate the child's problems. This assumption is based on several factors,

including the great amount of time parents spend with their children, the parents' control over the child's access to desired reinforcers, and the parents' understanding of the child's behavior because of their past relationship with the child. Behavioral parent training (BPT) is the most common type of parent training program. In BPT, parents are taught ways to modify their children's environment to improve behavior.

The initial phase of this treatment process involves instructing parents in the basics of learning theory. They are taught that all behavior, adaptive or maladaptive, is maintained because it is reinforced. The application of learning theory to the correction of children's misbehavior involves three principles. First, positive reinforcement should be withdrawn from children's maladaptive behavior. For example, a father who meets the demands of his screaming preschooler who throws a temper tantrum in the checkout line of the grocery store because she wants a piece of candy is unwittingly reinforcing the child's screaming behavior. Second, appropriate behavior that is incompatible with the maladaptive behavior should be positively reinforced. In the case of the screaming preschooler, this would involve rewarding her for acting correctly. Third, aversive consequences should be applied when the problem behavior recurs. That is, when the child engages in the misbehavior, he or she should consistently experience negative costs. For example, the preschooler who has a temper tantrum in the checkout line should not be allowed money to purchase gum, which she had previously selected as a potential reward for good store behavior, as the cost for her tantrum. To produce the greatest effect, positive reinforcement and negative consequences should be administered as close as possible to the occurrence of the appropriate or inappropriate behavior.

Family Format. The final category of child psychotherapy, family therapy, focuses intervention on both the child and the child's family. Family therapy rests on the assumption that the child's psychological problems were created and are maintained by interactions among different family members. In this model, attention is shifted away from the individual child's problems toward the functioning of the entire family. For example, in structural family therapy, a widely practiced type of family therapy, the boundaries between different family members are closely examined. Family boundaries represent the degree of separation between different family members or subsets of members (for example, the parent-versus-child subset). According to Salvador Minuchin, the originator of structural family therapy, families in which there is little separation between parents and children may cause certain children to misbehave as a way to gain increased emotional distance from their parents. On the other hand, families characterized by too much separation between parents and children may cause certain children to become depressed because of the lack of a confiding relationship with a parental figure. Regardless of the child's specific disorder, all family members, not the child or parents alone, are the focus of treatment.

EFFICACY OF PSYCHOTHERAPY

The two large questions that can be asked regarding psychotherapy for children are whether it is effective and whether one type of treatment is more effective than others. The answer to the first question is very clear: psychotherapy is effective in treating the majority of children's psychological disorders. Two major studies in the 1980s reviewed the existing research examining the effects of child psychotherapy. The first of these studies was conducted by Rita Casey and Jeffrey Berman in 1985, and the second was conducted by John Weisz, Bahr Weiss, Mark Alicke, and M. L. Klotz in 1987. Both these studies found that children who received psychotherapy were better off than approximately 75 percent of the children who did not receive psychotherapy. Interestingly, Weisz and colleagues found that younger children (ages four to twelve) appeared to obtain more benefit from psychotherapy than older children (ages thirteen to eighteen). In addition, Casey and Berman found that girls tend to receive more benefit from psychotherapy than do boys.

As one might expect, some controversy exists in attempting to answer the second question, regarding which treatment is the most effective. Casey and Berman concluded that all treatments were equally effective; however, Weisz and colleagues found that behavioral treatments were more effective than nonbehavioral treatments. Disagreement regarding which type of psychotherapy is most effective should not be allowed to obscure the general conclusion that psychotherapy for children is clearly beneficial. Many investigators would suggest that the characteristics shared by all types of child psychotherapy are responsible for the relatively equivalent improvement produced by different treatments. For example, one of these common characteristics may be the therapist's and child's expectations that therapy will result in a reduction in the child's psychological problems. In spite of the treatments' apparent differences in rationale and method, it may be

that this component, as well as other common elements, accounts for much of the similarity in treatment outcomes.

The number of psychotherapeutic approaches available to treat children's psychological disorders has exploded since their introduction in the 1920s. Recent research has clearly demonstrated the effectiveness of psychotherapy for children. Controversy still remains, however, regarding which treatment approach is the most effective; continued research is needed to address this issue. Of greater urgency is the need to provide psychotherapy to the approximately five to ten million children with psychological disorders who are not being served. Perhaps even more cost effective, in terms of both alleviating human suffering and reducing costs, would be the development of programs to prevent children's psychological disorders.

BIBLIOGRAPHY

American Psychiatric Association. *Diagnostic and Statistical Manual of Mental Disorders*. 5th ed. Washington, DC: APA, 2013. Print.

American Psychiatric Association. *DSM-5 and Diagnoses for Children*. Washington, DC: APA, 2013. Digital file.

Ammerman, R. T., M. Hersen, and C. Last, eds. *Handbook of Prescriptive Treatments for Children and Adolescents*. Boston: Allyn, 1999. Print.

Axline, Virginia Mae. *Dibs: In Search of Self*. New York: Ballantine, 1990. Print.

Brems, C. *A Comprehensive Guide to Child Psychotherapy*. 3d ed. Long Grove: Waveland, 2008. Print.

Briesmeister, J. M., and C. E. Schaefer, eds. *Handbook of Parent Training: Parents as Cotherapists for Children's Behavior Problems*. Hoboken: Wiley, 2007. Print.

Centers for Disease Control and Prevention. "CDC Features: Children's Mental Health—New Report." *Centers for Disease Control and Prevention*. CDC, 21 May 2013. Web. 26 June 2014.

Gordon, Thomas. *Parent Effectiveness Training: The Proven Program for Raising Responsible Children*. Rev. ed. New York: Three Rivers, 2000. Print.

Kendall, Philip C., ed. *Child and Adolescent Therapy*. 3d ed. New York: Guilford, 2006. Print.

Minuchin, Salvador. *Families and Family Therapy*. London: Routledge, 1993. Print.

Monte, Christopher. "Anna Freud: The Psychoanalytic Heritage and Developments in Ego Psychology." *In Beneath the Mask: An Introduction to Theories of Personality*. 7th ed. Hoboken: Wiley, 2003. Print.

National Institute of Mental Health. "Use of Mental Health Services and Treatment among Children."

National Institute of Mental Health. NIMH, n.d. Web. 26 June 2014.

Nemiroff, Marc A., and Jane Annunziata. *A Child's First Book About Play Therapy.* Washington, DC: American Psychological Association, 1990. Print.

Perou, Ruth, et al. "Mental Health Surveillance among Children—United States, 2005–2011: Supplements." *Morbidity and Mortality Weekly Report.* CDC, 17 May 2013. Web. 26 June 2014.

Reinecke, M. A., F. M. Dattilio, and A. Freeman, eds. *Cognitive Therapy with Children and Adolescents.* New York: Guilford, 2007. Print.

R. Christopher Qualls;
updated by Ellen C. Flannery-Schroeder

SEE ALSO: Anxiety disorders; Attachment and bonding in infancy and childhood; Attention-deficit hyperactivity disorder; Bed-wetting; Child abuse; Childhood disorder; Children's mental health; Conduct disorders; Dyslexia; Family life: Children's issues; Father-child relationship; Juvenile delinquency; Learning disorders; Misbehavior; Mother-child relationship; Parental alienation syndrome; Piaget, Jean; Prenatal physical development; Schizophrenia: Highrisk children; Separation and divorce: Children's issues; Sibling relationships; Stepfamilies; Stuttering; Teenage suicide; Violence by children and teenagers.

Psychotherapy
Effectiveness

TYPE OF PSYCHOLOGY: Psychotherapy

Psychotherapy is a rapidly expanding field; it has been estimated that there are more than four hundred psychotherapeutic approaches. Research evaluating the effectiveness of psychotherapy serves a primary role in the development and validation of therapeutic approaches. Studies have examined the effectiveness of psychotherapy on thousands of patients. Although such studies often produce contradictory and perhaps even disappointing findings, there is clear evidence that psychotherapy is effective.

KEY CONCEPTS
- Case study
- Empathy
- Meta-analysis
- Neurotic disorders
- Placebo
- Randomization
- Relapse
- Spontaneous remission

INTRODUCTION

Although the roots of psychotherapy can be traced back to ancient times, the birth of modern psychotherapy is frequently targeted with the famous case of Anna O. in 1882. Physician Josef Breuer, who was a colleague of Sigmund Freud, described Anna O. as a twenty-one-year-old patient with multiple symptoms, including paralysis and loss of sensitivity in her limbs, lapses in awareness, problems in vision and speech, headaches, and dual personality. During treatment, Breuer found that if Anna discussed every occurrence of a symptom until she described its origin and vividly recalled its first appearance, the symptom would disappear. Hypnosis was also employed to help Anna O. eliminate the symptoms more rapidly. (Eventually, Breuer stopped working with this patient because of numerous difficulties, including his jealous wife and his patient's tendency to become hysterical.) Anna O., whose real name was Bertha Pappenheim, later became well known throughout Germany for her work with children, prostitutes, and Jewish relief organizations.

The case of Anna O. is not only important as perhaps representing the birth of modern psychotherapy but also characteristic of a method of investigation referred to as the case study or case report. A case report attempts to highlight descriptions of a specific patient and treatment approach, typically as reported by the therapist. Given the fact that most patients treated in psychotherapy are seen individually by a single therapist, it is not surprising that some of the most influential literature in the history of psychotherapy is based on case reports. Unfortunately, the majority of case reports are inherently problematic in terms of scientific merit and methodological rigor. Moreover, it is difficult to determine which factors are most effective in the treatment of any particular patient. Thus, whereas case reports are common in the history of psychotherapy research, their value is generally limited.

EARLY STUDIES

The earliest psychotherapy outcome studies were conducted from the 1930s to the 1960s. These initial investigations were concerned with one primary question: Does psychotherapy demonstrate positive effects? Unfortunately, the research methodology employed in these studies was typically flawed, and interpretations proved ambiguous. The most common area of disagreement in the early investigations was the concept of spontaneous remission. Psychotherapy was evaluated in comparison to the rates of improvement seen among patients who were not currently receiving treatment.

For example, British psychologist Hans Eysenck created a furor in the early 1950s, one that continued to trouble psychologists and mental health workers for several decades. Eysenck concluded, on the basis of his review of twenty-four studies, that psychotherapy produced no greater changes in individuals than did naturally occurring life events. Specifically, he argued that two-thirds of people with neurotic disorders improve over a two-year period with or without psychotherapy. Two particular problems with his review warrant comment, however. First, the studies that were included in his review rarely employed randomization, which raises significant concerns about subsequent interpretations. Second, later analyses of the same data set demonstrated that Eysenck's original estimates of improvements in the absence of treatment were inflated.

The manner in which research investigations were conducted (the research methodology) became more sophisticated in the 1970s. In particular, research designs included appropriate control groups to account for spontaneous improvements, randomly assigned experimental conditions, well-specified treatment protocols administered by well-trained therapists, and improved instruments and procedures to measure effectiveness. As a result, it became increasingly clear that many psychotherapies demonstrate statistically significant and clinically meaningful effects on patients. Not all patients reveal improvement, however, and many patients relapse following successful treatment.

In 1977, researchers Mary Smith and Gene Glass presented a review of 375 psychotherapy outcome studies carried out by means of a newly devised methodology called "meta-analysis." Meta-analysis literally means "analysis of analyses" and represents a statistical procedure used to summarize collections of research data. Meta-analysis is frequently regarded as more objective and more sophisticated than traditional review procedures such as those employed by Eysenck. Smith and Glass revealed that most patients who entered outpatient psychotherapy showed noticeable improvement. In addition, the average therapy patient improved more than did 75 percent of comparable control patients.

The results reported by Smith and Glass were controversial, and they stimulated much productive debate. In particular, the authors were criticized for certain procedural steps (for example, excluding particular studies and including others). In response to such criticism, many researchers conducted additional meta-analytic investigations to examine the empirical effectiveness of psychotherapy. Of particular importance is the large follow-up investigation that was conducted by Smith, Glass, and Thomas Miller in 1980. The authors presented many detailed analyses of their results and expanded the data set from 375 studies to 475 studies involving approximately twenty-five thousand patients treated by seventy-eight therapies over an average of sixteen sessions. Smith, Glass, and Miller revealed that the average therapy patient was better off than 80 percent of the control group.

To date, numerous studies have provided evidence for the general effectiveness of psychotherapy to produce positive changes in targeted problem areas; however, psychotherapy is not a unitary procedure applied to a unitary problem. Moreover, many of the nearly four hundred psychotherapeutic approaches have yet to be systematically evaluated. Thus, it is important to understand the empirical evidence for specific treatment approaches with specific patient populations. It is similarly important to note that each therapist is a unique individual who provides his or her own unique perspective and experience to the psychotherapeutic process. Fortunately, positive effects are generally common among psychotherapy patients, and negative (deterioration) effects, which are also observed regularly, often appear related to a poor match of therapist, technique, and patient factors.

PATIENT IMPROVEMENT AND TREATMENT EVALUATION

Recent research has focused on some of the factors associated with patient improvement, and several specific methods have been used to evaluate different treatments. Common research designs include contrasting an established treatment with a new treatment approach (for example, systematic desensitization versus eye movement desensitization for anxiety) or therapeutic format (group depression treatment versus individual depression treatment), separating the components of an effective treatment package (such as cognitive behavioral treatment of anxiety) to examine the relative effectiveness of the modules, and analyzing the interactions between therapist and patient during psychotherapy (process research).

The results from studies employing these designs are generally mixed and reveal limited differences between specific therapeutic approaches. For example, in the largest meta-analytic studies, some analyses revealed that behavioral and cognitive therapies were found to have larger positive changes when compared to other types of psychotherapy (psychodynamic and humanistic), while other analyses did not. Similarly, several large comparative studies revealed considerable patient improvement regardless of treatment approach. Such results must be carefully evaluated, however, because there are numerous reasons for failing to find differences between treatments.

All psychotherapy research is flawed; there are no perfect studies. Thus, studies should be evaluated along several dimensions, including rigor of methodology and adequacy of statistical procedures. Psychotherapy is both an art and a science, and it involves the complex interaction between a socially sanctioned helper (a therapist) and a distressed patient or client. The complexity of this interaction raises some significant obstacles to designing psychotherapy research. Thus, methodological problems can be diverse and extensive, and they may account for the failure to find significant differences among alternative psychotherapeutic approaches. Some researchers have argued that the combination of methodological problems and statistical limitations (such as research samples that are too small to detect differences between groups or inconsistency with regard to patient characteristics) plagued many of the studies completed in the 1980s.

Still, the search for effective components of psychotherapy remains a primary research question focused on several key areas, including patient characteristics, therapist characteristics, treatment techniques, common factors across different psychotherapies, and the various interactions among these variables. As highlighted in Sol Garfield and Allen Bergin's edited book entitled *Handbook of Psychotherapy and Behavior Change* (1986), some evidence reveals that patient characteristics (such as amount of self-exploration and ability to solve problems and express emotions constructively) are of primary importance in positive outcomes. Therapist characteristics such as empathy, interpersonal warmth, acceptance toward patients, and genuineness also appear to play a major role in successful therapy. Treatment techniques seem generally less important than the ability of the therapist and patient to form a therapeutic relationship.

Additional studies have asked patients at the conclusion of psychotherapy to identify the most important factors in their successful treatment. Patients have generally described such factors as gradually facing their problems in a supportive setting, talking to an understanding person, and the personality of their therapist as helpful factors. Moreover, patients frequently conclude that their success in treatment is related to their therapist's support, encouragement, sensitivity, honesty, sense of humor, and ability to share insights. In contrast, other research has examined negative outcomes of psychotherapy to illuminate factors predictive of poor outcomes. These factors include the failure of the therapist to structure sessions and address primary concerns presented by the patient, poorly timed interventions, and negative therapist attitudes toward the patient.

COMMON FACTORS

Taken as a whole, psychotherapy research reveals some consistent results about many patient and therapist characteristics associated with positive and negative outcomes. Yet remarkably few differences have been found among the different types of treatment. This pattern of evidence has led many researchers to conclude that factors that are common across different forms of psychotherapy may account for the apparent equality among many treatment approaches. At the forefront of this position is psychiatrist and psychologist Jerome D. Frank.

In various books and journal articles, Frank has argued that all psychotherapeutic approaches share common ingredients that are simply variations of age-old procedures of psychological healing, such as confession, encouragement, modeling, positive reinforcement, and punishment. Because patients seeking treatment are typically demoralized, distressed, and feeling helpless, all psychotherapies aim to restore morale by offering support, reassurance, feedback, guidance, hope, and mutual understanding of the problems and proposed solutions. Among the common factors most frequently studied since the 1960s, the key ingredients outlined by the person-centered school are most widely regarded as central to the development of a successful therapeutic relationship. These ingredients are empathy, positive regard, warmth, and genuineness.

Various factors should be considered when one chooses a therapist. To begin with, it may be wise to consider first one's objectives and motivations for entering treatment. A thoughtful appraisal of one's own goals can serve as a map through the maze of alternative treatments, therapy agencies, and diverse professionals providing psychotherapeutic services. In addition, one should learn about the professionals in one's area by speaking with a family physician, a religious adviser, or friends who have previously sought psychotherapeutic services. It is also important to locate a licensed professional with whom one feels comfortable, because the primary ingredients for success are patient and therapist characteristics. All therapists and patients are unique individuals who provide their distinctive perspectives and contributions to the therapy process. Therefore, the most important factor in psychotherapeutic outcome may be the match between patient and therapist.

RESULTS OF META-ANALYSIS

Although the roots of psychotherapy can be traced back to antiquity, psychotherapy research is a recent development in the field of psychology. Early evidence for the effectiveness of psychotherapy was limited and consisted of case studies and investigations with significant methodological flaws. Considerable furor among therapists followed psychologist Eysenck's claims that psychotherapy is no more effective than naturally occurring life events are. Other disagreements followed the rapid development of many alternative and competing forms of psychotherapy in the 1960s and 1970s. Claims that one particular approach was better than another were rarely confirmed by empirical research. Still, psychotherapy research is a primary method in the development, refinement, and validation of treatments for diverse patient groups. Advancements in research methodology and statistical applications have provided answers to many important questions in psychotherapy research.

Rather than examining the question of whether psychotherapy works, researchers are designing sophisticated research programs to evaluate the effectiveness of specific treatment components on particular groups of patients with carefully diagnosed mental disorders. Researchers continue to identify specific variables and processes among patients and therapists that shape positive outcomes. The quality of interactions between patient and therapist appear to hold particular promise in understanding psychotherapy outcome.

To address the complexity of psychotherapy, research must address at least two important dimensions: process (how and why does this form of therapy work?) and outcome (to what degree is this specific treatment effective for this particular client in this setting at this time?). In addition, empirical comparisons between psychotherapy and medications in terms of effectiveness, side effects, compliance, and long-term outcome will continue to shape clinical practice for many years to come. As one example, the National Institute of Mental Health (NIMH) sponsored a large comparative psychotherapy and drug treatment study of depression. In that investigation, the effectiveness of individual interpersonal psychotherapy, individual cognitive therapy, antidepressant medication, and placebo conditions were tested. While findings from initial analyses revealed no significant differences among any of the treatment conditions, secondary analyses suggested that severity of depression was an important variable. For the less severely depressed, there was no evidence for the specific effectiveness of active-versus-placebo treatment conditions. The more severely depressed patients, however, responded best to antidepressant medications and interpersonal therapy. Future reports from the NIMH team of researchers may reveal additional results that could further shape the ways in which depressed patients are treated.

BIBLIOGRAPHY

Beutler, Larry E., and Marjorie Crago, eds. *Psychotherapy Research: An International Review of Programmatic Studies.* Washington: APA, 1994. Print.

Eells, Tracy D., ed. *Handbook of Psychotherapy Case Formulation.* 2nd ed. New York: Guilford, 2007. Print.

Frank, Jerome David. *Persuasion and Healing.* 3rd ed. Baltimore: Johns Hopkins UP, 1993. Print.

Garfield, Sol L., and Allen E. Bergin, eds. *Handbook of Psychotherapy and Behavior Change.* 4th ed. New York: Wiley, 1994. Print.

Hansen, James T. *Philosophical Issues in Counseling and Psychotherapy: Encounters with Four Questions about Knowing, Effectiveness, and Truth.* Lanham: Rowman, 2013. Print.

Kazdin, Alan E. *Single-Case Research Designs: Methods for Clinical and Applied Settings.* New York: Oxford UP, 1982. Print.

Norcross, John C., ed. *Psychotherapy Relationships That Work: Evidence-Based Responsiveness.* 2nd ed. New York: Oxford UP, 2011. Print.

Sharf, Richard S. *Theories of Psychotherapy and Counseling: Concepts and Cases.* 5th ed. Belmont: Brooks/Cole, 2012. Print

Smith, Mary Lee, and Gene V. Glass. "Meta-analysis of Psychotherapy Outcome Studies." *American Psychologist* 32.9 (1977): 752–60. Print.

Smith, Mary Lee, Gene V. Glass, and Thomas I. Miller. *Benefits of Psychotherapy*. Baltimore: Johns Hopkins UP, 1996. Print.

Gregory L. Wilson

SEE ALSO: Adler, Alfred; Adlerian psychotherapy; Behavioral family therapy; Cognitive behavior therapy; Depression; Eye movement desensitization and reprocessing; Gestalt therapy; Group therapy; Obsessive- compulsive disorder; Phobias; Psychoanalytic psychology and personality: Sigmund Freud; Psychotherapy: Goals and techniques; Psychotherapy: Historical approaches; Self-help groups.

Psychotherapy
Goals and techniques

TYPE OF PSYCHOLOGY: Psychotherapy

The goals to be reached in the meetings between a psychotherapist and a client, or patient, and the techniques employed to accomplish them vary according to the needs of the client and the theoretical orientation of the therapist.

KEY CONCEPTS
- Behavioral therapy
- Corrective emotional experience
- Desensitization
- Eclectic therapy
- Humanistic therapy
- Interpretation
- Psychodynamic therapy
- Resistance
- Shaping
- Therapeutic alliance

INTRODUCTION

Psychotherapy is an interpersonal relationship in which clients present themselves to a psychotherapist to gain some relief from distress in their lives. It should be noted that although people who seek psychological help are referred to as "clients" by a wide range of psychotherapists, this term is used interchangeably with the term "patients," which is traditionally used more often by psychodynamically and medically trained practitioners. In all forms of psychotherapy, patients or clients must tell the psychotherapist about their distress and reveal intimate information for the psychotherapist to be helpful. The psychotherapist must aid clients in the difficult task of admitting difficulties and revealing themselves, since a client's desire to be liked and to be seen as competent can stand in the way of this work. The client also wants to find relief from distress at the least possible cost in terms of the effort and personal changes to be made, and therefore, clients often prevent themselves from making the very changes in which they are interested. This is termed resistance, and much of the work of the psychotherapist involves dealing with such resistance.

The goals of the client are determined by the type of life problems that are being experienced. Traditionally, psychotherapists make a diagnosis of the psychiatric disorder from which the client suffers, with different disorders presenting certain symptoms to be removed for the client to gain relief. The vast majority of clients suffer from some form of anxiety or depression, or from certain failures in personality development, which produce deviant behaviors and rigid patterns of relating to others called personality disorders. Relatively few clients suffer from severe disorders, called psychoses, which are characterized by some degree of loss of contact with reality. Depending on the particular symptoms involved in the client's disorder, psychotherapeutic goals will be set, although the client may not be aware of the necessity of these changes at first. In addition, the diagnosis allows the psychotherapist to anticipate the kinds of goals that would be difficult for the client to attain. Psychotherapists also consider the length of time they will most likely work with the client. Therefore, psychotherapeutic goals depend on the client's wishes, the type of psychiatric disorder from which the client suffers, and the limitations of time under which the psychotherapy proceeds.

Another factor that plays a major role in determining psychotherapeutic goals is the psychotherapist's theoretical model for treatment. This model is based on a personality theory that explains people's motivations, how people develop psychologically, and how people differ from one another. It suggests what occurred in life to create the person's problems and what must be achieved to correct these problems. Associated with each theory is a group of techniques that can be applied to accomplish the goals considered to be crucial within the theory used. There are three main models of personality and treatment: psychodynamic therapies, behavioral therapies, and humanistic therapies. Psychodynamic therapists seek to make clients aware of motives for their actions of which they were previously unconscious or unaware. By becoming aware of their motives, clients can better control the balance between desires for pleasure and the need to obey one's conscience. Behavioral therapists attempt to increase the frequency of certain behaviors and decrease the frequency of others by reducing anxiety associated with certain behavior, teaching new behavior, and rewarding and punishing certain behaviors. Humanistic therapists try to free clients to use their innate abilities by developing relationships with clients in which clients can be assured of acceptance, making the clients more accepting of themselves and more confident in making decisions and expressing themselves.

Most psychotherapists use a combination of theories, and therefore of goals and techniques, in their practice. These "eclectic" therapists base their decisions about goals and techniques on the combined theory they have evolved or on a choice among other theories given what applies best to a client or diagnosis. It also appears that this eclectic approach has become popular because virtually all psychotherapy cases demand attention to certain common goals associated with the various stages of treatment, and different types of therapy are well suited to certain goals and related techniques at particular stages.

THERAPEUTIC RELATIONSHIPS

When clients first come to a psychotherapist, they have in mind some things about their lives that need to be changed. The psychotherapist recognizes that before this can be accomplished, a trusting relationship must be established with clients. This has been termed the therapeutic alliance or a collaborative relationship. Establishing this relationship becomes the first goal of therapy. Clients must learn that the therapist understands them and can be trusted with the secrets of their lives. They must also learn about the limits of the therapeutic relationship: that the psychotherapist is to be paid for the service, that the relationship will focus on the clients' concerns and life experiences rather than the psychotherapist's, that the psychotherapist is available to clients during the scheduled sessions and emergencies only, and that this relationship will end when the psychotherapeutic goals are met.

The therapist looks early for certain recurring patterns in what clients think, feel, and do. These patterns may occur in the therapy sessions, and clients report about the way these patterns have occurred in the past and how they continue. These patterns become the focal theme for the therapy and are seen as a basic reason for the clients' troubles. For example, some clients may complain that they have never had the confidence to think

for themselves. They report that their parents always told them what to do without explanation. In their current marriage, they find themselves unable to feel comfortable with any decisions, and they always look to their spouse for the final say. This pattern of dependence may not be as clear to the clients as to psychotherapists, who look specifically for similarities across past and present relationships. Furthermore, clients will probably approach the psychotherapist in a similar fashion. For example, clients might ask for the psychotherapist's advice, stating that they do not know what to do. When the psychotherapist points out the pattern in the clients' behavior, or suggests that it may have developed from the way their parents interacted with them, the psychotherapist is using the technique of interpretation. This technique originated in the psychodynamic models of psychotherapy.

When clients are confronted with having such patterns or focal themes, they may protest that they are not doing this, find it difficult to do anything different, or cannot imagine that there may be a different way of living. These tendencies to protest and to find change to be difficult are called resistance. Much of the work of psychotherapy involves overcoming this resistance and achieving the understanding of self called insight.

One of the techniques the psychotherapist uses to deal with resistance is the continued development of the therapeutic relationship to demonstrate that the psychotherapist understands and accepts the client's point of view and that these interpretations of patterns of living are done in the interest of the achievement of therapeutic goals by the client. Humanistic psychotherapists have emphasized this aspect of psychotherapeutic technique. The psychotherapist also responds differently to the client from the way others have in the past, so that when the client demonstrates the focal theme in the psychotherapy session, this different outcome to the pattern encourages a new approach to the difficulty. This is called the corrective emotional experience, a psychotherapeutic technique that originated in psychodynamic psychotherapy and is emphasized in humanistic therapies as well. For example, when the client asks the psychotherapist for advice, the psychotherapist might respond that they could work together on a solution, building on valuable information and ideas that both may have. In this way, the psychotherapist avoids keeping the client dependent in the relationship with the psychotherapist as the client has been in relationships with parents, a spouse, or others. This is experienced by the client emotionally, in that it may produce an increase in self-confidence or trust rather than resentment, since the psychotherapist did not dominate. With the repetition of these responses by the psychotherapist, the client's ways of relating are corrected. Such a repetition is often called working through, another term originating in psychodynamic models of therapy.

Psychotherapists have recognized that many clients have difficulty with changing their patterns of living because of anxiety or lack of skill and experience in behaving differently. Behavioral therapy techniques are especially useful in such cases. In cases of anxiety, the client can be taught to relax through relaxation training exercises. The client gradually imagines performing new, difficult behaviors while relaxing. Eventually, the client learns to stay relaxed while performing these behaviors with the psychotherapist and other people. This process is called desensitization, and it was originally developed to treat persons with extreme fears of particular objects or situations, termed phobias. New behavior is sometimes taught through modeling techniques in which examples of the behavior are first demonstrated by others. Behavioral psychotherapists have also shown the importance of rewarding small approximations to the new behavior that is the goal. This shaping technique might be used with the dependent client by praising confident, assertive, or independent behavior reported by the client or shown in the psychotherapy session, no matter how minor it may be initially.

ALLEVIATING DISTRESS

The goals and techniques of psychotherapy were first discussed by the psychodynamic theorists who originated the modern practice of psychotherapy. Sigmund Freud and Josef Breuer are generally credited with describing the first modern case treated with psychotherapy, and Freud went on to develop the basis for psychodynamic psychotherapy in his writings between 1895 and his death in 1939. Freud sat behind his clients while they lay on a couch so that they could concentrate on saying anything that came to mind to reveal themselves to the psychotherapist. This also prevented the clients from seeing the psychotherapist's reaction, in case they expected the psychotherapist to react to them as their parents had reacted. This transference relationship provided Freud with information about the client's relationship with parents, which Freud considered to be the root of the problems that his clients had. Later psychodynamic psychotherapists sat facing their clients and conversing

with them in a more conventional fashion, but they still attended to the transference.

Carl R. Rogers is usually described as the first humanistic psychotherapist, and he published descriptions of his techniques in 1942 and 1951. Rogers concentrated on establishing a warm, accepting, honest relationship with his clients. He established this relationship by attempting to understand the client from the client's point of view. By communicating this "accurate empathy," clients would feel accepted and therefore would accept themselves and be more confident in living according to their wishes without fear.

Behavioral psychotherapists began to play a major role in this field after Joseph Wolpe developed systematic desensitization in the 1950s. In the 1960s and 1970s, Albert Bandura applied his findings on how children learn to be aggressive through observation to the development of modeling techniques for reducing fears and teaching new behaviors. Bandura focused on how people attend to, remember, and decide to perform behavior they observe in others. These thought processes, or "cognitions," came to be addressed in cognitive psychotherapy by Aaron T. Beck and others in the 1970s and 1980s. Cognitive behavioral therapy became a popular hybrid that included emphasis on how thinking and behavior influence each other.

In surveys of practicing psychotherapists beginning in the late 1970s, Sol Garfield showed that the majority of therapists practice some hybrid therapy or eclectic approach. As it became apparent that no one model produced the desired effects in a variety of clients, psychotherapists used techniques from various approaches. An example is Arnold Lazarus's multimodal behavior therapy, introduced in 1971. It appears that such trends will continue and that, in addition to combining existing psychotherapeutic techniques, new eclectic models will produce additional ways of understanding psychotherapy as well as different techniques for practice.

BIBLIOGRAPHY

Garfield, Sol L. *Psychotherapy: An Eclectic Approach.* New York: John Wiley & Sons, 1980. Focuses on the client, the therapist, and their interaction within an eclectic framework. Written for the beginning student of psychotherapy and relatively free of jargon.

Goldfried, Marvin R., and Gerald C. Davison. *Clinical Behavior Therapy.* New York: Holt, Rinehart and Winston, 1976. An elementary, concise description of basic behavioral techniques. Includes clear examples of how these techniques are implemented.

Goldman, George D., and Donald S. Milman, eds. *Psychoanalytic Psychotherapy. Reading,* Mass.: Addison-Wesley, 1978. A very clear, concise treatment of complicated psychodynamic techniques. Explains difficult concepts in language accessible to the layperson.

Norcross, John C., and Marvin R. Goldfried, eds. *Handbook of Psychotherapy Integration.* 2d ed. New York: Oxford University Press, 2005. Filled with suggestions for therapists on ways to incorporate various therapeutic approaches in their client treatment. In addition, this resource provides the history of eclectic therapy, helpful to students.

Phares, E. Jerry. *Clinical Psychology.* 4th ed. Pacific Grove, Calif.: Brooks/Cole, 1997. An overview of clinical psychology that includes excellent chapters summarizing psychodynamic, behavioral, humanistic, and other models of psychotherapy. Written as a college-level text.

Rogers, Carl R. *Client-Centered Therapy.* 1951. Reprint. Boston: Houghton, 1965. A classic description of the author's humanistic psychotherapy, originally published in 1951, that is still useful as a strong statement of the value of the therapeutic relationship. Written for a professional audience, though quite readable.

Teyber, Edward. *Interpersonal Process in Psychotherapy: A Guide to Clinical Training.* 5th ed. Belmont, Calif.: Thomson-Brooks/Cole, 2006. An extremely clear and readable guide to modern eclectic therapy. Full of practical examples and written as a training manual for beginning psychotherapy students.

Wolpe, Joseph. *The Practice of Behavior Therapy.* 4th ed. Boston: Allyn & Bacon, 2008. Written by the originator of behavioral psychotherapy. Introduces basic principles, examples of behavioral interventions, and many references to research. Initial chapters are elementary, but later ones tend to be complicated.

Richard G. Tedeschi

SEE ALSO: Aversion therapy; Behavioral family therapy; Cognitive therapy; Drug therapies; Existential psychology; Feminist psychotherapy; Group therapy; Implosion; Music, dance, and theater therapy; Psychoanalysis; Psychoanalytic psychology; Psychotherapy: Effectiveness; Systematic desensitization.

Psychotherapy
Historical approaches

TYPE OF PSYCHOLOGY: Psychotherapy

Psychotherapy as a socially recognized process and profession emerged in Europe during the late nineteenth century. Although discussions of psychological or "mental healing" can be found dating back to antiquity, a cultural role for the secular psychological healer has become established only in modern times.

KEY CONCEPTS
- Catharsis
- Functional disorders
- Mental healing
- Mesmerism
- Nonspecific treatment factors
- Suggestion
- Transference

INTRODUCTION

The term "psychotherapy" (originally "psycho-therapy") came into use during the late nineteenth century to describe various treatments that were believed to act on the psychic or mental aspects of a patient rather than on physical conditions. It was contrasted with physical therapies such as medications, baths, surgery, diets, rest, or mild electrical currents, which, while they produced some mental relief, did so through physical means. The origins of psychotherapy have been variously traced. Some authors call attention to the practices of primitive witch doctors, to the exorcism rites of the Catholic Church, to the rhetorical methods of Greco-Roman speakers, to the naturalistic healing practices of Hippocrates, and to the Christian practice of public (and, later, private) confession.

One of the best argued and supported views claims a direct line of development from the practice of casting out demons all the way to psychoanalysis, the most widely recognized form of psychotherapy. The casting out of demons may be seen as leading to exorcism, which in turn led to the eighteenth century mesmeric technique (named for Franz Mesmer) based on the alleged phenomenon of "animal magnetism." This led to the practice of hypnosis as a psychological rather than a physiological phenomenon and finally to the work of Sigmund Freud, a late nineteenth century Viennese neurologist who, in his treatment of functional disorders (signs and symptoms for which no organic or physiological basis can be found), slowly moved from the practice of hypnosis to the development of psychoanalysis.

THERAPIST AS "HEALER"

There are two histories to be sought in the early forms of treatment by psychotherapy: One is an account of the relationship between a patient and a psychological healer; the other is the story of the specific techniques that the healer employs and the reasons that he or she gives to rationalize them. The latter began as religious or spiritual techniques and became naturalized as psychological or physiological methods. The prominence of spiritual revival during the mid- to late nineteenth century in the United States led to the rise of spiritual or mental healing movements (the healing of a disorder, functional or physical, through suggestion or persuasion), as demonstrated by the Christian Science movement. Religious healing, mental healing, and psychotherapy were often intertwined in the 1890s, especially in Boston, where many of the leading spokespersons for each perspective resided.

The distinction among these viewpoints was the explanation of the cure—naturalistic versus spiritualistic—and, to a lesser degree, the role or relationship between the practitioner and the patient. A psychotherapist in the United States or Europe, whether spiritualistic or naturalistic in orientation, was an authority (of whatever special techniques) who could offer the suffering patient relief through a relationship in which the patient shared his or her deepest feelings and most secret thoughts on a regular basis. The relationship bore a resemblance to that which a priest, rabbi, or minister might have with a member of the congregation. The psychotherapeutic relationship was also a commercial one, however, since private payment for services was usually the case. Freud came to believe that transference, the projection of emotional reactions from childhood onto the therapist, was a critical aspect of the relationship.

EVOLUTION OF PRACTICE

Initially, and well into the early part of the twentieth century, psychotherapists treated patients with physical as well as functional (mental) disorders, but by the 1920s, psychotherapy had largely become a procedure addressed to mental or psychological problems. In the United States, its use rested almost exclusively with the medical profession. Psychiatrists would provide therapy, clinical psychologists would provide testing and assess-

ment of the patient, and social workers would provide ancillary services related to the patient's family or societal and governmental programs. Following World War II, all three of these professions began to offer psychotherapy as one of their services.

One could chart the development of psychotherapy in a simplified, time-line approach, beginning with the early use of the term by Daniel H. Tuke in *Illustrations of the Influence of the Mind upon the Body in Health and Disease* in 1872, followed by the first use of the term at an international conference in 1889 and the publication of Freud and Josef Breuer's cathartic method in *Studien über Hysterie* (1895; *Studies in Hysteria*, 1950). Pierre Janet lectured on "The Chief Methods of Psychotherapeutics" in St. Louis in 1904, and psychotherapy was introduced as a heading in the index to medical literature (the Index Medicus) in 1906; at about the same time, private schools of psychotherapy began to be established. In 1909, Freud lectured on psychoanalysis at Clark University. That same year, Hugo Münsterberg published *Psychotherapy*. James Walsh published his *Psychotherapy* in 1912. During the 1920's, the widespread introduction and medicalization of psychoanalysis in the United States occurred. Person-centered therapy was introduced by Carl R. Rogers in 1942, and behavior-oriented therapy was developed by Joseph Wolpe and B. F. Skinner in the early 1950s.

HISTORIC TREATMENT OF ABNORMAL BEHAVIOR

Whatever form psychotherapy may take, it nearly always is applied to the least severe forms of maladjustment and abnormal behavior—to those behaviors and feelings that are least disturbing to others. When the patient has suffered a break with reality and experiences hallucinations, delusions, paranoia, or other behaviors that are socially disruptive, physical forms of treatment are often used. The earliest examples include trephining, a Stone Age practice in which a circular hole was cut into the brain cavity, perhaps to allow the escape of evil spirits. The best-known of the Greek theories of abnormal behavior were naturalistic and physicalistic, based on the belief that deviations in levels of bile caused mental derangement. The solution was bleeding, a practice that continued until the early nineteenth century. Rest, special diets, exercise, and other undertakings that would increase or decrease the relevant bile level were also practiced.

Banishment from public places was recommended by Plato. Initially, people were restricted to their own homes. Later, religious sanctuaries took in the mentally ill, and finally private for-profit and public asylums were developed. Institutions that specialized in the housing of the mentally ill began opening during the sixteenth century. Among the best-known institutions were Bethlehem in London (which came to be known as "Bedlam"), Salpêtrière in Paris, and later St. Elizabeth's in Washington, DC. Beyond confinement, treatments at these institutions included "whirling" chairs in which the patient would be strapped; the "tranquilizing" chair for restraining difficult patients; the straitjacket, which constrained only the arms; rest and diet therapies; and hot and cold water treatments.

By the 1930s, electroconvulsive therapy (shock therapy) was invented; it used an electric charge that induced a grand mal seizure. During the same period, the earliest lobotomy procedures were performed. These surgeries severed the connections between the brain's frontal lobes and lower centers of emotional functioning. What separates all these and other procedures from psychotherapy is the employment of physical and chemical means for changing behavior and emotions, rather than persuasion and social influence processes.

Periodic reforms were undertaken to improve the care of patients. Philippe Pinel, in the late eighteenth century, freed many mental patients in Paris from being chained in their rooms. He provided daily exercise and frequent cleaning of their quarters. In the United States, Dorothea Dix in the mid-1800s led a campaign of reform that resulted in vast improvement in state mental hospitals. In the 1960s and 1970s, some states placed restrictions on the use of electroconvulsive therapy and lobotomies, and the federal government funded many community mental health centers in an attempt to provide treatment that would keep the patient in his or her community. Since the 1950s, many effective medications have been developed for treating depressions, anxieties, compulsions, panic attacks, and a wide variety of other disorders.

FREUD'S PSYCHOANALYTIC CONTRIBUTIONS

Modern textbooks of psychotherapy may describe dozens of approaches and hundreds of specific psychotherapeutic techniques. What they have in common is the attempt of a person in the role of healer or teacher to assist another person in the role of patient or client with emotionally disturbing feelings, awkward behavior, or troubling thoughts. Many contemporary therapies are derivative of Freud's psychoanalysis. When Freud opened his practice for the treatment of functional disorders in Vienna in the spring of 1886, he initially employed the physical therapies common to his day. These included hydrotherapy, electrotherapy (a mild form of electrical stimulation), massage, rest, and a limited set of pharmaceutical agents. He was disappointed with the results, however, and reported feeling helpless.

He turned to the newly emerging procedure of hypnosis that was being developed by French physicians. Soon he was merely urging his patients to recall traumatic episodes from childhood rather than expecting them to recall such memories under hypnosis. In what he called his pressure technique, Freud would place his hand firmly on a patient's forehead, apply pressure, and say, "you will recall." Shortly, this became the famous method of free association, wherein the patient would recline on a couch with the instruction to say whatever came to mind. The psychoanalytic situation that Freud invented, with its feature of one person speaking freely to a passive but attentive audience about the most private and intimate aspects of his or her life, was unique in the history of Western civilization.

OTHER HISTORIC CONTRIBUTIONS

Psychoanalysis was not the only method of psychotherapy to emerge near the end of the nineteenth century, as an examination of a textbook published shortly after the turn of the century reveals. James Walsh, then dean and professor of functional disorders at Fordham University, published his eight-hundred-page textbook on psychotherapy in 1912. Only two pages were devoted to the new practice of psychoanalysis. For Walsh, psychotherapy was the use of mental influence to treat disease. His formulation, and that of many practitioners of his time, would encompass what today would be termed behavioral medicine. Thus, the chapters in his book are devoted to the different bodily systems, the digestive tract, cardiotherapy, gynecological psychotherapy, and skin diseases, as well as to the functional disorders.

The techniques that Walsh describes are wideranging. They include physical recommendations for rest and exercise, the value of hobbies as diversion, the need for regimentation, and varied baths, but it is the suggestion and treatment of the patient rather than the disease (that is, the establishment of a relationship with detailed knowledge of the patient's life and situation) that are the principal means for the relief and the cure of symptoms. A concluding chapter in Walsh's book compares psychotherapy with religion, with the view that considering religion simply as a curative agent lessens its meaning and worth.

BEHAVIOR THERAPY

In the mid-twentieth century, two new psychotherapies appeared that significantly altered the field, although one of them rejected the term, preferring to call itself behavior therapy to distinguish its method from the merely verbal or "talk" therapies. The first was found in the work of psychologist Carl R. Rogers. Rogers made three significant contributions to the development of psychotherapy. He originated nondirective or person-centered therapy, he phonographically recorded and transcribed therapy sessions, and he studied the process of therapy based on the transcripts. The development of an alternative to psychoanalysis was perhaps his most significant contribution. In the United States, psychoanalysis had become a medical specialty, practiced only by psychiatrists with advanced training. Rogers, a psychologist, created a role for psychologists and social workers as therapists. Thus, he expanded the range of professionals who could legitimately undertake the treatment of disorders through psychotherapy. The title of his most important work, *Counseling and Psychotherapy: Newer Concepts in Practice* (1942), suggests how other professions were to be included. In the preface to his book, Rogers indicated that he regarded these terms as synonymous. If psychologists and social workers could not practice therapy, they could counsel.

Behavior therapy describes a set of specific procedures, such as systematic desensitization and contingency management, that began to appear in the early 1950s, based on the work of Joseph Wolpe, a South African psychiatrist, Hans Eysenck, a British psychologist, and the American experimental psychologist and radical behaviorist B. F. Skinner. Wolpe's *Psychotherapy by Reciprocal Inhibition* appeared in 1958 and argued that states of relaxation and self-assertion would inhibit anxiety, since the patient could not be relaxed and anxious at the same time. It was argued that these were specific techniques based on the principles of learning and behavior; hence, therapeutic benefits did not depend on the nonspecific effects of mere suggestion or placebo. Behavior therapy was regarded by its developers as the first scientific therapy.

PSYCHOTHERAPY PERSPECTIVES AND CRITICISMS

The rise of psychotherapy in all of its forms may be explained in a variety of ways. The cultural role hypothesis argues that psychotherapists are essentially a controlling agency for the state and society. Their function is to help maintain the cultural norms and values by directly influencing persons at the individual level. This view holds that whatever psychotherapists might say, they occupy a position in the culture similar to that of authorities in educational and religious institutions. A related view argues that psychotherapy arose in Western culture to meet a deficiency in the culture itself. Such a view holds that if the culture were truly meeting the needs of its members, no therapeutic procedures would be required.

Psychotherapy has been explained as a scientific discovery, although exactly what was discovered depends on one's viewpoint. For example, behavior therapists might hold that the fundamental principles of behavior and learning were discovered, as was their applicability to emotional and mental problems. Others might hold that nonspecific or placebo effects were discovered, or at least placed in a naturalistic context. Another explanation follows the historical work of Henri Ellenberger and views psychotherapy as a naturalization of early religious practices: exorcism transformed to hypnotism transformed to psychoanalysis. The religious demons became mental demons and, with the rise of modern psychopharmacology in the 1950s, molecular demons.

More cynical explanations view psychotherapy as a mistaken metaphor. Recalling that the word was originally written with a hyphen, they argue that it is not possible to perform therapy, a physical practice, on a mental or spiritual object. Thus, psychotherapy is a kind of hoax perpetuated by its practitioners because of a mistaken formulation. Others suggest that the correct metaphor is that of healing and hold that psychotherapy is the history of mental healing, or healing through faith, suggestion, persuasion, and other rhetorical means. Whatever one's opinion of psychotherapy, it is both a cultural phenomenon and a specific set of practices that did not exist prior to the nineteenth century and that have had enormous influence on all aspects of American culture.

BIBLIOGRAPHY

Bowen, Murray, and J. Butler. *The Origins of Family Psychotherapy: The NIMH Family Study Project.* Lanham: Aronson, 2013. Print.

Corsini, Raymond J., comp. *Current Psychotherapies.* 8th ed. Belmont: Thomson, 2008. Print.

Cushman, Philip. *Constructing the Self, Constructing America: A Cultural History of Psychotherapy.* Cambridge: Perseus, 1997. Print.

Ellenberger, Henri. *The Discovery of the Unconscious: The History and Evolution of Dynamic Psychiatry.* New York:

Basic, 2006. Print.

Freedheim, Donald, Jane Kessler, and Donald Peterson, eds. *History of Psychotherapy: A Century of Change.* 5th ed. Washington, DC: Amer. Psychological Assn., 2003. Print.

Janet, Pierre. *Psychological Healing: A Historical and Clinical Study.* 2 vols. New York: Arno, 1976. Print.

Lebow, Jay. *Twenty-First Century Psychotherapies: Contemporary Approaches to Theory and Practice.* Hoboken, NJ: Wiley, 2008. Print.

Masson, Jeffrey Moussaieff. *Against Therapy: Emotional Tyranny and the Myth of Psychological Healing.* Monroe: Common Courage, 1994. Print.

Norcross, John C., Gary R. VandenBos, and Donald K. Freedheim. *History of Psychotherapy: Continuity and Change.* Washington, DC: Amer. Psychological Assn., 2011. Print.

Pande, Sashi K. "The Mystique of 'Western' Psychotherapy: An Eastern Interpretation." *About Human Nature: Journeys in Psychological Thought.* Ed. Terry J. Knapp and Charles T. Rasmussen. Dubuque: Kendall, 1989. Print.

Rogers, Carl R. *Counseling and Psychotherapy: Newer Concepts in Practice.* Boston: Houghton, 1960. Print.

Torrey, E. Fuller. *The Mind Game: Witchdoctors and Psychiatrists.* New York: Harper, 1986. Print.

Valenstein, Elliot S. *Great and Desperate Cures: The Rise and Decline of Psychosurgery and Other Radical Treatments.* New York: Basic, 1986. Print.

Wolpe, Joseph. *Psychotherapy by Reciprocal Inhibition.* Stanford: Stanford UP, 1980. Print.

Terry J. Knapp

SEE ALSO: Abnormality: Psychological models; Analytical psychotherapy; Cognitive therapy; Conditioning; Lobotomy; Mental illness: Historical concepts; Operant conditioning therapies; Psychoanalysis; Psychology: History; Psychosurgery; Shock therapy.

Psychotic disorders

TYPE OF PSYCHOLOGY: Psychopathology

Psychotic disorders are mental illnesses that are characterized by a breakdown in reality. Psychotic symptoms include delusions, hallucinations, and disorganized speech. Psychotic disorders, which may occur throughout the life span, vary in their etiology, onset, course, and treatment. Typically, psychotic disorders are treated with medication.

KEY CONCEPTS

- Antipsychotic medication
- Bipolar disorder
- Delusion
- Delusional disorder
- Dementia
- Dissociative identity disorder
- Hallucination
- Major depression
- Schizoaffective disorder
- Schizophrenia
- Thought disorder

INTRODUCTION

Psychotic disorders are a group of mental illnesses that share psychosis as one of their clinical features. Psychosis involves a gross impairment in one's sense of reality, as evidenced by symptoms such as delusions, hallucinations, thought disorder, and bizarre behavior. These psychotic symptoms may be a primary component of illness or may be secondary to a mental or physical condition.

TYPES OF PSYCHOTIC SYMPTOMS

Delusions are false beliefs that are associated with misinterpretations of perceptions or experiences. There are different types of delusions. The most common are persecutory delusions and grandiose delusions. Persecutory delusions are delusions in which the person believes that he or she is being spied on or plotted against. Grandiose delusions are delusions in which the person believes that he or she possesses special abilities or is related to a famous person or deity.

Hallucinations are false perceptions in the absence of any real stimulus. Hallucinations may involve any of the five senses. There are auditory hallucinations, such as hearing voices; visual hallucinations, such as seeing faces or flashes of light; tactile hallucinations, such as feeling a tingling, electrical, crawling, or burning sensation; and olfactory hallucinations, such as smelling something not perceived by others. Gustatory hallucinations, or false tastes, are very rare. Most hallucinations are auditory hallucinations.

Thought disorder is defined as a disturbance in the form or content of thought and speech. In psychosis, the person's speech may be incomprehensible or remotely related to the topic of conversation. Examples of formal thought disorder are neologisms, which are made-up words whose meaning is only known to the psychotic person, and loose associations, in which the person's ideas shift from one subject to another, loosely related topic, without the person seeming aware of the shift. Delusions are examples of disorders of thought content. Psychotic behavior is typically bizarre or grossly disorganized.

Psychotic symptoms can appear at any point during the life course, though it is difficult to diagnose psychotic symptoms in preverbal children (prior to age five or six). Psychotic disorders can appear for the first time in individuals over age sixty-five.

CONCEPTUALIZATIONS OF PSYCHOTIC DISORDERS

In 1896, the German clinical psychiatrist Emil Kraepelin proposed that there were two broad yet fundamental categories of psychotic disorder: manic-depressive illness, which is now referred to as bipolar disorder; and dementia praecox, which was labeled schizophrenia by the Swiss psychiatrist Eugen Bleuler in 1908. Kraepelin delineated dementia praecox on the basis of course and outcome, noting that it was associated with a deteriorating course and poor outcome. According to Kraepelin, manic-depressive illness was associated with a more episodic and less deteriorating course relative to dementia praecox.

Psychotic disorders are currently classified on the basis of presenting symptoms rather than on the basis of underlying etiological processes. Episodes of psychosis can be brief or chronic in duration, lasting from a few days to many years, and psychotic symptoms may be mild, moderate, or severe in form. Although the various types of psychotic disorders have some common symptoms, their onset, course, and development are often substantially different.

Ongoing research efforts to clarify the cognitive and physiological mechanisms associated with different psychotic illness will hopefully help to aid in future diagnosis. According to the *Diagnostic and Statistical Manual of Mental Disorders: DSM-5* (5th ed., 2013), published by the American Psychiatric Association, psychotic symptoms are a central feature of schizophrenia and other psychotic disorders. Schizophrenia, which is often a severe and debilitating mental illness, is found in approximately 1 percent of the general population and affects more than 2.5 million Americans. Onset of the disorder is most likely to occur between the ages of fifteen and thirty-five; the average age of onset is eighteen for men and twenty-five for women. Schizophrenia can occur in childhood, although this is rare, and can also have a late onset after the age of forty-five. Rates of schizophrenia do not vary substantially in terms of gender, race, or ethnicity, but the disorder is more prevalent in urban than in rural areas.

The DSM-5 outlines other psychotic disorders, known as schizophrenia spectrum disorders, that differ from schizophrenia primarily in terms of illness duration and severity. Schizophreniform disorder is diagnosed when the individual shows symptoms of schizophrenia that last less than six months. As the term implies, the psychotic symptoms in schizophreniform disorder are identical in form to schizophrenia but they have a briefer duration. Some individuals with schizophreniform disorder will eventually develop schizophrenia. Schizoaffective disorder contains features of a mood disturbance, with manic or depressive episodes, as well as the symptoms of schizophrenia. For a diagnosis of schizoaffective disorder, rather than schizophrenia or a mood disorder with psychotic features, both schizophrenia and mood disorder symptoms must be present the majority of the time. Schizoaffective disorder is less common than schizophrenia and may be associated with better functional outcome. Brief psychotic disorder, which is diagnosed if psychotic symptoms last for more than one day but no longer than four weeks, may develop in response to severe environmental stress or psychological trauma. Delusional disorder (paranoia) is less common and less severe than schizophrenia. In delusional disorder, the person has one or more delusions for at least one month. Other than the delusions, the person does not share any of the other psychotic symptoms typically observed in people with schizophrenia. As of the DSM-5, schizotypal personality disorder is listed under this category as well as under its original category of personality disorders. Schizotypal personality disorder is characterized by eccentric behavior, odd beliefs, and difficulty or lack of interest in forming social relationships.

Psychotic symptoms may also be present in bipolar disorder and major depression, though they are not typically categorized as psychotic disorders. Bipolar disorder is characterized by periods of elevated, expansive, or irritable mood that may alternate with periods of depressed mood. In 1990, Frederick K. Goodwin and Kay R. Jamison reported that approximately 58 percent of individuals with bipolar disorder have at least one psychotic symptom during their lifetimes, which is most likely to occur during a manic episode. Psychotic symptoms may also accompany major depression. Psychotic symptoms are most likely to be associated with severe episodes of affective disturbance and could be either mood congruent or mood incongruent. Mood congruent psychotic symptoms contain themes that are consistent with the current affective state, such as a depressed individual with delusional thoughts about death. Mood incongruent psychotic symptoms involve content that is inconsistent with the current mood state, such as a depressed individual with delusional ideas about possessing special powers.

Some psychotic disorders are the direct result of external or environmental factors. Psychotic symptoms that result from psychoactive substance use or toxin exposure are classified as a substance-induced psychotic disorder. For example, some people may appear at hospital emergency rooms because of amphetamine-induced psychosis or cocaine-induced psychosis. In these cases, psychotic symptoms appear to arise because of the ingestion of a psychoactive (psychomimetic) substance. However, it is not known whether the people who experience psychotic symptoms while using a drug were already prone to psychosis (diathesis) and the drug was the additional stressor, or whether the drug was the proximal causal agent in the development of the psychosis.

Psychotic symptoms can be present in other disorders but are not considered to be defining features of the illness. Psychotic symptoms, especially paranoid delusions, are observed in people with dementia. Dementia is any condition in which there is a progressive deterioration of one's memory, abstract thinking, and judgment and decision-making abilities. The most common types of dementia are Alzheimer's disease and vascular dementia. Psychotic symptoms may also accompany a disorder known as dissociative identity disorder. Dissociative identity disorder (formerly known as multiple personality disorder) is associated with a failure to integrate various aspects of identity, memory, and consciousness.

DIFFERENTIAL DIAGNOSIS

Because the symptoms found across psychotic disorders greatly overlap, differential diagnosis of these conditions is often challenging. If a patient presents with psychotic symptoms, each of the psychotic disorders is considered when making a differential diagnosis. When diagnosing a psychotic disorder, it is important for mental health professionals to first obtain a thorough personal and family history of the patient. Information about the onset and course of presenting symptoms should also be obtained. If necessary, a physical examination or laboratory tests

may be required to rule out other causes of the symptoms, such as brain injury.

Often, other psychotic disorders, such as schizoaffective disorder or schizophreniform disorder, must be ruled out from schizophrenia. The duration of psychotic symptoms will help differentiate whether the disorder is schizophrenia, schizophreniform disorder, or brief psychotic disorder. The length of affective impairment as well as the overlap between mood and psychotic symptoms is often helpful when distinguishing between schizoaffective disorder and psychotic mood disorder. The presence of other conditions, such as dementia or amnesic episodes, along with psychotic symptoms may aid in differential diagnosis as well.

ETIOLOGICAL FACTORS

Diathesis-stress models have been proposed as a way to explain the onset and development of many of the psychotic disorders. In this view, the diathesis, or underlying predisposition to illness, remains latent and unexpressed until it interacts with a sufficient amount of environmental stress. Individuals may vary in terms of the amount of their underlying diathesis and the stress required to bring about disorder. If an individual has a large diathesis, less stress is required to bring about illness onset. Conversely, if an individual with a substantial genetic diathesis is in a relatively low-stress environment, he or she may be protected from developing the illness. Diathesis-stress models have formed the basis for research on the role of genetic and environmental factors in the development of schizophrenia and related psychotic disorders.

TREATMENT APPROACHES

Antipsychotic medications are considered an effective means of alleviating psychotic symptoms. Conventional (typical) antipsychotics were used to treat psychotic symptoms beginning in the 1950s. More recently, novel (atypical) antipsychotics, such as clozapine, risperidone, and olanzapine, have been introduced, which greatly reduce the severity of extrapyramidal side effects and are more effective at reducing negative or deficit symptoms relative to the typical antipsychotics. The optimal medication dose required is often obtained through a series of judgments made by the psychiatrist, who gradually increases or tapers the dosage based on observed treatment response. Psychopharmacological treatment has been found to be very effective in reducing symptoms during acute psychotic episodes and in preventing future relapses.

Typically, the treatment of choice for individuals with mood disorders, such as bipolar disorder or major depression, is a mood stabilizer or antidepressant. If psychotic features are present, an antipsychotic medication may be added to the treatment regimen.

Psychotherapy may also be helpful to individuals with psychotic disorders to assist them in medication compliance and other aspects of having a chronic mental illness. Psychosocial treatments, such as social skills training and family psychoeducation, can enhance the daily functioning and quality of life of individuals with psychotic disorders. By strengthening social support networks and teaching life skills, such interventions could improve social and vocational functioning, enhance one's ability to cope with life stressors, and potentially protect against illness exacerbation.

BIBLIOGRAPHY

Cardinal, Rudolf N., and Edward T. Bullmore. *The Diagnosis of Psychosis.* Cambridge: Cambridge UP, 2011. Print.

Goodwin, Frederick K., and Kay R. Jamison. *Manic Depressive Illness.* 2d ed. New York: Oxford UP, 2007. Print.

Gottesman, Irving I. *Schizophrenia Genesis: The Origins of Madness.* New York: Freeman, 1991. Print.

Lucas, Richard. *The Psychotic Wavelength: A Psychoanalytic Perspective for Psychiatry.* London: Routledge, 2009. Print.

Moskowitz, Andrew, Ingo Schafer, and Martin J. Dorahy. *Psychosis, Trauma, and Dissociation: Emerging Perspectives on Severe Psychopathology.* Chichester: Wiley, 2009. Print.

Oltmanns, Thomas F., and Richard E. Emery. *Abnormal Psychology.* 5th ed. Upper Saddle River: Pearson, 2009. Print.

Weiden, Peter J., Patricia L. Scheifler, Ronald J. Diamond, and Ruth Ross. *Breakthroughs in Antipsychotic Medications.* New York: Norton, 1999. Print.

Diane C. Gooding and Kathleen A. Tallent

SEE ALSO: Antidepressant medications; Antipsychotic medications; Bipolar disorder; Dementia; Dissociative disorders; Drug therapies; Family systems theory; Hallucinations; Mood stabilizer medications; Paranoia; Psychopharmacology; Schizophrenia: Background, types, and symptoms; Schizophrenia: Theoretical explanations.

Punishment

TYPE OF PSYCHOLOGY: Developmental psychology; Learning; Motivation; Psychopathology; Social psychology

Punishment is an action taken in response to a person's unwanted behavior. The history of punishment describes the more popular trends in punishment, from attacks on the person's body to rehabilitation. Punishment plays a role in socialization.

KEY CONCEPTS
- Control
- Deterrence
- Learning process
- Moral development
- Philosophies of punishment
- Rehabilitation
- Reinforcement
- Retribution

INTRODUCTION

Punishment can be defined as an action taken based on a person's undesired behavior. It is intended to prevent future occurrence of the unwanted behavior by changing how the person behaves. It is a social mechanism used to help ensure the balanced functioning of a family, group, organization, or a society.

There are two main elements to punishment. First, appropriate behavior is arbitrary; it is determined by communal agreement regarding right and wrong behavior. Punishment attempts to foster and ensure what the group has determined to be appropriate, moral behavior. Second, punishment symbolizes power. The French philosopher Michel Foucault argued that punishment should be understood as an expression of power because, without the power to punish a person behaving in an undesirable manner, chaos could occur.

When a member of any social unit, small or large, goes against the group's accepted norms, it disrupts the unit. To regain balance or homeostasis, action may be needed, and a member of the social unit may punish the wrongdoer. Punishment may take the form of making some kind of amends. This could range from a token act to exile (temporary or permanent) or even to death.

A BRIEF HISTORY

One of the earliest records of punishments levied by a society can be found in a legal code developed in Babylon in about 2000 BCE, during the reign of Hammurabi, which listed corrective measures for wrongdoing. The Mosaic law recorded in the Pentateuch of the Old Testament is another early set of codes. Near the end of the first century CE, corporal punishment was increasingly applied to slaves and lower-class citizens, while punishments for higher-class citizens generally took the form of compensation.

During the reign of the Roman emperor Justinian in the sixth century, an attempt was made to match the severity of punishment to the level of the offense. More than a century later, laws became increasingly localized, although they generally followed the dictates of the Roman Catholic Church. Many of these laws were centralized during the reign of Charlemagne.

When William the Conqueror became king of England following the Norman invasion, he centralized power around himself as monarch. Any wrongdoing therefore became a crime against the king. He established the process of trial by ordeal to address those who violated the law, who were known as enemies of the king. Much of the punishment, official and unofficial, was directed at the offenders' bodies, through forms of torture.

It was not until the age of reason that major changes began to occur. With the development of social contracts, crimes were considered to have been committed against society, and people began to be viewed as rational beings able to make rational choices. It was during this period that the classical school offered new foundations of punishment as represented in the writings of Cesare Beccaria and Jeremy Bentham. These scholars believed that a person had free will and could make a rational choice whether to commit an offense. People made their choices by weighing the pleasure of the action against the punishment for it. Therefore, the punishment should fit the crime; be proportionate to the violation; be uniform and equal; be certain, swift, and severe; and deter and prevent.

Over the centuries, scholars have continued to debate what is effective punishment. For if punishment does not bring about the desired changes, then it does not serve its purpose.

PHILOSOPHIES OF PUNISHMENT

Most punishments are designed to prevent wrongdoers from repeating their acts and to deter people from committing undesired acts. There are four main philosophies of punishment. They are retribution (just deserts), deterrence, rehabilitation, and control (incapacitation).

Retribution has often been linked to revenge, taking an eye for an eye. Under this philosophy of punishment, justice is served if the punishment is equivalent to the wrongdoing: offenders get what they deserve (their just deserts). This has been the basis of much legal code.

As a philosophy of punishment, deterrence attempts to either restrict certain behaviors or encourage people to avoid them. Punishments aimed at deterring crime are designed to cause people to lose as much or more from committing an undesired behavior as they stand to gain from the behavior. Such punishments should cause a person to chose not to engage in the undesired behavior. However, punishment should not be excessive, as this might have negative overall results.

Rehabilitation seeks to change the offender so the person will not repeat the act. Under this philosophy, it is believed that the offender suffers from some sort of needs or deficiencies, and these deficiencies need to be addressed for the individual to change. Punishment should be individualized to address the offender's needs and deficiencies.

Control is based on the rationale that if the offender is incapacitated, the person cannot repeat the unacceptable behavior. Although establishing control over an offender does not keep the individual from desiring to commit an undesirable act, it effectively contains the person and prevents the individual from acting inappropriately. Control may take the form of restricting the person's movement or simply supervising the person.

MORAL DEVELOPMENT

An important consideration of punishment is whether the offender knows right from wrong. The process of learning what society has deemed right and wrong requires the moral development of the individual. This learning process is described differently by various psychological schools.

The psychoanalytic school describes this as a child learning to act in a manner in which the child will experience positive feelings and avoid negative feelings. Sigmund Freud focused on the development of the child's personality during the learning process, whereas Erik H. Erikson examined how children internalize the teachings of both parents to win and keep their love.

The cognitive school is represented by the theorists Jean Piaget and Lawrence Kohlberg. Piaget presented his theory that as children develop, they gain respect for rules and justice. The development process begins in a premoral period, a period in which children have little awareness of rules but simply act in a way that gives them pleasure. Then at about school age, children begin to develop an awareness of rules that they regard as absolute. They believe that either an act is right or wrong; they also believe in imminent justice, or that any wrong act will be punished in some way.

In the final stage in Piaget's process of cognitive development, children begin to surrender the absoluteness of rules for a more relative understanding of the nature of rules. This change comes from an awareness that rules are arbitrary social agreements and on occasion can be challenged, as rules should serve human needs. As a result, rules can be violated to serve the needs of a person. After experiencing and seeing others violate rules and go unpunished, children begin to accept the idea of reciprocal punishment, which is a more rehabilitative form of punishment.

Kohlberg developed on Piaget's theory by extending the development process. He created a three-level development process in which each level had two stages. This development process was unidirectional. Once a person has moved to a higher level of development, the individual could not regress to a lower level.

Kohlberg's first level was preconventional morality. At this level, a child follows rules to avoid punishment and to receive rewards. The punishment determines how bad an act is: The more severe the punishment, the worse the wrong. A child conforms to rules to seek rewards and self-satisfaction.

In conventional morality, a child seeks approval of others and tries to avoid shame. A child begins to experience understanding of others (empathy) and to conform to rules out of a desire to cooperate with others.

In postconventional morality, the third level, the child's moral reasoning is based on a broader understanding of justice and right and wrong. Sometimes the child's understanding of right and wrong is in conflict with the established rules and therefore justifies challenging rules. In the second stage within the third level, universal justice, the child is able to transcend any conflict through an ideal reasoning process.

LEARNING
Behaviorists and cognitivists have applied principles of reinforcement and punishment to change behavior. Both reinforcement and punishment can be positive or negative and are used to condition a person to act within the range of acceptable or desired behavior.

Reinforcement is a reward people receive for performing the desired or appropriate behavior. It is intended to increase the possibility of people's adopting the behavior. A positive reward is receiving something the person wants and a negative reward is having something removed that the person does not want. In identifying appropriate reinforcers, an individual's personal economy—the value a person places on an item or an action—must be determined. Individualizing reinforcers makes them more effective in accomplishing the goal of change.

Punishment is used to prevent or change undesired behavior and to decrease the possibility of it recurring. A positive punishment is the gaining of something unwanted, and a negative punishment is the loss of something wanted. Either punishment is undesirable for the recipient.

A major difference between behaviorists, such as B. F. Skinner, and cognitivists, such as Albert Bandura, is the cognitive factor of learning. Skinner did not accept that humans have free will but believed that their actions are environmentally determined. Bandura argued the value of observation and modeling. He proposed that a person could learn by observing the rewards and punishments another person received for behavior. Some studies, including that by Robert E. Larzelere and his associates, have suggested that a more effective disciplinary response can be produced by combining reasoning and punishment rather than using reasoning alone.

BIBLIOGRAPHY
Castro, Nicolas. *Psychology of Punishment: New Research.* Hauppage: Nova, 2013. Digital file.

Cusac, Anne-Marie. *Cruel and Unusual: The Culture of Punishment in America.* New Haven: Yale UP, 2010. Print.

Horne, Christine. *The Rewards of Punishment: A Relational Theory of Norm Enforcement.* Stanford: Stanford UP, 2009. Print.

Larzelere, Robert E., et al. "Punishment Enhances Reasoning's Effectiveness as a Disciplinary Response to Toddlers." *Journal of Marriage and the Family* 60 (1998): 388–430. Print.

Miltenberger, Raymond G. *Behavior Modification: Principles and Procedures.* 5th ed. Belmont: Wadsworth, 2012. Print.

Molm, Linda D. "Is Punishment Effective: Coercive Strategies in Social Exchange." *Social Psychology Quarterly* 57.2 (1994): 75–94. Print.

Oswald, Margit E., Steffen Bieneck, and Jorg Hupfeld-Heinemann, eds. *Social Psychology of Punishment of Crime*. Malden: Wiley, 2009. Print.

Russo, Jennifer P., and Nicholas M. Palmetti. *Psychology of Punishment*. New York: Nova, 2011. Digital file.

Sparks, Richard, and Jonathan Simon. *The SAGE Handbook of Punishment and Society*. Los Angeles: SAGE, 2013. Digital file.

Richard L. McWhorter

See Also: Bandura, Albert; Cognitive behavior therapy; Erikson, Erik H.; Kohlberg, Lawrence; Motivation; Motivation: Intrinsic and extrinsic; Piaget, Jean; Reinforcement; Skinner, B. F.

Q

Qualitative research

TYPE OF PSYCHOLOGY: Psychological methodologies

Qualitative research is an exploratory methodological approach used to study complex phenomena by collecting and analyzing nonnumerical data. Qualitative research grew out of naturalistic inquiries conducted in the disciplines of sociology, anthropology, and linguistics, but is now readily applied across the social sciences.

KEY CONCEPTS
- Case study
- Confirmability
- Credibility
- Dependability
- Grounded theory
- Historical foundations
- Phenomenology
- Transferability

INTRODUCTION

Qualitative methodology is a type of scientific inquiry that emphasizes the qualities or essences of the phenomenon under study. This type of research relies on nonnumerical data, such as words and images. For example, Rosemarie Rizzo Parse in *Qualitative Inquiry: The Path of Sciencing* (2001) defined qualitative research as "the systematic study of phenomena with rigorous adherence to a design, the data of which comprises oral, written, or artistic descriptions of human experiences, and for which there are no digital findings."

HISTORICAL FOUNDATIONS

Qualitative research grew out of naturalistic inquiries conducted in the disciplines of sociology, anthropology, and linguistics, but is now readily applied across the social sciences. This methodological approach has been used to investigate research questions in psychology and has been widely used in the fields of anthropology, sociology, nursing, social work, administration, community services, management, education, and medicine.

Qualitative methods have been used to investigate research questions ill-suited to quantitative methods, provide rich descriptions of particularly complex or multidimensional phenomena, give voice to traditionally marginalized groups, serve as an initial exploration toward the development of theories or quantitative measures, illuminate the diverse perspectives and experiences of several people experiencing a similar event, and connect research to applied practice.

FEATURES OF QUALITATIVE RESEARCH

Qualitative investigations contain several common features that distinguish them from other types of scientific inquiry. For example, in *Qualitative Research and Evaluation Methods* (3d ed., 2002), Michael Quinn Patton has outlined ten primary characteristics of qualitative research: naturalistic inquiry, inductive analysis, holistic perspective, qualitative data, personal contact and insight, dynamic systems, unique case orientation, context sensitivity, empathic neutrality, and design flexibility. Psychology's interest in qualitative approaches has grown in the twenty-first century. Several events have occurred that are examples of the emergence of qualitative methods in psychology. Psychology journals (such as the *Journal of Counseling Psychology*) have published special issues devoted to qualitative methods. There has also been an increased appreciation for how qualitative methods can be used to bridge the science-practice gap within the field of psychology. Researchers have also expressed a growing understanding of how such methods are congruent with the paradigms that characterize the helping professions. Psychological researchers have also increasingly begun using mixed models. Common qualitative approaches include phenomenology, case study, and grounded theory.

PHENOMENOLOGY

Phenomenology seeks to describe the meaning individuals give their life experiences and is based on the philosophy that observable, measurable, duplicable (that is, quantitative) approaches to psychological inquiry are prone to missing, or even altogether eliminating, the most important phenomenon under study, human experience. It concerns itself not with explanation and control but rather with understanding and description.

According to Paul F. Colaizzi in his essay "Psychological Research as the Phenomenologist Views It," in *Existential-Phenomenological Alternatives for Psychology* (1978), it is "a refusal to tell the phenomenon what it is, but a respectful listening to what the phenomenon speaks of itself."

There is no single phenomenological method, but most approaches fall under one of two major methodological umbrellas: hermeneutic or empirical. Hermeneutic phenomenological approaches are concerned with analyzing and understanding written narratives to understand and describe human experience. The goal is to produce a rich, deep description of a phenomenon as it emerges within a text, which can be done by analyzing the life texts, or written experience, of participants, or by studying previously written historical or literary narratives. The researcher works to overcome personal assumptions to understand and describe the phenomenon itself, as viewed in context from the text's perspective. Phenomenology seeks to explore and describe the unique meaning assigned to experience by persons who have lived through a common phenomenon. Phenomenology also provides a flexible step-by-step process for data analysis, the result of which is a description of the essence of participants' experience in terms of both their common and unique experiences.

CASE STUDY

Case study research has a long and rich history, especially within the disciplines of medicine, law, business, and the social sciences. Yet, this form of qualitative research was not conceptualized as a specific approach until the late 1970s and 1980s. The emphasis of case study research is on understanding phenomena from a specific case or cases within a bounded system. According to Patton, the primary function of case study research is "to gather comprehensive, systematic, and in-depth information about each case of interest." Robert E. Stake suggests that there are three different types of case studies. The primary investigation into one specific case is known as an intrinsic case study. In an instrumental case study, researchers study a particular case as a means to better understanding a specific issue. A collective case study involves the use of numerous cases to understand a particular phenomenon.

Case study research differs from other qualitative methods in several ways. It seeks to determine and describe the prevailing processes of the phenomena under investigation. Another key characteristic of case study research is that it makes a comparison of all the data sources, such as interviews, documents, and observations, within a contextual and historical framework. Case study research also attempts to integrate empirical data with theory. According to Sharan B. Merriam in *Case Study Research in Education: A Qualitative Approach* (1988), this approach to research also focuses on "thick" descriptions of the phenomena being studied; case study research uses "complete, literal description of the incident or entity being investigated." In addition, case study procedures engage the researcher in examining the data from the onset of the investigation.

Several basic assumptions are innate to case study research. First, a case may be chosen because it is unique and therefore is of interest. Second, the phenomenon under study is bound to a specific system, consisting of complex and interrelated elements. Third, an emphasis should be placed on understanding the intrinsic particulars of a phenomenon. Fourth, the research process is influenced by the perceptions of the researcher. Moreover, through careful comparative analysis of the data, and theory, a greater understanding of the phenomenon can be obtained.

GROUNDED THEORY

Grounded theory is a major qualitative tradition. Sociologists Barney G. Glasser and Anselm L. Strauss introduced this qualitative tradition in *Discovery of Grounded Theory: Strategies for Qualitative Research* (1967). The goal of grounded theory is to discover and develop comprehensive theories. It is a general methodology for theory development that comes from systematically gathered and analyzed data. The emphasis of grounded theory is on theory generation (developing theory from data) rather than on theory confirmation, or hypothesis testing. As a result, researchers have the freedom to modify procedures (for example, sampling changes) and methods (for example, reworking interview protocols) in accordance with the data.

Several basic assumptions are unique to grounded theory. The social phenomenon under study is seen as both complex and repeatedly adapting to the environment. Through a systematic approach, researchers can understand, predict, and control human behavior. Grounded theory also recognizes that the research process is subjective in nature and views the researcher as an active participant. Theory emerges through careful comparative analysis of the data.

EVALUATIVE CRITERIA

The criteria that should be used to evaluate qualitative research have been the cause of great debate among many qualitative researchers. Several researchers have attempted to evaluate qualitative research in terms of internal validity, external validity, reliability, and objectivity, which have traditionally been used in quantitative approaches. Kelly J. Devers states, in his 1999 article on qualitative research, that these criteria largely evolved out of the positivistic paradigm, which judged the scientific method suitable for researching all forms of knowledge (natural and social) and defined what that method should entail. Yet, qualitative research is based in postpositivistic philosophy, which proposes "reality is dynamic, contextual, and socially constructed." The differences in philosophical perspectives lead to a split between many quantitative and qualitative researchers.

During the late 1970s and mid-1980s, several qualitative researchers started challenging the positivistic criteria that had been used to evaluate qualitative research and began calling for a new set of criteria. Out of this dialogue came several diverse sets of evaluative criteria. Among these new advances were the criteria set forth by Norman Lincoln and Yvonna Guba: credibility, transferability, dependability, and confirmability. Credibility refers to the degree to which the results of a study have merit and accurately represent the experienced reality of its participants. Transferability is the qualitative counterpart of the quantitative concept of external validity or generalizability. It refers to the degree to which findings can be generalized or transferred to people, settings, and times similar to those found in the original study. Dependability is the qualitative counterpart to quantitative reliability. Dependable investigations can be relied on to accurately and impartially report the findings that emerged. Confirmability refers to the degree to which the results of the investigation can be objectively corroborated by the obtained data.

BIBLIOGRAPHY

Bamberg, Paul M., Jean E. Rhodes, and Lucy Yardley, eds. *Qualitative Research in Psychology: Expanding Perspectives in Methodology and Design*. Washington, DC: Amer. Psychological Assn., 2003. Print.

Creswell, John W. *Qualitative Inquiry and Research Design: Choosing Among the Five Traditions*. Thousand Oaks: Sage, 1998. Print.

Creswell, John W. *Research Design: Qualitative, Quantitative, and Mixed Methods Approaches*. Thousand Oaks: Sage, 2002. Print.

Denzin, Norman K., and Lincoln Yvonna, eds. *Handbook of Qualitative Research*. Thousand Oaks: Sage, 2000. Print.

Devers, Kelly J. "How Will We Know 'Good' Qualitative Research When We See It? Beginning the Dialogue in Health Services Research." *Health Services Research* 34 (1999): 1153–88. Print.

Forrester, Michael A., ed. *Doing Qualitative Research in Psychology*. Thousand Oaks: Sage, 2010. Print.

Frost, Nollaig. *Qualitative Research Methods in Psychology: Combining Core Approaches*. Maidenhead: Open UP, 2011. Print.

Glasser, Barney G., and Anselm L. Strauss. *The Discovery of Grounded Theory: Strategies for Qualitative Research*. New York: Aldine de Gruyter, 1967. Print.

Patton, Michael Quinn. *Qualitative Research and Evaluation Methods*. 3rd ed. Thousand Oaks: Sage, 2002. Print.

Willig, Carla. *Introducing Qualitative Research in Psychology*. 3rd ed. New York: McGraw, 2013. Print.

Jamie D. Aten and Ryan M. Denney

SEE ALSO: Case study methodologies; Complex experimental designs; Experimentation: Independent, dependent, and control variables; Field experimentation; Quasi-experimental designs.

Quality of life

DATE: 1930s forward
TYPE OF PSYCHOLOGY: Cognition; Consciousness; Emotion; Motivation; Personality; Sensation and perception

Quality of life research was not a priority until the 1980s, when concerns regarding treatment outcomes and the aging American society gained national attention. Inherently a murky concept, quality of life is simultaneously a self-report and an objective measure of general health and well-being, as well as a measure of treatment for specific illness and an overall standard-of-living index.

KEY CONCEPTS
- Ecological momentary assessments
- Life satisfaction
- Self-report measurement
- Standard of living
- Treatment outcomes
- Well-being

INTRODUCTION

Quality of life is a multidimensional concept encompassing several subcategories. Life satisfaction, well-being, happiness, meaning, and economic indices are but a few of the components of the broader concept of quality of life (QOL), yet no concept alone can adequately capture the complexity of quality of life. Instruments designed to measure QOL permit individuals to assess their overall health subjectively rather than using purely objective medical assessments such as body temperature or weight gain or loss. QOL questionnaires are generally either generic or illness specific; administering both types presents a more complete picture than using either alone.

Because QOL represents both a subjective and objective rating of a person's overall health and well-being, researchers or medical personnel are able to use it to capture an encompassing view of a single individual, groups or cultures, or entire nations. QOL is often used in scientific research to assess overall health as it relates to other variables of interest (for example, QOL after chemotherapy). Some of the areas where QOL is most frequently examined are health QOL, economic QOL, and specific illnesses and QOL.

HEALTH QOL

Perhaps the most widely investigated area of QOL involves the various facets that make up overall health. Health quality of life (HQOL) questionnaires measure a number of subcategories that are related to general health and well-being, broadly defined: limitations in physical and social activities, limitations in usual role activities because of physical health problems, bodily pain, general mental health (psychological distress and well-being), limitations in usual role activities because of emotional problems, vitality (energy and fatigue), and general health perceptions.

HQOL's importance, especially in an aging society, is in determining quality-adjusted life years (QALYs), which measure QOL as a person's age increases. This measure emphasizes living in health and independently instead of just the number of years added to a person's life. Overall health is not just the absence of illness but includes ensuring that life's meaning and richness continue with advancing age.

The difference between subjective and objective ratings of HQOL can be quite startling at times; examinations of fatigue is one such example. Two individuals can report the same overall level of fatigue yet report differing levels of fatigability, or how fatigue affects their daily lives. For example, one individual may retain an active and meaningful life, despite suffering great fatigue, whereas another individual, suffering the same fatigue, may be homebound. HQOL begins to unravel this heretofore neglected aspect of patient expectations. This disparity in subjective versus objective ratings is more pronounced when examining the aging population. Despite multiple comorbidities, most seniors report their health as good or better. Shoring up these discrepant ratings is an important contribution of HQOL measurements.

ECONOMIC QOL

Determining economic QOL generally involves assessing the gross domestic product (GDP), or total market value of all goods and services produced in a country in a given period (usually a year), and the material well-being of individuals within a culture or nation, which is often referred to as the standard of living. Other QOL indices are the Economist Intelligence Unit's (EIU) quality-of-life index and human development index, which represent numerous health factors of a country, such as GDP, life expectancy, employment rate, and political stability. Accurately measuring economic QOL is quite important. Often outcomes from such research structure public policy, legislation, and community-based programs, and because wealth creation does not always lead to concomitant increases in overall QOL, it is imperative that a multipronged assessment approach is used to create any economic QOL rating.

In 2008, the United States ranked thirteenth, out of 111 countries, in the EIU quality-of-life index. GDP usually explains around 50 percent of country variation in life satisfaction, suggesting factors other than income affect QOL ratings. Ireland, for example, has the number-one rating despite having low scores in health and climate. In Ireland, family cohesiveness and intact communities increase the nation's overall QOL. Education level, often a predictor of income, shows a modest correlation with life satisfaction; this finding reinforces the subjective nature and variation among what adds quality to life. In 2012, the EIU published its "Where-to-Be-Born Index, 2013," which ranked Switzerland as the number one place to be born out of eighty countries; the United States was ranked sixteenth.

SPECIFIC ILLNESSES AND QOL

Assessing QOL has long been of interest to researchers and clinicians examining patients' subjective ratings of their health before and after treatment for specific diseases. Because illness-specific QOL questionnaires can demonstrate treatment effectiveness, a growing concern of researchers, clinicians, and insurance companies, their use has increased significantly in the clinical setting. In one study, newly diagnosed lung cancer patients with lower socioeconomic status reported lower health-related QOL, but the differences disappeared at follow-up, suggesting that improved QOL can, in fact, be an outcome of treatment.

Often the effectiveness of treatment is gauged solely on the patient's self-reported QOL; for example, chemotherapy might have been marginally successful in tumor reduction, but if the patient reports a higher QOL, clinicians will gauge the treatment to be a success. Patients undergoing two different types of colorectal surgery, one widely accepted as superior in objective results, produced identical QOL ratings postsurgery. These often confounding results have pushed assessing patients' perceptions of the impact of their disease and its treatment on their lives to the top of clinical treatment paradigms.

THE FUTURE OF QOL

Because culture, expectancies, personality, and many other factors can affect individual ratings of QOL, clinical and research investigations are continually in flux, each searching for the most valid and reliable methods to capture QOL. Emerging research is focusing on ecological momentary assessments, or tracking QOL ratings randomly throughout the day via portable electronic devices, such as cell phones or personal digital assistants (PDAs). At random points throughout the day, a chime sounds, prompting the individual to answer a question about his or her current mood or state (for example, "Right now, are you experiencing any body pain?"). Such real-world data collection allows researchers to track QOL subcategories throughout the day to determine stability and fluctuations of health variables of interest. As personality, expectancies, self-efficacy, and other social cognitive factors can influence QOL, it is paramount that new and innovative ways are continually designed to capture this complex concept.

BIBLIOGRAPHY

Economist Intelligence Unit. *Economist Intelligence Unit.* Economist Intelligence Unit, 2014. Web. 26 June 2014. <http://www.eiu.com/>.

Guyatt, Gordon H., David H. Feeny, and Donald L. Patrick. "Measuring Health-Related Quality of Life." *Annals of Internal Medicine* 118.8 (1993): 622–629.

Print.

International Society for Quality of Life Research. *ISOQOL.* International Society for Quality of Life Research, 2014. Web. 26 June 2014. <http://isoqol. org/>.

Michalos, Alex C., ed. *Encyclopedia of Quality of Life and Well-Being Research.* Dordrecht: Springer, 2013. Digital file, print.

Nussbaum, Martha Craven, and Amartya Kumar Sen, eds. *The Quality of Life: A Study Prepared for World Institute for Development Economics Research of the United Nations University.* Oxford: Clarendon, 2010. Print.

Rahtz, Don R., Rhonda Phillips, and Joseph M. Sirgy. *Community Quality-of-Life Indicators: Best Cases VI.* Dordrecht: Springer, 2013. Digital file.

United Nations *Development Programme. Human Development Reports.* United Nations Development Programme, 2014. Web. 26 June 2014. <http://hdr. undp.org/en/>.

Dana K. Bagwell

SEE ALSO: Assisted living; Coping: Chronic illness; Coping: Terminal illness; Death and dying; Elders' mental health; Hierarchy of needs; Hospice; Social support and mental health; Survey research: Questionnaires and interviews.

Quasi-experimental designs

TYPE OF PSYCHOLOGY: Psychological methodologies

The ideal psychological study is a true experiment that allows unequivocal causal judgments to be made about the variables being investigated; the goal is to have confidence in the validity of judgments made from the experimental data. Quasi-experimental designs are ways of collecting data that maximize confidence in causal conclusions when a true experiment cannot be done.

KEY CONCEPTS
- Control group
- Dependent variable
- External validity
- Hypothesis
- Independent variable
- Internal validity
- Plausible rival alternative hypothesis
- Post-test

- Pretest
- True experiment

INTRODUCTION

The feature that separates psychology from an area such as philosophy is its reliance on the empirical method for its truths. Instead of arguing deductively from premises to conclusions, psychology progresses by using inductive reasoning in which psychological propositions are formulated as experimental hypotheses that can be tested by experiments. The outcome of the experiment determines whether the hypothesis is accepted or rejected. Therefore, the best test of a hypothesis is one that can be interpreted unambiguously. True experiments are considered the best way to test hypotheses, because they are the best way to rule out plausible alternative explanations (confounds) to the experimental hypothesis. True experiments are studies in which the variable whose effect the experimenter wants to understand, the independent variable, is randomly assigned to the experimental unit (usually a person); the researcher observes the effect of the independent variable by responses on the outcome measure, the dependent variable.

For example, if one wanted to study the effects of sugar on hyperactivity in children, the experimenter might ask, "Does sugar cause hyperactive behavior?" Using a true experiment, one would randomly assign half the children in a group to be given a soft drink sweetened with sugar and the other half a soft drink sweetened with a sugar substitute. One could then measure each child's activity level; if the children who were assigned the sugar-sweetened drinks showed hyperactivity as compared to the children who received the other drinks, one could confidently conclude that sugar caused the children to show hyperactivity. A second type of study, called a correlational study, could be done if one had investigated this hypothesis by simply asking or observing which children selected sugar-sweetened drinks and then comparing their behavior to the children who selected the other drinks. The correlational study, however, would not have been able to show whether sugar actually caused hyperactivity. It would be equally plausible that children who are hyperactive simply prefer sugar-sweetened drinks. Such correlational studies have a major validity weakness in not controlling for plausible rival alternative hypotheses. This type of hypothesis is one that is different from the experimenter's preferred hypothesis and offers another reasonable explanation for experimental results. Quasi-experimental designs stand between true experiments and correlational studies in that they control for as many threats to validity as possible.

PLAUSIBLE ALTERNATIVE EXPLANATIONS

Experimental and Quasi-Experimental Designs for Research (1966), by Donald T. Campbell and Julian Stanley, describes the major threats to validity that need to be controlled for so that the independent variable can be correctly tested. Major plausible alternative explanations may need to be controlled when considering internal validity. ("Controlled" does not mean that the threat is not a problem; it means only that the investigator can judge how probable it is that the threat actually influenced the results.)

An external environmental event may occur between the beginning and end of the study, and this historical factor, rather than the treatment, may be the cause of any observed difference. For example, highway fatalities decreased in 1973 after an oil embargo led to the establishment of a speed limit of 55 miles per hour. Some people believed that the cause of the decreased fatalities was the 55-mile-per-hour limit. If the oil embargo caused people to drive less because they could not get gasoline or because it was higher priced, however, either of those events could be a plausible alternative explanation. The number of fatalities may have declined simply because people were driving less, not because of the speed-limit change.

Maturation occurs when natural changes within people cause differences between the beginning and end of the study. Even over short periods of time, for example, people become tired, hungry, or bored. It may be these changes rather than the treatment that causes observed changes. An investigation of a treatment for sprained ankles measured the amount of pain people had when they first arrived for treatment and then measured their pain again four weeks after treatment. Finding a reduction in reported pain, the investigator concluded that the treatment was effective. Since a sprained ankle will probably improve naturally within four weeks, however, maturation (in this case, the natural healing process) is a plausible alternative explanation.

Testing is a problem when the process of measurement itself leads to systematic changes in measured performance. A study was done on the effects of a preparatory course on performance on the American College Test (ACT), a college entrance exam. Students were given the ACT, then given a course on improving their scores, then tested again; they achieved higher scores, on the average, the second time they took the test. The investigator attributed the improvement to the prep course, when actually it may have been simply the practice of taking the first test that led to improvement. This plausible alternative explanation suggests that even if the students had not taken the course, they would have improved their scores on the average on retaking the ACT. The presence of a control group (a group assembled to provide a comparison to the treatment group results) would improve this study.

A change in the instruments used to measure the dependent variable will also cause problems. This is a problem particularly when human observers are rating behaviors directly. The observers may tire, or their standards may shift over the course of the study. For example, if observers are rating children's "hyperactivity," they may see later behavior as more hyperactive than earlier behavior not because the children's behavior has changed but because, through observing the children play, the observers' own standards have shifted. Objective measurement is crucial for controlling this threat.

Selection presents a problem when the results are caused by a bias in the choice of subjects for each group. For example, a study of two programs designed to stop cigarette smoking assigned smokers who had been addicted for ten years to program A and smokers who had been addicted for two years to program B. It was found that 50 percent of the program B people quit and 30 percent of the program A people quit. The investigators concluded that program B is more effective; however, it may be that people in program B were more successful simply because they were not as addicted to their habit as the program A participants.

Mortality, or attrition, is a problem when a differential dropout rate influences the results. For example, in the preceding cigarette study, it might be that of one hundred participants in program A, ninety of them sent back their post-test form at the end of the study; for program B, only sixty of the participants sent their forms back. It may be that people who did not send their forms back were more likely to have continued smoking, causing the apparent difference in results between programs A and B.

When subjects become aware that they are in a study, and awareness of being observed influences their reactions, reactivity has occurred. The famous Hawthorne studies on a wiring room at a Western Electric plant were influenced by this phenomenon. The investigators intended to do a study on the effects of lighting on work productivity, but they were puzzled by the fact that any change they made in lighting—increasing it or decreasing it—led to improved productivity. They finally decided it was the workers' awareness of being in an experiment that caused their reactions, not the lighting level.

Statistical regression is a problem that occurs when subjects are selected to be in a group on the basis of their extreme scores (either high or low) on a test. Their group can be predicted to move toward the average the next time they take the test, even if the treatment has had no effect. For example, if low-scoring students are assigned to tutoring because of the low scores they achieved on a pretest, they will score higher on the second test (a posttest), even if the tutoring is ineffective.

EXTERNAL THREATS TO VALIDITY

External threats to validity constitute the other major validity issue. Generally speaking, true experiments control for internal threats to validity by experimental design, but external threats may be a problem for true experiments as well as quasi-experiments. Since a scientific finding is one that should hold true in different circumstances, external validity (the extent to which the results of any particular study can be generalized to other settings, people, and times) is a very important issue.

An interaction between selection and treatment can cause an external validity problem. For example, since much of the medical research on the treatment of diseases has been performed by selecting only men as subjects, one might question whether those results can be generalized to women. The interaction between setting and treatment can be a problem when settings differ greatly. For example, can results obtained on a college campus be generalized to a factory? Can results from a factory be generalized to an office? The interaction of history and treatment can be a problem when the specific time the experiment is carried out influences people's reaction to the treatment. The effectiveness of an advertisement for gun control might be judged differently if measured shortly after an assassination or a mass murder received extensive media coverage.

EXAMINING SOCIAL PHENOMENA AND PROGRAMS

Quasi-experimental designs have been most frequently used to examine the effects of social phenomena and social programs that cannot be or have not been investigated by experiments. For example, the effects of the public television show *Sesame Street* have been the subject of several quasi-experimental evaluations. One initial evaluation of *Sesame Street* concluded that it was ineffective in raising the academic abilities of poor children, but a reanalysis of the data suggested that statistical regression artifacts had contaminated the original evaluation and that *Sesame Street* had a more positive effect than was initially believed. This research showed the potential harm that can be done by reaching conclusions while not controlling for all the threats to validity. It also showed the value of doing true experiments whenever possible.

Many of the field-research studies carried out on the effects of violent television programming on children's aggressiveness have used quasi-experimental designs to estimate the effects of violent television. Other social-policy studies have included the effects of no-fault divorce laws on divorce rates, of crackdowns on drunken driving on the frequency of drunken driving, and of strict speed-law enforcement on speeding behavior and accidents. The study of the effects of speed-law enforcement represents excellent use of the "interrupted time series" quasi-experimental design. This design can be used when a series of pretest and post-test data points is available. In this case, the governor of Connecticut abruptly announced that people convicted of speeding would have their licenses suspended for a thirty-day period on the first offense, sixty days on a second offense, and longer for any further offenses. By comparing the number of motorists speeding, the number of accidents, and the number of fatalities during the period before the crackdown with the period after the crackdown, the investigators could judge how effective the crackdown was. The interrupted time series design provides control over many of the plausible rival alternative hypotheses and is thus a strong quasi-experimental design. The investigators concluded that it was probable that the crackdown did have a somewhat positive effect in reducing fatalities, but that a regression artifact may also have influenced the results. The regression artifact in this study would be a decrease in fatalities simply because there was such a high rate of fatalities before the crackdown.

USE IN ORGANIZATIONAL PSYCHOLOGY

Organizational psychology has used quasi-experimental designs to study such issues as the effects of strategies to reduce absenteeism in businesses, union-labor cooperation on grievance rates, and the effects of different forms of employee ownership on job attitudes and organizational performance. The last study compared three different conversions to employee ownership and found that employee ownership had positive effects on a com-

pany to the extent that it enhanced participative decision making and led to group work norms supportive of higher productivity. Quasi-experimental studies are particularly useful in those circumstances where it is impossible to carry out true experiments but policymakers still want to reach causal conclusions. A strong knowledge of quasi-experimental design principles helps prevent incorrect causal conclusions.

RESEARCH APPROACH

Psychology has progressed through the use of experiments to establish a base of facts that support psychological theories; however, there are many issues about which psychologists need to have expert knowledge that cannot be investigated by performing experiments. There are not too many social situations, outside a university laboratory, where a psychologist can randomly assign individuals to different treatments. For example, psychologists cannot dictate to parents what type of television programs they must assign their children to watch, they cannot tell the managers of a group of companies how to implement an employee stock option plan, and they cannot make a school superintendent randomly assign different classes to different instructional approaches. All these factors in the social environment vary, and quasi-experimental designs can be used to get the most available knowledge from the natural environment.

The philosophy of science associated with traditional experimental psychology argues that unless a true experiment is done it is impossible to reach any causal conclusion. The quasi-experimental view argues that a study is valid unless and until it is shown to be invalid. What is important in a study is the extent to which plausible alternative explanations can be ruled out. If there are no plausible alternative explanations to the results except for the experimenter's research hypothesis, then the experimenter's research hypothesis can be regarded as true.

EVOLUTION OF PRACTICE

The first generally circulated book that argued for a quasi-experimental approach to social decision making was William A. McCall's *How to Experiment in Education*, published in 1923. Education has been one of the areas where there has been an interest in and willingness to carry out quasi-experimental studies. Psychology was more influenced by the strictly experimental work of Ronald A. Fisher that was being published at around that time, and Fisher's ideas on true experiments dominated psychological methods through the mid-1950s.

The quasi-experimental view gained increasing popularity during the 1960s as psychology was challenged to become more socially relevant and make a contribution to understanding the larger society. At that time, the federal government was also engaged in many social programs, sometimes collectively called the War on Poverty, which included housing programs, welfare programs, and compensatory educational programs. Evaluation of these programs was needed so that what worked could be retained and what failed could be discontinued. There was an initial burst of enthusiasm for quasi-experimental studies, but the ambiguous results that they produced were discouraging, and this has led many leading methodologists to re-emphasize the value of true experiments.

Rather than hold up the university-based laboratory true experiment as a model, however, they called for implementing social programs and other evaluations using random assignment to treatments in such a way that stronger causal conclusions could be reached. The usefulness of true experiments and quasi-experiments was also seen to be much more dependent on psychological theory: the pattern of results obtained by many different types of studies became a key factor in the progress of psychological knowledge. The traditional laboratory experiment, on which many psychological theories are based, was recognized as being very limited in external validity, and the value of true experiments—carried out in different settings, with different types of people, and replicated many times over—was emphasized. Since politicians, business managers, and other social policymakers have not yet appreciated the advantages in knowledge to be gained by adopting a true experiment approach to social innovation, quasi-experimental designs are still an important and valuable tool in understanding human behavior.

BIBLIOGRAPHY

Abbott, Martin, and Jennifer McKinney. *Understanding and Applying Research Design*. Hoboken: Wiley, 2013. Digital file.

Campbell, Donald Thomas, and Julian C. Stanley. *Experimental and Quasi-Experimental Designs for Research*. Chicago: Rand McNally, 1966. Reprint. Belmont: Wadsworth, 2011. Print.

Cook, Thomas D., and Donald T. Campbell. *Quasi-Experimentation: Design and Analysis Issues for Field Settings*. Chicago: Rand, 1979. Print.

Cronbach, Lee J. *Designing Evaluations of Educational and Social Programs*. San Francisco: Jossey, 1987. Print.

Kerlinger, Fred N., and Howard B. Lee. *Foundations of Behavioral Research*. 4th ed. Belmont: Wadsworth, 2000. Print.

Maruyama, Geoffrey. *Research Methods in Social Relations*. [N.p.]: Wiley, 2014. Digital file.

Thyer, Bruce A. *Quasi-Experimental Research Designs*. New York: Oxford UP, 2012. Digital file.

Trochim, William M. K., ed. *Advances in Quasi-Experimental Design and Analysis*. San Francisco: Jossey-Bass, 1986. Print.

Don R. Osborn

SEE ALSO: Archival data; Children's mental health; Complex experimental designs; Experimentation: Independent, dependent, and control variables; Field experimentation; Hypothesis development and testing; Organizational behavior and consulting; Psychotherapy: Effectiveness; Sampling; Scientific methods; Violence and sexuality in the media; Within-subject experimental designs; Violence: Psychological causes and effects.

R

Race and intelligence

TYPE OF PSYCHOLOGY: Biological bases of behavior; Intelligence and intelligence testing

The relationship between race and intelligence has long been the subject of heated debate among social scientists. At issue is whether intelligence is an inherited trait or is primarily attributable to environmental influences.

KEY CONCEPTS
- Intelligence quotient (IQ) tests
- Nature versus nurture
- Twin studies

INTRODUCTION

In 1969, educational psychologist Arthur R. Jensen published an article in the Harvard Educational Review entitled "How Much Can We Boost I.Q. and Scholastic Achievement?" He attempted to explain the consistent finding that whites, on the average, outperform blacks by about 15 points on intelligence quotient (IQ) tests. His major conclusion was that racial differences in intelligence are primarily attributable to heredity and that whites, as a racial group, are born with abilities superior to those of blacks.

Jensen, along with William Shockley, presents the hereditarian hypothesis of intelligence. It argues that some people are born smarter than others and that this fact cannot be changed with training, education, or any alteration in the environment. Because they believe that African Americans as a group are not as smart as whites, they suggest that special programs, such as Head Start, which are designed to help disadvantaged children improve in school achievement, are doomed to fail.

In contrast to the hereditarians, Urie Bronfenbrenner and Ashley Montagu can be described as environmentalists. They believe that although intelligence has some genetic component, as do all human characteristics, the expression of intelligent behavior is defined, determined, and developed within a specific cultural context. Therefore, what people choose to call intelligence is primarily caused by the interaction of genetics with environmental influences. Environmentalists believe that a person can improve in his or her intellectual functioning with sufficient changes in environment.

Richard Herrnstein and Charles Murray's *The Bell Curve* (1994) reopened the issue of heredity versus environment in the attainment of intelligence. The authors argue that whites are inherently superior to African Americans in IQ levels, presenting a mass of statistical evidence to support their position. Critics of *The Bell Curve* attack it on a number of fronts. There is a failure to separate hereditary from genetic variables. The definition of race proves a difficult one. The IQ tests themselves come into the same culture bias category. The statistical tests hide more than they reveal. There is difficulty replicating Herrnstein and Murray's results. The defects mount up rather quickly.

Much of the hereditarian argument is based on two types of studies: those comparing IQ test performance of twins and those of adopted children. Because identical twins have the same genetic endowment, it is thought that any differences observed between them should be attributable to the effects of the environment. Hereditarians also suggest that one should observe more similarities in the IQs of parents and their biological children (because they share genes) than between parents and adopted children (who are biologically unrelated and therefore share no genes).

Statistical formulas are applied to comparisons between family members' IQs to determine the relative contributions of heredity and environment. Using this method, Sir Cyril Burt in 1958 reported a heritability estimate of 0.93. This means that 93 percent of the variability in intelligence could be explained genetically. People have also interpreted this to mean that 93 percent of the intelligence level is inherited. Jensen has more recently reported heritability estimates of 0.80 and 0.67, depending on what formula is used. Hereditarians have also pointed out that when they compare African Americans and whites from similar environments (the same educational level, income level, or occupation), the reported IQ differences remain. This, they argue, supports their view that heredity is more important in determining intelligence. The same arguments have been made for the work of Herrnstein and Murray.

For environmentalists, it is not so much the reported IQ differences between different racial groups that are in question. Of more concern are the basic assumptions made by the hereditarians and the reasons they give for the reported differences. Not surprisingly, environmentalists challenge the hereditarian arguments on several levels. First, they point out that there is no evidence of the existence of an "intelligence" gene or set of genes. They say that scientists have been unsuccessful in distinguishing the genetic from the environmental contributions to intelligence.

Environmentalists also refute the assumption that IQ tests adequately measure intelligence. Although IQ has been noted to be a good predictor of success in school, it turns out to have little relationship to economic success in life. S. E. Luria reports an analysis that shows that the son of a white businessman with an IQ of 90 has a greater chance of success than an African American boy with an IQ of 120. This example calls into question what actually is being assessed. It is not at all clear that "intelligence" is being measured, especially since there is no generally accepted definition of intelligence among social scientists.

The definition of race is also problematic. Although most people may classify people into several racial groups, Montagu and many other social scientists agree that race is a pseudoscientific concept, used as a social or political category to assign social status and to subordinate nonwhite populations. Because of intermingling among different cultural groups, it is also difficult to identify strict biological boundaries for race, which in turn makes genetic interpretations of racial comparisons of IQ differences much less meaningful.

In addition to questioning what IQ tests measure, many psychologists have criticized IQ tests as being biased against individuals who are culturally different from the mainstream group (whites) and who have not assimilated the white, middle-class norms on which the tests were based. Tests developed in one culture may not adequately measure the abilities and aptitude of people from another culture, especially if the two cultures emphasize different skills, ways of solving problems, and ways of understanding the world.

Environmentalists have also criticized the research and statistical techniques used by the hereditarians. It is now widely acknowledged that the data reported by Burt, on which Jensen heavily relied, were false. In many different studies, he came up with the same figures (to the third decimal point) for the similarities between IQ scores for twins. This is statistically impossible. He also did not take into account how other variables, such as age and gender, might have produced higher IQ values in the twins he studied. Rather, he assumed that they shared genes for intelligence.

It is also charged that the concept of heritability is misunderstood by the hereditarians. This is a statistic that applies to groups, not to individuals. If one states that the heritability estimate of a group of IQ scores is 0.80, that does not mean that 80 percent of each IQ score is attributable to genetics, but that 80 percent of the difference in the group of scores can be attributed to genetic variation. Therefore, according to the environmentalists, it is incorrect for hereditarians to establish heritability within one group (such as white children) and then apply that figure to a different racial group (such as African American children).

CONSEQUENCES OF VARIOUS POSITIONS

Several examples may help clarify the relationships between heredity, environment, and characteristics such as IQ. The first example involves a highly heritable characteristic, height. A farmer has two fields, one rich in nutrients (field A) and the other barren (field B). The farmer takes seeds from a bag that has considerable genetic variety, plants them in the two fields, and cares for the two fields of crops equally well. After several weeks, the plants are measured. The farmer finds that within field A, some plants are taller than others in the same field. Since all these plants had the same growing environment, the variation could be attributed to the genetic differences in the seeds planted. The same would be the case with the plants in field B.

The farmer also finds differences between the two fields. The plants in field A are taller than the plants in field B, because of the richer soil in which they grew. The difference in the average heights of the plants is attributable to the quality of the growing environment, even though the genetic variation (heritability) within field A may be the same as that within field B. This same principle applies to IQ scores of different human groups.

Taking the example further, the farmer might call a chemist to test the soil. If the chemist was able to determine all the essential missing nutrients, the farmer could add them to the soil in field B for the next season. The second batch of plants would grow larger, with the average height being similar to the average height of plants in field A. Similarly, if one is comparing African Americans and whites, or any number of racial groups, on a characteristic such as IQ test scores, it is important to understand that unless the groups have equivalent growing environments (social, political, economic, educational, and so on), differences between the groups cannot be easily traced to heredity.

As another example, one might take a set of identical twins who were born in Chicago, separate them at birth, and place one of the twins in the !Kung desert community in Africa. The life experiences of the twin in Africa would differ significantly from those of his Chicago counterpart because of the differences in diet, climate, and other relevant factors required for existence and survival in the two environments. The twin in Africa would have a different language and number system; drawing and writing would likely not be an important part of daily life. Therefore, if one were to use existing IQ tests, one would have to translate them from English to the !Kung language so that they could be understood. The translation might not truly capture the meaning of all the questions and tasks, which might interfere with the !Kung twin's understanding of what was being asked of him. More problems would arise when the !Kung twin is asked to interpret drawings or to copy figures, since he would not be very familiar with these activities.

It is likely that the !Kung twin would perform poorly on the translated IQ test, because it does not reflect what is emphasized and valued in his society. Rather, it is based on the schooling in the society in which the Chicago twin lives. This does not mean that the !Kung twin is less intelligent than his Chicago twin. Similarly, the Chicago twin would do poorly on a test developed from the experience of !Kung culture, because the !Kung test would emphasize skills such as building shelter, finding water, and other activities that are not important for survival in Chicago. In this case, the !Kung test would not adequately measure the ability of the Chicago twin.

Studies done by psychologist Sandra Scarr show that evidence for a genetic basis for racial differences in IQ is far from clear. She looked at the IQ scores of African American children who were born into working-class families but were adopted and reared by white middle-class families. The IQ scores of these children were close to the national average and were almost 10 to 20 points higher than would have been expected had they remained in their birth homes.

Change in children's environments seems to be a critical factor in enhancing their ability to perform on the IQ tests, as seen in the research done by Scarr. Bronfenbrenner found similar results. He examined a dozen studies that looked at early intervention in children's lives; he found that whenever it was possible to change the environment positively, children's scores on IQ tests increased.

HISTORICAL DEVELOPMENT OF RACIAL CONTEXT

The notion of inherited differences is an ancient one; however, the concept of racial classifications is more recent. According to psychologist Wade Nobles, the Western idea of race emerged during the sixteenth century as Europeans began to colonize other parts of the world. As they came into contact with people who looked different from them, many Europeans developed the notion that some races were superior to others. This belief often was given as a justification for slavery and other oppressive activities.

Charles Darwin's theory of evolution was critical in promoting the belief that human differences were a result of heredity and genetics. His notion of the survival of the fittest led psychologists to research racial differences in intelligence to understand the successes and failures of different human groups. Francis Galton, Darwin's cousin, was instrumental in furthering the hereditarian perspective in psychology. In his book *Hereditary Genius: An Inquiry into Its Laws and Consequences* (1869), he attempted to illustrate that genius and prominence follow family lines. He also began the eugenics movement, which supported the use of selective mating and forced sterilization to improve racial stock. *The Bell Curve* is simply a more recent argument along the same lines. Nothing really new is added to the argument. There is a bit more sociobiological jargon and a mass of statistics that do not hold up to careful scrutiny.

Following Galton's lead, many psychologists embraced the notions of inherited racial differences in intelligence. The pioneering work of anthropologist Franz Boas, in attacking the popular conception of race, fostered research to attack the myths attached to that concept, including the myth of inherent superiority or inferiority. G. Stanley Hall, the founder of the American Psychological Association, believed that African people were at a lower evolutionary stage than whites. By the beginning of the 1900's, psychological testing was being widely used to support the view that intelligence was hereditary and was little influenced by the environment. More recently, Burt, Herrnstein, and Jensen have argued in favor of an overriding genetic factor in intelligence.

There were also early efforts to challenge the hereditarian perspective in psychology. During the 1920's and

1930's, Herman Canady and Howard Long, two of the first African Americans to receive graduate degrees in psychology, produced evidence showing the importance of environmental influences on IQ test performance. They were concerned about increasing scientific justifications for the inequality and injustice experienced by African Americans, Native Americans, and other groups. Fighting racism was a major reason Leon Kamin became involved in the debate about race and intelligence. He gathered the original information that had been reported by scientists and reexamined it; Kamin was responsible for discovering that Burt had reported false information. He also noted that many hereditarians misused and misinterpreted their statistics.

Hereditarians maintain that racial differences in IQ test scores are primarily caused by genetics and that these scores do reflect differences in intelligence; environmentalists say no. It has not been proved definitively that IQ tests measure intelligence; however, the evidence does suggest that performance on IQ tests is determined by the interaction between genetic and environmental influences. The quality of the environment will determine how well people will fulfill their potential. In a society where the history of certain groups includes oppression, discrimination, and exclusion from opportunity, it is difficult to explain differences in achievement as being primarily inherited. Instead, it would seem to be a more important goal to eliminate injustices and to change the conditions of life so that all people could do well.

BIBLIOGRAPHY

Devlin, Bernie, et al., eds. *Intelligence, Genes, and Success: Scientists Respond to "The Bell Curve."* New York: Springer, 1997. A number of psychologists and social scientists respond to the claims of Herrnstein and Murray.

Fancher, Raymond E. *The Intelligence Men: Makers of the IQ Controversy.* New York: W. W. Norton, 1987. Examines the historical contexts of the IQ controversy. The life experiences of the major hereditarians and environmentalists and how these experiences influenced their perspectives are emphasized. This book is easy to read and does an excellent job of making complex statistics understandable.

Goldsby, Richard. *Race and Races.* 2d ed. New York: Macmillan, 1977. Provides straightforward and accurate information about issues of race, racial differences, and racism. There is a balanced discussion of both the hereditarian and environmentalist perspectives of the IQ controversy. Enjoyable and easy to read for high school and college students alike.

Gould, Stephen Jay. *The Mismeasure of Man.* Rev. ed. New York: W. W. Norton, 2008. Gould replies to the work of Herrnstein and Murray, questioning both their motives and their methods.

Guthrie, Robert V. *Even the Rat Was White.* 2d ed. Boston, Mass.: Pearson/Allyn & Bacon, 2004. Provides an excellent historical view of how psychology has dealt with race as an issue. The first section of the book focuses on methods of study, early psychological testing, and the development of racism in the profession of psychology.

Herrnstein, Richard, and Charles Murray. *The Bell Curve.* New York: Free Press, 1997. This book argues that differences in black and white IQ scores are genetically based.

Jensen, Arthur R. *Bias in Mental Testing.* New York: Free Press, 1980. An attempt to deal comprehensively with the issues of IQ testing and bias. Jensen challenges the criticisms against IQ tests and offers research to support his view that group differences in IQ test scores are not attributable to bias.

Kamin, Leon J. *The Science and Politics of IQ.* New York: Halstead Press, 1974. Discusses the political nature of the role psychologists have played in support of IQ testing and the role of psychologists in the eugenics movement and in education. Includes strong critiques of the work done by Burt and Jensen.

Montagu, Ashley, ed. *Race and IQ.* Expanded ed. New York: Oxford University Press, 2002. Written to challenge the interpretations offered by the hereditarians. Most of the articles were previously published in professional journals or popular magazines. Some of the chapters contain very technical material; however, the writers generally do an effective job translating this into more understandable language.

Derise E. Tolliver; updated by Frank A. Salamone

SEE ALSO: Ability tests; Bronfenbrenner, Urie; College entrance examinations; Hall, G. Stanley; Intelligence; Intelligence quotient (IQ); Intelligence tests; Prejudice; Racism; Testing: Historical perspectives.

Racism

TYPE OF PSYCHOLOGY: Social psychology

Those studying racism examine the phenomenon of negative attitudes and behavior by members of the majority toward those who belong to racial and ethnic minorities. The topic of racism, which straddles the boundaries between social psychology and sociology, is connected with the study of intergroup relations, cognition, and attitudes in general..

KEY CONCEPTS
- Attribution theory
- Discrimination
- Prejudice
- Scapegoating
- Social construction of race
- Stereotypes

INTRODUCTION

The social and psychological study of prejudice and discrimination, including prejudice and discrimination against African Americans, has a long history; the term "racism," however, did not enter the language of social psychology until the publication of the Kerner Commission Report of 1968, which blamed all-pervasive "white racism" for widespread black rioting in American cities. While usually applied to black-white relations in the United States, the term is also sometimes used with regard to white Americans' relations with other minority groups, such as Asians or Latinos, or to black-white relations outside the United States, for example, in Britain, Canada, or South Africa. Most of the studies and research on racism have focused on white racism against blacks in the United States.

Racism is seen by many social psychologists not as mere hatred but as a deep-rooted habit that is hard to change; hence, subvarieties of racism are distinguished. Psychoanalyst Joel Kovel, in his book *White Racism: A Psychohistory* (1970), distinguishes between dominative racism, the desire to oppress blacks, and aversive racism, the desire to avoid contact with blacks. Aversive racism, Samuel L. Gaertner and John Dovidio find, exists among those whites who pride themselves on being unprejudiced. David O. Sears, looking at whites' voting behavior and their political opinions as expressed in survey responses, finds what he calls symbolic racism: a resentment of African Americans for making demands

in the political realm that supposedly violate traditional American values. Social psychologist James M. Jones distinguishes three types of racism: individual racism, the prejudice and antiblack behavior deliberately manifested by individual whites; institutional racism, the social, economic, and political patterns that impersonally oppress blacks regardless of the prejudice or lack thereof of individuals; and cultural racism, the tendency of whites to ignore or to denigrate the special characteristics of black culture.

Where Dovidio and Gaertner find aversive racism, Irwin Katz finds ambivalence. Many whites, he argues, simultaneously see African Americans as disadvantaged (which creates sympathy) and as deviating from mainstream social norms (which creates antipathy). Such ambivalence, Katz contends, leads to exaggeratedly negative reactions to negative behaviors by an African American, but also to exaggeratedly positive reactions to positive behaviors by an African American. He calls this phenomenon ambivalence-induced behavior amplification.

The reasons suggested for individual racism are many. John Dollard, Neal E. Miller, and others, in *Frustration and Aggression* (1939), see prejudice as the scapegoating of minorities to provide a release for aggression in the face of frustration; in this view, outbursts of bigotry are a natural response to hard economic times. Muzafer and Carolyn Sherif, in *Groups in Harmony and Tension* (1953) and later works, see prejudice of all sorts as the result of competition between groups. Theodor Adorno and others, in *The Authoritarian Personality* (1950), view prejudice, whether directed against blacks or against Jews, as reflective of a supposedly fascist type of personality produced by authoritarian child-rearing practices. *In Racially Separate or Together?* (1971), Thomas F. Pettigrew shows that discriminatory behavior toward blacks, and the verbal expression of prejudices against them, can sometimes flow simply from a white's desire to fit in with his or her social group. Finally, both prejudice and discrimination, many psychologists argue, are rooted in those human cognitive processes involved in the formation of stereotypes.

RACISM AND STEREOTYPES

Stereotypes are ideas, often rigidly held, concerning members of a group to which one does not belong. Social psychologists who follow the cognitive approach to the study of racism, such as David L. Hamilton, Walter G. Stephan, and Myron Rothbart, argue that racial stereotyping (the tendency of whites to see blacks in some roles and not in others) arises, like any other kind of stereotyping, from the need of every human being to create some sort of order out of his or her perceptions of the world. Although stereotypes are not entirely impervious to revision or even to shattering in the face of disconfirming instances, information related to a stereotype is more efficiently retained than information unrelated to it. Whites, it has been found, tend to judge blacks to be more homogeneous than they really are, while being more aware of differences within their own group: This is called the out-group homogeneity hypothesis. Whites who are guided by stereotypes may act in such a way as to bring out worse behavior in blacks than would otherwise occur, thus creating a self-fulfilling prophecy.

Why is stereotypical thinking on the part of whites about African Americans so hard to eliminate? The history of race relations in the United States deserves some of the blame. Some mistakes in reasoning common to the tolerant and the intolerant alike—such as the tendency to remember spectacular events and to think of them as occurring more frequently than is really the case (the availability heuristic)—also occur in whites' judgments about members of minority groups. In addition, the social and occupational roles one fills may reinforce stereotypical thinking.

Pettigrew contends that attribution errors —mistakes in explaining the behavior of others—may have an important role to play in reinforcing racial stereotypes. The same behavioral act, Pettigrew argues, is interpreted differently by whites depending on the race of the actor. A positive act by a black might be ascribed to situational characteristics (for example, luck, affirmative action programs, or other circumstances beyond one's control) and thus discounted; a positive act by a white might be ascribed to personality characteristics. Similarly, a negative act might be ascribed to situational characteristics in the case of a white, but to personality characteristics in the case of a black. The tendency of whites to view the greater extent of poverty among blacks as solely the result of lack of motivation can be seen as a form of attribution error.

POLICY GUIDES

Institutional racism occurs when policies that are nonracial on their face have differential results for the two races. For example, a stiff educational requirement for a relatively unskilled job may effectively exclude blacks, whose educational preparation may be weaker, at least in part because of past racial discrimination. The policy of hiring friends and relatives of existing employees may also exclude blacks, if blacks have not historically worked in a particular business. In both cases, the effect is discriminatory even if the intent is not.

Somewhat connected with the concept of institutional racism is Pettigrew's notion of conformity-induced prejudice and discrimination. A classic example is that of the precivil-rights-era southern United States, where urban restaurant owners, regardless of their personal feelings about blacks, refused them service out of deference to local norms. Another example is the case of the white factory worker who cooperates with black fellow workers on the job and in union activities but strenuously opposes blacks moving into his neighborhood; norms of tolerance are followed in one context, norms of discrimination in the other.

The concept of symbolic (sometimes called "modern") racism, a form of covert prejudice said to be characteristic of political conservatives, arose from a series of questions designed to predict whether white Californians would vote against black political candidates. It has been used to explain opposition to school busing to achieve integration and support for the 1978 California referendum proposition for limiting taxes. John B. McConahay shows that white experimental subjects who score high on the modern racism scale, when faced with hypothetical black and white job candidates with identical credentials, are more likely than low scorers to give a much poorer rating to the black candidate's résumé.

Aversive racism cannot be detected by surveys. Since aversive racists wish to maintain a nonprejudiced self-image, they neither admit to being prejudiced nor discriminate against blacks when social norms clearly forbid it; when the norms are ambiguous, however, they do discriminate. In a New York City experiment, professed liberals and professed conservatives both got telephone calls from individuals identifiable from their speech patterns as either black or white. At first, the caller said he had the wrong number; if the recipient of the call did not hang up, the caller then asked for help regarding a disabled car. Conservatives were less likely to offer help to the black, but liberals were more likely to hang up when they were told by the black that a wrong number had been called. In another experiment, white college students proved just as willing to accept help from a black partner as from a white one when the help was offered. When the subjects had to take the initiative, however, discomfort with the reversal of traditional roles showed up: More asked for help from the white partner than from the black one.

Both symbolic and aversive, but not dominative, racists manifest ambivalence in their attitudes toward blacks. Katz's concept of ambivalence-induced behavior amplification has been tested in several experiments. In one experiment, white college student subjects were told to insult two individuals, one black and one white. After they had done so, they proved, when asked for assistance in a task later on, more willing to help the black they had insulted than the white person.

The effect of the availability heuristic in reinforcing stereotypes is seen in the case of a white who is mugged by a black criminal. If the victim knows no other blacks, he or she may well remember this one spectacular incident and forget the many blacks who are law-abiding. The effect of occupational roles in reinforcing stereotypes can be seen in the example of a white police officer who patrols a black slum neighborhood and jumps to the conclusion that all blacks are criminals.

Experiments on stereotyping indicate that white subjects remember the words or actions of a solo black in an otherwise all-white group better than they do words or actions of one black in a group of several blacks. With a mixed group of speakers, some white and some black, white experimental subjects proved later to be more likely to confuse the identities of the black speakers than those of the white speakers, while remembering the race of the former. The self-fulfilling prophecy concept has been tested in experiments with white subjects interviewing supposed job candidates. The white subjects were more ill at ease and inarticulate interviewing a black candidate than in interviewing a white one; in turn, the black candidate was more ill at ease than the white one and made more errors.

Since most such experiments use college students as subjects, there is inevitably some doubt about their generalizability to the outside world. Nevertheless, it seems likely that the evidence from social psychology experiments of just how deeply rooted racial bias is among white Americans has played at least some role in leading governments to adopt affirmative action policies to secure fairer treatment of blacks and other minorities in hiring procedures.

HISTORY AND DEVELOPMENTS

Although the study of racism per se began with the racial crisis of the 1960s, the study of prejudice in general goes back much further; as early as the 1920s, Emory Bog-

ardus constructed a social distance scale measuring the degree of intimacy members of different racial and ethnic groups were willing to tolerate with one another. At first, psychologists tended to seek the roots of prejudice in the emotional makeup of the prejudiced individual rather than in the structure of society or in the general patterns of human cognition. For many years, the study of antiblack prejudice was subsumed under the study of prejudice in general; those biased against blacks were thought to be biased against other groups, such as Jews, as well.

In the years immediately following World War II, American social psychologists were optimistic about the possibilities for reducing or even eliminating racial and ethnic prejudices. Adorno's *The Authoritarian Personality*, and *The Nature of Prejudice* (1954), by Gordon Allport, reflect the climate of opinion of the time. Allport, whose view of prejudice represented a mixture of the psychoanalytic and cognitive approaches, used the term "racism" to signify the doctrines preached by negrophobe political demagogues; he did not see it as a deeply ingrained bad habit pervading the entire society. Pettigrew, who wrote about antiblack prejudice from the late 1950s on, cast doubt on the notion that there was a specific type of personality or pattern of child rearing associated with prejudice. Nevertheless, he long remained in the optimistic tradition, arguing that changing white people's discriminatory behavior through the enactment of civil rights laws would ultimately change their prejudiced attitudes.

The more frequent use by social psychologists of the term "racism" from the late 1960s onward indicates a growing awareness that bias against blacks, a visible minority, might be harder to uproot than that directed against religious and ethnic minorities. Social psychologists studying racial prejudice shifted their research interest from the open and noisy bigotry most often found among political extremists (for example, the Ku Klux Klan) to the quiet, everyday prejudices of the average apolitical individual. Racial bias against blacks came to be seen as a central, rather than a peripheral, feature of American life.

Responses to surveys taken from the 1940s to the end of the 1970s indicated a steady decline in the percentage of white Americans willing to admit holding racist views. Yet in the 1970s, the sometimes violent white hostility to school busing for integration, and the continuing social and economic gap between black and white America, gave social psychologists reason to temper their earlier optimism. The contact hypothesis, the notion that contact between different racial groups would reduce prejudice, was subjected to greater skepticism and ever more careful qualification. Janet Schofield, in her field study of a desegregated junior high school, detected a persistence of racial divisions among the pupils; reviewing a number of such studies, Stephan similarly discerned a tendency toward increased interracial tension in schools following desegregation. The pessimism suggested by field studies among younger teenagers was confirmed by experiments conducted in the 1970s and 1980s on college students and adults; such studies demonstrated the existence, even among supposedly nonprejudiced people, of subtle racism and racial stereotyping.

Yet while social psychological experiments contribute to an understanding of the reasons for negative attitudes toward blacks by whites, and for discriminatory behavior toward blacks even by those whites who believe themselves to be tolerant, they do not by any means provide the complete answer to the riddle of racial prejudice and discrimination. Unlike many other topics in social psychology, racism has also been investigated by journalists, historians, economists, sociologists, political scientists, legal scholars, and even literary critics. The techniques of social psychology—surveys, controlled experiments, and field studies—provide only one window on this phenomenon.

BIBLIOGRAPHY

Allport, Gordon W. *The Nature of Prejudice.* 1954. Reprint. Cambridge: Addison, 1990. Print.

Augoustinos, Martha. "Psychological Perspectives on Racism." *InPsych.* Australian Psychological Society, Aug. 2013. Web. 25 June 2014.

Barndt, Joseph. *Understanding and Dismantling Racism: The Twenty-First Century Challenge to White America.* Minneapolis: Fortress, 2007. Print.

Bell, Derrick. *Faces at the Bottom of the Well: The Permanence of Racism.* New York: Basic, 1992. Print.

Campbell, Duane. *Choosing Democracy: A Practical Guide to Multicultural Education.* 4th ed. Boston: Allyn, 2009. Print.

Dovidio, John F., and Samuel L. Gaertner, eds. *Prejudice, Discrimination, and Racism.* 1986. Rpt. San Diego: Academic, 1992. Print.

Gilroy, Paul. *Against Race: Imaging Political Culture beyond the Color Line.* Cambridge: Belknap, 2001. Print.

Katz, Irwin. *Stigma: A Social Psychological Analysis.* Hillsdale: Lawrence Erlbaum, 1981. Print.

Katz, Phyllis A., and Dalmas A. Taylor, eds. *Eliminating Racism: Profiles in Controversy.* New York: Plenum, 1988. Print.

Marsh, Jason, Rodolfo Mendoza-Denton, and Jeremy Adam Smith. *Are We Born Racist? New Insights from Neuroscience and Positive Psychology.* Boston: Beacon, 2010. Print.

Oshodi, John Egbeazien. *History of Psychology in the Black Experience: Perspectives Then and Now—A Psychology in the Perspective of the History of the Africans and People of African Descent.* Lanham: UP of America, 2012. Print.

Pettigrew, Thomas F., et al. *Prejudice.* Cambridge: Belknap, 1982. Print.

Steele, Shelby. *The Content of Our Character: A New Vision of Race in America.* New York: HarperPerennial, 1998. Print.

Stephan, Walter G., and David Rosenfield. "Racial and Ethnic Stereotypes." *In the Eye of the Beholder: Contemporary Issues in Stereotyping.* Ed. Arthur G. Miller. New York: Praeger, 1982. Print.

Sue, Derald Wing, and David Sue. *Counseling the Culturally Diverse: Theory and Practice.* Hoboken: Wiley, 2013. Print.

Trepagnier, Barbara. *Silent Racism: How Well-Meaning White People Perpetuate the Racial Divide.* Boulder: Paradigm, 2007. Print.

West, Cornell. *Race Matters.* 2d ed. Boston: Beacon, 2001. Print.

Paul D. Mageli; updated by Frank A. Salamone

SEE ALSO: African Americans and mental health; Ageism; Asian Americans/Pacific Islanders and mental health; Attitude formation and change; Groups; Latinos and mental health; Native Americans/ Alaskan Natives and mental health; Prejudice; Prejudice reduction; Race and intelligence; Sexism; Social identity theory.

Radical behaviorism
B. F. Skinner

TYPE OF PSYCHOLOGY: Personality

Radical behaviorism describes the views of B. F. Skinner, an influential figure in American psychology since the 1930s. Skinner argued that most behavior is controlled by its consequences; he invented an apparatus for observing the effects of consequences, advocated a technology of be-

havior control, and believed that everyday views about the causes of behavior were an obstacle to its true understanding.

KEY CONCEPTS

- Contingency of reinforcement
- Discriminative stimulus
- Experimental analysis of behavior
- Mentalism
- Operant
- Private events
- Rule-governed behavior
- Shaping

INTRODUCTION

According to B. F. Skinner, the behavior of an organism is a product of current and past environmental consequences and genetic endowment. Since little can be done, at least by psychology, about genetic endowment, Skinner focused on those things that could be changed or controlled: the immediate consequences of behavior. By consequences, Skinner meant the results or effects that a particular behavior (a class of responses, or "operant") produces. There are many ways to open a door, for example, but since each one allows a person to walk to the next room, one would speak of a "door-opening" operant. The consequences not only define the class of responses but also determine how often members of the class are likely to occur in the future. This was termed the law of effect by early twentieth century American psychologist Edward L. Thorndike, whose work Skinner refined.

Skinner analyzed behavior by examining the antecedents and consequences that control any specific class of responses in the individual organism. From this view, he elaborated a psychology that encompassed all aspects of animal and human behavior, including language. By the late 1970s, historians of psychology ranked Skinner's work as the second most significant development in psychology since World War II; the general growth of the field was ranked first. Three journals arose to publish work in the Skinnerian tradition: *Journal of the Experimental Analysis of Behavior, Journal of Applied Behavior Analysis,* and *Behaviorism.* Moreover, an international organization, the Association for Behavior Analysis, was formed, with its own journal.

CONTROLLING VARIABLES

Skinner theorized that there are several kinds of consequences, or effects. Events that follow behavior and produce an increase in the rate or frequency of the behavior are termed reinforcers. In ordinary language, they might be called rewards, but Skinner avoided this expression because he defined reinforcing events in terms of the effects they produced (their rate of occurrence) rather than the alleged feelings they induced (for example, pleasure). To attribute the increase in rate of response produced by reinforcement to feelings of pleasure would be regarded by Skinner as an instance of mentalism—the attribution of behavior to a feeling rather than to an event occurring in the environment. Other consequences that follow a behavior produce a decrease in the rate of behavior. These are termed punishers. Skinner strongly objected to the use of punishment as a means to control behavior because it elicited aggression and produced dysfunctional emotional responses such as striking back and crying in a small child. Consequences (reinforcers and punishers) may be presented following a behavior (twenty dollars for building a doghouse, for example, or an electric shock for touching an exposed wire) or taken away (a fine for speeding, the end of a headache by taking aspirin). Consequences may be natural (tomatoes to eat after a season of careful planting and watering) or contrived (receiving a dollar for earning an A on a test).

Reinforcing and punishing consequences are one example of controlling variables. Events that precede behaviors are also controlling variables and determine under what circumstances certain behaviors are likely to appear. Events occurring before a response occurs are called discriminative stimuli because they come to discriminate in favor of a particular piece of behavior. They set the occasion for the behavior and make it more likely to occur. For example, persons trying to control their eating are told to keep away from the kitchen except at mealtimes. Being in the kitchen makes it more likely that the person will eat something, not simply because that is where the food is kept but also because being in the kitchen is one of the events that has preceded previous eating and therefore makes eating more likely to occur. This is true even when the person does not intend to eat but goes to the kitchen for other reasons. Being in the kitchen raises the probability of eating. It is a discriminative stimulus (any stimulus in the presence of which a response is reinforced) for eating, as are the table, the refrigerator, or a candy bar on the counter. Any event or stimulus that occurs immediately before a response is reinforced becomes reinforced with the response and makes the response more likely to occur again if the discriminative stimulus occurs again. The discriminative stimulus comes to gain some control over the behavior.

DISCRIMINATIVE AND REINFORCING STIMULI

Discriminative stimuli and reinforcing stimuli are the controlling variables Skinner used to analyze behavior. These events constitute a chain of behavior called a contingency of reinforcement. It is a contingency because reinforcement does not occur unless the response is made in the presence of the discriminative stimuli. Contingencies of reinforcement are encountered every day. For example, a soda is purchased from a machine. The machine is brightly colored to act as a discriminative stimulus for dropping coins in a slot, which in turn yields a can or bottle of soft drink. The machine comes to control a small portion of a person's behavior. If the machine malfunctions, a person may push the selector button several times repeatedly, perhaps even putting in more coins, and, still later, strike the machine. By carefully scheduling how many times an organism must respond before reinforcement occurs, the rate of response can be controlled as is done in slot or video machines, or gambling devices in general. Responses are made several hundred or thousand times for very little reinforcement—a near win or a small payoff. Schedules of reinforcement are another important set of controlling variables that Skinner explored.

Contingencies are relationships among controlling variables. Some of the relationships become abstracted and formulized, that is, put in the form of rules. When behavior is under the control of a rule, it is termed rule-governed behavior, as opposed to contingency-shaped behavior. As a person first learns any skill, much of his or her behavior is rule governed, either through written instructions or by the person's repeating the rule to himself or herself. For example, a novice golfer might review the rules for a good swing, even repeating them aloud. Eventually, though, swing becomes automatic; it seems to become "natural." The verbal discriminative stimuli have shifted to the very subtle and covert stimuli associated with swing without the golfer's thinking about it, and the natural consequences of a successful swing take over.

OPERANT CHAMBER EXPERIMENTS

The operant chamber is a small experimental space or cage that Skinner invented to observe the effects that consequences have on behavior. A food-deprived organism (Skinner first used rats and later switched to pigeons) is placed in the chamber containing a lever that, when depressed, releases a small piece of food into a cup from which the organism eats. The first bar-press response is produced through the process of shaping, or reinforcing approximations to bar pressing (for example, being near the bar, having a paw above the bar, resting a paw on the bar, nearly depressing the bar) until bar pressing is regularly occurring. Once the operant of bar pressing is established, an experimental analysis of the variables that influence it can be done. The schedule of reinforcement can be changed, for example, from one reinforcer for each response to five responses required for each reinforcer. Changes in the rate of response can be observed on a device Skinner invented, a cumulative record, which automatically displays the rate at which the operant is occurring. A discriminative stimulus can be introduced in the form of a small light mounted on the wall of the chamber. If bar presses are reinforced only when the light is turned on, the light will come to have some control over the operant. Turning the light on and off will literally turn bar pressing on and off in a food-deprived rat.

Skinner controlled his own behavior in the same fashion that he had learned to control the behavior of laboratory organisms. He arranged a "writing environment," a desk used only for that purpose; wrote at a set time each day; and kept careful records of time spent writing. Other examples of self-management may be found in Skinner's novel of his research, *Walden Two* (1948). In this fictionalized account, children learn self-control through a set of exercises that teach ways to tolerate increasing delays of reinforcement.

BEHAVIORAL ANALYSIS OF LANGUAGE

Skinner also performed a behavior analysis of language (*Verbal Behavior*, 1957). For example, a behavioral analysis of the word "want," "believe," or "love," an operational definition in Skinner's sense, would be all those circumstances and situations that control the use of the word, that is, the discriminative stimuli for the verbal response. Skinner tried to show in *Verbal Behavior* that speaking and writing could be explained with the same principle he had used to explain animal behavior. Many of Skinner's works and much of his private notebooks are taken up with the recording of how words are used. His purpose was to dementalize them, to show that what controls their use is some aspect of the environment or some behavioral practice on the part of the verbal community, rather than some internal or mental event. The earliest uses of the word "to know," for example, referred to action, something the individual could do, rather than something he or she possessed or had stored inside the mind.

UNDERSTANDING SKINNER'S CONTRIBUTIONS

So much has been written about Skinner, some of it misleading or false, that it is important to clarify what he did not do. He did not rear either of his daughters in a Skinner box. His younger daughter was reared during her infancy with the aid of an aircrib, a special enclosed crib Skinner built that allowed control of air temperature and humidity, and in which the infant could sleep and play without the burden of clothes. Aircribs were later available commercially. Skinner did not limit his analysis of behavior only to publicly observable events, as did the methodological behaviorists. Part of what made Skinner's behaviorism radical was his insistence that a science of behavior should be able to account for those private events to which only the individual has access, such as the pain of a toothache. He demonstrated how the community teaches its members to describe covert events such as toothaches and headaches. He did not regard such events as anything other than behavior. That is, he did not give them a special status by calling them mental events.

Skinner did not argue that reinforcement explains everything. He allowed, especially in his later works, that genetic endowment plays a role in the determination of behavior, as do rules and antecedent events. He did not reject physiological explanations of behavior when actual physiology was involved. He did object to the use of physiological terms in psychological accounts, unless the physiological mechanisms were known. For Skinner, physiology was one subject matter and behavior was another. Finally, he did not ignore complex behavior. Many of his works, particularly *Verbal Behavior* and *The Technology of Teaching* (1968), offered behaviorist analyses of what in other psychologies would be termed cognitive phenomena, such as talking, reading, thinking, problem solving, and remembering.

Skinner made many contributions to psychology. Among them was his invention of the operant chamber and its associated methodology. Operant equipment and procedures have been employed by animal and human experimental psychologists in laboratories around the world. Most of these psychologists do not adhere to

Skinner's radical behaviorism or to all the features of his science of behavior. They have, however, found the techniques that he developed to be productive in exploring a wide variety of problems, ranging from the fields of psychopharmacology to learning in children and adults and experimental economics. Skinner and his followers developed a technology of behavior that included techniques for working with the developmentally disabled, children in elementary classrooms, and persons with rehabilitation or health care problems; they also considered approaches to public safety, employee motivation and production, and other fields that involved the management of behavior. Although the technology developments never reached the vision he described in Walden Two, the efforts are ongoing.

Skinner may have exhausted the law of effect. The idea that consequences influence behavior can be found in many forms in the literature of psychology and philosophy, especially since the middle of the nineteenth century, but it is only in the work of Skinner that one sees how much of human and animal behavior can be brought within its purview. Because Skinner took behavior as his subject matter, he greatly expanded what could be regarded as being of interest to psychologists. Behavior was everywhere: in the classroom, at the office, in the factory. Nearly any aspect of human activity could become the legitimate object of study by a Skinnerian psychologist, a point well illustrated in Skinner's description of a utopian community that takes an experimental attitude toward its cultural practices and designs a culture based on a science of behavior (*Walden Two*). Finally, Skinner conceptualized an epistemology, a way of understanding what it means for humans to know something, that is perhaps his lasting contribution.

RELATIONSHIP WITH DARWINISM AND PRAGMATISM

In placing the radical behaviorism of Skinner in historical context, two nineteenth-century doctrines are often invoked. One view, shared by Skinner, is that operant psychology represents an extension of the principle of natural selection that Charles Darwin described at the level of the species. Natural selection explained the origin of species; contingencies of reinforcement and punishment explain the origin of classes of responses. The environment selects in both cases. In operant psychology, the role of the environment is to reinforce differentially and thereby select from among a pool of responses that the organism is making. The final effect is one particular operant that has survival or adaptive value for the individual organism. Skinner has suggested that cultural evolution occurs in a similar fashion.

It is also observed that Skinner's psychology resembles nineteenth-century pragmatism. The pragmatists held that beliefs are formed by their outcome, or practical effect. To explain why someone does something by reference to a belief would be regarded as mentalism by Skinner; he would substitute behavior for beliefs. Yet he comes to the same doctrine: one in which environmental consequences act in a Darwinian fashion. Finally, Skinner's philosophy shows the influence of the nineteenth -century positivism of physicist Ernst Mach. Skinner desired a description of behavior and its causes, while avoiding mental states or other cognitive or personality entities that intervene between behavior and the environment.

BIBLIOGRAPHY

Adams, Nelson. "Skinner's Walden Two: An Anticipation of Positive Psychology?" *Review of General Psychology* 16.1 (2012): 1–9. PsycARTICLES. Web. 25 June 2014.

Kazdin, Alan E. *Behavior Modification in Applied Settings.* 7th ed. Long Grove: Waveland, 2013. Print.

Madden, Gregory J. *APA Handbook of Behavior Analysis: Volume 2—Translating Principles into Practice.* Washington, DC: APA, 2013. Print.

Modgil, Sohan, and Celia Modgil, eds. *B. F. Skinner: Consensus and Controversy.* New York: Falmer, 1987. Print.

O'Donohue, William, and Kyle E. Ferguson. *The Psychology of B. F. Skinner.* Thousand Oaks: Sage, 2001. Print.

Rutherford, Alexandra. *Beyond the Box: B. F. Skinner's Technology of Behavior from Laboratory to Life, 1950s–1970s.* Toronto: U of Toronto P, 2009. Print.

Skinner, B. F. *About Behaviorism.* Reprint. London: Penguin, 1993. Print.

Skinner, B. F. *Particulars of My Life.* Rpt. New York: New York UP, 1984. Print.

Skinner, B. F. *The Shaping of a Behaviorist.* Rpt. New York: New York UP, 1984. Print.

Skinner, B. F. *A Matter of Consequences.* Rpt. New York: New York UP, 1985. Print.

Skinner, B. F. *Science and Human Behavior.* Rpt. New York: Macmillan, 1999. Print.

Skinner, B. F. *Walden Two.* Indianapolis: Hackett, 2005. Print.

Staddon, John. *The New Behaviorism.* 2nd ed. Hoboken: Taylor, 2014. Print.

Vargas, Julie S. "B. F. Skinner, Father, Grandfather, Behavior Modifier." *About Human Nature: Journeys in Psychological Thought.* Ed. Terry J. Knapp and Charles T. Rasmussen. Dubuque: Kendall/Hunt, 1987. Print.

Terry J. Knapp

SEE ALSO: Behavioral family therapy; Behaviorism; Cognitive behavior therapy; Conditioning; Genetics and mental health; Learning; Operant conditioning therapies; Punishment; Rule-governed behavior; Skinner, B. F.; Skinner box.

Rape

TYPE OF PSYCHOLOGY: Counseling; Clinical; Psychotherapy, Psychopathology

Rape, the sexual penetration of a person without his or her consent, has been documented for as long as written accounts of human experiences are available; however, it has increasingly been a topic of interest for modern researchers since the 1970's. This criminal act leads to significant emotional consequences for its victims, who are at risk for psychiatric conditions, such as Post Traumatic Stress Disorder and depression, which can last for decades despite many modern psychotherapeutic treatments.

KEY CONCEPTS
- Fight-or-flight response
- Parasympathetic nervous system
- Post traumatic stress disorder
- Rape scripts
- Sexual assault
- Trauma

INTRODUCTION

In the United States, rape is defined as the oral, anal, or vaginal penetration of another person without his or her consent. The penetration can be penile, digital, or with any other object or material. Rape is a specific form of sexual assault, which refers to any unwanted sexual contact with another person—touching, kissing, or revealing private parts—without consent. The concept of consent is crucial to the definition of rape. New York State law defines lack of consent as resulting from the following situations: forcible compulsion, incapacity to consent, a lack of expressed or implied acceptance, and clear expression of non-consent. A person is deemed incapable of consent when he or she is any of the following: less than seventeen years old (commonly known as statutory rape or childhood sexual abuse), mentally disabled, mentally incapacitated, physically helpless, or committed to the care or custody of the perpetrator (i.e., inmates in jail or prison cannot provide consent to prison employees, and patients cannot give consent to health care providers during treatment). Therefore, rape is not limited to situations in which one person physically forces another to have sexual intercourse. It also includes the sexual penetration of people who are unable to agree soundly to the acts. These include the following: individuals who are incapacitated by alcohol or drugs, individuals with cognitive impairments such as dementia or intellectual disabilities, children and teens who are considered too young to understand the implications of sex with an adult, and people in a relationship in which they may be unduly influenced because they rely on the other person for their care and wellbeing.

Rape is a type of trauma, which is an event that threatens a person or a loved one's life or bodily integrity, leading to intense fear, helplessness, or horror. Traumatic events such as rape are considered harmful to the victims because they can have long lasting physical and emotional consequences. Unlike many other forms of trauma, such as car accidents or natural disasters, rape is an interpersonal trauma that is committed by other people. As a result, rape victims often experience significant challenges to their social functioning, such as difficulty trusting other people. One common misconception of rape is that it is motivated by sexual desire; for example, a man sees an attractive woman and is sexually aroused, leading him to have forced sexual intercourse with her. Research has shown, however, that those who commit rape are motivated by power and control and not by sexual desire.

MISCONCEPTIONS ABOUT RAPE
In a series of studies beginning in the 1980's, Mary Koss demonstrated that rape is widely misunderstood and underestimated. She elucidated three important facts about rape that have since served as the foundation of rape research. First, rape was much more common than most people assumed: One in four women had an experience that met the legal definition of rape in her lifetime. Second, the majority of rapes were not committed by strangers, but by someone known to the victim, such as an acquaintance, a date, a romantic part-

ner, or a spouse. Third, more than 90% of rape victims did not report their experience to police, and more than half did not tell friends or family. These statistics challenged many people's commonly held ideas about what constitutes rape, which are known as rape scripts. When people are asked to describe rape, they typically describe a woman who is physically attacked by a stranger and subsequently forced to have vaginal sexual intercourse with him. Afterwards, the woman reports this assault to the police like she would a robbery or other crime. Although this "stranger rape" scenario is the most common description of rape, it only accounts for a minority of women's reported rape experiences. Three out of four victims of rape report experiencing what is now known as "acquaintance rape" because they knew their assailant prior to the assault. Often, they were interested in some form of romantic or sexual contact with the perpetrator, such as dating or kissing, but did not consent to sexual intercourse. Another discrepancy between a typical rape script and many women's experience is the lack of physical force. In nearly half of rapes, victims reported drinking alcohol. When a person uses alcohol or drugs to the extent that she is passed out or too drunk or high to be aware of her actions, unwanted sex is considered "incapacitated rape." The substance use can be voluntary or involuntary, but the consequences of substance use are the same: Typical cognitive functioning, such as thinking clearly and making decisions, is impaired under the influence of alcohol. Therefore, consent is not possible.

These common misconceptions about rape create unique challenges for people who have experienced this form of sexual trauma. They are at risk for increased stigma and self-blame compared to victims of other trauma, leading to increased negative experiences when disclosing the rape to friends, family, or law enforcement officials. Because many people think of rape as a crime committed by strangers that leaves bruises and clear signs of force, women who experienced acquaintance rape or incapacitated rape are less likely to be believed by others. As a result, many women do not feel comfortable telling other people about their assault for fear of being accused of lying or blamed for the experience. Very few report their experiences to law enforcement, and among those that do, conviction rates are exceedingly low. The "just world hypothesis" is often used to explain why rape victims are susceptible to blame and shame from others. According to the just world hypothesis, good things happen to good people, and bad things happen to bad people. As a result, people are able to feel safer because

Photo: iStock

reminders of the rape, including internal reminders such as thoughts and feelings pertaining to the event, and external reminders such as people, places, activities, situations, or objects that remind the person of the rape. Avoidance symptoms may be a conscious effort to not experience the distress that occurs from intrusive symptoms. The third cluster refers to negative alterations in thinking or mood: inability to remember key aspects of the rape, strong negative beliefs about oneself or the world, a distorted sense of blame for the rape, persistent negative trauma-related emotions (e.g., fear, helplessness, horror, anger, and shame), significantly reduced interest in activities or other people, and difficulty experiencing positive emotions such as happiness. The last symptoms cluster refers to changes in arousal and reactivity: inability to concentrate or sleep soundly, a heightened startle response when surprised or afraid, hypervigilance (e.g., feeling on edge and in danger more frequently), and aggressive or reckless behavior. PTSD is associated with changes to the areas of the nervous system responsible for responding to threats. Traumas such as rape trigger survival instincts that take over the bodily response by increasing blood circulation to major muscle groups that are used in the "Fight, Flight, or Freeze" response in an effort to maximize our chances of escaping by fighting back, running away, or staying completely still. Mental capacities are often diminished in an effort to maximize this physical response, leading to difficulties thinking logically or forming memories. With PTSD, survivors continue to respond as though the threat is still present even in situations they used to consider safe. Thus, their autonomic nervous system continues to be triggered by perceived threats, leading to the symptoms described above.

In addition to PTSD, victims of rape often experience depression; in fact, when PTSD is present, a depressive diagnosis is also present in approximately half of trauma survivors. Suicidality, anxiety, alcohol and substance abuse, somatic complaints, sleep and eating disturbances, sexual difficulties, relationship difficulties, and physical problems are also common emotional consequences of rape. These symptoms tend to begin immediately and last a long time: More than 90% of rape survivors report many of these symptoms within a week of their assault, three-quarters have significant symptoms one year later, and one in six women report symptoms nearly decades after their assault. Furthermore, the intensity of psychological symptoms is comparable for

they consider themselves good people who are subsequently protected from negative events. A woman who is raped, therefore, must have done something to deserve it, because bad things do not happen to good people. As a result, people often assume that victims were sexually promiscuous or provocative prior to their sexual assault, and thus sent mixed signals of consent to the perpetrator.

THE PSYCHOLOGICAL CONSEQUENCES OF RAPE

Rape victims often endure significant emotional distress as a result of their traumatic experiences. Post-traumatic Stress Disorder (PTSD) is a psychological condition that may occur after any traumatic event. PTSD is a series of anxious symptoms that develop in the aftermath of trauma including rape. There are four symptoms clusters that characterize it. The first is intrusive symptoms: individuals continue to re-experience aspects of the rape through repeated, involuntary memories of the rape, nightmares about the rape, flashbacks (during which one feels as though the rape is happening again), and significant distress when reminded of the event. Intrusive symptoms cause significant distress for the person experiencing them. The second cluster of symptoms are those pertaining to avoidance: persistent efforts to avoid women who were raped by a stranger or an acquaintance, and for women who were incapacitated due to drugs or alcohol or were physically forced.

TREATMENT OPTIONS FOR RAPE SURVIVORS

During the last three decades, a number of treatments have been created, researched and identified as effective for survivors of rape. Individual psychotherapy is the most common treatment modality for the reduction of symptoms of PTSD and psychological distress. Many of the empirically supported treatments to reduce PTSD and other symptoms following rape incorporate similar therapeutic components. First, survivors are provided psychoeducation about trauma and PTSD so that they have a better understanding of their symptoms and its impact on the way they think, feel, and behave. Second, they learn and practice specific techniques to reduce overwhelming fear and anxiety and increase relaxation. Third, principles of exposure therapy are utilized. Survivors, with the help of their therapists, are asked to consciously recall the rape in vivid detail, either through writing or describing it aloud in therapy, so that the traumatic memories can be organized and processed in a safe, controlled manner, and cognitive distortions such as self-blame can be identified and challenged. Coping skills are utilized to reduce the distress that conscious recollection triggers, and this process is repeated until it is much less distressing for the individual to think about the rape in detail. In addition to individual therapy, there are forms of group therapy that have demonstrated effectiveness in treating posttraumatic symptoms of rape survivors. Psychopharmacology (i.e., medication) may be utilized to treat posttraumatic symptoms as well, as certain antidepressants and anti-anxiety medications are approved for the treatment of PTSD or concurrent depressive and anxious symptoms.

BIBLIOGRAPHY

American Psychiatric Association. (2013). *Diagnostic and Statistical Manual of Mental Disorders* (5th ed.). Arlington, VA: American Psychiatric Publishing. Diagnostic manual with criteria for trauma and for Post-Traumatic Stress Disorder.

Frazier, P. A., & Seales, L. M. (1997). Acquaintance Rape is Real Rape. In M. D. Schwartz (Ed.), *Researching Sexual Violence Against Women: Methodological and Personal Perspectives* (p. 54-64). Thousand Oaks, CA: Sage. Explains rape scripts and their impact on labeling rape experiences.

Groth, A.N. (1979). *Men Who Rape: The Psychology of the Offender.* New York, NY: Basic Books. Discusses psychological and motivational factors that shed light on the psyche of the offenders in rape.

Jackson, T.L. (Ed). (1996) *Acquaintance Rape: Assessment, Treatment, and Prevention.* Sarasota, FL: Professional Resource Press. A comprehensive compilation that discusses a wide range of research on acquaintance rape, especially how to assess when it occurs and types of therapies available to treat symptoms.

Katz, B., & Burt, M. (1988). Self-blame in Recovery from Rape: Help or Hindrance. In A.W. Burgess (Ed.), *Sexual Assault* (Vol. II, p. 151-168). New York, NY: Garland. This book chapter highlights the impact of self-blame and stigma in healing from rape.

Kilpatrick, D.G., Resnick, P.A. Ruggiero, Conoscenti, and McCauley. (2007). *Drug-facilitated, Incapacitated, and Forcible Rape: A National Study.* Final report submitted to the National Institute of Justice, NCJ 219181. A summary of the results of one of the largest studies about rape in the United States; it demonstrates rates of PTSD and depression in victims.

Koss, M.P. (1985). "The Hidden Rape Victim: Personality, Attitudinal, and Situational Characteristics". *Psychology of Women Quarterly*, 9, 192-212. The first of a series of papers by Dr. Koss and colleagues that set the groundwork for research on women who do not report rape experiences and the infrequency of reporting to authorities.

Koss, M.P. (1988). Hidden rape: Sexual aggression and victimization in the national sample of students in higher education. In M.A. Pirog-Good & J.E. Stets (Eds.), *Violence in Dating Relationships: Emerging Social Issues* (p. 145-168). New York, NY: Praeger. Further early work of Dr. Koss that elucidated the frequency of acquaintance and incapacitated rape on college campuses.

Koss, M.P., Dinero, T.E., Siebel, C.A & Cox, S.L. (1988). "Stranger and Acquaintance Rape: Are There Differences in the Victim's Experience?" *Psychology of Women Quarterly*, 12, 1-24. Demonstrated that acquaintance rape victims suffer similar psychological consequences as stranger rape victims.

Lerner, M.J. & Miller, D.T. (1977). "Just World Research and the Attribution Process: Looking Back and Ahead". *Psychological Bulletin*, 85, 1030-1051. Article that further explains the "just world phenomenon."

N.Y. Const. §130.05. The law that defines "rape" and "consent" for New York State.

Rothbaum, B.O., Foa, E.B., Riggs, D.S., Murdock, T., and Walsh, W. (1992). "A Prospective Examination of Post-Traumatic Stress Disorder in Rape Victims. *Journal of Traumatic Stress*, 5(3), 455-274. Examines when PTSD symptoms develop in the aftermath of rape as well as their longevity over time.

Vasterling, J.J., and Brewer, C.R., (Eds.). (2005). Neuropsychology of PTSD: *Biological, Cognitive, and Clinical Perspectives.* New York, NY: The Guilford Press. This book provides a comprehensive examination of the effects that rape and other psychological traumas have on the brain, including the role of fight, flight, and freeze on memory and information processing.

Linda Smith

SEE ALSO: Abuse; Crime; Sex offenses; Sexual abuse; Trauma; Victimization

Rape and sexual assault

TYPE OF PSYCHOLOGY: Psychopathology

The study of rape and sexual assault examines the relationship of sexually disordered persons and nonconsensual sexual activity with others. Rape is an assaultive behavior of one person on another, where the assault involves sexual activity and the behavior involves one person fulfilling sexual desires by using a nonconsenting person.

KEY CONCEPTS
- Rape
- Rapist profiles
- Sexual paraphilias
- Stalking behavior

INTRODUCTION

Sexual assault is the threat or actual act of sexual physical endangerment of a nonconsensual person or legally defined minor child, regardless of consent. Rape is forced sexual penetration of a nonconsensual person or legally defined minor child, regardless of consent. Definitions of sexual assault and rape are further delineated by states' criminal codes. *The Crime Classification Manual* (1992) notes that "definitions of what constitutes rape and sexual assault vary from state to state, resulting in marked differences in the reported frequencies of offense and behavior categories in different samples reported in the literature."

According to the Office of Justice Programs of the US Department of Justice, 287,100 attempted or completed rapes or sexual assault victimizations against adolescents and adults were reported to law-enforcement agencies in 2010. This figure represents a victim ratio of 2.1 females in every 1,000 persons over age twelve and 0.1 males in every 1,000 persons over age twelve. However, it is significant to note that rape and sexual assault are the most underreported of the index crimes. Aggravated assault, robbery, and murder are commonly reported at near incidence level, but sex-related crimes are often not reported or are charged inaccurately.

Married or cohabiting people may be victims of forced sexual activity but do not report the behavior of their partner, or if they do report the behavior, it is commonly considered domestic violence and the formal legal charge is reduced to simple assault and does not represent the true, sexual nature of the assault. The question as to whether a husband can rape his wife has been debated in many courtrooms. The cross-examination of the victim is often a humiliating experience, and consequently, many victims choose not to press charges against the offender. Many women choose not to report forcible intercourse if they had previously been a consensual partner with the offender. It is also common that while children who are sexually molested by a parent are removed from the home under an order of child abuse, the offending parent is not charged with rape or sexual assault.

SEXUAL PARAPHILIAS

The American Psychiatric Association's *Diagnostic and Statistical Manual of Mental Disorders* (DSM-5) recognizes a group of disorders known as sexual paraphilias. The essential features of a paraphilia are recurrent, intense, sexually arousing fantasies, sexual urges, or behaviors, generally involving nonhuman objects or the suffering or humiliation of oneself or one's partner or children or other nonconsenting persons. Paraphilic disorders are paraphilias that occur over a period of at least six months and cause distress or impairment to the individual or cause harm to others. For some individuals, paraphilic fantasies or stimuli are obligatory for erotic arousal and are always included in the sexual activity.

It is significant to note that not all sexual paraphilias result in sexual assault or rape, and it is the preference of individuals who have paraphilias to identify consensual adult partners. It is also significant to note that the majority of those with known sexual paraphilias are male. However, some of the paraphilias are specific to nonconsensual parties and children. Children, because of their age, by law cannot consent to sexual activity. There are a handful of paraphilias that are commonly associated with nonconsensual partners.

Exhibitionism. Exhibitionism is defined as "behaviors involving the exposure of one's genitals to an unsuspecting stranger." The nature of this paraphilia requires a nonconsensual relationship with a stranger; consequently, it must be considered a form of sexual assault.

Frotteurism. Frotteurism is defined as "touching and rubbing against a nonconsensual person." A frotteur (usually a man) rubs his genitals against the victim, often in a crowded public place, or fondles the victim. Like exhibitionism, the nature of this paraphilia requires a nonconsensual victim and, consequently, must be considered a sexual assault.

Voyeurism. Voyeurism is defined as "the act of observing unsuspecting individuals, usually strangers, who are naked, in the process of disrobing, or engaging in sexual activity." A voyeur (usually a man) is sexually excited by looking ("peeping"), sometimes masturbating to orgasm either in the process of peeping or later while retrospectively reviewing what he has seen, but does not seek actual sexual contact with the victims. As in the previous paraphilias, the nature of voyeurism requires a nonconsenting person and, consequently, is considered a sexual assault.

Pedophilia. Pedophilia is defined as "recurrent, intense sexually arousing fantasies, sexual urges, or behaviors involving sexual activity with a prepubescent child or children (generally age thirteen years or younger)." State statutes define the minimum age at which a person may consent to sexual relations. Pedophilic behavior is by definition a violation of law and consequently is a sexual assault.

Sexual Sadism. Sexual sadism is defined as "recurrent, intense, sexually arousing fantasies, sexual urges, or behaviors involving acts (real, not simulated) in which the psychological or physical suffering (including humiliation) of the victim is sexually exciting to the person." Persons with this sexual paraphilia are continuously looking for a consensual partner. The practice of sexual sadism is commonly comorbid with sexual masochism. Sexual masochism is defined as "recurrent, intense, sexually arousing fantasies, sexual urges, or behaviors involving the act (real, not simulated) of being humiliated, beaten, bound, or otherwise made to suffer."

People with one or both of these sexual paraphilias frequent bars and social clubs where sadists and masochists congregate. They are able to establish consensual relationships and mutually satisfy their sexual urges. In the absence of a consensual partner, or when a masochistic party refuses to proceed as far as the sadist desires, the sadist may force compliance and a sexual assault takes place. Sexual assaults that occur because the masochist refuses to continue to participate are rarely reported. When no consensual partners are available and the sadist is experiencing intense sexual arousal, the sadist may forcibly rape a nonconsensual stranger party.

RAPE

The concept of rape has a historical and common definition of a man forcing a nonconsenting woman to engage in sexual intercourse. The definition is no longer contemporary. Men and women engage in sexual intercourse with children under the legal age of consent and, consequently, meet the statutory definition of rape. Men and women also engage in same-sex relationships that may result in behaviors that may be, in fact, forcible sexual assault or may be rape as defined by statute. Some hate-motivated crimes involve rape and sodomy. Consequently, the entire legal and philosophical concept of rape must be viewed from an expanded, inclusive definition.

The *Crime Classification Manual* includes a taxonomy of rape and sexual assault that outlines numerous categories: child pornography; criminal-enterprise rape; felony rape; personal cause sexual assault; nuisance offenses; domestic sexual assault; opportunistic rape, including social acquaintance rape, authority rape, power-reassurance rape, and exploitative rape; anger rape; sadistic rape; abduction rape; group-cause sexual assault; formal gang sexual assault, informal gang sexual assault; military sexual harassment; and military sexual assault/rape. The manual also classifies rapists based on motivations.

The taxonomic studies that describe the styles of convicted rapists focus on the interaction of sexual and aggressive motivations. Although all rape clearly includes both motivations, for some rapists, the need to humiliate and injure through aggression is the most salient feature of the offense, whereas for others the need to achieve sexual dominance is the most salient feature of the offense. John Douglas and Robert Ressler, both retired Federal Bureau of Investigation (FBI) agents who were the initial founders of the FBI's Behavioral Sciences Unit, identified four primary subcategories of rapists: power-reassurance, exploitative, anger, and sadistic.

Power-Reassurance Rapist. Referred to as a "compensatory rapist," this individual is commonly afflicted with one or more of the sexual paraphilic disorders, and these paraphilias are clearly demonstrated in the method in which the rape is preformed. These rapists are preoccupied with their particular sexual fantasies and commonly have a vision of their "perfect" victim. They are highly sexually aroused as they attempt to locate their "perfect" victim and may demonstrate voyeurism, exhibitionism, masturbation practices, and pedophilia. They are delusional, believing that their victim truly loves them in return. These individuals commonly cannot achieve and maintain normal, age-appropriate heterosexual or homosexual relationships and compensate for their personal perception of inadequacy by stalking and assaulting a younger or older, and weaker, victim.

Exploitative Rapist. The exploitative rapist, also referred to as an "impulsive rapist," commits the crime of rape as an afterthought while committing another crime. These rapes generally occur when a victim is found at the site of a burglary or armed robbery. There is no premeditation in this rape, and the motivation is purely coincidental to the original intended criminal activity. It is not uncommon for persons to take hostages during an armed robbery or carjacking and then impulsively rape the hostage.

Anger Rapist. The anger rapist, also referred to a "displaced aggressive rapist," commits sexual assault because of anger. This rapist is commonly not angry with the victims, because they are usually strangers. Rather, the displaced aggressive rapist is angry with someone or something else, perhaps a boss, a spouse, or just a set of circumstances. Unable to express anger at the source, he displaces his anger on the victim. The rape is characterized by very violent behavior, and the victim is commonly severely injured and may be killed.

Sadistic Rapist. The sadistic rapist, also referred to as a "sexually aggressive rapist," possesses the sexual sadism paraphilia and cannot achieve sexual arousal or satisfaction unless inflicting pain on a victim. The rapist believes that the victim likes his or her sex rough and, consequently, will demonstrate a variety of torturous behaviors during the rape. While the rape is violent, it does differ from the rape by the displaced aggression rapist. The sexually aggressive rapist will demonstrate behaviors that have sexual overtones, while the displaced aggressive rapist will demonstrate unrestrained violence, more violence than is necessary to subdue the victim.

Other Rapist Classifications. Other classifications of rapists include gang rapists motivated by retaliation, intimidation, or juvenile impulsivity. Persons who use drugs to incapacitate their victims are generally compensating for their inability to achieve normal sexual relations and are commonly personality disordered.

BIBLIOGRAPHY

American Psychiatric Association. *Diagnostic and Statistical Manual of Mental Disorders: DSM-5.* Washington: Amer. Psychiatric Assn., 2013. Print.

Bartol, Curt, and Anne M. Bartol. *Criminal Behavior: A Psychosocial Approach.* 10th ed. Upper Saddle River: Pearson Education, 2012. Print.

Dobbert, Duane, ed. *Forensic Psychology.* Columbus: McGraw, 1996. Print.

Douglas, John E., Ann W. Burgess, Allen G. Burgess, and Robert K. Ressler. *Crime Classification Manual.* 3rd ed. Hoboken: Wiley, 2013. Print.

Goode, Erich. *Deviant Behavior.* 10th ed. Upper Saddle River: Pearson, 2014. Print.

Planty, Michael, et al. *Female Victims of Sexual Violence, 1994–2010.* Ed. Catherine Bird and Jill Thomas. Office of Justice Programs, US Dept. of Justice, Mar. 2013. PDF file.

Duane L. Dobbert

SEE ALSO: Battered woman syndrome; Children's mental health; Domestic violence; Elder abuse; Juvenile delinquency; Law and psychology; Sadism and masochism; Sexual variants and paraphilias; Violence by children and teenagers; Violence: Causes and effects; Violence and sexuality in the media; Women's mental health.

Rational emotive therapy

TYPE OF PSYCHOLOGY: Psychotherapy

Developed by psychologist Albert Ellis, rational emotive therapy aims to minimize the client's self-defeating cognitive style by helping the client acquire a more rational and logical philosophy of life. It has been successfully applied to marital couples, family members, individual patients, and group clients across a host of psychological difficulties, including alcoholism, depression, anxiety disorders, and sexual dissatisfaction.

KEY CONCEPTS
- A-B-C theory of personality
- Irrational beliefs
- Long-range hedonism
- Rational emotive treatment
- Scientific thinking

INTRODUCTION

Rational emotive behavior therapy (REBT), originally called rational emotive therapy, was founded in 1955 by Albert Ellis following his disappointment with traditional methods of psychoanalysis. From 1947 to 1953, Ellis had practiced classical analysis and analytically oriented psychotherapy, but he came to the conclusion that psychoanalysis was a superficial and unscientific form of treatment. Specifically, rational emotive therapy was developed as a combined humanistic, cognitive, and behavioral form of therapy. Although Ellis initially used REBT primarily in individual formats, group and workshop formats followed quickly. Ellis published approximately fifty books and more than five hundred articles on REBT, and he presented more than fifteen hundred public workshops.

According to Ellis (in 1989), the philosophical origins of rational emotive therapy include the Stoic philosophers Epictetus and Marcus Aurelius. In particular, during the first century c.e. in *The Encheiridion,* Epictetus wrote that "people are disturbed not by things, but by the view which they take of them." Ellis also gives much credit for the development of rational emotive therapy to the theory of human disturbance highlighted by psychotherapist Alfred Adler. Specifically, Ellis was persuaded by Adler's conviction that a person's behavior originates from his or her ideas. As Ellis began writing about and describing REBT in the 1950s and 1960s, clinical behavior therapy was conceptually distinct and distant from Ellis's ideas. The primary similarity was that Ellis employed a host of behavioral techniques in his approach.

As time passed, however, behavior therapy engaged in a controversial yet productive broadening of what was meant by behavior and started to include cognition as a form of behavior that could be learned, modified, and studied. Ellis's REBT approach shares many similarities with other common cognitive behavior approaches to treatment. These include Donald Meichenbaum's cognitive behavior modification (focusing on self-instructional processes and adaptive coping statements), Maxie C. Maultsby, Jr.'s, rational behavior therapy (which is essentially REBT with some adaptations, including written

self-analysis techniques and rational emotive imagery), and Aaron T. Beck's cognitive therapy. Cognitive therapy has many similarities to REBT but was developed independently; it uses fewer "hard-headed approaches." For example, Beck advocates the use of collaborative empiricism and a focus on automatic thoughts and underlying cognitive schemas. REBT strongly emphasizes irrational beliefs (unreasonable evaluations that sabotage an individual's goals and lead to increased likelihood of experiencing needless pain, suffering, and displeasure), especially "unconditional shoulds" and "absolutistic musts," as the root of emotional and behavioral disturbances.

PRINCIPAL PROPOSITIONS

There are six principal propositions of rational emotive therapy as Ellis described them in 1989. First, people are born with rational and irrational tendencies. That is, individuals may be either self-helping or self-defeating, short-range hedonists or long-range hedonists; they may learn by mistakes or repeat the same mistakes, and they may actualize or avoid actualizing their potentials for growth. Second, cultural and family experiences may exacerbate irrational thinking. Third, individuals may seem to think, act, and feel simultaneously. Thinking, however, appears actually to precede actions and feelings. For example, the process of "appraising" a situation usually triggers feelings.

Fourth, REBT therapists differ from person-centered therapists in that REBT practitioners do not believe that a warm interpersonal relationship between therapist and patient is a sufficient or even necessary condition for effective change. REBT therapists also do not believe that personal warmth is necessary to accept clients fully. In fact, it is important in REBT treatment to criticize and point out the deficiencies in a person's behavior and thinking style. Moreover, Ellis argues that REBT therapists often need to use "hard-headed methods" to convince clients to employ more self-discipline.

Fifth, rational emotive therapists use a variety of strategies, including assertiveness training, desensitization, operant conditioning, support, and role-playing. The usual goal of REBT is to help rid clients of symptoms and modify underlying thinking styles that create symptoms. Ellis further identifies two basic forms of REBT: general REBT, which is similar to other forms of cognitive behavior therapy; and preferential REBT, which includes general REBT but also emphasizes philosophic restructuring and teaches clients how to dispute irrational thoughts and inappropriate behaviors via rules of logic and the scientific method. Sixth, all emotional problems are caused by people's tendencies to interpret events unrealistically and are maintained by irrational beliefs about them.

CONNECTIONS WITH IRRATIONALITY

Thus, the basic underlying tenet of REBT is that emotional disturbances are primarily the result of irrational thinking. Specifically, REBT argues that people upset themselves with "evaluative irrational beliefs"(rather than with "nonevaluative" irrational beliefs). For example, in an essay published in 1987, Ellis described the following scenario:

> If you devoutly believe that your fairy godmother looks out for you and is always ready to help you, you may live happily and undisturbedly with this highly questionable and unrealistic belief. But if you evaluate your fairy godmother's help as extremely desirable and go even further to insist that because it is desirable, you absolutely must at all times have her help, you will almost certainly make yourself anxious (whenever you realize that her magical help that you must have may actually be absent) and you will tend to make yourself extremely depressed (when you see that in your hour of need this help does not actually materialize).

Although many forms of irrationality exist, rational emotive therapy focuses on a client's strong "desires" and "commands." Ellis has developed various lists of irrational beliefs that highlight the most common thinking difficulties of patients. These include such beliefs as "I must do well or very well"; "I am a bad or worthless person when I act weakly or stupidly"; "I need to be loved by someone who matters to me a lot"; "People must treat me fairly and give me what I need"; "People must live up to my expectations or it is terrible"; "My life must have few major hassles"; and "I can't stand it when life is unfair."

Ellis has refined his ideas about irrational thoughts to three primary beliefs. These are: "I *must* do well and be approved by *significant* others, and if I don't do as well as I *should* or *must,* there is something really rotten about me. It is terrible that I am this way and I am a pretty worthless, rotten person"; "You (other humans with whom I relate, my original family, my later family that I may have, my friends, relatives, and people with whom I work) *must, ought,* and *should* treat me considerately and fairly and even *specially* (considering what a doll I am)!"; and "Conditions under which I live—my environment, social conditions, economic conditions, political conditions—must be arranged so that I easily and immediately, with no real effort, have a free lunch and get what I command." In summary, Ellis defines the three primary irrationalities as "I *must* do well; you *must* treat me beautifully; the world *must* be easy."

ORIGIN OF IRRATIONAL BELIEFS AND ACTIONS

Psychological disturbances are based on irrational thinking and behaving. The origin of irrational beliefs and actions stems from childhood. Irrational beliefs are shaped in part by significant others (parents, relatives, and teachers), as well as from misperceptions on the part of children (such as superstitions and overinterpretation). Rational emotive therapy also maintains that individuals have tendencies, which are both biologically and environmentally determined, for growth and actualization of their potential. Ellis argues that people also have powerful innate tendencies to condemn themselves, others, and the world when they do not get what they "childishly need." This pattern of self-sabotage is argued by Ellis to be both inborn and acquired during childhood. Moreover, via repetitive self-talk and self-evaluative tendencies, false beliefs are continually reindoctrinated by the individual. From the REBT perspective, self-blame and self-condemnation are the cornerstones of most emotional disturbances. By challenging self-blame and self-condemnation, via an analysis and refutation of irrational beliefs, a client can be helped.

ASSESSING MENTAL HEALTH

Ellis defines mental health as incorporating self-interest, social interests, self-direction, tolerance, acceptance of ambiguity and uncertainty, scientific thinking, commitment, risk taking, self-acceptance, long-range hedonism (the idea that well-adjusted people seek happiness and avoid pain today, tomorrow, and in the future), nonperfectionism, and self-responsibility for one's emotional disturbances. Three primary processes seem to be associated with mental functioning and mental disorders: self-talking, self-evaluating, and self-condemning. That is, individuals are constantly engaged in an internal dialogue (self-talk) with themselves, appraising and commenting on events that occur in their lives. Individuals also are self-evaluating in that humans seek meaning and constantly evaluate events and themselves, frequently placing blame on themselves for events. Self-evaluating is thus often associated with self-condemnation. As Ellis pointed out in an essay published in 1989, this condemnation may start in response to evaluating oneself as doing poorly at work or in school, which in turn leads to feeling guilty. This vicious cycle then leads to condemning oneself for condemning oneself, condemning oneself for not being able to stop condemning oneself, and finally condemning oneself for entering psychotherapy and not getting better.

Emotional and behavioral difficulties often occur when simple preferences are chosen above thoughtful decisions. Ellis believes that individuals have inborn growth and actualization tendencies, although they may become sabotaged through self-defeating and self-condemning patterns. Based on the REBT model, clients benefit from exposure to three primary insights. Insight number one is that a person's self-defeating behavior is related to antecedent and understandable causes. Specifically, an individual's beliefs are more important in understanding emotional upset than are past or present activating events. Insight number two is that individuals make themselves emotionally disturbed by reindoctrinating themselves with irrational and unproductive kinds of beliefs. Insight number three is that through hard work and practice, irrational beliefs can be corrected.

TREATMENT STEPS

As detailed by Gerald Corey in 1986, practitioners of rational emotive therapy actively teach, persuade, and direct clients to alter irrational styles of thinking and behaving. REBT can be defined as a process of reeducation in which clients learn to think differently and solve problems. The first step in treatment often focuses on distinguishing rational (or reasonable) thoughts from irrational (or unreasonable) beliefs. Educational approaches are employed to highlight for the client that he or she has acquired many irrational "shoulds, oughts, and musts." The second step in treatment emphasizes an awareness of how psychological disturbances are maintained through a client's repeated reindoctrination of illogical and unreasonable beliefs. During the third phase of treatment, therapists assist clients in modifying maladaptive thinking styles and abandoning irrational beliefs. Via a variety of cognitive, emotive, and behavioral approaches, self-condemnation and self-blame are replaced with more rational and logical views. Finally, the fourth step in REBT involves developing a rational lifestyle and philosophy. Specifically, from internalizing rules of logic and scientific thinking, individuals may prevent future psychological disturbances and live more productive lives.

A-B-C THEORIES

The A-B-C theory of personality and the A-B-C (D-E) theory of emotional change are also central to REBT approaches. "A" refers to an activating event. Activating events can include facts, events, behaviors, or perceived stimuli. "B" refers to beliefs triggered by the event or beliefs about the event. "C" refers to the consequential emotional (behavioral or cognitive) outcomes that proceed directly from beliefs. "D" is the application of methods to dispute or challenge irrational beliefs, and "E" refers to the effect of disputing beliefs on the emotional (behavioral or cognitive) reaction of the client.

Activating events are generally regarded as inherently neutral, and they have no particular emotional meaning in and of themselves. Thus, activating events do not directly cause emotions. Instead, beliefs about events primarily cause emotional reactions. For example, a woman who had been depressed for more than twelve months following the death of her husband from terminal cancer was participating in a hospice therapy group and had demonstrated little or no improvement over the last year. She reasoned that because her husband was dead, she would never feel happy again (nor "should" she feel happy again, since he was dead and she was "not entitled" to experience pleasure without him). She added, "He was the center of my life and I can never expect to feel happiness without him." Her resulting emotional reaction was severe depression, which accompanied her complicated grief and underlying anger.

In an effort to uncover and dispute her unreasonable beliefs, several strategies were employed. First, group members provided feedback about her reasonable and unreasonable ideas following (and during) her husband's death. In particular, group members pointed out that she could expect to experience happiness again in her life since she had experienced pleasure on many occasions before she met her husband, while her husband was away during military service, and while they were married and she enjoyed activities in which he did not share. Next, her emotional reaction was examined and viewed as being caused not by her husband's death, but instead by the manner in which she interpreted his death (as awful), her own ability to cope and change (as limited), and her future (as hopeless). A variety of behavioral and cognitive strategies were employed to challenge her irrational and self-condemning assumptions. Behavioral homework assignments included increasing activity levels and engaging in pleasurable activities to challenge the notion that she could never experience happiness again. Self-confidence and hope were fostered via strategies that highlighted her ability to cope with stress. This client also found cognitive homework assignments, wherein she listed her irrational beliefs on a daily log and then disputed those beliefs or replaced or modified them with more reasonable statements, to be helpful.

LIMITATIONS

Rational emotive therapy and its various techniques have been evaluated in at least two hundred studies. Although many of these studies have been associated with various methodological flaws, the effectiveness of REBT with a broad range of psychological disturbances is impressive. At the Evolution of Psychotherapy Conference in Phoenix, Arizona, in 1985, Ellis identified several limitations of REBT (and other therapies). These included several key "irrationalities." Because individuals falsely believe that they are unchangeable, they fail to work to change themselves. Because individuals falsely believe that activating events cause emotional reactions, they blame the activating events and fail to change their beliefs about them. Individuals falsely believe that unpleasant emotional reactions must be good or useful and should be cherished instead of minimized. Individuals are often confused about emotional reactions (for example, concern and caution versus anxiety and panic) and experience difficulty surrendering the inappropriate negative feelings. Because some REBT techniques require subtle and discriminative styles of thinking by clients, some clients are not capable of succeeding in therapy. REBT is not particularly useful for young children or developmentally delayed individuals (typically REBT requires a chronological age of at least eight years and average intelligence).

CRITICISMS

Ellis is regarded by many psychologists as the most prominent theorist in the cognitive behavioral school of psychotherapy. His insight and conceptualizations are evident in many of the various cognitive behavioral psychotherapeutic approaches. Specifically, the A-B-C theory of personality is well regarded among cognitive behavioral therapists, and many of Ellis's treatment strategies are frequently used by clinicians across other schools of psychotherapy. Ellis's interpersonal style in treatment has been criticized by many authors. Specifi-

cally, a warm, confiding relationship between therapist and client is often deemphasized in Ellis's writings, and confrontational interactions may be commonly observed in videotapes of rational emotive therapy. It also appears, however, that more attention is being paid to the quality of the interpersonal relationship between REBT practitioner and client. Moreover, the strengths of the REBT approach are not based on the style of any particular therapist but instead are evident in its underlying theory and therapeutic strategies.

Undoubtedly, the influence of rational emotive therapy in the field of psychotherapy will continue to be prominent. Ellis has written extensively on the application of REBT principles to diverse psychological disturbances. The Institute for Rational Emotive Therapy in New York continues to train hundreds of therapists and serves as a distribution center for most of the books and pamphlets developed by REBT therapists.

BIBLIOGRAPHY

Corey, Gerald. *Theory and Practice of Counseling and Psychotherapy.* 8th ed. Belmont: Thomson, 2009. Print.

Dryden, Windy. *Rational Emotive Behavior Therapy: Distinctive Features.* London: Routledge, 2009. Print.

Dryden, Windy, Daniel David, and Albert Ellis. "Rational Emotive Behavior Therapy." *Handbook of Cognitive-Behavioral Therapies.* Ed. Keith S. Dobson. 3rd ed. New York: Guilford, 2010. 226–76. Print.

Dryden, Windy, and Raymond Digiuseppe. *A Primer on Rational-Emotive Behavior Therapy.* Champaign: Research, 2003. Print.

Ellis, Albert. *Better, Deeper, and More Enduring Brief Therapy: The Rational Emotive Behavior Therapy Approach.* New York: Brunner, 1996. Print.

Ellis, Albert. *Overcoming Destructive Beliefs, Feelings, and Behaviors: New Directions for Rational Emotive Behavior Therapy.* Buffalo: Prometheus, 2001. Print.

Ellis, Albert, and Robert A. Harper. *A New Guide to Rational Living.* 3d rev. ed. North Hollywood: Wilshire, 1998. Print.

Robertson, Donald. *The Philosophy of Cognitive-Behavioral Therapy (CBT): Stoic Philosophy as Rational and Cognitive Psychotherapy.* London: Karnac, 2010. Print.

Gregory L. Wilson

SEE ALSO: Behavior therapy; Cognitive behavior therapy; Cognitive therapy; Couples therapy; Depression; Ellis, Albert; Environmental factors and mental health; Genetics and mental health; Group therapy; Hospice; Person-centered therapy; Psychotherapy: Effectiveness; Psychotherapy: Goals and techniques; Self-actualization; Strategic family therapy.

Reactive attachment disorder (RAD)

TYPE OF PSYCHOLOGY: Developmental psychology; Psychopathology

Reactive attachment disorder (RAD) is a variant of a general condition of impoverished psychosocial and physical development found in infants and children deprived of appropriate caretaking. The symptoms of RAD are believed to remit in an improved environment with a responsive caregiver.

KEY CONCEPTS
- Attachment theory
- Attachment therapy
- Developmental delays
- Failure to thrive
- Hospitalism
- Psychosocial development

INTRODUCTION

Since the 1940s, a substantial body of literature has documented the adverse effects of deprivation and institutionalization on infants and young children. Physical, cognitive, and social developmental delays are often present in such children. In a classic study published in 1945, René Spitz examined a group of children in an orphanage and compared them with children reared in a more attentive foster home setting. His results revealed slowed physical, motor, and intellectual development and high mortality in the orphanage group compared with essentially normal development in the comparison children. Several terms have been used to describe the diverse clinical features of this condition, including failure to thrive, psychosocial dwarfism, maternal deprivation, anaclitic depression, and, most recently, reactive attachment disorder (RAD). This plethora of different terms probably reflects a deeper confusion regarding this syndrome's symptom picture and etiology.

DESCRIPTION

RAD was first included in the third edition of the *Diagnostic and Statistical Manual of Mental Disorders* (DSM-III), published in 1980. In subsequent editions, the criteria were altered to reflect an emphasis on psychosocial maladjustment rather than on disrupted physical development. The fifth edition, DSM-5 (2013), describes the cardinal feature of RAD as disturbed and developmentally inappropriate social relations produced by persistent neglect or abuse on the part of the child's caregiver. Prior to the DSM-5, RAD was considered to have two subtypes, inhibited and disinhibited, but in the DSM-5, the disinhibited type was split into a separate disorder, disinhibited social engagement disorder.

Children with RAD are emotionally withdrawn and fail to initiate social relations, particularly with caregivers. They rarely express positive emotions and often do not seek or respond to comfort when distressed. This contrasts with disinhibited social engagement disorder, which is characterized by indiscriminate sociability and a lack of selectivity in seeking out attachment figures. RAD is believed to be the more common of the two, although trustworthy estimates of its prevalence are difficult to come by. Some researchers estimate that RAD occurs in approximately 1 percent of the population, while the DSM states only that it is "very uncommon."

The onset of RAD occurs before five years of age. Prior to the fourth edition of the DSM, it was required that RAD emerge before six months, but this criterion was altered in response to researchers' objections that selective attachments are not formed at such an early age. Nevertheless, the current criteria still allow clinicians to diagnose infants with RAD if they see fit.

Associated features of RAD include the physical signs of an impoverished rearing environment, such as developmental delays, feeding disorders, growth delays (that is, failure to thrive), physical abuse, and malnutrition. With the provision of a supportive environment and adequate caretaking for the child, the behavioral difficulties associated with RAD should ostensibly remit.

Other disorders that emerge in childhood can be difficult to distinguish from RAD. Children with RAD may manifest subnormal intellectual functioning comparable to that of children with developmental disabilities, but RAD can be differentiated by the improvement that typically occurs with an enriched environment. Autistic children often exhibit impaired communication and repetitious patterns of movement, but RAD children are much more socially oriented. Although adverse environmental conditions and pathogenic relationships in childhood may increase the risk for later antisocial behavior, no direct etiological links have been established between these behaviors and the characteristics of RAD.

CONTROVERSIES

Controversies abound concerning the conceptualization, diagnosis, and treatment of RAD. Foremost is the striking paucity of evidence for the validity of this diagnosis. For example, there is little controlled research examining the family history, course, and outcome, biological correlates, or laboratory performance of children with RAD. Such validity research will be essential to justify the continued inclusion of RAD in the diagnostic system.

With respect to the DSM-5 criteria, some researchers, such as Fred Volkmar, object to the stipulation that RAD must be the product of adverse caretaking. This requirement renders it impossible to ascertain the prevalence of RAD among children not subjected to pathogenic care.

Another diagnostic controversy concerns the labeling of RAD as an attachment disorder. Some developmental psychologists suggest that RAD is best conceptualized as a developmental disorder or a maltreatment syndrome. As conceptualized in the developmental literature, the prominent feature of disordered attachment is a disturbance in the child's use of a primary caregiver as a base of safety and security. From this point of view, evidence of an attachment disorder would require assessment of the child on a number of dimensions not included in the RAD criteria (such as comfort seeking, exploratory behavior, or affectionate responses). Moreover, findings in the child maltreatment literature suggest that although maltreated children often develop insecure or disorganized relational patterns to cope with the erratic care they receive, this is not necessarily synonymous with disordered attachment. Lastly, some developmental researchers note that the organic correlates of the conditions from which RAD derived (such as hospitalism or failure to thrive) have not been causally linked to attachment problems.

A third area of controversy surrounding RAD is the emergence of unvalidated and potentially dangerous attachment therapies, which are sometimes used with disruptive children and adolescents believed to be traumatized by early adverse emotional experiences or adoption. Attachment therapies include rebirthing (a procedure in which several adults simulate the birth process by constricting children in blankets and pillows and pushing them down the makeshift "birth canal"), holding therapy (in which the therapist forcefully restrains the child to achieve "rage reduction" and ostensibly correct aberrations in the "bonding cycle"), and therapeutic parenting (a strict regimen approved by attachment therapists by which parents exert their authority and impose rigid controls on the child). Rebirthing has been linked to several tragic incidents, including the 2000 death in Colorado of Candace Newmaker, a ten-year-old girl who suffocated during the process as her therapists ignored her cries for help. Despite the absence of well-controlled studies in peer-reviewed journals supporting the efficacy of attachment therapies, many proponents of these techniques claim that they are effective and safe. Responsible mental health professionals must take further steps to protect the public from the ever-growing industry of attachment therapies and similar unvalidated treatments.

BIBLIOGRAPHY

Brisch, Karl Heinz. *Treating Attachment Disorders: From Theory to Therapy.* Trans. Kenneth Kronenberg. New York: Guilford, 2004. Print.

Cain, Catherine Swanson. *Attachment Disorders: Treatment Strategies for Traumatized Children.* Lanham: Aronson, 2006. Print.

Davis, Andrew S. *Psychopathology of Childhood and Adolescence: A Neuropsychological Approach.* New York: Springer, 2013. Print.

Gleason, Mary Margaret, et al. "Validity of Evidence-Derived Criteria for Reactive Attachment Disorder: Indiscriminately Social/Disinhibited and Emotionally Withdrawn/Inhibited Types." *Journal of the American Academy of Child and Adolescent Psychiatry* 50.3 (2011): 216–31. Print.

Mercer, Jean. "'Attachment Therapy' Using Deliberate Restraint: An Object Lesson on the Identification of Unvalidated Treatments." *Journal of Child and Adolescent Psychiatric Nursing* 14.2 (2001): 105–114. Print.

Money, John. *The Kaspar Hauser Syndrome of "Psychosocial Dwarfism": Deficient Statural, Intellectual, and Social Growth Induced by Child Abuse.* Amherst: Prometheus, 1992. Print.

Richters, Margot Moser, and Fred R. Volkmar. "Reactive Attachment Disorder of Infancy or Early Childhood." *Journal of American Academy of Child and Adolescent Psychiatry* 33.3 (1994): 328–332. Print.

Shreeve, Daniel F. *Reactive Attachment Disorder: A Case-Based Approach.* New York: Springer, 2012. Print.

Spitz, René. "Hospitalism: An Inquiry into the Genesis of Psychiatric Conditions in Early Childhood."

Psychoanalytic Study of the Child 1 (1945): 53–74. Print.

Volkmar, Fred R. "Reactive Attachment Disorder." *DSM-IV Sourcebook*, ed. Thomas A. Widiger, Allen J. Frances, Harold Alan Pincus, Ruth Ross, Michael B. First, and Wendy Davis. Vol. 3. Washington, DC: Amer. Psychological Assoc., 1997. Print.

Katherine A. Fowler and Scott O. Lilienfeld

SEE ALSO: Attachment and bonding in infancy and childhood; Children's mental health; Family life: Children's issues; Mother-child relationship.

Reality therapy

TYPE OF PSYCHOLOGY: Psychotherapy

Reality therapy is a system of counseling or psychotherapy that attempts to help clients accept responsibility for their behavior. Its aim is to teach clients more appropriate patterns of behavior. Its significance is that it helps clients meet their basic needs more effectively.

KEY CONCEPTS
- Freedom
- Morality of behavior
- Responsibility
- Success identity

INTRODUCTION

William Glasser, the founder of reality therapy, believes that people are motivated to fulfill five basic needs: belonging, power, freedom, fun, and survival. When these needs are not met, problems begin. Individuals lose touch with the objective reality of life (what is appropriate behavior and what is not) and often stray into patterns of behavior that are self-defeating or destructive. The reality therapist attempts to help such people by teaching them more appropriate patterns of behavior. This, in turn, will enable individuals to meet their basic needs more effectively.

Reality therapy differs from conventional theories of counseling or psychotherapy in six ways. Reality therapy rejects the concept of mental illness and the use of diagnostic labels; it works in the present, not the past; it rejects the concept of transference (the idea that clients relate to the therapist as an authority figure from their past); it does not consider the unconscious to be the basis of present behavior; the morality of behavior

is emphasized; and, finally, reality therapy teaches individuals better ways to fulfill their needs and more appropriate (and more successful) ways to deal with the world.

THERAPY PROCESS

In practice, reality therapy involves eight steps. First the therapist gains makes friends with or establishes a rapport with the client and asks the client what he or she wants. Then the client is asked to focus on his or her current behavior. With help, the client makes a realistic evaluation of his or her behavior. Therapist and client make a plan for the client to do better, which consists of finding more appropriate (realistic) ways of behaving. The therapist gets a commitment from the client to follow the plan that has been worked out. The therapist accepts no excuses from the client if the plan is not followed. No form of punishment is used, however, if the client fails to follow through. Finally, the therapist must never give up on the client.

Paramount to the success of reality therapy is the planning stage, consisting of discovering ways to change the destructive or self-defeating behavior of the client into behavior oriented toward success. Success-oriented behavior leads to a success identity: the feeling that one is able to give and receive love, feel worthwhile, and meet one's needs appropriately. Glasser states that putting the plan into writing, in the form of a contract, is one way to help ensure that the client will follow through. The client, not the therapist, is then held accountable for the success or failure of follow-through. Commitment is, in many ways, the keystone of reality therapy. Resolutions and plans of action become meaningless unless there is a decision (and a commitment) to carry them out.

ROLE OF THERAPISTS

Reality therapists usually see their clients once weekly, for between forty-five minutes and one hour per visit. Therapists come from a variety of disciplines, including psychiatry, psychology, counseling, and social work. It is important in applying reality therapy that the therapist adopt no rigid rules. The therapist has a framework to follow, but within that framework he or she should be as free and creative as possible.

Like behavior therapists, reality therapists are basically active, directive, instructive, and oriented toward action. Reality therapists use a variety of techniques, including role-play, humor, question-and-answer sessions, and confrontation. They do not employ some commonly accepted therapeutic techniques, such as interpretation, insight, free association, analysis of transference and resistance, and dream analysis. In addition, reality therapists rarely recommend or promote the use of drugs or medications in treatment.

Confrontation is one technique of special consideration to reality therapy. Through confrontation, therapists force clients to evaluate their present behavior and to decide whether they will change it. Reality therapy maintains that the key to finding happiness and success is accepting responsibility. Thus the therapist neither accepts any excuses from the client for his or her self-defeating or destructive behavior nor ignores the reality of the situation (the consequences of the client's present behavior). The client is solely responsible for his or her behavior. Conventional psychotherapy often avoids the issue of responsibility; the client (or "patient") is thought to be "sick" and thus not responsible for his or her behavior.

Throughout reality therapy, the criterion of what is "right" plays an important role in determining the appropriateness of behavior; however, the therapist does not attempt to state the morality of behavior. This is the task and responsibility of the client. Clients are to make these value judgments based on the reality of their situation. Is their current behavior getting them what they want? Does their current behavior lead to success or to failure? The basic philosophy of reality therapy is that people are ultimately self-determining and in charge of their lives. People are, in other words, free to choose how they act and what they will become.

STRENGTHS AND WEAKNESSES

The strengths of reality therapy are that it is relatively short-term therapy (not lasting for years, as classical psychoanalysis does), consists of simple and clear concepts that can be used by all types of helpers, focuses on present behavioral problems, consists of a plan of action, seeks a commitment from the client to follow through, stresses personal responsibility, can be applied to a diverse population of clients (including people in prison, people addicted to drugs and alcohol, and juvenile offenders), and accepts no excuses, blame, or rationalizations.

The weaknesses of reality therapy are that it fails to recognize the significance of the unconscious or of intrapsychic conflict, minimizes the importance of one's past in present behavior, appears overly simplistic (problems are rarely simplistic in nature), may give the therapist an inappropriate feeling of power or control, minimizes the existence of biological or biochemical factors in mental

illness, and fails to recognize the significance of psychiatric drugs in the treatment of mental illness.

PRACTICAL APPLICATIONS

Reality therapy can be applied to individuals with many sorts of psychological problems, from mild to severe emotional disorders. It has been used in a variety of counseling situations, including individual and group counseling, marriage and family counseling, rehabilitation counseling, and crisis intervention. The principles of reality therapy have been applied to teaching, social work, business management, and community development. Reality therapy is a popular method of treatment in mental hospitals, correctional institutions, substance abuse centers, and facilities for delinquent youth.

Marriage therapy is often practiced by reality therapists; the number of sessions ranges from two to ten. Initially, it is important to clarify the couple's goals for marriage counseling: Are they seeking help to preserve the marriage, or have they already made the decision to end the relationship? In marriage counseling, Glasser recommends that the therapist be quite active, asking many questions while trying to understand the overall patterns of the marriage and of the interrelationship.

EVALUATION OF CURRENT BEHAVIOR

Reality therapists stress current behavior. The past is used only as a means of enlightening the present. The focus is on what a client is doing now. Through skillful questioning, clients are encouraged to evaluate current behavior and to consider its present consequences. Is their current behavior getting them what they want or need? If not, why? As this process of questioning and reflecting continues, clients begin to acknowledge the negative and detrimental aspects of their current behavior. Slowly, they begin to accept responsibility for these actions.

Once responsibility is accepted, much of the remaining work consists of helping clients identify specific and appropriate ways to fulfill their needs and wants. This is often considered the teaching stage, since the therapist may model or teach the client more effective behavioral patterns.

It is difficult to discuss the application of reality therapy to specific problems, since reality therapists do not look at people as objects to be classified according to diagnostic categories. Reality therapists, like others in the holistic health movement, believe that most ailments—whether physical or psychological—are manifestations of the way people choose to live their lives. Glasser has stated: It makes little difference to a reality therapist what the presenting complaint of the client is; that complaint is a part of the way the client is choosing now to deal with the world. . . . When the client begins to realize that instead of being the victim of some disease or diagnostic category he is a victim of his own ineffective behavior, then therapy begins and diagnosis becomes irrelevant.

CASE STUDY

The following example shows how the eight steps of reality therapy can be applied to a real-life situation. The client's name is Jim; he is thirty-five years old. For years, Jim has been unable to hold a job. He is twice divorced and is subject to angry outbursts. He has been arrested three times for disorderly conduct. Recently Jim has lost his driver's license because of alcohol intoxication; he has been referred by the court for counseling.

In step one, the therapist makes friends and asks the client what he or she wants. Here the reality therapist, David, will make himself available to Jim as a caring, warm individual but not as someone whom Jim can control or dominate. David will ask, "What is it that you want?" Jim says, "Well, what I want is a job." Once the client states what he or she wants, the therapist can move to step two, asking the client to focus on his or her current behavior. Together David and Jim talk about Jim's behavior—his tendency for angry outbursts, his arrests, and his problems with alcohol.

The third step attempts to get clients to evaluate their present behavior and to see whether what they are now doing is getting them what they want. David asks Jim whether getting in fights is helping him find a job. As this step unfolds, Jim begins to understand that what he is doing is not helping him to become employable. Paramount at this step is that the clients see that their current behavior is within their control: They "choose" to act this way.

Once clients begin to see that what they are doing is not working (not getting them what they want), then the next step (step four) is to help them make a plan to do better. Once Jim realizes that getting in fights and drinking is ineffective and self-defeating, then David will begin to talk with him about a plan to change his behavior and find more appropriate ways of behaving. They plan a course of action. To "cement" this plan, a contract is made. The contract might state that Jim will not get in fights, Jim will control his anger, and Jim will stay out of bars and refrain from alcohol. David may also advise Jim on how to get a job: where to look for work, whom to contact, even what to wear and say during a job interview. Throughout this job search, which may be long and frustrating, David needs to be encouraging and supportive.

Step five involves getting a commitment from the client to follow through. David now asks Jim, "Are you going to live up to the contract? Are you going to change your behavior?" David needs to stress that commitment is the key to making this plan a success. David also must accept only a yes or no answer from Jim. Reality therapy does not accept excuses or reasons why plans are not carried through; this is step six. David's response to excuses should be that he is not interested in why Jim cannot do it; he is interested in when Jim will do it.

Step seven holds that David needs to be "tough" with Jim, but must not punish him if he does not follow through. Instead of finding ways to punish Jim, David may ask instead, "What is it that will get you to follow through?" Reality therapy recognizes that punishment is, in the long run, rarely effective. Step eight is simply never giving up. For most people, change does not come naturally, nor is it easy. A good therapist, like a good friend, does not give up easily. David needs to persevere with Jim. Through perseverance, Jim's life can change.

CONTRIBUTIONS OF GLASSER

The tenets of reality therapy were formed in the 1950s and 1960s as a reaction to the dominant psychotherapeutic approaches of the times, which were closely based on Freudian psychoanalysis. Glasser, the founder of reality therapy, was trained as a physician and psychoanalyst, but during his psychiatric training in the early 1950s, he became more and more dissatisfied with the psychoanalytic approach. What disturbed him was the insistence of psychoanalysis on viewing the patient as a victim of forces beyond his or her control. In other words, the person was not considered responsible for his or her current behavior.

In 1956, Glasser became a consultant to a school for delinquent female adolescents in Ventura, California, developing a new therapeutic approach that was in sharp opposition to classical psychoanalysis. In 1962, he spoke at a meeting of the National Association of Youth Training Schools and presented his new ideas. The response was phenomenal; evidently many people were frustrated with the current mode of treatment.

Initially Glasser was hesitant to state his dissatisfaction with the conventional approach to treatment, psychoanalysis; however, his faculty supervisor, G. L.

Harrington, was supportive. This started a long relationship in which Harrington helped Glasser formulate many of the ideas that became reality therapy.

In 1965, Glasser put his principles of counseling into a book entitled *Reality Therapy: A New Approach to Psychiatry*. Since then, he has written extensively, including *Schools Without Failure* (1968), *The Identity Society* (1972), *Positive Addiction* (1976), *Stations of the Mind: New Directions for Reality Therapy* (1981), *Control Theory: A New Exploration of How We Control Our Lives* (1985), and *The Quality School* (1990). The Institute for Reality Therapy, in Canoga Park, California, offers programs designed to teach the concepts and practice of reality therapy. *The Journal of Reality Therapy* publishes articles concerning the research, theory, and application of reality therapy. Reality therapy has seen remarkable success since its conception, and many consider it one of the important approaches to counseling and psychotherapy.

BIBLIOGRAPHY

Corey, Gerald. *Theory and Practice of Counseling and Psychotherapy*. 9th ed. Belmont: Brooks, 2013. Print.

Ellsworth, Laura. *Choosing to Heal: Using Reality Therapy in Treatment with Sexually Abused Children*. New York: Routledge, 2007. Print.

Glasser, Naomi, ed. *What Are You Doing? How People Are Helped Through Reality Therapy*. New York: Harper, 1986. Print.

Glasser, William. *Control Theory: A New Explanation of How We Control Our Lives*. New York: Perennial Lib., 1990. Print.

Glasser, William. *Quality School*. 3d ed. New York: Harper, 1998. Print.

Glasser, William. *Reality Therapy: A New Approach to Psychiatry*. 1965. Reprint. New York: Harper, 1989. Print.

Glasser, William. *Reality Therapy in Action*. New York: Harper, 2001. Print.

Glasser, William. *Stations of the Mind: New Directions for Reality Therapy*. 1981. [S.I.]: Harper, 2014. Digital file.

Wubbolding, Robert E. *Reality Therapy*. Washington, DC: APA, 2012. Digital file. Theories of Psychotherapy.

Ted Eilders

SEE ALSO: Abnormality: Psychological models; Behavioral family therapy; Cognitive behavior therapy; Cognitive therapy; Existential psychology; Psychoanalysis; Psychoanalytic psychology; Rational emotive therapy.

Reality TV

TYPE OF PSYCHOLOGY: Cross-cultural; Social

Reality TV is a genre of television programming that is unscripted and based upon real life scenarios. Documentaries, sports programming, news shows, talk shows and game shows are generally not considered reality television. Reality television has early roots, starting in the 1950's with the show Candid Camera. Reality TV gained much popularity as a genre of television programming in the 1990's and 2000's.

KEY CONCEPTS:
- Cable networks
- Nonfiction
- Reality television
- Subcultures

Television programming has come a long way since the variety shows and newscasts that were a staple in the 1950's and 1960's. Scripted fiction based television dramas and comedies still exist, but room has been made for nonfiction based programming, specifically "reality television." Reality television is a genre of television programming that is unscripted and based upon real life scenarios. The cast of reality tv shows are generally "regular" people who do not consider themselves actors or actresses of any sort. The genre generally does not include documentaries, talk shows, game shows, and sports programming, even though these shows have many of the same characteristics as reality television shows.

REALITY TV HISTORY

Many consider the first reality television show to be *Candid Camera*, a show that gained syndication and much popularity in the early 1950's. The first episodes of *Candid Camera* were hosted by Allen Funt, and were focused on playing jokes on people that assumed that they were in real life situations. For example, a classic episode of *Candid Camera* focuses on a human resource manager who believes he is interviewing a prospective employee. He asks the prospective employee to tell him something about herself, and she says that she feels like recently, she has been followed by a woman who has a monkey on her head. The human resource manager becomes uncomfortable and dismisses the prospective employee. Another woman then walks in with a monkey on her head. The human resource manager is baffled.

Later on, a camera man walks in and states "You're on *Candid Camera!"*

In 1973, The Public Broadcasting Service (PBS), followed and filmed the Loud Family in Santa Barbara, California for seven months in a one season series called *An American Family.* Several landmark events happened during filming. First, the Loud's oldest son came out as a homosexual man. Second, the filming chronicled the Loud's separation and divorce. Although meant to be a documentary, this television series inspired many producers of modern day reality television, including the producers of MTV's *Real World.*

MTV's *Real World* focuses on a group of young adults who have been placed in a living situation together. They go through their daily lives, wearing microphone packs and surrounded by camera men and women almost 24 hours a day. Similar to everyday life, these young adults are taped dealing with relationship problems, issues of sexual identity, chronic illness, eating disorders, religious issues, and death. It is currently in its 30th season on the network.

Since the success of MTV's *Real World*, the genre of reality television has boomed. Traditional networks have found great success in reality television shows such as *The Bachelor, The Bachelorette, The Apprentice,* and *Big Brother*; and many cable networks such as *The History Channel, TLC, Bravo, Lifetime,* and *E!* primarily focus their programming on reality television shows. The Academy of Television Arts and Sciences also gave nod to the popularity of reality television, adding a Reality Television Award to the Emmy's in 2001, and expanding those awards to include an award for Outstanding Reality Competition Program (2003), and an award for Outstanding Host of a Reality Show or Reality Competition Program (2008).

GENRES

Numerous researchers of psychology and popular media have spent time categorizing the varied genres of reality television as it has increased in popularity. These categorizations have resulted in various genres and subgenres of reality television, many of which will be outlined below.

Documentary Style/Special Living Environment. This type of reality television show was introduced by MTV's *Real World.* Participants audition and are selected to live in a house/living environment together. Conflict and tension usually ensue. Social experiment based - special living environment shows have also become popular. In *Big Brother,* participants chosen to live in the same house are not allowed contact with the outside world. In ABC's *Wife Swap,* two women from very different households swap homes and families for a week.

Celebrity Reality Television. Follows celebrities going about their everyday life. For example, *The Osbournes* (MTV) followed rock singer Ozzy Osborne, his wife Sharon, and their children for three years from 2002 to 2005. *Keeping Up with the Kardashians* (E! network, 2007 to the present) focuses on talk show host Kris Jenner, Bruce Jenner, their adult and teenage children, and their grandchildren.

Professional Activity Reality Television. Profiles individuals in their daily work. Examples include *Deadliest Catch* (Discovery Channel), *Ice Road Truckers* (History Channel), *Pawn Stars* (History Channel), and *Duck Dynasty* (A & E).

Photo: iStock

Reality Legal Programming. Includes courtroom based shows as well as programming focused on law enforcement activity. Examples include *COPS* (Fox); *The People's Court* (Warner Brothers), and *Judge Judy* (CBS).

Reality Competition Based Shows. Comprised of shows where there is a clear winner. The concept of "immunity" is present within these shows. Immunity is usually gained when a contestant gets a break from weekly judging because of something they have done. For example, on *The Biggest Loser* (ABC), if a contestant wins a particular race or obstacle course, they may receive immunity for the week. On *The Bachelor* (ABC), immunity is gained in the form of a rose, which the Bachelor may give a woman after a promising individual or group date. Music based reality competition shows such as *American Idol* (Fox), *The X Factor* (Fox) and *The Voice* (NBC) are also highly popular in the United States, although some believe these shows are more variety based than reality television based. *Dancing with the Stars* (ABC) is a reality show where professional ballroom dancers are paired with celebrity non-dancers in competition for the coveted "Mirror Ball Trophy".

Self-Improvement or Makeover Shows. There are two basic types of self-improvement/makeover shows. The first type focuses on an individual who needs help with their weight (*Extreme Weight Loss*, ABC) style, (*What Not to Wear*, TLC), or particular obsession (*Hoarders*, A & E). The second type of makeover show focuses on a person's home. *This Old House* (PBS) was one of the first home improvement based reality shows. Newer home improvement based reality shows include *Extreme Makeover: Home Edition* (ABC) and *Love it or List it* (HGTV).

Reality Television Shows featuring Subcultures. The purpose of a subculture-based show is to document different lifestyles and subgroups. For example, the MTV series *16 and Pregnant* documents the lives of pregnant teenage girls from a couple of months into their pregnancy to halfway through their babies' first year. The TLC series *The Little Couple* follows two professional adults who have dwarfism through marriage and subsequent parenthood. *19 Kids and Counting* (TLC), follows the Duggar Family, a conservative Christian family with 19 children. The Lifetime network's show *Sisterhood* features four young women discerning to become Catholic nuns.

WHY PEOPLE WATCH REALITY TELEVISION

There are many reasons why people may watch reality television. Subculture based reality television shows allow individuals to learn about and be exposed to a new culture or lifestyle. Competition based reality shows allow audiences to assist in "picking a winner." Robert Galinsky, founder of the New York Reality TV School, states that the reason why people watch (and audition for) reality TV shows is anthropological in nature. People have an intrinsic interest in telling and listening to stories about people. People also like to live vicariously through others, and reality TV helps them do that. Many reality shows feature ordinary people in different or exotic locations. They are traveling, dating, or improving their home or appearance. Reality television allows individuals to experience their transformation or journey, albeit passively.

CRITICISMS OF REALITY TELEVISION

Critics of reality television, however, will say that reality TV is more scripted than viewers believe. In many reality television shows, situations are contrived or set up. Camera footage is edited in order to show the most extreme or most sensitive moments, and some producers may even instigate drama in order to make the overall show more exciting. Although many reality TV shows tape "confessionals" or "in the moment" (ITM) interviews, many former cast members report that the producers made sure that they caught them in a highly emotional moment when taping the confessional, enhancing dramatic effect and heightening audience interest.

Critics have also lambasted certain reality television shows as exploitive. ABC's *The Bachelor* reminds many of pre-feminist days by focusing on 27 to 30 women vying for one wealthy man. TLC's reality show *Toddlers and Tiaras* showcases the children's beauty pageant industry, which has been accused of sexualizing young girls and making them feel that their self-worth is based on appearance. NBC's *The Biggest Loser* was embroiled in controversy in 2014, when 5 foot 4 inch Rachel Frederickson weighed in at 105 pounds to win the competition, a weight considered "underweight" by the Body Mass Index (BMI) calculator.

REALITY TELEVISION AND SOCIAL CHANGE

Whether completely realistic or mostly contrived, reality television has changed not only the way individuals watch television, but also the way individuals live their lives. Even amid controversy, *The Biggest Loser* has inspired many to live a healthier lifestyle. Eighteen months after *16 and Pregnant* debuted, teen pregnancy in the United States decreased 5.7 percent. The cast of the *Sister Wives* helped Utah citizens maintain their first amendment right to free speech; allowing polygamous families in that state to be able to freely say "I have multiple spouses." Finally, shows like *COPS* and *Judge Judy* have allowed many a glimpse of the criminal and civil justice system, inspiring careers in the legal field and law enforcement.

BIBLIOGRAPHY

Burton, N.K. (2012, October 22). Reality TV is here to stay. *The New York Times.* Retrieved from http://www.nytimes.com/roomfordebate/2012/10/21/are-reality-shows-worse-than-other-tv/reality-tv-is-here-to-stay. Article one in a debate on the current status and future of reality television.

Galinsky, R. (2012, October 21). Reality TV is still storytelling. *The New York Times.* Retrieved from http://www.nytimes.com/roomfordebate/2012/10/21/are-reality-shows-worse-than-other-tv/reality-tv-is-still-storytelling. Focuses on the anthropological basis of reality television. This article is written by the founder of the NY Reality TV School, an educational institution that focuses on training individuals interested in auditioning for reality television shows.

Murray, S. & Ouelette, L. (2008). *Reality TV: Remaking Television Culture.* New York: NYU Press. A comprehensive compilation of research based articles on the history, culture, politics, and significance of reality television.

Reiss, S. & Wiltz, J. (2004). Why people watch reality TV, *Media Psychology,* 6, 363 – 378. Reiss and Wiltz questioned 239 people about their reality television watching habits. Results suggested that people watch reality television mostly to feel a level of self-importance, but also to feel friendly, secure, and romantic.

Robinson, C. (2014). *I Didn't Come Here To Make Friends: Confessions of a Reality Show Villain.* New York: It books. Autobiography of Courtney Robinson, who was portrayed as a "villain" by the media during her tenure on Season 16 of *The Bachelor.* Includes personal vignettes from her time on television as well as insights into the production process of a reality television show.

Rose, R.L. & Wood, S.L. (2005). The paradox and the consumption of authenticity through reality television. *Journal of Consumer Research,* 32, pp. 284 – 296. Discusses why individuals watch reality television from the perspectives of consumer research, literary criticism, and the social sciences. Hypothesizes that individuals watch reality television to blend fantasy with reality, and to create a type of "hyper-authenticity" within their own self.

Gina Riley

SEE ALSO: Audiences; Culture; Entertainment; Mass media; Popular culture; Television.

Recency effects

TYPES OF PSYCHOLOGY: cognitive, consumer, educational, social, testing and measurement

The position, or order, that items appear in a list affects everything from which results people are likely to click on during a web search, to which brands are remembered after a series of commercials. When presented with a series of items people are most likely to recall those that appear in the beginning and those that appear in the end. Items that appear in the middle tend to be forgotten. This tendency to remember items that appear at the end of a list is known as the Recency Effect.

KEY CONCEPTS:
- Memory for list items
- Position effect
- Primacy effect
- Serial order position

INTRODUCTION: WHAT ARE RECENCY EFFECTS?

There is a saying that history is written by the winners. History, at least in the mind's eye, is also determined by how events are remembered and recorded. Generally speaking, events that happen at the beginning or end of a series are better remembered than those that happen in the middle. This tendency for people to remember things that appear at the beginning of a series is referred to as primacy effects. The tendency to remember things that appear at the end of a series is known as recency effects. When given a list of words or items to remember, experimental subjects in the laboratory will largely remember items that appeared at the beginning of the list and items that appeared at the end of the list. This phenomenon has also been demonstrated in the real world in a variety of circumstances including hiring and talent acquisition to performance judging and even food preferences.

WHAT CAUSES RECENCY EFFECTS?

It is widely held that memory has two storage resources. One of these resources is permanent and is often referred to as long term memory. This is where all permanently retained information is stored. This permanent store contains episodic memory, or memory for life events; semantic memory, which is memory for the meanings of things, and procedural memory, or, memory for how to do things such as knowing how to drive a car. The second memory resource is not permanent but acts as a temporary storage mechanism. It is essentially a working buffer used to hold information that may be imminently needed for some task or function. Incoming information first enters the working memory, or short-term store. After use in the short-term buffer, the information is either passed to the permanent long-term store, or is lost (i.e., forgotten).

The conventional thinking for a long period was that recency effects occurred because people had fairly easy access to the last few items in a series. In theory, the information was more likely to still be retained in one's working memory. While there it is readily available for recall when a memory test is taken immediately after the series of items. However, new evidence suggests that this is not the case. Indeed, long-term recency effects have been found when there was no possibility for a short-term memory buffer to have contributed information to the recall process. In fact, evidence has shown that there may actually be different properties for recency effects that happen in the short term and those that happen in the long term.

WHY DO RECENCY EFFECTS MATTER? SEARCH AND ONLINE BEHAVIOR.

A common practice was for small businesses to name their companies so they would appear at the top of the list in phone books. While printed phone books published by the local phone company (i.e., the Yellow pages) are rapidly becoming obsolete, they were once the only way an individual had to locate a company that provided a certain service. Companies commonly adopted names such as "ABC Plumbing" or "Apple Realty" in order to appear at the top of the list of their given specialty. Without any prior knowledge or specific experience consumers simply opened the phone book and chose a company, seemingly at random, from there. Not surprisingly,

a company that appeared at the top of the list for a given service was far more likely to be chosen than one that appeared farther down. Now that searching for information and services often happens online there is similar effect of item position when choosing from options on a computer screen. Researchers have found that people are far more likely to choose from a link that appears at the top of the page than one that appears further down; a primacy effect. The popular search engine company Google is aware of this and awards websites with the most number of "hits," or visitors, on a topic with rank ordered link placement near the top. However, recent research has shown that online clicking behavior is also affected by recency effects. That is, given a list of about six items in a list of search results, internet searchers are nearly as likely to click on the very bottom link as they are to click on the link positioned second from the top.

TELEVISION ADVERTISING.

Television viewers are now less tolerant of advertising and commercials than at any other time in the medium's history. The advent of "on demand" viewing, the astounding number of choices, instant videos available on smart phones, and streaming services that eliminate advertising altogether make commercials more avoidable and less effective. However, there remains one outlet during which television commercials very nearly take center stage: the Super Bowl for which the role of advertising has taken on a life of its own. Some viewers report only tuning in to witness the airing of commercials. Nearly 50% of American households tuned in during the 2014 competition and advertisers paid the network airing the contest $4 million dollars for just 30-second spots. Super Bowl Ads that appear near the beginning of the broadcast, as well as at the start of a segment of commercials, are far more likely to have their brands recognized. However, recency effects may be more likely to determine which brands viewers recall during normal viewing patterns. Normal TV viewers tend to engage in a strategy of avoiding commercial advertising. This leads them to change channels, engage in conversation, and leave the room once commercials have begun. Furthermore, those who disengage, physically or otherwise, when a commercial segment appears also return just prior to the show's continuation. They are therefore only exposed to advertising that appears when they return at the end of a commercial break. When they do recall brands they are for products and services for which the advertisements appeared near the end of a commercial break. Therefore, because of the positioning of commercials with respect to one another, those that appear last in this new age of lower ad tolerance are better remembered. The casual viewer can easily observe that networks have caught on to this tendency and tend to place non-product non-brand, network commercials for new shows and other network events at the very end of an advertising segment.

JUDGMENTS OF PREFERENCE

Food choices. Those measuring food choices have long known the benefit of placing one option in the first position; the first food sample is usually most memorable because it is experienced most strongly. However, more recent findings show that enjoyment of food that appears near the end of a meal when one is satisfied interferes with memories of the initial moments of food consumption. Not only does the memory for the end moments interfere with the initial experience but these end moments are also more likely to determine when a particular food is consumed once again. That is, if a satisfying meal ends with consumption of a delicious cherry pie; consumers are more likely to remember the dessert portion and are more likely to have cherry pie again soon. Other researchers have found strong recency effects for preferences during a random series of wines during tasting. That is, when sequences of four and five wines were presented tasters were more likely to rate those that appeared near the end favorably. Primacy effects for the wines were found for both high-knowledge and low-knowledge tasters. However, what is interesting about this tendency for recency effects in wine tasting is that only high-knowledge wine-tasters demonstrated this preference. Low-knowledge wine-tasters only showed a preference for the first wines they tasted. One possibility suggested by the researchers is that those with a lot of experience at wine-tasting may have been using a more rigorous strategy of comparing each wine to the one they had recently deemed as their favorite (usually the one tasted first) and then updating as they proceeded through the sequence of flavors. The recency effect they thus attribute to high-knowledge tasters being more persistent about finding a better wine. Compared to the low-knowledge tasters they were thus more willing and able expend the extra effort to search for a better wine because of their greater expertise. Interestingly, for all the industry touts the quality and flavor of different wines the researchers found no difference at all in tasters' preference for any particular wine.

Judging Sports. Preferences for food and drink may seem relatively innocuous, but recency effects have also been found to occur in certain competitive arenas. The Olympics is held every four years in either winter or summer domains. It features international competitors in a variety of sports where the outcome is determined by a time-clock, as it is in swimming, bobsledding, and track, and sports where the outcome is determined by judges such as gymnastics, snow-boarding, and figure-skating. Some have argued that "clock sports" are easier to compete in fairly. This is because athletes in sports that are judged obviously have no control over the moods and whims of judges from one contestant to the next. Even the common man knows that extra points are given when competitors "stick the landing." However, there are many other nuances and subtleties of performance art that judges are expected to appreciate and rate. To have one's career in the hands of a set of judges who have watched countless others before their own performance or will watch many others after they are finished literally has the potential to change the outcome of the judging.

International figure skating organizers are presumably aware of this possibility and account for judging differences across a series of competitors by randomizing the order of participant appearance. Contestants are judged over two rounds with a performance near the end of the second round being awarded to those with better scores in the first round. Despite this, however, recency effects persist in International Figure Skating judging. That is, skaters whose performance takes place later near the end of the first round tend to receive better scores in both the first and final rounds. This is troubling, at best, as contestant fate seems literally in the hands of chance. However, the unavoidable reality is that when judging a serially occurring sequence of performances judges can only compare the most recent performance to any one that preceded it but cannot compare to any performance that will occur afterward. Recency effects, it seems, are a necessary artifact of certain types of performance and competition.

CONCLUSION:

The order that things appear affects everything from whether people will remember them to how well or poorly they are rated. There are a number of things that individuals can do, when armed with this knowledge, to increase their own odds when something important is at stake. During a job interview or other performance rating present the most favorable information near the end.

It is more like to take precedence as the last thing the other party remembers. This is also the case for any type of presentation and possibly even evidence given during legal proceedings. If you are the recipient of some set of information or data that you need to remember, place the most important portions to study at the beginning or end of the list and/or the beginning or end of the study period. And, if you are judging a series of choices involving preference you may benefit from a) putting the one you are least likely to prefer at the beginning or end so that it has a fair chance, and b) trying to make pairwise comparisons between items rather than judging every subsequent item based on the first. In addition, formal competition that involves judges viewing a series of contestants might benefit from spreading it out over a longer period so that smaller groups can be judged, or having a larger pool of judges and rotating some judges in and out so that for each competitor there are a number of judges who are not comparing their performance to every contestant who preceded them.

BIBLIOGRAPHY

Gabrinsky, E.N., Morewedge, C.K., & Shiv, B. (2014) "Interference of the End: Why Recency Bias in Memory Determines When a Food Is Consumed Again". *Psychological Science Online* First, 1 – 9. A brief but interesting read that describes novel findings on the issue of serial order position effects in the realm of food tasting.

Murphy, J., Hofacker, C., & Mizerski, R. (2006) "Primacy and Recency Effects on Clicking Behavior". *Journal of Computer-Mediated Communication*, 11, 522–535. An up-to-date source of information that demonstrates how the important of serial list position, formerly important in the traditional printed phone books, is now just as important as much of consumer information is available on line.

Mantonakis, A., Rodero, P., Lesschaeve, I., & Hastie, R. (2009). "Order in Choice Effects of Serial Position on Preferences". *Psychological Science*, 20 (11) 1309-1321. A concise, interesting, and thorough resource that describes an interesting set of results on the topic. The only difference in wine-tasting judgments researchers found was based on the serial order of the presentation.

Jacquelyn H. Berry

SEE ALSO: Association; Free recall; Memory; Recall; Recognition; Short term memory; Working memory.

Reflexes

TYPE OF PSYCHOLOGY: Biological bases of behavior

A reflex is one of the most basic types of behavior that can be elicited; over the years, psychologists and physiologists have studied the behavioral and biological processes associated with reflex production in the hope of understanding principles and processes involved in generating both simple behaviors and a variety of more complex behaviors such as learning, memory, and voluntary movement.

KEY CONCEPTS
- Classical (Pavlovian) conditioning
- Infantile reflexes
- Monosynaptic reflex
- Polysynaptic reflex
- Spinal reflex

INTRODUCTION

The reflex is undoubtedly the simplest form of behavior that has been studied widely by psychologists and neuroscientists. Reflexes involve two separate yet highly related events: the occurrence of an eliciting stimulus and the production of a specific response. Most organisms are capable of displaying a variety of complex behaviors; however, because these behaviors are complex, it has been very difficult, if not impossible, to understand biological or psychological processes involved in generating or modifying the variety of complex behaviors that most organisms can display. In attempts to study these complex behaviors, a number of researchers have adopted a strategy of studying simpler behaviors, such as reflexes, that are thought to make up, contribute to, or serve as a model of the more complex behavior.

SPINAL REFLEX

A number of reflexes can be generated in the mammalian spinal cord even after it has been surgically isolated from the brain. The stretch reflex is an example of a spinal reflex. When a muscle is stretched, such as when a tendon is tapped or when an attempt is made to reach for an object, sensory "detectors" or receptors within the muscle are activated to signal the muscle stretch. These receptors are at the end of very long nerve fibers that travel from the muscle receptor to the spinal cord, where they activate spinal motor neurons. The motor neurons control the same muscle on which the stretch receptor that initiated the stretch signal is located. When activated, the spinal motor neurons signal the muscle, causing it to contract. In this manner, when a muscle stretch is detected, the stretch reflex ensures that a contraction is generated in the muscle to counteract and balance the stretch. This type of reflex is referred to as a monosynaptic reflex because it involves only one synapse: the synapse between the sensory receptor neuron and the motor neuron (where a synapse is the junction between two neurons).

Another example of a spinal reflex is the flexion or withdrawal reflex. Anyone who has accidentally touched a hot stove has encountered this reflex. Touching a hot stove or applying any aversive stimulus to the skin activates pain receptors in the skin. These receptors are at the end of long sensory fibers that project to neurons in the spinal cord. The spinal neurons that receive input from the sensory fibers are not motor neurons, as in the stretch reflex, but rather very small neurons called spinal interneurons. The interneurons make synaptic contact on other interneurons as well as on motor neurons that innervate flexor muscles. When activated, the flexor muscles typically cause limb withdrawal. The flexor reflex ensures that a relatively rapid withdrawal of one's hand from a hot stove will occur if it is accidentally touched. The flexor reflex is an example of a polysynaptic reflex because there are two or more synapses involved in the reflex (the presence of at least one synapse between a sensory neuron and an interneuron and a second synapse between the interneuron and a motor neuron).

One functional difference between monosynaptic and polysynaptic reflexes is the amount of information processing that can take place in the two reflex systems. The monosynaptic reflex is somewhat limited, because information flow involves only the synapse between the sensory and motor neurons. This type of reflex is ideal for quick adjustments that must be made in muscle tension. Conversely, polysynaptic reflexes typically involve a number of levels of interneurons. Hence, convergence and divergence of information can occur as information flows from sensory to motor elements. In essence, the polysynaptic system, in addition to having afferent and efferent components, has a "processor" of sorts between the sensory and motor elements. In intact organisms, the integration that takes place within the processor allows information to be shared by other regions of the nervous system. For example, some of the interneurons send information upward to the brain. When a hot stove is touched, the brain is informed. This sensory experience is likely to be evaluated and stored by the brain, therefore making it less likely that the hot stove will be touched a second time.

MUSCULATURE REFLEXES

Reflexes are not limited to the spinal cord. Responses involving the musculature of the face and neck can also be reflexive in nature. For example, a puff of air that strikes the cornea of the human eye elicits a brisk, short-latency eyelid closure. Like the polysynaptic spinal reflexes, this eyeblink reflex appears to involve three elements: a sensory nerve, called the trigeminal nerve, that carries information from receptors in the cornea of the eye to the trigeminal nucleus (a cranial nerve nucleus); interneurons that connect the trigeminal nucleus with several other brain-stem neurons; and a motor nerve that originates from brain-stem motor neurons and contracts the muscles surrounding the eye to produce the eyeblink. This reflex is defensive in nature because it ensures that the eyeball is protected from further stimulation if a stimulus strikes the cornea.

USE OF AUTONOMIC NERVOUS SYSTEM

Not all reflexes involve activation of skeletal muscles. For example, control of the urinary bladder involves a spinal reflex that activates smooth muscles. In addition, temperature regulation is partially the product of a reflexive response to changes in external or internal environments. Many of these types of reflexes engage the autonomic nervous system, a division of the nervous system that is involved in regulating and maintaining the function of internal organs.

Not all reflexes involve simple, local, short-latency responses. The maintenance of posture when standing upright is a generally automatic, reflexive system that one does not think about. This system includes neurons in the spinal cord and brain stem. The body's equilibrium system (the vestibular or balance system) involves receptors in the middle ear, brain-stem structures, and spinal motor neurons, while locomotion requires the patterned activation of several reflex systems. Finally, a number of behavioral situations require a rapid response that integrates the motor system with one of the special senses (such as quickly applying the car brakes when a road hazard is seen). These are generally referred to as reaction-time situations and require considerable nervous system processing, including the involvement of the cerebral cortex, when engaged. Nevertheless, these responses are considered reflexive in nature because they involve an eliciting stimulus and a well-defined, consistent response.

ROLE IN LEARNING AND MEMORY

Reflexes have also been widely studied by psychologists and biologists interested in learning and memory. Russian physiologists Ivan Sechenov and Ivan Petrovich Pavlov have generally been credited with the first attempts to study systematically how reflexes could be used to examine relationships between behavior and physiology. Pavlov in particular had a huge influence on the study of behavior. Most students are familiar with the story of Pavlov and his successful demonstration of conditioned salivation in dogs produced by pairing a bell with meat powder. Over the years, the Pavlovian conditioning procedure (also known as classical conditioning) has often been used to study the behavioral principles and neural substrates of learning. The conditioning of a variety of reflexes has been observed, including skeletal muscle responses such as forelimb flexion, hindlimb flexion, and eyelid closure, as well as autonomic responses such as respiration, heart rate, and sweat gland activity.

One of the most widely studied classical conditioning procedures is classical eyelid conditioning. This reflex conditioning procedure has been studied in a variety of species, including rabbits, rats, cats, dogs, and humans. Mostly because of the research efforts of Isadore Gormezano and his colleagues, which began in the early 1960s, much is known about behavioral aspects of classical eyelid conditioning in rabbits. In this paradigm, a mild electric shock or air puff is presented to elicit reliably a reflexive blink from the rabbit. The blink is typically measured by means of devices that are attached to the nictitating membrane, a third eyelid that is present in a variety of species, including the rabbit. During training sessions, a neutral stimulus such as a tone or light is delivered 0.3 to 1.0 second prior to the air puff. After about one hundred of these tone and air-puff pairings, the rabbit learns to blink when the tone or light is presented (the rabbit begins to use the tone to signal the impending air-puff presentation).

This preparation has yielded a wealth of data concerning the parameters of behavioral training that produce the fastest or slowest learning rates (such as stimuli intensities, time between stimuli, and number of trials per day). Furthermore, this simple reflexive learning situation has been used to study how the brain codes simple forms of learning and memory. A number of researchers (most notably Richard F. Thompson) have studied the activity of a variety of brain structures during learning and performance of the classically conditioned eyelid response. These studies have shown that discrete brain regions such as the cerebellum and hippocampus alter their activity to generate or modify the conditioned response. In brief, these researchers have used the conditioning of a very simple reflex to advance the understanding of how the brain might code more complex learning and memory processes.

INNATE REFLEXES

The study of reflexes has not been limited to learning and memory. Developmental psychologists have studied a variety of innate reflexes in newborn infants. Sucking is a very prominent reflex that is readily observed in newborns. Related to feeding is the rooting reflex, which can be elicited when the cheek of an infant is stroked softly. The skin stimulation causes the infant to open his or her mouth and turn toward the point of stimulation. This reflex has obvious applications in helping the infant locate food. The infant's ability to hold on to objects is, in part, attributable to the presence of the grasp reflex. When an object touches the palm of a newborn's hand, the newborn's fist will close immediately around the object, thus allowing the infant to hold the object for a short period of time. The infantile reflexes disappear within a few months after birth and are replaced by voluntary responses. Most developmental researchers believe that the infantile reflexes are temporary substitutes for the voluntary responses. Apparently, the voluntary responses are not present during the first few months of life because various parts of the infant nervous system, including the cerebral cortex, have not matured sufficiently to support the behavior. Therefore, the disappearance of the infantile reflexes serves as an important marker of neural and behavioral development.

CONTRIBUTIONS TO PSYCHOLOGY

The study of reflexes has played a prominent role in shaping the field of psychology. During the late nineteenth century and early twentieth century, Sir Charles Sherrington, a British physiologist, conducted an extensive series of studies concerned with spinal reflexes. He showed that a number of skin stimulations, such as pinching or brushing, produced simple responses even when a spinal transection separated the spinal cord from the rest of the nervous system. From these experiments, he argued that the basic unit of movement was the reflex, which he defined as a highly stereotyped, unlearned response to external stimuli. This work created a flurry of activity among physiologists and psychologists, who tried to trace reflexes throughout the nervous system and assemble them into more complex behaviors.

Early in the twentieth century, many psychologists and physiologists, including Sherrington and Pavlov, adopted the reflex as the basic unit of behavior to study, in part because of the relative simplicity of the behavior and in part because of the ease with which the behavior could be reliably elicited by applying external stimuli. Based on his research, Sherrington believed that complex behaviors were produced by chaining together simple reflexes in some temporal order. This basic idea provided the framework for much of the physiological and behavioral work completed early in the twentieth century. Sechenov and Pavlov also believed that the concept of the reflex could explain more complex behaviors. Pavlov, for example, showed that not all reflexes were innate; rather, new reflexes could be established by associating a "neutral" stimulus (a stimulus that did not initially produce a reflex) with a stimulus that reliably elicited a reflex. As a result of this demonstration, Pavlov proposed an elaborate theory of reflex learning that involved forming associations between stimuli in the cerebral cortex.

In the latter half of the twentieth century, many psychologists interested in studying overt behavior and physiologists interested in studying nervous system function adopted the study of reflexes as a means of simplifying behavior or nervous system activity. Psychologists such as Gormezano, Robert Rescorla, and Allan Wagner, who have studied classical conditioning phenomena, are developing a comprehensive understanding of the learning process that occurs when simple paradigms such as classical conditioning are used. Behavioral neuroscientists and neurobiologists (such as Thompson and Eric R. Kandel) who study nervous system function have used reflexes as the basic unit of behavior in the hope of catching a glimpse of nervous system function when a fairly simple behavioral response is being generated and modified by learning experiences. In both cases, a major reason for using the reflex as the unit of behavior is to simplify the experimental situation. Indeed, researchers are not likely to understand complex behavioral processes without first understanding how simpler behaviors and nervous system functions are generated, modified, and maintained. The study of reflexes, from both a behavioral and biological standpoint, has provided and should continue to provide a valuable approach for understanding human behavior as well as understanding how the nervous system generates activity to produce the behavior.

BIBLIOGRAPHY

Carlson, Neil R. *Foundations of Physiological Psychology.* 7th ed. Boston: Allyn, 2008. Print.

Domjan, Michael, and Barbara Burkhard. *The Principles of Learning and Behavior.* 7th ed. Stamford: Cengage, 2015. Print.

Fancher, Raymond E. *Pioneers of Psychology.* 4th ed. New York: Norton, 2012. Print.

Gleitman, Henry, James J. Gross, and Daniel Weisberg. *Psychology.* 8th ed. New York: Norton, 2011. Print.

Joseph E. Steinmetz

SEE ALSO: Brain structure; Nervous system; Neurons; Pavlovian conditioning; Reflexes in newborns.

Reflexes in newborns

TYPE OF PSYCHOLOGY: Developmental psychology

Human infants are born with a repertoire of skills that help them adapt to their new environment immediately after birth. By exploring the nature and bases of these early abilities, researchers have gained a better understanding of processes that govern development during the earliest periods of the human life cycle.

KEY CONCEPTS
- Cortical brain centers
- Homeostasis
- Primitive reflex
- Reflex
- Subcortical brain centers
- Sudden infant death syndrome (SIDS)
- Survival reflex

INTRODUCTION

For many years, it was thought that newborns were completely helpless, fragile and hardly ready for survival in the relatively unprotected world into which they were born. Extensive research has now shown that healthy neonates are born with a set of prepared reactions to the environment that aid their survival. These prepared, inborn reactions are referred to as reflexes.

From the moment of birth, breathing must be self-sufficient, requiring that newborns use their lungs for the first time. They must actively approach, consume, and digest food. During the prenatal period, a fetus receives nutrients passively from the mother, and it discharges waste into the mother's bloodstream. For the first time, newborns must use their lungs, skin, kidneys, and gastrointestinal tract to regulate digestion and waste elimination.

In addition, newborns are much less protected in the extrauterine environment than they were in the uterus from which they emerged. The developing fetus experiences a world of constancy because of the insulating effects of life in amniotic fluid. At birth, however, newborns first experience fluctuations in air temperature, light, sound, and touch. Neonates will therefore need to be prepared to maintain a relatively constant body temperature and a degree of internal homeostasis—the tendency to maintain internal stability by responding in a coordinated fashion to any changes in the external world—immediately after birth. Reflexes assume many of these functions automatically. From the moment of birth, reflexes are elicited by stimuli in the extrauterine environment. Reflex action is controlled largely by subcortical brain centers in the central nervous system.

ROLE OF CENTRAL NERVOUS SYSTEM

The human central nervous system (CNS) is organized hierarchically. Simple, uncoordinated actions are controlled by lower, or subcortical, brain centers; coordinated, planned actions are controlled by higher, or cortical, brain centers. Reflexes are among the simplest patterns of action exhibited by humans and are controlled by lower brain centers. The lower brain centers are the most highly developed at birth, and they control the majority of human behavior until they are supplanted by higher cortical brain centers. A few months after birth, the cortical brain centers begin to assume control of the previously reflexive behaviors. That is, as humans develop voluntary control over their behavior, reflexes previously elicited automatically by stimulation no longer respond. This is evidenced by the disappearance of many reflexive behaviors between three and nine months after birth.

EARLY SURVIVAL RESPONSES

The most fundamental reflexes exhibited in newborns involve reactions to unpleasant or life-threatening stimuli. These reflexes protect them from further aversive or possibly life-threatening situations. For example, several reflexes allow newborns to maintain a clear airway for normal breathing. This is important because regular

breathing rhythms are not firmly established in newborns; normal, healthy newborns occasionally neglect to breathe for brief periods of time. When this occurs, carbon dioxide builds up in their bloodstreams, and the breathing reflex is triggered. This causes the neonates to start breathing again. Should neonates experience a clogged airway because of mucus or some other obstruction, a reflexive sneeze or cough may serve to remove the obstruction. If something covers a newborn's face, threatening the passage of air, the defensive reflex is activated, whereby the newborn swats at the object.

Similarly, neonates respond reflexively to the presence of food. At birth, lightly stroking the cheek of an infant will produce a rooting reflex. The rooting reflex is characterized as a head turn accompanied by mouth opening. This turn positions the baby for nutrient seeking via sucking. The sucking and swallowing reflexes enable neonates to consume nutrients, a process that is aided significantly by the activation of other parts of the human digestive tract.

Neonates respond reflexively to changes in temperature and touch. For example, heat causes neonates' blood vessels to expand so that more heat can be dispersed through the skin. Conversely, cold causes neonates' blood vessels to contract so that heat can be conserved inside their bodies. Neonates respond to painful physical stimulation such as a pinprick on the foot by reflexively withdrawing the limb. Similarly, neonates respond to loud noises or bright lights by turning away from the source of the aversive stimulus.

Perhaps one of the most general reflexes is the crying reflex. Crying is an important reflex that alerts caregivers that all is not well. Crying is especially important for maintaining homeostasis. Infants cry when they are overstimulated, understimulated, hungry, too cold or hot, in pain, or otherwise uncomfortable. Crying serves to communicate to caregivers as well as to release energy, ward off danger, and possibly clear an air passage.

PRIMITIVE REFLEXES

Newborns also exhibit a variety of reflexive actions that have no clear survival value. These nonadaptive reflexes are referred to as primitive reflexes. Primitive reflexes disappear early in the first year of life. Several of these primitive reflexes are interesting precursors of abilities that will be exhibited later in life. For example, neonates exhibit an early stepping reflex that closely resembles mature walking. This quickly disappears at about eight weeks of life and reemerges at about twelve to fifteen months as infants take their first true steps. Similarly, newborns will reflexively swim if placed in a prone position on a water surface. Newborns also grasp when the palm is touched. Early versions of both swimming and grasping will disappear in the first three months and, in the case of grasping, will give way first to slapping movements and then to progressive dexterity and the gripping with the palm and fingers at about six months.

Evolutionary accounts of the existence of primitive reflexes in humans suggest that they are remnants of survival reflexes that exist in humans' evolutionary ancestors. For example, the Moro reflex is a startle reflex observed when an infant is held in a supine position on his or her back and is then suddenly lowered several centimeters. The infant opens his or her arms and then pulls them toward the center of the chest as if grabbing onto something. The Moro reflex serves as a very adaptive clinging response among primates (for example, chimpanzees), which require their infants to hold on to their mother as they travel. For modern humans, however, it is a primitive reflex with no apparent survival value, though its presence in newborns and disappearance within the first six months of life is indicative of normal neurological development.

PRACTICAL APPLICATIONS

Reflex integrity is an important component of several newborn screening instruments. The Brazelton Neonatal Behavior Assessment Scale explores a newborn's responsiveness to several environmental stimuli as a function of neurological functioning. The Brazelton scale assesses the strength of twenty reflexes as well as a newborn's ability to respond to twenty-six situations such as orienting to and from a tester's voice. If an infant is extremely unresponsive, a low Brazelton score may indicate the existence of brain damage or other neurological dysfunction.

Lewis Lipsitt, a researcher studying newborn reflexes, found an important relationship between the integrity of a child's nervous system and the development of reflexes. Lipsitt conducted research on sudden infant death syndrome (SIDS), a complication in which apparently healthy infants suddenly stop breathing and die in their sleep. The cause of this disorder is unknown. Lipsitt noted that up to 95 percent of SIDS deaths occur when the infants are between two and five months of age, just the time when the neonatal reflexes are moving from subcortical to cortical control. Lipsitt therefore proposed that some infants have a specific disability that keeps

them from assuming voluntary control of previously involuntary survival reflexes. As a result, they fail to defend against blockages to their airways in some situations, especially when sleeping. Lipsitt's work has led to worldwide recognition that the safest sleeping posture for babies in the first six months of life is on the back, because it reduces the risk of airway blockage.

DEVELOPMENT IN INFANCY

The focus on reflexes in newborns has grown because of interest in understanding the rapid development of humans during infancy. Infancy is now understood as the period of most rapid development in a human's entire life span. During the first two years of life, an infant's brain will reach 75 percent of its eventual weight. Physical growth will accompany brain growth to enable an infant to display an array of complex motor and cognitive skills that emerge in rapid succession. Developmental psychologists have made considerable progress in understanding this period of development. This progress has been aided by advances in technology and research methods, primarily in the area of brain physiology and function.

Researchers now understand, in contrast to earlier thinking, that humans are born with a variety of skills that aid their survival during this particularly vulnerable developmental period. Previously, researchers, physicians, and parents had assumed that infants were fragile and helpless. Infants are indeed more prepared for life than was previously thought. All major sense organs are functioning at birth, and newborns are capable of learning and experiencing their world actively very shortly after birth.

Nineteenth century psychologist William James described infants as born into a blooming, buzzing confusion. This is clearly far from the truth. Reflexes play an important role in the realization of many early developing abilities. Researchers have used them as a window on the developing nervous system and have understood significant variation in neurological development from the pattern of reflexes. Infants interact with the world reflexively until they have matured enough to engage in more active exploration of their world.

BIBLIOGRAPHY

Brazelton, T. B. *Neonatal Behavioral Assessment Scale.* Clinics in Developmental Medicine 50. London: Heinemann, 1973. Print.

Domjan, Michael, and Barbara Burkhard. *The Principles of Learning and Behavior*. 7th ed. Stamford: Cengage, 2015. Print.

Fogel, Alan. *Infancy: Infant, Family, and Society*. 6th ed. New York: Sloan, 2014. Print.

Gleitman, Henry, James J. Gross, and Daniel Weisberg. *Psychology*. 8th ed. New York: Norton, 2011. Print.

Lipsitt, L. P. "Crib Death: A Biobehavioral Phenomenon." Current Directions in *Psychological Science* 12.5 (2003): 164–70. Print.

Maurer, Daphne, and Charles Maurer. *The World of the Newborn*. New York: Basic, 1989. Print.

Piek, J. *Infant Motor Development*. Champaign: Human Kinetics, 2006. Print.

Richard J. Ricard; updated by Virginia Slaughter

SEE ALSO: Birth: Effects on physical development; James, William; Motor development; Physical development: Environment versus genetics; Prenatal physical development; Sensation and perception.

Reinforcement

TYPE OF PSYCHOLOGY: Learning; Memory; Motivation

Reinforcement is one of the most pervasive concepts in psychology, ranging from basic research to applications in psychotherapy. Modern usage of the term is limited to specific consequences of behavior that lead to increases in the future probability of that same behavior. A great deal of effort has been dedicated to discovering various types of reinforcers, the effects of varying delivery patterns, and what makes consequences effective reinforcers.

KEY CONCEPTS
- Bliss point
- Establishing operation
- Intermittent reinforcement
- Negative reinforcers
- Positive reinforcers
- Premack principle
- Primary reinforcers
- Punishment
- Secondary reinforcers
- Social reinforcers

INTRODUCTION

The casual, everyday use of the word "reinforcement" generally refers to the granting of a reward for some behavior. While the use of this term by psychologists is more formal, a great deal of research has been dedicated to studying the effects of rewards on behavior. The most influential of the early studies were those done in the 1890s by American psychologist Edward L. Thorndike. Thorndike created a problem box from which a hungry cat could escape by performing a specific action, such as pulling on a wire, stepping on a pedal, or some similar behavior, thereby gaining access to food. From these studies Thorndike proposed his famous law of effect; that is, actions that are followed by satisfying events are more likely to recur while actions that are followed by discomfort will become less likely. The more satisfying or the more discomfort, the greater the effect on subsequent behavior.

Not all psychologists have used the word "reinforcement" to describe the same processes. In research where he conditioned dogs to salivate upon hearing certain tones, the Russian physiologist Ivan Petrovich Pavlov called pairing a stimulus (food) that automatically elicits a response (salivation) to a second stimulus (a tone) reinforcing; that is, the food reinforced the ability of the tone to generate the same response. This process has come to be known as Pavlovian conditioning. Unlike Thorndike, who was referring to consequences after the organism emitted some specific behavior, Pavlov was describing an effect that occurred during the presentation of stimuli before the organism responded. Another difference was that Thorndike studied an animal's voluntary behavior while Pavlov studied a reflexive, glandular response.

Most psychologists followed Thorndike and reserved the term "reinforcer" for voluntary behavior and its consequences. For many, though, it meant any consequence to a behavior, whether it increased or decreased the behavior's future probability. In this usage, a reinforcer could mean any kind of motivation, whether it was to seek a pleasant or to avoid an unpleasant set of circumstances. To be sure, there were modifying words for these specific situations. Thus, if a behavior resulted in the acquisition of some desired commodity (such as food), reducing a need or a drive state, it was said to be positive reinforcement. On the other hand, if the behavior caused an unpleasant situation to be terminated or avoided, it was called negative reinforcement. Both of these consequences would increase the rate of the behavior.

To make matters more confusing, some psychologists employed the term "reinforcement" even when the consequence reduced the likelihood of a specific behavior. In the 1960s, American psychologist Gregory A. Kimble described omission training as withholding a positive reinforcer when a specified response occurs. Conversely, Kimble said that if a negative reinforcer is given when the response occurs, this is punishment.

MODERN DEFINITIONS

To maintain a reasonable degree of consistency, most psychologists use the term "reinforcement" exclusively for a process of using rewards to increase voluntary behavior. The field of study most associated with this technique is instrumental conditioning. In this context, the formal definition states that a reinforcer is any consequence to a behavior that is emitted in a specified situation that has the effect of increasing that behavior in the future. It must be emphasized that the behavior itself is not sufficient for the consequence to be delivered. The circumstances in which the behavior occurs are also important. Thus, standing and cheering at a basketball game will likely lead to approval (social reinforcement), whereas this same response is not likely to yield acceptance if it occurs at a funeral.

A punisher is likewise defined as any consequence that reduces the probability of a behavior, with the same qualifications as for reinforcers. A behavior that occurs in response to a specified situation may receive a consequence that reduces the likelihood that it will occur in that situation in the future, but the same behavior in another situation would not generate the same consequence. For example, drawing on the walls of a freshly painted room would usually result in an unpleasant consequence, whereas the same behavior (drawing) in one's coloring book would not.

The terms "positive" and "negative" are also much more tightly defined. Former use confused these with the emotional values of good or bad, thereby requiring the counterintuitive and confusing claim that a positive reinforcer is withheld or a negative reinforcer presented when there is clearly no reward, and, in fact, the intent is to reduce the probability of that response (such as described by Kimble). A better, less confusing definition is to consider "positive" and "negative" as arithmetic symbols, as for adding or subtracting. They therefore are the methods of supplying reinforcement (or punishment) rather than descriptions of the reinforcer itself. Thus, if a behavior occurs, and as a consequence something

is given that will result in an increase in the rate of the behavior, this is positive reinforcement. Giving a dog a treat for executing a trick is a good example. One can also increase the rate of a behavior by removing something on its production. This is called negative reinforcement. A good example might be when a child who eats his or her vegetables does not have to wash the dinner dishes. Another example is the annoying seat belt buzzer in cars. Many people comply with the rules of safety simply to terminate that aversive sound.

The descriptors "positive" and "negative" can be applied to punishment as well. If something is added on the performance of a behavior which results in the reduction of that behavior—that is positive punishment. On the other hand, if this behavior causes the removal of something that reduces the response rate—negative punishment. A dog collar that provides an electric shock when the dog strays too close to the property line is an example of a device that delivers positive punishment. Loss of television privileges for rudeness is an example of negative punishment.

TYPES OF REINFORCERS

The range of possible consequences that can function as reinforcers is enormous. To make sense of this assortment, psychologists tend to place them into two main categories: primary reinforcers and secondary reinforcers. Primary reinforcers are those that require little, if any, experience to be effective. Food, drink, and sex are common examples. While it is true that experience will influence what would be considered desirable for food, drink, or an appropriate sex partner, there is little argument that these items, themselves, are natural reinforcers. Another kind of reinforcer that does not require experience is called a social reinforcer. Examples are social contact and social approval. Even newborns show a desire for social reinforcers. Psychologists have discovered that newborns prefer to look at pictures of human faces more than practically any other stimulus pattern, and this preference is stronger if that face is smiling. Like the other primary reinforcers, experience will modify the type of social recognition that is desired. Still, it is clear that most people will go to great lengths to be noticed by others or to gain their acceptance and approval.

Though these reinforcers are likely to be effective, most human behavior is not motivated directly by primary reinforcers. Money, entertainment, clothes, cars, and computer games are all effective rewards, yet none of these would qualify as natural or primary reinforcers.

Because they must be acquired, they are called secondary reinforcers. These become effective because they are paired with primary reinforcers. The famous American psychologist B. F. Skinner found that the sound of food being delivered was sufficient to maintain a high rate of bar pressing in experienced rats. Obviously, under normal circumstances the sound of the food only occurred if food was truly being delivered.

How a secondary reinforcer becomes effective is called two-factor theory and is generally explained through a combination of instrumental and Pavlovian conditioning (hence the label "two-factor"). For example, when a rat receives food for pressing a bar (positive reinforcement), at that same time a neutral stimulus is also presented, the sound of the food dropping into the food dish. The sound is paired with a stimulus that naturally elicits a reflexive response; that is, food elicits satisfaction. Over many trials, the sound is paired consistently with food; thus, it will be conditioned via Pavlovian methods to elicit the same response as the food. Additionally, this process occurred during the instrumental conditioning of bar pressing by using food as a reinforcer.

This same process works for most everyday activities. For most humans, money is an extremely powerful reinforcer. Money itself, though, is not very attractive. It does not taste good, does not reduce any biological drives, and does not, on its own, satisfy any needs. However, it is reliably paired with all of these things and therefore becomes as effective as these primary reinforcers. In a similar way, popular fashion in clothing, hair styles, and personal adornment, popular art or music, even behaving according to the moral values of one's family or church group (or one's gang) can all come to be effective reinforcers because they are reliably paired with an important primary reinforcer, namely, social approval. The person who will function most effectively as the approving agent changes throughout life. One's parents, friends, classmates, teachers, teammates, coaches, spouse, children, and colleagues at work all provide effective social approval opportunities.

WHY REINFORCERS WORK

Reinforcers (and punishers) are effective at influencing an organism's willingness to respond because they influence the way in which an organism acquires something that is desired, or avoids something that is not desired. For primary reinforcers, this concerns health and survival. Secondary reinforcers are learned through experience and do not directly affect one's health or survival,

yet they are adaptive because they are relevant to those situations that are related to well-being and an improved quality of life. Certainly learning where food, drink, receptive sex partners, or social acceptance can be located is useful for an organism. Coming to enjoy being in such situations is very useful, too.

An American psychologist, David Premack, has argued that it is the opportunity to engage in activity, and not the reinforcer itself, that is important; that is, it is not the food, but the opportunity to eat that matters. For example, he has shown that rats will work very hard to gain access to a running wheel. The activity of running in the wheel is apparently reinforcing. Other researchers have demonstrated that monkeys will perform numerous boring, repetitive tasks to open a window just to see into another room. This phenomenon has come to be known as the Premack principle. Premack explains that any high-probability activity can be used to reinforce a lower-probability behavior. This approach works for secondary reinforcers, too. The opportunity to spend money may be the reinforcer, not the money itself. Access to an opportunity to eat, to be entertained, to be with others who are complimentary about one's taste are all highly probable behaviors; thus, they reinforce work for which one may be paid.

According to Premack's position, a child might eat vegetables to gain access to apple pie, but not vice versa. Obviously, for most children getting apple pie is a far more effective reward than getting vegetables. Nonetheless, as unexpected as this is, such a reversal is possible. For this to work two conditions must be met: The child must truly enjoy eating the vegetables (though apple pie could still be preferred), and the child must have been deprived of these vegetables for a fair amount of time. This may make more sense when considering what happens to a child who overindulges in a favored treat. The happy child who is allowed to dive into a bag of Halloween candy, after having polished off a few pounds of sweets, would not find candy all that attractive.

A newer view of Premack's position that incorporates situations such as these is called the bliss point. That is, for each organism there is a particular level of each activity that is most desirable (that is, the bliss point). If one is below that level, that activity has become more probable and can be used as a reinforcer for other behaviors, even those that normally have a higher probability. Thus, if a child has not had vegetables in quite a while and has become tired of apple pie, the vegetables would be effective as reinforcers to increase pie eating, though only temporarily. Once the child has acquired the bliss point for vegetable eating (which is likely to be fairly quickly), its effectiveness is ended.

The bliss point idea addresses some of the confusion about positive and negative reinforcers as well. Intuitively, it seems that positive reinforcement should be the addition of a pleasant stimulus, and that negative reinforcement would be the removal of an unpleasant stimulus. However, as anyone who has overindulged in some favored activity knows, there are times when what is normally very pleasant becomes distinctly unpleasant. Thus, adding this stimulus would not be reinforcing, even though in general it seems that it should be. It is as if the organism conducts a cost-benefit analysis concerning its current state. If the consequence is preferable to the alternative, even one that is not particularly attractive, it will function as a reinforcer. Therefore, adding what would normally be an unpleasant stimulus is positively reinforcing if it is better than going without.

Another useful idea about what makes a particular situation reinforcing is called the establishing operation. This concept describes the process of creating a need for the particular stimulus. After a large meal, food is not an effective reinforcer, but after a period of not eating, it is. Denying an organism food establishes food as an effective reinforcer. The organism is below its bliss point. Secondary reinforcers can be explained by this concept as well. By pairing neutral stimuli with primary reinforcers, one is establishing their effectiveness. Finally, that different organisms find different situations or stimuli satisfying is no surprise. Ducks find the opportunity to swim satisfying; chickens do not. A species' natural history establishes what will be effective as well.

PATTERNS OF REINFORCER DELIVERY

It is not necessary to deliver a reinforcer on every occurrence of a behavior to have the desired effect. In fact, intermittent reinforcement has a stronger effect on the stability of the response rate than reinforcing every response. If the organism expects every response to be reinforced, suspending reinforcement will cause the response to disappear very quickly. If, however, the organism is familiar with occasions of responding without reinforcement, responding will continue for much longer on the termination of reinforcers.

There are two basic patterns of intermittent reinforcement: ratio and interval. Ratio schedules are based on the number of responses required to receive the reinforcer. Interval schedules are based on the amount of time that must pass before a reinforcer is available. Both schedules have fixed and variable types. On fixed schedules, whatever the rule is, it stays that way. If five responses are required to earn a reinforcer (a fixed ratio 5, or FR 5), every fifth response is reinforced. A fixed interval of ten seconds (FI 10) means that the first response after ten seconds has elapsed is reinforced, and this is true every time (responding during the interval is irrelevant). Variable schedules change the rule in unpredictable ways. A VR 5 (variable ratio 5) is one in which, on the average, the fifth response is reinforced, but it would vary over a series of trials. A variable interval of ten seconds (VI 10) is similar. The required amount of time is an average of ten seconds, but on any given trial it could be different.

An example of an FR schedule is pay for a specific amount of work, such as stuffing envelopes. The pay is always the same; stuffing a certain number of envelopes always equals the same pay. An example of an FI is receiving the daily mail. Checking the mailbox before the mail is delivered will not result in reinforcement. One must wait until the appropriate time. A VR example is a slot machine. The more attempts, the more times the player wins, but in an unpredictable pattern. A VI example would be telephoning a friend whose line is busy. Continued attempts will be unsuccessful until the friend hangs up the phone, but when this will happen is unknown.

Response rates for fixed schedules follow a fairly specific pattern. Fixed ratio schedules tend to have a steady rate until the reinforcer is delivered; then there is a short rest, followed by the same rate. A fixed interval is slightly different. The closer one gets to the required time, the faster the response rate. On receiving the reinforcer there will be a short rest, then a gradual return to responding, becoming quicker and quicker over time. This is called a "scalloped" pattern. (Though not strictly an FI schedule, it does have a temporal component, so it illustrates the phenomenon nicely.) Students are much more likely to study during the last few days before a test and very little during the days immediately after the test. As time passes, study behavior gradually begins again, becoming more concentrated the closer the next exam date comes.

BIBLIOGRAPHY

Flora, Stephen Ray. *The Power of Reinforcement*. Albany: State U of New York P, 2004. Print.

Hilgard, Ernest Ropiequet. *Psychology in America: A Historical Review*. San Diego: Harcourt, 1987. Print.

Kimble, Gregory A. *Hilgard and Marquis' Conditioning and Learning*. 2nd ed. New York: Appelton-Century-Crofts,

1968. Print.

Kimble, Gregory A., Michael Wertheimer, and Charlotte L. White, eds. *Portraits of Pioneers in Psychology.* Washington: APA, 1991. Print.

Lieberman, David A. *Learning: Behavior and Cognition.* 3rd ed. Belmont: Wadsworth, 2000. Print.

Ormrod, Jeanne E. *Human Learning.* 6th ed. Boston: Pearson, 2012. Print.

"Positive Reinforcement: A Self-Instructional Exercise." *Athabasca University.* Athabasca University, 2013. Web. 7 July 2014.

Salvador Macias III

SEE ALSO: Aversion therapy; Behaviorism; Conditioning; Habituation and sensitization; Implosion; Learned helplessness; Learning; Operant conditioning therapies; Pavlovian conditioning; Phobias; Punishment; Radical behaviorism: B. F. Skinner; Reflexes; Skinner box; Systematic desensitization.

Relaxation response
Herbert Benson

TYPE OF PSYCHOLOGY: Biological bases of human behavior; Clinical; Counseling; Health; Psychotherapy

The relaxation response is a "deep state of relaxation" according to Dr. Herbert Benson and can be learned through a process of using psychological meditational strategies to allow the body to return to baseline homeostasis after stress activates the fight, flight response. The Benson-Henry Mind-Body Medicine Institute at Massachusetts General Hospital which is affiliated with Harvard Medical School is led by Dr. Herbert Benson. Dr. Benson is the physician who conducted the initial research on what he called the relaxation response in the 1970's. He and his colleagues continue to publish on its methods and health benefits.

KEY CONCEPTS
- Homeostasis
- Mind-body
- Parasympathetic nervous system
- Relaxation
- Stress
- Sympathetic nervous system

INTRODUCTION

Human beings worldwide have used various strategies for achieving relaxation that date back centuries. Early methods used for relaxation included prayer, warm baths, listening to soft music, various herbal remedies and drinking tea or drinking warm milk before bedtime to name just a few. Some of these relaxation methods have endured overtime and are still used today. However, research on the benefits of relaxation started in the 1970's. Dr. Herbert Benson is credited with discovering and naming the phenomenon known as the relaxation response through empirical research on this process of calming the body. This normally autonomic response controlled by the parasympathetic division of the autonomic nervous system, which can be learned with practice, essentially involves training oneself to relax through dedicated and repeated practice, which now has evolved to encompass a number of relaxation strategies ranging from repeating a word or a mantra (special phrase) to repeating any phrase that is experienced as neutral by the person. Typically under stress humans will respond with the fight (fight back against an aggressor), flight (run away from danger), freeze (freeze or immobilize as in feigning death), faint (collapse) or submit (defer to the threat as dogs do when they roll over in submission) response. As Steven Porgess theorizes, humans may respond to stress utilizing three ways as described in Polyvagal theory: Immobilization, mobilization or social engagement if no threat is perceived.

Our bodies once stressed will return to homeostasis automatically when the threat has passed after a period of time. The stress response happens at the autonomic nervous system level and was thought to be solely under unconscious control. The sympathetic division of the autonomic nervous system responds when we are under stress to help mobilize our bodies via stress hormones or glucocorticoids to face the perceived threat. The parasympathetic division of the autonomic nervous system helps our bodies return to homeostasis. It is the parasympathetic nervous system that is in play when we experience relaxation (or return to homeostasis).

EFFECTS OF CHRONIC STRESS

Chronic stress exposure has been known to disrupt this automatic homeostatic pattern. In fact even though short-term sympathetic responsivity can be helpful at times of danger allowing us to escape and or mobilize ourselves to fight a predator, chronically elevated stress hormones can actually be damaging to the health of the individual. Some researchers have called the total stress burden on an individual the "allostatic load" which represents the total accumulated burden of stress that is potentially damaging to one's health especially over the long term.

The damage to health from long term stress can include lower immune system functioning resulting in increased susceptibility to illness, impaired sleep or insomnia, reduced cellular production or cellular size (lower volume) in the hippocampus that stores our emotional or autobiographical memories. It also enlarges the amygdala (a cluster of small almond shaped brain structures that processes stressors), causes hypertension (high blood pressure) and produces an over-sensitized fight-flight reaction.

INITIAL RESEARCH

Doctor Herbert Benson carried out research showing that being able to train our autonomic nervous system to facilitate the relaxation response could improve health. This was a groundbreaking discovery as autonomic nervous system functions are largely operating at the unconscious level, happen automatically, and were not previously thought of as being capable of being brought under conscious control.

CRITIQUE OF APPROACH

Christian religious groups have critiqued the meditational approach for achieving the relaxation response as being void of content and rooted in Eastern philosophy and religious beliefs. These groups have warned of the underlying Eastern influence of the meditation methods used to elicit the relaxation response. As a result, some colleges and meditation centers offer students and the public access to both Mindfulness Meditation groups and Christian Meditation groups. Benson has written in his 1998 book coauthored by Margaret Stark titled *Timeless Healing: The Biology and Power of Belief* on how the approach for achieving the relaxation response can be integrated with religious/spiritual belief in God.

RELAXATION TRAINING

There are many forms of relaxation training available today that can potentially elicit the relaxation response. Benson provided steps for eliciting the relaxation response in his 1975 book, *The Relaxation Response*. He recommended that the method be practiced twice a day for ten to twenty minutes each time in order to achieve full parasympathetic relaxation. However there are a number of methods or combinations of relaxation training methods that can be used to elicit this response and Benson utilized elements from some of these methods (primarily focused meditation and deep breathing) in his protocol. One of these relaxation training methods is called Jacobsen's progressive muscle relaxation (PMR) in which a person is encouraged to alternately tense and relax targeted muscle groups in the body while pairing that process with slow, deep breathing (slow inhale on count of 5 and slow exhale on count of 5). The person will start tensing and releasing the muscle groups in the head or neck and then move to the lower extremities to achieve total body relaxation. Another method he utilized is yoga which is more physically oriented. There are of course, various schools of yoga and meditation that have also been shown to elicit this response.

The Mind-Body Institute, and similar wellness centers, provides resources for achieving relaxation. Benson's institute specifically offers audio instruction in Basic Relaxation Exercise/Mindfulness Mediation, Basic Relaxation Response Exercise, Advanced Relaxation Response, Guided Visualization with Ocean Sounds and Breath and Body Awareness among others.

RECENT RESEARCH

The importance of regular stress reduction or self-care has been validated by ongoing research and the health and mental health benefits cannot be underestimated. Some of the recent work coming out of the Mind Body Institute at Massachusetts General Hospital includes a pilot investigation of a culturally adapted 8-week group mind-body approach to relaxation for American immigrants from China suffering from depression. This study was effective and shows promise for utilizing the relaxation response in conjunction with other tools for addressing both mood and anxiety or stress related disorders.

In addition, functional Magnetic Resonance Imagery (fMRI, a neuroimaging method that highlights changes in brain function) investigations have shown the neurological effects of the relaxation response on the brain. Changes in the brain due to meditation include increases in activity in areas of the brain that govern the autonomic nervous system and attention.

THE NATIONAL INSTITUTE OF HEALTH (NIH)

National Center for Complementary and Alternative Medicine (NCCAM) has taken a large role in educating the public on relaxation methods and supporting empirical investigation of various relaxation techniques including the various methods used for eliciting the relaxation response. There is a disclaimer on the website that alternative medicine methods should not replace conventional medical care. Information from NIH, NCCAM outlines not only health and mental health benefits of validated methods of relaxation training but also highlights associated risks and side effects. For example physicians must advise those suffering from heart conditions to see if progressive muscle relaxation can be used with individuals from that population.

Adverse effects of the relaxation response are thought to be rare. However, there are some individuals especially those with certain psychological disorders such as dissociative disorders, or survivors of childhood trauma or abuse, or epilepsy for whom any kind of relaxation or meditation training may aggravate symptoms. They may even experience increased anxiety and discomfort or increased dissociation (an uncomfortable mental state that disconnects feelings, thoughts and aspects of conscious processing of experience) showing the approach is not for everyone.

BIBLIOGRAPHY

Benson, Herbert (1975). *The Relaxation Response*. New York: William Morrow and Company. The original book showing the importance of using a mind-body approach to achieve the relaxation response. This book has been globally distributed and showed the promise of using psychological strategies (meditation) for achieving relaxation. Steps for eliciting the response is given. There is a new forward written in 2000, available in the 2009 Adobe digital e-book edition that gives a glimpse on the historical significance of the discovery of the relaxation response and its' promise if integrated into an approach with traditional medicine, published 25 years after the original book.

Benson, Herbert & Stark, Margaret (2014). *Timeless Healing*. (e book). New York: Scribner. Herbert Benson and Margaret Stark coauthors of this eBook version of an earlier hard copy edition title. *Timeless Healing: The Biology and Power of Belief* (1998) that is available in paperback version. Ullustrates how believing in God or a higher power can benefit both spiritual and physical well-being or overall health. In this book. Benson emphazises how integrating belief (which he proposes is neurobiologicall pre-hardwired into the brain/body), self-care and care from one's own physician can contribute to overall wellbeing.

No author. *National Institute of Health (NIH)* National Center for Complementary and AlternativeMedicine (NCAAM). Website. http://nccam nih.gov/health/stress/relaxation.htm Provides information and oversight and federal grant sponsorship of empirical research on alternative and complementary medicine focusing on health benefits of relaxation training techniques including biofeedback, progressive muscle relaxation, guided imagery, deep breathing and other breathing techniques, autogenic training, massage therapy, acupuncture and self-hypnosis. Health benefits range across many conditions from reducing insomnia, to stopping smoking.

The Benson-Henry Institute for Mind- Body Medicine at Massachusetts General Hospital. Website. http://www.massgeneral.org/bhi/ The nationally ranked hospital based center founded by Dr. Herbert Benson educates and trains individuals in stress reduction to achieve the relaxation response. The center sponsors research on the relaxation response and adaptations of relaxation response training to various populations and disorders. The center also teaches physicians mind body approaches to health and wellness that can be integrated with traditional medicine.

Levey, Joel & Levey, Michelle (2003). *The Fine Art of Relaxation, Concentration and Meditation: Ancient Skills For Modern Minds*. Massachusetts: Wisdom Publications. A manual that shows how modern distractions take away from our inner awareness and balance in life and the toll it takes on our health. Encourages people to take charge of their inner world through focused relaxation and meditation strategies.

Karen Wolford

SEE ALSO: Emotional arousal; Emotional states; Harvard; Mind body medicine; Mind/body institute; Relaxation.

Religion and psychology

TYPE OF PSYCHOLOGY: Cognition; Developmental psychology; Emotion; Motivation; Social psychology

The relationship between religion and psychology usually involves the study of religious belief and behavior from a psychological perspective. The psychological study of religion includes a focus on both religious behavior and religious belief and uses various models of human nature and many psychological concepts.

KEY CONCEPTS
- Extrinsic religious orientation
- Intrinsic religious orientation
- Moral behavior
- Quest religious orientation
- Religion
- Religious conversion
- Spirituality

Photo: iStock

INTRODUCTION

Both religion and psychology are broad topics that encompass a vast array of human experience. The study of the psychology of religion is the effort to understand and predict the thoughts, feelings, and actions of persons as they act religiously. (The psychology of religion is different from the idea of psychology itself as a religion, which suggests that the field of psychology, with its own interpretation of the meaning of personal existence, be granted the status of an alternative worldview or a secular religion.) The psychology of religion is also distinct from religious psychology, which usually attempts to integrate the tenets of a faith system (such as Judaism, Islam, or Christianity) with the findings of psychological science.

The word "religion" is rooted in two Latin words: legare and religio. Legare denotes a process of rebinding or reconnecting. Religio means to restrain or hold back, which implies that one purpose of religion is to bridle human motives and impulses. Religion can be understood, then, as a force that reconnects human fragmentation to a sense of wholeness and restrains problematic drives and impulses. It should be noted that a supernatural deity is not mentioned or even implied in this definition. Thus, religion may involve a reconnection to God, nature, the self, some cosmic force, or almost anything else as one strives to be complete or whole.

Some research in the psychology of religion considers the function that religion serves for the individual. From this perspective, religion may be seen as a confirmation of hope, a conservation of values, a means by which to establish goals and measure personal development, a source of comfort, or a quest for the ideal relationship. Sigmund Freud, for example, considered religious experience to be a search for an external source of control to supersede the ambivalent feelings that individuals have toward their parents. Thus, Freud viewed God as nothing more, psychologically, than an exalted father. He further maintained that the root of all religion is a longing for a father figure.

Another example of the perceived functional value of religion is in the study of religious conversions. A religious conversion may be understood as simply a transformation or a turning from one belief to another. Conversions may occur within religious contexts that are traditionally accepted by society (such as any major religious tradition) or may occur in cults or sects outside society's mainstream. Psychologists and other social scientists have often focused on the functional value of cultic conversions. One model, for example, suggests that the potential cultic convert must first experience enduring and strongly felt tensions that have not been met by traditional religious institutions. Once the cult movement is encountered, strong emotional bonds are established, and attachments to individuals outside the cult begin to diminish. Eventually, there is an intensive interaction between the new convert and the cult. Through these processes, the individual may believe that his or her needs are being met, while at the same time the control of the cult over the individual becomes substantially stronger.

Thus, the religious practices of the cult serve a particular function both for the individual and for the group.

While some psychologists stress the functional aspects of religion, others view the study of religious experience more in terms of its substance by investigating such topics as different ways of being religious, whether religiousness is related to social compassion, participation in religious behaviors such as church attendance and prayer, the importance of religion, and believers' openness to doubt. For example, Gordon Allport wanted to investigate the characteristics of mature religion. He distinguished between those with an intrinsic religious orientation that is characterized by an inner, personal, and meaningful faith and those with an extrinsic religious orientation, in which faith is used for some other self-interest. In the mature intrinsic orientation, the person's faith is a master motive that will be given priority over other motives, especially those that may conflict (such as a particular economic or sexual motive). In the immature extrinsic religious orientation, religion provides some sort of payoff or gain outside the self, such as the protection of social or economic well-being.

Allport's notion of religious orientation has generated considerable interest among psychologists of religion, and his theory has undergone some revision. It appears that intrinsic and extrinsic religiousness are not totally opposite. That is, some people may have both religious orientations, while others may have neither orientation. Furthermore, some psychologists have questioned whether the intrinsic orientation is really a mature religion. In part, this debate revolves around ways in which religious orientation is measured by means of self-reported responses to questions on a scale. The concern is that some people may respond a certain way to appear "good." An alternative religious orientation that has been proposed as a truly mature religion has been called the "quest" orientation. This orientation is characterized by an active searching for existential truth that may sometimes involve a certain degree of doubt or questioning. Defenders of Allport's notion of mature religion as an intrinsic orientation suggest that a quest orientation may be a necessary step in religious development but should not be understood as mature religion.

PSYCHOLOGICAL IMPLICATIONS OF RELIGION
While a psychological study of religion is of interest to many in its own right, others question the value of such research: Why bother with a psychological analysis of religious behavior?

One reason is that religion is apparently an important dimension in the life of many people. Religious conversions, for example, are very prevalent in Western society, and evidence indicates that in 1970 about 39 of the African population was Christian; by 2020, the Christian population in Africa is projected to be almost 50 percent. Data from a 2005 Gallup Poll indicate that 41 percent of US adults consider themselves to be "born-again" or evangelical Christians. The extent to which these percentages reflect genuine personal conversions is unclear; however, the indications are quite clear that religious conversion of some type, even if it means simply the confirmation of parental upbringing, occurs in the lives of many people.

Religion has other important psychological implications as well. Studies in the 1940s and 1950s showed repeatedly that religious people, as measured by frequency of church attendance, scored higher on measures of racial prejudice than did nonreligious people. This may be a disturbing finding to some, given that most religious teaching, regardless of tradition, stresses compassion, patience, and love for humanity. Yet there were also some notable exceptions to this general pattern. Allport decided to apply the intrinsic-extrinsic religious orientation concept to the study of prejudice. His reasoning was that "extrinsics" may be most likely to demonstrate prejudice, since their religious approach is one in which an individual seeks security and comfort, which are also byproducts of prejudice (as when one sees oneself as superior to others). Hence, the person who attends church because it is psychologically comforting or because it increases his or her status in the community is more likely, for similar reasons, to have prejudicial attitudes. Research has generally supported Allport's reasoning. Extrinsically oriented individuals (identified as those with immature religion) demonstrate higher levels of prejudice than either intrinsics or nonreligious individuals. People who score indiscriminately high on both intrinsic and extrinsic measures of religion, however, demonstrate the highest prejudice levels of all. Evidence suggests that these people tend to see things in blanket categories (such as "all religion is good"). Because prejudice is a negative prejudgment based on a stereotype, such people may also tend to see, for example, all minorities as bad.

The relationship between religion and prejudice is actually a part of a much broader question: Does religion have a positive effect on human behavior? Unfortunately, a simple, straightforward answer cannot be provided. One creative study at Princeton Theological Seminary was conducted to see if people with religion on their minds would be more likely to help someone in need. In the study, based on the New Testament parable of the Good Samaritan, in which only the Samaritan, not the religiously minded priest or the Levite, helped a victim along a roadside, it was discovered that theological students were no more likely to help someone in need if they were about to give a talk on the Good Samaritan than if they were to give a talk on the job market for seminary graduates. Rather, the more crucial issue was how much time they had. Those who thought they were late were far less likely to help.

This one study certainly does not determine whether religion is a good predictor of moral behavior. In some cases, research has shown what some may think is intuitively obvious. Most studies indicate that religious individuals are less likely to engage in extramarital sexual behavior or to use illicit drugs. Those with an intrinsic religious orientation, compared to extrinsics and the nonreligious, are less likely to cheat on an exam if given an opportunity to do so. Similarly, those who are highly committed to their faith are less likely blindly to obey an authority figure who orders them to hurt someone. It appears that religion can be an important predictor of some significant human behaviors.

Another common question involves religion and mental health. Religious symbolism is frequently found in the speech of those who are seriously disturbed, so this is a legitimate concern. Albert Ellis, an outspoken atheist and the creator of rational emotive therapy (which suggests that irrational beliefs are at the heart of most psychological problems), considers religion harmful to one's well-being. The idea that one needs some supernatural power on which to rely, insists Ellis, is an irrational belief. Freud, who also saw religion as unhealthy, identified it as a neurosis of the masses. Certainly, the 1997 Heaven's Gate mass suicide in Rancho Santa Fe, California, as well as a number of other incidents, indicates that people may often engage in bizarre behavior in the name of religion. Yet research on a number of mental health variables—including fear of death, anxiety, loneliness, sense of well-being, dogmatism, and authoritarianism—generally indicates that religious people are neither better nor worse off than other persons.

HISTORICAL BACKGROUND

Psychology and religion have had an intermittent relationship. William James's classic book *The Varieties of Religious Experience: A Study in Human Nature* (1902)

provided the early impetus for the psychology of religion. G. Stanley Hall, the first president of the American Psychological Association, wrote *Jesus, the Christ, in the Light of Psychology* (1917), which dealt with the underlying motivations of religious conversion. From 1920 to 1960, however, there was little interest in the field. Annual reviews on the subject in the *Psychology Bulletin* appeared less regularly from 1904 to 1920 and ceased altogether after 1933. Probably the greatest reason for the demise of the psychology of religion during this period was the idea that psychology should become an established science like the natural sciences. The study of religious experience, reasoned most experts, does not lend itself well to the scientific enterprise. Another reason that psychologists steered away from religion was the rise, during this period, of Freud's psychoanalytic theory, which many believed undermined the legitimacy of religious experience.

During the late 1950s and early 1960s, however, organizations such as the Christian Association for Psychological Studies and the Society for the Scientific Study of Religion were founded. The Catholic Psychological Association became Division 36 (Psychologists Interested in Religious Issues) of the American Psychological Association. At the same time, professional journals such as the *Journal for the Scientific Study of Religion* were established. In part, this about-face was caused by the changing religious patterns of society. Western culture has become increasingly religious since the 1950s. In addition, psychology's infatuation with the prevailing view of science during the 1930s and subsequent decades waned. No longer do many psychologists believe that psychology should (or can) become a science in the same way that physics, for example, is a science. This means that psychology is open to new methods and new areas of study, including religion.

An even more radical step since the 1970s has been the attempt by some psychologists to integrate theology with psychology. Though theology includes Judaism, Islam, Hinduism, and other major world religions, most of the effort at reconciliation has been directed toward Christian theology (particularly evangelical or conservative theology). Journals such as the *Journal of Psychology and Christianity* and the *Journal of Psychology and Theology* have been established as mechanisms of scholarly interchange on the relationship between psychological and theological understandings of the person. Even accredited graduate programs espousing an integrated study have opened and flourished.

Despite these dramatic changes by psychologists with regard to the study of religion, research has indicated that psychologists remain among the least religious of all scientists. Nevertheless, it is of interest to many to see whether these changes will affect the study of religious experience in the decades ahead.

BIBLIOGRAPHY

Benner, David G., and Peter C. Hill, eds. *Baker Encyclopedia of Psychology and Counseling*. Grand Rapids: Baker, 1999. Print.

Carter, John D., and Bruce Narramore. *The Integration of Psychology and Theology: An Introduction*. Grand Rapids: Zondervan, 1979. Print.

Fuller, Andrew R. *Psychology and Religion: Classical Theorists and Contemporary Developments*. 4th ed. Lanham: Rowman, 2008. Print.

Guirdham, Arthur. *Christ and Freud: A Study of Religious Experience and Observance*. London: Routledge, 2014. Print.

Hill, Peter C., et al. "Conceptualizing Religion and Spirituality: Points of Commonality, Points of Departure." *Journal for the Theory of Social Behavior* 30.1 (2000): 51–77. Print.

Hood, Ralph W., Jr., et al. *The Psychology of Religion: An Empirical Approach*. 4th ed. New York: Guilford, 2009. Print.

Knoop, Hans Henrik, and Antonella Delle Fave. *Well-Being and Cultures: Perspectives from Positive Psychology*. New York: Springer, 2013. Print.

Leeming, David A. *Encyclopedia of Psychology and Religion*. Boston: Springer, 2014. Print.

Merkur, Daniel. *Relating to God: Clinical Psychoanalysis, Spirituality, and Theism*. Lanham: Aronson, 2014. Print.

Paloutzian, Raymond F. *Invitation to the Psychology of Religion*. 2nd ed. Boston: Allyn, 1996. Print.

Pargament, Kenneth I. *The Psychology of Religion and Coping: Theory, Research, and Practice*. New York: Guilford, 1997. Print.

Peck, M. Scott. *The Road Less Traveled: A New Psychology of Love, Traditional Values, and Spiritual Growth*. 1978. Rpt. New York: Simon, 2003. Print.

Stern, E. Mark, ed. *The Other Side of the Couch: What Therapists Believe*. New York: Pilgrim, 1981. Print.

Wulff, David M. *Psychology of Religion: Classic and Contemporary Views*. 2nd ed. New York: Wiley, 1997. Print.

Peter C. Hill; updated by Tanja Bekhuis

SEE ALSO: Altruism, cooperation, and empathy; Attitude-behavior consistency; Attitude formation and change; Coping: Social support; Hall, G. Stanley; Helping; James, William; Moral development; Religiosity: Measurement; Spirituality and mental health.

Religiosity

TYPE OF PSYCHOLOGY: Cognition; Developmental psychology; Motivation; Psychological methodologies; Social psychology

The study of religiosity (religious feelings, beliefs, and behaviors) by psychologists and other scholars involves a variety of quantitative and qualitative methods. The traditional measurement approach is psychometric and rests on substantive or functional scales of various aspects of religiosity.

KEY CONCEPTS
- Denomination
- Extrinsic religious orientation
- Functional scales
- Intrinsic religious orientation
- Psychometric theory
- Qualitative method
- Quantitative method
- Quest orientation
- Religiosity
- Substantive scales

INTRODUCTION

During the twentieth century, academic psychologists were concerned with developing an empirical science that would compare favorably with other natural sciences. Hence, the constructs in models of human behavior were operationalized with the goal of yielding numeric data that could be analyzed statistically. Quantitative methods (experiments, quasi-experiments, surveys, correlational studies) superseded the earlier descriptive, qualitative methods (Oedipal interpretations, clinical and literary case studies, introspective reports) and required relatively objective measurement of psychological attributes or traits. A fundamental notion in psychometric theory is that measurements taken on people should at the very least allow ordering along some continuum or dimension, such as intelligence or anxiety. However, measurement also may connote appraisal or understanding. Thus, the early explorations of religious experience (such as those of Sigmund Freud, Carl Jung, or William

James) may be very broadly considered as involving, in some sense, the "measure" of religious experience.

The development of models and methods in the study of religiosity (religious feelings, beliefs, and behaviors) parallels this general timeline, although the emphasis on empiricism occurred in the latter half of the twentieth century. Since then, most psychologists of religion have been academic social psychologists who relied heavily on psychometric measures of religiosity, such as self-report questionnaires. However, since the 1980s, a resurgent interest in narrative or interpretive methods has competed with the psychometric tradition. Additionally, psychology of religion has become an international enterprise more open to qualitative methods. For example, Europeans are not averse to phenomenological interpretations of religious experience. The result of these diverging views is a broadening of the methodological base for testing models and theories of religion and an increasing sophistication with respect to measurement of religiosity. Many psychologists welcome this development, as they feel that more meaningful research is possible. For example, Kenneth I. Pargament, a renowned psychologist who studies coping behavior and religious beliefs, maintains that empirical methods must be balanced with phenomenological or interpretive methods, since religious experience is often private and symbolic and, therefore, not observable.

SOCIAL PSYCHOLOGY, ATTITUDES, AND SURVEYS
Mainstream social psychologists regard attitudes as learned habits for responding to social stimuli and attempt to identify the cognitive, affective (emotional), and behavioral components of the attitude. Religiosity (also known as religiousness) is generally understood as a person's essential attitude toward religion. The word "religion" has a Latin root that implies binding and restraining. Religion is therefore a personal and social force that serves to bind people together in a community of worshipers, unite them in reverence with a spiritual dimension of existence, and restrain their inappropriate impulses via moral commandments.

The form of attitude surveying with which the average American would be most familiar is the national opinion poll as conducted by George Gallup, Louis Harris, a major newspaper or magazine, or a marketing research firm. For example, the Gallup Poll measures a person's overall religiosity by asking, "How important would you say religion is in your own life?" Nationally, more than half of the adults surveyed in 2012 respond "very important,"

where importance tends to increase with age. In addition, there are gender, ethnic, and church affiliation differences; for example, the subgroups comprising women, African Americans, or Protestants are most likely to say that religion is very important.

Pollsters usually break down religion into specific behavioral, cognitive, and affective components. An important behavioral component is affiliation with a particular denomination (a religious organization within the host culture usually referred to as a church). In 2013, according to Gallup, about 83 percent of all adults in the United States claimed a religious affiliation (such as Protestant, Catholic, or Jewish), but only about 69 percent said they were actually members of a specific denomination. The largest single denomination in the United States in 2013 was Roman Catholic (27 percent), followed by Baptists (12 percent), then Methodists (5 percent). However, taken in the aggregate, 41 percent of the adults surveyed were Protestant.

Attending worship services is another behavior that may be measured. In 2013, 39 percent of US adults attended a service during the last seven days. Since 1939, this figure has been very stable. Other measurable religious activities include reading the Bible and praying: 47 percent of U.S. adults have read the Bible in the last week and 75 percent pray daily.

Another approach would be to measure people's level of acceptance or endorsement of specific church policies (or of government laws relating to religion). For example, 59 percent of American Catholics disagree with the official teachings of their church of not allowing divorced people to remarry in the church and 79 percent disagree with not permitting people to use artificial means of birth control, according to 2014 poll conducted by Univision. Polls have also discovered that about three-quarters of all Americans would accept teaching about world religions and the Bible (as literature and history) in the public schools.

Cognitive dimensions of religiousness include beliefs about God or a spiritual reality, as well as what people believe about religion. According to a 2014 Gallup poll, 86 percent of US adults believe in God or in a higher power. As of 2011, 85 percent believe in heaven and 75 percent believe in hell. In 2013, 56 percent believed that religion, rather than being out of date, could answer most of the day's problems; 21 percent believed that religion is increasing its influence on American life, while 76 percent believed it is losing influence. According to Gallup, in 2014, about 45 percent of adults surveyed had a "Great

PSYCHOLOGY & BEHAVIORAL HEALTH

deal" or "Quite a lot" of confidence in the church and organized religion.

The affective components of religiosity deal with emotions, priorities, values, and evaluations. For example, in evaluating the overall priority they give to religion in their lives, 56 percent of Americans state that religion is "very important," while only 22 percent say it is "not very important."

RELIGIOUS ORIENTATION SCALES

In the 1960s, a dominant theme in research on religiosity emerged in response to the work of Gordon Allport, who had developed a model of religious orientation characterized by intrinsic and extrinsic dimensions. The former type of religiosity is interiorized, private, devotional, and based on individual commitment. Some items purporting to measure intrinsic religiosity have dealt with personal piety, church attendance, and the importance of religion. Extrinsic religiosity is more institutional, public, and pragmatic. Some of the items on scales designed to measure the extrinsic dimension include seeing religion as a vehicle for social relationships, consolation of grief, maintenance of order, and adherence to tradition. Many psychometric scales have been developed to assess orientation, an aspect of religiosity. Some measure orientation with a single intrinsic/extrinsic, bipolar scale, others with two distinct subscales. In contrast, in 1991, C. Daniel Batson and P. Schoenrade developed the Quest Scale to measure a third type. A quest orientation recognizes the positive value of doubt in the face of complex, existential questions regarding the meaning of life. What is particularly interesting is that Quest Scale scores tend to correlate negatively with prejudice measures.

OTHER MEASURES OF RELIGIOSITY

Peter C. Hill and Ralph W. Hood, Jr., edited a much-needed compendium of scales titled *Measures of Religiosity* (1999). There are 126 scales grouped in seventeen chapters, thematically arranged. For example, there are measures of beliefs, attitudes, orientation, development, commitment, experience, values, and coping. Scales are presented along with information about the measured variable or dimension; scoring; psychometric properties, including evidence for reliability and validity; characteristics of people studied during the test development phase (norming samples); documentation regarding where the measure appeared in the research literature; and references for follow-up study. By identifying measures of similar constructs with different names or, con-

versely, measures of dissimilar constructs with the same name, Hill and Hood hope to promote a better understanding of the constructs measured. Richard Gorsuch also has suggested that construct and convergent validity could be improved if different researchers would use the same measures in well-developed, theoretically driven programs of research.

It is rare for scales used in the measurement of religiosity to meet well-known criteria for psychological tests. For example, few researchers publish standardized norms or even basic descriptive statistics for the samples used, such as measures of central tendency (means or medians) and variability (standard deviations or ranges). While reliability may be good, information regarding validity is often inadequate. Validity is further compromised by the inherent sampling bias of many American religiosity scales, since most were developed using samples of convenience comprising US Protestants. Therefore, scales may be invalid for groups other than US Protestants. Traditional criteria and standards for scales may be found in texts such as *Psychological Testing* (1997) by Anne Anastasi and Susana Urbina or in the *Standards for Educational and Psychological Testing* (1999).

Religiosity measures may be classified as substantive scales or functional scales. If the former, the focus is on content; and if the latter, the focus is on process. For example, measures of religious beliefs tend to be substantive and are about what is believed, whereas measures of religious orientation tend to be functional and are variants or departures from Allport and Ross's Religious Orientation Scale (1967).

Although social psychologists still dominate the field, developmental, cognitive, and evolutionary psychologists are contributing measures that correspond to their models of religious experience. While measures across these domains are primarily paper-and-pencil questionnaires, some are structured or semistructured interviews and some, as in the evolutionary approach, measure neurophysiological variables as indicators of religious or spiritual states.

HOW RELIGIOSITY MEASURES ARE USED

Numerous applications of the various measures of religiosity are possible. Researchers can correlate any of these to other attitudes, personality traits, or demographic variables. Questions such as whether religious people are more superstitious, how religiosity differs between Democrats and Republicans, and whether religion helps people cope with marital problems can be addressed. For example, depending on how one decides to measure religion (and how one measures superstition), there is a slight tendency for more religious people to be a little less superstitious, but there are many people who are neither very religious nor very superstitious, and there are some who are both.

Using data from political polls, it can be verified that Jews, Catholics, and black Baptists tend to vote for Democrats, while most mainline white Protestant groups tend to vote for Republicans. Much of this correlation can be explained by historical and social-class features, however, in addition to the religious positions of the denominations.

Whether (and how) religion helps people cope with marital or other real-life problems is a difficult question to resolve. True experimentation, with random assignment of people to experimental and control conditions, would be necessary to confirm a cause-and-effect relationship. What seems to be apparent, however, is that religious people have a lower incidence of divorce and report slightly higher levels of marital satisfaction. This could be attributable to the fact that religious people feel more obligated to report that they have better marital relations, or it could be attributable to the fact that people who have problems in staying with a spouse also have problems in staying with their religion. When parents are asked whether religion has helped strengthen their family relationships, nearly four in five report that it has.

Clinical applications of the measurement of religiosity are also numerous. Very religiously committed individuals may have a problem with entering purely secular psychotherapy. The therapist may be seen as a nonbeliever who will challenge the patient's worldview. Depending on the denomination, patients' motivation for change may be tempered by the belief that their sufferings are a punishment inflicted by God.

From a more positive perspective, a patient's religion can both serve as a source of impulse control (for example, as a check on suicidal tendencies) and provide a wide range of formal and informal social supports. For all these reasons, it is necessary for clinicians to assess the religiosity of their patients. Tolerant therapists can then use the patient's worldview as a reference point. Therapists who cannot tolerate a given patient's religiosity can make an appropriate referral (to another therapist who can) before the therapist is frustrated and the psychotherapeutic relationship has been damaged.

Other applications are possible in social and applied psychology. By understanding the religiosity of their

"target segment," for example, advertisers can tailor commercial and political messages to synchronize them with the values and worldviews of potential customers or voters.

HISTORICAL BACKGROUND

In the late nineteenth century, psychologists turned to the field of religion and speculated about its origins and importance. William James was one of the foremost scholars of this period. His approach was chiefly that of the case study. The strength of his qualitative and narrative approach was that religion was embedded within the broader context of human life. The weakness was that two different investigators could look at the same religious person or phenomenon and come to very different conclusions, for there were no quantitative data.

The psychoanalyst Erik H. Erikson also employed the case study approach. For example, he wrote about the lives of Martin Luther and Mahatma Gandhi in terms of his eight-stage, epigenetic theory. Other theorists with a positive view of religion included neo-Freudians such as Carl Jung and Erich Fromm, and humanistic "third force" representatives such as Abraham Maslow. However, for these theorists, religion was secondary to their studies of personality, and their work was, therefore, seen by academic psychologists of religion as more philosophical than scientific.

For these reasons, the quantitative approach of the pollsters and psychologists dominates academic psychology. Yet doubt may be cast on the scientific status of this approach as well. A serious problem has to do with social desirability—people often respond in a way they think they should respond. Even though responses may be anonymous, people may (unconsciously or not) seek to portray themselves in a favorable light (in other words, as more religious than they really are). Another concern is the use of ambiguous terms in questions. Each denomination tends to define terms in its own way. What one denomination calls "services" might be called "worship" or "mass" by another. The Lord's Supper is also known as Holy Communion and the Eucharist. Terms such as "God" and "personal commitment" may be so vague as to preclude construct validity.

The same item may have a different meaning for different people. For example, a person answering "rarely or never" to the question "How often do you ask God to forgive your sins?" may be an atheist who sees no purpose to the confession or a pious individual who rarely sins. Someone who disagrees with the statement "The word of

God is revealed only in the Scriptures" may be an atheist or someone who believes in the possibility of present-day revelation. Certainly, national polls and measures of religiosity have ignored the importance of the context of the respondent's denomination. Religiosity, as measured by the same scale, may mean one thing for an Orthodox Jew and another for a Jehovah's Witness.

Many social scientists predicted the demise of religion during the twentieth century. Karl Marx believed that religion was the "opiate" of the people: a social institution used by the ruling classes to control and placate the exploited masses. After a proletarian revolution and the establishment of a just (Communist) social order, reasoned Marx, there would be no need for religion or, for that matter, the other instruments of state repression. Freud contended that, as psychoanalysis became more prevalent, people would turn away from religion; society would be composed of self-restrained individuals in control of their sexual and aggressive drives. The behaviorist B. F. Skinner regarded religious behavior as the result of accidental reinforcement, a superstitious approach to life that would diminish as humanity developed better technology for controlling the contingencies of its own reinforcement.

Instead, religion remains in myriad forms. For example, many intellectuals have moved away from institutionalized religion toward secular humanism. This requires those who study religion to rethink certain definitions, such as whether secular humanism can be defined as a religion and whether its religiosity can be measured. A more relevant question is not whether religion will continue to exist, but whether qualitative methods can attain the precision that science demands and whether quantitative methods can ever adequately measure the richness of human religious experience.

BIBLIOGRAPHY

Allport, Gordon W. *The Individual and His Religion: A Psychological Interpretation*. 1950. Reprint. New York: Macmillan, 1970. Print.

American Educational Research Association, American Psychological Association, and National Council on Measurement in Education. *Standards for Educational and Psychological Testing*. Washington: American Psychological Association, 1999. Print.

Anastasi, Anne, and Susan Urbina. *Psychological Testing*. 7th ed. Upper Saddle River: Prentice Hall, 1997. Print.

Cook, Kaye V., et al. "The Complexity of Quest in Emerging Adults' Religiosity, Well-Being, and Identity." *Journ. of the Scientific Study of Religion* 53.1 (2014): 73–89. Print.

DeBono, Kenneth, and Anja Kuschpel. "Gender Differences in Religiosity: The Role of Self-Monitoring." *North American Journ. of Psychology* 16.2 (2014): 415–26. Print.

Erikson, Erik H. *Gandhi's Truth: On the Origin of Militant Nonviolence*. New York: Norton, 1993. Print.

Erikson, Erik H. *Young Man Luther: A Study in Psychoanalysis and History*. New York: Norton, 1993. Print.

Gallup, George, Jr., and D. Michael Lindsay. *Surveying the Religious Landscape: Trends in U.S. Beliefs*. Harrisburg: Morehouse, 1999. Print.

Hill, Peter C., and Ralph W. Hood, Jr., eds. *Measures of Religiosity*. Birmingham,: Religious Education, 1999. Print.

Hood, Ralph W., Jr., Bernard Spilka, Bruce Hunsberger, and Richard Gorsuch. *The Psychology of Religion: An Empirical Approach*. 4th ed. New York: Guilford, 2009. Print.

Meadow, Mary Jo, and R. D. Kahoe. *Psychology of Religion: Religion in Individual Lives*. New York: Harper, 1984. Print.

Van Slyke, James A. *The Cognitive Science of Religion*. Burlington: Ashgate, 2011. Print.

Whitehouse, Harvey. *Modes of Religiosity: A Cognitive Theory of Religious Transmission*. Walnut Creek, Calif.: AltaMira, 2004. Print.

Wulff, David M. *The Psychology of Religion: Classic and Contemporary*. 2d ed. New York: Wiley, 1997. Print.

T. L. Brink; updated by Tanja Bekhuis

SEE ALSO: Archetypes and the collective unconscious; Attitude-behavior consistency; Attitude formation and change; James, William; Maslow, Abraham; Religion and psychology; Spirituality and mental health; Survey research: Questionnaires and interviews.

Repressed memories

TYPE OF PSYCHOLOGY: Consciousness; Memory; Psychopathology; Psychotherapy

A repressed memory is a memory loss that is brought on by psychological processes responsible for protecting the

mind from potentially harmful experiences. Both memory theorists and clinical therapists have acknowledged that individuals can have recollections of prior traumatic experiences that are later shown to be totally false.

KEY CONCEPTS
- Childhood sexual abuse
- Defense mechanism
- Forgetting
- Traumatic experiences
- Unconscious mind

INTRODUCTION

Sigmund Freud was the first to introduce the concept that memories of traumatic experiences or harmful desires could be "repressed" and kept from conscious awareness for years or even an entire lifetime. In 1896, Freud presented an essay to the Viennese Society for Psychiatry and Neurology stating that he believed certain kinds of hysterical symptoms such as the temporary paralysis of a hand or the inability to speak could be brought on by previously experienced trauma that had been blocked out of consciousness. If these repressed memories were not recollected but continued to fester in the unconscious mind, then they could produce harmful psychological effects on the individual. Freud used hypnosis as a means to gain access to repressed memories with the hope that once the traumatic memory surfaced, it could be processed and analyzed within the confines of psychoanalysis. However, Freud soon learned that many of the memories that hypnosis uncovered were found to be false.

DEBATE

The concept of repression represents an explanation for how past traumatic events could be forgotten over long periods of time. Repression is seen as a type of defense mechanism, providing protection to the psychological health and well-being of the individual. The forgetting associated with repression is not due to an organic problem with the brain, such as a traumatic brain injury or a neurological illness such as Alzheimer's disease, which results in observable brain damage. Repression is seen as cognitive mechanism at the psychological level of processing that denies the conscious mind access to the preserved, intact memory that resides in the unconscious mind.

One question that current memory theorists debate is exactly how people remember or forget a traumatic experience. Contemporary theorists question whether traumatic events, such as childhood sexual abuse, involve cognitive mechanisms that differ from those that process mundane childhood memories. Most researchers agree that the empirical evidence in support of Freud's repressed memory construct is rather scant.

Several alternative theories have been proposed to explain how an individual can go for years without being aware of a previous traumatic experience. One rival explanation is to view memory loss as a function of a problem with how memories are processed and eventually converted into long-term memories. Neuroscientist James McGaugh has argued that the abnormally high levels of anxiety associated with trauma interfere with the consolidation of a recent experience into a more permanent representation. Altered brain chemistry, as a result of the highly charged emotions that are present, could result in deficient memory processing for the details of a previous event, while both emotional and perceptual elements are processed normally. This alternative theory could help explain the difficulty an individual has in recollecting a traumatic event experienced years earlier, without relying on the notion of repression. Memory theorist Elke Geraerts and his colleagues point out that it has only been recently that research has focused on the cognitive functioning of individuals who have recovered memories of previous trauma.

FALSE MEMORIES

During the 1980s and 1990s, the number of people who reported recovered memories of prior childhood sexual abuse increased dramatically. These recovered memories typically emerged in two different contexts. In some instances, the recovered memory came spontaneously, perhaps being triggered by cues within the environment that could have resembled cues present during the original assault. In other instances, recovered memories emerged during sessions of psychotherapy, particularly with therapists who relied on techniques such as hypnosis, guided imagery, and dream interpretation. Although it is difficult to determine the accuracy of a memory for a sexual assault in the absence of independent corroborating evidence, there have been many documented cases that appear to indicate that the recovered memory for childhood sexual abuse never occurred. A study published in 2013 indicated that skepticism about the validity of repressed memories among research psychologists and memory experts had grown significantly since the 1990s.

BIBLIOGRAPHY

Geraerts, Elke, et al. "Cognitive Mechanisms Underlying Recovered-Memory Experiences of Childhood Sexual Abuse." *Psychological Science* 20.1 (2009): 1–7. Print.

Goodman, Gail S., et al. "A Prospective Study of Memory for Child Sexual Abuse: New Findings Relevant to the Repressed-Memory Controversy." *Psychological Science* 14.2 (2003): 113–18. Print.

Loftus, Elizabeth F., and Katherine Ketcham. *The Myth of Repressed Memory: False Memories and Allegations of Sexual Abuse.* New York: St. Martin's, 1996. Print.

Patihis, Lawrence, et al. "Are the 'Memory Wars' Over? A Scientist-Practitioner Gap in Beliefs about Repressed Memory." *Psychological Science* 25.2 (2014): 519–30. Print.

Pettus, Ashley. "A Cultural Symptom? Repressed Memory." *Harvard Magazine.* Harvard Magazine, Jan.–Feb. 2008. Web. 27 June 2014.

Radvansky, Gabriel. *Human Memory.* New York: Pearson, 2006. Print.

Schacter, Daniel L. *Searching for Memory: The Brain, the Mind, and the Past.* New York: Basic, 1996. Print.

Sifferlin, Alexandra. "Study: Freud Was Wrong about Repressed Memories." *Time.* Time, 19 Mar. 2014. Web. 27 June 2014.

Bryan C. Auday

SEE ALSO: Child abuse; Defense mechanisms; Ego defense mechanisms; Forgetting and forgetfulness; Hypnosis; Memory; Memory: Animal research; Memory: Empirical studies; Memory: Physiology; Memory storage.

Research ethics

TYPE OF PSYCHOLOGY: All

Research ethics are part of a broader set of general principles operating in the field of the social sciences that focus on maintaining certain standards of behavior for psychologists who conduct or supervise research.

KEY CONCEPTS
- Animal testing
- Confidentiality
- Consent
- Control groups
- Data
- Deception
- Release of information
- Side effects

INTRODUCTION

To advance knowledge about human behavior, individuals in the field of psychology conduct research. Such endeavors involve both human and nonhuman participants. The use of nonhuman participants is usually understood to mean that there will be animal testing in the research. With either type of participant, lawful conduct and efforts to protect the welfare of the research participants are always of the utmost concern. The field of psychology, through the work of the American Psychological Association (APA), has devised a set of general ethical principles that apply to research to protect the participant and the data, or information, derived from such work.

In addition, ethical guidelines are designed to protect the interests of involved others, such as students and colleagues, who may be active in the research process as assistants and coinvestigators rather than as research participants. Protections for these individuals come in the form of guidelines regarding professionalism, honesty among colleagues, proper supervision, vigilance against plagiarism, and the maintenance of appropriate professional boundaries.

Guidelines for ethical research exist to protect all involved in psychology research, the public at large, and the field of psychology as a whole.

PROTECTING ANIMAL PARTICIPANTS

The protection of research participants is a key element of research ethics in psychology. Separate guidelines for protections exist for nonhuman and human participants. Animal research participants must be treated with respect and care. The research must be purposeful and have benefits that clearly outweigh the cost of involving the animals. Nonanimal alternatives must have been explored. The type of animal selected must be best suited to answer the research question, based on the most current literature. The animals used must be treated in a humane way so as to reduce the risk of pain or suffering as much as possible. The animals must be properly monitored to ensure that they are free from pain and suffering and kept in good care. No work may be conducted on the animals until a research plan has been approved by an appropriate committee overseeing animal care.

In addition, any staff members assisting with animal research must be familiar with these guidelines, as well as with all the laws and regulations involved in the conduct of this work. They must be adequately trained and supervised in the conduct of such work, which includes having knowledge of any behavioral or other indicators that suggest that an animal might be distressed or in need of health care. Further, very strict guidelines exist regarding the quality of housing provided for the animals, how animals may or may not be selected for use, and the types of experimental procedures permitted. If animal studies are conducted outside the laboratory, in the animals' natural habitat, researchers must also follow guidelines designed to minimize disturbance of the animals and their environment.

PROTECTING HUMAN PARTICIPANTS

Human participants must be treated with respect, and all commitments to them must be honored. Their privacy and confidentiality must be maintained, meaning that their participation and the information that they reveal are kept secret, known only to the researchers and their staff, and protected in the way in which they are presented in written descriptions of the study. Human subjects must be exposed to as little risk as is necessary. Research procedures should be as minimally invasive as possible.

Participants must be adequately informed about the purposes of the research and the relative risks and benefits of participating. They are formally asked to consent, or give permission, for their participation, a process known as informed consent. They must be free to withdraw from participation for any reason with no negative consequences to them.

Some special issues deserving discussion are the use of deception, limits to confidentiality, and use of control groups. Deception is the obscuring or withholding of information that is vital to the experiment but that may mislead participants to some degree. Psychologists are never to deceive participants about matters that might affect their willingness to serve as participants, such as physical risks, discomfort, or unpleasant emotional experiences. Psychologists also cannot use deception unless it is absolutely necessary to the study and judged to outweigh the costs of the manipulation. Finally, when deception is used, participants must be debriefed about the deception as soon as possible.

Limits to confidentiality are also important. While efforts are made to keep data and research findings separate from the identity of the research participants, in some cases confidentiality is limited, such as when the participant reports a plan of self-harm or harm to another person. It is the duty of the psychologist to act on such knowledge to protect the general good by reporting the information to the appropriate authorities or individuals. Therefore, as part of the consent process, researchers must explain the limits of confidentiality to potential participants.

Finally, control groups in research deserve a special mention. Control groups provide a special experimental condition in which research participants receive as little assessment and intervention as possible. These groups may be used to allow researchers to see experimentally the results of the simple passage of time or the simple effect of assessment on research participants. In research involving the treatment of mental health conditions, particularly where there are known effective treatments for the disorder in question, the use of a true control group is controversial and discouraged. Participation in research where random assignment to a control group might occur could be seen as a way of delaying or withholding treatment from someone who needs it. In such cases, researchers have had to resort to other means to establish experimental control. For instance, waiting-list controls might be used under the logic that it is typical for individuals to have to wait for treatment under normal circumstances, so doing so under an experimental paradigm does not constitute undue harm. Researchers have also employed minimal treatment controls, where a minimum level of treatment is provided to the control group. In such cases, participants might be allowed to receive the experimental treatment later if it were found to be more effective than the minimal treatment. Finally, in some cases, researchers must provide a full-fledged active treatment to participants, such as standard care, when trying to assess the utility of a new treatment strategy. In such cases, the negative consequences of receiving no care outweigh the benefits of comparing the new treatment to a no-care situation.

In addition to these issues, many provisions are related to the training of research staff and the maintenance and care of the data collected to support these general goals. Just as guidelines prohibit research on animals until the work plan has been reviewed, no research with humans should be conducted until the research plan is assessed by an institutional review board (IRB). This committee oversees the identification of risks and benefits of the research, the communication of this information to the participants, and the overall safety and ethical soundness of the research plan.

PROTECTING DATA

Once data have been collected, the information and any files related to it must receive special protections. This is primarily important for data from human participants because of confidentiality issues, but it can also be important for animal data because of procedural and other information that may be contained in the data records or research files.

A basic consideration is that the raw data, such as data collected from a human participant, must be kept in a secure location and in a manner that protects the identity of the participant. This requirement usually means that questionnaires and other data are identified by code numbers rather than by individual participant names. In addition, any links among code numbers and participant identities must be minimized and stored in a place separate from the data or any representation of them, such as electronic files.

Data should be retained for five years after the publication of any reports so that colleagues may examine the information to determine whether the conclusions were properly pursued and represented. This is done by the assigned owner of the data, a designation usually agreed on by all senior investigators involved in the research planning. If the data are to be collected using monies from the federal government, however, the government may require a longer maintenance period, such as ten years after collection. In addition, the government may require that the data be made public for any related request, rather than only collegial requests.

Finally, prior to their presentation in research reports, the data should be verified, meaning that errors should be processed out to avoid the presentation of misleading findings. Data on discrete research questions should not be published in duplicate form to avoid misrepresenting the findings or placing them out of context. In addition, the presentation of data collected for research purposes should be limited to those purposes. A scientist may present the data for some other use, such as training or education, but, as with all presentations, care to protect the confidentiality and welfare of the research participants must take priority.

PROFESSIONALISM AND PUBLICATIONS

Another set of issues related to research ethics involves publications. For those serving as professional reviewers, ethical guidelines apply because new research reports are privileged information. Therefore, reviewers are bound to treat the information reviewed as highly confidential. In deciding to serve as a reviewer, a psychologist must acknowledge any conflicts of interest that might be present regarding a relationship with the author, any companies connected to the research, or any other relationships that might affect the ability to be impartial. When a conflict exists, the potential reviewer must resign from the process.

Similar disclosures of conflicts of interest are required of the authors of research reports. For example, when an individual receives money from a drug company or a health maintenance organization (HMO) to conduct a study that could affect how that drug or that HMO is perceived, it is important for the researcher to acknowledge that financial relationship, as well as any other influence that the company or the HMO might have had on the findings and their presentation in the research report. This disclosure allows for fair review of the findings for readers.

In general, psychologists are advised to avoid taking multiple roles; this is true for those in research as well. For instance, a psychologist would not seek to enroll friends and family members in his or her own research and would be advised against becoming a stockholder in a drug company when conducting research on a drug made by that company. Such dual relationships might make it difficult to be impartial or to be seen as impartial by others in the reporting of any data collected.

A final issue regarding research ethics relates to publication credit: who is included as an author on papers and presentations as well as the order of authorship. In general, persons who substantially contribute to the production of the research report in ways that directly apply to the intellectual content should be included as authors. Typically, authorship on papers is decided before the research is started as part of the research plan. This agreement allows each person to anticipate his or her contributions and to input effort to the process fairly. Additionally, it facilitates the ownership of responsibility for the authors to ensure that all ethical guidelines for research in the field were adhered to in the conduct of the study. Typically, assurances to this effect are required by many journals in order for the report to be accepted for publication.

NEW CHALLENGES

As the human population grows, so, too, do the complexities of human life and the potential for problems. The human community is no longer simply a local tribe but a global force composed of different peoples with different languages, cultural customs, histories, and resources. As communication among different peoples increases, the potential for miscommunication is likely to increase as well. Research in psychology will remain quite important as it—combined with knowledge from such fields as sociology, anthropology, and political science—will be key in the untangling of such miscommunications. Research ethics and guidelines will encourage proactive communications about research endeavors and their potential impact.

It is important to realize, however, that not all countries demand the same standard of ethics for research in general, or research in psychology more specifically, as do the legal and professional governing bodies in the United States. For the most part, the research ethics standards observed in the United States are among the highest worldwide. American researchers conducting research or collaborating in other countries may be permitted or even encouraged by local authorities to act in accord with somewhat different standards. The researchers will be encouraged to maintain the highest of standards while striving to understand and respond to the local standards. In such cases, consultation with senior colleagues is important to ensure that the issues at hand are thoroughly considered.

An example of an issue that might require consideration involves the use of incentives to encourage participation. For a study of health behavior, for instance, each participant might be offered $100 for five hours of participation. By American standards, this amount might not seem like much for that period of time. If the study were done in a very poor country, however, this incentive could be astronomical in relation to what most people earn in a year. Such an incentive could cause problems that the researcher might not anticipate without the review of a local IRB. In this example, a local IRB might recommend that they researchers pay only $1 as an incentive, which might seem absurdly low from an American perspective. It is in such circumstances that culture and research ethics and methods must continue to grow to allow work to advance without causing disruption.

Another complexity affecting contemporary psychological research is scientific knowledge in the field of genetics research ethics and the increasing use of personal medical records and data sharing for research purposes. For instance, one must ask what constitutes adequate consent to participate in a research project that includes genetic testing and the use of personal medical records. While the individual participant may weigh the costs and benefits of participating, what about the family members? Should they be asked to sign a release allowing the individual to give information to researchers? This question arises because such research may expose the participant's entire family to problems unwanted information about health risks and loss of privacy. The question becomes how extensive consent to participation should be. While provisions may be written into the management of the data collected to protect individual participants, side effects or unanticipated consequences may arise that have deleterious effects. A scenario involving genetic research may prompt conversations among family members about the information, including potential miscommunications. It also might lead to accidental loss of privacy, particularly if family members report information in a pedigree format, in which a family tree is described. In such cases, one family member may reveal information about other family members that those members do not want revealed and that could expose them to unanticipated risks. These examples provide food for thought regarding how research ethics in psychology and other areas of science will need to grow in the future to address the complexities brought about by modern life.

BIBLIOGRAPHY

American Psychological Association. *Publication Manual of the American Psychological Association*. 5th ed. Washington: Author, 2008.

American Psychological Association. Committee on Animal Research and Ethics (CARE). *Guidelines for Ethical Conduct in the Care and Use of Animals*. Washington: Author, 2002.

Banyard, Philip, and Cara Flanagan. *Ethical Issues in Psychology*. London: Routledge, 2011. Print.

Carroll, Marilyn E., and J. Bruce Overmier, eds. *Animal Research and Human Welfare: Advancing Human Welfare Through Behavioral Science*. Washington: American Psychological Association, 2001.

Coolican, Hugh. *Research Methods and Statistics in Psychology*. 6th ed. East Sussex: Psychology, 2014. Print.

"Ethical Principles of Psychologists and Code of Conduct." *American Psychological Association*. American Psychological Association, 1 June 2010. Web. 23 July 2014.

Josselson, Ruthellen, ed. *Ethics and Process in the Narrative Study of Lives*. Thousand Oaks: Sage, 1996. Print.

Kitchener, Karen S., and Sharon K. Anderson. *Foundations of Ethical Practice, Research, and Teaching in Psychology and Counseling.* New York: Routledge, 2011. Print.

Koocher, Gerald P., and Patricia Keith-Spiegel. *Ethics in Psychology: Professional Standards and Cases.* 2nd ed. New York: Oxford UP, 1998. Print.

Sales, Bruce D., and Susan Folkman, eds. *Ethics in Research with Human Participants.* Washington: American Psychological Association, 2005. Print.

Street, Linda L., and Jason B. Luoma, eds. *Control Groups in Psychosocial Intervention Research: Ethical and Methodological Issues.* Hillsdale: Erlbaum, 2002. Print.

Zucchero, Renee A. "Psychology Ethics in Introductory Psychology Textbooks." *Teaching of Psychology* 38.2 (2011): 110–13. Print.

Nancy A. Piotrowski

SEE ALSO: Animal experimentation; Archival data; Complex experimental designs; Confidentiality; Data description; Experimental psychology; Experimentation: Ethics and subject rights; Experimentation: Independent, dependent, and control variables; Field experimentation; Observational methods; Qualitative research; Quasi-experimental designs; Scientific methods; Survey research: Questionnaires and interviews; Within-subject experimental designs.

Reticular formation

TYPE OF PSYCHOLOGY: Biological bases of behavior

The reticular formation is a system of interneurons in the brain stem that receives and integrates sensory information from all parts of the body. It influences almost all functions of the nervous system but is especially known for its effects on attentiveness, waking, and sleeping.

KEY CONCEPTS
- Afferent
- Arousal
- Brain stem
- Efferent
- Epilepsy
- Integration
- Interneuron
- Nucleus
- Reticular activating system
- Sleep circuit

INTRODUCTION

The term "reticular formation" is used to refer to one of several so-called reticular structures of the central nervous system. A reticulum is a mesh or network, and reticular formation designates a specific grouping of more than ninety nuclei of interneurons that have common characteristics in the area of the brain stem. The nuclei are clusters of cell bodies of neurons that form a network of their dendritic and axonal cellular processes, those extensions that bring information into the cell and transmit information from the cell.

The mesh reaches throughout the brain stem, as well as to higher and lower regions of the central nervous system as far as the cerebral cortex and spinal cord, serving both sensory and integrative functions. Anatomically, the reticular formation is continuous from the medulla oblongata, the lowest part of the brain stem, through the pons to the midbrain. It connects with the intermediate gray region of the spinal cord and sends processes into the higher brain areas of the thalamus and hypothalamus.

Neurons of the reticular formation contain many dendritic processes, afferent cytoplasmic extensions that carry electrical stimuli toward the cell nucleus, arranged perpendicular to the central axis of the body. Each cell also contains a single long axon, with numerous collateral branches, that extends along the body's axis, going to the higher or lower regions of the central nervous system. The axon carries impulses away from the nucleus of the neuron toward the synapse, where it passes information on to the next neighboring cell. The axons and dendrites, present in large numbers, make up the mesh, or reticulum, that gives the reticular formation its name. The many aggregated processes make it extremely difficult to identify the clustered groups of neurons (nuclei) to which the individual cells belong.

INFORMATION AND AROUSAL

The reticular formation is a portion of an important informational loop in the brain that allows the modification and adjustment of behavior. This loop extends from the cerebral cortex to subcortical areas (lower brain regions), including the reticular formation, and then back to the cortex. The reticular formation makes connections with all the portions of the loop and plays an important role in exciting or inhibiting the functions of the lower motor neuron centers. This loop is important in practically all functions of the nervous system and behavior, particularly sleep/wakefulness, emotional stress, depression and distress, the induction of rapid eye movement (REM) sleep, and even sleepwalking.

The process of arousal appears to take place as the reticular formation sends impulses to an area of the thalamus occupied by the midline thalamic nuclei. These nuclei then pass the information on to the cortex, which is stimulated to become more aware that information is coming and more attentive to receiving the information. This is an oversimplification of the process, however, as other areas of the brain also seem to be involved in arousal. The neurotransmitters involved in the reticular formation's connection to the cortex are thought to include both cholinergic and monoamine systems in the arousal process, although these are still not well understood.

The basic functions of the reticular formation are two-fold: to alert the higher centers, especially in the cortex, that sensory information is coming into the processing areas and to screen incoming information being passed upward on sensory (afferent) pathways toward the higher centers of the brain, blocking the passage of irrelevant information and passing along the information that should be acted on by the higher brain. All sensory information must be passed through the lower regions of the brain before reaching the associative regions of the cerebral cortex. The cortex is unable to process incoming information unless it has been alerted and aroused and unless the information is channeled through the proper lower brain regions. Besides the reticular formation, the thalamus is also involved in this function, taking information from the reticular formation and passing it on to the cortex, where it is then processed and coordinated to produce motor behavior.

INFORMATION INHIBITION

Because the reticular formation has so many pathways from each cell leading to many other cells, it is very quickly inhibited by anesthetics that act by inhibiting the transfer of information between cells at the synapse. This inhibition of activity leads to unconsciousness from a general lack of sensation and loss of alertness and arousal as polysynaptic pathways are shut down. Under proper medical control, use of anesthesia to turn off the reticular formation can be lifesaving, allowing surgical procedures that could not be tolerated without it.

Lesions of the brain stem may damage the reticular formation, producing the uncontrolled unconsciousness of coma if they occur above the level of the pons on both sides. Coma that results from drug overdose or drug reaction occurs mainly as the result of depression of the reticular formation. Any lesion of the brain stem that affects the reticular formation directly will also have a secondary effect on other structures on the brain stem, causing disappearance of its reflex reactions. Damage to ascending efferent pathways from the reticular formation to the cortex sometimes can also cause coma. Because the reticular formation aids the brain stem in regulating critical visceral vital functions such as breathing and blood circulation, damage to this area may threaten life itself.

The actions of alcohol on behavior also are the result of its effects on the reticular formation. Alcohol blocks the actions of this area, allowing a temporary loss of control over other brain regions. This lack of behavioral inhibition from higher brain centers produces a feeling of excitement and well-being at first. Later effects of continued alcohol intake lead to depression of emotions and behavior, followed by depression of basic body functions that can produce unconsciousness.

The production of unconsciousness through sleep is also associated with the reticular formation, particularly the part that is in the pons and another center in the lower medulla. The lower medullary sleep/waking center seems to work with the basal forebrain to modulate the induction of sleep. Rapid eye movement (REM) sleep may be controlled, at least in part, by specific nuclei in the pontine reticular formation.

BEHAVIORAL EFFECTS

Stimulation of the reticular formation and other areas (the hippocampus and amygdala) improves memory retention (memory consolidation) if electrical current is applied directly to the reticular cells immediately after a training session. It is difficult to understand how this stimulation operates, however, since in some cases stimulating these same areas instead produces retrograde amnesia, causing the loss of memory retention. It is thought that the level of electrical stimulation may cause these different results. The highest and lowest stimulation levels reduce memory consolidation in some cases, and intermediate stimulation seems to be the most effective. The nature of the training process is also important in the results, as learning seems to be more difficult with high stimulation levels associated with aversive conditioning.

Another aspect of the reticular formation and its possible effects on behavior is the theory that many (or perhaps most) convulsive epileptic seizures originate there. Since this area can be stimulated by electrical impulses and by convulsive drugs to produce seizures, it is thought that the reticular formation may be the site from which stimulation of the cerebral cortex starts. It is difficult to establish the origins of epilepsy conclusively, since there are no adequate animal models for this disorder, but antiepileptic drugs are shown to depress neuron function in the reticular formation. The actual source of the convulsive behavior is thought to be the nonspecific reticular core of this formation.

RESEARCH AND EXPERIMENTATION

The reticular formation influences nearly all aspects of nervous system function, including sensory and motor activities and somatic and visceral functions. It is important in influencing the integrative processes of the central nervous system, acting on the mind and behavior. Included in this influence are the stimulatory aspects of arousal, awakening, and attentiveness, as well as the inhibitory aspects of drowsiness, sleep induction, and general disruption of the stimulatory functions. To understand how this region of the brain can be so important in such contradictory functions, it is important to consider the integration of excitatory and inhibitory inputs and the consolidation of their overall influences. Depending on which type of stimulus has the greatest effect, the net result on behavior can be alertness or drowsiness, active function or the inactivity of sleep.

Research on anesthetized cats in the late 1940s produced an increased understanding of the activities of the reticular formation. It was shown that electrical stimulation of the brain stem caused changes in the cats' electroencephalograph (EEG) readings that were similar to changes occurring in humans when they were aroused from a drowsy state to alertness. From these observations and others, it has been concluded that the ascending reticular system of the brain stem acts as a nonspecific arousal system of the cerebral cortex.

In the 1950s, Donald Lindsley and his colleagues studied the reticular formation as the source of arousal. They showed that two discrete flashes of light shown to a monkey produced discrete electrical responses (evoked potentials) in the visual cortex. If the pulses were very close together, only one potential was evoked, showing that the cortex could not distinguish both within that time. If two electrical stimulations were applied directly to the reticular formation at the short interval, however, two discrete flashes were expressed in the cortex, showing the influence of the reticular formation on the threshold level of the cortex's response to stimuli. J. M.

Fuster, one of Lindsley's coworkers, examined the behavioral responses that resulted from electrical stimulation of the reticular formation in monkeys trained to discriminate between two objects. Reducing the time of visual exposure to the objects also reduced the correct responses, but stimulation of the reticular formation at the same time as the visual exposure reduced the error level. This indicated that increased arousal and attentiveness to the visual stimuli were produced by electrical activation of the reticular formation.

J. M. Siegal and D. J. McGinty's work on stimulation of the reticular formation in cats in the 1970s showed that individual neurons seem to have a role in controlling various motor functions of the body. Other studies show that various autonomic responses, such as vomiting, respiration, sneezing, and coughing, may also originate at least in part from the reticular formation.

It is thought that the period of sleep known as rapid eye movement sleep, or paradoxical sleep, is a time of memory consolidation. During this time, the reticular formation, the hippocampus, and the amygdala are stimulated to activate the higher brain centers, and arousal occurs. REM sleep is considered paradoxical because the brain waves produced during this time are similar to those produced during stimulation of the awake brain. Vincent Bloch and his colleagues have shown that laboratory animals and human subjects deprived of REM sleep display decreased memory consolidation. During this process, short-term memories are converted somehow into long-term memories, which withstand even disruptions of the electrical activities of the brain. The reticular formation is an important part of memory function, but much remains to be discovered about this and other reticular activities.

BIBLIOGRAPHY

Carlson, Neil R. *Physiology of Behavior.* 10th ed. Boston: Allyn, 2009. Print.

Fromm, Gerhard H., Carl L. Faingold, Ronald A. Browning, and W. M. Burnham, eds. *Epilepsy and the Reticular Formation: The Role of the Reticular Core in Convulsive Seizures.* New York: Liss, 1987. Print.

Hobson, J. Allan, and Mary A. B. Brazier, eds. *The Reticular Formation Revisited: Specifying Function for a Nonspecific System.* New York: Raven, 1980. Print.

Klemm, W. R., and Robert P. Vertes, eds. *Brainstem Mechanisms of Behavior.* New York: Wiley, 1990. Print.

Mai, Juergen K., and George Paxinos. *The Human Nervous System.* Burlington: Elsevier Science, 2011.

Print.

Romero-Sierra, C. *Neuroanatomy: A Conceptual Approach*. New York: Churchill, 1986. Print.

Sadock, Benjamin J., and Virginia Sadock, eds. *Kaplan and Sadock's Comprehensive Textbook of Psychiatry*. 8th ed. Philadelphia: Lippincott , 2005. Print.

Siegel, Alln, and Hreday N Sapru. *Essential Neuroscience*. Philadelphia: Lippincott, 2011. Print.

Steriade, Mircea, and Robert W. McCarley. *Brainstem Control of Wakefulness and Sleep*. 2d ed. New York: Springer, 2005. Print.

Yogarajah, Mahinda, and Christopher Turner. *Neurology*. Edinburgh: Mosby, 2013. Print.

Jean S. Helgeson

SEE ALSO: Attention; Brain structure; Consciousness; Dreams; Insomnia; Nervous system; Neurons; Sleep; Sleep apnea; Narcolepsy.

Retirement

TYPE OF PSYCHOLOGY: Developmental psychology

With increased longevity and improved health, many older workers are living long and healthy lives after retirement. Longitudinal studies have explored a wide range of contextual factors that influence life satisfaction during retirement.

KEY CONCEPTS

- Activity theory
- Disengagement theory
- Leisure
- Longitudinal studies
- Retired population
- Role differentiation

INTRODUCTION

Retirement only became an accepted part of modern life in the first half of the twentieth century, due to increasing longevity and the introduction of pension and retirement benefits. Many workers choose to retire when they become eligible for pension or social security benefits. In the United States, the possibility of retirement became more accessible with the passage of the Social Security Act in 1935. From 1900 to 2000, the percentage of men over the age of sixty-five who continued to work declined as much as 70 percent in the United States.

At the same time, the percentage of all adults over sixty-five who worked at least part-time steadily increased from 1960. Although the majority of older Americans do not choose to work after reaching retirement age, more than 18 percent of Americans older than sixty-five were working in 2012 (compared to less than 11 percent in 1985). Psychologist Frank Floyd and his colleagues, in their 1992 Retirement Satisfaction Inventory, found four primary reasons for retirement: job stress, pressure from employer, desire to pursue one's own interests, and circumstances such as health problems. With an increasing number of older workers delaying retirement, psychologist Towers Watson and his colleagues at Boston College's Center on Aging and Work looked at the reasons why American workers postpone retirement and found that the most common reasons included high debt loads; reluctance to lose employer-provided benefits, particularly health insurance; insufficient savings for retirement; care-taking or financial responsibilities for children and elderly parents; and a desire to remain active and engaged in the work force.

The retired population is defined as all people aged sixty-five and over. Traditionally, sixty-five has been the age at which people could retire and receive full Social Security and Medicare benefits in the United States, although a law is in place to gradually raise the retirement age to sixty-seven. Approximately seventy-eight million people belong to the large cohort of baby boomers who will begin to reach the traditional age of retirement in 2010. In 1900, only about three million were retired at sixty-five, in 2000 the number increased to thirty-five million, and it is projected that, by 2050, the number will be increased to sixty-seven million. If future projections are anywhere close to accurate, it can be assumed that it will take approximately four working Americans to provide for every retiree in 2050.

WORKING DURING RETIREMENT

Even as individuals near retirement age, the decision to continue working in some form after retirement or to discontinue work altogether is a complex one. Many people feel that they have sufficient finances to comfortably exist without working if that is their preference. The primary determiner for most is their health status. Employer pension benefits were found to reduce the probability of future employment in some form, while part-time work was more likely for those who were limited to Social Security benefits. Spousal influence is often cited by retirees as a major factor in deciding whether to choose future employment, although spouses report that they perceive themselves as having little influence on the decision. Specific training and the job opportunities that are available within a community are also important in determining postretirement work.

One survey reported that 80 percent of baby boomers expect to work during their retirement years. More than one-third wanted part-time work because they would personally find it interesting or enjoyable. A little less than one-fourth planned to work for financial reasons. In another study, nearly 70 percent planned to work for pay during postretirement because they wanted to stay active and involved.

The probability of working after retirement has a positive correlation with educational attainment and being married to a working spouse. The primary characteristics associated with men who work in their seventies and eighties are good health, a strong psychological commitment to work, and a distaste for retirement.

RETIREES IN THE WORK FORCE

The Retirement History Study by the Social Security Administration identified four career job exits for postretirement employment: part-time employment in one's career job, part-time employment in a new job, full-time employment in a new job, and full-time retirement. The Age Discrimination in Employment Act of 1967 prohibited firing people because of their age before they retired, and in 1978, the mandatory retirement age was extended from sixty-five to seventy. Mandatory retirement was banned altogether in 1986, except for a few occupations where safety is at issue.

Studies have found older adults tend to be productive participants in the workforce. They have lower rates of absenteeism, show a high level of job satisfaction, and experience fewer accidents. There is a cyclic relationship between higher cognitive ability and complex jobs. Older adults who work in more complex job settings demonstrate higher cognitive ability, and those with a higher level of intellectual functioning are more likely to continue working as older adults. It is also important to note that ageist stereotypes of workers and their ability can encourage early retirement or have an adverse effect on the career opportunities given to older adults.

ADJUSTMENT TO RETIREMENT

Retirement may represent golden years for some, but not necessarily for all. Certain factors have been found to have an impact on the degree of satisfaction retirees ex-

perience. Some of these factors are found within society and have an indirect influence on how life is experienced for those who retire. Other factors are directly related to specifics in the individual's life.

Data from longitudinal studies have identified factors that influence adjustment to retirement. Those who adjust best are more likely to be healthy, active, better educated, satisfied with life before retirement, have an adequate level of financial resources, and have an extended social network of family and friends. Factors that contribute to a less positive adjustment to retirement are poor health, inadequate finances, and general or specific stress in various areas of life. Those who demonstrate flexibility typically function better in the retirement setting in which the structured environment of work is missing. Individuals who have cultivated interests and friends unrelated to work show greater adaptation to retirement.

A primary factor in adjustment is whether retirement was voluntary or involuntary. Forced retirement has been ranked as one of the top ten crisis situations that cause stress. When retirement is voluntary, adjustment is more positive. Those who do not voluntarily retire are more likely to be unhealthy and depressed.

An important aspect of successful adjustment is preretirement planning. Those who are most satisfied with retirement are those who have been preparing for it for several years. Adults can begin preparing psychologically for retirement in middle age. Decisions need to be made relative to activities that will be used to stay active, socially involved, and mentally alert. Of most importance during this time is the task of finding constructive and fulfilling leisure activities that can be continued into retirement. Individuals who are already involved in a number of leisure activities will experience less stress when they make the transition from work to retirement.

During the middle of the twentieth century, disengagement theory was proposed as the approach older adults used to withdraw from obligations and social relationships. It was suggested that this would provide enhanced life satisfaction. Retirement was viewed as part of the disengagement process. Although this theory has not been considered acceptable for some time, it would be fair to say that it represented a prevailing belief about older adults during the first half of the twentieth century.

Researchers have since found support for the activity theory, which is the exact opposite of disengagement theory. The activity theory proposes that the more active and involved older adults are, the more likely they are to experience life satisfaction. Supporting research suggests that activity and productivity cause older adults to age more successfully and to be happier and healthier than those who disengage. The theory further suggests that greater life satisfaction can be expected if adults continue their middle-adulthood roles into late adulthood. For those who lose their middle-adulthood roles, it is important that they find substitute roles to keep them active.

MARRIAGE AND FAMILY RELATIONSHIPS

Retirement is often a time when adults have sufficient time to develop their social lives. Aging expert Lillian Troll found that older adults who are embedded in family relationships have less distress than those who are family deprived. There is a gender difference in the perspectives of older parents relative to the importance of support from family members. Women perceived support from children as most important whereas men considered spousal support as most important.

For married couples, retirement may bring changes for both spouses. When retirement allows a spouse to leave a high-stress job, marital quality is improved. In dual-income families, couples may choose to retire simultaneously or to retire at separate times to ease into the financial changes that retirement may bring. However, studies have suggested that both husbands and wives report greater marital satisfaction if they retire at the same time. Retirement may bring about a significant disruption to established patterns within the home and family, and couples need to work together to establish new patterns and habits that are satisfactory to both partners. Some studies have likened the first two years of retirement to the first two years of marriage or parenthood, in that couples need to actively renegotiate their roles, plans, dreams, and habits to adapt to the lifestyle and role changes that retirement brings. Nevertheless, nearly 60 percent of retired couples report improved marital satisfaction following retirement, after a period of adjustment.

WORK, RETIREMENT, AND LEISURE

The perception of retirement is affected by work and leisure experiences during the preretirement years. Leisure refers to the activities and interests one chooses to engage in when free from work responsibilities. Many find it difficult to seek leisure activities during the height of their work careers because of the value placed on productivity and the pressures of many modern jobs. They may view leisure activities as boring and lacking challenge. Many workers fear a loss of identity or status with the loss of their jobs; by engaging in enjoyable activities, volunteer or part-time work, or family, retirees can establish new, meaningful facets to their identity.

Midlife is the first opportunity many adults have to include leisure activities in their schedule. This can be an especially appropriate time if they are experiencing physical changes in strength, endurance, and health as well as changes in family responsibilities. Those who are able to find constructive and fulfilling leisure activities during this time are psychologically prepared from the middle adult years for retirement. Some developmentalists believe that middle adults tend to reassess priorities and that this becomes a time of questioning how their time should be spent.

Late adulthood, with its possibility of representing the years from sixty-five to more than one hundred years, is the longest span of any period of human development. The improved understanding of the nature of life after sixty-five and the greater commitment on the part of medical and mental health personnel to the improvement of health and living conditions for the older adult are giving all retirees a better chance of being satisfied with the years beyond their work experience.

BIBLIOGRAPHY

Bamberger, Peter, and Samuel B. Bacharach. *Retirement and the Hidden Epidemic: The Complex Link between Aging, Work Disengagement, and Substance Misuse—And What to Do about It*. New York: Oxford UP, 2014. Print.

Bengtson, Vern L., and K. Warner Schaie. *Handbook of Theories of Aging*. 2nd ed. New York: Springer, 2009. Print.

Knoll, Melissa A. "Behavioral and Psychological Aspects of the Retirement Decision." *Social Security Bulletin* 71.4 (2011): 15–32. PDF file.

Maddox, H. George L., Caleb E. Finch, Robert C. Atchley, and J. Grimley Evans, eds. *The Encyclopedia of Aging*. 3rd ed. New York: Springer, 2001. Print.

Milne, Derek. *The Psychology of Retirement: Coping with the Transition from Work*. West Sussex: Wiley, 2013. Print.

Pipher, Mary Bray. *Another Country: Navigating the Emotional Terrain of Our Elders*. New York: Riverhead, 2000. Print.

Ryff, Carol D., and Victor W. Marshall, eds. *The Self and Society in Aging Processes*. New York: Springer, 1999.

Print.

Vaillant, George E. *Aging Well: Surprising Guideposts to a Happier Life from the Landmark Harvard Study of Adult Development*. Boston: Little, 2003. Print.

Wang, Mo, ed. *The Oxford Handbook of Retirement*. Oxford: Oxford UP, 2013. Print.

Lillian J. Breckenridge

SEE ALSO: Ageism; Aging: Cognitive changes; Aging: Physical changes; Aging: Theories; Assisted living; Coping: Social support; Death and dying; Ego psychology: Erik H. Erikson; Elders' mental health; Hospice; Midlife crises.

Risk assessments

TYPE OF PSYCHOLOGY: Psychopathology; Psychotherapy

Risk assessments are tests conducted by professionals to determine the likelihood of a specific event or behavior occurring or reoccurring during a specified time period. Most risk assessments are made by experts in mental health or criminal justice.

KEY CONCEPTS
- Actuarial risk
- Clinical risk
- Fluid risk factors
- Forensic setting
- Static risk factors
- Sex offender risk
- Suicide risk

INTRODUCTION

Risk assessments are conducted by a variety of specialists within their respective fields of mental health. The primary reason for a risk assessment is to offer a qualified professional opinion as to the probable rate of risk for a specific event or behavior occurring or reoccurring during a certain time period.

Although the need for a risk assessment can arise in any area of human services, it is most common in the areas of mental health and criminal justice. A common area of inquiry in mental health, for example, might revolve around knowing a client's risk for suicide or violence. In criminal or juvenile justice, for example, a parole board might be interested in a prospective parolee's risk of recidivism.

TYPES OF RISK ASSESSMENT

In the field of mental health, there are primarily two types of risk assessment: clinical and actuarial. Clinical risk assessment is the older of the two types of assessment. A mental health professional conducts an interview with and observes the subject, then makes a prediction of risk based on the professional's experience working with similar individuals. Unfortunately, research has shown that basing a risk assessment simply on an interview and observations is not much more accurate than making a guess. In forensic settings (jails, prisons, hospitals for the criminally insane, locked units in general hospitals) especially, clinical risk assessments have often been very inaccurate.

Actuarial risk assessment has developed out of the need to make risk assessment more accurate and predictive. It involves the use of valid and reliable risk assessment instruments and statistical models to predict the likelihood of a future event. The best of these instruments examine the static and fluid risk factors associated with the probability of repeating a behavior. Static risk factors (for example, gender and race) are those that do not change, and fluid risk factors (for example, substance use) are those that change. A wide variety of risk assessment instruments can be used, depending on the question to be answered.

A good actuarial risk assessment instrument has been standardized and empirically validated based on a sample population that mirrors the target population. The instrument should have validity scales. In a forensic setting, there are a variety of commonly used risk assessment instruments available to practitioners. Some of these instruments are appropriate for a general offender population: the Psychopathy Checklist-Revised (PCL-R), the Violence Risk Appraisal Guide (VRAG; which can also be used with sexual offenders), and the Historical Clinical Risk Management scale (HCR-20). A number of risk assessment instruments have been especially designed for use with sexual offenders, including the Rapid Risk Assessment of Sexual Offense Recidivism (RRASOR), Static-99, Sex Offender Need Assessment Rating (SONAR), and Minnesota Sex Offender Screening Tool-Revised (MnSOST-R).

Risk assessment instruments have also been developed for use with the general juvenile population and the juvenile sex offender population. These include the Juvenile Sex Offender Assessment Protocol (J-SOAP), the Estimate of Risk of Adolescent Sexual Offender Recidivism (ERASOR), the Youth Level of Service/Case

Management Inventory (YLS/CMI), the Structured Assessment of Violence Risk in Youth (SAVRY), the Psychopathy Checklist: Youth Version (PCL:YV), and the Child and Adolescent Functional Assessment (CAFAS).

MACARTHUR STUDY

The MacArthur Violence Risk Assessment Study was a groundbreaking study of the risk of violence in a mental health population. The study was conducted between 1992 and 1995, and initial findings were published in 1998. The study led to the surprising conclusion that discharged mental patients as a whole were not more likely than the general population to become violent. (Since the initial study was conducted, the original data has been further analyzed by a variety of researchers.)

The MacArthur study also identified risk factors associated with and predictive of violence in the community after release. The study concluded that prior violence, seriousness and frequency of having been abused as a child, a diagnosis of substance abuse, hallucinations of voices commanding a violent act, persistent daydreams and thoughts of violence, and high levels of anger were all associated with future violence.

From the study, the first violence risk assessment software, the Classification of Violence Risk (COVR) was developed and released in 2005. This interactive software measures forty risk factors to determine the risk of a patient's becoming violent.

SUICIDE RISK

Although risk assessment for possible violence or repeat offending behavior presents many challenges, risk assessment for suicide is even more complex. Some researchers have stated that it is almost impossible to predict suicidal behavior with any great accuracy, and many suicide assessment instruments and psychological tests have not proven to be very useful. Most clinicians make a judgment of suicide risk based on a clinical interview and observation. Yet, like all risk assessments based on clinical interviews, these assessments are not reliably accurate.

Many of the available suicide risk assessment instruments are not theoretically based. Studies have looked at risk factors (such as depression) and risk mediators (such as moral objections against suicide and strong social support), yet many clinicians use self-reported suicidal ideation (thoughts of suicide) and previous attempts as predictors of future suicidal behavior.

A few instruments have been noted as being valuable to use with a student population. These include the Suicide Probability Scale (SPS), the Self-Reporting Depression Scale (SDS), the Suicidal Behaviors Questionnaire (SBQ), the Reasons for Living Inventory (RFL), and the Multi-Attitude Suicide Tendency Scale (MAST). Several have been successfully used with adult populations, including the Suicide Probability Scale (SPS), the Adult Suicidal Ideation Questionnaire (ASIQ), the Beck Scale for Suicide Ideation (BSI), and the Beck Depression Inventory II (BDI-II).

BIBLIOGRAPHY

Cramer, Robert J., et al. "Suicide Risk Assessment Training for Psychology Doctoral Programs: Core Competencies and a Framework for Training." *Training and Education in Professional Psychology* 7.1 (2013): 1–11. Print.

Gardner, W., C. W. Lidz, E. P. Mulvey, and E. C. Shaw. "A Comparison of Actuarial Methods for Identifying Repetitively Violent Patients with Mental Illnesses." *Law & Human Behavior* 20 (1996): 35–48. Print.

Hall, Harold V. *Forensic Psychology and Neuropsychology for Criminal and Civil Cases.* Boca Raton: CRC, 2008. Print.

Hart, Chris. *A Pocket Guide to Risk Assessment and Management in Mental Health.* Abindon: Routledge, 2014. Print.

Heilbrun, Kirk, David DeMatteo, Stephanie Brooks Holliday, and Casey LaDuke. *Forensic Mental Health Assessment: A Casebook.* 2nd ed. Oxford: Oxford UP, 2014. Print.

Huss, Matthew T. *Forensic Psychology: Research, Practice, and Applications.* Malden: Blackwell, 2009. Print.

Monahan, J., et al. *Rethinking Risk Assessment: The MacArthur Study of Mental Disorder and Violence.* New York: Oxford UP, 2001. Print.

Sellars, Carol. *Risk Assessment in People with Learning Disabilities.* Chichester: Blackwell, 2011. Print.

Werth, James L., Jr., Elizabeth Reynolds Welfel, and G. Andrew H. Benjamin, eds. *The Duty to Protect: Ethical, Legal, and Professional Considerations for Mental Health Professionals.* Washington: American Psychological Assoc., 2009. Print.

Ayn Embar-Seddon O'Reilly and Allan D. Pass

SEE ALSO: Assessment; Beck Depression Inventory (BDI); Child abuse; Children's Depression Inventory (CDI); Domestic violence; Elder abuse; Forensic psychology; Juvenile delinquency; Suicide; Violence by children and teenagers; Violence: Psychological causes and effects.

Road rage

TYPE OF PSYCHOLOGY: Personality; Sensation and perception; Social psychology; Stress

Road rage is a phrase indicating impulsive aggression by enraged operators of motor vehicles who lose emotional control and intentionally intimidate other drivers.

KEY CONCEPTS
- Aggressive drivers
- Antisocial
- Driver violence
- Frustration
- Impulsiveness
- Stress

Photo: iStock

INTRODUCTION

A global problem, road rage became a concern for social psychologists in the late 1980s, when the term first began to be used. Although incidents of driver violence occurred in previous decades, they were considered isolated events based on factors unrelated to driving. By the 1980s, cases became more frequent and were directly tied to stimuli surrounding motorists. Violence intensified because more people carried weapons and used them impulsively in traffic incidents. As aggressive drivers compromised public transportation safety, researchers sought to understand why some drivers become enraged, lose control, and commit hostile actions against strangers over disputed traffic behavior. The American Psychiatric Association's *Diagnostic and Statistical Manual of Mental Disorders* (DSM-5, 2013) does not include a specific diagnosis for road rage. However, some psychologists describe road rage as a pathological condition related to intermittent explosive disorder. Intermittent explosive definition is characterized by repeated episodes of impulsive, aggressive, angry, or violent behavior that is disproportional to the situation that triggered the reaction; in addition to road rage, domestic abuse and temper tantrums may be signs of an intermittent explosive disorder. Some authorities have argued that the media exaggerates road casualty statistics to sensationalize coverage of driving behavior and that politicians, the US

Department of Transportation, and other groups rely on scientifically unsound studies, particularly an American Automobile Association (AAA) report cited as evidence of an overwhelming threat, to seek funding and publicity. Nevertheless, surveys report that up to one-third of drivers admit to being perpetrators of road rage, indicating that experiencing road rage is not uncommon.

However, less than 2 percent of road-rage incidents result in damage to individuals or vehicles. The majority of road-rage perpetrators report shouting or gesturing at other drivers and speeding, while only a small number of incidents involve direct contact, such as verbal threats or acts of violence. Psychologists note that road rage is not confined to individuals suffering mental illnesses such as intermittent explosive disorder, antisocial personality disorder, or narcissistic personality disorder, but road rage may also be triggered by substance use, exhaustion, and physiological ailments.

DIAGNOSING ROAD RAGE

Degrees of road rage range from name-calling and obscene gesturing to threats, physical confrontations, and murder. Feeling empowered by the strength, anonymity, and speed of their cars, angry drivers committing road rage challenge other drivers for such perceived slights as driving too slowly, cutting them off, or taking a parking space. Drivers often feel compelled to punish other motorists. Many drivers consider their cars as personal territory and can become temperamental and vengeful if they believe that their space has been violated.

Some out-of-control drivers cut others off in traffic, stare menacingly, throw things, honk, flash headlights, brake unexpectedly, or bump from behind to express anger. Other furious drivers chase their victims, forcing them to stop or crash, and then engage in screaming, punching, breaking windows, and even assaulting other drivers. Road rage assailants mostly become angry with people they do not know.

ROAD RAGE PROFILES

E. Scott Gellar, a Virginia Polytechnic Institute and State University psychology professor, examined why drivers succumb to road rage. Gellar differentiated between aggressive driving, which constitutes risky behavior such as speeding, tailgating, and passing dangerously, and road rage, which is the lack of emotional control while driving and the development of aggression that can escalate into violence. Arnold Nerenberg, a Los Angeles traffic psychologist, explained that the human psyche seeks to release its aggression on anonymous people that it feels have purposefully interfered with it. While people may become equally frustrated when someone cuts them in line at the grocery store, it is more easy to ignore the humanity of the other person when in a car. Yale University psychiatrist John

Larson ranked degrees of road rage, emphasizing that vigilante driving is the most extreme. He attributed some road rage cases to assumptions based on automobile types that drivers often associate with certain personalities. Specific conditions often exacerbate road rage because of physiological or psychological arousal. Rush-hour traffic and construction zones frustrate people already prone to emotional outbursts, who misdirect their anger at others.

Societal pressures for speed push hurried drivers to reach destinations quickly and to become overwhelmed by delays. Some impatient drivers consider sitting in traffic because of road repairs or holiday congestion as a personal threat to their time and plans. Personal stress related to work and family security can cause feelings of powerlessness and intensify drivers' sense of entitlement to roads.

Drivers of all ages commit road rage, and women and men can be equally aggressive behind the wheel. Various studies identify a gender, ethnicity, or age group as being more likely to participate in road rage, but a specific profile cannot be compiled. Some people commit a single act of road rage, while others are perpetually hostile motorists. Some personality traits that enraged drivers might share include being emotionally immature, intolerant, impulsive, self-righteous, and competitive.

TREATMENT OPTIONS

Few drivers feel regret after initiating acts of road rage. Most assert they were correct and rationalize their actions. They do not view road rage as problematic and blame other drivers for enraging them. Hostile drivers perceive themselves as more competent drivers than those who offend them and consider their anger to be an inborn personality trait that cannot be changed. Personalizing driving situations, they seek apologies from drivers who they believe have wronged them and become argumentative when denied such submissive responses.

To defend against road rage, psychologists advise drivers confronted by angry motorists to remain calm and ignore gestures to avoid being drawn into a confrontation. Most psychologists suggest that enraged drivers should admit they have a problem, assume responsibility, and try to alter their behavior and control their anger to avoid being provoked into road rage patterns. Psychotherapist Barry Markell recommends that drivers who are prone to road rage give themselves plenty of time to arrive at their destinations, to play soothing music, to get sufficient sleep, to limit their alcohol intake, and to remind themselves of the potential consequences of succumbing to road rage, including traffic tickets, damage to vehicles, and rising insurance rates.

University of Hawaii psychologist Leon James promotes supportive driving by acting courteously, yielding as necessary, and forgiving other drivers' mistakes. Nerenberg counsels his patients by riding in cars and mimicking their aggressive behavior. His therapy also involves visualization and relaxation techniques to overcome self-defeating and potentially dangerous behavioral patterns.

BIBLIOGRAPHY

Carroll, Linda J., and Peter J. Rothe. "Viewing Vehicular Violence through a Wide Angle Lens: Contributing Factors and a Proposed Framework." *Canadian Journal of Criminology and Criminal Justice* 56.2 (2014): 1–25. Print.

Fong, G., D. Frost, and S. Stansfeld. "Road Rage: A Psychiatric Phenomenon?" *Social Psychiatry and Psychiatric Epidemiology* 36 (2001): 277–86. Print.

Fumento, Michael. "Road Rage Versus Reality." *Atlantic Monthly* 282 (1998): 12–17. Print.

Galovski, Tara E. , Loretta S. Malta, and Edward B. Blanchard. *Road Rage: Assessment and Treatment of the Angry, Aggressive Driver*. Washington: American Psychological Assoc., 2006. Print.

James, Leon, and Diane Nahl. *Road Rage and Aggressive Driving: Steering Clear of Highway Warfare*. Amherst: Prometheus, 2000. Print.

Larson, John A., and Carol Rodriguez. *Road Rage to Road-Wise*. New York: Forge, 1999. Print.

Michael, Mike. "The Invisible Car: The Cultural Purification of Road Rage." *Car Cultures*. Ed. Daniel Miller. New York: Berg, 2001. Print.

Penrod, Maurice G., and Scott N. Paulk, eds. *Psychology of Anger: New Research*. New York: Nova, 2014. Print.

Sansone, Randy A., and Lori A. Sansone. "Road Rage: What's Driving It?" *Psychiatry* 7.7 (2010): 14–18. Print.

Vallières, Evelyne F., et al. "Intentionality, Anger, Coping, and Ego Defensiveness in Reactive Aggressive Driving." *Journal of Applied Social Psychology* 44.5 (2014): 354–63. Print.

Vanderbilt, Tom. *Traffic: Why We Drive the Way We Do (And What It Says about Us)*. New York: Knopf, 2008. Print.

Elizabeth D. Schafer

SEE ALSO: Aggression; Aggression: Reduction and control; Air rage; Anger; Impulse control disorders.

Rogers, Carl R.

BORN: January 8, 1902
DIED: February 4, 1987
BIRTHPLACE: Oak Park, Illinois
PLACE OF DEATH: La Jolla, California
IDENTITY: American founder of person-centered therapy
TYPE OF PSYCHOLOGY: Psychotherapy

Carl R. Rogers is best known as the founder of person-centered therapy.

Carl R. Rogers was the fourth of six children. His parents were living monuments to the Protestant work ethic, which had a lifelong effect on Rogers's character. Rogers proved to be a bright and able student in school, though he was given to daydreaming. Still, there was never any question in his family that Rogers would attend college. He completed his undergraduate work at the University of Wisconsin and took his doctoral degree in clinical and educational psychology at Teachers College, Columbia University.

Rogers held a number of important positions during his professional career. After finishing graduate school, he worked in human services for the state of New York. His first academic position was at the Ohio State University. He then became director of the Guidance Center at the University of Chicago. In 1957, he accepted a teaching position at the University of Wisconsin, where he served until he moved to the Western Behavioral Science Institute in California.

Rogers is best known as the founder of person-centered therapy. He outlined seven principles that characterize the approach. The first is facilitation. The client is responsible for his or her own healing. The therapist is merely the facilitator, mirroring back what the client says. The second principle is problem. The client's personal problem is the focal point around which therapy sessions are organized. The client has to decide what is the correct course of action for addressing his or her problem. The third principle is realness. The therapist must set aside any artificial guise that he or she may wear and become a "real person." The client must follow suit and drop any pretenses during the therapy sessions. The fourth principle is prizing. The therapist must express unconditional regard for the client. Each person is of inherent worth. The fifth principle is empathy. The therapist must become a nonjudgmental listener. He or she must come to view the world through the client's eyes. The sixth principle is trust. The therapist must trust the client's judgment. Whatever decision the client makes regarding his or her problem, the therapist must support the decision because it represents the "right" one for the client at the time. The seventh principle is congruence. The process of psychotherapy is a two-sided coin. Just as the therapist must express empathy, trust, and prizing for the client, so the client must reciprocate and express the same qualities for the therapist. When everything falls into place—all seven principles are acted on—real change can take place in human character.

BIBLIOGRAPHY

Kirschenbaum, Howard. *Life and Work of Carl Rogers*. Alexandria: Amer. Counseling Assn., 2009. Print.

Lux, Michael, Renate Motschnig-Pitrik, and Jeffrey H. Cornelius-White. *Interdisciplinary Handbook of the*

Person-Centered Approach: Research and Theory. New York: Springer, 2013. Digital file.

Rogers, Carl R., and David E. Russell. *Carl Rogers—The Quiet Revolutionary: An Oral History.* Granite Bay: Penmarin, 2002. Print.

Rogers, Carl R., Reinhard Tausch, and Harold C. Lyon. *On Becoming an Effective Teacher: Person-Centred Teaching, Psychology, Philosophy, and Dialogues with Carl R. Rogers.* Abingdon, Oxon: Routledge, 2013. Digital file.

Thorne, Brian, and Pete Sanders. *Carl Rogers.* 3rd ed. Thousand Oaks: Sage, 2013. Print.

Stanley D. Ivie

SEE ALSO: Person-centered therapy; Psychotherapy: Goals and techniques.

Romantic addiction

TYPE OF PSYCHOLOGY: Addiction; Biological bases of human behavior; Clinical; Counseling; Developmental; Family; Social

Heartbreak due to the dissolution of a romantic relationship and withdrawal from an addictive substance share many similar psychological and neurobiological symptoms. Increasing awareness regarding the similarities across both conditions and conceptualizing the process of getting over a romantic relationship from an addiction framework may be helpful from a treatment/recovery standpoint. Using an addiction model to understand the common thoughts, emotions, and behaviors individuals experiencing heartbreak have can promote consideration of strategies that have been shown to be effective in treating substance use conditions.

KEY CONCEPTS
- Addictions
- Addictive behaviors
- Break-up
- Heartbreak
- Loss of relationships

INTRODUCTION

The end of a romantic relationship, whether through a break-up or divorce, is a profoundly emotional but common occurrence. The majority of individuals experience the hurt of heartbreak at least once in their lifetime. Although grief is a key symptom following a break-up, a simple bereavement model of recovery from heartbreak may not address the myriad symptoms individuals experience when a relationship ends, particularly when the relationship is terminated by the other partner. An abundance of literature suggests that heartbreak can lead to a wide range of multiple mental health issues such as depression, anxiety, and insomnia. Additionally, individuals suffering from the loss of a relationship may be at risk for using alcohol or drugs as a maladaptive coping behavior to help alleviate the pain. In fact, the process of trying to get over a former romantic partner can often look very similar to the process of individuals struggling to overcome a substance related addiction; research has found many neurological and psychological similarities among these two conditions. Conceptualizing a person's struggle of getting over a romantic partner as recovery from an addiction can help integrate techniques that may not be utilized if this process is only viewed as bereavement.

PSYCHOLOGICAL SIMILARITIES BETWEEN ROMANTIC RELATIONSHIPS, HEARTBREAK, AND ADDICTION

Two researchers, Burkett and Young, report that from "initial encounters to withdrawal" love, heartbreak, and addiction share similar psychological features and symptoms. They describe the experience of love as leading to experiences of "exquisite euphoria, loss of control, loss of time, and a powerful motivation to seek out the partner" and the experience of getting over a former partner as a withdrawal from an addiction. For example, the substance use disorder criterion, which states that individuals experience "a persistent desire or unsuccessful efforts to cut down or control substance use" and spend "a great deal of time . . . us[ing] the substance, or recover[ing] from its effects," appears to capture the symptoms experienced by individuals suffering from heartbreak. A study conducted on participants currently struggling to get over their former partner found that participants reported routinely thinking about their ex-partner at least 85% of the day. In the same study, Fisher and colleagues also found that many participants reported yearning to reunite romantically with their ex-partner through inappropriate contact (i.e. phone, email, in person), they were unable to stop crying, and often drank excessively.

Research has found that found that people going through a break-up had made strenuous attempts to reunite with their ex-partner and reported extreme distress and preoccupation related to the ex-partner. The tendency for the individuals to desperately attempt to reestablish the relationship post breakup appears to parallel the common struggle individuals experience when they try to refrain from using a substance. In addition, the distress and preoccupation associated with the former partner is also analogous to the distress and preoccupation many substance abusers report experiencing due to their addiction.

Substance-related withdrawal symptoms such as autonomic hyperactivity, increased hand tremor, insomnia, nausea/vomiting, psychomotor agitation, and anxiety have also been observed in individuals who experience heartbreak. For example, three researchers, Gilbert, Gilbert and Schultz found a high degree of similarity with regard to withdrawal symptoms between individuals with addictive behaviors and relationship loss. Additionally, separation anxiety, another condition that is triggered by separation from others, overlaps with substance abuse withdrawal symptoms for the following: sleep difficulty, anxiety, and nausea/vomiting. Although the separation anxiety and heartbreak following the dissolution of a romantic relationship are different, they are both triggered by the separation from a loved one and as such, provide additional support that experiencing a breakup may lead to substance-like withdrawal symptoms.

NEUROLOGICAL SIMILARITIES BETWEEN ROMANTIC RELATIONSHIPS, HEARTBREAK, AND ADDICTION

Romantic relationships and addictions also appear to share similar biochemical pathways. In their review article, Burkett and Young suggest that attachment, love, and addiction share commonalities in brain regions and neurochemical activity across conditions. More specifically, they found the following neurochemicals to be highly involved in both drug addiction and romantic relationship bonding: dopamine, opioids, oxytocin, corticotrophin-releasing hormones, and arginine vasopressin. For example, corticotrophin-releasing hormones are activated both during withdrawal from drugs of abuse and during separation and/or the end of a relationship from a loved one. The presence of withdrawal symptoms in both substance disorders and break-ups, and the finding that the same hormones are activated during both withdrawal processes supports the concept that going through a break-up and suffering from an addiction share underlying commonalities.

Further support for the neurological similarities between addiction and romantic relationships comes from a study by Fisher and colleagues that assessed the brain activity of individuals who experienced the loss of a romantic relationship and reported difficulty in getting over a former partner. Their results found an increase in neural activity within specific brain areas (the nucleus accumbens and the orbitofrontal/prefrontal cortex) when participants were presented with the picture of their former partner. These same brain regions are activated during periods of drug craving.

CLINICAL IMPLICATIONS

Conceptualizing romantic relationships as a form of addiction may provide important in trying to overcome the struggle of ending it. Given the neurological and psychological commonalities shared by addictive behaviors and romantic relationships, it may be therapeutically beneficial to conceptualize the loss of a romantic relationship as withdrawal from a substance and guide treatment from this framework. While symptoms of depression, anxiety and substance use are associated with relationship loss, the underlying processes that precipitate and maintain these symptoms may be attributed to both neurobiological and psychological factors that are remarkably similar to those associated with addiction.

Conceptualizing the process of "getting over an ex" as similar to the process of substance cessation may lead to treatment benefits for individuals who suffer extreme distress and experience impairment in functioning. Clinicians may draw from strategies that have demonstrated efficacy in treating individuals suffering from substance use. Psychoeducation regarding common symptoms associated with addictive behaviors (e.g., withdrawal symptoms, unsuccessful attempts to control use (like not contacting the ex-partner), continued use despite awareness of negative consequences (like looking at pictures of the ex-partner or mentally reviewing past experiences with the ex-partner) may be helpful during the initial phase of therapy. Framing lapses as both normal and to-be-expected can help individuals to accept these episodes without viewing them themselves as failures or personally weak may also be helpful. In addition, psychoeducation regarding urges and cravings to reach out to the ex-partner or to ruminate about him or her, can outline specific coping strategies to use during times of when urges become intense. Similarly, identifying and self-monitoring specific triggers, like past shared locations, foods, people, smells, movies, to be avoided has the benefit of promoting behavioral and emotional detachment, and thereby reduce personal suffering.

Another strategy might be use of a sponsor system as is commonly associated with individuals in AA and other substance support groups. One can contact an established family member or friend when the urge to initiate contact with the ex-partner is heightened.

FUTURE DIRECTIONS

Though nascent research supports the idea that ending romantic relationships and surviving the resulting heartbreak may have similarities to forms of behavioral addiction, the state of psychosocial research is as yet insufficient to determine that these underlying similarities are true in all cases. Recognizing the similarities, when they exist, can help those suffering, to suffer less and cope better.

BIBLIOGRAPHY

Durayappah, A. (February 23, 2011). "5 Scientific Reasons Why Breakups Are Devastating". *Huffington Post*. Retrieved from: http://www.huffingtonpost.com/adoree-durayappah-mapp-mba/breakups_b_825613.html This article reviews five reasons why people have so much difficulty moving on from a break-up. More specifically they discuss how rejection causes physiologically responses within an individual and how recovering from a breakup is similar to trying to overcome a drug addiction.

Heussner, K.M. (July 8, 2010). "Addicted To Love? It's Not You, It's Your Brain". *ABC News*. Retrieved from: http://abcnews.go.com/Technology/addicted-love-brain/story?id=11110866 This article discusses how going through a break-up is very similar to suffering from an addiction. Furthermore, the author discusses how beneficial it may be to treat individuals suffering from heartbreak as though you are treating an addiction.

Lachmann, S. (June 4, 2013). "How To Mourn a Breakup To Move Past Grief and Withdrawal". *Psychology Today*. Retrieved from: http://www.psychologytoday.com/blog/me-we/201306/how-mourn-breakup-move-past-grief-and-withdrawal This article focuses on the physical and emotional withdrawal symptoms that many people going through a breakup experience. The author provides examples of ways individuals can overcome the acute withdrawal symptoms.

Luscombe, B. (July 9, 2010). "The Cruelest Study: Why Breakups Hurt". *TIME*. Retrieved from: http://content.time.com/time/health/article/0,8599,2002688,00.html This article reviews a study that assessed

individuals' brain activity after being exposed to a picture of their ex-partner who they were still mourning. The study found similarities in brain activity between looking at the pictures and physical pain, craving and addiction, reward and motivation.

Kimberly Glazier and Lata K. McGinn

SEE ALSO: Addiction; Attachment; Dependency; Love Psychosexual behavior; Relationships.

Rorschach, Hermann

BORN: November 8, 1884, in Zurich, Switzerland
DIED: April 2, 1922, in Herisau, Switzerland
IDENTITY: Swiss psychiatrist
TYPE OF PSYCHOLOGY: Personality; Psychological methodologies; Psychopathology

Rorschach developed the inkblot personality test.

Hermann Rorschach's father was an art teacher. As a result, Rorschach developed an avid interest in art. During his childhood, he was fascinated with inkblots. In school, he was often preoccupied drawing random inkblot designs, which earned him the nickname "Kleck," German for "inkblot."

Rorschach studied for five years at the University of Zurich, earning an undergraduate degree in 1907. While in school, he worked at the university hospital's psychiatric ward, taking a residency at a mental institution in Munsterlingen, Switzerland, in 1909. In 1912, Rorschach earned his doctorate in medicine from Zurich. In 1914, he took a job as a resident physician at the Waldau Mental Hospital in Bern. Two years later, he was hired at the Krombach Mental Hospital in Appenzell, Switzerland. He was elected as the vice president of the Swiss Psychoanalytic Society in 1919.

Between 1911 and 1921, Rorschach worked on inkblot experiments that would yield meaningful results for understanding a subject's personality traits. He presented his inkblot method in his book *Psychodiagnostik* (1921). The book also contained his more general theories of human personality. Hermann Rorschach Rorschach designed ten Rorschach inkblot cards, each with a different symmetrical pattern. He argued that, by recording a subject's responses to this series of inkblots, the amount of introversion and extroversion that a person possessed could be determined, as well as clues about intelligence, emotional stability, and mental abnormalities. In 1942, his book appeared in English translation as *Psychodiagnostics: A Diagnostic Test Based on Perception*.

Although Rorschach's inkblots do not depict any particular objects, they contain shapes that suggest physical items. Five of the cards are black and white, two are primarily black and white with some color, and three are in color. Subjects describe what they see in each inkblot. The responses are then analyzed in terms of what part of the picture was focused on, the content and originality of the response, and the subject's attention to details. Before he could make planned improvements to his inkblot test, Rorschach died of appendicitis in 1922.

After Rorschach's death, colleagues applied his inkblot test to a number of subjects, and it rapidly gained popularity. The test is still considered a valuable tool in the fields of psychology and psychiatry and is still used as a standard testing method for compiling a personality profile. However, it is no longer used as an absolute diagnosis, but only to provide indicators of potential psychiatric traits or problems.

BIBLIOGRAPHY

Dana, Richard Henry, ed. *Handbook of Cross-cultural and Multicultural Personality Assessment*. Hillsdale, N.J.: Laurence Erlbaum, 2000. Discusses use of Rorschach's inkblot test for assessing personality traits in different ethnic groups and cultures.

Inman, Sally, Martin Buck, and Helena Burke, eds. *Assessing Personal and Social Development: Measuring the Unmeasurable*. London: Falmer, 1999. Addresses the use of the inkblot test in assessing child development.

Shrout, Patrick E., and Susan T. Fiske, eds. *Personality Research, Methods, and Theory*. Hillsdale, N.J.: Laurence Erlbaum, 1995. Insights on how the inkblot test is used in personality assessment.

Alvin K. Benson

SEE ALSO: Personality rating scales; Personality theory; Rorschach inkblots

Rorschach inkblots

DATE: 1921 forward
TYPE OF PSYCHOLOGY: Personality

The Rorschach inkblot test is widely used to assess various aspects of a person's personality. It consists of ten standardized inkblots, always given in the same order. The subject relates to the examiner what he or she sees in the blots as well as what it is about the blot that suggests that particular thing. Although several scoring systems have been developed, today most clinicians use the Exner Comprehensive System to score and interpret the Rorschach inkblot test.

KEY CONCEPTS
• Ambiguous stimuli
• Norms
• Personality assessment
• Projective techniques

INTRODUCTION

Personality assessment is the measurement of affective aspects of a person's behavior, such as emotional states, motivation, attitudes, interests, and interpersonal relations. One type of personality assessment measurement is the use of projective techniques. These techniques require that the client respond to a relatively unstructured task that permits a variety of possible responses. The fundamental assumption is that the individual's responses to the ambiguous stimuli will reflect significant and relatively enduring personality characteristics. The Rorschach inkblot test is one such technique.

The idea that associations with ambiguous visual stimuli provide a key to personality is an ancient one, going back to the classical period in early Greece. The use of inkblots as stimuli for imagination achieved popularity in Europe during the nineteenth century. A parlor game called Blotto required players to create responses to inkblots. Although the Swiss psychiatrist Hermann Rorschach, who created the test with the intention of using it to diagnose schizophrenia, was not the first to involve inkblots in the study of psychological processes, his work was qualitatively different in establishing the framework from which personality descriptions could be made. Rorschach's work became known with the publication of *Psychodiagnostik* (1921; *Psychodiagnostics: A Diagnostic Test Based on Perception*, 1942). Tragically, he died within a year, at the age of thirty-eight, of complications of appendicitis.

The test was adopted by five American psychologists of very different backgrounds. Each developed a scoring system based on his or her theoretical background, but all five saw the data as having perceptual-cognitive and symbolic components. In the early 1970s, the American psychologist John Exner developed the Comprehensive System to provide the Rorschach community with a common methodology, language, and literature base. Today the Exner Comprehensive System is the most widely used system to administer, score, and interpret the Rorschach. Doctoral-level psychologists require advanced training and supervision to administer, score, and interpret the Rorschach inkblot test. Some clinicians have raised concerns about the validity and reliability of the Rorschach test, but the test has many strong proponents and remains widely used among psychologists in the United States.

ADMINISTRATION, SCORING, AND INTERPRETATION

The Rorschach uses ten cards, on one side of which is printed a bilaterally symmetrical inkblot. Five of the blots are in shades of gray and black only; two add additional touches of bright red; and the remaining three combine several pastel shades. The Rorschach inkblot test may be administered to preschool children through adults. The client is shown each card in a specific order and asked to relate what the blot could represent. The examiner keeps a verbatim record of what is said and done, including spontaneous remarks, position of the card, and expressions of emotion.

After all ten cards are presented, the examiner questions the client systemically regarding the location of the responses and aspects of the blot to which the associations were given. The examiner then scores the test, usually using the Exner Comprehensive System. Examples of variables scored include content (What did the client see?), location (In what part of the blot did he or see she it?), and quality of the response (Can it be seen easily by others?). The scores are then compared with norms that are the test performance of the standardization sample. Thus, an adult outpatient would be compared with a large group of other adult outpatients to discover where he or she falls on each variable in relation to the comparison group, and a nine-year-old child would be compared to other nine-year-olds. Each score would be examined to determine if it would be considered an average, below average, or above average score.

Finally, the psychologist interprets the test, focusing on those scores or combinations of scores that vary from the average performance of the standardization group. The interpretations focus on many aspects of personality, including affective features, capacity for control and stress tolerance, cognitive processes, interpersonal perception, self-perception, and situation-related stress. Information from other tests, interviews, and case history records is also utilized in formulating the interpretations. For example, if the Rorschach shows a high amount of situational stress, a clinical interview can determine what the situational stress is about. An alternative interpretative approach to the Rorschach is a clinical one. In this approach, the focus is on the interpretation of content rather than a strict analysis of scores. Most psychologists combine both approaches as a means of enhancing the interpretations.

BIBLIOGRAPHY

Anastasi, Anne, and Susan Urbina. *Psychological Testing*. 7th ed. Upper Saddle River: Prentice, 1997. Print.

Butcher, James Neal. *Oxford Handbook of Personality Assessment*. New York: Oxford UP, 2009. Print.

Drayton, Mike. "What's Behind the Rorschach Inkblot Test?" *BBC News Magazine*. BBC, 24 July 2012. Web. 26 June 2014.

Erdberg, Philip. "Rorschach Assessment." *Handbook of Psychological Assessment*. Ed. Gerald Goldstein and Michel Hersen. 2d ed. New York: Pergamon, 2000. Print.

Exner, John E. *The Rorschach: A Comprehensive System Volume 1, Basic Foundations*. 4th ed. Hoboken: Wiley, 2003. Print.

Hardman, David. *Judgment and Decision Making: Psychological Perspectives*. Chichester: Blackwell, 2009. Print.

Gacono, Carl B., and Barton Evans, eds. *The Handbook of Forensic Rorschach Assessment*. New York: Routledge, 2008. Print.

Karen D. Multon

SEE ALSO: Beck Depression Inventory (BDI); California Psychological Inventory (CPI); Children's Depression Inventory (CDI); Clinical interviewing, testing, and observation; Depression; Diagnosis; Minnesota Multiphasic Personality Inventory (MMPI); Personality: Psychophysiological measures; Personality interviewing strategies; Personality rating scales; Rorschach, Hermann; State-Trait Anxiety Inventory (STAI); Thematic Apperception Test (TAT).

Rosenhan experiment

DATE: 1973

TYPE OF PSYCHOLOGY: Social psychology

KEY CONCEPTS
- Bias
- Labeling
- Participant-observation research
- Psychiatric diagnosis
- Sanity

INTRODUCTION

In a powerful and illuminating study of the validity of psychiatric diagnoses, David L. Rosenhan of Stanford University persuaded eight people who had no history of psychiatric illness to present themselves at various mental hospitals in five states on the East and West Coasts. Each of these imposters, or pseudopatients, falsely reported a single psychiatric symptom: vague auditory hallucinations. For example, imposters stated that they occasionally heard the words "thud," "empty," and "hollow." Aside from lying about the occasional voices, everything else these imposters said and did was honest, including the responses they gave during extensive admission interviews and large batteries of tests. Rosenhan wanted to see how long it would take for the hospital staff to recognize the normality of the imposters.

Hospital staff never did. On the basis of the one complaint alone, all eight people were admitted to twelve different hospitals (some did it twice) and kept there from seven to fifty-two days. Their average length of stay was nineteen days, despite the fact that after they were admitted, each person responded honestly to questions about significant life events, said that they no longer heard voices, and attempted to interact normally with staff members. Indeed, the imposters had a hard time convincing the staff that they were well and no longer needed to be hospitalized.

On the basis of the behavior that they observed, hospital personnel diagnosed each person as severely abnormal. Most diagnoses were schizophrenia, which is a severe disorder. Even when they were discharged, most of these imposters left with the label "schizophrenia—in remission." Labeling had a powerful, long-lasting effect.

Although the hospital staff never detected any of the imposters, many of the other inpatients did. Patients came forward and said something like, "You're not crazy. You're a journalist or a professor checking up on the hospital." In part, patients figured out the ruse because the imposters openly kept notes about their experiences on the psychiatric ward.

These notes, a typical aspect of participant-observation research, provided much information about the daily activities on a psychiatric ward. These imposters noted that the hospital staff spent surprisingly little time interacting with patients, an average of only 6.8 minutes per day. Mostly, staff members segregated themselves from patients in a glassed-off enclosure, where they could observe but did not have to respond to patients. When staff did interact with patients, treatment was often depersonalizing, including avoiding patients and ignoring their questions. Staff often behaved in an authoritarian manner, and the imposters grew to feel powerless, invisible, and bored. Hospital staff interpreted every behavior as a symptom of a mental disorder. For example, note taking was seen as a sign of obsession, and pacing the corridor out of boredom was viewed as a sign of nervousness. Further, these imposters noted the largely normal quality of the real patients' behavior, concluding that people with genuine mental illness act normally most of the time.

In a follow-up experiment, Rosenhan alerted hospital staff to the possibility that people who presented for admission were imposters. In this follow-up study, staff judged about 10 to 20 percent of new admissions to be faking. However, none of those identified was actually an experimental imposter.

LONG-TERM IMPLICATIONS

In Rosenhan's study, the label "schizophrenic" distorted how hospital staff viewed each of the imposters on the ward. Rosenhan concluded that hospitals impose a special environment in which mental health professionals can easily misunderstand the meanings of behavior. Attitudes can bias how people view others' behavior.

The results illustrate several important points. One, labels have a powerful influence on the way mental health workers perceive and interpret actions. Two, the mental health system is biased toward seeing pathology in anyone who walks in the door. Three, determining who is psychologically disordered is not always clear. Four, psychiatric diagnoses have questionable validity.

Rosenhan's controversial study stimulated a lot of critical discussion and examination of psychiatric institutions. Rosenhan actually proposed that psychiatrists and other mental health professionals stop diagnosing personality and instead label specific behaviors. The mental health field did not make this step, but psychiatry moved to improve the reliability of diagnoses in subsequent editions of the *Diagnostic and Statistical Manual of Mental Disorders* (DSM), the fifth edition of which was published by the American Psychiatric Association in 2013. According to the DSM-5, most psychiatric disorders can be diagnosed only if the symptoms occur over a long period of time and interfere significantly with the patient's life, which, if the standards were correctly applied, would rule out Rosenhan's pseudopatients.

The study was also used at the time as a basis for suggestions of reforms of inpatient psychiatric care facilities, though that was not Rosenhan's aim in conducting the study. In the twenty-first century, the Rosenhan experiment has inspired a number of studies involving pseudopatients—or, as they are sometimes called, "mystery shoppers"—intended to evaluate the quality of patient life and care in various facilities, rather than to evaluate the validity of psychiatric diagnoses in general.

Rosenhan's original experiment is often listed as one of the classic psychology experiments of the twentieth century. The original article, "On Being Sane in Insane Places," which was published in the journal *Science* in 1973, has been reprinted in books listing key readings in psychology, introductory readings in sociology, and examples of participant-observation in qualitative health research. The extensive discussion of this study in other fields such as social work and law reflects tremendous breadth across disciplines.

BIBLIOGRAPHY

Crown, Sidney. "'On Being Sane in Insane Places': A Comment from England." *Journal of Abnormal Psychology* 84.5 (Oct. 1975): 453–55. Print.

Goddard, Murray J. "Personal Accounts: On Being Possibly Sane in Possibly Insane Places." *Psychiatric Services* 62.8 (2011): 831–32. Print.

Lazarus, Arthur. "Improving Psychiatric Services through Mystery Shopping." *Psychiatric Services* 60.7 (2009): 972–73. Print.

Millon, Theodore. "Reflections on Rosenhan's 'On Being Sane in Insane Places.'" *Journal of Abnormal Psychology* 84.5 (Oct. 1975): 456–61. Print.

Polak, Paul R., et al. "On Treating the Insane in Sane Places." *Journal of Community Psychology* 5.4 (Oct. 1977): 380–87. Print.

Rhodes, Karin. "Taking the Mystery out of 'Mystery Shopper' Studies." *New England Journal of Medicine* 365.6 (2011): 484–86. Print.

Rosenhan, David L. "On Being Sane in Insane Places." *Science* 179 (Jan. 1973): 250–58. Print.

Slater, Lauren. *Opening Skinner's Box: Great Psychological Experiments of the Twentieth Century.* New York: Norton, 2004. Print.

Lillian M. Range

SEE ALSO: Abnormality: Psychological models; Culture and diagnosis; Diagnosis; Experimentation: Ethics and subject rights; Mental illness: Historical concepts; Research ethics; Schizophrenia: Background, types, and symptoms.

Rule-governed behavior

TYPE OF PSYCHOLOGY: Learning

A rule (or instruction) is a verbal stimulus that describes a behavior and its consequences. Rules can establish even complicated behaviors quickly and effectively, but they may produce insensitivity to changing contingencies. The study of rules allows an operant analysis of processes that are often termed cognitive.

KEY CONCEPTS
- Contingency
- Discriminative stimulus
- Rule
- Schedule of reinforcement
- Shaping
- Stimulus control

INTRODUCTION

Following the tradition of B. F. Skinner, the famous Harvard University psychologist who pioneered the study of operant conditioning, behavior analysts initially examined the behavior of rats and pigeons because nonhuman subjects could be studied under well-controlled conditions in the experimental laboratory. This made it possible for operant psychologists to discover a number of important behavioral principles and to demonstrate that much of the behavior of their experimental subjects was shaped and maintained by contingencies of reinforcement. "Contingencies" can be thought of as cause-effect relations between a context (in operant terms, a "discriminative stimulus"), an action ("response"), and the consequence ("reinforcement") it produces. For example, if pressing a bar is followed by food only when a light is on and never when it is off, a rat's behavior is gradually shaped by these contingencies until the rat presses the lever only when the light is on.

When operant researchers began to bring human subjects into the laboratory, however, the analysis went beyond behavior directly shaped by contingencies to include behavior under the control of instructions or rules. According to Skinner, a rule is a "contingency-specifying stimulus." It functions as a discriminative stimulus (SD), but it differs from other SDs in that it is a description of a behavior-outcome relation. Other SDs are stimuli in the environment that acquire control over behavior only through specific training; rules, in contrast, have an immediate effect on behavior because they make use of an already existing language repertoire. For example, through a history of careful shaping, a seeing-eye dog can be trained to stop at red lights and cross the street only when the light is green. A verbal child, however, can be taught the same discrimination simply by being told, "Go when the light is green; don't go when the light is red."

Proverbs, maxims, advice, instructions, commands, and so forth all function as rules when they control behavior. In complete form, rules specify an antecedent condition, an action, and its consequences, and often take the form of if-then statements, as in "If you want to get to the other side safely, then cross the street only when the light is green." Most rules, however, are only partial statements of contingencies, specifying exclusively the antecedent (such as a male figure or the word "men" on a door), the behavior (a sign reading do not enter), or the consequence ("Lose twenty-five pounds in one month!"), and it is left to the individual to fill in the blanks.

Despite an abundance of rules in the human environment, many people are not reliable rule-followers. Control by rules is often deficient because rules only determine the topography, or form, of behavior, but they do not impart the motivation to act. Stated differently, rules tell people what to do, but whether people actually do it depends on other circumstances.

ROLE OF CONTINGENCIES
For a rule to be followed, it must be part of an effective contingency: Either the outcome specified in the rule must function as a reinforcer, or the rule giver must be able to mediate aversive consequences (punishment) for noncompliance. Psychologists Steven C. Hayes and Robert D. Zettle have drawn an important distinction between contingency-shaped and rule-governed behavior. They assert that contingency-shaped behavior is con-

trolled by one set of contingencies, usually consisting of a situation, an action, and a consequence (such as being offered a beer, drinking, and feeling relaxed).

In contrast, rule-governed behavior involves two sets of contingencies. One of them is the behavior-outcome relation specified in the rule itself ("If you want to avoid addiction, just say no"). The second involves social consequences for rule following, such as praise or criticism from significant others or social pressure to comply with peer norms. As the following examples will show, at times both sets of contingencies support rule following, but sometimes they compete with each other. In one example, a man is lost and his wife insists that he ask for directions. He is told to "turn left at the light and then follow the signs to the interstate." The man is likely to follow these directions, because both sets of contingencies surrounding rule following are congruent: The natural consequences of finding the highway are indeed reinforcing to him, and the social consequences are reinforcing because following the directions will satisfy his wife and spare him criticism. In another example, however, a child is given a box of candy. Her mother says, "You may have only one piece of candy before dinner, or else you will spoil your appetite." The contingency specified in the rule may be ineffective, because eating only one piece of candy if there is more may never have been reinforcing to the child. Hence, if the child obeys, it is not for the contingency specified in the rule but for the parental consequences that would result from noncompliance.

Behavior under the control of a description of contingencies does not involve a new process but is consistent with an operant framework postulating that the probability of behavior is controlled by its outcome. Rule governance results from an extensive history of reinforcement in which rule-following has directly led to contact with the contingencies specified in the rule, to social consequences associated with compliance and noncompliance, or both.

ROLE IN LEARNING
Teaching people to follow rules is important for a number of reasons, which B. F. Skinner outlined in his book *About Behaviorism* (1974). Most important, many behaviors can be acquired much more quickly through rules than through shaping by the contingencies described in the rules. For example, it is easier to teach a boy the basics of a card game by explaining the rules to him than by playing with him until he gradually (if at all) figures out the rules for himself. Furthermore, there are cases when

the contingencies are so complex or vague that most people would never understand them without the help of rules. Learning to type with ten fingers illustrates such a case. Without appropriate instruction, the immediate success accruing from a hunt-and-peck method will reinforce typing with two fingers, and the person will never learn to use ten fingers, even though in the long run this would have been much more efficient.

According to Roger L. Poppen in a 1989 essay, initially people learn rules from a multitude of external sources such as parents, peers, teachers, television, and books, and eventually they learn to extract rules from interacting with and observing environmental contingencies. Parents encourage the rehearsal and internalization of rules so that these self-instructions then help children guide their own behavior in similar circumstances.

BEHAVIOR-ANALYTIC THEORY

The effects of rules on behavior have been extensively studied within a behavior-analytic methodology. A summary of this research can be found in a chapter by Margaret Vaughan in the book *Rule-Governed Behavior: Cognitions, Contingencies, and Instructional Control*, edited by Steven C. Hayes (1989). Most of these human operant studies use a method in which subjects press a button that, according to some schedule of reinforcement (an arrangement that specifies which responses within an operant class will be reinforced), occasionally produces points exchangeable for money. Depending on the preparation, button pressing may be controlled by the contingency between pressing and point delivery; in this case, the behavior would be contingency-shaped. Button pressing may also be controlled by experimenter instructions, in which case the behavior would be rule-governed.

A number of studies showed that experimenter-provided instructions quickly bring the behavior under stimulus control (behavior occasioned by a stimulus because the stimulus signals some consequence of responding) but also create insensitivity to the scheduled contingencies. For example, telling subjects that "the best way to earn points is to press the button fast" (a fixed-ratio contingency) immediately allows them to respond correctly and earn points. When the contingencies are then surreptitiously changed, however, subjects continue to follow the instructions for long periods of time although they have become obsolete and no longer produce rewards. In contrast, when subjects receive no instructions and their responses are shaped, sensitivity to changing

contingencies develops; that is, when the schedule of reinforcement changes, subjects adjust their behavior to the new schedule and continue to earn points. This observation has led operant researchers to conclude that insensitivity to contingencies may be an inherent property of instructional control.

EFFECT OF IRRATIONAL BELIEFS

The insensitivity effect of rules has intriguing implications: Instructing people how to solve problems is immediately effective, but it may be counterproductive in the long run, because individuals may come to act in accordance with outdated rules. Their behavior may come to be guided by what cognitive psychologists call irrational beliefs or unrealistic expectations, which from an operant perspective would be considered inaccurate statements about contingencies resulting from broad overgeneralizations of old rules. The following example illustrates how an irrational belief may come to control behavior. A mother might tell her child, "Stop making noise! I don't love you when you are bad." This rule may quiet the child immediately, and because it is effective, the parent may use it in other situations. Over the course of her development, the child learns many instances of what her parent considers "bad" (perhaps disobeying instructions, perhaps asserting herself, showing anger, and so on). Gradually she internalizes a generalized rule, "I am only lovable when others approve of me," and evolves into an adult who tries to please everybody and feels unworthy at any sign of disapproval, however ineffective this behavior may be.

Humans live in a world in which rules abound, in the form of instructions, advice, warnings, manuals, cookbooks, self-help books, laws, and social norms. They are intended to provide guidelines for effective behavior. Even when no external rules are available, most people can formulate their own plans of action. The greatest advantage of rules is that they can be extremely helpful and can establish effective behavior quickly. Their greatest disadvantages are that rules do not produce behavior unless other contingencies support rule following and (as Skinner has pointed out) that they may be troublesome rather than helpful when the contingencies change but the rules do not.

EVOLUTION OF STUDY

Originally, behavioral researchers attempted to replicate findings from experimental work with rats and pigeons to demonstrate the generality of the principles of behavior discovered in the animal laboratory. It soon became apparent that people often showed response patterns not comparable to those of animal subjects on the same schedules of reinforcement. For example, a cumulative record of responding on a fixed-interval schedule for animals typically shows "scallops" (a pause after reinforcement, followed by a gradually accelerating response rate until delivery of the next reinforcer). In contrast, human subjects typically time the interval by counting; toward the end, they respond as few times as necessary to obtain the reinforcer.

Behavior analysts suspected that the differences between human and animal responding mainly stemmed from people's prior conditioning history and from instructions, both experimenter-provided and self-generated, with which they approached the experimental tasks. These assumptions began to focus the attention of operant researchers on the role of instructions. By the mid-1970s, instruction following became synonymous with rule-governed behavior and began to evolve into a field of study in its own right.

IMPORTANCE OF APPROACH

One importance of rule governance lies in the possibility of a rapprochement between behaviorist and cognitivist positions. Behaviorists have often been accused of disregarding or failing to acknowledge the importance of higher mental processes. Although such accusations are polemic and extremely misleading, it is true that it was not until the mid-1970s that operant psychologists began a systematic empirical analysis of cognitive-verbal processes. The study of rule-governed behavior marked the beginning of the experimental analysis of phenomena that until then pertained to the domain of cognitive psychology.

The analysis of rule-governed behavior is important for another reason. It provides some insights into causal mechanisms that may underlie current cognitive therapies. For example, in 1987 Poppen presented an excellent theoretical analysis of a self-efficacy approach and of rational emotive therapy, while in 1982, Zettle and Hayes presented a similar analysis of cognitive restructuring and cognitive therapy for depression. The common denominator of these diverse cognitive approaches is their assertion that people's reactions to their environment are mediated by covert verbal statements, which, when dysfunctional, are given labels such as irrational beliefs, low self-efficacy, and negative expectancies. From an operant perspective, such formal categorizations are considered not very useful because formally distinct verbal statements may all have the same function, while statements identical in form may have different functions (one person might say "I can't do it; I'm too dumb" to avoid an unpleasant task, while another person may say the same thing to request assistance).

Within a framework of rule-governed behavior, all these dysfunctional cognitions are considered partial statements of contingencies, and the behavior they produce is rule-governed. Hence, findings from basic experimental research on rule-governed behavior could conceivably be brought to bear on clinical phenomena, which eventually might lead to a better understanding of psychological dysfunctions and to the development of more effective therapies.

BIBLIOGRAPHY

Catania, A. Charles. *Learning*. 4th ed. Cornwall-on-Hudson: Sloan, 2006.Print.

Freeman, Arthur, ed. *Encyclopedia of Cognitive Behavior Therapy*. New York: Springer, 2005. Print.

O'Hora, Denis, Dermot Barnes-Holmes, and Ian Stewart. "Antecedent and Consequential Control of Derived Instruction-Following." *Journal of the Experimental Analysis of Behavior* 102.1 (2014): 66–85. Print.

Pierce, W. David, and Carl D. Cheney. *Behavior Analysis and Learning*. 5th ed. New York: Psychology, 2013. Print.

Poppen, Roger L. "Some Clinical Implications of Rule-Governed Behavior." *Rule-Governed Behavior: Cognitions, Contingencies, and Instructional Control*. Ed. Steven C. Hayes. Reno: Context, 2004. Print.

Skinner, B. F. *About Behaviorism*. 1974. Reprint. London: Penguin, 1993. Print.

Skinner, B. F. "An Operant Analysis of Problem Solving." *Problem-Solving: Research, Method, and Theory*. Ed. Benjamin Kleinmuntz. New York: Wiley, 1966. Print.

Vaughan, Margaret. "Rule-Governed Behavior in Behavior Analysis: A Theoretical and Experimental History." *Rule-Governed Behavior: Cognitions, Contingencies, and Instructional Control*. Ed. Steven C. Hayes. New York: Plenum, 1989. Print.

Watts, Amanda C., et al. "The Effect of Rules on Differential Reinforcement of Other Behavior." *Journal of Applied Behavior Analysis* 46.3 (2013): 680–84. Print.

Zettle, Robert D., and Steven C. Hayes. "Rule-Governed Behavior: A Potential Theoretical Framework for Cognitive-Behavioral Therapy." *Advances in*

Cognitive-Behavioral Research and Therapy. Ed. Philip C. Kendall. Vol. 1. New York: Academic, 1982. Print.

Edelgard Wulfert

SEE ALSO: Behavior therapy; Behavioral family therapy; Behaviorism; Cognitive behavior therapy; Conditioning; Gender differences; Radical behaviorism: B. F. Skinner; Skinner, B. F.

S

S-R theory
Neal E. Miller and John Dollard

TYPE OF PSYCHOLOGY: Personality

Miller and Dollard developed a personality theory that was based on Clark L. Hull's stimulus-response learning theory. They used this theory and a number of psychoanalytic concepts to explain how neurosis develops. They also showed how psychotherapy could be conceptualized as a learning process by using an S-R model of higher mental processes.

KEY CONCEPTS
- Conflict
- Cue
- Cue-producing response
- Drive
- Habit
- Imitation
- Reinforcement
- Response
- Response hierarchy
- Secondary drive

INTRODUCTION

Much, if not most, human behavior is learned. How human beings learn is one of the central, and most controversial, topics in psychology. Neal E. Miller and John Dollard used principles of learning developed by Clark L. Hull, who studied how animals learn, and applied them to explain complex human behavior.

According to Miller and Dollard, human behavior occurs in response to cues. A red traffic light, for example, is a cue to stop, whereas green is a cue to go. A cue is simply any stimulus that is recognized as different from other stimuli. A cue may bring about a variety of responses, but some responses are more likely to occur than others. The response to a cue most likely to occur is called the dominant response. Responses to a cue are arranged in a response hierarchy, from the dominant response to the response least likely to occur. A person's response hierarchy can change. The hierarchy that a person has originally is called the initial hierarchy. If the

initial hierarchy is inborn, it is known as the innate hierarchy. When a hierarchy changes, the result is known as the response hierarchy.

RESPONSE HIERARCHY AND LEARNING

Change in a response hierarchy occurs as a result of learning. There are four fundamental considerations in the explanation of how learning occurs: drive, cue, response, and reinforcement.

A drive is an intense stimulus, such as hunger, that motivates a response. The cue is the stimulus that elicits the response. If the dominant response in the hierarchy results in a reduction in the drive, then reinforcement will occur. Reinforcement means that the association, or connection, between the cue (stimulus) and response is strengthened; the next time the cue occurs, therefore, that response will be even more likely to occur. Reinforcement occurs when a person realizes that the response has led to a reward, although such awareness is not always necessary; reinforcement can also occur automatically. In other words, Miller and Dollard's theory states that for people to learn, they must want something (drive), must do something (response) in the presence of a distinct stimulus (cue), and must get some reward for their actions (reinforcement).

If the dominant response does not result in a reward, the chance that the dominant response will occur again is gradually lessened. This process is called extinction. Eventually, the next response in the hierarchy will occur (in other words, the person will try something else). If that response results in reward, it will be reinforced and may become the dominant response in the hierarchy. In this way, according to Miller and Dollard, humans learn and change their behavior. According to this theory, connections between stimulus and response are learned; these are called habits. Theories that view learning in this way are called stimulus-response, or S-R, theories. The total collection of a person's habits makes up the individual's personality.

ROLE OF DRIVES

Drives, as previously noted, motivate and reinforce responses. Some drives, such as hunger, thirst, sex, and pain, are inborn and are known as primary drives. These drives are naturally aroused by certain physiological conditions; through learning, however, they may also be aroused by cues to which they are not innately connected. For example, one may feel hungry when one sees a favorite restaurant even though one has recently eaten. Drives aroused in this way (that is, by previously neutral cues) are called secondary, or learned, drives.

The natural reaction to an aversive stimulus is pain. Pain is a primary drive; it motivates a person to act, and any response that reduces pain will be reinforced. Neutral cues associated with pain may also produce a response related to pain called fear or anxiety). Fear motivates a person to act; a response that reduces fear will be reinforced. Fear is therefore a drive; it is a drive that is especially important for understanding neurotic behavior, according to Miller and Dollard. For example, a fear of a harmless cue such as an elevator (an elevator phobia) will motivate a person to avoid elevators, and such avoidance will be reinforced by reduction of fear.

CUE RESPONSES

A response to one cue may also occur to cues that are physically similar to that cue; in other words, what one learns to do in one situation will occur in other, similar situations. This phenomenon is called stimulus generalization.

Many responses are instrumental responses; that is, they act on and change some aspect of the environment. Other responses are known as cue-producing responses; the cues from these responses serve to bring about other responses. Words are especially important cue-producing responses; someone says a word and another person responds, or one thinks a word and this is a cue for another word. Thinking can be considered as chains of cue-producing responses—that is, as a sequence of associated words; in this way Miller and Dollard sought to describe the higher mental processes such as thinking, reasoning, and planning.

SOCIAL ROLE OF LEARNING

In their book *Social Learning and Imitation* (1941), Miller and Dollard pointed out that to understand human behavior, one must know not only the process of learning but also the social conditions under which learning occurs. Human learning is social—that is, it occurs in a social context, which can range from the societal level to the interpersonal level. The process of imitation is one

example of how what an individual learns to do depends on the social context.

Imitation involves matching, or copying, the behavior of another person. If the matching behavior is rewarded, it will be reinforced, and the individual will therefore continue to imitate. The cue that elicits the imitating response is the person being imitated (the model), so that the imitative behavior, in Miller and Dollard's analysis, is dependent on the presence of the model. In this way, Miller and Dollard used S-R theory to explain how individuals learn what to do from others and thereby learn how to conform to society.

PSYCHOANALYTIC APPROACH TO NEUROSIS

In their best-known work, *Personality and Psychotherapy: An Analysis in Terms of Learning, Thinking, and Culture* (1950), Dollard and Miller applied S-R theory to explain how neurosis is learned and how it can be treated using learning principles. They pointed out three central characteristics of neurosis that require explanation: misery, stupidity, and symptoms. The misery that neurotics experience is a result of conflict. Conflict exists when incompatible responses are elicited in an individual. An approach-approach conflict exists when a person has to choose between two desirable goals; once a choice is made, the conflict is easily resolved. An avoidance-avoidance conflict exists when an individual must choose between two undesirable goals. An approach-avoidance conflict exists when an individual is motivated both to approach and to avoid the same goal. The last two types of conflicts may be difficult to resolve and under certain conditions may result in a neurosis.

Dollard and Miller tried to explain some aspects of psychoanalytic theory in S-R terms; like Sigmund Freud, the founder of psychoanalysis, they emphasized the role of four critical childhood training situations in producing conflicts that can result in neurosis. These are the feeding situation, cleanliness training, sex training, and anger-anxiety conflicts. Unfortunate training experiences during these stages of childhood may result in emotional problems. Childhood conflicts arising from such problems may be repressed and may therefore operate unconsciously.

The "stupidity" of the neurotic is related to the fact that conflicts that produce misery are repressed and unconscious. Dollard and Miller explained the psychoanalytic concept of repression in terms of S-R theory in the following manner. Thinking about an experience involves the use of cue-producing responses (that is, the use of words) in thinking. If no words are available to label an experience, then a person is unable to think about it—that is, the experience is unconscious. Some experiences are unconscious because they were never labeled; early childhood experiences before the development of speech and experiences for which the culture and language do not provide adequate labels are examples of experiences that are unconscious because they are unlabeled. Labeled painful experiences may also become unconscious if a person stops thinking about them. Consciously deciding to stop thinking about an unpleasant topic is called suppression. Repression is similar to suppression except that it is automatic—that is, it occurs without one consciously planning to stop thinking. For Dollard and Miller, therefore, repression is the automatic response of stopping thinking about very painful thoughts; it is reinforced by drive reduction and eventually becomes a very strong habit.

The third characteristic of neuroses requiring explanation is symptoms. Phobias, compulsions, hysteria, and alcoholism are examples of symptoms. Symptoms arise when an individual is in a state of conflict-produced misery. This misery is a result of the intense fear, and of other intense drives (for example, sexual drives), involved in conflict. Because the conflict is unconscious, the individual cannot learn that the fear is unrealistic. Some symptoms of neurosis are physiological; these are direct effects of the fear and other drives that produce the conflict. Other symptoms, such as avoidance in a phobia, are learned behaviors that reduce the fear or drives of the conflict. These symptoms are reinforced, therefore, by drive reduction.

THERAPEUTIC TECHNIQUES

Dollard and Miller's explanation of psychotherapy is largely a presentation of key features of psychoanalysis described in S-R terms. Therapy is viewed as a situation in which new learning can occur. Because neurotic conflict is unconscious, new learning is required to remove repression so that conflict can be resolved. One technique for doing this, taken directly from psychoanalysis, is free association; here, neurotic patients are instructed to say whatever comes to their consciousness. Because this can be a painful experience, patients may resist doing this, but, because the therapist rewards patients for free associating, they eventually continue. While free associating, patients become aware of emotions related to their unconscious conflicts and so develop a better understanding of themselves.

Another technique borrowed from psychoanalysis involves a phenomenon known as transference. Patients experience and express feelings about the therapist. Such feelings really represent, in S-R terms, emotional reactions to parents, teachers, and other important persons in the patient's past, which, through stimulus generalization, have been transferred to the therapist. The therapist helps the patient to recognize and label these feelings and to see that they are generalized from significant persons in the patient's past. The patient in this way learns how she or he really feels. The patient learns much about herself or himself that was previously unconscious and learns how to think more adaptively about everyday life. The patient's symptoms are thereby alleviated.

EXTENDING THE BEHAVIORIST APPROACH

The S-R theory used by Miller and Dollard had its intellectual roots in the thinking of the seventeenth century, when human beings were thought of as being complicated machines that were set in motion by external stimuli. At the beginning of the twentieth century, the stimulus-response model was adopted by John B. Watson, the founder of behaviorism. Watson used the S-R model to explain observable behavior, but he avoided applying it to mental processes because he believed that mental processes could not be studied scientifically.

Miller and Dollard extended the behaviorism of Watson to the explanation of mental events through their concept of the cue-producing response and its role in the higher mental processes. This was an S-R explanation: Mental processes were seen as arising from associations between words that represent external objects; the words are cues producing responses. Miller and Dollard's approach, therefore, represented a significant departure from the behaviorism of Watson. Miller and Dollard tried to explain mental events in their book Personality and Psychotherapy, in which they attempted to explain many psychoanalytic concepts in S-R terms. Because psychoanalysis is largely a theory of the mind, it would have been impossible for them not to have attempted to describe mental processes.

CONTRIBUTIONS TO MENTAL PROCESSES RESEARCH

The approach to explaining mental processes used by Miller and Dollard, though it represented a theoretical advance in the 1950s, was gradually replaced by other explanations beginning in the 1960s. The drive-reduction theory of learning that they advocated came under criticism, and the S-R view that humans passively react to external stimuli was criticized by many psychologists. As a result, new theories of learning emphasizing cognitive (mental) concepts were developed.

New ways of thinking about mental processes were also suggested by fields outside psychology; one of these was computer science. The computer and its program were seen as analogous to human mental processes, which, like computer programs, involve the input, storage, and retrieval of information. The computer and its program, therefore, suggested new ways of thinking about the human mind. Miller and Dollard's S-R theory has largely been replaced by concepts of contemporary cognitive science.

Miller and Dollard's theory still exercises an important influence on contemporary thinking in psychology. Their analysis of psychoanalysis in terms of learning theory made the important point that neuroses could be unlearned using the principles of learning. Behaviorally oriented treatments of emotional disorders owe a debt to the intellectual legacy of Miller and Dollard.

BIBLIOGRAPHY
Bouton, Mark E. *Learning and Behavior: A Contemporary Synthesis.* Sunderland: Sinauer, 2007. Print.
Dollard, John, et al. *Frustration and Aggression.* 1939. London: Routledge, 1998. Print.
Dollard, John, and Neal E. Miller. *Personality and Psychotherapy: An Analysis in Terms of Learning, Thinking, and Culture.* New York: McGraw-Hill, 1950. Print.
Hall, Calvin S., Gardner Lindzey, and John B. Campbell. *Theories of Personality.* 4th ed. New York: Wiley, 1998. Print.
Klein, Stephen B. *Learning: Principles and Applications.* 6th ed. Thousand Oaks: Sage, 2012. Print.
Merriam, Sharan B., Rosemary S. Caffarella, and Lisa M. Baumgartner. *Learning in Adulthood: A Comprehensive Guide.* 3rd ed. San Francisco: Jossey-Bass, 2007. Print.
Miller, Neal E. "Studies of Fear as an Acquirable Drive: I. Fear as a Motivator and Fear-Reduction as Reinforcement in the Learning of New Responses." *Journal of Experimental Psychology* 38 (1948): 89–101. Print.
Miller, Neal E., and John Dollard. *Social Learning and Imitation.* 1941. Westport: Greenwood, 1979. Print.
Pear, Joseph J. *The Science of Learning.* New York: Psychology, 2014. Digital file.
Sternberg, Robert J., and Li-Fang Zhang, eds. *Perspectives on Thinking, Learning, and Cognitive Styles.* New York: Routledge, 2011. Print.

Sanford Golin

See Also: Bandura, Albert; Behaviorism; Conditioning; Drives; Learning; Miller, Neal E., and John Dollard; Observational learning and modeling therapy; Social learning: Albert Bandura; Watson, John B.

Sadism and masochism

Type of psychology: Psychopathology

Sadism and masochism can exist as normal sexual variations, but "sexual sadism" and "sexual masochism" refer to specific paraphilic disorders, as defined by modern psychiatry. The causes for these disorders are not known, and treatments have not been very effective.

Key Concepts
• Antisocial personality disorder
• Paraphilia
• Sadistic personality disorder
• Self-defeating personality disorder
• Sexual masochism
• Sexual sadism

INTRODUCTION
The terms "sadism" and "masochism" have been used to refer to a variety of behaviors by both clinicians and laypersons, resulting in considerable confusion as to what they actually are. Although sadism and masochism can fall within the range of normal variations in sexual behavior, the medical terms "sexual sadism disorder" and "sexual masochism disorder" refer to paraphilic disorders, as defined in the American Psychiatric Association's *Diagnostic and Statistical Manual of Mental Disorders* (DSM-5).

Sexual sadism disorder, as defined in the manual, consists of recurrent sexual fantasies, urges, or behaviors involving the psychological or physical suffering of another. To meet the clinical diagnostic criteria, these behaviors must be ongoing and have been present for at least a period of six months. Behaviors engaged in may include, but are not limited to, dominating, beating, restraining, whipping, burning, cutting, strangulation, torture, mutilation, and killing. Also, to meet the diagnostic criteria, the fantasies, urges, or behaviors must cause significant distress, interpersonal difficulty, employment disruption, or have been inflicted on a nonconsenting person.

Sexual masochism disorder, as defined in the manual, consists of recurrent sexual fantasies, urges, or behaviors. These must occur over a period of at least six months, and the fantasies, urges, or behaviors must cause significant distress, interpersonal difficulty, or employment disruption. Sexual sadism and sexual masochism are frequently seen in the same individual.

Sexual sadism and sexual masochism disorders are both classified as paraphilias, which means that the individual is sexually attracted to deviant stimuli. Among other paraphilic disorders are pedophilic (arousal from children), exhibitionistic (arousal from exposing one's genitals), fetishistic (arousal from objects such as shoes or leather), and frotteuristic (arousal from rubbing up against strangers) disorders. It has been noted in clinical practice that an individual is likely to exhibit not only both sexual sadism and sexual masochism but also other paraphilias as well.

HISTORY OF THE DISORDERS

The terms "sadism" and "masochism" were first introduced by Richard von Krafft-Ebing in his work *Psychopathia Sexualis: Mit besonderer Berücksichtigung der conträren Sexualempfindung—Eine klinisch-forensische Studie* (1886; *Psychopathia Sexualis: With Especial Reference to Contrary Sexual Instinct—A Medico-legal Study,* 1892). He discussed a variety of sexual perversions. According to Krafft-Ebing, a sexual perversion was any action that could not result in procreation. He saw a basic tendency toward sadism in men and masochism in women. Interestingly, both "sadism" and "masochism" were derived from the names of authors (the marquis de Sade and Leopold von Sacher-Masoch) whose writing seems to exemplify the terms. Although the terms are derived from the writing of these individuals, it should be noted that behavior that could be labeled "sadistic" or "masochistic" was known long before this time.

The marquis de Sade was born to a noble family in France. He served in the military but spent much of his life living as a libertine. He enjoyed the company of many prostitutes and apparently physically and psychologically abused a number of them. Although best known for his sexual writings that exemplified his lifestyle, *Les 120 journées de Sodome*(written 1785, published 1904; *The 120 Days of Sodom,* 1954) and *Justine* (1791; English translation, 1889), he also wrote on philosophical topics.

Due to his lifestyle and the condemnation of his family, Sade spent much of his life incarcerated.

Leopold von Sacher-Masoch was born in the Austrian Empire. He was a professor and wrote extensively on the history of his homeland; however, he is most known for his stories that dealt with his fetishes of dominant women. Like the marquis de Sade, Sacher-Masoch attempted to live out his fantasies during his life with a number of women. It is believed that Sacher-Masoch spent the end of his life insane.

Sigmund Freud expanded on masochism and, to a lesser extent, sadism in his psychosexual theory. He postulated that masochism was a perversion that arose out of guilt caused by sexual desire for the opposite-sexed parent. Because the child could not have the parent sexually, he or she desired to be beaten by that parent. This served both as punishment for the inappropriate feelings but also as sexual satisfaction. Freud's theory held that masochism was a common perversion and indicative of improper sexual development. He viewed women as inherently masochistic.

Philosopher Jean-Paul Sartre saw both sadism and masochism as being examples of what he termed "bad faith," which consists of misleading the self about relationships. Both sadism and masochism are part of what he termed "being-for-the-other." In masochism, the self becomes an object of the other. In sadism, the other becomes an object for the self.

POSSIBLE CAUSES

There is no known definitive cause of sexual sadism and sexual masochism disorders. Researchers have looked to the areas of genetic predisposition, biophysical influences, personality development, learned behavior, and brain studies. Freud believed that masochism and sadism were the result of improper psychosexual development, generally in the anal stage of development. Object-relations theorists maintain that all paraphilias are caused by domineering and frustrating parenting. The child responds to being powerless with a need for power.

Learning and reinforcement may play a significant role in sadistic and masochistic behavior. Children who grow up in an environment with sadistic or masochistic models may themselves repeat such behaviors. Orgasm is a strong reinforcer, and any behavior that accompanies an orgasm is likely to be repeated.

Some brain studies show that individuals may seek to give or receive pain to increase stimulation in a brain that is not receiving enough stimulation. Individuals who are sensation seekers engage in dangerous behaviors to increase their level of stimulation and arousal.

DIAGNOSING SEXUAL SADISM AND SEXUAL MASOCHISM

Previously all forms of sadism and masochism were considered mental disorders. Now only sadistic acts practiced on unwilling partners or sadistic and masochistic acts that cause mental anguish to the individual are considered to be pathological. Masochistic behavior generally is brought to clinical attention when it has resulted in patient self-harm, which may result from acts of consent or from self-induced harm to the point wherein the patient can no longer self-regulate the sexual experience.

Sadistic behavior is considered pathological only once it crosses certain legal and medical boundaries of harm with nonconsenting partners, children, or animals. Illegal behaviors include coercing partners through acts of rape and molestation. Sexual sadists may even kill a partner—either accidentally or intentionally.

Individuals who practice sadism and masochism as forms of sexual expression seem to be significantly different from those individuals who are seen clinically for treatment of sexual sadism and sexual masochism disorders. These sadists do not seek to hurt others outside of sexual play and administer only forms of pain that the masochist has agreed on. Masochists enjoy pain only in a sexual setting, but it is not coercive pain—such as rape—and it is generally pain that they maintain control over through agreement with a partner. Sadists and masochists can engage in a wide range of behaviors, which are often referred to as "play." Very often their fantasies are highly structured and, in fact, very safe. Some individuals may engage in sadomasochistic fantasies only and not act them out. Others may use playful spanking or light bondage; some may engage in whipping and even forms of minor mutilation. Like any other interest, individuals' involvement levels vary. There are those who only engage in some sadomasochistic activities with their partner, and others who live a master-slave relationship full time. Sadists and masochists can find others who share their interests at clubs in most major cities, on websites and chatrooms, and through magazines.

One potentially very dangerous practice of sadists and masochists is erotic asphyxiation (referred to as "autoerotic asphyxiation" when practiced alone). In erotic asphyxiation, one partner deprives the other of oxygen to increase sexual pleasure during orgasm. However, the inability to judge when to stop oxygen deprivation has resulted in accidental deaths. In some instances, when the evidence is inconclusive, the surviving partner has been charged with murder.

CLINICAL ISSUES

A variety of personality disorders have been associated with sexual sadism and sexual masochism disorders. Although not an official diagnosis, self-defeating personality disorder, also referred to as "masochistic personality disorder," has been used by some clinicians and researchers to describe a cluster of extremely self-defeating personality traits. People with this disorder may interpret positive events and actions in a negative light or behave in such a way as to engender a negative response from others and then feel unreasonably hurt when that response is forthcoming. These individuals seem to choose situations or relationships that are disappointing, self-defeating, negative, and even harmful. They are drawn to abusive, hateful individuals. In some cases, they will avoid pleasurable experiences or experiences that are likely to lead to success and even react negatively to individuals who treat them well.

Sadistic personality disorder was classified as a disorder in the revised third edition of the *Diagnostic and Statistical Manual of Mental Disorders* (DSM-III-R) but does not appear in the revised fourth or fifth editions. People with sadistic personality disorder are cruel, manipulative, and aggressive. They can be physically violent and enjoy harming others. Individuals with sadistic personality disorder may enjoy humiliating others and use intimidation and violence to get what they want. The behavior must be directed toward more than one person and is not used for sexual arousal.

Antisocial personality disorder (ASPD) is found in the DSM-5. People with this disorder are marked by a disregard for the rights and feelings of others. They may break laws and may be deceitful, impulsive, aggressive, and irresponsible. Although they are often superficially charming, they have difficulty maintaining a job or relationship. They tend to lack remorse for their behaviors. These individuals have often been diagnosed with conduct disorder in childhood.

Some clinicians and researchers have created a subcategory of rapists known as "sadistic rapists." Although some might argue that all rapists, because of the act of coerced sex, are sexual sadists, many rapists use little force during their crimes. Sadistic rapists are more deviant than other rapists. They seem to reoffend more rapidly than other rapists. They tend to use much more force than is necessary to control their victims. However, caution should be taken when assigning rapists to this category. Just because force was used during a rape—or even if the victim was killed—it cannot be assumed that the rapist is a sadistic rapist. Also, some rapists who do not use extreme force still engage in sadistic fantasies that would classify them as sadistic rapists.

TREATMENT OPTIONS

Sexual sadists and sexual masochists rarely present themselves for treatment unless their behavior is causing them significant psychological distress or they are mandated into treatment for coercing others into sexual behavior. Although there are treatment options, none has had overwhelming success. Pharmacological treatment options include antiandrogen steroids and gonadotropin-releasing hormone agonists, which use medications that act on testosterone and other androgen hormones. Psychotherapeutic approaches may use operant conditioning or cognitive behavioral therapy. These approaches aim to improve the patient's self-control and self-regulation of behavior; whether paraphilic interests, such as sadism or masochism, can change remains subject to debate. Involving a sexual partner in treatment can increase the chances of success, but overall, these patients are difficult to treat.

BIBLIOGRAPHY

Assumpção, Alessandra Almeida, et al. "Pharmacologic Treatment of Paraphilias." *Sexual Deviation: Assessment and Treatment.* Ed. John M. W. Bradford and A. G. Ahmed. Philadelphia: Elsevier, June 2014. 173–81. Digital file.

Baumeister, Roy F. *Masochism and the Self.* Hillsdale: Lawrence Erlbaum, 1989. Print.

Briken, Peer, Dominique Bourget, and Mathieu Dufour. "Sexual Sadism in Sexual Offenders and Sexually Motivated Homicide." *Sexual Deviation: Assessment and Treatment.* Ed. John M. W. Bradford and A. G. Ahmed. Philadelphia: Elsevier, June 2014. 215–30. Digital file.

Freud, Sigmund. *Three Essays on the Theory of Sexuality.* Rpt. Mansfield: Martino, 2011. Print.

Gosselin, Christopher C. "The Sado-Masochistic Contract." *Variant Sexuality.* Ed. Glenn Wilson. New York: Routledge, 2014. 229–57. Digital file.

"The Relevance of Sigmund Freud for the Twenty-First Century". Spec. issue of *Psychoanalytic Psychology* 23.2 (2006): 215–455. Print.

Stekel, Wilhelm, and Louise Brink. *Sadism and Masochism: The Psychology of Hatred and Cruelty.* Vol. 2. New York: Liveright, 1953. Print.

Von Krafft-Ebing, Richard. *Psychopathia Sexualis: With Especial Reference to Contrary Sexual Instinct—A Clinical-Forensic Study.* 1886. Burbank: Bloat, 1999. Print.

Sampling

TYPE OF PSYCHOLOGY: Psychological methodologies

Probability sampling is a scientific method that uses random selection to generate representative samples from populations. It enables researchers to make relatively few observations and to generalize from those observations to a much wider population. Nonprobability sampling does not ensure the representativeness of selected samples.

KEY CONCEPTS
- Element
- Observation unit
- Parameter
- Population
- Sample
- Sampling error
- Sampling frame
- Sampling unit
- Statistic
- Validity

INTRODUCTION

A critical part of social research is the decision as to what will be observed and what will not. It is often impractical or even impossible to survey or observe every element of interest. Sampling methodology provides guidelines for choosing from a population some smaller group that represents the population's important characteristics. There are two general approaches to selecting samples: probability and nonprobability sampling.

Probability sampling techniques allow researchers to select relatively few elements and generalize from these sample elements to the much larger population. For example, before the 1984 US presidential election, George Gallup's poll correctly predicted that the popular vote would split 59 percent to 41 percent in favor of Ronald Reagan. This accurate prediction was based on the stated voting intentions of a tiny fraction—less than 0.01 percent—of the 92.5 million people who voted in the election. Accuracy was possible because Gallup used probability sampling techniques to choose a sample that was representative of the general population. A sample is representative of the population from which it is chosen if the aggregate characteristics of the sample closely approximate those same aggregate characteristics in the population. Samples, however, need not be representative in all respects; representativeness is limited to those characteristics that are relevant to the substantive interests of the study. The most widely used probability sampling methods are simple random sampling, systematic sampling with a random start, stratified sampling, and multistage cluster sampling.

Nonprobability sampling methods, such as purposive, convenience, and quota sampling, do not ensure a representative sample. These samples are not useful for drawing conclusions about the population because there is no way to measure the sampling error. Purposive and convenience sampling allow the researcher to choose samples that fit his or her particular interest or convenience; quota sampling aims to generate a representative sample by developing a complex sampling frame (a quota matrix) that divides the population into relevant subclasses. Aside from being cumbersome, however, the nonrandom selection of samples from each cell of the quota matrix decreases the likelihood of generating a representative sample.

Probability theory is based on random selection procedures and assumes three things: that each random sample drawn from a population provides an estimate of the true population parameter, that multiple random samples drawn from the same population will yield statistics that cluster around the true population value in a predictable way, and that it is possible to calculate the sampling error associated with any one sample. The magnitude of sampling error associated with any random sample is a function of two variables: the homogeneity of the population from which the random sample is drawn and the sample's size. A more homogeneous parent population will have a smaller sampling error associated with a given random sample. Moreover, sampling error declines as the size of one's random sample increases, since larger samples are more likely than smaller ones to capture a representative portion of the parent population. In fact, for small populations (less than fifty members), it is often best to collect data on the entire population rather than use a sample because this often improves the reliability and credibility of the data.

FORMULATING THE SAMPLE

When sampling is necessary, it is essential that the researcher first consider the quality of the sampling frame. A sampling frame is the list or quasi list of elements from which a probability sample is selected. Often, sampling frames do not truly include all of the elements that their names might imply. For example, telephone directories are often taken to be a listing of a city's population. There are several defects in this reasoning, but the major one involves a social-class bias. Poor people are less likely to have telephones; therefore, a telephone directory sample is likely to have a middle- and upper-class bias. To generalize to the population composing the sampling frame, it is necessary for all of the elements to have equal representation in the frame. Elements that occur more than once will have a greater probability of selection, and the overall sample will overrepresent those elements.

Regardless of how carefully the researcher chooses a sampling frame and a representative sample from it, sample values are only approximations of population parameters. Probability theory enables the researcher to estimate how far the sample statistic is likely to diverge from population values, using two key indices called confidence levels and confidence intervals. Both of these are calculated by mathematical procedures that can be found in any basic statistics book.

A confidence level specifies how confident the researcher can be that the statistics are reliable estimates of population parameters, and a confidence interval stipulates how far the population parameters might be expected to deviate from sample values. For example, in the 1984 presidential election, *The Washington Post* polled a sample of 8,969 registered voters; based on their responses, the newspaper reported that 57 percent of the vote would go to Ronald Reagan and 39 percent would go to Walter Mondale. The poll in *The Washington Post* had a confidence level of 95 percent, and its confidence interval was plus or minus three percentage points. This means that pollsters could be 95 percent confident that Reagan's share of the 92.5 million popular votes would range between 54 percent and 60 percent, while Mondale's vote would vary between 36 percent and 42 percent. When reporting predictions based on probability sampling, the researcher should always report the confidence level and confidence interval associated with the sample.

SAMPLING TECHNIQUES

A basic principle of probability sampling is that a sample will be representative of the population from which it is selected if all members of the population have an equal chance of being selected in the sample. Flipping a coin is the most frequently cited example: The "selection" of a head or a tail is independent of previous selections of heads or tails. Instead of flipping a coin, however, researchers usually use a table of random numbers.

A simple random sample may be generated by assigning consecutive numbers to the elements in a sampling frame, generating a list of random numbers equal to one's desired sample size and selecting from the sampling frame all elements having assigned numbers that correspond to one's list of random numbers. This is the basic sampling method assumed in survey statistical computations, but it is seldom used in practice because it is often cumbersome and inefficient. For that reason, researchers usually prefer systematic sampling with a random start. This approach, under appropriate circumstances, can generate equally representative samples with relative ease.

A systematic sample with a random start is generated by selecting every element of a certain number (for example, every fifth element) listed in a sampling frame. Thus, a systematic sample of one hundred can be derived from a sampling frame containing one thousand elements by selecting every tenth element in the frame. To ensure against any possible human bias, the first element should be chosen at random. Although systematic sampling is relatively uncomplicated, it yields samples that are highly representative of the populations from which they are drawn. The researcher should be alert, however, to the potential systematic sampling problem called sampling frame periodicity, which does not affect simple random methods. If the sampling frame is arranged in a cyclical pattern that coincides with the sampling interval, a grossly biased sample may be drawn.

SAMPLING FRAME PERIODICITY

American sociologist Earl Babbie described a study of soldiers that illustrates how sampling frame periodicity can produce seriously unrepresentative systematic samples. He reports that the researchers used unit rosters as sampling frames and selected every tenth soldier for the study. The rosters, however, were arranged by squads containing ten members each, and squad members were listed by rank, with sergeants first, followed by corporals and privates. Because this cyclical arrangement coincid-

ed with the ten-element sampling interval, the resulting sample contained only sergeants.

Sampling frame periodicity, although a serious threat to sampling validity, can be avoided if researchers carefully study the sampling frame for evidence of periodicity. Periodicity can be corrected by randomizing the entire list before sampling from it or by drawing a simple random sample from within each cyclical portion of the frame.

The third method of probability sampling, stratified sampling, is not an alternative to systematic sampling or simple random sampling; rather, it represents a modified framework within which the two methods are used. Instead of sampling from a total population as simple and systematic methods do, stratified sampling organizes a population into homogeneous subsets and selects elements from each subset, using either systematic or simple random procedures. To generate a stratified sample, the researcher begins by specifying the population subgroups, or stratification variables, that are to be represented in a sample. After stipulating these variables, the researcher divides all sampling frame elements into homogeneous subsets representing a saturated mix of relevant stratification characteristics. Once the population has been stratified, a researcher uses either simple random sampling or systematic sampling with a random start to generate a representative sample from the elements falling within each subgroup. Stratified sampling methods can generate a highly useful sample of any well-defined population and may have a smaller sampling error than any other sampling method.

COMPREHENSIVE SAMPLING

Simple random sampling, systematic sampling, and stratified sampling are reasonably simple procedures for sampling from lists of elements. If one wishes to sample from a very large population, however, such as all university students in the United States, a comprehensive sampling frame may not be available. In this case, a modified sampling method, called multistage cluster sampling, is appropriate. It begins with the systematic or simple random selection of subgroups or clusters within a population, followed by a systematic or simple random selection of elements within each selected cluster. For example, if a researcher were interested in the population of all university students in the United States, it would be possible to create a list of all the universities, then sample them using either stratified or systematic sampling procedures. Next, the researcher could obtain lists of students from each of the sample universities; each of those lists would then be sampled to provide the final list of university students for study.

Multistage cluster sampling is an efficient method of sampling a very large population, but the price of that efficiency is a less accurate sample. Although a simple random sample drawn from a population list is subject to a single sampling error, a two-stage cluster sample is subject to two sampling errors. The best way to avoid this problem is to maximize the number of clusters selected while decreasing the number of elements within each cluster.

STATISTICAL THEORY

As statistician Raymond Jessen pointed out, the theory of sampling is probably one of the oldest branches of statistical theory. It has only been since the early twentieth century, however, that there has been much progress in applying that theory to, and developing a new theory for, statistical surveys. One of the earliest applications for sampling was in political polling, perhaps because this area provides researchers with the opportunity to discover the accuracy of their estimates fairly quickly. This area has also been useful in detecting errors in sampling methods. For example, in 1936, the *Literary Digest*, which had been accurate in predicting the winners of the US presidential elections since 1920, inaccurately predicted that Republican contender Alfred Landon would win 57 percent of the vote over incumbent President Franklin D. Roosevelt's 43 percent. The *Literary Digest's* mistake was an unrepresentative sampling frame consisting of telephone directories and automobile registration lists. This frame resulted in a disproportionately wealthy sample, excluding poor people who predominantly favored Roosevelt's New Deal recovery programs. This emphasized to researchers that a representative sampling frame was crucial if the sample were to be valid.

In the 1940s, the US Bureau of the Census developed unequal probability sampling theory, and area-probability sampling methods became widely used and sophisticated in both theory and practice. The 1945 census of agriculture in the United States was collected in part on a sample, and the 1950 census of population made extensive use of built-in samples to increase its accuracy and reduce costs.

One of the most important advances for sampling techniques has been increasingly sophisticated computer technology. For example, once the sampling frame is entered into the computer, a simple random sample can be selected automatically. In the future, computer technology, coupled with increasingly efficient and accurate information-gathering technology, will enable researchers to select samples that more accurately represent the population.

Sampling techniques are essential for researchers in psychology. Without relying on sampling as the basis for collecting evaluative data, the risk and cost involved with adopting new methods of treatment would be difficult to justify. Evaluating the effectiveness of new programs would be prohibitive, and some populations are so large and dispersed that observing each element is impossible.

Probability sampling is the most effective method for the selection of study elements in the field of psychology for two reasons. First, it avoids conscious or unconscious biases in element selection on the part of the researcher. If all elements in the population have an equal chance of selection, there is an excellent chance that a sample so selected will closely represent the population of all elements. Second, probability sampling permits estimates of sampling error. Although no probability sample will be perfectly representative in all respects, controlled selection methods permit the researcher to estimate the degree of expected error in that regard.

BIBLIOGRAPHY

Babbie, Earl R. *The Practice of Social Research*. 13th ed. Belmont: Wadsworth, 2012. Print.

Blalock, Hubert M., Jr. *Social Statistics*. 2nd ed. New York: McGraw-Hill, 1981. Print.

Henry, Gary T. *Practical Sampling*. Newbury Park: Sage, 1998. Print.

Jessen, Raymond James. *Statistical Survey Techniques*. New York: Wiley, 1978. Print.

Kish, Leslie. *Survey Sampling*. 1965. Reprint. New York: Wiley, 1995. Print.

Lohr, Sharon L. *Sampling: Design and Analysis*. Pacific Grove: Duxbury, 2009. Print.

Panik, Michael J. *Statistical Inference: A Short Course*. Hoboken: Wiley, 2012. Print.

Thompson, Steven K. *Sampling*. 3rd ed. Hoboken: Wiley, 2012. Print.

Uprichard, Emma. "Sampling: Bridging Probability and Non-Probability Designs." *International Journal of Social Research Methodology* 16.1 (2013): 1–11. Print.

Karen Anding Fontenot

SEE ALSO: Data description; Experimentation: Independent, dependent, and control variables; Hypothesis development and testing; Scientific methods; Statistical significance tests; Survey research: Questionnaires and interviews.

Satir, Virginia

BORN: June 26, 1916
DIED: September 10, 1988
BIRTHPLACE: Neillsville, Wisconsin
PLACE OF DEATH: San Mateo, California
IDENTITY: American psychotherapist
TYPE OF PSYCHOLOGY: Psychological methodologies; Psychotherapy

Satir was a pioneer in the psychology of human growth and family systems theory.

Virginia (Pagenkopf) Satir was the oldest of five children born to Alfred and Minnie Pagenkopf. She developed a keen interest in reading at a very young age. By the age of five, she had decided that she would eventually pursue a career that would involve helping families face and solve problems.

During her teenage years, Satir's family moved to Milwaukee, Wisconsin, so that she could attend high school. In 1936, she earned a BA in education from Milwaukee State Teachers College (now a part of the University of Wisconsin). In 1948, Satir received an MA in social work from the University of Chicago. After her first marriage ended in divorce, she married Norman Satir in 1951. They divorced in 1957.

During much of the 1950s, Satir worked with families at the Dallas Child Guidance Center and at the Illinois State Psychiatric Institute. In 1959, Satir, Don Jackson, Jules Ruskin, and Gregory Bateson started the Mental Research Institute (MRI) in Palo Alto, California, and created the first formal program in family therapy in the United States. Recognized for her insights into human communication and her understanding of interpersonal relationships and development of self-esteem, Satir became known as the Columbus of family therapy and the mother of family system therapy. She strongly believed that if families could be healed and united, then the problems of the world would be solved, and world peace would eventually be established.

In her efforts to teach people how to cope with their problems, Satir presented hundreds of workshops and training seminars throughout the world. Her change-process model focused on personal growth, health, and the worth of each individual. She authored or coauthored twelve books, including *Conjoint Family Therapy* (1964), *Peoplemaking* (1972), and *The New Peoplemaking* (1988), all three of which achieved international success.

In 1976, Satir was awarded the Gold Medal for "outstanding and consistent service to mankind" by the University of Chicago. The following year, she organized the Avanta Network to implement the Satir model to help people develop coping skills that would change their lives and help them handle problems in their relationships. In 1982, the West German government recognized Satir as one of the twelve most influential leaders in the world at that time. When Satir died in 1988, she had become internationally acclaimed as a therapist, educator, and author.

BIBLIOGRAPHY

"About Virginia Satir." *Virginia Satir Global Network.* Satir Global, n.d. Web. 12 June 2014.

Andreas, Steven. *Virginia Satir: The Patterns of Her Magic.* Palo Alto.: Science and Behavior, 1991. Print.

Friedlander, Myrna L. *Therapeutic Alliances in Couple and Family Therapy: An Empirically Informed Guide to Practice.* Washington, DC: Amer. Psychological Assn., 2006. Print.

Jones-Smith, Elsie. *Theories of Counseling and Psychotherapy: An Integrative Approach.* London: Sage, 2012. Print.

Rambo, Anne Hearon. *Family Therapy Review: Contrasting Contemporary Models.* New York: Routledge, 2013. Print.

Wilcoxon, S. Allen. *Ethical, Legal, and Professional Issues in the Practice of Marriage and Family Therapy.* Upper Saddle River: Pearson, 2007. Print.

Alvin K. Benson

SEE ALSO: Coping: Strategies; Couples therapy; Family life: Adult issues; Family life: Children's issues; Family systems theory; Group therapy; Humanistic psychology.

Schizoid personality disorder (SPD)

TYPE OF PSYCHOLOGY: Biological bases of behavior; Developmental psychology; Emotion; Personality; Psychopathology; Psychotherapy

Schizoid personality disorder is grouped in the Cluster A odd and eccentric personality disorders, along with paranoid and schizotypal personality disorders. The individual with schizoid personality is detached from social relationships and displays a restricted range of emotional expressions in interpersonal settings. Those with schizoid personality disorder are primarily treated with psychotherapy.

KEY CONCEPTS
- Avoidant personality disorder
- Comorbidity
- Differential diagnosis
- Homelessness
- Personality disorder
- Schizophrenia
- Schizophrenia spectrum

INTRODUCTION
A personality disorder is defined as an inflexible, long-term, and pervasive pattern of perceiving, interpreting, and responding to a variety of personal, social, and historical situations that leads to clinically significant distress or functional impairment. Schizoid personality disorder (SPD) is characterized by emotional coldness, solitariness, and general apathy towards the outside world. Unlike the similar schizotypal personality disorder, schizoid personality disorder is not accompanied by psychotic-like cognitive or perceptual distortions.

DIAGNOSIS
Eugen Bleuler first introduced the term "schizoid" to describe a tendency of a person to direct inward, away from the outside world, accompanied by an absence of expressivity. Bleuler noted that the individual with a schizoid personality appeared indifferent both to other people and to pleasure. The fifth edition of the *Diagnostic and Statistical Manual of Mental Disorders* (DSM-5) lists seven criteria: avoidance of close relationships, preference for solitary activities, avoidance of sexual intimacy, anhedonia, lack of close friends, indifference to praise or criticism, and emotional detachment. The individual must have four or more of these criteria to receive the

diagnosis of schizoid personality disorder. Schizoid personality disorder is frequently comorbid with other disorders such as major depressive disorder, social phobia, and schizophrenia.

DIFFERENTIAL DIAGNOSIS
Many people who are given this diagnosis are also likely to meet the diagnostic criteria for at least one additional personality disorder, typically schizotypal, paranoid, or avoidant personality disorder; this is known as comorbidity. Indeed, some experts question whether schizoid personality disorder is a valid independent diagnosis.

Schizoid personality disorder can be particularly difficult to differentiate from avoidant personality disorder. The schizoid personality and avoidant personality share the clinical feature of social withdrawal. Although neither may have intimate relationships, the schizoid personality has no interest or desire in having them. Because individuals with schizoid personality are indifferent to interpersonal relationships, they appear less anxious regarding the criticism of others and show little sensitivity to rejection.

Schizoid personality disorder is diagnosed more often in men, whereas avoidant personality disorder is diagnosed more frequently in women. It is unclear whether these sex differences reflect true gender differences in psychopathology or gender differences in the expression of the same disorder.

PREVALENCE
Schizoid personality disorder is the least frequently diagnosed personality disorder of all the personality disorders. Prevalence rates of schizoid personality disorder in nonclinical populations and community studies have ranged from 0.8 to 4.9 percent. Prevalence rates estimated from clinical settings such as psychiatric hospitals may not be representative, because schizoid patients are unlikely to seek help unless they are in a crisis.

One special population in which there is a high prevalence of individuals with schizoid personality disorder and schizoid personality traits is the homeless mentally ill, a group that typically fails to use mental health and social services. In one recent study of homeless mentally ill persons in Chicago, 14 percent of the sample were diagnosed with schizoid personality disorder. Although this significantly elevated prevalence rate suggests an association between schizoid traits and homelessness, individuals who are both homeless and have schizoid personality disorder may also be more likely to have other serious and persistent mental illnesses, such as schizo-phrenia and post-traumatic stress disorder; this is known as the third variable problem.

Some studies have also found schizoid personality disorder to be more common in people with relatives who are schizophrenic.

CAUSE

According to object relations theorists Ronald Fairbairn and Harry Guntrip, the schizoid person has an underlying need for social contact with others and is interested in intimate relationships. Because of an early history of neglect or mistreatment by others, the schizoid person's needs have gone unmet. To avoid future frustration, the schizoid person avoids interpersonal contact and relationships. In the 1990s, both Melanie Klein and L. A. Clark wrote about schizoid personality disorder as a compromise between fear of losing oneself and fear of being completely cut off from all others. For the schizoid individual, interpersonal isolation is the only way to guarantee autonomy.

Data regarding whether schizoid personality disorder is genetically related to schizophrenia is equivocal. An exhaustive review by Joel T. Nigg and H. Hill Goldsmith reveals that several family studies of schizophrenia either fail to include schizoid personality disorder or combine schizoid personality disorder with schizotypal personality disorder, thereby confounding interpretation of the findings. If schizoid personality disorder is truly part of the schizophrenia spectrum, then individuals with the diagnosis have an underlying genetic diathesis, or susceptibility, to schizophrenia.

Michael Rutter has asserted that schizoid personality disorder may be etiologically related to autism spectrum disorders, which are characterized by severe impairments in social interactions. Some cross-sectional research also suggests a relationship between schizoid personality disorder and autism spectrum disorders. However, schizoid personality disorder is associated with an onset in late adolescence or early adulthood, and little is known regarding the developmental histories of adults with schizoid personality disorders.

TREATMENT

Comorbid mood disorders are often the reason an individual with schizoid personality disorder seeks treatment. Treatment for schizoid personality disorder typically involves either individual psychotherapy or individual supportive therapy plus group psychotherapy. Intervention

for schizoid personality disorder involves educating the person, providing feedback, and fostering social skills and communication, with the goal of increasing the person's social contact. Therapists employ various techniques such as role-playing, videotaping, and cognitive behavior techniques involving homework assignments of gradual involvement with social activities. Group therapy for people with schizoid personality disorder may be useful in terms of providing an opportunity to observe social interactions and practice social skills.

Psychopharmacological agents are seldom used in the treatment of symptoms associated with schizoid personality disorder. However, medications may be prescribed for comorbid disorders such as depression or anxiety disorders.

IMPACT

The impact of schizoid personality disorder can vary considerably. The extent of functional impairment that may result from schizoidal traits and symptoms depends in part on the extent to which the person's job involves interpersonal interactions and how much intimacy is demanded by the person's partner or family. The schizoid personality may encounter job difficulties or may not benefit from job advancement because of an inability to successfully negotiate social situations. The schizoid personality may continually feel frustrated or misunderstood by others.

Although schizoid personality disorder seems to be stable over time, little is known regarding its course and prognosis. Clearly, the study of schizoid personality disorder is in its infancy.

BIBLIOGRAPHY

Dobbert, Duane L. *Understanding Personality Disorders: An Introduction.* Westport: Praeger, 2007. Print.

Dumont, Frank. *A History of Personality Psychology: Theory, Science, and Research from Hellenism to the Twenty-First Century.* Cambridge: Cambridge UP, 2010. Print.

Lenzenweger, Mark F. "Epidemiology of Personality Disorders." *Psychiatric Clinics of North America* 31 (2008): 395–403. Print.

Lenzenweger, Mark F., Michael C. Lane, Armand W. Loranger, and Ronald C. Kessler. "DSM-IV Personality Disorders in the National Comorbidity Survey Replication." *Biological Psychiatry* 62.6 (2007): 553–64. Print.

Nigg, Joel T., and H. Hill Goldsmith. "Genetics of Personality Disorders: Perspectives from Personality and Psychopathology Research." *Psychological Bulletin* 115 (1994): 346–380. Print.

Nirestean, Aurel, Emese Lukacs, Dana Cimpan, and Livia Taran. "Schizoid Personality Disorder—The Peculiarities of Their Interpersonal Relationships and Existential Roles." *Personality and Mental Health* 6.1 (2012): 69–74. Print.

Robinson, David J. *Disordered Personalities*. 3d ed. Port Huron: Rapid Psychler, 2005. Print.

Silverstein, Marshall L. *Disorders of the Self: A Personality-Guided Approach*. Washington, DC: Amer. Psychological Assn., 2007. Print.

Triebwasser, Joseph, Eran Chemerinski, Panos Roussos, and Larry J. Siever. "Schizoid Personality Disorder." *Journal of Personality Disoders* (2012): 1–8. Print.

Diane C. Gooding

SEE ALSO: Avoidant personality disorder; Comorbidity; Homelessness: Psychological causes and effects; Personality disorders; Schizophrenia: Background, types, and symptoms; Schizotypal personality disorder.

Schizophrenia
Background, types, and symptoms

TYPE OF PSYCHOLOGY: Psychopathology

Schizophrenia is a severe mental illness that interferes with a person's ability to think and to communicate. Researchers have studied the illness for decades, and while genetic factors contribute to the illness, the specific genetic mechanisms and how they interact with environmental factors remain unknown.

KEY CONCEPTS
- Affect
- Antipsychotic medication
- Delusions
- Genetic factors
- Hallucinations
- Insight
- Neuroleptics
- Psychosis
- Tardive dyskinesia

INTRODUCTION

According to the National Alliance on Mental Illness (NAMI) in 2013, approximately 1.1 US adults (about 2.4 million people) lived with schizophrenia. It is considered to be one of the most severe mental illnesses, because its symptoms can have a devastating impact on the lives of patients and their families. The patient's thought processes, communication abilities, and emotional expressions are disturbed. As a result, many patients with schizophrenia are dependent on others for assistance with daily life activities.

Schizophrenia is often confused, by the layperson, with dissociative identity disorder (commonly known as multiple personality disorder), is an illness defined as having two or more distinct personalities existing within the person. The personalities tend to be intact, and each is associated with its own style of perceiving the world and relating to others. Schizophrenia, in contrast, does not involve the existence of two or more personalities; rather, it is the presence of psychotic symptoms and characteristic deficits in social interaction that define schizophrenia.

The diagnostic criteria for schizophrenia have changed over the years; however, certain key symptoms for a diagnosis as noted by the *Diagnostic and Statistical Manual of Mental Disorders: DSM-5* (2013) include delusions, hallucinations, disorganized speech (such as frequent incoherence or connecting a sequence of unrelated ideas), completely disorganized or catatonic behavior, and such negative symptoms as diminished emotional expression or avolition (general lack of motivation or drive). The DSM-5 is published by the American Psychiatric Association and is periodically revised to incorporate changes in diagnostic criteria.

Of the five symptoms listed above and in the DSM-5, at least two of the symptoms must be present in an individual for at least one month. One of two of the symptoms must include delusions, hallucinations, or disorganized speech. Further, the presence of other disorders, such as drug reactions or organic brain disorders associated with aging, must be ruled out. Thus, the diagnosis of schizophrenia typically involves a thorough physical and mental assessment. Although no single individual symptom is necessary for a person to receive a diagnosis of schizophrenia, according to the DSM-5, the persistent and debilitating presence of hallucinations, a hallucinated voice commenting on the individual, or hallucinated conversations between two voices is a strong indication of schizophrenia. The presence of delusions or hallucinations and loss of contact with reality is referred to as psychosis and is often present in schizophrenia, but psychotic symptoms can be seen in other mental disorders (for example, bipolar disorder or substance-induced psychotic disorder), so the term "psychosis" is not synonymous with the diagnosis of schizophrenia. The DSM-5 also notes that not one single symptom denotes a diagnosis of schizophrenia. In other words, two individuals may be diagnosed with the disorder and have different symptoms, which then make them look and act completely different from one another.

Although not emphasized by the DSM-5, international and cross-cultural study of the symptoms of schizophrenia has noted that the most frequently observed symptom in schizophrenia is patients' lack of insight. That is, despite sometimes overwhelming evidence of gross abnormalities in perception and behavior, patients with schizophrenia are likely to deny that those problems are symptomatic of a disorder.

Each of these symptoms can take a variety of forms. Delusions are defined as false beliefs based on incorrect inferences about external reality. Delusions are classified based on the nature of their content. For example, grandiose delusions involve false beliefs about one's importance, power, or knowledge. The patient might express the belief that he or she is the most intelligent person in the world but that these special intellectual powers have gone unrecognized. As another example, persecutory delusions involve beliefs of being persecuted or conspired against by others. The patient might claim, for example, that there is a government plot to poison him or her.

Hallucinations are sensory experiences that occur in the absence of a real stimulus. In the case of auditory hallucinations, the patient may hear voices calling or conversing when there is no one in physical proximity. Visual hallucinations may involve seeing people who are deceased or seeing inanimate objects move on their own accord. Olfactory (smell) and tactile (touch) hallucinations are also possible.

The term "affect" is used to refer to observable behaviors that are the expression of an emotion. Affect is predominantly displayed in facial expressions. "Flat" affect describes a severe reduction in the intensity of emotional expressions, both positive and negative. Patients with flat affect may show no observable sign of emotion, even when experiencing a very joyful or sad event.

Among the symptoms of schizophrenia, abnormalities in the expression of thoughts are a central feature. When speech is incoherent, it is difficult for the listener to comprehend because it is illogical or incomplete. As an example, in response to the question "Where do you live?" one patient replied, "Yes, live! I haven't had much time in this or that. It is an area. In the same area. Mrs. Smith! If the time comes for a temporary space now or whatever." The term "loose associations" is applied to speech in which ideas shift from one subject to another subject that is completely unrelated. If the loosening of associations is severe, speech may be incoherent. As an illustration of loose associations, a patient described the meaning of "A rolling stone gathers no moss" by saying, "Inside your head there's a brain and it's round like a stone and when it spins around it can't make connections the way moss has little filaments."

With regard to speech, a variety of other abnormalities are sometimes shown by patients. They may use neologisms, which are new words invented by the patient to convey a special meaning. Some show clang associations, which involve the use of rhyming words in conversation: "Live and let live, that's my motto. You live and give and live-give." Abnormalities in the intonation and pace of speech are also common.

In addition to these symptoms, some patients manifest bizarre behaviors, such as odd, repetitive movements or unusual postures. Odd or inappropriate styles of dressing, such as wearing winter coats in the summer, may also occur in some patients. More deteriorated patients frequently show poor hygiene. To meet the diagnostic criteria for schizophrenia, the individual must show signs of disturbance for at least six months.

TYPES AND TREATMENT OF SCHIZOPHRENIA

Prior to the release of the DSM-5, clinicians recognized five subtypes of schizophrenia when making a diagnosis (the differentiation among these subtypes was based on the symptom profile, and the criteria for subtype designation were described in DSM-IV-TR). They were catatonic schizophrenia, disorganized schizophrenia, paranoid schizophrenia, residual schizophrenia, and undifferentiated schizophrenia. Because no one symptom is sufficient for a diagnosis of schizophrenia, patients vary in the numbers and the intensity of their symptoms. It was for this reason as well as the low reliability and poor validity in diagnosing and treating schizophrenics when using the subtypes that the subtypes were eliminated in the DSM-5.

In his writings shortly after the turn of the twentieth century, Eugen Bleuler often used the phrase "the group of schizophrenias," because he believed the disorder could be caused by a variety of factors. In other words, he believed that schizophrenia may not be a single disease entity. Today, some researchers and clinicians who work in the field take the same position. They believe that the differences among patients in symptom patterns and the course of the illness are attributable to differences in etiology.

Because schizophrenic symptoms have such a devastating impact on the individual's ability to function, family members often respond to the onset of symptoms by seeking immediate treatment. Clinicians, in turn, often respond by recommending hospitalization so that tests can be conducted and an appropriate treatment can be determined. Consequently, almost all patients who are diagnosed with schizophrenia are hospitalized at least once in their lives. The majority experience several hospitalizations.

Research on the long-term outcome of schizophrenia indicates that the illness is highly variable in its course. A minority of patients have only one episode of illness, then go into remission and experience no further symptoms. Unfortunately, however, the majority of patients have recurring episodes that require periodic rehospitalizations. The most severely ill never experience remission but instead show a chronic course of symptomatology. For these reasons, schizophrenia is viewed as having the poorest prognosis of all the major mental illnesses.

Prior to the 1950s, patients with schizophrenia were hospitalized for extended periods of time and frequently became institutionalized. There were only a few available somatic treatments, and those proved to be of little efficacy. Included among them were insulin coma therapy (the administration of large doses of insulin to induce coma), electroconvulsive therapy (the application of electrical current to the temples to induce a seizure), and prefrontal lobotomy (a surgical procedure in which the tracts connecting the frontal lobes to other areas of the brain are severed).

Also, in the 1950s, a class of drugs referred to as antipsychotic medications were discovered to be effective in treating schizophrenia. Antipsychotic drugs significantly reduce some of the symptoms of schizophrenia in many patients. The introduction of antipsychotic medications (also called neuroleptics) in combination with changes in public policy led to a dramatic decline in the number of patients in public mental hospitals. Antipsychotic medications have freed many patients from confinement in hospitals and have enhanced their chances for functioning in the community. Not all patients benefit from typical antipsychotic medications, and the discovery of new classes of medications has offered hope to patients and families. Despite the benefits of antipsychotic medications, they can also produce serious side effects, particularly tardive dyskinesia, a movement disorder associated in some patients with chronic use of typical antipsychotic medications.

The public policy that has contributed to the decline in the number of hospitalized patients with schizophrenia is the nationwide policy of deinstitutionalization. This policy, which has been adopted and promoted by most state governments in the years since 1970, emphasizes short-term hospitalizations, and it has involved the release of some patients who had been in institutions for many years. Unfortunately, the support services that were needed to facilitate the transition from hospital to community living were never put in place. Consequently, the number of homeless schizophrenic patients has increased dramatically. Some of these are patients whose family members have died or have simply lost touch with them. Other patients have withdrawn from contact with their families, despite efforts by concerned relatives to provide assistance. The plight of the homeless mentally ill is of great concern to mental health professionals.

HISTORY AND FUTURE DIRECTIONS

Writing in the late 1800s, the eminent physician Emil Kraepelin was among the first to document the symptoms and course of this illness, referring to it as dementia praecox (dementia of early life). Subsequently, Bleuler applied the term "schizophrenia," meaning splitting of the mind, to the disorder. Both Kraepelin and Bleuler assumed that organic factors were involved in developing schizophrenia. Contemporary research has confirmed this assumption; brain scans reveal that a significant proportion of schizophrenia patients do have organic abnormalities. The precise nature and cause of these abnormalities remain unknown.

In the majority of cases, the onset of schizophrenic symptoms occurs in late adolescence or early adulthood. The major risk period is between twenty and twenty-five years of age, but the period of risk extends well into adult life. The majority of individuals to not develop schizophrenia after the age of forty-five. For some patients, there are no readily apparent abnormalities prior to the development of illness. For others, however, the onset of schizophrenia is preceded by impairments in social, academic, or occupational functioning. Some are described by their families as having had adjustment problems in childhood. Childhood schizophrenia, which is defined as onset of schizophrenic symptoms prior to age thirteen, is relatively rare. It is estimated to occur in about one out of every ten thousand children. When schizophrenia is diagnosed in childhood, the same diagnostic criteria and treatments are applied.

Schizophrenia shows no clear pattern in terms of its distribution in the population. It occurs in both males and females, although it tends to have a slightly earlier onset in males than in females. The illness strikes individuals of all social, economic, and ethnic backgrounds. Some patients manifest high levels of intelligence and are excellent students prior to becoming ill; others show poor academic performance and signs of learning disability. Although the specific pathophysiology associated with schizophrenia remains obscure, the preponderance of evidence demonstrates a significant role for genetic factors in the risk for developing schizophrenia. According to the National Institute of Mental Health, schizophrenia occurs in roughly 1 percent of the general population, but it occurs in roughly 10 percent of individuals with a first-degree relative (parent, sibling) with the disorder. The risk increases when one has an identical twin with schizophrenia; that individual then has a 40–60 percent chance of developing the disorder.

Schizophrenia is an illness that has been recognized by medicine for more than a hundred years. During this time, only modest progress has been made in research on its etiology. Some significant advances have been achieved in treatment, however, and the prognosis for schizophrenia is better now than ever before. Moreover, there is reason to believe that the availability of new technologies for studying the central nervous system will speed the pace of further discovery.

BIBLIOGRAPHY

Bleuler, Eugen. *Dementia Praecox: Or, The Group of Schizophrenias*. 1911. Albuquerque: American Institute for Psychological Research, 1990. Print.

Diagnostic and Statistical Manual of Mental Disorders: DSM-5. Washington: American Psychological Association, 2013. Print.

Duckworth, Ken. "Mental Illness Facts and Numbers." *NAMI*. National Alliance on Mental Illness, Mar. 2013. Web. 21 July 2014.

Gottesman, Irving I. *Schizophrenia Genesis: The Origins of Madness*. New York: W. H. Freeman, 1991. Print.

Herz, Marvin I., Samuel J. Keith, and John P. Docherty. *Psychosocial Treatment of Schizophrenia*. New York:

Elsevier, 1990. Print.

Hirsch, Steven R., and Daniel R. Weinberger. *Schizophrenia*. Oxford: Blackwell Science, 2002. Print.

Kingdon, David G. , and Douglas Turkington. *Cognitive Therapy of Schizophrenia*. New York: Guilford Press, 2008. Print.

Kraepelin, Emil. *Clinical Psychiatry*. Translated by A. Ross Diefendorf. Delmar, N.Y.: Scholars' Facsimiles & Reprints, 1981. Print.

Maj, Mario, and Norman Sartorius. *Schizophrenia*. 2d ed. Hoboken, N.J.: John Wiley & Sons, 2003. Print.

Marder, Stephen R., and Vandra Chopra. *Schizophrenia*. New York: Oxford UP, 2014. Print.

Mueser, Kim T., and Dilip V. Jeste. *Clinical Handbook of Schizophrenia*. New York: Guilford Press, 2008. Print.

Neale, John M., and Thomas F. Oltmanns. *Schizophrenia*. New York: John Wiley & Sons, 1980. Print.

"Numbers of Americans Affected by Mental Illness." *NAMI*. National Alliance on Mental Illness, June 2014. Web. 20 July 2014..

Walker, Elaine F., ed. *Schizophrenia: A Life-Span Developmental Perspective*. San Diego, Calif.: Academic Press, 1991. Print.

"What is Schizophrenia?" *National Institute of Mental Health*. US Department of Health and Human Services, n.d. Web. 20 July 2014.

Elaine F. Walker; updated by Loring J. Ingraham

See Also: Abnormality: Biomedical models; Abnormality: Psychological models; Antipsychotic medications; Diagnosis; Drug therapies; Elders' mental health; Genetics and mental health; Lobotomy; Mental illness: Historical concepts; Psychopharmacology; Psychosurgery; Schizophrenia: High-risk children; Schizophrenia: Theoretical explanations.

Schizophrenia
High-risk children

Type of psychology: Psychopathology

Researchers have been conducting studies of children of parents with schizophrenia to identify the indicators of risk for this psychiatric illness; preliminary findings indicate that it may someday be possible to prevent the onset of schizophrenia. Longitudinal studies of high-risk children may provide information regarding developmental precursors of adult schizophrenia. A recent outgrowth of the high-risk method has been the development of early intervention programs that involve the administration of preventive medication to targeted at-risk individuals.

KEY CONCEPTS
- Early intervention
- Etiology
- Genetics
- Longitudinal study
- Premorbid
- Preventive medication
- Schizophrenia

INTRODUCTION

By the 1960s, it had been well established that schizophrenia often ran in families. The general population rate for the disorder is about 1 percent. In contrast, it has been estimated that children who have one biological parent with schizophrenia have a 10 to 15 percent chance of developing the disorder. When both biological parents are diagnosed with schizophrenia, the risk rate is thought to be around 40 percent. It is apparent, therefore, that offspring of schizophrenic parents are indeed at heightened risk for developing the disorder.

The term "high risk" has been applied to biological offspring of schizophrenic parents, because they are known to be at genetic risk for the disorder shown by their parents. Numerous researchers have studied high-risk children and adolescents to shed light on the origins of schizophrenia. Traditional studies focused on the high-risk children of schizophrenic parents, and the second generation of high-risk studies studied adolescents and young adults with a family history of schizophrenia and treated them in early intervention programs.

The importance of research on children at risk for schizophrenia stems from a need to understand the precursors of the illness. Over the years, researchers have studied schizophrenia from many different perspectives and with a variety of methods. Despite many decades of work, however, investigators have been unsuccessful in identifying the causes or developing a cure. Some progress has been made in clarifying the nature and course of schizophrenia, and there have been considerable advances in the pharmacological treatment of symptoms; however, the precursors and the origins remain a mystery.

Because the onset of schizophrenia usually occurs in late adolescence or early adulthood, patients typically do not come to the attention of investigators until they have been experiencing symptoms for some period of time. At that point, researchers have to rely on the patient and other informants for information about the nature of the individual's adjustment before the onset of the illness. These retrospective accounts of the patient's functioning are often sketchy and can be biased in various ways. Yet it is well accepted that progress toward the ultimate goal—the prevention of schizophrenia—will not be achieved until researchers are able to identify individuals who are vulnerable to the disorder.

In response to this concern, several investigators emphasized the importance of studying the development of individuals known to be at heightened statistical risk for schizophrenia. Specifically, it was proposed that repeated assessments should be conducted so that data on all aspects of the development of at-risk children would be available by the time they enter the adult risk period for schizophrenia. In this way, it might be possible to identify precursors of the illness in subjects who had not yet received any treatment for the disorder. Another major advantage of studying subjects before the provision of treatment is that it makes it possible to differentiate true precursors of the illness from the consequences or side effects of treatment for the illness.

METHODOLOGICAL ISSUES

One of the major challenges in conducting high-risk research is locating the sample. As previously stated, schizophrenia is a relatively rare disorder in that it occurs in about 1 percent of the general population. Moreover, because most schizophrenic patients experience an onset of illness in late adolescence or early adulthood, they are less likely to marry or have children. This is especially true of male schizophrenic patients. Consequently, the majority of the subjects of high-risk research are offspring of schizophrenic mothers. Further, of the schizophrenic women who do have children, a substantial portion do not keep their children but instead give them up for adoption. This further complicates the task of identifying samples of high-risk children. To be assured of identifying a sample of adequate size, researchers in this field establish formal arrangements with local treatment facilities to increase their chances of identifying all the high-risk children in their geographic area.

Another important issue confronted by high-risk researchers is the question of when the study should be initiated. Most investigators are interested in identifying the very earliest signs of vulnerability for schizophrenia. Therefore, it is desirable to initiate a high-risk study with infant subjects. In this way, investigators will be able to examine the entire premorbid life course of patients. If there are any markers of vulnerability apparent in infancy, they will be able to identify them. The investigator who initiates a study of infant subjects, however, must wait an extended period of time to gather any information about their adult psychiatric outcomes. To reduce the period between the initiation of the study and the entry of the subjects into the major risk period for schizophrenia, most investigators have initiated high-risk projects on subjects who are in middle or late childhood.

The problem of attrition (loss of subjects) is another aspect of concern to high-risk researchers. As mentioned, the long-term goal is to compare those high-risk children who succumb to schizophrenia to those who do not. Consequently, the most crucial information will be provided only when the researchers are knowledgeable about the adult psychiatric outcome of the subjects. Because a sample of one hundred high-risk children may eventually yield only ten to fifteen schizophrenic patients, it is of critical importance to investigators that they maintain contact with all subjects so that they can determine their adult psychiatric outcomes.

The question of how to select an appropriate comparison group is salient to high-risk researchers. One of the ultimate goals is to identify specific signs of vulnerability to schizophrenia. An important question is whether the signs identified by researchers are simply manifestations of vulnerability to any adult psychiatric disorder or signs of specific vulnerability to schizophrenia. To address this question, it is necessary to include groups of children whose parents have psychiatric disorders other than schizophrenia.

EARLY STUDIES

Conducting longitudinal studies of these high-risk children is an efficient way of studying individuals who are most likely to develop schizophrenia. The first large-scale prospective longitudinal study of high-risk children was initiated in Denmark in the mid-1960s by Sarnoff Mednick and Fini Schulsinger. They followed a group of one hundred children who had at least one schizophrenic parent and two hundred comparison children whose parents had no psychiatric disorder. Since the Danish study was initiated, a number of other research groups have started similar high-risk research programs.

A second longitudinal study of particular note is the New York High-Risk Project, led by L. Erlenmeyer-Kimling. Erlenmeyer-Kimling and her associates followed two independent series of three groups of

children: children with at least one schizophrenic parent, children with one or two parents with major affective disorder (typically depression), and children whose parents were not diagnosed with or described having a mental illness. One notable feature of the New York High-Risk Project is that the investigators included an at-risk comparison group, consisting of offspring of other psychiatrically disturbed individuals. Comparisons between high-risk offspring (children with at least one schizophrenic parent) and offspring of mood-disordered parents is especially useful in identifying behavioral precursors that are specifically associated with the later development of schizophrenia rather than an adult psychiatric outcome in general.

RESEARCH FINDINGS

The results from studies of high-risk children suggest that the predisposition for schizophrenia may be detectable at an early age. Reports on the developmental characteristics of high-risk children have revealed some important differences between children of schizophrenic parents and children whose parents have no mental illness. The differences that have been found tend to fall into three general areas: motor functions, cognitive functions, and social adjustment. When compared with children of parents without reported or diagnosed mental illness, high-risk subjects have been found to show a variety of impairments in motor development and motor abilities. Infant offspring of schizophrenic parents tend to show delays in the development of motor skills, such as crawling and walking. Similarly, studies of high-risk subjects in their middle childhood and early adolescent years reveal deficits in fine and gross motor skills and coordination. It is important to emphasize, however, that these deficiencies are not of such a severe magnitude that the child would be viewed as clinically impaired in motor skills. However, the deficiencies are apparent when high-risk children, as a group, are compared with children of parents without mental illness.

Numerous studies have found that children at high risk for schizophrenia also show impairments in cognitive functions. Although their scores on standardized tests of intelligence are within the normal range, they tend to be slightly below those of children of parents who are not high-risk. With regard to specific abilities, investigators have found that high-risk children show deficiencies in their capacity to maintain and focus attention. These deficiencies are apparent as early as the preschool years and involve the processing of both auditory and visual information. Recall that the New York High-Risk Project included a comparison group of offspring of individuals with affective illnesses such as depression. The results of the project, which started in 1971 and has now followed the offspring from childhood to mid-adulthood, indicated that attention deviance, impairments in gross motor skills, and memory deficits were relatively unique to risk for schizophrenia. That is, these deficits were more prevalent in high-risk children (offspring of schizophrenic parents) than among offspring of affectively ill parents. Erlenmeyer-Kimling and associates have noted that among all the neurobehavioral predictors of later development of schizophrenia, attention deviance appears to be the most specifically related to genetic risk for schizophrenia. In the New York High-Risk Project, the offspring of schizophrenic parents showed more attention deviance than either the offspring of affectively ill parents or the offspring of parents who were not considered high-risk. Because attention deficits have been found so consistently in high-risk children, some researchers in the field have suggested that these deficits may be a key marker of risk for schizophrenia.

When compared with children of parents without psychiatric disorders, offspring of schizophrenic parents tend to manifest a higher rate of behavioral problems. These include a higher rate of aggressive behaviors, as well as an increased frequency of social withdrawal. In general, children of schizophrenic parents are perceived as less socially competent than comparison children. It is important to take into consideration, however, that children of parents with other psychiatric disorders are also found to show problems with social adjustment. Consequently, it is unlikely that behavioral adjustment problems are uniquely characteristic of risk for schizophrenia.

RESEARCH APPLICATIONS

The goal of high-risk research is to identify factors that can successfully predict those who are most likely to develop subsequent cases of schizophrenia or schizophrenia-related disorders. Only a subgroup—in fact, a minority—of high-risk children will eventually manifest schizophrenia. The most significant question, therefore, is not what differentiates high-risk children from a comparison group, but rather what differentiates high-risk children who develop schizophrenia from high-risk children who do not. Even those individuals who are predicted to be at heightened risk who do not eventually develop schizophrenia are interesting and potentially informative. The high-risk offspring who do not develop schizophrenia can inform investigators about resiliency factors that are likely to be important. Only a few high-risk research projects have followed their subjects all the way into adulthood. Only limited data are thus available regarding the childhood characteristics that predict adult psychiatric outcome. The findings from these studies confirm the predictions made by the researchers. Specifically, the high-risk children who eventually develop schizophrenia show more evidence of motor abnormalities, memory deficits, and attention dysfunction in childhood than those who do not.

The findings of neurobehavioral abnormalities in preschizophrenic individuals during childhood are consistent with the etiologic hypotheses held by most researchers in the field. Specifically, such abnormalities would be expected in a disorder that is presumed to be attributable to a central nervous system impairment that is, at least in part, genetically determined. These findings are consistent with the hypothesis that an early brain insult may manifest itself in neurobehavioral abnormalities early on but can remain latent (unexpressed) as clinical symptoms for many years.

LIMITATIONS

Like all approaches to research, the high-risk method has some limitations. One limitation concerns whether the findings from these studies can be generalized to a wider population. Although it is true that schizophrenia tends to run in families, it is also true that the majority of schizophrenic patients do not have a schizophrenic parent; children of schizophrenic parents may represent a unique subgroup of schizophrenic patients. The fact that they have a parent with the illness may mean that they have a higher genetic loading for the disorder than do schizophrenic patients whose parents have no mental illness. Moreover, there are undoubtedly some environmental stresses associated with being reared by a schizophrenic parent. In sum, high-risk children who become schizophrenic patients may differ from other schizophrenic patients both in terms of genetic factors and in terms of environment. Some other problems with the method mentioned above include subject attrition and the extensive waiting period required before adult psychiatric outcome is determined.

Some investigators have attempted to address the issue of identifying markers of vulnerability with alternative methodologies. For example, one group has used childhood home movies of adult-onset schizophrenic patients as a database for identifying infant and early childhood precursors. Up to this point, the findings from these studies are consistent with those from high-risk research. Others have studied siblings of schizophrenic individuals who are within the period of greatest risk for the development of the disorder (ages eighteen through thirty). Biological siblings of individuals with schizophrenia are at heightened risk for the development of schizophrenia, typically approximately ten to fourteen times greater than the general population.

IMPLICATIONS OF GENETIC HIGH-RISK STUDIES

Based on the research findings, there is good reason to believe that individuals who develop schizophrenia in adulthood manifested signs of vulnerability long before the onset of the disorder, perhaps as early as infancy. These findings have some important implications. First, they provide some clues to etiology; they suggest that the neuropathological process underlying schizophrenia is one that begins long before the onset of the clinical symptoms that define the illness. Therefore, the search for the biological bases of this illness must encompass the entire premorbid life course. Second, the findings suggest that it may be possible to identify individuals who are at risk for schizophrenia so that preventive interventions can be provided.

EARLY INTERVENTION AND PREVENTIVE MEDICATION

Findings based on the first generation of high-risk studies provide the framework for establishing the validity of prodromal clinical indicators and for understanding the nature of the premorbid as well as the earliest prodromal (prepsychotic) phases of schizophrenia.

Since the late 1990s, several clinicians and investigators in North America, Europe, and Australia have begun to identify and treat adolescents and young adults at clinical risk for schizophrenia or in the prodromal phase of the disorder. In nearly all these programs, targeted at-risk individuals are treated preemptively with low doses of atypical antipsychotic medications such as risperidone (Risperdal) and olanzapine (Zyprexa). The goal of this treatment is to prevent the onset of the illness, or at least to halt the progression to illness. However, because no one is certain how many individuals in the clinically at-risk group would actually develop schizophrenia if left untreated, early intervention in schizophrenia is an ethically complex issue that has met with some controversy.

Patrick McGorry and Alison Yung, leaders of the Australian research group, one of the first to initiate an early intervention program, have been outspoken proponents of the preventive medication strategy. They argue that the premorbid phase and the prodromal phase are windows of opportunity for intervention. Indeed, some research suggests that the longer the duration of untreated psychosis, the poorer the disease outcome. However, the prodromal phase—the period directly preceding the onset of psychosis—can be determined only retrospectively. Development of schizophrenia is neither inevitable or predetermined for any of the at-risk individuals enrolled in these early intervention programs. Therefore, there will be individuals in the treatment group who would have never developed the illness; these are known as false positives.

DEFINING AT-RISK CLINICAL STATUS

To minimize the number of false positives, careful screening and identification of the at-risk population is critical. McGorry, Yung, and associates consider individuals meeting any of their definitions of at-risk mental state as being at ultra-high risk. They define at-risk mental status as attenuated (subsyndromal) psychotic symptoms; transient psychotic symptoms that resolve within one week; or genetic risk for schizophrenia that was accompanied by marked decline in functioning over a six-month period. Other clinical research teams, such as the one led by Barbara Cornblatt and Todd Lencz, have adopted additional criteria for defining at-risk mental status. The expanded criteria include subsyndromal negative symptoms of schizophrenia such as social withdrawal, depressed mood, reduced motivation, sleep disturbance, and anxiety. The advantage of this approach is that it enables earlier identification of clinical high-risk individuals and therefore possible earlier enrollment in the preventive treatment program. The researchers note that many, but not all, of the at-risk individuals may later show attenuated psychotic symptoms. Regardless of their definition of at-risk mental status, there is consensus among the early intervention researchers that individuals who enroll in these programs must be either symptomatic or subjectively distressed, be seeking treatment, and equally important, must give their informed consent.

TREATMENT ISSUES

Early intervention programs have been criticized because although the predictive accuracy of presumed prodromal signs and symptoms has not been established, many research clinicians are treating at-risk individuals with antipsychotic medications. Although the newer antipsychotic medications have lower risks of extrapyramidal symptoms and tardive dyskinesia, they are nonetheless associated with significant weight gain, sexual side effects, and long-term medical complications such as diabetes and cardiovascular problems. Others point out that the effects of long-term treatment with atypical antipsychotic medications on the developing adolescent brain are unknown. One distinctive aspect of Cornblatt and Lencz's early intervention program in New York is that the first line of treatment offers alternatives to antipsychotic medications. According to preliminary reports, treatment with antidepressants, antianxiety medications, and mood stabilizers has been equally effective as antipsychotics in terms of improving the functioning of the clinically at-risk participants.

PRELIMINARY OUTCOMES

The interim findings of early intervention studies have become available. Overall, the studies are consistent in terms of the percentage of at-risk individuals who had developed a psychotic disorder within approximately two years. The results of a multisite longitudinal study of at-risk individuals in North America revealed that 35 percent of the group developed psychosis. McGorry's group reported that 40 percent of their at-risk participants developed psychosis. Genetic risk with functional decline was a strong predictor of later psychotic outcome. The possibility that the percentage of at-risk individuals who developed schizophrenia or another psychotic disorder over that time period might have been considerably higher had they not been enrolled in an early intervention program cannot be ruled out.

Clearly, there are potential advantages and disadvantages associated with this second generation of high-risk research. The advances in high-risk research indicate that there are several methods for viewing the developmental course of schizophrenia. These methods include not only prospectively following genetically high-risk individuals through the age of risk, but also following clinically high-risk individuals and intervening preemptively, while collecting information regarding their neurocognitive, social, psychophysiological, and clinical functioning.

BIBLIOGRAPHY

Carlisle, L. Lee, and Jon McClellen. "Psychopharmacology of Schizophrenia in Children and Adolescents." *Pediatric Clinics of North America* 58.1 (2011):205–18. Print.

Corcoran, Cheryl, Dolores Malaspina, and L. Hercher. "Prodromal Interventions for Schizophrenia Vulnerability: The Risks of Being 'At Risk.'" *Schizophrenia Research* 73 (2005): 173–84. Print.

Erlenmeyer-Kimling, L., et al. "Attention, Memory, and Motor Skills as Childhood Predictors of Schizophrenia-Related Psychoses: The New York High-Risk Project." *American Journal of Psychiatry* 157 (2000): 1416–22. Print.

Goode, Erica. "Doctors Try a Bold Move Against Schizophrenia." *The New York Times,* December 7, 1999, pp. F1, F6. Print.

Gooding, Diane C., and William C. Iacono. "Schizophrenia Through the Lens of a Developmental Psychopathology Perspective." *In Risk, Disorder, and Adaptation.* Vol. 2 in Manual of Developmental Psychopathology, edited by D. Cicchetti and D. J. Cohen. New York: John Wiley & Sons, 1995. Print.

Masi, Gabriele, and Francesca Liboni. "Management of Schizophrenia in Children and Adolescents." *Drugs* 71.2 (2011): 179–208. Print.

Mednick, Sarnoff A., and Thomas F. McNeil. "Current Methodology in Research on the Etiology of Schizophrenia: Serious Difficulties Which Suggest the Use of the High-Risk Group Method." *Psychological Bulletin* 70, no. 6 (1968): 681–93. Print.

Schofield, Michael. *January First: A Child's Descent into Madness and Her Father's Struggle to Save Her.* New York: Broadway. 2013. Print.

Seidman, Larry J., et al. "Neuropsychological Performance and Family History in Children Age 7 Who Develop Adult Schizophrenia or Bipolar Psychosis in the New England Family Studies." *Psychological Medicine* 43.1 (2013): 119–31. Print.

Torrey, E. Fuller. *Surviving Schizophrenia: A Family Manual.* 6th ed. New York: Harper Perennial, 2013. Print.

Diane C. Gooding and Elaine F. Walker

SEE ALSO: Abnormality: Biomedical models; Abnormality: Psychological models; Antipsychotic medications; Children's mental health; Diagnosis; Drug therapies; Mental illness: Historical concepts; Psychopharmacology; Psychosurgery; Schizoid personality disorder; Schizophrenia: Background, types, and symptoms; Schizophrenia: Theoretical explanations; Schizotypal personality disorder.

Schizophrenia
Theoretical explanations

TYPE OF PSYCHOLOGY: Psychopathology

Schizophrenia is one of the most severe and potentially devastating of all psychological disorders. Over the years, a variety of theoretical explanations, sometimes poorly supported by direct experimental evidence, have been proposed. Current empirical research supports the operation of genetic factors in schizophrenia and suggests that such factors may act in concert with environmental factors during early development to elevate the risk for subsequent illness.

KEY CONCEPTS
- Environment
- Genetic factors
- Interaction
- Neurodevelopment
- Neurotransmitter
- Organic
- Schizophrenia spectrum
- Schizotypal

INTRODUCTION

Schizophrenia, an illness that strikes 1 percent of adults, involves changes in all aspects of psychological functioning. Thinking disorders, perceptual distortions and hallucinations, delusions, and emotional changes are the most prominent of such changes. Although some people recover completely, in many others, the illness is chronic and deteriorative. For many years, because the causes of schizophrenia were poorly understood, a wide range of theories was proposed to account for the development of schizophrenia. These early theories about schizophrenia can be classified into four types: psychodynamic, family interaction, learning/attention, and organic. Current theories of schizophrenia focus primarily on genetic factors and their interaction with environmental conditions, particularly the environment experienced before birth and during early development.

PSYCHODYNAMIC THEORIES

Psychodynamic theories originated with Sigmund Freud, who believed that schizophrenia results when a child fails to develop an attachment to his or her parent of the opposite sex. This causes a powerful conflict (called an Oedipal conflict in males) in which unconscious homo-sexual desires threaten to overwhelm the conscious self. To prevent these desires from generating thoughts and feelings that cause painful guilt or behaviors that would be punished, the ego defends itself by regressing to a state in which awareness of the self as a distinct entity is lost. Thus, the person's behavior becomes socially inappropriate; the person mistakes fantasies for reality and experiences hallucinations and delusions.

Harry Stack Sullivan, a follower of Freud, believed that failure of maternal attachment creates excessive anxiety and sets the pattern for all future relationships. Unable to cope in a world seen as socially dangerous, the individual retreats into fantasy. Having done so, the individual cannot grow socially or develop a sense of trust in or belonging with others. By late adolescence or early adulthood, the person's situation has become so hopeless that all pretense of normality collapses and he or she withdraws totally and finally into a world of fantasy and delusion.

FAMILY AND LEARNING THEORIES

Family interaction theories dwell even more intensely on parent-child, especially mother-child, relationships. Theodore Lidz and coworkers, after conducting studies on families with a schizophrenic member, concluded that one or both parents of a future schizophrenic are likely to be nearly, if not overtly, psychotic. They proposed that the psychotogenic influence of these parents on a psychologically vulnerable child is most likely the cause of schizophrenia.

Gregory Bateson and colleagues proposed a family interaction theory called the double-bind theory. Bateson suggested that schizophrenia results when parents expose a child to a family atmosphere in which they never effectively communicate their expectations, and therefore the child is unable to discover which behaviors will win approval. Scolded for disobeying, for example, the child changes his or her behavior only to be scolded for being "too obedient." Subjected to such no-win situations constantly, the child cannot develop an attachment to the family, and this failure generalizes to all subsequent relationships.

Learning theories propose that failure of operant conditioning causes the bizarre behavior of schizophrenia. In one version, conditioning fails because mechanisms in the brain that support operant learning, such as reinforcement and attention, are faulty, thus preventing the learning of appropriate, adaptive behaviors.

For example, a person who is unable to focus attention on relevant stimuli would be unable to learn the stimulus associations and discriminations necessary for successful day-to-day behavior. Such an individual's behavior would eventually become chaotic. This learning/attention theory proposes a defect in perceptual filtering, a function of the brain's reticular formation. This system filters out the innumerable stimuli that impinge on one's senses every moment but are unimportant. In schizophrenia, the theory proposes, this filtering system fails, and the individual is overwhelmed by a welter of trivial stimuli. Unable to cope with this confusing overstimulation, the person withdraws, becomes preoccupied with sorting out his or her thoughts, and becomes unable to distinguish internally generated stimuli from external ones.

ORGANIC THEORIES

Organic theories of schizophrenia are influenced by the knowledge that conditions known to have organic causes (that is, causes stemming from biological abnormalities) often produce psychological symptoms that mimic the psychotic symptoms of schizophrenia. Among these are vitamin-deficiency diseases, viral encephalitis, temporal-lobe epilepsy, and neurodegenerative disease such as Huntington's disease and Wilson's disease. In contradistinction to historical theories of schizophrenia that have little empirical support, considerable research supports the operation of genetic factors in schizophrenia; such factors are most often assumed to influence the development of the brain and its resilience to a variety of physiological and psychological stressors. In the diathesis-stress model, such a genetic defect is necessary for the development of chronic schizophrenia but is not sufficient to produce it. Stressful life events must also be present. The genetic abnormality then leaves the person unable to cope with life stresses, the result being psychosis. Research demonstrating the operation of genetic factors in schizophrenia in no way implies the absence of environmental factors that operate to influence the course of the disorder.

Many brain abnormalities have been proposed as causes of schizophrenia. One suggestion is that schizophrenia results from generalized brain pathology. For example, some researchers suggest that widespread brain deterioration caused by either environmental poisoning or infection by a virus causes schizophrenia.

Alternatively, some biochemical abnormality may be at fault. The endogenous psychotogen theory proposes that abnormal production of a chemical substance either inside or outside the brain produces psychotic symptoms by affecting the brain in a druglike fashion. Substances similar to the hallucinogenic drugs lysergic acid diethylamide (LSD) and mescaline are popular candidates for the endogenous psychotogen. The dopamine theory, however, proposes that schizophrenia results when a chemical neurotransmitter system in the brain called the dopamine system becomes abnormally overactive or when dopamine receptors in the brain become abnormally sensitive to normal amounts of dopamine. In addition to dopamine, other neurotransmitters have been proposed as important in the development and maintenance of schizophrenia.

NEUROLOGICAL AND GENETIC STUDIES

Theories of schizophrenia are instrumental in generating experiments that provide definite knowledge of the condition. Experimental support for psychodynamic theories of the development and progression of schizophrenia has not been forthcoming. Therefore, most empirical researchers regard psychodynamic theories of schizophrenia as having little scientific merit. Family interaction theories also have not been supported by subsequent experiments. Although studies have found disturbed family relationships, the evidence suggests that these are most likely the result of, not the cause of, having a schizophrenic individual in the family. Family interaction has, however, been shown to be influential in modifying the course of illness and the risk of relapse. Studies consistently fail to find that parent-child interactions are psychotogenic, and the once-popular notion of the schizophrenogenic parent has been discarded. Only learning/attention and organic theories are strongly supported by experimental evidence. The evidence for attentional or learning deficits resulting from a fault in the reticular formation is strong, and it stems from electrophysiological and behavioral studies.

The electroencephalogram (EEG) is often found to be abnormal in schizophrenic patients, showing excessive activation that indicates overarousal.

Furthermore, studies of evoked potentials, electrical events recorded from the cortex of the brain in response to specific sensory stimuli, often find abnormalities. Significantly, these occur late in the evoked potential, indicating abnormality in the brain's interpretation of sensory stimuli rather than in initial reception and conduction.

Behavioral studies show that schizophrenic patients often overreact to low-intensity stimuli, which corresponds to their complaints that lights are too bright or sounds are too loud. In addition, patients are often unusually distractible—unable to focus attention on the most relevant stimuli. Orienting responses to novel stimuli are deficient in about half of schizophrenic patients. Patient self-reports also indicate that, subjectively, the individual feels overwhelmed by sensory stimulation.

Thus, considerable evidence suggests that, at least in many patients, there is an abnormality in the sensory/perceptual functioning in the brain, perhaps in the perceptual filtering mechanism of the reticular formation.

Franz J. Kallmann's twin studies of the 1940s provided convincing evidence of a genetic factor in schizophrenia. He found that genetically identical monozygotic twins are much more likely to be concordant for schizophrenia (that is, both twins are much more likely to be psychotic) than are dizygotic twins, who are not genetically identical. Studies using genealogical techniques also showed that schizophrenia runs in families.

The criticism of these studies was that twins not only are genetically similar but also are exposed to the same family environment, and therefore genetic and environmental factors were confounded. Seymour Kety and colleagues, working with adoption records in Scandinavia, effectively answered this criticism by showing that adoptees with schizophrenia are more likely to have biological relatives with schizophrenia or related illnesses than the biological relatives of unaffected adoptees. These studies showed that schizophrenia is more closely associated with genetic relatedness than with family environment. In addition, these studies showed that the genetic liability is not a liability to psychopathology in general (that is, relatives of individuals with schizophrenia are not at elevated risk for all forms of mental disorder) but that there is a range of severity of illness observed in the relatives of individuals with schizophrenia. The range of less severe schizophrenia-like conditions observed is called the schizophrenia spectrum of illness; schizotypal personality disorder is the most frequently studied form. Schizotypal personality disorder occurs more frequently than schizophrenia itself among the relatives of individuals with schizophrenia.

Presumably, this genetic predisposition works by producing some organic change. Studies using advanced brain-imaging techniques indicate that, in many patients, there is nonlocalized brain degeneration, which is revealed by the increased size of the ventricles, fluid-filled spaces within the brain. What causes this degeneration is unknown, but some researchers suggest that it is caused by a virus and that a genetic factor increases susceptibility to infection and the subsequent damaging effects of a viral disease. Although direct evidence of a virus has been found in a minority of patients, the viral theory is still considered speculative and unproved. There is no evidence that schizophrenia is contagious.

BIOCHEMICAL STUDIES

Experimental evidence of biochemical abnormalities in the brain's dopamine neurotransmitter systems is, however, impressive. Antipsychotic drugs are effective in relieving the symptoms of schizophrenia, especially positive symptoms such as hallucinations and delusions. These drugs block dopamine receptors in the brain. Furthermore, the more powerfully the drugs bind to and block dopamine receptors, the smaller the effective dose that is necessary to produce a therapeutic result.

Further evidence comes from a condition called amphetamine psychosis, which occurs in people who abuse amphetamine and similar stimulants such as cocaine. Amphetamine psychosis so closely mimics some forms of schizophrenia that misdiagnoses have been common. Furthermore, amphetamine psychosis is not an artifact of disturbed personality; experiments show that normal control subjects will develop the condition if they are given high doses of amphetamines every few hours for several days. Amphetamine psychosis, which is believed to result from the overactivation of dopamine systems in the brain, is treated with antipsychotic drugs such as chlorpromazine.

Direct evidence of abnormality in the dopamine systems comes from studies using advanced techniques such as positron emission tomography (PET) scanning. These studies show that the brains of schizophrenic patients, even those who have never been treated with antipsychotic medications, may have abnormally large numbers of dopamine receptors in an area called the limbic system, which is responsible for emotional regulation.

Dopamine-blocking drugs, however, help only a subset of patients. Studies show that those most likely to benefit from medication are patients who display primarily positive symptoms. Patients who show negative symptoms—such as withdrawal, thought blocking, and catatonia—are less likely to be helped by medication.

HISTORY OF THE CONCEPT OF SCHIZOPHRENIA

The disorders that are now called schizophrenia were first characterized in the nineteenth century. Emil Kraepelin first grouped these disorders, referring to them by the collective name dementia praecox, in 1893.

Many early neurologists and psychiatrists thought these dementias were organic conditions. This view changed, however, after Swiss psychiatrist Eugen Bleuler published his classic work on the disorder in 1911. Bleuler proposed that the primary characteristic of the condition was a splitting of intellect from emotions. He introduced the term "schizophrenia" (literally, "split mind"). Bleuler, influenced by the psychodynamic theories of Freud, believed that the bizarre content of schizophrenic thoughts and perceptions represented a breaking away from an external reality that was too painful or frightening. His ideas became especially influential in the United States.

Attempts to treat schizophrenia with traditional psychotherapies were, however, unsuccessful. Success rates rarely surpassed the rate of spontaneous recovery, the rate at which patients recover without treatment. Because medical interventions such as lobotomy, insulin shock therapy, and electroconvulsive therapy were also ineffective, psychiatric hospitals were filled with patients for whom little could be done.

The discovery of antipsychotic drugs and changing public policy about institutionalization in the 1950s changed things dramatically. Hospital populations declined. The surprising effectiveness of these medications, in concert with the discovery of amphetamine psychosis in the 1930s and the genetic studies of the 1940s, renewed the belief that schizophrenia is an organic condition.

Two problems impeded further understanding. First, techniques available for investigating the brain were primitive compared with modern techniques. Therefore, reports of organic changes in schizophrenia, although common, were difficult to confirm. Second, since the routinely administered medications powerfully influenced brain functioning, it became a problem to distinguish organic changes that were important in causing the disorder from those that were merely secondary to the action of antipsychotic drugs in the brain.

Indeed, it became common wisdom among many psychologists that organic factors identified by researchers were not primary to the disorder but were, rather, side effects of medication. Soft neurological signs such as eye-movement dysfunctions, abnormal orienting responses, and unusual movements were considered drug related even though Kraepelin and others had described them decades before the drugs were discovered. The drugs

came to be called major tranquilizers, implying that medication allowed patients to function more effectively by relieving the overwhelming anxiety that accompanied the disorder but that the drugs did not influence the schizophrenic process itself.

The fact that antipsychotic drugs have little usefulness as antianxiety agents in nonschizophrenics did not shake this opinion. Neither did the discovery of more powerful antianxiety agents such as chlordiazepoxide (Librium) and diazepam (Valium), even after they were shown to be almost useless in treating schizophrenia.

The next dramatic change in understanding schizophrenia came in the 1960s with the discovery of monoamine neurotransmitters, including dopamine, and the discovery that these chemical systems in the brain are strongly affected in opposite ways by psychotogenic drugs, such as cocaine and amphetamine, and antipsychotic drugs, such as chlorpromazine. Carefully conducted twin and adoption studies confirmed the role of genetic factors in schizophrenia and encouraged the search for the mechanism by which genes influenced the risk for developing schizophrenia. In the following decades, evidence that prenatal and perinatal factors are instrumental in the development of schizophrenia has led to the emerging consensus that schizophrenia should be considered from a neurodevelopmental perspective.

BIBLIOGRAPHY

Bowers, Malcolm B. *Retreat from Sanity: The Structure of Emerging Psychosis*. New York: Human Sciences, 1974. Print.

Brown, Alan S., and Paul H. Patterson. *The Origins of Schizophrenia*. New York: Columbia UP, 2012. Print.

Gottesman, Irving I. *Schizophrenia Genesis: The Origins of Madness*. New York: Freeman, 1991. Print.

Gottesman, Irving I., James Shields, and Daniel R. Hanson. *Schizophrenia: The Epigenetic Puzzle*. Cambridge: Cambridge UP, 1984. Print.

Hirsch, Steven R., and Daniel R. Weinberger. *Schizophrenia*. Oxford: Blackwell Science, 2002. Print.

Maj, Mario, and Norman Sartorius. *Schizophrenia*. 2d ed. Hoboken: Wiley, 2003. Print.

Marder, Stephen R., and Vandra Chopra. *Schizophrenia*. New York: Oxford UP, 2014. Print.

Myslobodsky, Michael S., and Ina Weiner. *Contemporary Issues in Modeling Psychopathology*. Boston: Kluwer Academic, 2000. Print.

Raine, Adrian, Todd Lencz, and Sarnoff A. Mednick. *Schizotypal Personality.* Cambridge: Cambridge UP, 2006. Print.

Roberts, David L., and David L. Penn. *Social Cognition in Schizophrenia: From Evidence to Treatment.* New York: Oxford UP, 2013. Print.

Snyder, Solomon H. *Madness and the Brain.* New York: McGraw, 1975. Print.

Torrey, E. Fuller. *Surviving Schizophrenia: A Family Manual.* 5th ed. New York: Collins, 2006. Print.

William B. King; updated by Loring J. Ingraham

SEE ALSO: Abnormality: Biomedical models; Abnormality: Psychological models; Antipsychotic medications; Diagnosis; Drug therapies; Environmental factors and mental health; Genetics and mental health; Mental illness: Historical concepts; Psychopharmacology; Psychosurgery; Schizophrenia: Background, types, and symptoms; Schizophrenia: High-risk children.

Schizotypal personality disorder

DATE: 1960s forward
TYPE OF PSYCHOLOGY: Personality; Psychopathology

Schizotypal personality disorder is a personality disorder that shares clinical features with schizophrenia. Because of the eccentric behaviors and unusual thinking patterns that accompany this disorder, mental health professionals often conceptualize it as a mild form of schizophrenia. This conceptualization has helped researchers to better understand schizotypal personality disorder and develop potential treatments.

KEY CONCEPTS

- Antipsychotics
- Five-factor model of personality
- Negative schizotypy
- Neuropsychology
- Schizophrenia
- Schizotaxia

INTRODUCTION

According to the *Diagnostic and Statistical Manual of Mental Disorders: DSM-5* (5th ed., 2013) of the American Psychiatric Association (APA), schizotypal personality disorder (SPD) is characterized by interpersonal deficits, such as suspiciousness and difficulty establish-

ing and maintaining close relationships; cognitive or perceptual distortions; and eccentric behavior, all of which are pervasive throughout much of an individual's lifetime. Individuals with SPD are not psychotic (out of touch with reality), although others typically perceive them as odd or strange. They often harbor strange ideas, such as magical thinking, which is the belief that merely thinking about an event (such as that their mother will die) can trigger that event. SPD typically begins in early adulthood and is present in about 3 to 5 percent in the general population.

POSSIBLE CAUSES

To help explain the causes of SPD, researchers have attempted to identify genetic markers of the disorder. In the 1960s, University of Minnesota psychologist Paul Meehl introduced the term "schizotaxia" to describe the genetic predisposition to schizophrenia, which he believed to reflect a single gene of large effect. Meehl regarded schizotaxia as a neural deficit that could be expressed as either schizophrenia or what Hungarian psychoanalyst Sandor Rado termed schizotypy—presumably a milder version of schizophrenia—depending on environmental circumstances and other modifying characteristics, such as personality traits and intelligence. Nevertheless, Meehl hypothesized that schizotypy rather than schizophrenia would result from schizotaxia and that only about 10 percent of schizotypes (individuals with schizotypy) develop schizophrenia. In later research, Harvard University psychiatrist Ming Tsuang and his colleagues modified Meehl's concept of schizotaxia to reflect a condition caused by multiple genes acting in concert rather than a single gene. Although Meehl's concept of schizotaxia has been refined over the years, his original concept has encouraged researchers to investigate genetic, neurobiological, and clinical similarities between SPD and schizophrenia.

Twin studies suggest that the heritability of clinically assessed schizotypal features is approximately 0.60, meaning that about 60 percent of the differences among people in their levels of these features are caused by differences in their genes. Several other twin studies, including those conducted by Virginia Commonwealth University's Kenneth Kendler and his colleagues, have demonstrated substantial genetic contributions to SPD.

DIAGNOSING SPD

Psychiatrists and psychologists added SPD to the third version of the DSM in 1980 to describe individuals who display mild psychotic features and interpersonal deficits, such as social isolation and poor rapport. Certain features of SPD are easily confused with those of other personality disorders. For instance, the psychotic-like features of SPD overlap with the psychotic features of borderline personality disorder (such as brief periods of loss of contact with reality), while the socially inappropriate features of SPD, such as social withdrawal, overlap with those of schizoid personality disorder.

Researchers have raised questions about whether SPD is dimensional or categorical in nature: That is, does SPD differ only in degree from normal functioning (a dimensional model) or in kind (a categorical model)? Studies using sophisticated statistical analyses generally support a categorical view of SPD, in which this condition is underpinned by two core features: oddness of speech and interpersonal dysfunction.

SIMILARITIES BETWEEN SPD AND SCHIZOPHRENIA

Certain clinical features of SPD are especially related to schizophrenia. In particular, negative schizotypy, that is, such features as odd speech, restricted emotional expression, and aloofness, is closely related to schizophrenia and tends to respond positively to antipsychotic medications. Because certain features of SPD are more related to schizophrenia than others, researchers have investigated whether SPD may contain two or more subtypes. University of Pennsylvania psychologist Adrian Raine hypothesized that two subtypes of schizotypy exist. The first subtype, neurodevelopmental schizotypy, is a condition that is genetically related to schizophrenia and largely influenced by biological factors such as prenatal stress, influenza exposure, and birth complications. The second subtype, pseudoschizotypy, is generally unrelated to schizophrenia, and is largely influenced by environmental adversity such as impaired familial relationships. Although both subtypes share similar clinical features, neurodevelopmental SPD is thought to be more likely to lead to schizophrenia.

Researchers have observed similar neuropsychological problems, such as deficits in attention, memory, and higher-level thought processes, among patients with schizophrenia and SPD. Moreover, they have investigated potential personality similarities between SPD and schizophrenia. Several researchers have applied the influential five-factor model (FFM) of personality, which proposes that personality consists of five major personality traits (extraversion, neuroticism, agreeableness, conscientiousness, and openness to experience) to identify personality characteristics associated with SPD. Researchers using the FFM have found that individuals with SPD and schizophrenia exhibit significantly higher levels of neuroticism and lower levels of extraversion, agreeableness, and conscientiousness than individuals without schizophrenia or SPD. Despite SPD individuals' high levels of neuroticism, their scores on this dimension tend to be lower than those of individuals with schizophrenia, at least among outpatients.

In the fifth edition of the DSM, SPD was added to the chapter on psychotic disorders as a schizophrenia-spectrum disorder, although it remained cross-listed in the chapter on personality disorders.

TREATMENT OPTIONS

Results from studies on neuropsychology, clinical symptoms, and personality support the hypothesis that SPD is a mild form of schizophrenia. This hypothesis has assisted researchers in formulating pharmacological and psychotherapeutic treatments for this condition. In general, the closer the patient's symptoms are to those of schizophrenia and related conditions, the more likely that medication will be effective. Small dosages of antipsychotic medications have been effective in ameliorating the symptoms of SPD. In one study, neuropsychological deficits, such as problems with information processing, improved following the administration of guanfacine (Tenex), a medication that works on receptors in the frontal areas of the brain. Another study using olanzapine (Zyprexa; an atypical antipsychotic) with SPD patients found improvements in psychosis, depression, and overall functioning.

In conclusion, SPD shares many clinical, neuropsychological, and personality characteristics with schizophrenia, and may be a mild form of that disorder. SPD is influenced by a host of genetic and environmental factors, most of which remain to be ascertained. Given that SPD may be more than one condition, more research is needed on its causes and effective treatments, both psychotherapeutic and pharmacological.

BIBLIOGRAPHY

Camisa, Kathryn, et al. "Personality Traits in Schizophrenia and Related Personality Disorders." *Psychiatry Research* 133 (2005): 23–33. Print. Chemerinski, Eran, et al. "Schizotypal Personality Disorder." *Journal of Personality Disorders* 27.5 (2013): 652–79.

Lenzenweger, Mark F., Brendan A. Maher, and Theo C. Manschreck. "Paul E. Meehl's Influence on Experimental Psychopathology: Fruits of the Nexus of Schizotypy and Schizophrenia, Neurology, and Methodology." *Journal of Clinical Psychology* 61, no. 10 (2005): 1295–1315.

Print.Meehl, Paul E. "Schizotaxia, Schizotypy, Schizophrenia." *American Psychologist* 17 (1962): 827–38. Print.

Pulay, Attila J., et al. "Prevalence, Correlates, Disability, and Comorbidity of DSM-IV Schizotypal Personality Disorder: Results from the Wave 2 National Epidemiologic Survey on Alcohol and Related Conditions." *Primary Care Companion to the Journal of Clinical Psychiatry* 11.2 (2009): 53–67. Print.

Raine, Adrian. "Schizotypal Personality: Neurodevelopmental and Psychosocial Trajectories." *Annual Review of Clinical Psychology* 2 (2006): 291–326. Print.

Torgersen, Svenn, et al. "Schizotypal Personality Disorder Inside and Outside the Schizophrenic Spectrum." *Schizophrenia Research* 54, nos. 1/2 (2002): 33–38. Print.

Torti, Maria, et al. "Schizotypy and Personality Profiles of Cluster A in a Group of Schizophrenic Patients and Their Siblings." *BMC Psychiatry* 13.1 (2013): 245. Print.

Tsuang, Ming, William S. Stone, Sarah I. Tarbox, and Steven V. Farone. "An Integration of Schizophrenia with Schizotypy: Identification of Schizotaxia and Implication for Research on Treatment and Prevention." *Schizophrenia Research* 54 (2002): 169–75. Print.

April D. Thames and Scott O. Lilienfeld

SEE ALSO: Abnormality: Biomedical models; Abnormality: Psychological models; Antipsychotic medications; Attention; Borderline personality disorder; Dissociative disorders; Drug therapies; Neuropsychology; Personality disorders; Personality theory; Psychopharmacology; Psychotic disorders; Schizoid personality disorder; Schizophrenia: Background, types, and symptoms; Schizophrenia: High-risk children; Schizophrenia: Theoretical explanations.

Scientific methods

TYPE OF PSYCHOLOGY: Psychological methodologies

Scientific methods refer to the techniques psychologists use to study psychological and behavioral processes in humans and animals. Although there are many variations to each, there are generally five scientific methods on which psychologists rely. These include the experiment, correlation, survey, naturalistic observation, and case study. Each of the five approaches has special features, along with limitations, that help psychologists make inferences about the phenomenon under study.

KEY CONCEPTS
- Between- and within-subject designs
- Conditions or levels of the independent variable
- Confounding or extraneous variable
- Dependent variable
- Experimental and control groups
- Experimental design
- Independent variable
- Operational definitions
- Placebo effect
- Population
- Positive and negative correlations
- Sample
- Subject selectivity

INTRODUCTION

Since its inception as an identifiable discipline in the 1870's, psychology has relied on scientific methods for studying psychological and behavioral processes in both humans and animals. Embracing such an approach represented a significant landmark in the history of psychology. The use of these methods helped identify psychology as a separate and distinct discipline, allowing it to break away from its roots in philosophy.

Historians have credited the German physician and psychophysiologist Wilhelm Wundt as being the first to employ scientific methods in the study of psychological processes. For doing so, Wundt is often known as the father of psychology. Although his methods were crude by modern-day standards, Wundt examined how perceptions were formed in the mind by simply asking subjects to look within themselves and reflect on what they were thinking when he exposed them to a variety of sensory stimuli such as different intensities of light or sound. This approach, known as introspection, in the end proved to be too unreliable in characterizing psychological processes and was eventually abandoned. Despite its failure as a scientific method, the use of introspection by Wundt represented the first attempt at studying mental events objectively and laid the foundation for the scientific methods used by psychologists today.

Since the time of Wundt, psychologists have developed a variety of methodological approaches. Although variations exist, generally there are five scientific methods on which psychologists rely. They are experiment, correlation, survey, naturalistic observation, and case study. The selection of an appropriate method will depend on a number of issues such as the nature, intensity, and duration of the phenomena under investigation; the species, gender, age, weight, and other variables associated with the individuals being studied; the number of individuals available for study; the sensitivity, reliability, and validity of the measures and devices used to study the phenomenon; and ethical and/or legal concerns that might limit or alter the specific methodological procedures and tactics employed.

GENERAL ISSUES

Regardless of the particular method used, the researcher must be concerned about a variety of general issues before conducting the investigation. Paramount among them is the identification of the population of interest, selecting a sample from the population, ethical guidelines in conducting the research, and statistical analysis of the research data.

The population is the entire universe of individuals about whom the researcher wishes to identify some law of nature or relationship. The researcher should be clear as to exactly which individuals constitute the population. Because it is almost always impossible to study every individual in the population, the researcher is left with the next best thing: selecting a subgroup from the population, called a sample. The individuals selected for the sample are called subjects. Subjects are almost always selected in a nonbiased, random fashion that ensures that each individual in the population has an equal chance of being included in the sample. Researchers must be certain that the sample represents accurately the characteristics of the population so that the data collected can be confidently applied to the population at large.

As researchers conduct their investigations, they must follow a number of ethical guidelines that ensure that subjects are protected from risk or harm. Many professional organizations, such as the American Psychological Association and the Society for Neuroscience, have published guidelines that help researchers meet the ethical standards of using human and animal subjects. In addition, researchers must conform to many federal and state laws and peer-review institutional committees (such as the Institutional Review Board and Institutional Animal Care and Use Committee) that regulate and oversee research activities and ensure the protection of research subjects. Once the data are collected, the researcher must summarize and analyze the results with statistical tests and procedures to help determine whether relationships or trends exist and to draw conclusions from the study.

EXPERIMENT

The experiment is one of the most frequently used techniques for studying psychological and behavioral processes. It is the only method of the five techniques discussed that allows for the determination of cause-effect relationships. Its rationale lies in the active manipulation by the experimenter of a Variablesdependent and independentvariable called the independent variable and the effects of it on an outcome measure called the dependent variable. Crucial to the experimental method, also, is the control of other variables, called confounding or extraneous variables. Confounding or extraneous variables are those that are not intentionally manipulated by the experimenter but somehow influence the results. The entire plan for the experiment, including techniques for controlling or eliminating confounding variables, is referred to as theExperimental designexperimental design. Well-conceived experimental designs are crucial for allowing the experimenter to make clear and concise conclusions from the data that are collected in the experiment. In fact, constructing the experimental design is the most crucial aspect of the experiment. Once a well-designed experiment is conceived, it is only a matter of following the "game plan."

A simple experimental design illustrates the nuances that are involved in the conception of the experimental design: A researcher wants to determine whether a new drug, "Drug A," improves memory. The experimenter would have some subjects in the experiment ingest or be injected with the drug shortly before learning some task on which a test of retention would be given at a later time. Because Drug A is the variable that is being actively manipulated by the experimenter to determine its effects on memory, it is referred to as the independent variable, and those individuals exposed to it are collectively referred to as the experimental group.

However, by definition, a variable is something that exists in more than one form. To compare the effects of the drug on memory, the experimenter needs to include another group of participants who are not exposed to the drug. This latter group of subjects is collectively referred to as the control group, since their performance on the memory test will provide a baseline measurement of how well individuals who are not given the drug remember the information. Comparing the performance of the experimental subjects with those in the control group is the only way to assess the effect of Drug A on memory. Without the inclusion of the control subjects there would be no way to determine whether the drug had any beneficial (or deleterious) effects on memory.

The inference of causality in the experiment relies on the fact that the experimental and control subjects should differ only on the independent variable. That is, to infer that the drug improves or worsens memory, it is necessary that the only variable that can account for effects on memory is the drug itself. The possibility of any other variable accounting for differences among the performance of the two groups on the test of retention represents a confounding variable. A closer examination of the experimental design described above, however, does reveal the presence of a confounding variable. The control subjects were simply not given any "drug," while the experimental subjects received an active dose of the drug. It is a real possibility that the performance of the experimental subjects might have been affected simply by the fact that they received something and that they expected that their performance would be altered in some way. This is referred to as the placebo effectPlacebo effect—the effect of psychological expectation on performance.

To eliminate or control for the influence of a placebo effect, it is crucial that the control subjects also receive a "drug," but that the substance that they receive contain an inactive substance. In fact, to assess whether the active dose of the drug does indeed affect memory and what role, if any, a placebo effect has, it might be wise also to include a control group of subjects that do not receive anything. Thus, three groups of participants would constitute the experimental design, with one group receiving the active dose of the drug, another receiving a placebo, and a third group receiving nothing at all. If all three groups of subjects were included, then the experimental design would have one independent variable (Drug A) with three different variations of it. The different variations of the independent variable are referred to as the conditions or levels of the independent variable.

Confounding variables can take many forms and must be carefully evaluated when constructing any experimental design. Other factors, such as gender, body weight, general intelligence, age of the subjects, ambient temperature, humidity, lighting, distracting sounds in the testing room, and purity and consistency of the drug might represent possible sources of confounding variables in this experiment. To ensure that confounding variables are not affecting the outcome measure, the general rule of thumb is to ensure that the subjects in the experiment are the same or similar with regard to all variables except the independent variable. It is only when this rule is met that inferences of causality can be made with any degree of certainty.

COMPLEX DESIGNS

Conducting experiments is time-consuming and costly. Therefore, it is prudent that the experimental design be constructed in such a way as to maximize the information gained from the enterprise. In this regard, researchers often will study more than one independent variable in an experiment. In the experimental design already described, the researchers might wish to determine whether the time of drug administration has any effect on the drug's ability to influence memory processes. The experimental design would then necessitate the inclusion of other groups of subjects, some of whom would be given the drug, placebo, or nothing at all during the morning while others would be given the drug, placebo, or nothing at all in the afternoon. If this were the design, then six, rather than three, groups of participants would be needed and "time of administration" would be another independent variable with two levels (morning versus afternoon). In this case, since each level of each independent variable is combined with each level of the other independent variable to form six groups of subjects, the experimental design would represent a factorial design as opposed to a single-variable design. The number of levels of each independent variable is used when identifying factorial designs. Thus, this study with three levels of Drug A and two levels of time of administration would be described as a "3 × 2" design (said "three by two").

Adding more independent variables to the experimental design does have its drawbacks. In addition to increasing the complexity of the experimental design and the time required to complete the study, it also requires the recruitment of additional subjects. In the above 3 × 2 study, six groups of subjects would be required. If there were twelve subjects in each of the six groups (the number of subjects in a group usually ranges from eight to twelve), then seventy-two subjects in total would be needed, with both independent variables being between-subject variables. (A between-subject variable is in effect when subjects serve in one and only one level of the independent variable.) Since both variables in this case are between-subject variables, then the experimental design is identified as a "3 × 2 between-subject design."

However, there exists another way of assigning subjects to the six groups. It is possible that each subject could be tested under the influence of the drug, the placebo, and nothing at all both in the morning and in the afternoon on separate days. In this case all participants would serve as subjects in all six groups, thus requiring only twelve subjects in total. In this instance, each of the two independent variables would be described as within-subject variables and the design referred to as a "3 × 2 within-subject design." (A within-subject variable is in effect when subjects serve in more than one level of the independent variable. "Repeated measures" is often used as a synonymous term.)

Within-subject designs, although having the advantage of requiring fewer subjects, do have their disadvantages. Chief among them is the fact that subjects are exposed to the test situation multiple times, thus making their performance on subsequent tests potentially tainted by the virtue of being exposed earlier to other conditions, a confounding variable referred to as order effect. To help minimize order effects in within-subject designs, it is prudent to expose subjects to the various conditions in different sequences. This will help to prevent the introduction of any specific order effects on the dependent variable and thus allow for a more reliable inference of causality.

Another confounding variable associated with within-subject designs is called the carry-over effect. This confounding variable is related to the possibility that treatments made to the subjects under earlier conditions might still exist and affect performance under later conditions of the independent variable. In the experiment described above, for example, the drug may still be physiologically active in the body at the time when subjects are tested in the placebo or nothing-at-all conditions, and thus might influence performance under those conditions. Elimination of this confounding variable, often by waiting a sufficient amount of time before the next

condition is tested, is critical to any design in which exposure to one level of the independent variable might influence performance when subjects are exposed to other levels of the independent variable.

A compromise between within- and between-subject designs is the mixed design. Mixed designs have at least one between- and one within-subject variable. In the example being discussed, independent groups of subjects might serve in the drug, the placebo, and nothing-at-all groups, but all subjects would be administered their respective treatments both in the morning and in the afternoon on different days. Fewer subjects, therefore, are needed, while at the same time avoiding or at least minimizing some of the confounding variables associated with repeatedly testing subjects. In the present example, thirty-six subjects would be recruited, with twelve individuals serving in each of the three levels of the drug, and all subjects receiving their respective treatments both in the morning and in the afternoon on separate days. The design would thus be described as a "3 × 2 mixed design with repeated measures on the last variable."

Another important aspect of experimental designs is accurately and precisely defining the phenomenon under study in terms of how it is measured—what is known as creating operational definitions. Regardless of the phenomenon under study, experimenters must precisely communicate to others in the scientific community how they measured the phenomenon. For example, memory might be measured by counting the number of words recalled from a list of words learned previously. It can also be measured in many other ways. Selecting the exact way in which the phenomenon is measured (that is, selecting the dependent variable) is entirely up to the experimenter, but the method must meet generally accepted criteria in the field and must be described in detail sufficient to enable other competent researchers to use the same method.

CORRELATION

In addition to the experiment, psychologists also frequently use the correlation method. Unlike the experiment, the correlation methodCorrelational studies does not allow for conclusions of causality. It does, however, allow researchers to identify relationships among variables. More specifically, the correlation approach allows the researcher to determine whether variables change in some consistent manner over time.

Although many variables can be simultaneously examined using the method of correlation (multiple regression), the simplest correlation method examines two variables and thus is called bivariate correlation. In bivariate correlation, subjects are studied with regard to their performance on two variables, designated the X and the Y variables. Thus, each subject provides two scores, and the scores from all the subjects in the study are then statistically analyzed to determine whether a relationship between the two variables exists. A statistical technique used to analyze bivariate data is the Pearson Product Moment Correlation Coefficient, better known as Pearson r. Pearson r yields a coefficient value that lies between −1.00 and +1.00. The absolute value of Pearson r indicates the magnitude of the relationship, with values close to or equal to the absolute value of 1.00 indicating a strong relationship and values close to or equal to zero indicating little or no relationship. The sign of Pearson r, on the other hand, indicates whether the change in the two variables occurs in the same (positive values) or opposite (negative values) directions.

Bivariate data are often graphically presented in a scatter plot. A scatter plot is a graph with X and Y axes, on which each subject's X and Y scores are plotted. Consider a set of students' scores on an exam and the number of hours students studied for the exam (figure 1) along with the scatter plot that graphs the relationship between these two variables (figure 2). As can be seen in the scatter plot, there is a positive relationship (positive correlation) between the number of hours studied and the student's exam score. Generally speaking, as the number of hours increases, so do exam scores. In fact, the value for the Pearson r coefficient for these data is +.92.

Now consider another set of data that correlates the number of alcoholic drinks and the number of words remembered from a list of twenty-five words (figure 3) and its associated scatter plot (figure 4). These data also indicate a strong bivariate relationship, with the value of the Pearson r coefficient equal to −.96. However, the direction of the relationship is negative (as reflected in the value of Pearson r), indicating that as the number of alcoholic drinks increases, the number of words remembered decreases—an example of a negative correlation.

Correlations can be helpful to researchers in a number of ways. First, they may provide suggestions for variables that ought to be studied using experiments, since the experiment is the only method that can establish cause-effect relationships. Correlations are also useful when active manipulation of a variable cannot be performed because of ethical, legal, or practical limitations (such as exposure to lead paint in children,

exposure to environmental radiation, or exposure to job stress). Finally, correlations are used to identify trends in large groups of individuals in the population suggestive of interesting or potentially dangerous social or medical phenomena (such as the relationship between smoking cigarettes and the development of cancer, or exposure to sources of drinking water and development of bacterial illness).

SURVEY

The survey method relies on questionnaires administered to a fairly large number of subjects to determine their opinions, reactions, and views. The most critical aspect of survey research is developing the questions that will be asked of subjects. Constructing the questions ought to be done in a manner that does not increase the likelihood of biased responses. Thus, the researcher must always be aware of how each question is phrased. The questions should not contain language that would make the respondents more or less likely to answer in a particular manner. Another critical aspect of survey research is the recruitment of subjects. The manner in which subjects are recruited—such as by telephone, in a shopping mall, or in a classroom—might affect the type of individual participating in the survey. In essence, what researchers must ask themselves is, "Who is participating in my survey and why are they participating in my survey?" For example, if a survey is administered over the telephone, who is more likely to take the time to answer questions, and might individuals who do participate have a special interest in the survey and/or have a vested interest in the survey's outcome? As discussed above, all research methods use samples, and the subjects who form the sample should be representative of the population at large. Therefore, if only a specialized segment of the population is willing to participate, researchers must question whether they have a confounding variable called subject selectivity.

Although there are many ways in which questions can be asked, the most frequently used ways of constructing questionnaires involve closed-ended questions, open-ended questions, or Likert scale responses. Closed-ended questions limit the responses subjects can make to discrete categories, such as "agree," "disagree," "no opinion," "yes," or "no." The advantage of closed-ended questions is that the data collected are much more amenable to categorizing and statistical analysis. The disadvantage, however, is that subjects' responses are limited to predetermined discrete categories.

Open-ended questions, on the other hand, allow subjects more freedom in expanding or qualifying their responses. For example, a subject may respond "yes" to a question, but that response may only apply to certain conditions. For example, subjects may qualify a response to the question "Are you in favor of abortion?" by saying, "Only in the case of rape or incest." This flexibility does come with a price; open-ended questions often make responses difficult to categorize and analyze statistically. It is therefore crucial that the researcher decide ahead of time on operational definitions that set clear criteria for categorizing responses.

Likert scales responses involve asking subjects to rate their response intensities on a scale typically from 0 to 7 or 10, with low values indicating a small degree of intensity or agreement and greater values indicating a large degree of intensity or agreement. For example, the item, "On a scale of 0 to 10, rate your feeling toward abortion, with 10 indicating total support" might yield a score of 4 if the subject is against abortion except in cases of rape or incest. In this manner, subjects are allowed somewhat more freedom to qualify their responses but still need to stay within the confines of a limited number of response categories. This objectification of the data facilitates scoring and categorizing responses, making the data more amenable to statistical analysis.

NATURALISTIC OBSERVATION

Although the experiment, survey, and correlation methods are useful, they do suffer from the problem that subjects are aware that they are being studied and thus their behavior or responses might be altered in some manner. Observing the behavior of subjects in their natural environment, such as observing ape behavior in the wild, is an attempt to minimize this confounding variable. Moreover, it has been argued that results derived from naturalistic observation are more reliable since they are obtained outside the artificial environment of the laboratory.

The general rule of thumb with naturalistic observations is that the researcher must be an unobserved observer. If subjects are consciously aware that they are being observed, then the entire rationale for using this method is undermined. Although naturalistic observation has the advantage of allowing a wider range of behaviors to be exhibited, it does require special attention to operational definitions. As with other methods, researchers must clearly construct operational definitions and scoring systems that will guide their observations

and will allow other competent researchers to confirm their findings. Similarly, the data collected from naturalistic observational studies are organized and analyzed with statistics in order for trends to be identified and conclusions to be drawn.

CASE STUDY

Sometimes individuals exhibit rare disorders or behaviors that are notable or illustrate some special feature of a disease. In this instance, psychologists might employ the case study method to characterize and describe this individual to the research community. Case study methodology necessitate providing an intense and highly descriptive profile of the individual being studied. The major drawback of the case study method is that only one rare individual from the population is studied, thus limiting the degree to which the findings can be generalized to the larger population. However, case studies are informative especially in the field of clinical psychology, where previously known disorders or diseases of the brain or the mind can be further characterized, or new disorders or diseases can be identified.

BIBLIOGRAPHY

Allen, Mary J. *Introduction to Psychological Research*. Itasca, Ill.: F. E. Peacock, 1995. This book provides a simple and highly accessible overview of research methods.

Crawford, Helen J., and Larry B. Christensen. *Developing Research Skills: A Laboratory Manual*. 3d ed. Needham Heights, Mass.: Allyn & Bacon, 1995. This workbook contains several exercises that help students hone their research skills.

Heiman, Gary W. *Basic Statistics for the Behavioral Sciences*. 5th ed. Boston: Houghton Mifflin, 2006. A very good introduction to the various statistical procedures used in research.

Kirk, Roger E. *Experimental Design: Procedures for the Behavioral Sciences*. 3d ed. Pacific Grove, Calif.: Brooks/Cole, 1995. Originally published in 1965, this book has remained the standard guide for researchers in the field. It is recommended only to seasoned researchers.

Smith, Randolph A., and Stephen F. Davis. *The Psychologist as Detective: An Introduction to Conducting Research in Psychology*. 5th ed. Upper Saddle River, N.J.: Prentice Hall, 2009. A very good undergraduate textbook providing broad coverage of psychological methods and related statistical issues.

Anthony C. Santucci

SEE ALSO: Animal experimentation; Archival data; Case study methodologies; Complex experimental designs; Data description; Experimental psychology; Experimentation: Ethics and participant rights; Experimentation: Independent, dependent, and control variables; Field experimentation; Hypothesis development and testing; Observational methods; Placebo effect; Quasi-experimental designs; Sampling; Statistical significance tests; Survey research: Questionnaires and interviews; Within-subject experimental designs.

Seasonal affective disorder

TYPE OF PSYCHOLOGY: Personality; Psychopathology

Seasonal affective disorder is a form of major depressive disorder believed to exhibit two forms: winter depression, beginning in late fall or winter, and spring-onset, which continues through summer and fall.

KEY CONCEPTS
- Double-blind study
- Hypersomnia
- Libido
- Lux
- Placebo

INTRODUCTION

Seasonal affective disorder (SAD) became the focus of systematic scientific research in the early 1980's. Research originally focused on seasonal changes in mood that coincided with the onset of winter and became known as winter depression. Symptoms consistently identified by Norman Rosenthal and others as indicative of winter depression included hypersomnia, overeating, carbohydrate craving, and weight gain. Michael Garvey and others found the same primary symptoms and the following secondary ones: decreased libido, irritability, fatigue, anxiety, problems concentrating, and premenstrual sadness. Several researchers have found that winter depression is more of a problem at higher latitudes. Thomas Wehr and Rosenthal report on a description of winter depression by Frederick Cook during an expedition to Antarctica in 1898. While winter depression was the form of seasonal affective disorder that received the most initial attention, there is another variation that changes with the seasons.

Summer depression affects some people in the same way that winter depression affects others. Both are examples of seasonal affective disorder. According to Wehr and Rosenthal, symptoms of summer depression include agitation, loss of appetite, insomnia, and loss of weight. Many people with summer depression also have histories of chronic anxiety. As can be seen, the person with a summer depression experiences symptoms that are almost the opposite of the primary symptoms of winter depression.

To diagnose a seasonal affective disorder, there must be evidence that the symptoms vary according to a seasonal pattern. If seasonality is not present, the diagnosis of SAD cannot be made. In the Northern Hemisphere, the seasonal pattern for winter depression is for it to begin in November and continue unabated through March. Summer depression usually begins in May and continues through September. Siegfried Kasper and others reported that people suffering from winter depression outnumber those suffering from summer depression by 4.5 to 1. Wehr and Rosenthal reported that as people come out of their seasonal depression they experience feelings of euphoria, increased energy, less depression, hypomania, and possibly mania.

Philip Boyce and Gordon Parker investigated seasonal affective disorder in Australia. Their interest was in determining whether seasonal affective disorder occurs in the Southern Hemisphere and, if so, whether it manifests the same symptoms and temporal relationships with seasons as noted in the Northern Hemisphere. Their results confirmed the existence of seasonal affective disorder with an onset coinciding with winter and remission coinciding with summer. Their study also provided evidence that seasonal affective disorder occurs independently of important holidays and celebrations, such as Christmas. There is also a subsyndromal form of seasonal affective disorder. This is usually seen in winter depression and represents a milder form of the disorder. It interferes with the person's life, although to a lesser degree than the full syndrome, and it is responsive to the primary treatment for seasonal affective disorder.

HYPOTHESES OF ETIOLOGY

Three hypotheses are being tested to explain seasonal affective disorder: the melatonin hypothesis, the circadian rhythm phase shift hypothesis, and the circadian rhythm amplitude hypothesis.

The melatonin hypothesis is based on animal studies and focuses on a chemical signal for darkness. During darkness, the hormone melatonin is produced in greater quantities; during periods of light, it is produced in lesser quantities. Increases in melatonin level occur at the onset of seasonal affective disorder (winter depression) and are thought to be causally related to the development of the depression.

The circadian rhythm phase shift hypothesis contends that the delay in the arrival of dawn disrupts the person's circadian rhythm by postponing it for a few hours. This disruption of the circadian rhythm is thought to be integral in the development of winter depression. Disruptions in the circadian rhythm are also related to secretion of melatonin.

The third hypothesis is the circadian rhythm amplitude hypothesis. A major tenet of this hypothesis is that the amplitude of the circadian rhythm is directly related to winter depression. Lower amplitudes are associated with depression and higher ones with normal mood states. The presence or absence of light has been an important determinant in the amplitude of circadian rhythms.

The melatonin hypothesis is falling out of favor. Rosenthal and others administered to volunteers in a double-blind study a drug known to suppress melatonin secretion and a placebo. Despite melatonin suppression, there was no difference in the degree of depression experienced by the two groups (drug and placebo). In addition, no difference was observed in melatonin rhythms when persons with SAD were compared with those not suffering from the disorder.

Nevertheless, scientists have continued to investigate the role played by neurological chemicals in the etiology of the disorder. Some of these studies have focused on the possible role of neurotransmitters such as serotonin, dopamine, and norepinephrine. It is known that these chemicals may play a role in some forms of depression. For example, low levels of serotonin have been linked with some disorders; similar depressed levels have been observed in SAD patients during the winter months. If at least some forms of SAD are linked to reduction in serotonin production or uptake, this would explain the craving for carbohydrates observed in some patients.

Association of SAD with reduced pharmacological agents does not exclude other possible causes. It is certainly possible that diagnosis of SAD encompasses a variety of disorders associated with several causes. Evidence for a genetic predisposition is also undergoing investigation and cannot be eliminated as a contributing factor. At least one study using adult twins has suggested that nearly 30 percent of SAD cases may have a genetic basis.

DIAGNOSIS OF SAD

Diagnosis is based on the description of the disorder as updated in the *Diagnostic and Statistical Manual of Mental Disorders: DSM-IV-TR* (rev. 4th ed., 2000). According to the manual, the presence of five specific symptoms typical of depression constitutes the criteria for diagnosis; these symptoms must have been present during a two-week interval prior to diagnosis. Symptoms include general daily depression, loss of interest in normal activities, significant loss of appetite, fatigue, insomnia, decreased ability in thinking or reasoning, and thoughts of suicide or death. To be diagnosed with SAD, the patient must exhibit among the symptoms either depression or loss of interest in normal activities. To

DSM-IV-TR CRITERIA FOR SEASONAL AFFECTIVE DISORDER

SEASONAL PATTERN SPECIFIER FOR MOOD DISORDERS

Specify with Seasonal Pattern

Can be applied to pattern of Major Depressive Episodes in the following:
- Bipolar I Disorder
- Bipolar II Disorder
- Major Depressive Disorder, Recurrent

Regular temporal relationship between the onset of Major Depressive Episodes in Bipolar I or Bipolar II Disorder or Major Depressive Disorder, Recurrent, and a particular time of the year (such as regular appearance of Major Depressive Episode in fall or winter)

Cases excluded involving an obvious effect of seasonal-related psychosocial stressors (such as regularly being unemployed every winter)

Full remissions (or change from depression to mania or hypomania) also occur at a characteristic time of the year (for example, depression disappears in spring)

In the last two years, two Major Depressive Episodes have occurred demonstrating temporal seasonal relationships and no nonseasonal Major Depressive Episodes have occurred

Seasonal Major Depressive Episodes substantially outnumber nonseasonal Major Depressive Episodes that may have occurred over individual's lifetime differentiate SAD from other forms of depression, these symptoms must exhibit a seasonal pattern that has been experienced over a period of at least three years, with at least two of these periods occurring consecutively. Two forms of SAD have been described. The more common type, affecting approximately 15 percent of the population at some period within their lifetime, is referred to as fall-onset or winter depression. Generally this form appears in late fall and lasts until the following spring. A less common form of SAD is typically a spring-onset form of depression. This form generally lasts throughout the summer into the following season.

Regardless of the form of SAD, for diagnostic purposes the depressed person must experience the beginning and ending of the depression during the sixty-day window of time at both the beginning and the ending of the seasons. The patient must not have been diagnosed with other forms of depression, though the incidence of SAD appears highest among patients with a history of mood disorders.

TREATMENT

Historically, light therapy or phototherapy has been the principal method of treatment for SAD. Studies have repeatedly shown that exposure of patients to bright light, at least 2,500 lux, has had some success in relieving the depression associated with the disorder. Such phototherapy sessions have generally consisted of two to four hours of exposure per day; similar results have been observed if the light intensity is increased to 10,000 lux, using treatment sessions as short as thirty minutes.

The major advantage of phototherapy is that it represents a nonpharmacological approach to treatment of the problem. However, as many as one-third of the patients exhibiting SAD do not respond to light therapy. Frequently, those patients who responded least well were those suffering from the highest degree of depression. The inclusion of negative air ionization in conjunction with light therapy has resulted in some degree of success with such patients.

A variety of pharmacological agents have been developed for treatment of SAD patients who show no response to conventional treatments. These includeSelective serotonin reuptake inhibitorsselective serotonin reuptake inhibitors (SSRIs) such as fluoxetine, paroxetine, and sertraline. Trials have been most successful when using these agents in combination with phototherapy, rather than either treatment alone.

EPIDEMIOLOGY OF SAD

Boyce and Parker, two Australian scientists, studied SAD in the Southern Hemisphere. Since the Southern Hemisphere has weather patterns reversed from those in the Northern Hemisphere, and since holidays occurring during the winter in the Northern Hemisphere occur during the summer in the Southern Hemisphere, these researchers were able to reproduce Northern Hemisphere studies systematically while eliminating the possible influence of holidays, such as Christmas. Their findings support those of their colleagues in the Northern Hemisphere. There is a dependable pattern of depression beginning during autumn and early winter and ending in the late spring and early summer. The incidence of SAD is significantly greater in North America than in Europe, suggesting a possible genetic or climatic influence on appearance of the disorder.

It is important to study the prevalence of SAD to understand how many people are affected by it. Kasper and others investigated the prevalence of SAD in Montgomery County, Maryland, a suburb of Washington, D.C. The results of their study suggested that between 4.3 percent and 10 percent of the general population is affected to some extent. Mary Blehar and Rosenthal report data from research in New York City that between 4 percent and 6 percent of a clinical sample met the criteria for SAD. More significantly, between 31 percent and 50 percent of people responding to a survey reported changes to their life that were similar to those reported by SAD patients. There are strong indications that the overall prevalence rate for SAD is between 5 percent and 10 percent of the general population. As much as 50 percent of the population may experience symptoms similar to but less intense than those of SAD patients.

Prevalence studies have found that the female-to-male ratio for SAD is approximately 4 to 1.Gender differencesseasonal affective disorder The age of onset is about twenty-two. The primary symptoms of SAD overlap with other diagnoses that have a relatively high female-to-male ratio. For example, people diagnosed with winter depression frequently crave carbohydrate-loaded foods. In addition to carbohydrate-craving obesity, there is another serious disorder, bulimia nervosa, which involves binging on high-carbohydrate foods and has a depressive component. Bulimia nervosa is much more common in females than it is in males.

While most of the research has focused on SAD in adults, it has also been found in Childrenseasonal affective disorderchildren. Children affected with SAD seem to experience a significant decrease in their energy level as their primary symptom rather than the symptoms seen in adults. This is not unusual; in many disorders, children and adults experience different symptoms.

The winter variant of SAD is much more common than the summer variant. It appears that winter depression is precipitated by the reduction in light that accompanies the onset of winter. As a result, it is also quite responsive to phototherapy. Summer depression, the summer variant of SAD, is precipitated by increases in humidity and temperature associated with the summer months. This suggests a different (and currently unknown) mechanism of action for the two variations.

The importance of light in the development and treatment of the winter variant of SAD has been demonstrated in a variety of studies worldwide. The general finding is that people living in the higher latitudes are increasingly susceptible to SAD in the winter.

EARLY HISTORY OF SAD

The observation that seasons affect people's moods is not new. Hippocrates, writing in 400 b.c.e., noted in section 3 of his "Aphorisms" that, "Of natures (temperaments?), some are well- or ill-adapted for summer, and some for winter." What Hippocrates noticed (and many others since have noticed) is that there are differences in the way people experience the various seasons. Summer and winter are the most extreme seasons in terms of both light and temperature and, not surprisingly, are the seasons in which most people have problems coping.

As noted above, the physician Cook, on an expedition to Antarctica in 1898, noted that the crew experienced symptoms of depression as the days grew shorter. This same report (mentioned by Wehr and Rosenthal) revealed that "bright artificial lights relieve this to some extent." Emil Kraepelin reported in 1921 that approximately 5 percent of his patients with manic-depressive illness (bipolar disorder) also had a seasonal pattern to their depressions. The data from antiquity to the present strongly favor the existence of a form of mood disturbance associated with seasonal variation. Just as the observation of seasonal variations in mood and behavior dates back to antiquity, so does the use of light as a treatment. Wehr and Rosenthal report that light was used as a treatment nearly two thousand years ago. Not only was light used but also it was specified that the light was to be directed to the eyes.

In summary, seasonal affective disorder seems to have some degree of relationship to carbohydrate-craving

obesity, bulimia nervosa, bipolar disorder, and premenstrual syndrome. It affects women more often than men and is more frequently seen covarying with winter than with summer. The winter variant is probably caused by changes in light; it is more severe in the higher latitudes. The summer variant seems to be attributable to intolerance of heat and humidity and would be more prevalent in the lower latitudes. Whether the cause is related to variation in circadian rhythms, abnormal levels of neurotransmitters, genetics, or combinations of these, reduced exposure to sunlight appears to be a major contributor.

BIBLIOGRAPHY

Boyce, Philip, and Gordon Parker. "Seasonal Affective Disorder in the Southern Hemisphere." *American Journal of Psychiatry* 145, no. 1 (1988): 96-99. This study surveyed an Australian sample to determine the extent to which the people experienced symptoms of seasonal affective disorder and to see if the pattern was similar to that of people in the Northern Hemisphere. The results are presented as percentages and are easily understood. Addresses the issue of separating holidays from climatic changes and presents a table of symptoms for seasonal affective disorder.

Kasper, Siegfried, Susan L. Rogers, Angela Yancey, Patricia M. Schulz, Robert A. Skwerer, and Norman E. Rosenthal. "Phototherapy in Individuals with and Without Subsyndromal Seasonal Affective Disorder." *Archives of General Psychiatry* 46, no. 9 (1989): 837-844. This study extends research into seasonal variants of affective disorder to people who have less intense forms. Addresses issues of the difficulty of establishing adequate experimental control and practical implications for people with these disorders.

Kasper, Siegfried, Thomas A. Wehr, John J. Bartko, Paul A. Gaist, and Norman E. Rosenthal. "Epidemiological Findings of Seasonal Changes in Mood and Behavior." *Archives of General Psychiatry* 46, no. 9 (1989): 823-833. A thorough description of the major prevalence study on seasonal affective disorder. The statistics are fairly advanced, but the authors' use of figures and tables makes the results understandable. An extensive reference list is provided.

Lam, R. W. "An Open Trial of Light Therapy for Women with Seasonal Affective Disorder and Comorbid Bulimia Nervosa." *Journal of Clinical Psychiatry* 62, no. 3 (2001): 164-168. A discussion of the use of light therapy in the treatment of two of the more common psychiatric/mood disorders.

Partonen, Timo, ed. *Seasonal Affective Disorder: Practice and Research*. New York: Oxford University Press, 2001. Emphasis is on the clinical disorder of SAD. The first portion of the book deals primarily with presentation of the illness in a clinical situation; the second half of the text addresses research into SAD, including evidence for its physiological basis.

Rohan, Kelly J. *Coping with the Seasons: A Cognitive Behavioral Approach to Seasonal Affective Disorder Workbook*. New York: Oxford University Press, 2009. For the layperson, a simple but thorough description of "winter blues" and guidelines on how to deal with SAD symptoms.

Rosenthal, Norman E. *Winter Blues: Seasonal Affective Disorder—What It Is and How to Overcome It*. Rev. ed. New York: Guilford Press, 2006. A thorough description of SAD by an expert in the field. The author describes the clinical patterns associated with various degrees of the disorder.

Singer, Ethan. "Seasonal Affective Disorder: Autumn Onset, Winter Gloom." *Clinician Reviews*, November, 2001. The author provides an updated overview of the condition. In addition to epidemiological references, various physiological explanations for the disorder are discussed, as well as alternative treatments.

Wileman, S., et al. "Light Therapy for Seasonal Affective Disorder in Primary Care." *British Journal of Psychiatry* 178 (2001): 311-316. A clinical description of the disorder that includes a summary of the most popular method of treatment as well as a discussion of the efficacy of light therapy.

Wurtman, Richard J., and Judith J. Wurtman. "Carbohydrates and Depression." *Scientific American* 260 (January, 1989): 68-75. The authors provide a good review of seasonal affective disorder and the relationships that may exist between it and maladaptive behaviors. They also review the more important theories about the cause and treatment of seasonal affective disorder.

James T. Trent; updated by Richard Adler

SEE ALSO: Abnormality: Biomedical models; Bipolar disorder; Circadian rhythms; Depression; Genetics and mental health; Placebo effect.

Self

TYPE OF PSYCHOLOGY: Personality; Developmental psychology; Social psychology; Consciousness

The self is a term that is widely used and variously defined. It has been examined by personality theorists as a central structure. Social cognitive psychology has explored the individual and interpersonal processes that influence such dimensions as self-systems, self-concept, self-consciousness, and self-efficacy. Recent research has challenged psychologists to rethink concepts of the self.

KEY CONCEPTS
- Being-in-the-world
- Identity
- Identity crisis
- Narrative
- Self-awareness
- Self-concept
- Self-efficacy
- Self-in-relation
- Self-system
- Subjectivity

INTRODUCTION

The concept of the self was invoked in Western thought long before the advent of the discipline of psychology. During the Renaissance and Enlightenment, scholars often depicted humans as having a soul, spirit, or metaphysical essence. The famous argument by French Renaissance philosopher René Descartes, "I think, therefore I am," placed its fundamental confidence in the assumption that the "I"—an active, unique identity—could be directly experienced through introspection and therefore trusted to exist. Descartes's dualistic formulation of the mind-body relation set the stage for a number of assumptions about the self: that the self is an active, unitary, core structure of the person that belongs to and is consciously accessible to the individual.

During the Enlightenment, empiricist and associationist philosophers retained mind-body dualism but emphasized the material, objectively observable behaviors of the body, with more stress on observable information, as seen in the rephrasing of Descartes by Scottish philosopher David Hume: "I sense, therefore I am." William James, philosopher and founder of American scientific psychology, recognized that the personal experience of one's own stream of consciousness—the sense of "I" or subjectivity—is fleeting and fluid and less measurable than the objective "me" with its body, relationships, and belongings. However, he considered the self to be made up of both subjective and objective components, a perspective reflected in the various theories of the self present in contemporary psychology.

Many psychologists believe that there is an internal self in potentia that takes shape and grows as long as an adequate environment is provided. Others emphasize a social component, suggesting that a person's sense of self develops directly out of interpersonal interactions.

PSYCHOANALYTIC AND PSYCHODYNAMIC THEORIES

Sigmund Freud, Austrian founder of psychoanalysis at the turn of the twentieth century, had little use in his tripartite theory of the psyche for the idea of self as one's central identity. He conceptualized the ego as an important but secondary structure that mediates between the instincts of the id and the strictures of the superego. However, other psychodynamic theorists of the first half of the twentieth century returned to the idea of a center of personality. Carl Jung, a Swiss psychiatrist, thought of the self as an important archetype—an energized symbol in the collective unconscious—that organizes and balances the contradictory influences of other archetypes and in fact transcends opposing forces within the psyche. The archetype is an inborn potential, while its actual development is informed by personal experiences. Karen Horney, a German psychiatrist, believed that each individual is born with a real self, containing healthy intrinsic potentials and capabilities. However, because of basic anxiety and a belief that one is unlovable, some individuals become alienated from their real selves and pursue an unrealistic idealized self. Margaret Mahler, Hungarian-born pediatrician and psychoanalyst, described the separation-individuation process of the first three years of life, by which a child achieves individual personhood through psychologically separating from other people.

In contrast, Harry Stack Sullivan, an American psychiatrist, believed that personality and self can never be fully disconnected from interpersonal relations. His concept of the self-system is thus a set of enduring patterns of relating to others that avoids anxiety by striving for others' approval (the "good-me"), avoiding their disapproval (the "bad-me"), and dissociating from whatever causes their revulsion (the "not-me"). Heinz Kohut, Austrian founder of self psychology, also stressed that healthy selfhood is only attained through satisfying, empathically attuned interactions between infants and caregivers. Caregivers initially provide the self with a sense of goodness and strength and are therefore termed self-objects. The healthy self then develops its own ambitions, ideals, and skills, while deprivation from self-objects results in an injured self.

DEVELOPMENTAL THEORIES

While these psychodynamic theorists focused on the emotional and relational dimensions of early development, others, such as German-born Erik H. Erikson, who trained in psychoanalysis with Anna Freud, also emphasized cognitive and identity development over the entire life span. Erikson's theory of the stages of development, in which the ego confronts a series of psychosocial crises, recognized such childhood stages as autonomy versus shame and doubt, initiative versus guilt, and industry versus inferiority as important to ego development. However, it was his conceptualization of the identity crisis during adolescence that has been highly influential on contemporary research on self-concept and self-esteem. By searching out and eventually choosing life strategies, values, and goals, the adolescent establishes a sense of inner assuredness and self-definition, which serves to promote healthy intimacy, productivity, and integration later in life. James Marcia, an American developmental psychologist, demonstrated in the 1960s, 1970s, and 1980s that adolescents who actively explore the question "Who am I?" and achieve their own sense of identity are more likely to have positive outcomes, including high self-esteem, self-direction, and mature relationships. Erikson, Marcia, and other developmental scholars recognize that the task of establishing identity can be facilitated or hampered by the values and traditions presented in families and social structures.

HUMANISTIC AND EXISTENTIAL PERSPECTIVES

Since the 1920s, humanistic and existential traditions have focused on the human being as a whole, and division into parts or structures is resisted insofar as it leads to dehumanizing the person. Thus, the self as such is often renamed or deemphasized in these theories. Gordon Allport, an American psychologist, used the concept of "proprium" to describe the unique, holistic organization of personality and awareness that develops over the life span, culminating in ownership of one's own consciousness in adulthood. American psychologist Carl R. Rogers also deemphasized the role of self, which he thought was merely one differentiated aspect of one's phenom-enological, conscious experience. Rogers's self-image was a complex representation of the total organism as perceived through self-reflection. Abraham Maslow, an-other American psychologist, proposed that one of the most advanced human needs was the pull to be true to one's own nature. While he called this pull "self-actu-alization," he did not theorize the self to be a central structure but a unique range of capacities, talents, and activities.American existentialist psychologist Rollo May suggested that instead of thinking of a person as having a central, internal self that is separated from the world, a person should be considered to be a being-in-the-world (Dasein in German), who is in all ways related to the physical and especially the social environment.

THE SELF AS A REGULATOR OF INDIVIDUAL PROCESSES

Beginning in the 1950s and accelerating through the turn of the twenty-first century, much research on per-sonality has moved away from extensive personality theo-ries toward empirically testable hypotheses. Models of the self focus on describing and observing the mental mechanisms by which individuals moderate and control their internal processes and their interactions with the world within specific social traditions and expectations.

Albert Bandura, the American founder of social cog-nitive psychology, conceptualizes the person as part of an interactive triad consisting of individual, behavior, and environment. Like radical behaviorism, social cog-nitive theory assumes that all human behavior is ulti-mately caused by the external environment. However, Bandura also describes individuals as having cognitions with which they regulate their own behavior, through the establishment of guiding performance standards. His idea of the self-system consists of internal motiva-tions, emotions, plans, and beliefs that are organized into three processes: self-observation, judgmental processes, and self-reaction. In self-observation, the individual con-sciously monitors his or her own behavior and describes it. Through judgmental processes, values are placed on the observations, according to personal standards inter-nalized from past experience and comparisons to others. The self-reaction is the self-system's way of punishing, rewarding, changing, or continuing with renewed moti-vation the behavior that has been self-observed.

Bandura's concept of self-observation has been further refined in research on self-awareness, self-conscious-ness, and self-monitoring. American social psychologists such as Robert Wicklund, Arnold Buss, Mark Davis, and Stephen Franzoi have defined self-awareness as a state of focusing attention on oneself, while self-consciousness is defined as a traitlike tendency to spend time in the state of such self-awareness. Most such research distinguishes between private self-awareness or self-consciousness, in which a person attends to internal aspects of self such as thoughts and emotions, and public self-awareness or self-consciousness, in which a person attends to external aspects of self that can be observed by others, such as appearance, physical movements, and spoken words. Private self-awareness and self-consciousness have been associated with intense emotional responses, clear self-knowledge, and actions that are consistent with one's own attitudes and values. Self-monitoring is related pri-marily to public self-consciousness and is described by American psychologist Mark Snyder as the tendency to engage in attempts to control how one is perceived in social interactions. Snyder's research suggests that high self-monitors use current situations to guide their reac-tions more than do low self-monitors, which can lead to the relationships of high self-monitors being dependent on situations or

Social cognitive theory has also directed research on self-efficacy, the belief that one will be capable of using one's own behavior, knowledge, and skills to master a situation or overcome an obstacle. For example, Bandura showed in 1986 that people in recovery from a heart at-tack were more likely to follow an exercise regimen when they learned to see themselves as having physical efficacy. Perceived self-efficacy was demonstrated throughout the 1980s and 1990s as contributing to a wide range of behaviors, from weight loss to maternal competence to managerial decision making.

A final theme coming to prominence since the 1970s relates to identity and self-concept. Self-concept has been defined by American psychologist Roy Baumeister as one's personal beliefs about oneself, including one's at-tributes and traits and one's self-esteem, which is based on self-evaluations. American developmental psycholo-gists such as Jerome Kagan, Michael Lewis, and Jeanne Brooks-Gunn found that by their second year, children become capable of recognizing and cognitively repre-senting as their own their actions, intentions, states, and competencies. With further development, people ap-pear to form not one unitary self-concept but a collec-tion of self-schemas or ideas about themselves in relation to specific domains such as school or work. American psychologist Hazel Markus has also found time to be a relevant dimension of self-concept, in that persons develop possible selves: detailed concepts of who they hope and fear to become in the future.

Identity is defined as who a person is, including not only the personal ideas in the self-concept but also the public perceptions of a person in his or her social context (for instance, birth name or roles in cultural institutions). Identity consists of two major features: continuity or sameness of the person over time, and differentiation of the person as unique compared to others and groups of others. As mentioned with regard to Erikson's theory and Marcia's research, adolescence has been demonstrated to be a primary stage for exploring the values, beliefs, and group memberships that constitute identity. However, identity continues to evolve during adulthood with changes in roles (such as student versus parent) and activities (work versus retirement).

NEUROPSYCHOLOGICAL PERSPECTIVES

From a neuropsychological perspective, brain functions underlie all dimensions and activities of the self. Yet an important question is how the functioning of biophysical structures such as the brain and the nervous system can give rise to the self, which can be consciously experienced, either directly or through its activity. This question relies on the same mind-body problem that first arose with Descartes. One solution to this mental-physical divide proposed by such neuroscientists as Australian Sir John Eccles and Hungarian-born Michael Polanyi is the concept of emergent systems, or marginal control of lower systems by the organizational rules of higher systems. As the nervous system evolved into a complex set of structures, neural circuitry gained a concomitant complexity of organized functioning such that a new property, consciousness, emerged. This emergent property has capabilities and activities (such as the experience of mental images) that are a result of the organization of neural patterns but are not reducible to its component neural parts, much as water molecules have different qualities from those of hydrogen and oxygen atoms alone. Yet consciousness and thus experience of the self are necessarily embodied in and constrained by these patterned brain and biological processes.

Thus, the sense of self as having continuity relies on the capacity of several structures of the brain (such as the hippocampus and specialized areas of the association cortex) for forming, storing, and retrieving personal memories, as well as representations of background bodily and emotional states. A specific self-concept, as explored in social cognitive research, can only be developed through the organizational capacity of the prefrontal cortex to self-observe and construct cognitive schemas. The prefrontal cortex is also involved in carrying out many actions attributed to the self, such as the planned action of self-efficacy and the techniques of presenting the self in a particular light, as in self-monitoring. Research such as that by Antonio Damasio, an American neurologist, indicates that when normal functioning of specific neural circuits is disturbed, deficits also occur in these experiences of self as knower and owner of mental and physical states. For example, with anosognosia, damage to the right somatosensory cortices impairs a person's ability to be aware of damage to the body or associated problems in the functioning of the self. The body itself may become completely disowned by the person, and the unified sense of "me" is fractured.

CULTURE AND GENDER DIFFERENCES

Empirical and theoretical scholarship since the 1970s has presented alternatives to the universality of the self across culture and gender and has challenged the utility of the construct as heretofore defined. Humans' experiences of self have been found to vary substantially across cultures and gender, especially regarding the importance of independence and separation versus interdependence and relationship. For example, American psychologist Markus, Japanese psychologist Shinobu Kitayama, and their colleagues found in their 1991 and 1997 studies that the concept of an individualized self as uniquely differentiated from others is descriptive of Americans' psychological experience. In contrast, Japanese personal experience is often more consistent with collective, relational roles, a conclusion that has been replicated with other predominantly collectivist cultures.

Feminist psychologists working at the Stone Center in Massachusetts have drawn on the developmental psychological work of Americans Nancy Chodorow and Carol Gilligan, observing that many women find the notion of a discrete and individualized self places too much emphasis on separation between people. This research group proposed the concept of self-in-relation to capture the extent to mwhich one's core sense of being is defined by one's relationships with and commitments to other individuals. Likewise, as American developmental psychologist Mary Field Belenky and her colleagues interviewed women about their learning processes, they found that the sense of self as an individual, separate knower and speaker is only one stage of development.

The individualist stage is often followed by respect for the ways one's subjectivity is informed by empathy and intimacy with others. These empirical observations suggest that theories of the self should attend more carefully to the interplay of individual and interpersonal or social experience.

POSTMODERN, DIALOGICAL, AND NARRATIVE THEORIES

The advancement since the 1970s of postmodernism has led many psychologists to recognize that persons construct their own realities through social rules, roles, and structures. Kenneth Gergen, an American social psychologist, proposes that the self gains its unity and identity from the consistency of the social roles a person plays. He points out that the more a person's roles multiply and conflict, as is common in fast-paced technological societies, the less cohesive and the more obsolete the concept of self becomes.

New Zealand-born cognitive psychologist Rom Harré and American psychologists Edward Sampson and Frank Richardson have each advanced alternative theories in which the concept of self is still viable but that emphasize the necessity of recognizing the multiplicity of perspectives within a self. Drawing on the sociological traditions of symbolic interactionism, especially the looking-glass self of American sociologists George Herbert Mead and Charles Cooley, these theorists see the self as constructed only through intimate involvement in interpersonal interaction and especially language, which allow one to reflect on oneself and create the social bonds that define one as a self. The unique and specific manner with which one articulates one's self appears to reflect not only one's culture and social audience but also one's beliefs and commitments about identity.

American developmental psychologist Dan McAdams has led research on the narratives people tell to describe and explain their lives to themselves and others, concluding that the linguistic construction of the self is a continuous and central task of the entire life span. Jerome Bruner, an American cognitive psychologist, suggested that through narrative, the various dimensions of self—public and private, structure and activity—become interrelated in meaningful stories and serve to promote both the growth of the individual and the survival of human culture.

BIBLIOGRAPHY

Bak, Waclaw. "Self-Standards and Self-Discrepancies: A Structural Model of Self-Knowledge." *Current Psychology* 33.2 (2014): 155–73. Print.

Bandura, Albert. "The Self-System in Reciprocal Determinism." *American Psychologist* 33 (1978): 344–58. Print.

Coburn, William J., ed. *Transformations in Self Psychology.* Hoboken: Taylor, 2013. Print.

Damasio, Antonio R. *Descartes' Error: Emotion, Reason, and the Human Brain.* New York: Penguin, 2005. Print.

Derlega, Valerian J., Barbara A. Winstead, and Warren H. Jones. *Personality: Contemporary Theory and Research.* 3rd ed. Belmont: Wadsworth, 2005. Print.

Gana, Kamel. *Psychology of Self-Concept.* Hauppauge: Nova Science, 2012. Print.

Gergen, Kenneth J. *The Saturated Self.* New York: Basic, 2000. Print.

Hall, Calvin S., Gardner Lindzey, and John B. Campbell. *Theories of Personality.* 4th ed. New York: Wiley, 1998. Print.

Kitayama, Shinobu, Hazel Rose Markus, Hisaya Matsumoto, and Vinai Norasakkunkit. "Individual and Collective Processes in the Construction of the Self: Self-Enhancement in the United States and Self-Criticism in Japan." *Journal of Personality and Social Psychology* 72.6 (1997): 1245–1267. Print.

Lewis, Michael, and Jeanne Brooks-Gunn. *Social Cognition and the Acquisition of Self.* New York: Plenum, 1979. Print.

Martin, Raymond, and John Barresi. *The Rise and Fall of Soul and Self: An Intellectual History of Personal Identity.* New York: Columbia UP, 2008. Print.

Snodgrass, Joan Gay, and Robert L. Thompson, eds. *The Self Across Psychology.* New York: New York Academy of Sciences, 1997. Print.

Stevens, Richard. *Understanding the Self.* Thousand Oaks: Sage, 1997. Print.

Mary L. Wandrei

SEE ALSO: Analytic psychology: Jacques Lacan; Analytical psychology: Carl Jung; Attitude-behavior consistency; Cognitive psychology; Consciousness; Crosscultural psychology; Crowd behavior; Death and dying; Ego psychology: Erik H. Erikson; Ego, superego, and id; Gender differences; Gender identity formation; Identity crises; Intimacy; Introverts and extroverts; James, William; Maslow, Abraham; May, Rollo; Multiple personality; Personality theory; Philosophy and psychology; Projection; Psychoanalytic psychology and personality: Sigmund Freud; Selfactualization; Self-disclosure; Self-efficacy; Self-esteem; Self-perception theory; Self-presentation; Social identity theory; Social psychological models: Erich

Fromm; Social psychological models: Karen Horney; Thought: Study and measurement.

Self-actualization

TYPE OF PSYCHOLOGY: Personality

Self-actualization, a constructive process of functioning optimally and fulfilling one's potentials, is perhaps the central concept and most influential model within humanistic psychology. The self-actualization theory and model have had important applications in the fields of counseling, education, and business and hold significant implications for basic conceptions of humankind and for society.

KEY CONCEPTS
- Actualizing tendency
- Existentialism
- Humanistic psychology
- Organismic theory
- Phenomenology
- Self
- Synergy

INTRODUCTION

Self-actualization—as a concept, a theory, and a model—has extended the domain and impact of psychology. Humanistic psychology—a branch of psychology that emphasizes growth and fulfillment, autonomy, choice, responsibility, and ultimate values such as truth, love, and justice—has become an important paradigm for understanding personality, psychopathology, and therapy. Applications have been extensive in education, counseling, religion, and business. Suggesting action and implying consequences, self-actualization holds clear and significant implications regarding the dimensions of psychology, the basic conception of humankind, and the functions and organization of society.

Self-actualization is often defined as a process of growing and fulfilling one's potential, of being self-directed and integrated, and of moving toward full humanness. The most complete description of the self-actualizing person has been provided by the psychologist Abraham Maslow, who devoted much of his professional life to the study of exceptional individuals. Maslow abstracted several ways in which self-actualizing people could be characterized.

CHARACTERIZING SELF-ACTUALIZERS

Compared with ordinary or average persons, self-actualizing persons, as Maslow describes them, may be characterized as follows: They show a more efficient and accurate perception of reality, seeing things as they really are rather than as distortions based on wishes or neurotic needs. They accept themselves, others, and nature as they are. They are spontaneous both in behavior and in thinking, and they focus on problems outside themselves rather than being self-centered. Self-actualizing persons enjoy and need solitude and privacy; are autonomous, with the ability to transcend culture and environment; have a freshness of appreciation, taking pleasure and finding wonder in the everyday world; and have peak experiences or ecstatic, mystic feelings that provide special meaning to everyday life. They show social interest, which is a deep feeling of empathy, sympathy, identification, and compassionate affection for humankind in general, and have deep interpersonal relationships with others. They carry a democratic character structure that includes humility, respect for everyone, and an emphasis on common bonds rather than differences; they distinguish between means and ends, and they possess a clear sense of ethics. Self-actualizers have a philosophical and unhostile sense of humor, and they are creative and inventive in an everyday sense. They are resistant to enculturation, with a degree of detachment and autonomy greater than that found in people who are motivated simply to adjust to and go along with their own in-groups or society. Their value system results from their great acceptance of self and others and easily resolves or transcends many dichotomies (such as work/pleasure, selfish/unselfish, good/bad) that others view as absolute opposites.

Carl R. Rogers, another influential humanistic psychologist, characterized the fully functioning person in ways that parallel Maslow's description. Rogers's theory holds that people have an actualizing tendency, which is an inherent striving to actualize, maintain, and enhance the organism. When people function according to valuing processes based within them and are therefore following their actualizing tendency, experiences can be accurately symbolized into awareness and efficiently communicated. Thus, according to Rogers, full humanness involves openness to experiences of all kinds without distorting them. People thus open to experience will show a flexible, existential kind of living that allows change, adaptability, and a sense of flow. These people trust their own internal feelings of what is right, and they use the self as their basis for and guide to behavior. Rogers, like Maslow, holds that such people do not necessarily adjust or conform to cultural prescriptions, but nevertheless they do live constructively.

Rogers, Maslow, and most self-actualization theorists present an optimistic and favorable view of human nature. Unlike Sigmund Freud and classical psychoanalysts, who believed humans to be basically irrational and human impulses to require control through socialization and other societal constraints, self-actualization theorists regard human nature as constructive, trustworthy, positive, forward moving, rational, and possessing an inherent capacity to realize or actualize itself.

POSITIVE AND NEGATIVE REACTION

Although Maslow approached his study of growing individuals from a somewhat more absolute, rational theoretical perspective than Rogers, who came from a more relativistic, phenomenological, and clinical direction, the theorizing and empirical observations of both psychologists converge on a similar description of a self-actualizing or a fully functioning person who makes full use of capacities and potentialities. Such descriptions have aroused much positive as well as negative reaction. One reason is the implicit suggestion that humankind can or should be self-actualizing. The values of actualizing one's self—of fulfilling one's potentials and possessing the characteristics described by Maslow and Rogers—are always implied. Thus, self-actualization is more than a psychological construct; it becomes a possible ethic. Many humanistic proponents have viewed values as necessary in their theorizing; Maslow made an impassioned plea that values, crucial to the development of humanistic psychology, be integrated into science.

Critics of self-actualization theory have argued that it reflects the theorists' own values and individualist ideology; that it neglects sociohistorical and cultural changes by being rooted in unchanging biology; that there may be social-class or cultural bias in the descriptions; that the concept may be misused and encourage the creation of a cultural aristocracy of "superior" people; and that many people may well choose an ideal self that does not match Maslow's characterization. In addition, critics have misunderstood the concept by erroneously thinking that self-actualizing is synonymous with selfishness and self-indulgence or is consistent with asocial or antisocial behavior. In fact, Maslow and Rogers described self-actualizers as not being overly concerned with themselves, but as typically engaged in larger issues and problems such as poverty, bigotry, warfare, and environmental concerns; as having a highly ethical nature; and as having relationships with others that have a positive and even therapeutic quality.

The various criticisms and arguments surrounding self-actualization have led to clarifications and improvements in understanding the concept, and they attest to the vitality of this major, provocative, and influential psychological construct.

A POSITIVE GROWTH MODEL

Self-actualization presents a growth model that can be and has been used in diverse areas such as counseling, education, and business. In addition, there are implications for people's way of conceptualizing humankind and for structuring institutions and organizing society.

As a model for therapists and counselors and their clients, self-actualization is an alternative to the medical or illness model, which implies that the person coming to the therapist is beset by disease and requires a cure, often from some external source or authority. The self-actualization model represents a positive process, a fostering of strengths. It is concerned with growth choices, self-knowledge, being fully human, and realizing one's potential; yet it also encompasses an understanding of anxiety, defenses, and obstacles to growth. Psychological education, facilitation of growth, self-help and self-learning, and counseling to deal with problems of living and with dysfunctional defenses all are implied in the self-actualization model for human fulfillment and actualization of potentials. This model also avoids problems associated with an adjustment model, in which therapists may socialize conformity or adjustment to a particular status quo or societal mainstream.

Rogers employed the model in his nondirective, person-centered therapy, later called the person-centered approach. Grounded in trust and emphasizing the therapist's unconditional positive regard, empathy, and genuineness, this therapy system allows the client's natural and healthy growth tendencies and organismic valuing processes to determine choices and behaviors. Much research has supported the importance of these therapist characteristics and has documented the increased congruence and process of growth of clients, beginning with Rogers's own empirical research explorations. Rogers's approach to counseling has become one of the most influential in the psychotherapy field.

USE IN WORKPLACE MANAGEMENT

Maslow's application of self-actualization theory to management represents another very influential contribution. Douglas McGregor described a humanistic theory of management (theory Y) that respects human rights and treats workers as individuals. This theory was contrasted with theory X, a managerial view that holds that people dislike work and must therefore be controlled, coerced, conditioned, or externally reinforced to obtain high work productivity. Maslow's own book on management assumes the existence of higher needs in all workers that, if met in the world of work, would demonstrate the inherent creativity and responsibility of workers and result in greater satisfaction, increased self-direction, and also greater work productivity. Many influential management theorists, including McGregor, Rensis Likert, and Chris Argyris, have acknowledged Maslow's influence. Many field and research studies have supported the value of the self-actualization model as applied to management. Maslow contended that such enlightened management policies are necessary for interacting with a growing, actualizing population; in the world of work, as elsewhere, the highest levels of efficiency can be obtained only by taking full account of the need for self-actualization that is present in everyone.

EXAMINING SYNERGIC SOCIETIES

One of the major conclusions and implications stemming from the self-actualization model is that a synergic society can evolve naturally from the present social system; such a society would be one in which every person may reach a high level of fulfillment.

Ruth Benedict tried to account for differences in societies that related to the overall human fulfillment they could afford their citizens. She prepared brief descriptions of four pairs of cultures. One of each pair was an insecure society, described as nasty, surly, and anxious, with low levels of moral behavior and high levels of hatred and aggression. The contrasting culture was a secure one, described as comfortable, showing affection and niceness. The concept of synergy differentiated these two groups. In high-synergy societies, social arrangements allowed for mutually reinforcing acts that would benefit both individual people and the group; these societies were characterized by nonaggression and cooperation. In low-synergy societies, the social structure provided for mutually opposed and counteractive acts, whereby one individual could or must benefit at the expense of others;

these were the cultures in which aggression, insecurity, and rivalry were conspicuous.

Roderic Gorney described how the absolute amount of wealth in a society did not determine the degree of synergy or quality of life in that society. More crucial, he found, were the economic arrangements within the society—whether the resources were concentrated among a "have" group (low synergy) or were dispersed widely to all (high synergy). Gorney argued that low-synergy arrangements in societies promoted higher levels of aggression and mental disorder. Thus, to minimize aggression and mental disorder and to promote self-development and zestful investment in living and learning, Gorney specified that a society should increase the degree of synergy fostered by its institutions.

Thus, the self-actualization model and theory have clear implications for societies and their political and economic structures. The model suggests action and implies consequences. It stresses a particular type of relationship between the society and the individual as a social being. The commingling of individual and social concerns and involvements translates self-actualization theory into practical consequences and is precisely what Maslow described as characterizing his self-actualizers. Self-actualizing people easily resolve superficial dichotomies, and choices are not inevitably seen as "either/or." Work and play, lust and love, self-love and love for others need not be opposites. Maslow described the individual-societal holism by noting that self-actualizing people were not only the best experiencers but also the most compassionate people, the great reformers of society, and the most effective workers against injustice, inequality, and other social ills.

Thus, what self-actualization theory suggests is an integration of self-improvement and social zeal; Maslow held that both can occur simultaneously.

INFLUENCES AND CONTRIBUTORS

The development of the self-actualization concept was influenced by many sources. Carl Jung, Otto Rank, and Alfred Adler, departing from Freud's classical psychoanalytic formulations, emphasized the importance of individuality and social dimensions. Jung, credited with being the first to use the term "self-actualization," developed the concept of the self as a goal of life; self-actualization meant a complete differentiation and harmonious blending of the many aspects of personality. Rank emphasized the necessity of expressing one's individuality to be creative. Adler described self-actualization motives with the concept of striving for superiority or for perfection; this innate striving, or great upward drive, was a prepotent dynamic principle of human development. Adler also believed that a constructive working toward perfection (of self and society) would result from a loving, trustworthy early social environment.

Kurt Goldstein, the first psychologist who explicitly used self-actualization as the master motive or most basic sovereign drive, was a leading exponent of organismic theory; this approach emphasized unity, consistency, coherence, and integrity of normal personality. Goldstein held self-actualization to be a universal phenomenon; all organisms tend to actualize their individual capacities and inner natures as much as possible. Prescott Lecky also propounded the achievement of a unified and self-consistent organization as the one developmental goal; his concepts of self-consistency and unified personality have much in common with organismic theory. Later, Gordon Allport stressed methods for studying the unique and undivided personality; he described motivation for normal adults as functionally autonomous, and in the individual's conscious awareness. Fritz Perls's Gestalt therapy emphasized here-and-now awareness and integrated personality.

Sociology and cultural anthropology influenced other theorists. Karen Horney spoke of the real self and its realization; Erich Fromm wrote of the "productive orientation," combining productive work and productive love; and David Riesman described the autonomous person and theorized about inner- and other-directed personalities. Arthur Combs and Donald Snygg, influenced by the phenomenological approach, emphasized the maintenance and enhancement of the self as the inclusive human need motivating all behavior. Their description of the adequate self is quite similar to the contemporary description of self-actualization.

Existentialist views (existential psychology), emphasizing the present, free will, values and ultimate concerns, and subjective experience as a sufficient criterion of truth, influenced conceptualizing about self-actualization. Rollo May's description of existential being is important in this respect.

From all these sources came the backdrop for the modern description of self-actualization: the emphasis on the uniqueness of the individual; a holistic, organismic, and phenomenological approach to human experience and conduct; and the need to discover a real self and to express, develop, and actualize that self.

BIBLIOGRAPHY

Goble, Frank G. *The Third Force: The Psychology of Abraham Maslow*. New York: Pocket, 1978. Print.

Gold, Joshua M. "Spirituality and Self-Actualization: Considerations for Twenty-First-Century Counselors." *Journal of Humanistic Counseling* 52.2 (2013): 223–34. OmniFile Full Text Mega (H.W. Wilson). Web. 30 June 2014.

Johnson, David R. *Reaching Out: Interpersonal Effectiveness and Self-Actualization*. 11th ed. Upper Saddle River: Pearson, 2014. Print.

Jones, Alvin, and Rick Crandall, eds. "Handbook of Self-Actualization." *Journal of Social Behavior and Personality* 5 (1991). Print.

LeDoux, Joseph. *Synaptic Self: How Our Brains Become Who We Are*. New York: Penguin, 2003. Print.

Maslow, Abraham Harold. *Motivation and Personality*. 3rd ed. New York: Harper, 1987. Print.

Maslow, Abraham Harold. *Toward a Psychology of Being*. 3rd ed. New York: Wiley, 1999. Print.

Poorsheikhali, Fatemah, and Hamid Alavi. "Correlation of Parents' Religious Behavior with Family's Emotional Relations and Students' Self-Actualization." *Journal of Religion and Health Preprints* (2014): 1–7. E-Journals. Web. 30 June 2014.

Rogers, Carl R. *A Way of Being*. Boston: Houghton Mifflin, 1995. Print.

Sullivan, Bob, and Herbert H. Thompson. *Getting Unstuck: Break Free of the Plateau Effect*. New York: Penguin, 2014. Print.

Edward R. Whitson

SEE ALSO: Abnormality: Psychological models; Existential psychology; Gestalt therapy; Humanistic psychology; Humanistic trait models: Gordon Allport; Maslow, Abraham; May, Rollo; Person-centered therapy; Self-efficacy; Self-esteem; Workplace issues and mental health.

Self-disclosure

TYPE OF PSYCHOLOGY: Social psychology

Self-disclosure is the process of revealing personal information during communication with others. Progress in self-disclosure depends on personal skills and interpersonal intimacy; appropriate self-disclosure is important in communicating effectively and maintaining healthy close relationships.

KEY CONCEPTS
- Interdependence
- Intimacy
- Loneliness
- Reciprocity
- Social penetration

INTRODUCTION

Self-disclosure is the process of communicating personal information to another individual. It involves a willingness to reveal intimate thoughts and feelings rather than superficial or obvious characteristics. Scientists studying personal relationships have found that, as two people become acquainted and interact over time, they reveal more of themselves to each other. For example, when two people first know each other, their conversation may be limited to the weather, mutual interests, and similarly "safe" topics. The topics they discuss are neutral, and the feelings they express are matters of public knowledge. As their relationship develops, they feel comfortable disclosing more intimate feelings and experiences. Later in their friendship, their conversation may be entirely about their feelings, personal problems, and other experiences that are not public knowledge. Self-disclosure is the process by which communication in a relationship becomes more private and intimate.

The term "self-disclosure" was introduced by psychologist Sidney Jourard in his 1964 book *The Transparent Self: Self-Disclosure and Well-Being*. Early work by therapists and researchers speculated that self-disclosure is essential for the health and growth of personal relationships; however, not all self-disclosures serve to promote relationships. Disclosures can be distinguished as either appropriate or inappropriate. Healthy intimacy is promoted when one's self-disclosure suits the time and the place as well as the relationship. When two people are close friends, for example, it is appropriate for them to reveal personal information or feelings to each other.

In contrast, confessing intimate feelings or confiding personal experiences to a stranger or mild acquaintance is often considered inappropriate. Personal revelations are often too intimate for those interactions. Such inappropriate self-disclosure may elicit withdrawal or rejection by others. Self-disclosure can also be inappropriate because it is not intimate enough. For example, if two long-time friends converse about their lives and one refuses to tell the other about a problem because it is somewhat personal, the other may feel rejected or slighted.

Because of their history as friends, personal confidences are appropriate, while nondisclosure is not.

LEVELS OF COMMUNICATION

The quality of self-disclosure was considered in the 1973 book *Social Penetration: The Development of Interpersonal Relationships*, by Irwin Altman and Dalmas Taylor. Altman and Taylor argued that, as a relationship develops, communication between partners increases in two qualities or dimensions: breadth and depth. Breadth increases before depth. Communication becomes broader as partners add more topic areas to their conversation. Eventually the two people's communication also deepens: Their interaction becomes less superficial and more intimate. For example, two people whose early friendship is based on a common interest in music will discover other things in common (greater breadth) as they communicate. Eventually, they not only talk about what they mutually enjoy but also confide in each other and help each other solve problems (greater depth).

Altman and Taylor argue that most relationships develop in a more satisfactory way when self-disclosure proceeds (breadth before depth) over time; however, not all individuals conform to this model. For example, some persons are low revealers, unable to proceed to more personal levels of communication over time. Others are high revealers, indiscriminately disclosing too much to others, irrespective of the exact relationships or interactions between them. Disclosing too little prevents a relationship from becoming more intimate and may result in its termination. Disclosing too much signals intrusiveness rather than intimacy, and it usually causes others to withdraw rather than to respond with equal intimacy.

Healthy self-disclosure adheres to a norm of reciprocity—the expectation that partners will exchange disclosures, taking turns revealing similar levels of intimacy. For example, if one partner confides to the other, "I am worried that I might not succeed in reaching this goal," the other can reciprocate by admitting similar feelings or understanding the fear of failure. It would not be reciprocal to change the subject or offer superficial reassurance such as, "I know you will do just fine." Self-disclosure is risky, because it makes the revealer more vulnerable to the confidant's rejection or ridicule. Reciprocal self-disclosure establishes trust, since partners are confiding on similar levels and their knowledge of each other is balanced.

As relationships develop, Altman has argued, immediate reciprocity becomes unnecessary, because trust has already been established. Thus, long-time friends can have nonreciprocal conversations without threatening their level of intimacy.

In a particular interaction, one partner may confide while the other listens without reciprocating. They both know that their roles can be reversed in some future conversation. Disclosure depends on the style as well as the content of communication. An individual may wish to discuss a personal problem or concern with a friend but not know how to express himself or herself effectively. The complaint, "Sometimes things can be very hard for a person to deal with," is more vague and less disclosing than the statement, "I feel very frustrated and need help solving a problem." In this example, the former disclosure is closed and impersonal while the latter is more open and personal. To be open and personal, self-disclosing statements should be relevant to the immediate situation, expressed in personal terms ("I feel" rather than "People say"), specifically addressed to the listener, clearly explanatory rather than vague or hinting, and specific rather than general.

ROLE IN RELATIONSHIPS

Differences in patterns of self-disclosure can account for differences in relationship development, conflict, personal distress, and loneliness. Individual differences in self-disclosure—the fact that some people are high revealers and others low revealers—help explain why some relationships become more intimate while others never progress. For example, a low revealer may feel unable to reciprocate when a new friend confides a secret or problem. The nondiscloser may be unsure of the other's response to a personal revelation, fearful of rejection, or unable to express himself or herself. The friend who has confided in the nondiscloser is left feeling unsatisfied or mistrustful by the lack of response and may discourage future interactions.

In contrast, a high revealer's indiscriminate disclosures can offend others. Overdisclosing to a stranger can cause him or her to withdraw and terminate any further interaction. Even friends can be disturbed by a high revealer's willingness to confide inappropriately to others besides themselves. Their own confidences in the overdiscloser may also seem to be at risk. Differences in people's willingness and ability to engage in self-disclosure can affect the success and development of their relationships.

Research and theory on self-disclosure contribute to a larger body of work on communication in close relationships. The study of relationships combines the observations and perspectives of social psychology, sociology, counseling, and communication studies. Early work in this multidisciplinary field focused on how relationships begin, including motivations for affiliation and factors in interpersonal attraction. Researchers have since turned their attention to relationship development and maintenance, processes dependent on the quality and quantity of partners' communication. Self-disclosure is a central goal of intimate communication. An understanding of self-disclosure and its role in developing and maintaining intimacy is essential to improving and stabilizing the significant relationships in people's lives.

EXCEPTIONS TO SELF-DISCLOSURE RULES

Two kinds of interactions may appear to violate the rules of developing self-disclosure: brief intimate encounters and love at first sight. In the first case, a brief interaction with a stranger involves unusually deep self-disclosure. Psychologist Zick Rubin has dubbed this the Fort Lauderdale phenomenon, for the Florida city that is a popular destination for spring vacation travel. A college student on vacation may feel less inhibited about self-disclosure with others encountered there, because he or she will not see any of these people again. Thus, high levels of self-disclosure are possible because no future relationship is anticipated.

In love at first sight, two people may become quickly and mutually attracted and communicate intimately with each other with the intention of maintaining their relationship in the future. Altman and Taylor warn, however, that the two individuals have no history of communication, so no trust has been established between them. The risk of conflict is high, and conflict is likely to be more destructive than if the relationship had been established more gradually. Thus, disclosing too much too fast can doom a relationship even when disclosure is reciprocal and when both partners have similar motives.

ROLE IN PSYCHOLOGICAL WELL-BEING

The relationship between psychological adjustment and quantity or amount of self-disclosure has been explored by Valerian Derlega and Alan Chaikin in their 1975 book *Sharing Intimacy: What We Reveal to Others and Why.* Derlega and Chaikin suggest that adjustment is a curvilinear (changing) function of self-disclosure, rather than a linear (constant) one. A person's adjustment does not continually increase as the amount that he or she self-discloses increases. Initially, as self-disclosure increases from low to medium levels, adjustment also improves—up to a point. Beyond that optimal point, increasing from medium to high self-disclosure actually reduces psychological adjustment. In other words, disclosing too much can interfere with a person's well-being and relationship success.

Self-disclosure is important to psychological well-being. Friends value being able to talk to and be themselves with each other. Intimacy involves more than being honest and revealing secrets, however; it is possible to express oneself about personal concerns without participating in an intimate relationship. For example, one may keep a diary or confide in a pet. There are also some relationships that have no expectation of reciprocity. A patient or client must describe personal experiences and feelings to a physician or psychotherapist without expecting him or her to respond in kind. In these contexts, it is helpful to be able to express oneself honestly without fear of rejection or criticism. Research evidence confirms that the process of articulating and confiding one's concerns significantly helps in coping with stress and trauma. Diaries and professional relationships are not a substitute for real intimacy, however; genuine intimacy is an outcome of communication within relationships, not of one-sided expression. Confiding in others who are willing to listen is essential to gaining the benefits of social support.

ISSUES OF INTIMACY

Personal relationships are based on interdependence—the reliance of both parties on joint outcomes. Reciprocity in self-disclosure represents a mutual investment that builds such interdependence. Withholding a confidence at one extreme and overdisclosing at the other are both hindrances to satisfactory intimacy. People who fail to establish and maintain intimacy with others experience loneliness. Loneliness is defined as the experience of inadequate or insufficient relationships. People feel lonely when they have fewer relationships than are wanted or when existing relationships fail to meet their needs. A pattern of inappropriate or inexpressive self-disclosure can ultimately lead one to experience chronic loneliness.

Training in social skills may help those who suffer the consequences of unsatisfactory relationships or loneliness. Individuals could be taught, in psychotherapy or support groups, to modify their self-disclosure. Overdisclosers could become selective in choosing their confidants, and low revealers could learn how to express themselves more openly and personally. Like other relationship skills, self-disclosure requires motivation and competence but contributes to better communication and higher self-esteem.

INFLUENCES AND EVOLUTION OF STUDY

Research on self-disclosure was influenced by the human potential movement of the 1960s and 1970s. Early theorists such as Jourard argued that it is important to be able to reveal aspects of oneself to a few significant others. Work by Altman and Taylor and by Derlega and Chaikin extended the concept of self-disclosure into the context of personal relationships and communication. Work conducted in the 1970s and 1980s explored the ways people choose topics and levels in disclosing to others. Self-disclosure has come to be regarded more as an aspect of interpersonal communication than of self-development. Whether a disclosure is appropriate depends on the relationship of the discloser to the listener and on the expectations of both individuals.

Altman and Taylor's theory of social penetration recognizes that self-disclosure involves changes in both the quantity and quality of intimate communication. Later research has concentrated on identifying the qualities of appropriate and healthy communication. An understanding of how self-disclosure is developed and how it contributes to communication is important in the study of close relationships; identifying problems in self-disclosure can lead to solving those problems. Research on loneliness has led to the development of social-skills training programs. Similarly, self-disclosure skills can be improved with education based on an understanding of intimate communication.

BIBLIOGRAPHY

Adler, Ronald B., Lawrence B. Rosenfeld, and Neil Towne. *Interplay: The Process of Interpersonal Communication*. 11th ed. New York: Oxford UP, 2009. Print.

Altman, Irwin, and Dalmas A. Taylor. *Social Penetration: The Development of Interpersonal Relationships*. New York: Holt, 2006. Print.

Brehm, Sharon S. *Intimate Relationships*. 4th ed. New York: McGraw-Hill, 2006. Print.

Brewer, Gayle, Loren Abell, and Minna Lyons. "Machiavellianism, Competition, and Self-Disclosure in Friendship." *Individual Differences Research* 12.1 (2014): 1–7. Print.

Derlega, Valerian, Sandra Metts, Sandra Petronio, and

Steven Margulies, eds. *Self-Disclosure.* Thousand Oaks: Sage, 1993. Print.

Duck, Steve. *Relating to Others.* 2nd ed. Buckingham: Open UP, 1999. Print.

Eunjung Lee. "A Therapist's Self-Disclosure and Its Impact on the Therapy Process in Cross-Cultural Encounters: Disclosure of Personal Self, Professional Self, and/or Cultural Self?" *Families in Society* 95.1 (2014): 15–23. Print.

Knapp, Mark L., and Anita L. Vangelisti. *Interpersonal Communication and Human Relationships.* 6th ed. Boston: Allyn, 2009. Print.

Stoltz, Molly, Raymond W. Young, Kevin L. Bryant. "Can Teacher Self-Disclosure Increase Student Cognitive Learning?" *College Student Journal* 48.1 (2014): 166–72. Print.

Voncken M., and K. Dijk. "Socially Anxious Individuals Get a Second Chance after Being Disliked at First Sight: The Role of Self-Disclosure in the Development of Likeability in Sequential Social Contact." *Cognitive Therapy and Research* 37.1 (2013): 7–17. Print.

Ann L. Weber

SEE ALSO: Affiliation and friendship; Coping: Social support; Emotional expression; Intimacy; Psychotherapy: Goals and techniques; Rational emotive therapy; Self; Self-presentation.

Self-efficacy

DATE: 1970's forward

TYPE OF PSYCHOLOGY: Cognition; Learning; Motivation; Personality

Self-efficacy, a central concept in Albert Bandura's social cognitive theory, is one's belief or lack of belief that one can bring about a particular outcome or change. It has been shown to play an important role in a wide range of human endeavors.

INTRODUCTION

Self-efficacy is a person's belief that he or she can (or cannot) successfully organize and execute an action to achieve a desired outcome in a particular situation. According to psychologist Albert Bandura, a person's self-efficacy will strongly influence how that person approaches a task or goal. For example, if a woman has a strong belief that she can learn new dance steps, she will be more likely to say yes when asked if she wants to learn a new dance. She will also be more likely to persevere if at first she is not successful. However, if her belief in her ability to draw is weak, she will be less likely to say yes when asked if she wants to draw some pictures with her friends, and even if she agrees to try, she will be more likely to become frustrated and quit if she encounters difficulties. Thus, self-efficacy is situation specific. Although self-efficacy is situation specific, Bandura refers to a person's total set of self-efficacies as an individual's coping self-efficacy. Individuals with a strong coping self-efficacy will persevere even when faced with the most difficult circumstances because they have learned how to cope with initial failure.

LEARNING THEORY HISTORY

During the first half of the twentieth century, the psychological study of learning yielded three major principles: contingency, effect, and expectancy. Contingency was first demonstrated in Ivan Petrovich Pavlov's study, in which a dog learned to salivate at the sound of a buzzer that preceded the release of food. The law of effect was initially formulated by Edward L. Thorndike, when he noticed that the animals he studied would learn to repeat the behaviors that were rewarded.

Unlike contingency and effect, expectancy provides a cognitive explanation for behavior. Its initial proponent was Edward C. Tolman, who believed that an organism's behavior is based on what it expects to happen if it performs a particular action. Tolman believed that the simple stimulus-response connections that Pavlov and Thorndike used to explain behaviors were inadequate to explain complex behavioral choices. Tolman did not believe that organisms just reacted to a situation based on their past learning history. Instead, he argued that an organism's behavior is guided by its beliefs about the best way to achieve a desired goal, although the organism's beliefs are informed by its past stimulus-response history.

Bandura's concept of self-efficacy is a descendent of Tolman's expectancy principle. Bandura's social cognitive theory has become one of the most researched learning theories. According to his theory, although people can learn through direct experience, they also learn by observing the consequences of the behaviors of others and through symbolic modeling, such as when they read about characters in a book. From these direct and vicarious experiences, people learn abstract rules, such as "It is not good to hurt other people," that they can generalize to use in entirely new situations. This can lead to unpredictable, creative solutions to new situations.

Self-efficacy is an important part of Bandura's social cognitive theory. People with high self-efficacy for a particular action believe that they have the ability to exert control over their environment, at least in a particular situation. People's self-efficacies will affect what they choose to learn, how well they will learn it, and whether they will stick with it or give it up. In other words, these self-efficacies will affect how people interact with their world

CAUSES OF SELF-EFFICACY

According to Bandura, experiences of personal mastery most enhance the development of self-efficacy. The experience of having successfully learned something in the past will most likely cause people to believe that similar learning can be done again.

Another source of acquiring self-efficacy comes from observing others. The act of observing another person successfully complete a task causes people to believe that they can also learn to do the task. A third source of acquiring self-efficacy comes from other people's verbal encouragements or discouragements. If people who have no experience at a particular task are told by others that they can (or cannot) do the task, they tend to believe what they are told and develop a high or low self-efficacy in response.

Physiological factors can influence self-efficacy. For example, when people with low self-efficacy regarding a specific task attempt to accomplish that task, they may experience fear or anxiety, plus accompanying physiological symptoms such as nausea or shaking of the hands. These negative signals from the body may further reduce their self-efficacy. However, in a situation in which people have strong self-efficacy, they may ignore similar symptoms because they know that these symptoms will not prevent successful learning.

SELF-EFFICACY AND THOUGHT PATTERNS

A person's self-efficacy can influence the individual's thoughts. For example, if people with low self-efficacy visualize failing at a particular task, their already low self-efficacy may fall further. When these people are faced with the actual task, their lowered self-efficacy ensures defeat, acting like a self-fulfilling prophesy brought about by self-doubts.

Self-efficacy can be influenced by a person's understanding of the concept of ability. For example, if people believe that ability is an acquirable skill, they will be

more likely to take on a challenging task. Mistakes do not deter them because they think of mistakes as part of the learning process. However, if people believe that ability is inherited or innate, they will be less likely to take on a task because each mistake confirms their lack of ability. It would be easier to simply avoid such ego-threatening experiences.

The feedback that people receive about their performance affects their understanding of ability. When people are told that they did not perform as well as others, their self-efficacy drops, but when people are told that their performance improved, their self-efficacy increases.

SELF-EFFICACY, MOTIVATION, AND COPING

People are more likely to pursue and spend time and effort on goals for which they have high self-efficacy. Also, people are more likely to persevere in the face of failure when they have high self-efficacy.

When a person with low self-efficacy experiences difficulties, stress and anxiety may ensue. Stress and anxiety can impair performance, lowering self-efficacy even more. However, people who are high in what Bandura called coping self-efficacy are more capable and comfortable taking on threatening tasks, in which they will probably experience a great deal of failure, because they are not overcome by anxiety. They are confident in their ability to cope with difficult situations. These people believe that they are in control of their lives, while the people with low coping self-efficacy believe that their lives are out of their control. These beliefs become self-fulfilling prophesies because they influence how each person interacts with the world.

THE IMPACT OF SELF-EFFICACY

People select activities and situations they believe that they can handle. Therefore, self-efficacy plays an important role in the competencies people develop, the interests they pursue, and the social networks they grow—in short, self-efficacy plays a crucial role in who people become. Bandura and others have written extensively about the impact of people's self-efficacy on their achievement in academics, sports, and business; on their career choices; on their physical and mental health; and on their personality development over their life spans.

Many useful interventions have been created by Bandura and others that can be used to increase a person's self-efficacy. These interventions improve the quality of the recipients' lives by allowing them to achieve more and to feel better about themselves and more confident in their abilities.

POSSIBLE CULTURAL DIFFERENCES

Bandura makes a distinction between personal efficacy and collective efficacy. The former refers to an individual's belief in the potency of his or her own actions, while the latter refers to a group's belief in the potency of its actions. According to Bandura, group success depends on high collective efficacy. If group members do not believe in the group's capacity to succeed, they will not be motivated to act.

Although people may work more for group goals in collectivist societies, Bandura believed that beliefs in personal efficacy are as just as important for productivity in collectivist societies as they are in individualistic societies. In either type of society, if someone has low self-efficacy, Bandura believed that person will exert less effort.

However, four studies in 2001 conducted by Steven Heine and his associates uggest that self-efficacy may operate differently in traditionally collectivist cultures. In their studies, Japanese participants who failed at a task persisted much more than those who had succeeded at the same task. The American and Canadian participants who failed, however, showed less persistence, as predicted by previous self-efficacy research.

To explain these results, the authors suggested that Westerners selectively attend to the positive aspects of themselves and work hard on improving them, while Easterners selectively attend to the negative aspects of themselves and work hard on improving them. For example, if an Asian woman believes she is a capable dancer, she may choose to invest less energy in dancing so as not to stick out. There is an old Eastern saying that the tall flower gets cut down. However, if the Asian woman's class at school is working on a mural and the woman does not believe that she is good at drawing, then she may feel that her poor drawing efforts are letting her classmates down. Subsequently, she may work extra hard on her drawing. It appears that more cross-cultural research is needed to uncover how self-efficacy operates in different cultures.

BIBLIOGRAPHY

Bandura, Albert. *Self-Efficacy in Changing Societies.* New York: Cambridge UP, 1995. Print.

Bandura, Albert. *Self-Efficacy: The Exercise of Control.* New York: Freeman, 1997. Print.

Britner, Shari, ed. *Self-Efficacy in School and Community Settings.* New York: Nova Science, 2012. Print.

Changxiu Shi, and Xiaojun Zhao. "The Influence of College Students' Coping Styles on Perceived Self-Efficacy in Managing Inferiority." *Social Behavior and Personality: An International Journal* 42.6 (2014): 949–58. Print.

Eisenberger, Joanne, Marcia Conti-D'Antonio, and Robert Bertrando. *Self-Efficacy: Raising the Bar for All Students.* 2nd ed. Larchmont: Eye On Education, 2005. Print.

Heine, Steven J., et al. "Divergent Consequences of Success and Failure in Japan and North America: An Investigation of Self-Improving Motivation." *Journal of Personality and Social Psychology* 81.4 (2001): 599–615. Print.

Roos, Sarah M., Johan C. Potgieter, and Michael Q. Temane. "Self-Efficacy, Collective Efficacy and the Psychological Well-Being of Groups in Transition." *Journal of Psychology in Africa* 23.4 (2013): 561–67. Print.

Sedikides, Constantine, Lowell Gaertner, and Jack L. Vevea. "Pancultural Self-Enhancement Reloaded: A Meta-analytic Reply to Heine." *Journal of Personality and Social Psychology* 89.4 (2005): 539–51. Print.

Tolman, Edward C. *Purposive Behavior in Animals and Man.* 1972. Reprint. New York: Appleton-Century-Crofts, 1987. Print.

George B. Yancey

SEE ALSO: Attitude formation and change; Bandura, Albert; Cognitive social learning: Walter Mischel; Conditioning; Coping: Strategies; Groups; Learning; Multicultural psychology; Pavlov, Ivan Petrovich; Social learning: Albert Bandura; Stress: Behavioral and psychological responses; Stress: Physiological responses; Thorndike, Edward L.; Tolman, Edward C.

Self-esteem

TYPE OF PSYCHOLOGY: Social psychology

Self-esteem research examines how individuals come to feel about and perceive themselves. Psychologists seek to understand how self-esteem develops and what can be done to change negative views of the self once they have been established..

KEY CONCEPTS
- Attributions
- Identity negotiation
- Inheritable traits
- Self-concept
- Self-efficacy
- Self-esteem

INTRODUCTION

"Self-esteem" is a term with which almost everyone is familiar, yet it is not necessarily easily understood. Psychologist William James gave the first clear definition in 1892 when he said that self-esteem equals success divided by pretensions. In other words, feelings of self-worth come from the successes an individual achieves tempered by what the person had expected to achieve. If the person expected to do extremely well on an exam (his or her pretensions are quite high) and scores an A, then his or her self-esteem should be high. If, however, the person expected to do well and then scores a D, his or her self-esteem should be low.

This important but simplistic view of self-esteem started a movement toward a better understanding of the complex series of factors that come together to create the positive or negative feelings individuals have about who they are. Once a person has developed a self-concept (a global idea of all the things that define who and what a person is), that person is likely to exhibit behaviors that are consistent with that self-concept. If a young woman believes that she is a good tennis player, then she is likely to put herself in situations in which that factor is important. Once she behaves (in this case, plays her game of tennis), she is likely to receive feedback from others as to how she did. This feedback determines how she will feel about her tennis-playing ability. Over time, these specific instances of positive or negative feedback about tennis-playing ability will come together to create the more global feelings of positivity or negativity a person has about the self in general.

Even though an individual may believe that she is good at tennis, her ability may not live up to those expectations, and she may receive feedback telling her so (for example, losing in the early rounds of a tournament). In this case, the individual may come to feel somewhat negative about her tennis ability. If this continues to happen, she will adjust her view of her ability and come to believe that she is not a good tennis player after all. To the extent that the person truly wanted to be good, this realization can cause her to feel quite negative about all aspects of

her self. When this happens, the person is said to have developed low self-esteem.

ROLE OF ATTRIBUTIONS

The reality of how self-esteem develops, however, is more complicated than this example demonstrates. People do not always accept the feedback that others offer, and they may believe that their failure means nothing more than having an off day. To understand the impact that success and failure will have on self-esteem, it is important to understand the kinds of attributions people make for their successes and failures. When a person succeeds or fails, there are three levels of attributions that can be made for explaining the occurrence. First, the individual must decide if the event occurred because of something internal (something inside caused it to happen) or something external (something in the environment caused it to happen). Second, it must be decided whether the event occurred because of a stable factor (since it happened this time, it will happen again) or a temporary circumstance (it probably will not happen again). Finally, it must be decided whether the event occurred because of something specific (this failure resulted because of poor tennis ability) or something global (failure resulted at this undertaking because of lack of ability to do anything).

It is easy to see that the kinds of attributions individuals make for their successes and failures will have a profound impact on how a particular event influences their self-esteem. If a decision is made that a failure at tennis occurred because of something internal (lack of ability), stable (the ability will never be present), and global (lack of any ability), then a failure is going to damage self-esteem severely. Self-esteem is created through the blending of expectations for success, actual levels of success, and the kinds of attributions made for why success or failure occurred.

CYCLIC PERPETUATION

Once positive or negative self-esteem has developed, it will perpetuate itself in a cycle. If a person believes that he is a failure, he may put himself into situations in which he is destined to fail. If he does not think he can succeed, he may not put forth the amount of effort that success would require. Similarly, if a person believes that he is a success, he will not let one little failure cause him to change his entire opinion of his self. Self-esteem, once it is created, is very difficult to change. If a person dislikes who he is, yet someone else tries to tell him that he is wonderful, he probably will not believe that person. More likely, he will wonder what this person could possibly want from him that the person is willing to lie and be so nice to get it. On the other hand, if the person feels positive about himself, a single instance of failure will be written off as bad luck, poor effort, or a simple fluke. A negative self-esteem cycle, once it gets started, is very difficult to change, and learning how to break this cycle is the single greatest challenge to self-esteem therapists.

UNDERSTANDING NEGATIVE SELF-ESTEEM

Understanding self-esteem has considerable practical importance in daily life. If it is believed that all successes come from external sources (luck or someone else's effort), then good things coming from others can be seen as an attempt to degrade the individual or offer a bribe. People feeling this way relate to others in a judgmental way and cause them to turn away. When others turn away, the person takes it as a signal that he or she was correct about his or her unworthiness, and the negative self-esteem level is perpetuated.

If this negative self-esteem cycle is to be broken, it is important to convince the person of the critical point made by George Herbert Mead. According to Mead, self-esteem is a product of people's interpretation of the feedback that they receive from others. A person with low self-esteem often misinterprets that feedback. If someone with low self-esteem is told, "You look really nice today," he or she is likely to misinterpret that to mean, "You usually look terrible; what did you do different today?"

Ralph Turner has said that the self is not fixed and that the person with low self-esteem must be convinced that he or she is not at the mercy of a self: He or she can be, and is, the creator of a self. It helps to put the person into a situation in which he or she can succeed with no possibility for the wrong attributions to be made. If a person cannot read, this failure will generalize to other situations and is likely to be considered a stable and global deficiency. If this person is taught to read, however, even a person with low self-esteem would find it difficult to argue that the success was situational. In this way, the person begins to see that he or she can take control and that failures need not be catastrophic for the other self-conceptions he or she might hold.

A person with negative self-esteem can be difficult to help. It takes more than the providing of positive feedback to assist such a person. Imagine a series of circles, one inside the other, each one getting smaller. Take that smallest, innermost circle and assign it a negative value. This represents an overall negative self-esteem. Then assign negative values to all the outer circles as well. These represent how the person feels about his or her specific attributes.

If positive messages are directed toward a person with negative values assigned to all these layers of self-esteem, they will not easily penetrate the negative layers; they will be much more likely to bounce off. Negative messages, on the other hand, will easily enter the circles and will strengthen the negativity. Penetration of all the negative layers can, however, sometimes be achieved by a long-term direction of positive and loving messages toward the person with low self-esteem. In effect, the innermost circle, that of global self-esteem, will eventually be exposed. Self-esteem can then be improved if enough positive, loving messages can be directed at the level of the person's global self-esteem. This can be a long-term process, partly because as soon as the person's negative self-image comes into serious question, confusion about his or her identity results; living in self-hate, although often painful, is still more secure than suddenly living in doubt.

Once the negative signs have been replaced with positive ones, the new self-esteem level will be as impervious to change as the negative one was. Now, when the person enters a situation, he or she will have more realistic expectations as to what he or she can and cannot do. The person has been taught to make realistic attributions about success and failure. Most important, the individual has been taught that one need not succeed at everything to be a worthy person. James suggested in 1892 that striving does as much to alleviate self-esteem problems as actual success. Once the individual is convinced that setting a goal and striving rather than not trying at all is all it takes to feel good about him- or herself, the person is truly on the way to having high self-esteem.

IMPORTANCE OF CHILDHOOD AND ADOLESCENCE

An interest in self-esteem developed along with interest in psychological questions in general. Early psychologists such as Sigmund Freud, Carl Jung, James, and others realized that an important part of what makes individuals think and act the way they do is determined by the early experiences that create their sense of self and self-esteem. A very important aspect of psychological inquiry has been asking how and why people perceive and interpret the same event so differently. Self-esteem and self-concept play a big role in these interpretations. Knowing an individual's self-esteem level helps one to predict how others will be perceived, what kind of other individuals will be chosen for interaction, and the kinds of attitudes and beliefs the person may hold.

An understanding of childhood development and adolescence would be impossible without an understanding of the forces that combine to create a person's sense of self-esteem. Adolescence has often been described as a time of storm and stress because the teenager is trying to negotiate an identity (create a sense of self and self-esteem that he or she would like to have). Teenagers' own wishes and desires, however, are not the only things they must consider. They are receiving pressure from parents, peers, and society as a whole to be a certain kind of person and do certain kinds of things. Only when self-esteem development is fully understood will it be known how to alleviate some of the trials and tribulations of adolescence and ensure that teenagers develop a healthy and productive view of their worth.

ROLE IN CONTEMPORARY SOCIETY

The role of self-esteem will probably be even greater as psychological inquiry moves ahead. Contemporary society continues to tell people that if they want to succeed, they have to achieve more. Yet economic downturns and increasing competition make it even more difficult for young people to live up to those expectations and feel good about who they are. The role that psychologists with experience in self-esteem enhancement training will play in the future cannot be overemphasized. For adults to lead healthy, productive, and satisfied lives, they must feel good about who they are and where they are going. This requires an intimate understanding of the factors that combine to create people's expectations for success and the likelihood that they will be able to achieve that level of success. Self-esteem development must be kept in mind in helping young people create for themselves a realistic set of expectations for success and an ability to make realistic attributions for why their successes and failures occur.

BIBLIOGRAPHY

Butler, Gillian. *Overcoming Social Anxiety and Shyness: A Self-Help Guide Using Cognitive Behavioral Techniques*. New York: Basic, 2008. Print.

Coopersmith, Stanley. *The Antecedents of Self-Esteem.* Palo Alto: Consulting Psychologists, 1990. Print.

DeMarree, Kenneth G., and Kimberly Rios. "Understanding the Relationship between Self-Esteem and Self-Clarity: The Role of Desired Self-Esteem." *Journal of Experimental Social Psychology* 50 (2014): 202–09. Print.

Jones, Warren H., Jonathan M. Cheek, and Stephen R. Briggs. *Shyness: Perspectives on Research and Treatment*. New York: Plenum, 1986. Print.

Kernis, Michael. *Efficacy, Agency, and Self-Esteem*. New York: Plenum, 1995. Print.

Rosenberg, Morris. *Society and the Adolescent Self-Image*. Reprint. Collingdale: DIANE, 1999. Print.

Sharma, Shraddha, and Surila Agarwala. "Contribution of Self-Esteem and Collective Self-Esteem in Predicting Depression." *Psychological Thought* 6.1 (2013): 117–23. Print.

Sorensen, Marilyn. *Breaking the Chain of Low Self-Esteem*. 2nd ed. Sherwood: Wolf, 2006. Print.

Zeigler-Hill, Virgil, et al. "The Status-Signaling Property of Self-Esteem: The Role of Self-Reported Self-Esteem and Perceived Self-Esteem in Personality Judgments." *Journal of Personality* 81.2 (2013): 209–20. Print.

Randall E. Osborne

SEE ALSO: Affiliation and friendship; Attitude formation and change; Child abuse; Identity crises; James, William; Positive psychology; Self; Self-efficacy; Self-perception theory; Social perception.

Self-help groups

TYPE OF PSYCHOLOGY: Social psychology

Self-help groups provide an environment in which individuals with a common problem or interest can gather and discuss issues, share experiences, and assist one another with coping strategies. Groups may be led by peers or a mental health professional and may be disease-centered or situationally driven. Because participants have common problems, they find immediate acceptance and understanding. Cognitive restructuring as a result of the group process provides stress relief and enables participants to deal with the issues at hand.

KEY CONCEPTS
- Asynchronous self-help group
- Community of experiences
- Empathetic understanding
- Enhanced self-esteem
- Learned coping skills
- Social learning theory
- Synchronous self-help group

INTRODUCTION

A self-help group, also called a mutual help, mutual aid, or support group, is a gathering of individuals with a shared topic of interest, an issue, or a problem. Groups may be disease-related (for example, Alcoholics Anonymous or Parents of Children with Schizophrenia) or related to a situation such as bereavement or the stress of care-giving. Groups may be led by a mental health professional, but most self-help groups provide peer-to-peer support with a moderator who is a member of the group. Most self-help groups are free of charge to participants and are limited in size to facilitate enhanced interaction.

Groups provide social support by creating a shared community of experiences among members. Participants obtain experiential knowledge from peers who have gone through similar situations and, through trial and error, have determined the best action to take to address an issue. The ideal group is composed of experienced members who can assist newer members with expected challenges over time. The experienced members become role models for their peers, validating the social learning theory that learning can occur within a social context. Members who share experiences may eel a sense of normalcy within the group as it provides a sense of commonality that may not be present in their daily lives. Empathetic understanding occurs when experiences are shared. Comparing situations to those of others and finding them similar creates an environment of safety and security. Members who help others within the group find their self-esteem enhanced by the realization that their experiences are useful learning tools for other participants.

Self-help groups vary in success and effectiveness based on the members of the group and the skill of the moderator. There are many psychosocial processes that occur within self-help groups. Acceptance of others, catharsis, enhanced self-esteem, information sharing, learned coping strategies, openness, and self-disclosure are all examples of behaviors that may occur in healthy self-help groups. In less effective groups, members may have a sense of unrest, fail to recognize when a participant needs professional intervention, and learn bad behaviors from peers, leading participants to ignore professional mental health advice when needed. Selecting the appropriate self-help group is critical to obtaining benefits from the activity.

SELECTING A SELF-HELP GROUP

To select a self-help group, a patient may seek the assistance of a physician or health care professional. Different types of groups are available in most communities. The most common types are weekly groups that meet in an easily accessible location and are free of charge for attendees, but fee-based groups conducted by professionals are also available in many communities. It is important to understand that self-help groups are not group therapy and cannot replace prescribed group therapy. Groups such as Alcoholics Anonymous may be listed in the telephone book. Workshops with a specific focus may also be available on an interim basis and are often advertised in local newspapers or online. These are generally fee based and focus on a particular topic such as smoking cessation. Self-help groups can also be found by contacting local or national agencies.

Once a self-help group is selected, an ongoing evaluation of the group interaction and applicability to the member is important. Attendance on a regular basis will benefit the participant, assuming that the group is a healthy and effective one. The group should have a sense of structure but not to the point that the format feels rigid, the environment should feel safe and secure, and members should be respectful to one another. Learning opportunities should exist, and members should leave the group on a weekly basis feeling better than when they arrived. If at any point, participants feel uncomfortable in the group, they should discuss their feelings with the moderator and determine if leaving the group is necessary.

ALTERNATIVES TO TRADITIONAL FORMATS

An alternative to attending a weekly group is an online self-help group. If a person's community is too small to offer self-help groups, or if circumstances such as transportation or disability exist, then an online group may be an option. There are two types of online self-help groups, synchronous and asynchronous. A synchronous group allows participants to exchange comments in real time, similar to a chat room. An asynchronous group allows messages and responses to be posted, such as in an online forum, but no interactive dialogue occurs. Online groups are not difficult to find, but participants should verify the quality of the group. Online groups sponsored by reputable organizations tend to be of better quality and more effective.

BIBLIOGRAPHY

Klein, Linda L. *The Support Group Sourcebook: What They Are, How You Can Find One, and How They Can Help You*. New York: Wiley, 2000. Print.

Kurtz, Linda Farris. *Self-Help and Support Groups: A Handbook for Practitioners*. Thousand Oaks: Sage, 1997. Print.

MClay, Carrie-Anne, Jill Morrison, Alex McConnachie, and Christopher Williams. "A Community-Based Group-Guided Self-Help Intervention for Low Mood and Stress: Study Protocol for a Randomised Controlled Trial." *Trials* 14.1 (2013): 1–20. Print.

Miller, James E. *Effective Support Groups: How to Plan, Design, Facilitate, and Enjoy Them*. Fort Wayne: Willowgreen, 1998. Print.

Mowat, Joan. *Using Support Groups to Improve Behaviour*. Thousand Oaks: Sage, 2007. Print.

Nichols, Keith, and John Jenkinson. *Leading a Support Group: A Practical Guide*. New York: Open UP, 2006. Print.

Schulz, Ava, Timo Stolz, and Thomas Berger. "Internet-Based Individually versus Group Guided Self-Help Treatment for Social Anxiety Disorder: Protocol of a Randomized Controlled Trial." *BMC Psychiatry* 14.1 (2014): 1–15. Print.

Seebohm, Patience, et al. "The Contribution of Self-Help/Mutual Aid Groups to Mental Well-Being." *Health and Social Care in the Community* 21.4 (2013): 391–401. Print.

Patricia Stanfill Edens

SEE ALSO: Addictive personality and behaviors; Alcohol dependence and abuse; Coping: Strategies; Group therapy; Groups; Nicotine dependence; Support groups.

Self-perception theory (SPT)

TYPE OF PSYCHOLOGY: Social psychology

Self-perception theory examines how behavior can affect attitudes. Research stemming from the theory has led to increased understanding of attitude change, persuasion, and intrinsic motivation.

KEY CONCEPTS
- Attitude
- Attribution process
- Vounterattitudinal behavior
- Foot-in-the-door effect
- Induced-compliance paradigm
- Intrinsic motivation
- Overjustification effect
- Self-discrepancy theory
- Self-perception

INTRODUCTION

Self-perception theory, which was proposed by psychologist Daryl Bem in 1965, consists of two postulates. The first is that individuals learn about their own attitudes, emotions, and other internal states partially by inferring them from observations of their own behavior and the circumstances in which their behavior occurs. The second is that, to the extent that individuals' internal cues regarding their internal states are weak or ambiguous, they must infer those internal states in the same way that an observer would—based on external cues. Thus, the theory proposes that people's knowledge of their own feelings often comes from inferences based on external information rather than from direct internal access to their feelings.

To understand the self-perception process, one must first consider how an individual generally learns about another person's feelings. The person's behavior is observed, and possible external factors that might account for the behavior are considered. If powerful external inducements for the behavior are observed, the person's behavior is likely to be attributed to those external inducements. If, however, compelling external causes of the behavior are not observed, the person's behavior is likely to be attributed to some internal factor in the individual, such as an attitude or an emotion.

For example, if an observer watches a person give a speech supporting a certain political candidate, the observer may infer that the person likes that candidate. If, however, the observer knows that the person was forced to give the speech or was offered a large sum of money to give the speech, the observer is likely to attribute the speech to the external inducement rather than to the person's attitude toward the candidate. This process of determining the causal explanation for a behavior is called the attribution process.

Self-perception theory posits that when internal cues are not particularly informative, people act like observers of their own behavior and engage in this same attribution process. Thus, when people engage in a new behavior and perceive no external factors controlling their behavior, they are likely to infer an attitude that provides an explanation for that behavior. Through this process, an individual's behavior can affect his or her attitude. For example, if an individual eats pistachio ice cream for the first time with no external inducement and is then asked if he likes pistachio ice cream, he is likely to infer his attitude based on how much of the ice cream he ate and how fast he ate it.

The theory specifies two factors, however, that limit the extent to which an observed behavior will affect an attitude. First, if the individual has clear prior internal information regarding his or her attitude toward the behavior, a given instance of the behavior is not likely to affect that attitude. If a person has eaten and expressed a liking for pistachio ice cream many times before, a new instance of eating that ice cream is not likely to affect that person's attitude toward it. Second, if there is a strong external inducement for the behavior, the behavior will be attributed to that external factor rather than to an attitude. If a person was ordered at gunpoint to eat the ice cream or was offered a large sum of money to eat the ice cream, she would not infer from the behavior that she likes pistachio ice cream, but rather that she ate the ice cream because of the external inducement (the threat of punishment or the promise of reward).

RESEARCH SUPPORT

Self-perception theory has been supported by various lines of research. The critical assumption underlying the theory is that individuals sometimes do not have internal access to the causes of their own behavior. This notion has been supported by a variety of findings summarized by psychologists Richard Nisbett and Timothy Wilson. These studies have shown that people often do not have accurate knowledge of why they behave as they do. For example, female participants were asked to choose a favorite from among four pairs of virtually identical stockings hanging on a rack. The position of each pair of stockings was varied, and the researchers found that the rightmost pair (usually the last pair examined) was chosen 80 percent of the time. When the participants were asked to explain their choices, they had no trouble generating reasons; however, none of the

participants mentioned that the position of the pair of stockings affected the choice, even though it was clearly a major factor. Similar deficits in causal self-knowledge Self-knowledge have been shown in connection with a wide variety of phenomena, including why people feel the way they do about books and films, and what factors affect their moods.

The primary hypothesis derived from self-perception theory is that, when individuals engage in a new behavior that differs from their past behavior and there appears to be little or no external inducement, they will infer an attitude that is consistent with that behavior. Many studies using the induced-compliance paradigm have supported this hypothesis. In the typical study, individuals are led to write an essay expressing an attitude on an issue that is different from their own initial attitude. If the participants perceive that they can choose whether to write an essay and they are not offered a substantial external inducement (for example, a large amount of money) for doing so, their attitudes become more consistent with the attitudes expressed in their essays. If, however, the participants are not given a choice or are offered a substantial external inducement to write an essay, they do not change their attitudes. Thus, the participants in these studies infer their attitudes from their behavior unless their behavior appears to be controlled by a lack of choice or a large external inducement.

ATTITUDE CHANGE

Self-perception theory has implications for the development of attitudes and emotions, persuasion, compliance, and intrinsic motivation. According to Bem, the self-perception process begins in early childhood, when children are taught how to describe their internal states in much the same way that they learn to describe external objects and events. For example, if a child consumes large quantities of grape juice, the parent may tell the child, "You really like grape juice." Similarly, if a child has a temper tantrum, the parent may say, "You're really angry, aren't you?" In this way, children learn how to infer their own attitudes and emotions. The socialization process can thus be viewed as training in how to infer one's attitudes and emotions in a culturally appropriate manner.

Self-perception processes can continue to affect people's attitudes throughout their life spans. Induced-compliance research indicates that, whenever people are induced to behave in a way that is somehow different from their past behavior and do not perceive a strong external inducement for doing so, their attitudes will become more favorable toward that behavior. Thus, by subtly encouraging a change in a person's behavior, one can effect a change in that person's attitude formation and change

One application of this notion is to psychotherapy. Various techniques used in psychotherapy encourage the client to behave in new, more beneficial ways; it is hoped that such techniques also lead the client to develop new, more beneficial attitudes. Consistent with this idea, a number of studies have shown that, when participants are induced to write favorable statements about themselves or present themselves to an interviewer in self-enhancing ways and they perceive that they freely chose to do so, they experience an increase in self-esteem.

Self-perception theory has implications for compliance as well as for persuasion. Compliance is acceding to a request from another. Research has shown that one way to increase compliance with a particular request is to first gain compliance with a smaller request. This phenomenon is known as the foot-in-the-door effect, a name derived from the door-to-door sales strategy of first getting one's foot in the door. In the first demonstration of this phenomenon, some participants were asked to comply with a small request: to sign a safe-driving petition. All of them agreed to do so. Two weeks later, all the participants were asked to comply with a larger request: to place "Drive Carefully" signs in their front yards. Participants who had been asked to sign the petition were three times more likely to comply with the larger request than those participants who had not been asked to sign the petition. Many subsequent studies have confirmed this effect.

Self-perception theory provides the most widely accepted explanation of the foot-in-the-door effect. Compliance with the initial request is posited to lead individuals to infer either that they like to be helpful or that they like the requester or the type of request with which they have complied. The newly formed attitudes resulting from the initial compliance make the participant more receptive to the second, larger request. This technique is commonly used by salespeople, and it is also employed to increase compliance with requests made by charitable organizations, such as the Red Cross. More generally, the foot-in-the-door effect suggests that each small commitment people make to a personal, organizational, or career goal will lead to a larger commitment to that goal.

INTRINSIC MOTIVATION

All these applications of self-perception theory are based on the notion that, when behavior is not sufficiently justified by external inducements, an individual will infer that he or she is intrinsically motivated to engage in that behavior. Research on the overjustification effect has revealed a complementary tendency of people to infer that they are not intrinsically motivated to engage in an activity if there appears to be too much external justification for the behavior. From the perspective of self-perception theory, if an individual is initially intrinsically motivated to engage in a behavior but is offered a large external inducement for performing the behavior, the person may infer that he or she is performing the behavior for the external inducement; this attribution will lead the individual to conclude that he or she is not interested in the activity for its own sake. Thus, large external inducements for engaging in a previously enjoyable activity may overjustify the activity, thereby undermining intrinsic interest in that activity.

The classic demonstration of the overjustification effect was conducted by psychologists Mark Lepper, David Greene, and Richard Nisbett. Nursery school children were first given a chance to play with colorful felt-tip markers. The researchers noted the amount of time each child played with the markers and used this as a measure of intrinsic motivation. Two weeks later, the children were divided into three groups that were approximately equal in their initial levels of intrinsic motivation. Each child in the first group was simply asked to play with the markers. The children in the second group were told that, if they played with the markers, they would receive a "good player award," a gold star, and a ribbon when they were done. The third group of children was not offered rewards for playing with the markers; after they were done, however, the children were given the awards, stars, and ribbons anyway.

Approximately one week later, each child was observed in a free-play period in which he or she could play with the markers or engage in other activities. The group of children that had previously been offered and had received rewards for playing with the markers spent less free time engaged in that activity than the group that received no rewards and the group that unexpectedly received the rewards. Thus, intrinsic motivation to perform the activity was undermined in children who had previously been offered a substantial external inducement to engage in it. Probably because of their reduced intrinsic interest, these same children drew lower-quality pictures with the markers than the children in the other groups. Similar effects have been shown for both children and adults across a wide range of activities. In addition, over-justification effects have been shown to result from external inducements such as deadlines and competition as well as from various types of rewards.

Behaviorists such as B. F. Skinner popularized the strategy of using rewards to reinforce behavior. Based on the overjustification research, the wisdom of this strategy has been challenged. Rewards are commonly used in child-rearing, education, and work settings, yet in all three settings it is harmful to undermine the individual's intrinsic motivation to engage in the desired behaviors. For example, if a child has some intrinsic interest in doing homework, offering a reward for doing the homework is likely to motivate the behavior but is also likely to undermine the child's intrinsic interest in the activity; thus, when the reward is no longer offered, the child may be less likely to engage in the activity than before he or she was ever offered a reward for doing it.

If the individual has no intrinsic interest in the behavior, there is no problem with using rewards, because there is no intrinsic motivation to undermine. In addition, research has shown that rewards do not necessarily undermine intrinsic motivation; they do so only to the extent that the reward is perceived to be a factor controlling the behavior. Thus, if a behavior is subtly rewarded or the rewards are viewed as indicators of the quality of one's performance, they may actually increase rather than decrease intrinsic motivation. The key to the effective use of rewards is therefore to present them in such a way that they are perceived to be rewards for competence rather than efforts to coerce the individual into engaging in the task.

SELF-PERCEPTION THEORY VERSUS COGNITIVE DISSONANCE THEORY

Self-perception theory first gained prominence in 1967, when Bem argued that the theory could provide an alternative explanation for the large body of evidence supporting Leon Festinger's influential cognitive dissonance theory. From its inception in 1957, cognitive dissonance theory generated considerable supportive research. The theory proposed that, when an individual holds two cognitions such that one cognition logically implies the opposite of the other, the individual experiences a negative tension state, known as dissonance, and becomes motivated to reduce the dissonance; this can be done by changing one of the cognitions or by adding consonant cognitions, which reduces the overall level of inconsistency.

Most of the research on the theory utilized the induced-compliance paradigm. In these studies, participants would be induced to engage in a behavior contrary to their prior attitudes; if the participants engaged in such counterattitudinal behavior while perceiving that they had a choice and had no sufficient external justification for doing so, they were assumed to be experiencing dissonance. Study after study supported the prediction that these participants would change their attitudes so that they would be more consistent with their behavior, presumably to reduce dissonance.

Bem argued that self-perception theory could account for these findings more simply than dissonance theory by positing that, when participants in these studies observed themselves engaging in a behavior with little external inducement, they logically inferred an attitude consistent with that behavior. Thus, Bem offered a cognitive explanation for the most popular motivational theory of the time. Since then, it has virtually become a tradition in social psychology for cognitive theories to be pitted against motivational theories in attempting to account for social attitudes and behavior.

This challenge to dissonance theory was viewed as a major controversy in the field, and it generated much research that attempted to support one theory or the other. Finally, in the mid-1970s, research emerged that resolved the controversy. Evidence was obtained that supported dissonance theory by showing that, when people engage in counterattitudinal behavior with little external inducement, they do experience a negative psychological state, and this negative state does motivate the attitude change following counterattitudinal behavior. However, it was also found that, when individuals engage in behavior that is different from behavior that would be implied by their prior attitudes but not so different that it is really inconsistent with prior attitudes, an attitude change may still occur; this attitude change is best accounted for by self-perception theory. Self-perception theory is also still considered to be the best explanation for the foot-in-the-door and overjustification effects, effects that do not involve counterattitudinal behavior and therefore cannot be explained by cognitive dissonance theory.

BIBLIOGRAPHY

Bem, Daryl J. "Self-Perception Theory." In Advances in Experimental Social Psychology. Vol. 6, edited by Leonard Berkowitz. New York: Academic, 1972. Print.

Cialdini, Robert B. Influence: Science and Practice. 5th ed. Boston: Pearson, 2009. Print.

Fazio, R. H. "Self-Perception Theory: A Current Perspective." Social Influence: The Ontario Symposium. Vol. 5. Ed. M. P. Zanna, J. M. Olson, and C. P. Herman. Hillsdale.: Lawrence Erlbaum, 1987. Print.

Higgins, E. T. "Self-Discrepancy: A Theory Relating Self and Affect." Psychological Review 94 (1987): 319–40. Print.

Laird, James D. Feelings: The Perception of Self. New York: Oxford UP, 2007. Print.

Moskowitz, Gordon B., ed. Cognitive Social Psychology: The Princeton Symposium on the Legacy and Future of Social Cognition. Mahwah: Lawrence Erlbaum, 2001. Print.

Murdoch-Eaton, Deborah. "Feedback: The Complexity of Self-Perception and the Transition from 'Transmit' to 'Received and Understood.'" Medical Education 46.6 (2012): 538–40. Print.

Riding, Richard J., and Stephen G. Rayner, eds. Self Perception. Westport, Conn.: Ablex, 2001. Print.

Robak, Rostyslaw W. "Self-Definition in Psychotherapy: Is it Time to Revisit Self-Perception Theory?" North Amer. Journ. of Psychology 3.3 (2001): 529. Print.

Robak, Rostyslaw W., Alfred Ward, and Kimberly Ostolaza. "Development of a General Measure of Individuals' Recognition of Their Self-Perception Processes." North Amer. Journ. of Psychology 7.3 (2005): 337–44. Print.

Robins, Richard W., and Oliver P. John. "The Quest for Self-Insight: Theory and Research on Accuracy and Bias in Self-Perception." Handbook of Personality Psychology. Ed. Robert Hogan and John A. Johnson, et al. San Diego: Academic Press, 1997. Print.

Jeff Greenberg; updated by Michelle Murphy

See Also: Attitude-behavior consistency; Attitude formation and change; Attributional biases; Causal attribution; Cognitive dissonance; Emotions; Motivation; Motivation: Intrinsic and extrinsic; Radical behaviorism: B. F. Skinner; Work motivation.

Self-presentation

Type of psychology: Social psychology

Self-presentation is behavior with which people try to affect how they are perceived and judged by others; much social behavior is influenced by self-presentational motives and goals.

Key Concepts
- Impression management
- Ingratiation
- Intimidation
- Power
- Self-monitoring
- Self-promotion
- Social anxiety
- Supplication

INTRODUCTION

Although they may or may not be consciously thinking about it, people often try to control the information that others receive about them. When they are deliberately trying to make a certain impression on others, people may carefully choose their dress, think about what to say, monitor their behavior, pick their friends, and even decide what to eat. Self-presentation refers to the various behaviors with which people attempt to manage and influence the impressions they make on others. Nearly any public behavior may be strategically regulated in the service of impression management, and people may behave quite differently in the presence of others from the way they behave when they are alone. Moreover, self-presentation is not always a conscious activity; without planning to, people may fall into familiar patterns of behavior that represent personal habits of self-presentation.

The impressions of someone that others form substantially determine how they treat that person. Obviously, if others like and respect someone, they behave differently toward him or her from the way they would if the person were disliked or mistrusted. Thus, it is usually personally advantageous for a person to have some control over what others think of him or her. To the extent that one can regulate one's image in others' eyes, one gains influence over their behavior and increases one's interpersonal power. Self-presentational perspectives on social interaction assume that people manage their impressions to augment their power and maximize their social outcomes.

IMPRESSION MANAGEMENT AND STRATEGIES

Self-presentation, however, is usually not deceitful. Although people do occasionally misrepresent themselves through lying and pretense, most self-presentation communicates one's authentic attributes to others. Because frauds and cheats are rejected by others, dishonest self-presentation is risky. Instead, impression management usually involves the attempt to reveal, in a selective fashion, those aspects of one's true character that will allow one to attain one's current goals. By announcing some of their attitudes but not mentioning others, for example, people may appear to have something in common with almost anyone they meet; this simple tactic of impression management facilitates graceful and rewarding social interaction and does not involve untruthfulness at all. Over time, genuine, realistic presentations of self in which people accurately reveal portions of themselves to others are likely to be more successful than those in which people pretend to be things they are not.

Nevertheless, because most people have diverse interests and talents, there may be many distinct impressions they can honestly attempt to create, and people may seek different images in different situations. Psychologists Edward Jones and Thane Pittman identified four discrete strategies of self-presentation that produce disparate results. When people seek acceptance and likeability, they typically ingratiate themselves with others by doing favors, paying compliments, mentioning areas of agreement, and describing themselves in attractive, desirable ways. On other occasions, when they wish their abilities to be recognized and respected by others, people may engage in self-promotion, recounting their accomplishments or strategically arranging public demonstrations of their skills. Both ingratiation (a strategy of self-presentation in which one seeks to elicit liking and affection from others) and self-promotion create socially desirable impressions and thus are very common strategies of self-presentation.

In contrast, other strategies create undesirable impressions. Through intimidation, people portray themselves as ruthless, dangerous, and menacing so that others will do their bidding. Such behavior tends to drive others away, but if those others cannot easily escape, intimidation often works. Drill sergeants who threaten recalcitrant recruits usually are not interested in being liked; they want compliance, and the more fierce they seem, the more likely they may be to get it. Finally, using the strategy of supplication, people sometimes present themselves as inept or infirm to avoid obligations and elicit help and support from others.

People's choices of strategies and desired images depend on several factors, such as the values and preferences of the target audience. People often tailor their self-presentations to fit the interests of the others they are trying to impress. In one study of this phenomenon, college women were given job interviews with a male interviewer who, they were told, was either quite traditional or "liberated" in his views toward women. With this information in hand, the women dressed, acted, and spoke differently for the different targets. They wore more makeup and jewelry, behaved less assertively, and expressed a greater interest in children to the traditional interviewer than they did to the liberated interviewer.

Individuals' own self-concepts also influence their self-presentations. People typically prefer to manage impressions that are personally palatable, both because they are easier to maintain and because they help bolster self-esteem; however, self-presentations also shape self-concepts. When people do occasionally claim images they personally feel they do not deserve, their audiences may either see through the fraudulent claim and dispute the image or accept it as legitimate. In the latter case, the audience's approving reactions may gradually convince people that they really do deserve the images they are projecting. Because a person's self-concept is determined, in part, by feedback received from others, self-presentations that were once inaccurate can become truthful over time as people are gradually persuaded by others that they really are the people they were pretending to be.

FINESSING PUBLIC IMAGE

Studies of self-presentation demonstrate that people are capable of enormous subtlety as they fine-tune their public images. For example, psychologist Robert Cialdini and his colleagues have identified several ingenious, specific tactics of ingratiation. Observations of students at famous football colleges (such as Notre Dame, Ohio State, the University of Southern California, Arizona, Pittsburgh, and Louisiana State) revealed that after a weekend football victory, students were especially likely to come to class on Monday wearing school colors and insignia. If their team had lost, however, such identifying apparel was conspicuously absent. Further laboratory studies suggested that the students were strategically choosing their apparel to publicize their association with a winning team, a tendency Cialdini called "basking in reflected glory." By contrast, they were careful not to mention their connection to a loser. In general, people who seek acceptance and liking will advertise their association with other desirable images, while trying to distance themselves from failure and other disreputable images.

Furthermore, they may do this with precise sophistication. In another study by Cialdini, people privately learned that they had a trivial connection—a shared birth date—with another person who was said to have either high or low social or intellectual ability. The participants then encountered a public, personal success or failure when they were informed that they had either high or low social ability themselves. Armed with this information, people cleverly selected the specific self-descriptions that would make the best possible impression on the researchers.

If they had failed their social ability test, they typically mentioned their similarity with another person who had high intellect but did not bring up their connection to another person with higher social ability than themselves. They thus publicized a flattering link between themselves and others while steering clear of comparisons that would make them look bad. In contrast, if they had passed the social ability test and the researchers already thought highly of them, people brought up their connection to another person who had poorer social ability. By mentioning their resemblance to less talented others, people not only reminded their audiences of their superior talent, but seemed humble and modest as well.

Self-presentation can be ingenious, indeed. In general, if they wish to ingratiate themselves with others, people with deficient images try to find something good to communicate about themselves that does not contradict the negative information the audience already has. If they are already held in high esteem, however, people typically select modest, self-effacing presentations that demonstrate that they are humble as well as talented.

People do not go to such trouble for everyone, however; if people do not care what a particular audience thinks, they may not be motivated to create any impression at all. One experiment that illustrated this point invited women to "get acquainted" with men who were either desirable or undesirable partners. Snacks were provided; the women who were paired with attractive men ate much less than the women stuck with unappealing partners. Because women who eat lightly are often considered more feminine than those who eat heartily, women who wanted to create a favorable impression strategically limited their snack consumption; in contrast, those who were less eager to impress their partners ate as much as they liked.

ROLE IN SOCIAL ANXIETIES
On occasion, people care too much what an audience thinks. One reason that people suffer from social anxieties such as shyness or stage fright is that their desire to make a particular impression on a certain audience is too high. According to theorists Mark Leary and Barry

Schlenker, people suffer from social anxiety when they are motivated to create a certain impression but doubt their ability to do so. Any influence that increases one's motivation (such as the attractiveness, prestige, or power of an audience) or causes one to doubt one's ability (such as unfamiliar situations or inadequate personal social skills) can cause social anxiety. This self-presentation perspective suggests that, if excessive social anxiety is a problem, different therapies will be needed for different people. Some sufferers will benefit most from behavioral social skills training, whereas others who have passable skills simply need to worry less what others are thinking of them; cognitive therapies will be best for them.

ROLE OF SELF-MONITORING
Finally, people differ in their self-presentational proclivities. Those high in the trait of self-monitoring tend to be sensitive to social cues that suggest how one should act in a particular situation and are adept at adjusting their self-presentations to fit in. By comparison, low self-monitors seem less attentive and flexible and tend to display more stable images regardless of their situational appropriateness. High self-monitors are more changeable and energetic self-presenters, and, as a result, they create social worlds that are different from those of low self-monitors. Because they can deftly switch images from one audience to the next, high self-monitors tend to have wider circles of friends with whom they have less in common than do low self-monitors. Compared to high self-monitors, lows must search harder for partners with whom they share broader compatibilities. Over time, however, lows are likely to develop longer-lasting, more committed relationships with others; they invest more in the partners they have. High self-monitors are more influenced by social image than lows are, a self-presentational difference with important consequences for interaction.

THEORETICAL ROOTS AND INFLUENCES
The roots of self-presentation theory date back to the very beginnings of American psychology and the writings of William James in 1890. James recognized that the human self is multifaceted, and that it is not surprising for different audiences to have very different impressions of the same individual. After James, in the early twentieth century, sociologists Charles Horton Cooley and George Herbert Mead stressed that others' impressions of an individual are especially important, shaping that person's social life and personal self-concept. The most influ-

ential parent of this perspective, however, was Erving Goffman, who was the first to insist that people actively, consciously, and deliberately construct social images for public consumption. Goffman's book *The Presentation of Self in Everyday Life* (1959) eloquently compared social behavior to a theatrical performance staged for credulous audiences, complete with scripts, props, and backstage areas where the actors drop their roles.

As it emerged thereafter, self-presentation theory seemed to be a heretical alternative to established explanations for some social phenomena. For example, whereas cognitive dissonance theory suggested that people sometimes change attitudes that are inconsistent with their behavior to gain peace of mind, self-presentation theory argued that people merely report different attitudes that make them look consistent, without changing their real attitudes at all. Nevertheless, despite theoretical controversy, Goffman's provocative dramaturgical analogy gradually became more widely accepted as researchers demonstrated that a wide variety of social behavior was affected by self-presentational concerns. With the publication in 1980 of Barry Schlenker's book-length review of self-presentation research, impression management theory finally entered the mainstream of social psychology.

IMPORTANCE AND CONTRIBUTIONS
The lasting importance of self-presentation theory lies in its reminders that people are cognizant of the images they present to others and often thoughtfully attempt to shape those images to accomplish their objectives. As a result, much social behavior has a self-presentational component. An angry boss may have real problems controlling his temper, for example, but he may also occasionally exaggerate his anger to intimidate his employees. Even people suffering from severe mental illness may engage in impression management; research has revealed that individuals who have been institutionalized for schizophrenia sometimes adjust the apparent severity of their symptoms so that they seem well enough to be granted special privileges without seeming so healthy that they are released back into the threatening free world. In this case, self-presentation theory does not suggest that people with schizophrenia are merely pretending to be disturbed; obviously, people suffering from psychosis are burdened by real psychological or biological problems. Impression management, however, may contribute in part to their apparent illness, just as it does to many other social behaviors. In general, self-presentation theory

does not claim to replace other explanations for behavior, but it does assert that much of what people do is influenced by self-presentational motives and concerns.

BIBLIOGRAPHY
Baumeister, Roy F., ed. *Public Self and Private Self*. New York: Springer-Verlag, 1986. Print.

Brissett, Dennis, and Charles Edgley, eds. *Life as Theater: A Dramaturgical Sourcebook*. 2nd ed. Somerset: Aldine Transaction, 2005. Print.

Goffman, Erving. *The Presentation of Self in Everyday Life*. New York: Anchor, 2008. Print.

Jones, E. E., and Thane Pittman. "Toward a General Theory of Strategic Self-Presentation." *Psychological Perspectives on the Self*. Ed. Jerry Suls. Hillsdale: Erlbaum, 1993. Print.

Hadden, Benjamin W., Camilla S. Overup, and C. Raymond Knee. "Removing the Ego: Need Fulfillment, Self-Image Goals, and Self-Presentation." *Self and Identity* 13.3 (2014): 274–93. Print.

Leary, Mark R., and Rowland S. Miller. *Social Psychology and Dysfunctional Behavior: Origins, Diagnosis, and Treatment*. New York: Springer-Verlag, 1986. Print.

Schlenker, Barry R. *Impression Management: The Self-Concept, Social Identity, and Interpersonal Relations*. Monterey: Brooks/Cole, 1980. Print.

Schlenker, Barry R., ed. *The Self and Social Life*. New York: McGraw-Hill, 1985. Print.

Snyder, Mark. *Public Appearances, Private Realities: The Psychology of Self-Monitoring*. New York: Freeman, 1987. Print.

Svennevig, Jan. "Direct and Indirect Self-Presentation in First Conversations." *Journal of Language and Social Psychology* 33.3 (2014): 302–27. Print.

Weber, Robert. *The Created Self: Reinventing Body, Persona, and Spirit*. New York: Norton, 2001. Print.

Zach, Sima, and Yael Netz. "Self-Presentation Concerns and Physical Activity in Three-Generation Families." *Social Behavior and Personality: An International Journal* 42.2 (2014): 259–67. Print.

Rowland Miller

SEE ALSO: Attitude-behavior consistency; Cognitive dissonance; James, William; Self; Self-disclosure; Self-efficacy; Self-esteem; Self-perception theory.

Seligman, Martin E. P.

BORN: August 12, 1942
BIRTHPLACE: Albany, New York
IDENTITY: American clinical psychologist
TYPE OF PSYCHOLOGY: Motivation; Personality; Psychopathology

Seligman is the world's leading authority on positive psychology and optimism.

Martin E. P. Seligman earned a BA in psychology from Princeton University in 1964 and his doctorate in psychology from the University of Pennsylvania in 1967. Shortly thereafter, he accepted a position in the Department of Psychology at the University of Pennsylvania. In 1975, he published *Helplessness*, a book describing how to deal with the emotional distresses that can lead to depression, anxiety, and failure. A few years later, Seligman and David L. Rosenhan coauthored a popular textbook, *Abnormal Psychology* (1984), that included the latest nuclear technology for mapping the brain. For his work on preventing depression, Seligman received the Merit Award of the National Institute of Mental Health in 1991.

Seligman served as the director of the Clinical Training Program of the Psychology Department of the University of Pennsylvania for fourteen years. His primary emphasis and research efforts concentrated on learned depression and pessimism and learned optimism. In 1995, he was presented the Pennsylvania Psychology Association's award for Distinguished Contributions to Science and Practice. One year later, he was elected president of the American Psychological Association (APA) by the widest margin in history. His focus as APA president was on joining psychological practice and science in a united effort to combat mental illness. He is the founding editor-in-chief of *Prevention and Treatment Magazine*, the APA electronic journal.

In 1999, Seligman was appointed as the Robert A. Fox leadership professor of psychology at the University of Pennsylvania. Since 2000, he has advocated positive psychology, the study and implementation of positive emotions, positive character traits, and positive-oriented mental health institutions. His efforts have established a firm foundation for research that involves the study of human happiness as a basis for optimal human functioning.

Seligman has written twenty-two books and published more than two hundred articles dealing with learning, motivation, personality, and psychopathology. His books on positive psychology—including *Learned Optimism* (1991), *The Optimistic Child* (1995; with Karen Reivich, Lisa Jaycox, and Jane Gillham), and *Authentic Happiness: Using the New Positive Psychology to Realize Your Potential for Lasting Fulfillment* (2002)—have made him a best-selling author. In 2003, Seligman established the master of applied positive psychology program at the University of Pennsylvania as part of the Positive Psychology Center. In honor of his research, he has been awarded the APA Distinguished Scientific Contribution Award, the Laurel Award from the American Association for Applied Psychology and Prevention, and the William James Fellow Award and James McKeen Cattell Fellow Award from the American Psychological Society.

BIBLIOGRAPHY

Csikszentmihalyi, Mihaly, and Isabella Selega Csikszentmihalyi. *A Life Worth Living: Contributions to Positive Psychology.* Oxford, England: Oxford University Press, 2006. Print.

McNutty, James K, and Frank D. Fincham. "Beyond Positive Psychology? Toward a Contextual View of Psychological Process and Well-Being." *American Psychologist* 67.2 (2012): 101–10. Print.

Ong, Anthony D., and Manfred H. M. Van Dulmen. *Oxford Handbook of Methods in Positive Psychology.* Oxford, England: Oxford University Press, 2007. Print.

Seligman, Martin E. P., et al. "Mental Health Promotion in Public Health: Perspectives and Strategies from Positive Psychology." *American Journal of Public Health* 101.8 (2011): e1–e9. Print.

Sheldon, Kennon M., et al. *Designing Positive Psychology: Taking Stock and Moving Forward.* New York: Oxford UP, 2011. Print.

Simonton, Dean Keith. *Great Psychologists and Their Times: Scientific Insights into Psychology's History.* Washington, D.C.: American Psychological Association, 2002. Print.

Alvin K. Benson

SEE ALSO: Attitude formation and change; Depression; Learned helplessness; Positive psychology; Psychosomatic disorders.

Selye, Hans

BORN: January 26, 1907
DIED: October 16, 1982
BIRTHPLACE: Vienna, Austria
PLACE OF DEATH: Montreal, Quebec, Canada
IDENTITY: Austrian-born Canadian physician and endocrinologist
TYPE OF PSYCHOLOGY: Stress

Hans Selye, considered the founder of the stress field, devoted his entire professional life to the study of stress.

Hans Selye started medical school in 1925 at the University of Prague. While in medical school, he began his research into causes of stress and its effects on the body. He noticed that people undergoing a wide variety of stressors exhibited, in addition to those symptoms associated with the specific stressor, symptoms that were remarkably similar regardless of the type of stress being experienced. In other words, each stressor (for instance, cold) caused its own specific response (shivering) and a nonspecific set of symptoms which he described as "the syndrome of just being sick." He named this collection of nonspecific symptoms the general adaptation syndrome (GAS), also known as the "Selye syndrome." These nonspecific symptoms, over time, may lead to physical illness and, ultimately, death. In his own words, "Every stress leaves an indelible scar, and the organism pays for its survival after a stressful situation by becoming a little older."

Selye proposed three stages of the GAS: alarm, in which the body prepares for fight or flight when challenged by a stressor; resistance, in which the body returns to normal but requires enormous energy to maintain homeostasis; and exhaustion, when continued stress causes symptoms similar to the alarm stage. Because at this point the body's resources are depleted, physical illness ensues. Selye also later coined the term "eustress" for the positive, challenging type of stress that helps people grow and defined "distress" as the negative, destructive type of stress.

In 1936, he published his first scientific paper on the subject of stress. During his lifetime, he wrote thirty-nine books and more than 1,700 scholarly articles on this subject. Two of Selye's best-known works are *Stress without Distress* (1974) and *The Stress of Life* (1956). Stress without Distress was published in seventeen languages and is still widely available.

In addition to his medical studies in Prague, Selye studied in Paris and Rome, earning MD, PhD, and DSc degrees. He left Europe when he received a Rockefeller Research Fellowship and a position at the Johns Hopkins University in Baltimore, Maryland. In 1932, he became an associate professor of histology at McGill University in Montreal and, in 1945, the first director of the Institute of Experimental Medicine and Surgery at the University of Montreal, where he served until he retired in 1976. With Alvin Toffler, he founded the International Institute of Stress in 1979. Much honored for his scientific work, Selye was granted forty-three honorary doctorates during his lifetime. After his death, the Hans Selye Chair was established in 1989 at the University of Montreal.

Selye's lifework has not been without its detractors, however. In *Stress, Shock, and Adaptation in the Twentieth Century* (2014), Mark Jackson notes that critics, both during and after Selye's lifetime, have taken issue with his ethics, methodology, or emphasis on biology over cultural factors. Mark P. Petticrew and Kelley Lee, in a 2011 article, assert that the tobacco-industry funding Selye received and his lack of disclosure about it, as well as his role as expert witness in tobacco-related litigation and the industry's use of his findings, undermine the integrity of his scientific research. Nevertheless, Selye's work laid the foundation for the field of stress research.

BIBLIOGRAPHY

Jackson, Mark. "Evaluating the Role of Hans Selye in the Modern History of Stress." *Stress, Shock, and Adaptation in the Twentieth Century.* Ed. Edmund Ramsden and David Cantor. Rochester: U of Rochester P, 2014. 21–48. Print.

Petticrew, Mark P, and Kelley Lee. "The 'Father of Stress' Meets 'Big Tobacco': Hans Selye and the Tobacco Industry." *American Journal of Public Health* 101.3 (2011): 411–18. Print.

Selye, Hans. *The Stress of My Life: A Scientist's Memoirs.* 2nd ed. New York: Van Nostrand, 1979. Print.

Szabo, Sandor, Yvette Tache, and Arpad Somogyi. "The Legacy of Hans Selye and the Origins of Stress Research: A Retrospective 75 Years after His Landmark Brief 'Letter' to the Editor of Nature." *Stress* 15.5 (2012): 472–78. Print.

Viner, Russell. "Putting Stress in Life: Hans Selye and the Making of Stress Theory." *Social Studies of Science* 29.3 (1999): 391–410. Print.

Rebecca Lovell Scott

SEE ALSO: General adaptation syndrome; Stress: Behavioral and physiological responses; Stress-related diseases.

Sensation and perception

TYPE OF PSYCHOLOGY: Sensation and perception

The study of sensation and perception examines the relationship between input from the world and the manner in which people react to it. Through the process of sensation, the body receives various stimuli that are transformed into neural messages and transmitted to the brain. Perception is the meaning and interpretation given to these messages..

KEY CONCEPTS
- Absolute threshold
- Acuity
- Attention
- Sensory deprivation
- Sensory receptors

INTRODUCTION

Although the distinction between sensation and perception is not always clear, psychologists attempt to distinguish between the two concepts. Sensation is generally viewed as the initial contact between organisms and their physical environment. It focuses on the interaction between various forms of sensory stimulation and how these sensations are registered by the sense organs (nose, skin, eyes, ears, and tongue). The process by which an individual then interprets and organizes this information to produce conscious experiences is known as perception.

The warmth of the sun, the distinctive sound of a jet airplane rumbling down a runway, the smell of freshly baked bread, and the taste of an ice cream sundae all have an impact on the body's sensory receptors. The signals received are transmitted via the nervous system to the brain, where the information is interpreted. The body's sensory receptors are capable of detecting very low levels of stimulation. Eugene Galanter's studies indicated that on a clear night, the human eye is capable of viewing a candle at a distance of thirty miles (forty-eight kilometers), while the ears can detect the ticking of a watch twenty feet (six meters) away in a quiet room. He also demonstrated that the tongue can taste a teaspoon of sugar dissolved in 2 gallons (about 7.5 liters) of water. People can feel a bee wing falling on the cheek and can smell a single drop of perfume in a three-bedroom apartment. Awareness of these faint stimuli demonstrates the absolute thresholds, defined as the minimum amount of stimulus that can be detected 50 percent of the time.

SIGNAL RECOGNITION

A person's ability to detect a weak stimulus, often called a signal, depends not only on the strength of the signal or stimulus but also on the person's psychological state. For example, a child remaining at home alone for the first time may be startled by an almost imperceptible noise. In a normal setting, with his or her parents at home, the same noise or signal would probably go unnoticed. Scientists who study signal detection seek to explain why people respond differently to a similar signal and why the same person's reactions vary as circumstances change. Studies have shown that people's reactions to signals depend on many factors, including the time of day and the type of signal.

Much controversy has arisen over the subject of subliminal signals—signals that one's body receives without one's conscious awareness. It has long been thought that these subliminal signals could influence a person's behaviors through persuasion. Many researchers believe that individuals do sense subliminal sensations; however, it is highly unlikely that this information will somehow change an individual's behaviors. Researchers Anthony Pratkanis and Anthony Greenwald suggest that in the area of advertising, subliminal procedures offer little or nothing of value to the marketing practitioner.

ADAPTATION AND SELECTIVE ATTENTION

An individual's response to a stimulus may change over time. For example, when a swimmer first enters the cold ocean, the initial response may be to complain about the water's frigidity; however, after a few minutes, the water feels comfortable. This is an example of sensory adaptation—the body's ability to diminish sensitivity to unchanging stimuli. Sensory receptors are initially alert to the coldness of the water, but prolonged exposure reduces sensitivity. This is an important benefit to humans in that it allows an individual to not be distracted by constant stimuli that are uninformative. It would be very difficult to function daily if one's body were constantly aware of the fit of shoes and garments, the rumble of a heating system, or constant street noises.

The reception of sensory information by the senses, and the transmission of this information to the brain, is included under the term "sensation." Of equal importance is the process of perception: the way an individual selects information, organizes it, and makes an interpretation, thus achieving a grasp of one's surroundings. People cannot absorb and understand all the available sensory information received from the environment. Thus, they must selectively attend to certain information and disregard other material. Through the process of selective attention, people are able to maximize information gained from the object of focus, while at the same time ignoring irrelevant material. People are capable of controlling the focus of their attention to some degree; in many instances, however, focus can be shifted undesirably. For example, while one is watching a television show, extraneous stimuli such as a car horn blaring may change one's focus.

The fundamental focus of the study of perception is how people come to comprehend the world around them through its objects and events. People are constantly giving meaning to a host of stimuli being received from all their senses. While research suggests that people prize visual stimuli above other forms, information from all other senses must also be processed. More difficult to understand is the concept of extrasensory perception (ESP).

More researchers are becoming interested in the possible existence of extrasensory perception—perceptions that are not based on information from the sensory receptors. Often included under the heading of ESP are such questionable abilities as clairvoyance and telepathy. While psychologists generally remain skeptical as to the existence of ESP, some do not deny that evidence may someday be available supporting its existence.

FIVE LAWS OF GROUPING
Knowledge of the fields of sensation and perception assists people in understanding their environment. By understanding how and why people respond to various stimuli, scientists have been able to identify important factors that have proved useful in such fields as advertising, industry, and education.

Max Wertheimer discussed five laws of grouping that describe why certain elements seem to go together rather than remain independent. These laws include the law of similarity, which states that similar objects tend to be seen as a unit; the law of nearness, which states that objects near one another tend to be seen as a unit; the law of closure, which states that when a figure has a gap, the figure still tends to be seen as closed; the law of common fate, which states that when objects move in the same

direction, they tend to be seen as a unit; and the law of good continuation, which states that objects organized in a straight line or a smooth curve tend to be seen as a unit. These laws are illustrated in the figure.

USE IN ADVERTISING AND MARKETING
The laws of grouping are frequently utilized in the field of advertising. Advertisers attempt to associate their products with various stimuli. For example, David L. Loudon and Albert J. Della Bitta, after studying advertisements for menthol cigarettes, noted that the advertisers often show mentholated cigarettes in green, springlike settings to suggest freshness and taste. Similarly, summertime soft-drink advertisements include refreshing outdoor scenes depicting cool, fresh, clean running water, which is meant to be associated with the beverage; and advertisements for rugged four-wheel-drive vehicles use the laws of grouping by placing their vehicles in harsh, rugged climates, causing the viewer to develop a perception of toughness and ruggedness.

The overall goal of advertisers is to provide consumers with appropriate sensations that will cause them to perceive the products in a manner that the advertisers desire. By structuring the stimuli that reach the senses, advertisers can build a foundation for perceptions of products, making them seem durable, sensuous, refreshing, or otherwise desirable. By using the results of numerous research studies pertaining to perception, subtle yet effective manipulation of the consumer is achieved.

COLOR STUDIES
Another area that has been researched extensively by industry deals with color. If one ordered dinner in a restaurant and received an orange steak with purple french fries and a blue salad, the meal would be difficult to consume. People's individual perceptions of color are extremely important. Variations from these expectations can be very difficult to overcome. Researchers have found that people's perceptions of color also influence their beliefs about products. When reactions to laundry detergents were examined, detergent in a blue box was found to be too weak, while detergent in a yellow box was thought to be too strong. Consumers believed, based on coloration, that the ideal detergent came in a blue box with yellow accentuation. Similarly, when individuals were asked to judge the capsule color of drugs, findings suggested that orange capsules were frequently seen as stimulants, white capsules as having an analgesic action, and lavender capsules as having a hallucinogenic effect.

Studies have shown that various colors have proved more satisfactory than others for industrial application. Red has been shown to be typically perceived as a sign of danger and is used to warn individuals of hazardous situations. Yellow is also a sign of warning. It is frequently used on highway signs as a warning indicator because of its high degree of visibility in adverse weather conditions. Instrument panels in both automobiles and airplanes are frequently equipped with orange- and yellow-tipped instrument indicators, because research has demonstrated that these colors are easily distinguished from the dark background of the gauges. Finally, industry has not overlooked the fact that many colors have a calming and relaxing effect on people. Thus, soft pastels are often used in the workplace.

USE IN EDUCATION
The field of education has also benefited from research in the areas of sensation and perception. Knowing how young children perceive educational materials is important in developing ways to increase their skills and motivation. Textbook publishers have found that materials need to be visually attractive to children to help them focus on activities. Graphics and illustrations help the young learner to understand written materials. It is also important that the size of the printed text accommodate the developmental level of the student. For example, primers and primary-level reading series typically have larger print to assist the student in focusing on the text. As the child's ability to discriminate letters and numbers becomes more efficient with age, the print size diminishes to that of the size of characters in adult books. Similar techniques continue into high school and college; especially in introductory courses, texts are designed using a great deal of color and variation in page design. The reader's eyes are attracted by numerous stimuli to pictures, figures, definitions, and charts strategically placed on each page. This technique allows the author to highlight and accent essential points of information.

EARLY RESEARCH
The study of sensation and perception began more than two thousand years ago with the Greek philosophers and is one of the oldest fields in psychology. There are numerous theories, hypotheses, and facts dealing with how people obtain information about their world, what type of information they obtain, and what they do with this information once they obtain it. None of this information has been sufficient to account for human perceptual

experiences and perceptual behavior, so research in the area of sensation and perception continues.

The philosopher Thomas Reid made the original distinction between sensations and perceptions. He proposed that the crucial difference between them is that perceptions always refer to external objects, whereas sensations refer to the experiences within a person that are not linked to external objects. Many psychologists of the nineteenth century proposed that sensations are elementary building blocks of perceptions. According to their ideas, perceptions arise from the addition of numerous sensations. The sum of these sensations thus creates a perception. Other psychologists believed that making a distinction between sensations and perceptions was not useful.

The first psychologists saw the importance of perception when they realized that information from the senses was necessary to learn, think, and memorize. Thus, research pertaining to the senses was a central research component of all the psychological laboratories established in Europe and the United States during the late nineteenth and early twentieth centuries.

APPLICATIONS IN CONTEMPORARY SOCIETY
By studying perceptions, researchers can identify potential environmental hazards that threaten the senses. Studying perception has also enabled people to develop devices that ensure optimal performance of the senses. For example, on a daily basis, one's senses rely on such manufactured objects as telephones, clocks, televisions, and computers. To be effective, these devices must be tailored to the human sensory systems.

The study of sensations and perceptions has also made it possible to build and develop prosthetic devices to aid individuals with impaired sensory function. For example, hearing aids amplify sound for hard-of-hearing individuals; however, when all sounds are amplified to the same degree, it is often difficult for people to discriminate between sounds. From the work of British psychologist Richard Gregory, an instrument was developed that would amplify only speech sounds, thus allowing a person to attend more adequately to conversations and tune out background noise.

Finally, understanding perception is important for comprehending and appreciating the perceptual experience called art. When knowledge of perception is combined with the process of perceiving artistic works, this understanding adds an additional dimension to one's ability to view a work of art.

BIBLIOGRAPHY

Barth, Friedrich G., Patrizia Giampieri-Deutsch, and Hans-Dieter Klein, eds. *Sensory Perception: Mind and Matter.* New York: Springer, 2012. Print.

Blake, Randolph, and Robert Sekuler. *Perception.* 5th ed. New York: McGraw, 2006. Print.

Foley, Hugh J., and Margaret W. Matlin. *Sensation and Perception.* 5th ed. Boston: Allyn, 2009. Print.

Goldstein, E. Bruce. *Sensation and Perception.* 9th ed. Belmont: Wadsworth, 2014. Print.

Gregory, Richard L. *Eye and Brain: The Psychology of Seeing.* 5th ed. Princeton: Princeton UP, 1997. Print.

Harris, John. *Sensation and Perception.* Thousand Oaks: Sage, 2014. Print.

Schiff, William. *Perception: An Applied Approach.* Boston: Houghton, 1980. Print.

Wolfe, Jeremy M., et al. *Sensation & Perception.* 3rd ed. Sunderland: Sinauer, 2012. Print.

Eugene R. Johnson

SEE ALSO: Advertising; Attention; Depth and motion perception; Hearing; Kinesthetic memory; Senses; Signal detection theory; Smell and taste; Touch and pressure; Visual system.

Senses

TYPE OF PSYCHOLOGY: Sensation and perception

Humans process information using at least five sensory modalities: sight, sound, taste, smell, and the body senses, which include touch, temperature, balance, and pain. Because people's sensation and perception of external stimuli define their world, knowledge of these processes is relevant to every aspect of daily life.

KEY CONCEPTS

- Cutaneous
- Perception
- Proximate
- Receptor
- Sensation
- Ultimate studies
- Umwelt

INTRODUCTION

Humans have five sense organs: the eyes, the ears, the taste buds, the nasal mucosa, and the skin. Each sense organ is specialized to intercept a particular kind of envi-

ronmental energy and then to convert that energy into a message that the brain can interpret. Together, these two processes are called sensation.

The first step of sensation, the interception of external energy, is done by the part of the sense organ that is in direct contact with the environment. Each sense organ has a specialized shape and structure designed to intercept a particular form of energy. The second step, conversion of the captured energy into signals the brain can understand, is done by cells inside the sense organ called receptors. Receptors are structures to which physicists and engineers refer as transducers: They convert one form of energy into another. Artificial transducers are common. Hydroelectric plants, for example, intercept flowing water and convert it to electricity; then appliances convert the electricity into heat, moving parts, sound, or light displays. Receptors are biological transducers that convert environmental energy intercepted by the sense organ into neural signals. These signals are then sent to the brain, where they are interpreted through a process called perception.

The eye, the best understood of all the sense organs, consists of a lens that focuses light (a kind of electromagnetic energy) through a small hole (the pupil) onto a sheet of cells (the retina). The retina contains the eye's receptor cells: the rods, which are sensitive to all wavelengths of light in the visible spectrum, and three kinds of cones, which are sensitive to those wavelengths that the brain perceives as blue, green, and yellow.

The ear funnels air pressure waves onto the tympanic membrane (more commonly known as the eardrum), where vibrations are transmitted to the inner ear. In the inner ear, receptors called hair cells are stimulated by different frequency vibrations; they then send signals to the brain which are interpreted as different pitches and harmonics.

Taste buds are small bumps on the tongue and parts of the throat that are continuously bathed in liquid. Receptors in the taste buds intercept any chemicals that have been dissolved in the liquid. Molecules of different shapes trigger messages from different receptors. Humans have several kinds of taste receptors that send signals the brain interprets as bitter, at least two kinds of receptors that send signals interpreted as sweet, and one kind of receptor each that sends signals interpreted as salty and sour.

The nasal mucosa, the organ responsible for one's sense of smell, is a layer of cells lining parts of the nasal passageways and throat; it intercepts chemicals directly from inhaled air. Apparently, cells in the nasal mucosa can produce receptor cells (called olfactory receptors) throughout life. This way, people can develop the capacity to smell "new" chemicals that they could not smell before. New olfactory receptors seem to be created in response to exposure to novel chemicals, analogous to the production of antibodies when the immune system is exposed to foreign material. Because of this ability to create new olfactory receptors, it is not possible to list and categorize all the different types of smells.

The skin is the largest sense organ in the human body; its sense, touch, actually consists of several different senses, collectively referred to as the cutaneous senses. Receptors called mechanoreceptors are triggered by mechanical movements of the skin and send signals that the brain interprets as vibration, light or deep pressure, and stretching. Thermoreceptors intercept heat passing in or out of the body through the skin; their signals are interpreted by the brain as warmth and cold, respectively. Receptors that are triggered when skin cells are damaged are called nociceptors; their signals to the brain are interpreted as pain.

ANIMAL SENSES

Some animals have sense organs that humans do not and can thereby sense and perceive stimuli that humans cannot. Many birds and probably a variety of marine creatures can detect variations in the earth's magnetic field; some fish and invertebrates can detect electrical fields. Other animals have sense organs similar to, but more sensitive than, those of humans; they can intercept a broader range of energy or detect it at lower levels. Insects can see ultraviolet light, while pit vipers can sense infrared light. Elephants can hear infrasound, and mice can hear ultrasound. The olfactory sensitivity of most animals far surpasses that of humans. Because of differences in sensory apparatus, each animal experiences a different sensory reality; this is termed each animal's Umwelt.

BIOENGINEERING USES

One application of the knowledge of sensory modalities is in the field of bioengineering. Knowing that sense organs are biological transducers allows the possibility of replacing damaged or nonfunctional sense organs with artificial transducers, the same way artificial limbs replace missing ones. Today's most advanced artificial limbs can be connected directly to nerves that send information from the motor (movement) areas of the brain;

thus, a person can direct movement of the artificial limb with neural messages via thoughts. Similarly, bioengineers are researching the use of small sensors that can be set up to send electrical signals directly to a person's sensory nerves or the sensory cortex of the brain. Researchers have already developed the first version of a hearing aid to help people who have nerve deafness in the inner ear but whose auditory processing centers in the brain are still intact.

HUMAN FACTORS ENGINEERING

Another field that applies the findings of experimental sensory psychologists is called human factors engineering. People who design complicated instrument panels (for example, in jet cockpits or nuclear reactors) must have an understanding of what kinds of stimuli will elicit attention, what will be irritating, and what will fade unnoticed into the background. Using knowledge of how sound is transmitted and how the human brain perceives sound, human factors engineers have designed police and ambulance sirens that make one type of sound while the vehicle is moving quickly (the air-raid-type wailing sound) and another while the vehicle is moving slowly, as through a crowded intersection (alternating pulses of different pitches). These two types of sounds maximize the likelihood that the siren will be noticed in the different environmental settings. Research by human factors engineers has also prompted many communities to change the color of fire engines from red to yellow; since red is difficult to see in twilight and darkness and bright yellow can be seen well at all times of day, yellow makes a better warning color.

Research by human factors engineers and environmental psychologists is also used to improve commercial products and other aspects of day-to-day living, answering questions such as: How loud should the music be in a dentist's waiting office? What color packaging will attract the most buyers to a product? How much salt does a potato chip need? How much light is necessary to maximize production in a factory? Will noise in a domed stadium cause damage in the fans' ears? Research on sensation and perception is applied in almost every setting imaginable.

INFLUENCING ANIMAL BEHAVIOR

Knowledge of sensation and perception can also be used to influence the behavior of other animals. Since people visit zoos during the daytime, nocturnal animals are often housed in areas bathed in only red light. Most nocturnal animals are colorblind, and since red light by itself is so difficult to see, the animals are tricked into perceiving that it is nighttime and become active for the viewers. Knowing that vultures have an exceptionally good sense of smell and that they are attracted to the scent of rotting meat allowed scientists to find an invisible but dangerous leak in a long, geographically isolated pipeline; after adding the aroma of rotting meat into the pipeline fuel, they simply waited to see where the vultures started circling—and knew where they would find the leak.

LEARNING THEORY

The knowledge that sensation and perception differ across species has also influenced the biggest and perhaps most important field in all of psychology: learning theory. The so-called laws of learning were derived from observations of animals during the acquisition of associations between two previously unassociated stimuli, between a stimulus and a response, or between a behavior and a consequent change in the environment. These laws were originally thought to generalize equally to all species and all stimuli. This belief, along with the prevailing Zeitgeist that held that learning was the basis of all behavior, led to the assumption that studies of any animal could serve as a sufficient model for discovering the principles guiding human learning and behavior. It is now known that such is not the case.

Although laws of learning do generalize nicely in the acquisition of associations between biologically neutral stimuli, each animal's sensory apparatus is designed specifically to sense those stimuli that are relevant for its lifestyle, and how it perceives those stimuli will also be related to its lifestyle. Therefore, the meaning of a particular stimulus may be different for different species, so results from studies on one animal cannot be generalized to another; neither can results from studies using one stimulus or stimulus modality be generalized to another.

Finally, it is important to note that scientific inquiry itself is dependent on human understanding of the human senses. Scientific method is based on the philosophy of empiricism, which states that knowledge must be obtained by direct experience using the physical senses (or extensions of them). In short, all scientific data are collected through the physical senses; thus, the entirety of scientific knowledge is ultimately based on, and limited by, human understanding of, and the limitations of, the human senses.

EVOLUTION OF STUDY

In the late nineteenth and early twentieth centuries, Wilhelm Wundt, often considered the founder of scientific psychology, aspired to study the most fundamental units (or structures) of the mind. Wundt and other European psychologists (called structuralists) focused much of their attention on the description of mental responses to external stimuli—in other words, on sensation and perception. Around the same time, educational philosopher William James developed functionalism in the United States. Functionalists avoided questions about what was happening in the mind and brain and focused on questions about why people respond the way they do to different stimuli.

Today, both the structuralist and the functionalist methodologies have been replaced, but the fundamental questions they addressed remain. Psychologists who study sensation and perception still conduct research into how sense organs and the brain work together to produce perceptions (proximate studies) and why people and other animals have their own particular Umwelts (ultimate studies). Results from proximate and ultimate studies typically lead to different kinds of insights about the human condition. Proximate studies lead to solutions for real-world problems, while studies of ultimate functions provide enlightenment about the evolution of human nature and humans' place in the world; they help identify what stimuli were important throughout human evolutionary history.

For example, the human ear is fine-tuned so that its greatest sensitivity is in the frequency range that matches sounds produced by the human voice. Clearly, this reflects the importance of communication—and, in turn, cooperation—throughout human evolution. More specifically, hearing sensitivity peaks nearer to the frequencies produced by female voices than male voices. This suggests that human language capacity may have evolved out of mother-infant interactions rather than from the need for communication in some other activity, such as hunting.

STIMULI ADAPTATIONS FOR SURVIVAL

Knowing what kinds and intensities of stimuli the human sense organs can detect suggests what stimuli have been important for human survival; furthermore, the way the brain perceives those stimuli says something about their role. Most stimuli that are perceived positively are, in fact, good for people; food tastes and smells "good" because without some kind of psychological inducement to eat, people would not survive. Stimuli that are perceived negatively are those that people need to avoid; the fact that rotting foods smell "bad" is the brain's way of keeping one from eating something that might make one sick. To give an example from another sensory modality, most adults find the sound of a crying baby bothersome; to stop the sound, they address the needs of the infant. Cooing and laughing are rewards that reinforce good parenting.

BIBLIOGRAPHY

Ackerman, Diane. *A Natural History of the Senses*. Reprint. New York: Vintage, 1995. Print.

Baldwin, Carryl L. *Auditory Cognition and Human Performance: Research and Applications*. Boca Raton: Taylor & Francis, 2012. Print.

Bin He, ed. *Neural Engineering*. New York: Springer, 2013. Print.

Brown, Evan L., and Kenneth Deffenbacher. *Perception and the Senses*. New York: Oxford UP, 1979. Print.

Buddenbrock, Wolfgang von. *The Senses*. Ann Arbor: U of Michigan P, 1962. Print.

Gescheider, George. *Psychophysics: The Fundamentals*. 3d ed. Hillsdale: Lawrence Erlbaum, 1997. Print.

Hall, Edward Twitchell. *The Hidden Dimension*. 1966. Reprint. New York: Anchor, 1990. Print.

Lawless, Harry T. *Quantitative Sensory Analysis*. West Sussex: John Wiley & Sons, 2014. Print.

Meilgaard, Morten C., Gail Vance Civille, and B. Thomas Carr. *Sensory Evaluation Techniques*. 4th ed. Boca Raton: Taylor & Francis, 2007. Print.

Scharf, Bertram, ed. *Experimental Sensory Psychology*. Glenview: Scott, Foresman, 1976. Print.

Seligman, Martin E. P. "On the Generality of the Laws of Learning." *Psychological Review* 77.5 (1970): 406–18. Print.

Stone, Herbert, and Joel L. Sidel. *Sensory Evaluation Practices*. 3d ed. Boston: Elsevier, 2004. Print.

Linda Mealey

SEE ALSO: Hearing; Pain; Sensation and perception; Smell and taste; Touch and pressure; Vision: Brightness and contrast; Vision: Color; Visual system.

Separation and divorce
Adult issues

TYPE OF PSYCHOLOGY: Developmental psychology

Marriage is one of the most significant of all adult life structures, and so the experience of separation and divorce is a major change in the psychological life and subsequent development of the adults involved.

KEY CONCEPTS
- Acceptance
- Anger
- Bargaining
- Denial
- Depression
- Divorce
- Morbid dependency
- Parental alienation syndrome
- Preseparation
- Separation

INTRODUCTION

Separation and divorce occur when a husband and wife decide to cease living together. In some cases, separation is temporary, allowing a couple to resolve their problems and resume living together. A divorce is a permanent loss and the end of a marriage.

In the United States, divorce is very common, with approximately one divorce for every two marriages in an average year. This is among the highest divorce rates in the world (although rates of marriage and remarriage in the United States are also among the highest). This rate, however, varied considerably over the twentieth century. Factors contributing to these trends include the decreasing significance of religious and social stigma surrounding divorce, the increasing perception that marriage should be based on love and serve personal growth and self-fulfillment, and the attainment by women of economic self-sufficiency.

Demographically, divorce is more common in couples who married young, who experienced a premarital pregnancy, and who are financially downwardly mobile. Divorce is also more prevalent in couples who come from divorced families or have not resolved attachments or conflicts with their families of origin. Divorce is more frequent in subsequent marriages than in first marriages.

DIVORCE AS A LEGAL AND ECONOMIC REALITY

Divorce, like marriage, is a legal arrangement with significant economic consequences. The major legal issues include division of property, alimony, child support, custody, and visitation. Although these issues are settled by the divorcing couple through negotiation or litigation,

Photo: iStock

the courts of each state now have guidelines that specify certain parameters as generally appropriate. How these are handled will have a large impact on the psychological experience of divorce. The legal process establishes and promotes an adversarial relationship for the couple. Although this arrangement is to be expected of a jurisprudence system built on an adversarial pursuit of justice, an essentially combative relationship is profoundly antithetical to the goal of a psychologically healthy divorce. Rather than working together toward a mutually satisfying result, divorcing couples are trained to compete in a distinctly win-lose arena, often with disastrous consequences for both. As an appreciation of the psychological costs of these consequences has grown, mediation has emerged as an increasingly popular alternative way of resolving the legal issues.

THE PSYCHOLOGICAL PHASES OF DIVORCE

When a couple divorces, a great loss is experienced by all family members. This experience is not a momentary event. Its impact continues to unfold over time, as its meaning undergoes various transformations until it is gradually assimilated. There are predictable stages involved in letting go of a marriage and moving on in life. These stages appear in the experience of both members of the couple, regardless of who wanted the separation or divorce. The spouse who decides to live apart usu-

ally begins grieving the relationship while the couple is still living together. Although both spouses go through a mourning process, they often go through stages at different times and rates.

Much of the literature in the psychology of divorce has been devoted to mapping these phases. Some recognize that the steps of divorce actually begin in the period before separation. As Constance Ahrons demonstrated in *The Good Divorce* (1994), divorce is not entered into easily or quickly. Typically, the preseparation phase involves a protracted period of confused tension, and it is during this painfully drawn-out ending that the most serious psychological harm is inflicted on any children. Divorced couples frequently realize, in hindsight, that the marriage should have ended sooner. Sadly, it is this period of painful conflict that often provides the needed momentum for the separation to be enacted as welcome relief.

Craig and Sandra Everett in *Healthy Divorce* (1994) identify three preseparation stages. First, clouds of doubt gather, as one becomes increasingly disillusioned with one's partner and ambivalent about continuing in the marriage. One may become confused, with questions about what was initially attractive about one's partner. One becomes increasingly angry and critical and acts out that unhappiness. These early warning signs could lead the couple to make changes to save their marriage, especially with the help of marriage therapy, but the full significance of these signs is usually unrecognized and therapy entered into only later, when it is too late. The second preseparation stage is "the cold shoulder." Warmth and affection are withdrawn, and there is less talk, disclosure, or support as one becomes emotionally unavailable to one's partner. This pulling away is also evident in a declining interest or responsiveness in sexual relations and even in physical withdrawal, as more separate and independent activity is undertaken, excluding the partner. In stage three, fantasies of a life beyond the marriage emerge. Usually they are idealized sexual or romantic liaisons or adventurous escapes. Sometimes a spouse may act out these fantasies through extramarital affairs.

Once the actual physical separation takes place, the couple undergoes a grieving process, an experience of letting go of their marriage. As a form of grief work, this process is analogous to the phases people experience when mourning the death of a loved one, or when coming to terms with one's own impending death (a process first identified by Elisabeth Kübler-Ross in 1969).

Not everyone goes through all the stages, and sometimes people's grieving varies from the usual sequence. Some people get stuck in certain stages of the mourning process and need psychotherapy to help them move on.

STAGES OF GRIEVING

In the first phase, denial, people may completely deny the marital problem, or, in a more sophisticated form, they may minimize the import of the problem by a sort of magical thinking, an "if only" fantasy ("It could all be resolved if only . . . "). Such a fantasy can be held only in the mind (safe from any testing against reality), or it may lead to desperate, even self-destructive efforts to resurrect a dead relationship. In the extreme, this course can become a pathological morbid dependency on the partner. Unable to move on, such people may remain fixated on their former spouse for many years afterward. Even after it becomes evident that the partner has actually left, people can still use wishful thinking to minimize the real impact of this rupture. For example, they may think that the partner will come back once he or she realizes that no one else will be as suitable. The children of divorcing parents are prone to such fantasies of reconciliation as well. They will be very vulnerable to construing parents' words or actions as hopeful indicators of this possibility.

In the second phase, anger, people tend to blame the breakup on the other partner. Thoughts such as, "If he (or she) were not like this, we could still be married," are very common. Here, unlike the experience of grieving a death, there is an overwhelming sense of personal rejection by one who was loved dearly. It is this profound hurt that underlies the intense feelings of anger. In such a view, the marital breakdown is seen as completely the fault of the other, and people cannot see their own role in the unsatisfactory state of the marriage. In this phase, people are likely to become outspokenly critical of their partner to friends and children. Richard A. Gardner has described this "campaign of denigration" and the sad consequences that accrue when one parent successfully induces in the children a directive to carry this anger toward the other parent. Gardner identifies the subsequent withdrawing of affection by the child as the parental alienation syndrome: a loss, sometimes for years, of a close bond with that parent. In another extreme form, such anger can become pathologically overgeneralized. It is directed then to all men or women. Such a negative stereotype will preclude or sabotage any subsequent effort toward an intimate relationship with a person of that gender.

In the third phase, bargaining, the reality of the ending is still avoided, now by maneuvers designed to ward it off. Typically, they involve implicit or explicit offers to act differently to better suit the partner. The "bargain" involves a fantasy that change would eliminate the problem and stop the divorce. Like denial, these typically are formulated as "if only . . . ." In the extreme form, people make bargains with themselves, to enact changes designed to alter the situation. While all these bargaining ploys are unrealistic, their function is something deeper than warding off the divorce, for which they are ineffective. They serve to ward off the subjective experience of the reality and finality of the divorce by remaining focused on how to "fix" it.

In the fourth phase, depression, the reality of the divorce breaks through people's previous efforts to minimize or avoid its emotional impact. People feel the depressive weight of the loss without the cushioning provided by denial, anger, and bargaining. This initial despair is founded on a deep sense of shame for having a failed marriage and so is accompanied by feelings of guilt and low self-esteem. Then the demands of life and fears about the future can become overwhelming. People feel inadequate to handle the roles previously taken care of by their spouse (such as finances or social arrangements). Self-defeating thoughts further undermine functioning. People may cry frequently and experience a variety of somatic problems, including changes in appetite (either eating very little or overeating); changes in sleep (either insomnia or excessive sleeping); a marked decrease in level of energy; a tendency to become isolated from social contact; an increased use of addictive substances (such as alcohol, nicotine, television, computers); and a loss of pleasure in things that used to bring joy. These symptoms are manifestations of the crushing sadness that the reality of the divorce now brings as people begin to experience the true impact of the loss.

Beyond the sense of sheer loss, there is a final phase of this process. In the fifth phase, acceptance, resolution occurs. People accept that the marriage has ended and will not be revived and that they can survive and even thrive. People reorient to a single life, incorporating this reality into a new sense of identity and functioning. When this occurs, there is a renewed interest in life; regular patterns of sleeping, eating, and activity resume; and coping mechanisms (such as excessive drinking or television viewing) abate. As anger and guilt are released, people become able to speak about and relate to their former spouses without bitterness. They do not forget the painful experience of the divorce or the preceding unhappiness in the marriage. Rather, the marital failure is seen as an opportunity for personal growth, an occasion to learn lessons and to gain insights to integrate into subsequent relationships.

As negative overgeneralizations about the other gender and about the possibility of intimate relationships are released, people become available to form new interpersonal connections. Typically, divorced individuals do remarry, often to others who are themselves divorced. The resulting unions can involve a bewildering array of step-relationships with children of new partners. Their success will depend on whether the new couple has been able to work through the issues from their divorces.

BIBLIOGRAPHY

Ahrons, Constance. *The Good Divorce.* Rev. and updated. New York: HarperCollins, 1995. Print.

Clarke-Stewart, Alison, and Cornelia Brentano. *Divorce: Causes and Consequences.* New York: Yale UP, 2008. Print.

Demo, David H., and Cheryl Buehler. "Theoretical Approaches to Studying Divorce." *Handbook of Family Theories: A Content-Based Approach.* Ed. Mark A. Fine and Frank D. Fincham. New York: Routledge, 2013. Print.

Everett, Craig, and Sandra Everett. *Healthy Divorce.* San Francisco: Jossey-Bass, 1998. Print.

Gardner, Richard A. *The Parental Alienation Syndrome.* 2nd ed. Cresskill: Creative Therapeutics, 2000. Print.

Guttman, Joseph. *Divorce in Psychosocial Perspective.* Hillsdale: Erlbaum, 1993. Print.

Kaufman, Taube S. *The Combined Family.* New York: Plenum, 1993. Print.

Kübler-Ross, Elisabeth. *On Death and Dying.* 1969. Reprint. New York: Routledge, 2009. Print.

Margulies, Sam. *Getting Divorced without Ruining Your Life.* Rev. and updated. New York: Simon, 2001. Print.

Mercer, Diana, and Katie Jane Wennechuck. *Making Divorce Work.* New York: Perigee, 2010. Print.

Schaffer, Jill. "A Humanistic Approach to Mediation." *Humanistic Psychologist* 27.2 (1999): 213–20. Print.

Christopher M. Aanstoos and Judi Garland

SEE ALSO: Children's mental health; Computer and Internet use and mental health; Couples therapy; Family life: Adult issues; Intimacy; Kübler-Ross, Elisabeth; Love; Midlife crises; Parental alienation syndrome; Separation and divorce: Children's issues.

Separation and divorce
Children's issues

TYPE OF PSYCHOLOGY: Developmental psychology; Social psychology

Marital separation and divorce are stressful life transitions to which children must adapt in many ways. Several perspectives to explain the impact of divorce on children have been developed. Research identifies common issues for children of divorce, but individual adjustment may vary significantly as a result of a variety of factors.

KEY CONCEPTS
- Divorce-stress-adjustment model
- Family composition perspective
- Family process viewpoint
- Individual risk and vulnerability perspective
- Parental distress perspective
- Stress and socioeconomic disadvantage viewpoint
- Stressful family transition

INTRODUCTION

At the beginning of the twenty-first century, every year more than one million children in the United States experienced the divorce of their parents, according to the U.S. Bureau of the Census. It was estimated that about 40 percent of all children would experience divorce before they reached eighteen years of age.

Most studies regarding children's issues in divorce conceptualize the separation and divorce process as a stressful family transition to which children must adapt. These studies focus on the specific factors that children face in divorce, the protective factors that may assist them, and the range of outcomes experienced by all children of divorce. Divorce is not a discrete event but a process that begins with the specific sociological aspects in place in a particular family prior to the marital separation and continues through the divorce to the adjustment period afterward. Children are involved throughout the process and may experience a range of psychological, social, academic, and health issues as a result of the divorce. Children from different ethnic and cultural groups may experience different rates of parental divorce and remarriage and variations in specific effects.

The study of children's issues before, during, and after separation and divorce is controversial because of the different social and political viewpoints held by family life scholars. Some scholars believe that children need two-parent homes to achieve optimum development and that divorce and single-parent families have a negative impact on the institution of the family, resulting in many social problems. Other scholars believe that it is possible for children to develop well in different family structures, including single-parent families and stepfamilies. These scholars suggest that divorce may resolve home problems and ultimately benefit the development of children by creating more healthy and positive home environments. The differences among scholars can lead to alternative interpretations of research results and very different reports of the implications of research findings for families and society.

PERSPECTIVES ON CHILDREN'S ADJUSTMENT

American psychologist E. Mavis Hetherington identified five perspectives that help to explain the relationship between divorce and children's adjustment to it. The individual risk and vulnerability perspective proposes that some parents may have characteristics or psychological problems that make it more likely that they will experience divorce. These individual factors will also have an impact on the way the parents handle the divorce and the consequences of divorce for their children. On the other hand, children have individual characteristics that may safeguard them from the negative consequences of divorce or increase their vulnerability to negative outcomes.

The family composition perspective predicts that any family structure other than the two-biological-parent family may be related to increased problems for children. Research concerning the father's absence after divorce is related to this perspective.

The stress and socioeconomic disadvantage viewpoint notes that divorce may lead to an increased number of stressful life events, including new roles, change of residence, loss of social networks, child-care problems, conflict with the former spouse, and decreases in family finances. Children and parents may be affected negatively by these events. Research on the frequent financial problems of former spouses, especially custodial mothers, originates from this viewpoint.

The parental distress perspective indicates that tremendous variability exists in how individual parents handle all the issues and difficulties involved in divorce. Some parents are able to manage the events well and continue to provide consistent parenting to their children; other parents experience a noted deterioration in their parenting skills following divorce.

Finally, the family process viewpoint recognizes that divorced families may demonstrate disruptions in family relationships and interactions, having an impact on such processes as child discipline or child rearing. Hetherington suggests that the five perspectives complement each other and form a transactional model for understanding the impact of divorce on children.

Sociologist Paul R. Amato of Pennsylvania State University proposed a divorce-stress-adjustment model that incorporates the multiple perspectives noted by Hetherington into three factors: mediators, moderators, and adjustment. Amato noted that the divorce process may begin months or years prior to separation with a cycle involving overt conflict between the parents, attempts to renegotiate the relationship, or avoidance and denial of the problems. It is not unusual to note increased behavior problems in children at this early stage that reflect the marital discord.

Individual differences, however, may be noted between children. Some children may experience significant distress as a result of parental conflict prior to separation, so that the level of distress diminishes after marital separation. Other children may be unaware of the marital difficulties until the separation occurs, precipitating significant distress at that point. Children experience mediators or stressors that continue throughout the divorce process. They may include a decline in parental support and effective control, loss of contact with one parent, continuing conflict between parents, and economic decline.

In Amato's model, moderators or protective factors interact with the stressors throughout the process to determine the ultimate adjustment of the child. Moderators include individual resources (such as coping skills), interpersonal resources (such as extended family support), structural resources (such as school programs and services), and demographic characteristics (age, gender, race, ethnicity, and culture) that combine to determine how a particular child will respond to the stressors of divorce. Adjustment refers to the time and intensity of psychological, behavioral, and health problems for children before they adapt to the new roles required of them by the divorce.

MOST COMMON ISSUES FOR CHILDREN

Research on the effects of divorce on children between 1960 and 2000 consistently showed that children whose parents had divorced scored lower than children whose parents remained married on several outcome measures.

Amato analyzed the research several times and noted small but statistically significant differences on measures such as conduct, academic achievement, psychological adjustment, self-concept, social competence, and long-term health. These effects continue even though more children are experiencing family divorce, the social stigma of divorce appears to have diminished, and support services for children of divorce have increased. A few studies indicate that divorce has positive results for some children, especially when divorce ends chronic high-conflict marriages that had created negative home environments, but the number of children in this type of situation is relatively low.

Research conducted by sociologist Yongmin Sun at Ohio State University confirmed that divorce is a multistage process, beginning before separation. Sun studied 10,088 students and compared the results of 798 students (8 percent) whose parents divorced over a two-year period to students whose parents did not divorce. He found that families in the predisruption phase, the period when the family is still intact before disruption of the marriage, show evidence of different family processes than do families that remain intact. The families that eventually divorced experienced deterioration in relationships between the parents and the children at least one year before the divorce. These parents did fewer things with their children, had lower expectations for the children, and were not as involved in school issues and events. The children had lower school math and reading scores and exhibited more behavior problems than did children in families that did not experience divorce.

After divorce, children may experience a variety of effects. One major problem for children of divorce is the continuation of preseparation conflict between the parents into the postdivorce period. By the second year after separation, one-third of parent relationships are still conflicted, one-fourth have achieved a cooperative coparenting relationship, and one-third are disconnected and do not interact about parenting. Continuing conflict is a problem because exposure to angry exchanges and fighting is itself a stressor for children. Conflict may also result in decreases in the quality of the parent-child relationship, including less consistent discipline, less demonstration of affection toward the child, emotional dependence on the child, less ability to control parental anger, and using the child as a cocombatant in disputes with the former spouse. Conflict that involves the child directly (such as fights in the child's presence or arguments that focus on the child or child rearing or include

the child in the dispute) is most harmful to the child. In general, the greater the degree of conflict between the parents, the more likely it is that the child will experience psychological distress. Interventions that diminish conflict are likely to have beneficial results for children of divorce.

Many children have diminished contact with their fathers following the divorce. Studies indicate that when the mother has primary physical custody, more than one-fourth of all children report that they did not see their father in the last year and only about one-fourth saw their father at least weekly. More than half of fathers are not involved at all in making decisions about their children, and half did not pay any child support during the previous year. Fathers who have joint custody, live near their children, or had stronger emotional relations with their children prior to the divorce are more likely to have regular contact after the divorce.

The effects of divorce on children often continue over time, although the immediate emotional disruption and behavioral problems may be resolved within the first two years. Interview research by Judith Wallerstein with children of divorce over a twenty-five-year period suggested that even as children grow into adulthood, there is a continuing impact of divorce on their attitudes and behaviors toward relationships and marriage. Other researchers note a variety of effects later in life, including an increased probability of divorce for the children of divorce.

BIBLIOGRAPHY

Amato, Paul R. "The Consequences of Divorce for Adults and Children." *Journal of Marriage and the Family* 62 (2000): 1269–87. Print.

Baker, Amy J. L., and Paul R. Fine. *Surviving Parental Alienation: A Journey of Hope and Healing.* Lanham: Rowman & Littlefield, 2014. Print.

Emery, Robert E. *Marriage, Divorce, and Children's Adjustment.* 2nd ed. Thousand Oaks: Sage, 1999. Print.

Hetherington, E. Mavis, ed. *Coping with Divorce, Single Parenting, and Remarriage: A Risk and Resiliency Perspective.* Mahwah: Lawrence Erlbaum, 1999. Print.

O'Hagan, Kieran. *Filicide-Suicide: The Killing of Children in the Context of Separations, Divorce and Custody Disputes.* New York: Palgrave Macmillan, 2014. Print.

Teyber, Edward. *Helping Children Cope with Divorce.* Rev. ed. San Francisco: Jossey-Bass, 2001. Print.

Thompson, Ross A., and Paul R. Amato, eds. *The*

Postdivorce Family: Children, Parenting, and Society. Thousand Oaks: Sage, 1999. Print.

Wallerstein, Judith S., and Joan B. Kelly. *Surviving the Breakup.* 1980. New York: Basic Books, 1996. Print.

Wallerstein, Judith S., Julia Lewis, and Sandra Blakeslee. *The Unexpected Legacy of Divorce: A Twenty-five Year Landmark Study.* New York: Hyperion, 2002. Print.

Wallerstein, Judith, Julia Lewis, and Sherrin Packer Rosenthal. "Mothers and Their Children after Divorce: Report from a 25-Year Longitudinal Study." *Psychoanalytic Psychology* 30.2 (2013): 167–84. Print.

Mark Stanton

SEE ALSO: Children's mental health; Family life: Children's issues; Father-child relationship; Motherchild relationship; Parental alienation syndrome; Separation and divorce: Adult issues; Stepfamilies.

Separation anxiety

TYPE OF PSYCHOLOGY: Developmental psychology

Separation anxiety is characterized by fear on separation from home or parents/caretakers. Separation anxiety, while a normal part of the developmental process, can become a behavior of concern when it is persistent, intense, and impairing.

KEY CONCEPTS
- Behavioral inhibition
- Cognitive behavioral therapy
- School refusal
- Separation anxiety disorder

INTRODUCTION

Anxiety is often defined as apprehension related to the expectation of real or imagined danger. Many of the anxieties seen in childhood are expected in the course of normal development, cause mild discomfort, and have a quick resolution. Separation anxiety may be defined as fear on separation from home or parents/caretakers and has been identified and described both as a part of the normal developmental process and as a sign of disorder since the early 1900's. Sigmund Freud, John Bowlby, and other personality theorists have described the phenomenology and significance of this common fear. Separation anxiety usually begins between six and nine months of age, reaches a peak between ten and eighteen months, and often resolves by the end of the second year. Parents may first notice separation anxiety in their young child as clingy, crying, tearful, or protesting behaviors that begin on separation and typically disappear on reunion. Once children begin daycare or school (ages two through six), it is not uncommon to see a resurgence of separation anxiety during morning drop-offs or at bedtime. Typically, this separation anxiety is mild, and children calm down shortly after their parents' departure. While the anxious behaviors (such as crying) are a cause of discomfort and strain for the parents, generally, separation anxiety is not a cause for concern. Separation anxiety is considered a normal part of the developmental process.

There are times, however, when separation anxiety does become a cause for concern. Separation anxiety becomes a clinical concern when the anxiety is excessive, of relatively long duration, and a significant source of interference for the parents or the child. If the separation anxiety is disproportionate to the situation, persists beyond age-appropriate reactions, and keeps the child or family from doing the things they want or need to do, then the behavioral patterns are most likely outside the range of what is considered normal. When separation anxious behaviors become atypical given the child's age and developmental course, the behaviors may be characterized as symptoms of a clinical disorder.

SEPARATION ANXIETY DISORDER

Separation anxiety first made its appearance as a childhood anxiety disorder in 1980 with the American Psychiatric Association's publication of the third edition of the *Diagnostic and Statistical Manual of Mental Disorders* (DSM-III). Although the fourth edition text revision of the *Diagnostic and Statistical Manual of Mental Disorders* (DSM-IV-TR, 2000) recognizes the possibility of separation anxiety in adults, this presentation is regarded as rare. Separation anxiety disorder is characterized by developmentally inappropriate and excessive anxiety on separation from home or from attachment figures. Prevalence rates range from 2 to 5 percent of children.

Separation anxiety disorder is manifested as the refusal to be left alone. Children will actively, even vehemently, avoid separations with parents by refusing to stay home alone, go to school, go to sleepovers, or sleep by themselves. Children may demand that parents do not vacation, leave home, or even be in another area or room of the house without them. They anxiously anticipate separations (for instance, worrying weeks before the parents' vacation) and experience extreme distress during the separations. School refusal (frequent calls home during the school day or multiple trips to the school nurse) is not uncommon for children suffering from separation anxiety disorder. These children have difficulty not only separating for school in the morning but also separating at bedtime. Many children with this disorder sleep in their parents' beds or insist that a parent accompany them to bed.

Children with separation anxiety disorder frequently worry that during the separation, some danger or harm will befall their loved ones. They fear permanent separation, such as the parent being in an accident, the death of the parent, or their own abduction. The child often views the world as a dangerous place—a place where various and numerous untold, untoward events may occur. Children with this disorder often experience physical symptoms of anxiety. They complain of stomachaches, nausea, vomiting, headaches, hyperventilation, and rapid heartbeat.

POSSIBLE CAUSES

Little research has specifically targeted the origin or causes of separation anxiety disorder. However, a fair amount of research has been accumulated that has examined the origins of childhood anxiety more generally. Research has identified several risk factors for childhood anxiety disorder, including attachment style, parental anxiety, child temperament, negative life events, and parenting style. Attachment style anxiety (the style of relating to an attachment figure) has been identified as a potential risk factor for childhood anxiety. Parental anxiety has been demonstrated to be predictive of anxiety disorders in children. Anxious children are more likely than nonanxious peers to have an anxious parent. Additionally, children who possess the temperamental characteristic of behavioral inhibition (a shy, fearful personality style) and who experience negative life events are at increased risk for the development of a childhood anxiety disorder. Last, several parenting characteristics or styles have been associated with child anxiety. Researchers found parents of anxious children to be more overcontrolling, more overprotective, and more likely to allow or encourage their children to avoid feared situations than other parents.

DEVELOPMENTAL OUTCOMES AND TREATMENTS

Several researchers have noted the link between anxiety in childhood and anxiety in adulthood. More specifically, researchers have suggested a link between separation anxiety disorder in childhood and panic attacks and

---

DSM-IV-TR CRITERIA FOR SEPARATION ANXIETY

SEPARATION ANXIETY DISORDER (DSM CODE 309.21)

Developmentally inappropriate and excessive anxiety concerning separation from home or from those to whom the individual is attached

Evidenced by three or more of the following:
- recurrent excessive distress when separation from home or major attachment figures occurs or is anticipated
- persistent and excessive worry about losing, or about possible harm befalling, major attachment figures
- persistent and excessive worry that an untoward event (such as getting lost or being kidnapped) will lead to separation from a major attachment figure
- persistent reluctance or refusal to go to school or elsewhere because of fear of separation
- persistent and excessive fear or reluctance to be alone or without major attachment figures at home or without significant adults in other settings
- persistent reluctance or refusal to go to sleep without being near a major attachment figure or to sleep away from home
- repeated nightmares involving the theme of separation
- repeated complaints of physical symptoms (such as headaches, stomachaches, nausea, or vomiting) when separation from major attachment figures occurs or is anticipated

Duration of at least four weeks

Onset before eighteen years of age; early onset occurs before six years of age

Disturbance causes clinically significant distress or impairment in social, academic, or other important areas of functioning

Disturbance does not occur exclusively during the course of a pervasive developmental disorder, schizophrenia, or other psychotic disorder

In adolescents and adults, not better accounted for by Panic Disorder with Agoraphobia

Photo: iStock

agoraphobia in adulthood.

A number of approaches have been used to treat childhood separation anxiety, most notably behavioral (such as exposure-based techniques and contingency management) and cognitive (such as problem-solving training). Most often, however, these approaches are used in combination as cognitive behavioral therapy. Cognitive behavior therapy address both thoughts and behaviors while emphasizing their reciprocal relationship—thought affects behavior and behavior affects thought. In the 1990's, treatment research flourished, and cognitive behavioral interventions have shown real promise in helping children with clinical levels of separation anxiety.

BIBLIOGRAPHY

Bowlby, John. *A Secure Base: Parent-Child Attachment and Healthy Development*. London: Routledge, 2007. The author examines the nature and importance of parental bonding in early child development and presents a model for how such attachment promotes later psychological health and well-being.

_____. *Separation: Anxiety and Anger*. New York: Basic Books, 2000. The author examines the effect of separation on child development and discusses the psychopathology that may result from such separations.

McLeod, Bryce D., and Jeffrey J. Wood. *Child Anxiety Disorders: A Family-Based Treatment Manual for Practitioners*. New York: W. W. Norton, 2008. The authors claim that more than 10 percent of children can be diagnosed with anxiety disorder, and in this book they suggest therapeutic strategies that can be employed by doctors, schools, and parents to help these troubled youngsters. The second half of the book is a treatment manual.

March, J. S., ed. *Anxiety Disorders in Children and Adolescents*. 2d ed. New York: Guilford, 2004. Edited volume in which experts in child anxiety explore neurobiological foundations, risk factors, assessment strategies, current literature on specific disorders, and treatment approaches.

Rapee, Ronald M., Ann Wignall, Susan H. Spence, et al. *Helping Your Anxious Child: A Step-by-Step Guide for Parents*. Oakland, Calif.: Harbinger, 2008. This resource, designed for parents, offers suggestions for helping children who are suffering with anxiety, which may take the form of phobias, panic, shyness, or obsessive-compulsive disorder. There is practical advice for treating children who are troubled by separation anxiety.

Silverman, W., and P. Treffers, eds. *Anxiety Disorders in Children and Adolescents: Research, Assessment, and Intervention*. New York: Cambridge University Press, 2001. Edited text exploring the theory, research, and treatment of anxiety disorders in children and adolescents. Chapters include discussions of historical, genetic/biological, temperamental, and psychosocial perspectives, as well as current information on treatment techniques and prevention strategies.

Vasey, M., and M. Dadds, eds. *The Developmental Psychopathology of Anxiety*. New York: Oxford University Press, 2001. Edited volume in which authoritative experts in the field of child anxiety present factors that contribute to the etiology and maintenance of anxiety disorders in childhood, adolescence, and adulthood. Book sections include preliminary issues; predisposing, protective, maintaining, and ameliorating influences; and integrative examples.

Ellen C. Flannery-Schroeder

SEE ALSO: Anxiety disorders; Attachment and bonding in infancy and childhood; Bed-wetting; Childhood disorders; Children's mental health; Cognitive behavior therapy; Conduct disorder; Dyslexia; Family life: Children's issues; Father-child relationship; Learning disorders; Misbehavior; Mother-child relationship; Psychotherapy: Children; Separation and divorce:

Children's issues; Stuttering.

Sex addiction

TYPE OF PSYCHOLOGY: Addiction; Biological bases of human behavior; Clinical; Counseling; Psychopathology, Psychotherapy

Sex addiction is a label applied in both clinical settings and popular psychology circles, when people engage in sexual behavior that is excessive in frequency, intensity, or duration and that leads to adverse consequences, such as subjective distress or impairment in social or occupational roles. It is not a technical diagnosis. Common manifestations include excessive use of pornography, compulsive masturbation, intercourse with many casual partners or with prostitutes, and cybersex, including "sexting" (exchanging text messages and photographs for the purpose of sexual arousal).

KEY CONCEPTS
- Behavioral addiction
- Classical conditioning

- Dopamine
- Romantic attachment

WHAT ARE ITS CAUSES

The causes of sex addiction are not known. Nevertheless, as with substance addictions, most research focuses on the structures of the brain's mesolimbic reward system and the neurotransmitter (chemical messenger) dopamine. Most researchers believe that the mesolimbic reward system evolved to sustain behaviors that are necessary for survival and reproduction, namely the pursuit of food, water, and sex.

Normal sexual arousal and orgasm involve excitation in the brain's mesolimbic reward system. In sex addiction, repeated sexual behavior is hypothesized to result in excessive stimulation of dopamine pathways in structures of the mesolimbic reward system (for example, the striatum), thereby causing changes at the cellular level (fewer dopamine receptors) that lead to even greater desire and cravings to engage in the behavior.

As in substance addictions, classical conditioning appears to play a role in the development and maintenance of many sexually addictive behaviors. Stimuli that are present when an addict engages in the problem behavior, such as a computer that the person uses to view pornography or a street where the person has often visited a strip club, can become powerful triggers for the desire to engage in the addictive behavior.

THE RISK FACTORS

Men are at higher risk than women for sex addiction. Although high-quality epidemiological data are lacking, the substantial majority (80 percent or more) of sex addicts addressed in published work are male. Access to numerous sexual partners also may be a risk factor. Thus, men who are famous or socially powerful may be at especially heightened risk for sex addiction.

In 2010, tremendous media attention focused on the alleged sex addiction of golf superstar Tiger Woods, who was reportedly treated for the condition. In 2011, Anthony Weiner resigned from the US House of Representatives because of his alleged involvement in a sexting scandal. Although both Woods and Weiner and numerous other high profile persons with "excessive" sexual activity were labeled as sex addicts by much of the popular media, it is not known whether either men met any formal or informal criteria for sex addiction.

Some experts have suggested that childhood sexual abuse may play an important role in the development of sex addiction. Nevertheless, available research suggests that childhood sexual abuse is a nonspecific risk factor for a broad range of mental health difficulties during adulthood rather than a specific risk factor for sex addiction.

Although pornography viewing and masturbation are common manifestations of sex addiction, these behaviors are common among adult men, and the vast majority of these men will never develop behaviors that are compulsive or otherwise problematic. Thus, masturbation and pornography are not considered risk factors for sex addiction.

Some clinicians believe rates of sex addiction have increased in recent years because of the internet. They argue that the internet has made pornography, and connection with casual sex partners and prostitutes, far more accessible, anonymous, and affordable than ever before. This claim is plausible, but there are no firm data to support or refute it.

THE SYMPTOMS

The manifestations of sex addiction are diverse. Nevertheless, all manifestations involve a preoccupation with sexual thoughts, fantasies, or urges and sexual activity that is excessive in frequency or duration. The behavior is pursued despite obvious costs and consequences, such as loss of a job or relationship or getting a sexually transmitted disease. Many sex addicts have repeatedly attempted to discontinue or curb their behavior unsuccessfully.

There is controversy concerning whether sex addicts exhibit tolerance and withdrawal. In support of the view that tolerance develops, some have observed that many sex addicts take greater risks over time and engage in increasingly extreme or unusual sex acts. Similarly, some argue that withdrawal is evident in the frustration and anger sex addicts experience when they cannot engage in the desired sexual behaviors.

Many clinicians have reported that sex addicts use sexual behavior as a way to cope with unpleasant emotions; this possibility needs to be examined in systematic research. Data are limited, but preliminary information suggests that sex addiction is highly comorbid (overlapping), not only with substance addictions but also with anxiety and mood disorders.

Sex addiction may manifest differently in women than in men. Rather than focusing on fantasies and behaviors associated with sexual gratification, as do most men with sex addiction, some women who self-identify as sex addicts appear to experience an ongoing series of intense romantic attachments toward new partners. The romantic attachments may develop toward inappropriate persons (such as a coworker or boss) and despite possible negative consequences (such as the loss of one's marriage). Although no systematic data are available, there have been occasional reports of men who experience such a series of attachments to many partners over time. Some authors refer to this ongoing pattern of new romantic attachments as love addiction.

ITS SCREENING AND DIAGNOSIS

As noted, sex addiction is not yet recognized as a formal behavioral health diagnosis. Many clinicians believe there is a need for a diagnosis for sexual behaviors (intercourse or masturbation) that are excessive in frequency or duration and causes subjective distress or impairment in social or occupational functioning, and the term, hypersexuality is in common parlance and focuses on what most consider "normal" sexual behaviors that are habitual and cause distress or impairment. The term "sex addiction" encompasses both the "normal" sexual behaviors and what many consider "unusual" sexual behaviors like exhibitionism, fetishes, and paraphilias that are habitual, cause distress, and functional and/or relational impairment.

A clinician who suspects sex addiction should conduct a thorough interview, obtain a detailed history covering the person's sexual behaviors, urges, and fantasies and their frequency, duration, and consequences. Clinicians also may screen for sex addiction using various checklists and questionnaires.

TREATMENT AND THERAPY

Little research has been conducted on the efficacy of treatments for sex addiction. However, most treatment approaches for sex addiction parallel effective treatments for substance addictions and other behavioral addictions (e.g., gambling, gaming, exercise, shopping). These approaches include behavioral and cognitive-behavioral therapies. Such treatments teach addicts how to recognize and avoid stimuli that increase the risk of engaging in sexually inappropriate behavior. These stimuli generally include people, places, and internet sites associated with the addict's previous maladaptive sexual behavior.

Because many sex addicts engage in sexually inappropriate behaviors in response to negative emotions, sex addicts may be taught skills that enable them to cope with negative feelings more adaptively and to identify situations that may trigger unpleasant emotions, such as anger or feelings of loneliness. Cognitive-behavioral therapy interventions also seek to identify and correct erroneous beliefs (for example, "I will be miserable if I cannot have sex when I have the urge to do so") that the addict maintains about sex or romantic relationships.

In addition to embracing traditional psychotherapy, many clinicians and recovering sex addicts believe twelve-step programs like Sexaholic anonymous (SA) that are modeled after Alcoholic Anonymous (AA) are helpful to recovering sex addicts. A difference between traditional AA self-management and SA is that AA promotes complete abstinence from alcohol and SA and similar twelve-step groups for sex addicts promote responsible sexual behavior, not actual abstinence. Inpatient treatment programs for sex addiction exist and are typically used when outpatient treatments fail to curb life-threatening behaviors, such as frequent, unprotected sex with strangers.

In extreme cases in which a sex addict's behavior is illegal or harmful to others (such as with exhibitionism), anti-androgen medications like Depo-Provera or depot medroxyprogesterone acetate are sometimes prescribed to reduce the person's sex drive. Nevertheless, controlled studies to ascertain whether these medications are effective for sex addiction are lacking.

PREVENTION

No research has been conducted on the prevention of sex addiction.

BIBLIOGRAPHY

Carnes, Patrick J. *Don't Call It Love: Recovery from Sexual Addiction.* New York: Bantam, 1991. Provides an excellent description of the clinical features of sex addiction. However, Carnes based many of his claims on a survey that had low participation rates.

Cooper, Alvin. "Sexuality and the Internet: Surfing into the New Millennium." *Cyberpsychology and Behavior* 1.2 (1998): 187–93. Print. Argues that Internet accessibility, anonymity, and affordability create new risks for sex addiction.

Kafka, Martin P. "Hypersexual Disorder: A Proposed Diagnosis for DSM-V." *Archives of Sexual Behavior* 39.2 (2010): 377–400. Print. Provides rationale for including hypersexual disorder in the next version of the DSM, although the author does not argue that hypersexual disorder should be considered an addiction.

WEBSITES OF INTEREST

American Psychiatric Association, DSM-5 Development
http://www.dsm5.org
Sex Addicts Anonymous
http://www.sexaa.org

Scott O. Lilienfeld

SEE ALSO: Addiction; Pleasure; Psychosexual behavior; Sex; Sexuality.

Sex hormones and motivation

TYPE OF PSYCHOLOGY: Motivation

Sex hormones control sexual maturation and exert an important influence on sexual motivation. The role of the sex hormones varies across species; they play only a limited role in humans.

KEY CONCEPTS

- Androgens
- Antiandrogen drugs
- Estradiol
- Hormones
- Pheromone
- Progesterone
- Testosterone

INTRODUCTION

Sex hormones exert an important influence on behavior. These hormones control sexual maturation at puberty, and they have an impact on the sex drive and on sexual activity throughout the life span. In most animal species, sex hormones completely control sexual behavior. In humans, their role is more limited. Human sexual motivation is the result of the complex interplay of hormones, psychological factors, and social factors.

At puberty, the brain releases several hormones that travel through the bloodstream to target organs. In males, the targets are the testes; in females, the ovaries. In response to the hormones released from the brain, these targets begin to produce the sex hormones. The principal male sex hormone is testosterone (the name refers to the fact that it is produced by the testes). With the production of testosterone at puberty in human males, facial and body hair grows, bones and muscles develop more fully, the voice deepens, and the genitals enlarge. In females, two sex hormones are produced by the ovaries at puberty, estradiol (often called estrogen)and progesterone. Estradiol is responsible for breast development, changes in female appearance (for example, wider hips), and maturation of the genitals and uterus. Progesterone plays a major role in preparing the female body for menstruation and pregnancy. It should be noted that although testosterone is called the "male sex hormone," it is also found in females, though in much smaller quantities. The same applies to the female sex hormones, which are found in males.

After puberty is completed, the sex hormones continue to play a role in sexual motivation. In most mammal species, the female goes through a regular cycle, the Estrous cycleestrous cycle, during which sex hormones are released, causing an increase in sex drive. During this phase of the cycle, a female will seek a male partner with the goal of reproduction; she is said to be "in heat." In the presence of a female in estrus, the male experiences an increase in the sex hormone testosterone, and he will be sexually attracted to the female. For example, male rats will ignore a female whose ovaries have been removed and who thus cannot produce estradiol; however, an injection of estradiol will make the female interested in sex, and males will approach her for sexual activity. In these animals, sexual behavior is largely determined by the females' sexual readiness, which depends on the phase of estrus.

In most animal species, the male learns of a female's sexual readiness by the presence of a chemical she emits called a pheromone. Pheromones are usually derived from vaginal secretions during estrus. If pheromones are collected from an animal in estrus and applied to another that is not in estrus, males will approach the nonreceptive female and attempt sexual intercourse. In humans, pheromones do not appear to play a significant role in sexual attraction.

THE HUMAN CONDITION

Humans are quite different from other animals in other respects. While the sex hormones do have an important influence, they do not control sexual motivation and behavior. Research has shown that males who have abnormally low levels of testosterone have problems achieving erection and often have a very low sex drive. Injections of testosterone restore the ability to obtain normal erection in these cases. Abnormally high levels of testosterone, however, do not cause an unusually high sex drive. Apparently, there is a minimum level of testosterone necessary for normal sexual behavior, but higher levels do not seem to have any significant effect.

Like females of other animal species, the human female goes through a cycle during which levels of sex hormones are increased. This cycle in humans and primates is called the menstrual cycle. Although human females experience cyclic increases in the sex hormones estradiol and progesterone, there is no clear indication of change in sexual motivation during this phase. For most women, sex drive does not vary with sex hormone levels. For example, women who have had their ovaries removed continue to experience a normal sex drive. The same usually applies to women who have undergone menopause, the stage of the life in the late forties during which the ovaries cease producing sex hormones. Most postmenopausal women continue to enjoy a normal sex life in spite of their reduced sex hormone levels.

Though the role of the sex hormones in sexual motivation in women is limited, it appears that testosterone plays a role. In women, small amounts of testosterone are produced by the adrenal glands, small glands that secrete several hormones and are located atop the kidneys. Removal of the adrenal glands often abolishes the sex drive in women. In adult female monkeys whose adrenal glands and ovaries have been removed, injections of testosterone restore sex drive and sexual activity. In

women, while testosterone appears to play a role, many psychological factors such as attitudes and religious beliefs seem to be more important in understanding sexual motivation.

HORMONES AND SEXUAL DYSFUNCTIONS

Knowledge about sex hormones and their role in sexual motivation has been used in several ways. With the discovery that castration, or removal of the testes, drastically lowers sex drive, it was concluded that some cases of impaired sex drive in males may be caused by low levels of testosterone. For example, a soldier was castrated by an explosive during World War I. As a result, he lost interest in sex, was unable to obtain an erection, and lost significant muscle mass; his hips also expanded. After receiving five injections of high doses of testosterone, he was experiencing normal erections, his sex drive returned, and he began to gain weight and muscle mass. For males whose sexual difficulties are caused by abnormally low levels of testosterone, regular injections tend to restore a normal sex drive and the ability to achieve erections. Studies reveal, however, that not all individuals who are castrated experience changes in sexual behavior. For reasons that are unclear, some males appear capable of sexual behavior in spite of the removal of the testes.

Giving doses of estradiol or progesterone to men has several effects. First, excesses of these hormones cause a sharp decline in the production of testosterone, which may interfere with sex drive, erection, and ejaculation. Administering estradiol also causes breast enlargement in men. When given to men, progesterone causes a decrease in sex drive and erection ability. It does not tend to make males develop a female appearance, as estradiol does. This knowledge has been applied to treating sex offenders. Compulsive sex offenders, especially child molesters, are sometimes given injections of progesterone to help them control their sexual urges. When combined with counseling, this treatment may be useful in helping these persons gain some control over their sexual activity. While receiving the injections, the sex offenders often lose their sex drive and have trouble achieving erections. These effects are only temporary and disappear when progesterone is no longer given.

Women with unusually low levels of estradiol do not appear to suffer from direct sexual problems. They do experience difficulties with vaginal lubrication. Vaginal dryness makes sexual intercourse difficult and painful as a result of friction. One remedy for this problem is the use of a lubricant.

One early theory of homosexuality proposed that an imbalance in the sex hormones was responsible for sexual attraction to members of the same sex. According to the theory, male homosexuality was caused by a deficiency in testosterone or an excess of estradiol. This would explain why some men display the behavior expected of women: attraction to men and, according to popular stereotypes, effeminate mannerisms. Female homosexuality was believed to be caused by excess testosterone and, possibly, insufficient estradiol. Scientific tests of the theory have consistently failed to support it. Homosexuals, both male and female, do not differ from heterosexuals in their circulating sex hormone levels. Therefore, the hormone imbalance theory of homosexuality is no longer accepted. In fact, abnormally low levels of testosterone in men do not make them sexually attracted to men; the typical result is a decrease in sexual interest for any type of sexual partner. In women, excessively elevated levels of testosterone do not cause lesbianism; if anything, they tend to increase women's sexual interest in men. Factors other than levels of sex hormones are important in understanding homosexuality.

Another application involves the treatment of transsexuals. Transsexualism is a rare but interesting condition in which the person feels that nature made a mistake and placed him or her in the body of the wrong sex. A transsexual man is an anatomical male who firmly believes that he is a woman in a man's body. A transsexual woman believes that she is a male in a female body. Transsexuals who strongly desire to change their sex will sometimes receive hormone treatments. For a transsexual male, this consists of taking regular doses of estrogens. As a result, the male will experience breast growth, smoother skin, loss of muscle mass, and decreases in erection and sperm production. The treatment does not change facial and body hair or raise the pitch of the voice, but physical appearance will become femalelike. For transsexual women, testosterone is administered, which leads to growth of facial and body hair, deepening of the voice, and the end of menstruation. After living with these changes for two years, those who are seeking a sex change operation may do so at one of several specialized centers. The sex change surgery for males involves the removal of male genitals and creation of an artificial vagina. For females, the breasts and reproductive organs are removed, and an artificial penis and testes may be created. The results of these procedures are still controversial, as there are many possible problems, and not all transsexuals are satisfied with the outcome.

INSTINCTS AND CULTURE

The term "hormone" is derived from the Greek hormaein, which means "to set in motion." It was first used in 1904 to refer to those bodily substances that can have a profound influence on human development and behavior. All knowledge about the sex hormones is relatively new. Undoubtedly, much more will be discovered as medical technology continues to develop rapidly.

Knowledge about the effects of castration dates back to ancient China and Arabic countries. In these countries castration was practiced to provide safe guardians of the royal harem. The castrated guardians, or eunuchs, were considered safe since their sexual motivation was impaired as a result of testosterone deficiency. In Europe, up to the beginning of the nineteenth century, boys in church choirs were sometimes castrated to ensure their continued ability to sing soprano.

Thus, a general understanding about the importance of the testes in affecting human development and behavior is not new. Information about the exact nature and role of sex hormones, however, is relatively new. For example, the eighteenth century physician Simon Tissot believed that the results of castration were caused by impairments in semen production. According to his view, the loss of semen caused a decrease in strength, passivity, and a variety of other complications. It was not until the twentieth century that the loss of testosterone was identified as the mechanism underlying the effects of castration.

Although sexual motivation in lower animals is readily understood in terms of sex hormones and instincts, human sexual behavior is much more complex. A number of cultural and psychological factors, in combination with sex hormones, interact to determine human sexual motivation and behavior. The range of sexual activities in lower animals is limited and rigidly controlled by the phase of the female's estrous cycle. In humans, there is tremendous variability in types of sexual behavior, timing and frequency of sex, choice of partners, number of partners, and context of sexual activity. These variables are influenced by cultural standards regarding sexual activity. In permissive cultures, such as in Polynesia, sexual experimentation is encouraged and expected. Other cultures are more restrictive and discourage sex before marriage.

Within each culture, other factors such as peer group influence, familial and religious beliefs and values toward sexuality, and individual fears (such as pregnancy and sexually transmitted diseases) can also have an impact on human sexual behavior. For example, the threat of acquired immunodeficiency syndrome (AIDS) has led some individuals to change their sexual behavior. Abstinence and monogamy are advocated by some, while others, including many adolescents, have adopted few changes. On the other hand, the development of drugs such as sildenafil (Viagra) that overcome the effects of the normal decline of male sex hormones with age is part of a movement to increase conscious control of and prolongation of sexuality.

Thus, although sex hormones play an important role in human sexual behavior, especially with respect to sexual maturity and sex drive, several cultural and psychological influences are more important. To address the problems of teenage pregnancy and sexually transmitted disease, including AIDS, all factors that determine human sexual motivation and behavior must be explored in depth.

BIBLIOGRAPHY

Carlson, Neil R. *Foundations of Physiological Psychology.* 7th ed. Boston: Allyn & Bacon, 2008. One of the standard texts on the physiological basis of human and animal behavior. The importance of sex hormones in development and motivation is emphasized throughout the chapter on reproductive behavior.

Katchadourian, Herant A. *Fundamentals of Human Sexuality.* 5th ed. Fort Worth, Tex.: Holt, Rinehart and Winston, 1989. One of the best and most readable books on human sexuality. The discussion of sex hormones in chapter 4 is thorough and clear; psychological and cultural influences on sexual motivation are covered in chapters 8, 9, 20, and 21. The presentation is accessible to high school and college students.

Masters, William H., Virginia E. Johnson, and Robert C. Kolodny. *Human Sexuality.* 5th ed. New York: HarperCollins, 1995. An overview of human sexuality by some of the world's foremost sex researchers. Although the coverage of sex hormones is limited, the material on the other determinants of human sexual motivation is thorough, detailed, and understandable.

Pinel, John P. J. *Biopsychology.* 7th ed. Boston: Allyn & Bacon, 2008. Another good introductory text to the physiology of human and animal behavior. The chapter "Hormones and Sex" is detailed and clearly presented; several good case studies are offered to illustrate how hormonal problems can affect human sexual development.

Richard D. McAnulty

SEE ALSO: Gay, lesbian, bisexual, and transgender mental health; Gender differences; Gender identity disorder; Gonads; Homosexuality; Hormones and behavior; Psychosexual development; Sexual behavior patterns; Sexual dysfunction; Sexual variants and paraphilias.

Sexism

TYPE OF PSYCHOLOGY: Social psychology

Sexism is prejudice against persons on the basis of their gender. Sexism may exist at the interpersonal level, where it is expressed in individual beliefs and behaviors; alternatively, it may become institutionalized when social institutions and practices encourage gender bias.

KEY CONCEPT
- Discrimination
- Expressiveness
- Instrumentality
- Male-as-normative principle
- Prejudice
- Psychological trait
- Role
- Stereotype

INTRODUCTION

The psychological basis for sexism, as for other forms of prejudice, is the human tendency to form stereotypes about persons who are members of certain social groups. Stereotypes may be either positive or negative; they consist of sets of interrelated beliefs and expectations that a person holds about a particular social group. When these stereotypes affect people's interpersonal behavior, sexism can result, leading to prejudice—a negative attitude toward a social group—and discrimination.

Gender stereotypes are reflected in beliefs and attitudes about the general nature of men and women as members of distinct social groups. In addition, gender stereotypes are related to the development of expectations about men's and women's psychological characteristics, interests, aptitudes, and behaviors. For example, if a person believes that women are more nurturant than men, then he or she might expect that women are more likely than men to be employed as child-care workers. In turn, these expectations may affect how people behave in social situations. The presence of different expectations for male and female performance may lead to differential treatment on the basis of gender. For example, if the director of a child-care center expects women to be superior nursery school teachers, then he or she may be likely to discriminate against males who apply for an available teaching position.

AMERICAN GENDER STEREOTYPES

Psychological research has established that gender stereotypes are quite pervasive in American culture. Considerable attention has been directed toward identifying the content of gender stereotypes. Psychologists are interested in the particular nature of beliefs that individuals hold about men and women in American culture. In a classic study, Paul Rosenkrantz, Inge Broverman, and their colleagues asked Americans to describe characteristics of the typical American man and woman. Their findings, which were first reported in the late 1960s, have been supported by subsequent research. Thus, their research appears to provide an accurate portrayal of the gender stereotypes commonly held by American adults.

These researchers found that subjects tended to describe men and women in terms of two different clusters of psychological traits, or personality characteristics. Women were more likely to be characterized by a group of traits that could be summarized as representing an expressiveness cluster. That is, men and women agreed that, as a group, women were caring, warm, and emotionally expressive. In contrast, men were characterized by a group of traits that could be described as an instrumentality cluster. In this instance, the typical man was perceived to be assertive, dominant, and competent. Thus, perceptions of men and women, as members of social groups, were conceived in terms of opposing psychological characteristics.

In the early 1980s, Kay Deaux and Laurie Lewis conducted a series of studies that elaborated on this pioneering research. They hypothesized that instrumentality and expressiveness are only two possible distinctions between men and women. Deaux and Lewis believed that additional factors were likely to play an important role in gender stereotyping. In their research program, male and female subjects were given a list of gender-relevant characteristics. Subjects then were asked to estimate the likelihood that a man or woman possessed each

characteristic. The results of these studies indicated that gender stereotypes do in fact consist of a number of related components. Subjects reliably associated certain psychological traits, role behaviors, occupations, and physical characteristics with gender.

The male stereotype consisted of the instrumentality cluster coupled with masculine psychological and physical characteristics. Subjects perceived the typical male to be strong, masculine, likely to hide his feelings, sexy, and muscular. Men typically were described as breadwinners and as being likely to take the initiative in encounters with the opposite sex. The typical male roles included blue-collar worker, businessman, athlete, and "macho man." In contrast, the female stereotype consisted of the expressiveness personality cluster coupled with feminine psychological and physical characteristics. Subjects described the typical woman as being smart and attractive, but also feminine, sensitive, and emotional. Women often were stereotyped as housewives and were perceived to be likely to be engaged in domestic chores such as child rearing and cooking. On the other hand, female stereotypes were not simply relegated to the domestic role. Subjects also held stereotypes that were representative of female athletes, businesswomen, and "sexy women."

Although there appears to be some overlap between male and female categories, it is clear that gender stereotypes do parallel the common roles that men and women typically assume in society. In addition, men and women are perceived to be members of distinctly different social groups. For the most part, people expect men and women to display opposing psychological characteristics and role behaviors. Finally, it should be noted that psychologists have found remarkable cross-cultural similarity in the content of gender stereotypes.

THE CONSTRAINTS OF STEREOTYPES

A large body of psychological research has investigated the effects of sexism. Some psychologists have investigated how gender stereotypes may influence people's perceptions of women in certain social roles (for example, as leaders). Others have studied how the use of sexist language might be related to the formation and maintenance of gender stereotypes.

The effects of gender stereotypes are particularly pronounced when people must form first impressions and make social judgments about others on the basis of little information. Natalie Porter and her colleagues have studied the factors that persons consider when they are asked to identify the leader of a small group. They asked subjects to view a photograph of an all-male group, an all-female group, or a mixed-sex group. Subjects were then asked to guess which person in the photograph held the position of group leader.

First, Porter and her colleagues found that subjects were likely to rely on spatial configuration as an important cue in determining which person was the leader of the group. In the cases of all-male and all-female groups, the majority of subjects identified the person at the head of the table as the group leader. When the group consisted of both male and female members and a male was seated at the head of the table, this person also was designated as leader by a majority of subjects. When a female occupied the head position in a mixed-sex group, however, her position at the table was disregarded. In this situation, any of the other males in the group was selected. It is clear from these results that women are less likely than men to be seen as leaders of mixed-sex groups. The results of this study are consistent with the content of gender stereotypes described by Deaux and Lewis.

SEXISM AND LANGUAGE

Gender stereotypes are also apparent in the everyday use of language. For example, many linguists have pointed out that the English language traditionally has regarded the male linguistic forms as normative. The male-as-normative principle refers to the tendency for "man" to be used to refer to all human beings. Thus, the male is considered to be the representative, or prototype, of the human species. An example of the male-as-normative principle is the use of the pronoun "he" as a generic pronoun that is intended to refer to both males and females. An example is, "While stress is a normal concomitant of our daily lives, man's ever-increasing pace of life may in fact shorten his life span."

The use of the male-as-normative principle has been subjected to two primary criticisms. First, the use of a male-gendered pronoun is often ambiguous. When a writer asserts that "man's ever-increasing pace of life may in fact shorten his life span," the reader may assume that men are more susceptible to the negative effects of stress than women. An alternative interpretation is that humans, regardless of sex, are negatively affected by stress. The second criticism focuses on issues of gender equality. The use of the male-as-normative principle implies that women are exceptions to the general rule. Critics argue that the use of the male generic encourages people to think exclusively of males rather than including

females. Further, they claim that language and thought are closely related and that sexist language may foster gender stereotypes.

In the early 1980s, psychologist Janet Shibley Hyde investigated the effects of sexist language on children's thought processes. She was particularly interested in discovering whether children understood the male-as-normative principle. She asked elementary school children to complete a story about another child. Each of the children was given a sentence with which to begin his or her story (for example, "When a kid goes to school, _____often feels excited on the first day."). One-third of the sentences provided "he" in place of the blank, one-third included "they," and one-third included "he or she." Hyde found that children's stories indeed were influenced by the use of gender pronouns. When "he" or "they" was provided to the child, fewer than 20 percent of the stories were about females. This effect was especially pronounced when boys were tested. Not one boy who was provided with the pronoun "he" wrote a story about a girl. In contrast, when the pronouns "he or she" were supplied, 42 percent of the stories were about females. Hyde concluded that when children hear the word "he," even when used as a generic pronoun, they tend to think of males.

A number of practical suggestions have been made to avoid the use of sexist language. One simple change is to use the pronoun "they" in place of "he." The results of Hyde's study, however, would suggest that the use of "he or she" would be a better alternative. Others have argued that the single pronouns "he" and "she" might be used with equal frequency throughout written text. Such suggestions are not trivial. Since the 1970s, many textbook publishers have issued guidelines that forbid the use of sexist language. The American Psychological Association (APA) has provided similar guidelines for manuscripts that are submitted for publication in journals published by the APA.

DIFFERENTIAL PSYCHOLOGY

Psychological research investigating the causes and effects of sexism is rooted in the specialized field of differential psychology, which investigated ethnic and gender differences in psychological variables such as intelligence and mental abilities. As early as 1879, Gustave Le Bon provided a description of gender differences in which he noted women's innate inferiority to men, an observation echoed by many other differential psychologists of that period. Hence, the tendency to observe differences between social groups was reflected in both the attitudes and the research efforts of early psychological researchers and continues today.

Historically, social psychologists have studied people's beliefs about differences between social groups and their attitudes toward members of other social groups. The first study of stereotypes was conducted in 1922 by Walter Lippmann, a public opinion researcher. His identification of the stereotype concept provided a means for the scientific study of ethnocentrism. The rise of fascism and its thesis of group superiority and inferiority in pre-World War II Europe concerned many social scientists and provided an impetus for the development of systematic studies of intergroup relations. While perceptions of different ethnic groups were the focus of social psychological studies of stereotypes conducted before the 1940's, the study of gender stereotypes was initiated by the publication of a study conducted by Samuel Fernberger in 1948.

Social psychologists continued to study stereotypes and their relation to prejudice in the post-World War II era. Gordon Allport's *The Nature of Prejudice* (1954) provided a theoretical model that explained the process of stereotyping and the development and maintenance of prejudice. In Allport's view, stereotypes are negative attitudes toward the members of other groups that are accompanied by rigid, inflexible thought processes. His conceptualization of stereotypes and prejudice remained unchallenged until the late 1960s, when social psychological research demonstrated that categorization and stereotyping were normal consequences of human thought processes.

The political unrest that characterized American society during the Vietnam War era was reflected in an explosion of social psychological studies of racism and sexism. In addition, the prevailing societal concerns about political and social inequality coincided with demands among feminist scholars for the conduct of nonsexist psychological research. This resulted in the emergence of a new field in the early 1970s, the psychology of women. Nonsexist, gender-fair psychological research has been promoted as a legitimate field of study by the establishment of a specialized section within the APA (Division 35) that is dedicated to the psychology of women. Scholarship in this field is dedicated to the study of sexism, gender differences and similarities, and other aspects of gender role socialization.

BIBLIOGRAPHY

Bem, Sandra Lipsitz. *The Lenses of Gender: Transforming the Debate on Sexual Inequality.* New Haven, Conn.: Yale University Press, 1994. Print.

Calogero, Rachel M., and John T. Jost. "Self-Subjugation Among Women: Exposure to Sexist Ideology, Self-Objectification, and the Protective Function of the Need to Avoid Closure." *Journal of Personality and Social Psychology* 100.2 (2011): 211–28. Print.

Keonig, Anne M., et al. "Are Leader Stereotypes Masculine? A Meta-Analysis of Three Research Paradigms." *Psychological Bulletin* 137.4 (2011): 616–42. Print.

McClean, Vernon, and Cornelia Wells, eds. *Racism and Sexism: A Collaborative Study.* 2d ed. Dubuque, Iowa: Kendall/Hunt, 2006. Print.

Mills, Sara. *Language and Sexism.* New York: Cambridge University Press, 2008. Print.

Sleeter, Christine E., and Carl A. Grant. "Race, Class, Gender, and Disability in Current Textbooks." *The Textbook as Discourse: Sociocultural Dimensions of American Schoolbooks.* Eds. Eugene F. Provenzo, et al. New York: Routledge, 2011. 183–215. Print.

Swann, William B., Judith H. Langlois, and Lucie Albino Gilbert, eds. *Sexism and Stereotypes in Modern Society.* Washington, D.C.: American Psychological Association, 1998. Print.

Tavris, Carol, and Carole Wade. *The Longest War: Sex Differences in Perspective.* 2d ed. New York: Harcourt Brace Jovanovich, 1984. Print.

Thorne, Barrie, Cheris Kramarae, and Nancy Henley. *Language, Gender, and Society.* Rowley, Mass.: Newbury House, 1983. Print.

Walsh, Mary Roth, ed. *The Psychology of Women: Ongoing Debates.* New Haven, Conn.: Yale University Press, 1987. Print.

Williams, John E., and Deborah L. Best. *Sex and Psyche: Gender and Self Viewed Cross-culturally.* Newbury Park, Calif.: Sage Publications, 1990. Print.

Cheryl A. Rickabaugh

SEE ALSO: Ageism; Causal attribution; Cognitive ability: Gender differences; Feminist psychotherapy; Gender differences; Gender identity formation; Prejudice; Racism; Social schemata; Women's psychology: Carol Gilligan; Women's psychology: Karen Horney; Women's psychology: Sigmund Freud.

Sexual abuse
Impact

TYPE OF PSYCHOLOGY: Clinical; Counseling; Psychopathology, Psychotherapy

Sexual abuse is any kind of nonconsensual, sexual activity using force, threats, or coercion to take advantage of another. While both men and women can be victims, the vast majority are female. Sexual abuse includes unwanted touching, inflicting unwanted physical pain during sex, deliberately spreading sexual infections, using objects without consent, forcing sexual activity with others, forcing prostitution, refusing to use contraception, withholding sex, ridiculing others, and humiliating others. Immediate reactions to sexual abuse include shock, fear, or disbelief.

KEY CONCEPTS
- Molestation
- Rape
- Sexual assault/violence
- Sexual misconduct
- Sexual harassment
- Sexual exploitation

INTRODUCTION

Sexual abuse is a form of interpersonal violence that involves all forms of forced sexual activity on one person by another. Sexual abuse may include sexual acts that are consensual but illegal such as sex with minors, people with disabilities, or mentally incompetent individuals. It involves unwanted sexual contact between two or more adults, two or more minors, an adult and a minor, two minors with a significant age difference between them, or sexual contact initiated by a youth toward an adult.

Nonphysical sexual abuse includes indecent exposure, voyeurism, exhibitionism, exposure to pornographic material, a viewing of sexual intercourse, or masturbation in front of a victim. Physical sexual abuse involves direct contact and includes vaginal, anal, or oral sex, fondling, groping, touching genitalia, unwanted kissing, violent sex, rape, or sex with someone who is under the influence of drugs or alcohol.

To gain sexual control, abusers use intimidation, fraud, humiliation, verbal pressure, false promises to gain trust, nonphysical threats, threats of physical harm to cause pregnancy or transmit sexual infections, threats to reveal immigration status or sexual orientation, substances, disability exploitation, misuse of authority, bartering of sexual favors for basic needs, or the providing of drugs, alcohol, or other substances.

Many sexual abuse laws distinguish between sexual contact and penetration. Abuse laws in some states focus on nonphysical sexual abuse. Some states specifically address nonconsensual or illegal sexual penetration under state rape or assault laws. Though sexual abuse between partners and married couples is considered by some to be a form of domestic violence, for centuries, the law did not recognize sexual abuse or rape between partners and married couples because women were the property of male partners/husbands who had sexual rights to their female partners. Today, the concept of ownership has changed so that nonconsensual sexual activities are recognized as crimes even between partners and married couples.

It is estimated that only 30% of sexual assault cases are reported. The national prevalence of intimate partner violence, sexual violence, and stalking survey of the Centers for Disease Control and Prevention (CDC) reported that 81% of rape, stalking, or physical violence female victims reported short or long-term effects. In the United States, approximately 18% of women were raped during their lifetime though only 16% of these cases were reported to law enforcement. Thirty-five percent of women who were raped as minors were raped again as adults. Twenty-eight percent of male rape victims were first raped at 10 years of age or younger. In 2012, 26% of sexual abuse victims were between 10 to 12 years of age, and 34% were younger than 9. Almost two million adolescents in the United States have been victims of sexual assault. Eighty-two percent of juvenile sexual assault victims are female.

RISK FACTORS

The risks for being a victim of sexual abuse include being female, young, physically attractive, educated or economically empowered, and mentally disabled as well as having experiences of substance abuse, multiple sex partners, previous rape or sexual abuse, poverty, institutionalization, or incarceration. Among children, domestic violence, parents with low education, mental illness, substance abuse, social isolation, history of abuse, and poverty are risk factors.

The risk factors for becoming an abuser include being male, liking impersonal sex, or feeling hostile toward women as well as having experiences of a physically or sexually abusive family environment, impulsive antisocial personality, coercive sexual fantasies, peer associations, community tolerance for sexual violence, and lack of support.

SIGNS AND SYMPTOMS

Physical signs and symptoms of sexual abuse include bruising or bleeding around genitalia, breasts, or mouth, vaginal or anal bleeding, stained or bloody undergarments, sexually transmitted infection, pregnancy, difficulty walking or sitting, or reporting being sexually assaulted.

Psychological signs and symptoms of sexual abuse include anxiety, fear, depression, disassociation, and posttraumatic stress disorder (PTSD). Anxiety is often associated with depression. Its symptoms include excessive worry and negativity, hyper-alertness, apprehension, feeling unsafe, out of control, and an urgent need to escape. Depression symptoms include prolonged feelings of sadness, hopelessness, crying, changes in appetite, lack of energy, sleep disturbances, loss of interest in activities, and suicidal ideations. Fear is a psychological symptom of anxiety. It can manifest by social withdrawal, avoidance of reminders of a situation, person, or place, depersonalization, heightened restlessness, crying, lack of energy, shock, guilt, anxiety, loneliness, yearning, confusion, sadness, and hallucinations. Dissociation causes victims to feel detached from life. Symptoms include sleep disorders, depression, headaches, amnesia, dramatic mood swings, hallucinations, acting in socially inappropriate ways or insisting to be called by another name, a sense of lost time, self-harm, and suicidal ideations. PTSD results in response to a traumatic event. Its symptoms include anxiety, fear, flashbacks, and uncontrollable thoughts about an incident.

Children may exhibit inappropriate sexual behavior and/or sexual abuse toward other children. Sexually abused children may also exhibit changes in behavior. Children up to three years of age may fail to thrive, cry excessively, have extreme fear or sleep disturbances, and may have bowel, feeding, and vomiting issues. Children two to nine years of age may feel shame or guilt, be fearful of specific people or strangers, places, and activities, live in fear that the incident will recur, experience eating problems, nightmares, or sleep disturbances, revert to bedwetting, masturbate excessively, become withdrawn, or sexually abuse others. Preadolescent and adolescents may become depressed, promiscuous, aggressive, or angry and may experience powerlessness, eating issues, nightmares or sleep disturbances, fear that the incident

will recur, or poor academic performance. They may also run away, become pregnant, get married, substance abuse, act older than their age, or attempt suicide.

The psychological effects of child sexual abuse last into adulthood. Survivors may feel stigmatized and experience low self-esteem, depression, grief, guilt, shame, self-blame, rage, anxiety, fear, and panic attacks. They are often distrustful, have difficulty developing and maintaining relationships, have poor support systems, tend to be re-victimized, self-mutilate, or attempt suicide.

CONSEQUENCES

Not everyone who is sexually abused experiences negative effects. However, those who are negatively affected by sexual abuse suffer with feelings of distrust, guilt, depression, identity confusion, low self-esteem, and emotional and relationship issues. They may exhibit self-abuse and antisocial behavior. Some behaviors are consequences of sexual abuse at the same time that they are risk factors for re-victimization. Such behaviors include high-risk sexual activities like unprotected sex, multiple sexual partners, prostitution, substance abuse, and diet extremes like fasting, purging, and vomiting.

PREVENTION AND TREATMENT

Victims are often reluctant to report sexual abuse because they are afraid they will be harmed by their abuser again, do not want it to become public, feel ashamed, guilty or embarrassed, or fear they will be blamed or not believed. The Centers for Disease Control and Prevention (CDC) uses a four-step approach to address sexual violence. It includes defining the problem, identifying the risk and protective factors, developing and testing prevention strategies, and assuring widespread adoption. The goal is to stop sexual violence before it begins.

There are also psychological and pharmacological treatments available for victims of abuse. Stress management, emotional expression, exposure therapy, group therapy, and anti-depressants are available to assist in the recovery of victims. Victims should be provided information about the resources available to them so that they can be treated appropriately and effectively.

Children should be taught appropriate sexual behavior and to say "no" to touch in ways that make them uncomfortable. Child victims of sexual abuse need to be reassured that they are not responsible for what happened and that they should not feel shame or guilt. Awareness of sexual abuse should be provided to others through community programs. Any suspected abuse should be reported to local police and/or child protective agencies so that a child who is being sexually abused can be helped.

Actions taken by individuals that can lessen the chance of being sexually assaulted include not drinking too much alcohol, not taking drugs, parking in well-lit areas, keeping car and house doors locked, having keys ready when approaching the door, setting sexual limits, not sending mixed messages, and becoming educated about sexual abuse and assault by attending community, campus, or facility crime prevention programs.

Convicted sex offenders may be sentenced to correction or rehabilitation facilities. Afterward they are placed on probation or parole, based on their risk for sexually abusing again. They must report to their supervisor in addition to following restrictions that may include no contact with victims, no or limited contact with minors, and restricted geographic movement, Internet, workplace, and living access.

BIBLIOGRAPHY

Basile, K. (2005). Sexual violence in the lives of girls and women. In K. Kendall-Tackett (Ed.), *Handbook of Women, Stress, and Trauma* (101-122). New York, NY: Brunner-Routledge.

Basile, K., Smith, S., Breiding M., Blackman, M., & Mahendra, R. (2014). *Sexual Violence Surveillance:*

Uniform Definitions and Recommended Data Elements Version 2.0. Atlanta, GA: Centers for Disease Control and Prevention National Center for Injury Prevention and Control.

Field, T., & Winterfeld, A. (2003). *Abuse- Sexual Abuse. In Tough problems, Tough Choices: Guidelines For Needs-Based Service Planning in Child Welfare.* Englewood, CO: American Humane Association, Annie E. Casey Foundation, and Casey Family Programs.

Gilligan, L. (2008). *Fact Sheet: What You Need to Know About Sex Offenders.* Silver Spring, MD: Center for Sex Offender Management.

Jewkes, R., Sen, P., & Garcia-Moreno, C. (2002). "Sexual Violence." *World Report on Violence and Health,* (213-239). Geneva, Switzerland: World Health Organization.

U.S. Department of Health and Human Services, Administration on Children, Youth, and Families. (2007). *Child Maltreatment 2005.* Washington, DC: U.S. Government Printing Office.

Sharon W. Stark

SEE ALSO: Abuse; Crime; Rape; Sex offenses; Trauma; Victimization.

Sexual behavior patterns

TYPE OF PSYCHOLOGY: Motivation

Sexual behavior patterns help to ensure the survival of virtually all species. There is a rich diversity of patterns in the animal kingdom, each shaped by evolutionary, ecological, and environmental factors on one hand and hormonal and neural factors on the other.

KEY CONCEPTS
- Monogamy
- Pheromones
- Polyandry
- Polygyny
- Proximate cause
- Sex hormones
- Sexual selection
- Ultimate cause

INTRODUCTION

Sexual behavior patterns represent one of the most important aspects of an organism's life. These patterns not only provide for the successful perpetuation of the species but also allow the individual to contribute genetically to future generations. Sexual behavior is unlike other physical motives, such as feeding and drinking, which are required for the individual's survival and which are initiated to some extent by measurable changes in blood sugar and cellular hydration. Engaging in sexual behavior is neither necessary to live nor stimulated by the depletion of a bodily fluid or chemical substance.

Two types of questions, relating to ultimate and proximate causality, must be addressed when sexual behavior patterns are examined. The first question asks why the pattern developed; the second asks how it occurs. For example, many species breed only during particular seasons, and the onset of these periods is often associated with changes in plumage or coloration, or the growth of anatomical structures such as antlers. Why do these changes take place? This question of ultimate causality is really asking about purpose or function; in these examples, one answer could be that the alteration makes the animal more attractive to a potential mate.

The second question, concerning proximate causation, asks how these changes come about or what the more immediate cause is. In this case, the answer could be related to a change in the animal's hormonal secretions. Thus, the sexual behavior pattern of a given species is determined by many factors, each with ultimate and proximate causes.

SEXUAL SELECTION AND MATING SYSTEMS

One of these factors is sexual selection, a concept originated by Charles Darwin in *The Descent of Man and Selection in Relation to Sex* (1871) and related to the example mentioned above. There are two kinds of selection, intersexual and intrasexual. In the first, one sex's ability to secure a mate is related to its anatomical and behavioral traits. Examples that pertain to males include antlers, the peacock's feathers (and the way the male displays the fully fanned-out feathers for the female), and the songs of some bird species used to "advertise" the male's availability for mating as well as the fact that he has obtained a territory relatively free of intruders.

Intrasexual selection involves those anatomical and behavioral traits that are used to compete with members of the same sex for access to a member of the other sex. The battle between males to establish dominance that for the winner often leads to the opportunity to mate is a common example. A well-known phenomenon in mice, the Bruce effect, provides a different sort of intrasexual selection example. The presence of an unknown male during the early stages of pregnancy can cause a female to abort, which results in her becoming sexually receptive and hence a potential mate for the strange male. In this case, the ultimate cause is that this enables the male to sire more offspring, while the proximate cause is that his odor alters the female's hormone secretions in such a way as to terminate pregnancy.

Various mating systems have evolved that also determine the type of sexual behavior pattern. Monogamy represents a sexual relationship between one female and one male, sometimes for life. One advantage is that it precludes the effort necessary to search for a mate during each breeding cycle or season. It may, however, sometimes be more advantageous for a female to enter a good territory already inhabited by a male and one or more other females than to form a monogamous relationship with a male who lives in a dangerous territory or one with fewer resources. These systems are called polygynous, as opposed to those that are polyandrous, in which one female has a sexual relationship with more than one male. Although polyandrous systems are uncommon, polyandry does occur in situations in which the female can lay many eggs in various nests while the different males do most or all of the incubating.

Unlike some species, such as humans, who reproduce throughout the year, most species breed only during one or more restricted times of the year. The ultimate cause could be that hatching or birth occurs at a time when the environmental features are more optimal in terms of temperature, predators, or food availability. Proximate factors have been well studied, and it is known that changes in the amount of light per day or temperature can cause an animal's endocrine system to become reproductively active. In female mammals, these periods are called estrous cycles; it is only during these cycles that pregnancy can occur. Animals kept in laboratories and maintained with constant and optimal amounts of light and other environmental factors will breed all year long.

The changes in hormonal secretions that precede the onset of a breeding period are critical for several reasons. Physiological processes such as maturation of the egg or ovum, the formation of the hard shell of the egg in birds and reptiles, ovulation, preparation of the uterus for implantation of the ovum in mammals, and development of sperm depend on particular hormones.

Hormones are also important because they act directly on regions of the brain to increase an organism's motivation to reproduce. In addition, by affecting sensory processes, hormones directly or indirectly enable an animal to communicate its reproductive readiness over distances. Examples include pheromones, which are odors that are emitted by many species to attract a sexual partner, some types of singing in birds and croaking in frogs, and the increased swelling and reddening of the genital region in monkeys.

SEXUAL BEHAVIOR IN DOVES

Sexual behavior patterns are extremely varied; only by studying them in detail have scientists uncovered some general principles that apply to various groupings of species. Appreciating the differences between even closely related species prevents making oversimplified generalizations from one species to another.

Many species of birds have relatively prolonged and intricate courtship and mating patterns. The ring dove was extensively studied in the laboratory by Daniel Lehrman and his colleagues in the 1950s and 1960s and by a number of other scientists since then. Although the dove has breeding cycles in nature, it reproduces almost the entire year if kept in the laboratory under constant conditions of fourteen hours of light and ten hours of dark per day, at a temperature of 22 degrees Celsius.

The male dove's courtship begins with cooing sounds while in a bowing posture. This continues for a period of time until he selects a nest site and then coos from that location. When sufficiently aroused, the female also "nest coos," which tells the male that it is time to gather material for the nest. Eventually the female ovulates, and the birds mate. She lays two eggs; both parents incubate the eggs, and both participate in feeding the young squabs by regurgitation.

Experiments have shown that androgens, the male sex hormones secreted from the testes, stimulate the male dove's courtship behavior, which in turn stimulates the female's ovaries to release the female sex hormones estrogen and progesterone. Hearing her own nest coos affects the female's physiology by playing a major role in the development of the follicles, the ovarian structures that contain her gametes, or eggs, which will be fertilized by the sperm. These hormones are important for ovulation and for mating behavior. Behavioral participation in the building of the nest produces further hormonal changes, which increase each partner's motivation to sit on the eggs. Visual and tactile sensory input from the eggs stimulates prolactin from the pituitary gland in both sexes, which functions to keep the parents incubating until the eggs hatch; it also causes the production of crop milk, the partially digested food that is regurgitated for the hatchlings. These behavioral-hormonal interrelationships have been shown to exist in other species, and they point out the importance of particular sexual behavior patterns for successful reproduction.

SEXUAL BEHAVIOR IN RATS

Another example of the role of behavior patterns in the survival of the species comes from experiments on rats by Norman Adler. A female rat comes into "heat" or estrus on only one day during the latter portion of her four-day estrous cycle. Her period of heat begins several hours before ovulation and ends several hours afterward. It is only during this time that she will mate and can become pregnant. During the first few days of the estrous cycle, the female secretes hormones that cause growth of the follicles, ovulation, and sexual behavior. If her eggs or ova are fertilized, her estrous cycling stops until after delivery of the litter. As in the case of the dove, a female rat will continue to have estrous cycles all year long un-

der constant environmental conditions in the laboratory, unless she becomes pregnant.

Under those constant conditions, the male continues to secrete androgens and is almost always ready to mate. Placing a sexually receptive female and sexually active male together in a cage results in a predictable sequence of behaviors. The male will investigate the female and, on the basis of certain odors attributable to her estrogen and progesterone, will find her "attractive." In response to the male's interest in her and her attraction to him, she engages in proceptive behaviors—sexually stimulating activities that maintain the pair's interaction. In the rat, these behaviors include a "hopping and darting" form of locomotion and ear quivering. The male will mount the female, and if sufficiently motivated, she will show receptivity by adopting the lordosis posture (characterized by immobility, arched back, and raised genital region). On many of these mounts, the male will be able to intromit his penis into her vagina; after an average of ten to fifteen intromissions, he will ejaculate. A number of minutes will elapse and the sequence will begin again; it will be repeated several times in a single sexual session.

In one experiment, males were allowed to intromit a varying number of times with a first female; then, before ejaculating, they were each placed with a second female. In this way, various females received different numbers of intromissions prior to an ejaculation. The significant finding was that the female needs a number of intromissions plus an ejaculation to become pregnant. If she receives only one or two intromissions prior to an ejaculation, her likelihood of becoming pregnant is greatly reduced. The stimulation she receives from these intromissions is necessary to alter her hormonal secretions in preparation for pregnancy. Additionally, males who intromit fewer than six times prior to an ejaculation release fewer sperm, hence reducing the probability that their partners will become pregnant. This result is related to the fact that subdominant male rats have fewer intromissions and reduced fertility, but only when a more dominant male is nearby.

SEXUAL BEHAVIOR IN PRIMATES

Scientists study primate species both because they are interesting in their own right and because the researchers wish to gain some understanding of human behavior. The rhesus monkey, a commonly studied primate, is polygynous and native to India; it has a breeding season that begins in the fall and lasts about five months. Instead of an estrous cycle, it has a menstrual cycle that is almost identical to that of human females.

Mating behavior is not controlled as exclusively by hormones as it is in lower species, but the frequency of copulation is greatest around the time of ovulation. Attractivity of the female is enhanced by estrogen, but unlike in the rat, it is reduced by progesterone, the hormone that is at its highest level after ovulation in the second half of the menstrual cycle. Experiments have shown that for optimal mating behavior to occur, androgen is necessary for the male, and both estrogen and androgen are required in the female. Female monkeys, like female humans, normally secrete androgen, although at much lower levels than males do (just as male monkeys and humans secrete female sex hormones). Studies on human females have shown that levels of androgen during the menstrual cycle correlate with increased sexual motivation and gratification.

FROM EVOLUTION TO ETHOLOGY

Darwin was influential in convincing scientists and nonscientists alike that humans and other animals are products of evolution and that they share common ancestors. Further, Darwin and his successors have argued that behavior, like anatomy, has changed as a result of natural selection, the process whereby traits that allow an organism to produce more offspring will be inherited by subsequent generations.

In part because of Darwin's emphasis on the similarity between animals and humans, William James in the late nineteenth century and William McDougall in the early twentieth century proposed the instinct theory, that much of human behavior is based on instincts. Instincts are behaviors that are characterized by their lack of dependence on learning, fairly rigid performance, and presence in all members of at least one sex of a species.

The question of instincts is a key issue in the longstanding controversy in psychology between "nature" and "nurture," or the relative role of inborn versus environmental or learned factors in behavior. Over the years, some behaviors that were thought to be pure instincts have been shown to be affected by learning or experience, and other behaviors have been shown to be more inborn than originally thought. Advances in the field of genetics has enabled further study into which behaviors, including sexual behaviors, may be more inborn than others. Furthermore, simply calling a behavior an instinct does little to shed light on either its ultimate or its proximate causes.

Partly as a result of the debate over instincts, the study of animal and human behavior has taken two somewhat separate paths. On one side are primarily psychologists, psychobiologists, and neuroscientists who investigate the more proximate causes of sexual behavior patterns in the laboratory under controlled conditions. Their progress has helped to gather information on the nervous system, the endocrine system, the interaction between the two, and their relationship to environmental factors such as light, temperature, and the presence of potential mates.

Evolutionary biologists, animal behaviorists, sociobiologists, and ethologists tend to study sexual and other behaviors under natural conditions. Ethologists Konrad Lorenz and Nikolaas Tinbergen focused on more instinctive, species-specific behaviors emphasizing ultimate causation.

It is often difficult for a laboratory scientist to devote much attention to evolutionary concerns, and it is equally difficult for the animal behaviorist to focus on the nervous and endocrine systems. Information from one approach often complements the other, however, and a complete understanding of the effect of all relevant factors is necessary for the study of sexual behavior patterns.

BIBLIOGRAPHY

Crews, David, ed. *Psychobiology of Reproductive Behavior: An Evolutionary Perspective.* Englewood Cliffs: Prentice, 1987. Print.

Dixson, A. F. *Primate Sexuality: Comparative Studies of the Prosimians, Monkeys, Apes and Human Beings.* Oxford: Oxford UP, 2012. Print.

Gray, Peter B., and Justin R. Garcia. *Evolution and Human Sexual Behavior.* Cambridge: Harvard UP, 2013. Print.

Hutchison, John Bower, ed. *Biological Determinants of Sexual Behaviour.* New York: Wiley, 1979. Print.

Komisaruk, Barry R., et al., eds. *Reproduction: A Behavioral and Neuroendocrine Perspective.* New York: New York Acad. of Sciences, 1986. Print.

Lehrman, Daniel S. "The Reproductive Behavior of Ring Doves." *Scientific American* Nov. 1964: 48–54. Print.

Levay, Simon, and Janice Baldwin. *Human Sexuality.* 4th ed. Sunderland: Sinauer, 2011. Print.

Pincott, Jena. *Do Gentlemen Really Prefer Blondes? Bodies, Behavior, and Brains—The Science behind Sex, Love, and Attraction.* New York: Delacorte, 2008. Print.

Yasukawa, Ken. *Animal Behavior.* Vol. 2. Santa Barbara: ABC-CLIO, 2014. Print.

Harold I. Siegel

SEE ALSO: Animal experimentation; Endocrine system; Gender differences; Gonads; Hormones and behavior; Instinct theory; James, William; Psychosexual development; Sex hormones and motivation.

Sexual dysfunction

TYPE OF PSYCHOLOGY: Psychopathology

Sexual problems are influenced by both health-related and psychosocial factors. Stress-inducing situations, interpersonal communication problems, or chronic illness can affect sexual functioning in both men and women. Sex therapy is aimed at helping individuals and couples to understand the underlying causes of sexual distress and to adopt new behaviors conducive to a more satisfying sex life.

KEY CONCEPTS
- Arousal disorders
- Dyspareunia
- Feminist perspectives
- Hyperactive sexual desire
- Hypoactive sexual desire
- Orgasmic disorders
- Sexual aversion
- Sexual minorities
- Vaginismus

INTRODUCTION

A satisfactory sexual life is an integral component of a person's physical and psychological health. It plays an important role in both an individual's self-esteem and an enriching and fulfilling couple relationship. A strong association exists between sexual dysfunction and an impaired quality of life.

Sexual problems can be caused by various medical conditions, such as cardiovascular problems, diabetes, and hormonal imbalances. A majority of sexual disorders, however, are associated with significant psychological difficulties in an individual's personal and interpersonal life. Those suffering from sexual problems are also likely to experience distress, reduced self-esteem, and symptoms of anxiety and depression. In some cases, psychological problems are a consequence of sexual problems. In other cases, sexual problems reflect coexisting psychopathology. In still other cases, sexual problems may even result in other unspecified physical, psychological, interpersonal, or social problems.

Treatment strategies include a comprehensive assessment of the physiological and psychological factors contributing to the dysfunction, appropriate psychotherapeutic interventions, interpersonal intimacy training, and, in certain cases, surgical procedures such as penile implants.

In the early twentieth century, Sigmund Freud conceptualized sexual problems as symptoms of deep-rooted disturbances of personality originating from early childhood experiences. Treatment usually consisted of lengthy psychoanalysis that did not always alleviate the problem. In the early 1960's, behavior therapies such as systematic desensitization were used to treat sexual problems, specifically erectile dysfunction in men and so-called frigidity (lack of sexual desire) in women. These therapies, however, were mostly aimed at relieving symptoms rather than examining the underlying causes.

THE SEXUAL RESPONSE

In 1966, William H. Masters and Virginia E. Johnson proposed a comprehensive model of the sexual response cycle consisting of four stages: excitement, the initial stage of increasing arousal in which the skin becomes flushed, the penis or clitoris becomes engorged with blood, and vaginal lubrication increases; plateau, the stage of full arousal in which the penis becomes enlarged to maximum erection and the outer third of the vagina becomes engorged with blood; orgasm, the stage involving muscle contraction throughout the body in which men ejaculate sperm-filled semen and women's vaginal contractions facilitate conception by helping propel the semen into the vagina; and resolution, the stage during which the body gradually returns to an unaroused state in which muscles relax and engorged genital blood vessels release excess blood.

For the first time, Masters and Johnson documented the genital and extragenital physiological changes that typically occur during each of these stages. They argued not only that men's and women's physiological changes are remarkably similar as they approach and achieve orgasm but also that the physiological expression of an orgasm is similar regardless of how it is achieved. Based on their model, Masters and Johnson subsequently published the book *Human Sexual Inadequacy* (1970), which described a sex therapy combining behavioral and psychotherapeutic approaches. The focus of this therapy was mostly on the relationship between the couple. Their treatment of individuals using sexual surrogates raised certain ethical dilemmas.

During the late 1970's, Helen Singer Kaplan observed that many of her sexually troubled patients complained of a lack of interest in sex or even an aversion to sexual activity. She concluded from her observations that there is an important stage preliminary to the excitement phase, one that she labeled sexual desire. This stage involves an individual's cognitive and emotional readiness for and interest in participating in sexual activity. Masters and Johnson's original sexual response cycle has since been revised to include sexual desire as a primary component, and the cycle is now recognized of having five main stages: desire, excitement, plateau, orgasm, and resolution.

THE DEFINITION OF SEXUAL DYSFUNCTION

The revised fourth edition of the American Psychiatric Association's *Diagnostic and Statistical Manual of Mental Disorders* (2000), more commonly known as the DSM-IV-TR, defines sexual dysfunction as a disturbance in sexual desire and the psychophysiological changes that characterize the sexual response cycle that causes marked distress and interpersonal difficulties. While the DSM-IV-TR provides a clear framework for classifying sexual problems, decisions about the presence or absence of a dysfunction may often reflect the values and standards of both clinicians and patients, which in turn are affected by the constantly shifting cultural opinions regarding sexual mores and behavior. Thus, the defini-

---

DSM-IV-TR CRITERIA FOR SEXUAL DYSFUNCTIONS

SEXUAL AVERSION DISORDER (DSM CODE 302.79)

Persistent or recurrent extreme aversion to, and avoidance of, all (or almost all) genital sexual contact with sexual partner

Disturbance causes marked distress or interpersonal difficulty

Sexual dysfunction not better accounted for by another Axis I disorder (except another sexual dysfunction)

HYPOACTIVE SEXUAL DESIRE DISORDER (DSM CODE 302.71)

Persistently or recurrently deficient (or absent) sexual fantasies and desire for sexual activity; judgment of deficiency or absence made by clinician, taking into account factors affecting sexual functioning, such as age and life context

Disturbance causes marked distress or interpersonal difficulty

Sexual dysfunction not better accounted for by another Axis I disorder (except another sexual dysfunction) and not due exclusively to direct physiological effects of a substance or general medical condition

FEMALE SEXUAL AROUSAL DISORDER (DSM CODE 302.72)

Persistent or recurrent inability to attain, or to maintain until completion of sexual activity, an adequate lubrication-swelling response of sexual excitement

Disturbance causes marked distress or interpersonal difficulty

Sexual dysfunction not better accounted for by another Axis I disorder (except another sexual dysfunction) and not due exclusively to direct physiological effects of a substance or general medical condition

MALE ERECTILE DISORDER (DSM CODE 302.72)

Persistent or recurrent inability to attain, or to maintain until completion of sexual activity, an adequate erection

Disturbance causes marked distress or interpersonal difficulty

Erectile dysfunction not better accounted for by another Axis I disorder (other than a sexual dysfunction) and not due exclusively to direct physiological effects of a substance or general medical condition

FEMALE ORGASMIC DISORDER (DSM CODE 302.73)

Persistent or recurrent delay in, or absence of, orgasm following normal sexual excitement phase; diagnosis based on clinician's judgment that woman's orgasmic capacity is less than reasonable for her age and sexual experience and the adequacy of sexual stimulation

Disturbance causes marked distress or interpersonal difficulty

Orgasmic dysfunction not better accounted for by another Axis I disorder (except another sexual dysfunction) and not due exclusively to direct physiological effects of a substance or general medical condition

(continued)

MALE ORGASMIC DISORDER (DSM CDE 302.74)

Persistent or recurrent delay in, or absence of, orgasm following normal sexual excitement phase during sexual activity that clinician, taking into account person's age, judges to be adequate in focus, intensity, and duration

Disturbance causes marked distress or interpersonal difficulty

Orgasmic dysfunction not better accounted for by another Axis I disorder (except another sexual dysfunction) and not due exclusively to direct physiological effects of a substance or general medical condition

PREMATURE EJACULATION (DSM CODE 302.75)

Persistent or recurrent ejaculation with minimal sexual stimulation before, on, or shortly after penetration and before person wishes it; clinician takes into account factors affecting duration of excitement phase, such as age, novelty of sexual partner or situation, and recent frequency of sexual activity

Disturbance causes marked distress or interpersonal difficulty

Premature ejaculation not due exclusively to direct effects of a substance, such as withdrawal from opioids

DYSPAREUNIA (DSM CODE 302.76)

Recurrent or persistent genital pain associated with sexual intercourse in male or female

Disturbance causes marked distress or interpersonal difficulty

Disturbance not caused exclusively by Vaginismus or lack of lubrication, not better accounted for by another Axis I disorder (except another sexual dysfunction), and not due exclusively to direct physiological effects of a substance or general medical condition

VAGINISMUS (DSM CODE 306.51)

Recurrent or persistent involuntary spasm of musculature of outer third of vagina interfering with sexual intercourse

Disturbance causes marked distress or interpersonal difficulty

Disturbance not better accounted for by another Axis I disorder (such as Somatization Disorder) and not due exclusively to direct physiological effects of a general medical condition

SEXUAL DYSFUNCTION NOT OTHERWISE SPECIFIED (DSM CODE 302.70)

Specify for each disorder:
- Lifelong or Acquired
- Generalized or Situational
- Due to Psychological Factors or Due to Combined Factors

tion and understanding of sexual dysfunctions can be rather complex and, at times, controversial, particularly when the sexual behavior implies a reference to a perceived normal level of activity or interest.

Sexual dysfunctions can be classified under four major areas: sexual desire disorders, arousal disorders, orgasmic disorders, and physical pain experienced during intercourse. These dysfunctions are not always discrete, and specific problems may overlap as to their origin, presentation, and intensity.

SEXUAL DESIRE DISORDERS

Sexual desire disorders include hypoactive sexual desire, hyperactive sexual desire, and sexual aversion. Properly speaking, these disorders affect the brain's arousal capabilities rather than physiological responses. Individuals with sexual desire disorders have the ability to respond physically but have little or no emotional investment in sexual activities. It is as if the brain's erotic centers have shut down.

Hypoactive sexual desire, also known as inhibited sexual desire, is a low or absent sexual desire. The person suffering from hypoactive sexual desire has little or no interest in sexual matters, will not actively pursue sexual gratification, and, if a sexual situation presents itself, is not readily moved to avail himself or herself of the opportunity to engage in sexual activity. Hypoactive sexual desire generally stems from deeper, more intense sexual anxieties such as sexual performance anxiety. By developing a low interest in sexual activity, the person avoids the unpleasant feelings of embarrassment, loss of self-esteem, and frustration as a result of perceived sexual failure.

Depression can be one of the major causes of hypoactive sexual desire. Hypoactive sexual desire may also have roots in various unresolved relationship problems. Suppressed and unacknowledged anger and resentment toward one's partner can often manifest in hypoactive sexual desire. Stress, a traumatic marital separation or divorce, or loss of employment can also result in hypoactive sexual desire. Drugs, hormonal imbalance, and chronic illness are major contributors to hypoactive sexual desire. Some individuals may use lack of desire as a defense against a generalized anxiety around situations involving intimacy, closeness, and even physical touch.

Individuals with excessive desire disorder often experience uncontrollable sexual urges. They are obsessed with sexual thoughts that permeate all their actions and feelings, and they demand immediate gratification. These individuals are unable to control their sexual appetite and view sex as a magical cure for depression. Sex becomes an addiction for such people. Hypersexuality can occur with or without frequent masturbation. A person with excessive sexual desire uses sex as a substitute for involvement in other activities. For such a person, sex is impersonal, with few or no positive feelings or emotions associated with the sex act.

Sexual aversion is a consistently phobic response to sexual activities or even thoughts of such activities. A person suffering from sexual aversion experiences an overwhelming anxiety about any kind of sexual contact. A mere kiss, touch, or caress may create fear that the initial contact might lead to sexual arousal or activity. Anticipating the sex act may provoke greater anxiety than actual participation in the sexual activity. Sexual aversion may result from strict and authoritarian parental attitudes during childhood, from sexual trauma such as rape or sexual abuse, or from consistent and increasing sexual pressure from a long-term partner. Sexual aversion may also be a result of adolescent difficulties with self-esteem and perceived body image.

AROUSAL DISORDERS

Arousal disorders among males include disorders of the erectile process, such as dysfunctional arousal and plateau phases. Erectile difficulties may be defined as persisting or recurrent inability to attain or maintain a penile erection sufficient to permit vaginal penetration and satisfactory conclusion of sexual intercourse. Erectile difficulties in men are commonly known as impotence and are the most frequently occurring male sexual dysfunctions. Impotence can be of great concern to not only the patient but also his sexual partner.

Total erectile dysfunction is rare and is caused by serious disruption in the blood supply to the penis or the leakage of blood from penile cavernous bodies.

Cardiovascular problems and diabetes may sometimes cause nerve damage, leading to sexual arousal disorders. Situational erectile dysfunction, on the other hand, usually has a psychological basis. The man is able to obtain an erection but is unable to experience erection with his partner or cannot sustain his erection when sexual intercourse is attempted.

Among women, arousal disorders include failure of vaginal swelling, the lack of sufficient lubrication, and a lack of sensation that is usually associated with sexual excitement. For some women, the hormonal changes that occur after childbirth may impair the normal vaginal response to sexual stimulation.

ORGASMIC DISORDERS

Orgasmic disorders is defined as the building up and release of tension. During release of the tension, contractions are felt in the genital area and, after the peak of excitement, a period of relaxation follows. In women, rhythmic contractions occur in the uterus, the vaginal barrel, and the rectal sphincter, gradually diminishing in intensity, regularity, and duration.

Women who are diagnosed as having primary anorgasmia have never experienced an orgasm. Women suffering from secondary anorgasmia are those who have previously experienced orgasm in sexual intercourse but either are no longer able to do so or are able to have an orgasm only in certain situations, such as masturbation. These women suffer from orgasmic infrequency and are not always aware of the conditions that restrict them from being orgasmic.

Orgasmic disorders among males include inability to achieve orgasm and disturbances of ejaculation. Premature ejaculation in men is a persistent or recurrent ejaculation with minimal sexual stimulation before, during, or shortly after penetration and before the man's desire for it to occur. Men suffering from premature ejaculation fail to fully experience the orgasmic release, usually the most pleasurable sensation of the sexual activity. Failure to emit or eject seminal fluid can also raise concerns, primarily in those situations in which fertility is desired. A less common male sexual disorder is retarded ejaculation, which is the persistent or recurrent delay in, or absence of, orgasm following a phase of normal sexual excitement.

PHYSICAL PAIN DURING INTERCOURSE

In women, painful intercourse, or dyspareunia, often occurs because the woman is not entirely aroused before her partner attempts intercourse. Sexual inhibitions, lack of appropriate foreplay, a poor relationship with the partner, and hormonal imbalances can contribute to a woman's dyspareunia. Postmenopausal women may suffer from decreased vaginal lubrication and, as a result, lose much of the vaginal elasticity. Related to painful intercourse is vaginismus, a condition in which the muscles around the vaginal entrance go into involuntary spasmodic contractions, preventing the entrance of the penis. Vaginismus is essentially a conditioned response that reflects fear, anxiety, or pain. It may be a result of negative attitudes about sexuality, harsh early sexual experiences, sexual abuse or rape, or painful pelvic examinations.

SEXUAL MINORITIES

Sexual problems experienced by gay men, lesbians, and bisexuals are not significantly different from those experienced by heterosexuals except that the traditional concepts of monogamous sexual relationship cannot always be taken for granted when working with members of such populations. As in the general population, gay men and lesbians also suffer from desire, arousal, and orgasmic disorders. They also have a variety of problems that set them apart from the general heterosexual population. Gay men, for example, tend to experiment with various forms of sexuality that may include open and frequently changing relationships, which sometimes leads to insecurity and instability in their relationships. Some gay men entertain fantasies of domination and overpowering others in their sexual repertoire.

Many lesbian relationships are based on feminist principles that incorporate equality and nonexclusivity in their relationships. Some lesbians tend to prefer bisexual relationships. They appear to be looking for a sense of community and spirituality in their relationships. Frustration in attainment of those ideals can sometimes lead to a generalized lack of sexual desire.

A SYSTEMS APPROACH TO SEXUAL DYSFUNCTION

Psychologist David Schnarch advocates a combination of physical stimulus and internal focus that brings together the physiological experience of sex and the phenomenological meanings that people attach to it. He distinguishes between clinical and subjective arousal and creates a clinical framework that can accommodate such subjective constructs as sexual potential and intimacy. He attempts to explore the roots of human inability to tolerate high levels of eroticism and intimacy, and

he presents a model that integrates behavioral, object relations, and systematic approaches to help patients achieve the developmental maturity to tolerate a high level of emotional salience.

According to Schnarch, a couple's sexual problems are a window to latent unresolved issues in the individual, in the couple, or in the extended emotional system of the couple, including the family of origin as well as lovers and friends. These unresolved issues can inhibit satisfying sexual-marital functioning and the full exploration of sexual potential.

TREATMENT OF SEXUAL DYSFUNCTIONS

Sex therapists are nationally certified by the American Association of Sex Educators, Counselors, and Therapists on completion of the required training and supervision. Sexual dysfunctions are also treated by licensed marriage and family therapists, physicians, psychologists, psychiatrists, and social workers. Treatment usually begins with a comprehensive assessment of physiological and psychosocial factors that could be contributing to the presenting problem. In the absence of a significant medical finding, the therapist attempts to uncover the emotional and interpersonal issues underlying the sexual problem and helps the patients find ways to resolve them. In addition to office visits, some therapists may assign homework aimed at gaining greater awareness of one's own feelings and those of one's partner and enhancing interpersonal intimacy. Psychotherapeutic treatments may include cognitive behavior therapy, mental imagery, psychodynamic therapy, and systematic desensitization. For patients with physiological deficiencies, medical interventions may include the use of hormonal treatments, appropriate antidepressants, sildenafil (Viagra), and, where necessary, penile implants.

A FEMINIST PERSPECTIVE ON SEX THERAPY

Traditional sex therapists mostly use the diagnostic framework of sexual dysfunctions as articulated in the DSM-IV-TR, which many feminist therapists consider as very poorly suited to women's and sexual minorities' sexual reality. Because it ignores the social context of sexuality, these minorities assert that the DSM-IV-TR nomenclature perpetuates a dangerously naïve and false vision of how sex really works.

Feminist sex therapy encompasses the two domains of insight and skill. The first includes corrective genital physiology education, assertiveness training, body image reclamation, and masturbation education. The second rejects sexual drive in favor of contact comfort, mutual masturbation, and new ways of sexual understanding and exploration.

Feminist sex therapy attempts to move beyond restrictions and inhibitions created by the prevalent body/mind conflict, depreciation of women's sexuality, and preoccupation with procreation. It also attempts to bypass the restrictions and inhibitions embedded in gender roles and stereotypes. The focus in feminist sex therapy is on the personal meaning and subjective nature of sexual activity, feelings, and relationships.

BIBLIOGRAPHY

American Psychiatric Association. *Diagnostic and Statistical Manual of Mental Disorders: DSM-IV-TR.* Rev. 4th ed. Washington, D.C.: Author, 2000. A reference manual used as an aid in diagnosing mental disorders.

Balon, Richard, ed. *Sexual Dysfunction: The Brain-Body Connection.* New York: Karger, 2008. A collection of essays by experts in sexual dysfunction comprehensively covers such topics as hypoactive sexual disorder, premature ejaculation, and imaging.

Heiman, J., L. LoPiccolo, and J. LoPiccolo. *Becoming Orgasmic: A Sexual Growth Program for Women.* 2d ed. Rev. and expanded. New York: Simon & Schuster, 1996. The authors offer guidance for enhancing the emotional experience of sexual activity. Areas of discussion include sexual expectations, sexual awareness, communication with one's sexual partner, and the enhancement of intimacy.

IsHak, Waguih William. *The Guidebook of Sexual Medicine.* Beverly Hills, Calif.: A & W, 2008. Designed for professionals in mental health and doctors, this is a practical manual that offers guidelines on the assessment and treatment of sexual disorders.

Kaplan, Helen Singer. *Disorders of Sexual Desire and Other New Concepts and Techniques in Sex Therapy.* New York: Brunner/Mazel, 1979. Focuses on inhibited sexual desire, including its identification and treatment. Presents case histories and examines the effects of medical conditions and drug interactions on sexual function.

Masters, William H., and Virginia E. Johnson. *Human Sexual Inadequacy.* New York: Bantam Books, 1980. The authors present definitions of various sexual dysfunctions, based on direct observations of sexual activity in a clinical setting, and offer treatment approaches.

_____. *Human Sexual Response.* New York: Bantam Books, 1986. The authors propose a comprehensive model of the sexual response cycle based on their clinical research on the sexual activities of numerous volunteers.

Saral, Tulsi B. "Mental Imagery in Sex Therapy." In *Healing Images: The Role of Imagination in Health,* edited by A. A. Sheikh. Amityville, N.Y.: Baywood, 2003. This article explores the use of mental imagery in the diagnosis and treatment of sexual dysfunctions and presents a series of imagery exercises for use in treating specific sexual disorders.

Schnarch, David M. *Constructing the Sexual Crucible: An Integration of Sexual and Marital Therapy.* New York: W. W. Norton, 1991. Schnarch presents a framework for integrating biological functioning, emotional experience, and spiritual awareness to achieve optimum sexual gratification. The book also brings together individual and couple psychotherapies to propose an effective sex therapy model.

Tiefer, Leonore. "Towards a Feminist Sex Therapy." In *Sexualities,* edited by Marney Hall. Binghamton, N.Y.: Harrington Park Press, 1996. This article argues that traditional approaches of therapeutic intervention for sexual dysfunctions are biased toward the medical/symptomological model. Tiefer advocates a more holistic approach, integrating emotional factors, interpersonal skills, and social awareness.

Wincze, J. P., and M. P. Carey. *Sexual Dysfunction: A Guide for Assessment and Treatment.* 2d ed. New York: Guilford, 2001. The authors offer a biopsychosocial model of sexual behavior, discuss the main categories of sexual dysfunctions, and present guidelines for the assessment and treatment of sexual problems.

Tulsi B. Saral

SEE ALSO: Endocrine system; Gay, lesbian, bisexual, and transgender mental health; Gender differences; Gonads; Homosexuality; Hormones and behavior; James, William; Men's mental health; Nervous system; Psychobiology; Psychosexual development; Sex hormones and motivation; Sexual behavior patterns; Sexual variants and paraphilias; Women's mental health.

Sexual harassment
Psychological causes and effects

TYPE OF PSYCHOLOGY: Emotion; Motivation; Personality; Sensation and perception; Stress

Sexual harassment is unwelcome attention of a sexual nature and is illegal if it results in a tangible employment or academic action or creates a hostile environment. The psychological effects of sexual harassment can range from mild to severe, resulting in decreased work or school performance or job loss, symptoms of extreme personal distress such as depression, anxiety, and sleeplessness, and physical problems such as headaches, gastrointestinal upset, and raised blood pressure. Harassers are often motivated by a desire for personal power or social control or by actual sexual desire.

KEY CONCEPTS
- Climate of intimidation
- Harasser
- Hostile environment
- Opportunist
- Quid pro quo

INTRODUCTION

The term "sexual harassment" covers a broad spectrum of activity, from telling an off-color joke of a sexual nature to the display of sexually offensive pictures and from casual touching to actually propositioning another person for sex to sexual assault. Often what is included in the rubric "sexual harassment" depends on who is doing the harassing and who is being harassed. The behavior in question may be more offensive to one person's sensibilities than to another's, and the harasser's intent may also vary. The severity of sexual harassment, generally regarded as unwelcome attention of a sexual nature causing discomfort, humiliation, offense, or distress that interferes with one's schoolwork or job, is largely determined by its impact on the victim.

The law recognizes two forms of sexual harassment, that produced by a hostile environment and that which occurs as the result of a quid pro quo arrangement. The line between the two is often blurry. The former occurs when the gender-based conduct of anyone with whom an individual interacts creates an intimidating, hostile, or offensive environment, making it difficult for that individual to function. Some examples of such conduct include making lewd comments about a person's looks, using offensive language of a sexual nature, telling sexual jokes or stories, making sexual innuendoes, or displaying sexually suggestive materials. Quid pro quo (this for that) sexual harassment is when a person in a supervisory capacity threatens to take (or takes) an employment or academic action in response to a demand for a subordinate to submit to acts of a sexual nature. Examples of this form of harassment are a supervisor's pushing an employee to spend more personal time with him or her, making a romantic date a requisite of receiving a raise, or threatening to terminate an employee for refusing to have sexual relations with him or her. Threats of jeopardy to the subordinate's well-being or job security do not have to be carried out to be construed as quid pro quo sexual harassment; all that is necessary is that the subordinate is made to feel threatened.

THE DYNAMICS

Although the greatest numbers of harassers are men who harass women, women can also harass men, and same-sex harassment has also been reported. Much of the research on sexual harassment, however, focuses on male perpetrators and female victims, and much of what is known is based on these studies.

Sexual harassment stems from sexism, and it is a way to diminish the victim's status and power and to increase the harasser's feeling of power. High levels of sexual harassment have been found to exist when the number of female workers in a field is relatively low. Women in traditionally male occupations—whether professionals such as engineers, surgeons, and investment bankers, or blue-collar workers such as linemen and construction workers—are more likely to be harassed.

When women enter traditionally male fields, men are likely to feel threatened. Some men feel threatened by the career advancements of women or are uncomfortable with women's independence and assertiveness. Other men think that sexual harassment is a fringe benefit that comes with their higher position. A female victim of harassment may make mistakes, be absent from work with greater frequency, or fail to carry out her job in a satisfactory manner, leaving the harasser with the impression that women cannot perform in a man's world.

Those few women in a traditionally male occupations find themselves singled out for scrutiny and the focus of rumors. Their actions, particularly their mistakes, generate extreme responses from the men, who are in the majority. Mistakes that would be minor if made by men assume greater importance and elicit ridicule when made by women. In male-dominated workplaces, if a woman complains about a man's behavior toward her, it is the woman who is usually perceived to be the problem. Often the male worker either will remain undisciplined or will be disciplined only slightly. To try to alleviate these situations, some women may try to join in the stereotyping, becoming overly sexy or flirtatious, or telling dirty jokes so that they will fit in and not be ostracized.

Harassers remind their victims of their vulnerability, creating tension that makes job performance more difficult and making their victims hesitate to seek raises and promotions. Sexual harassment creates a climate of intimidation and is considered by the courts as part of sex discrimination. The sexually harassed woman endures pressure, degradation, and hostility, which her male coworkers do not experience. Consequently, the female victim finds it difficult to thrive in the workplace.

HARASSERS AND THEIR VICTIMS

Harassers vary, but when male, they often assume the role of "Mr. Macho" or "just one of the boys." They engage in acts of bravado, embarrassing women with personal comments, inappropriate compliments, lewd jokes or gestures, and the like. Inappropriate compliments and personal comments that embarrass the recipient are often regarded as patronizing or annoying. Other roles include the male opportunist, whose eyes and hands wander at every opportunity, public and private, and the power player, who insists on sexual favors in exchange for getting or keeping a job, a promotion, or other benefits.

Women of all ages and all races can be harassed, regardless of their looks, their manner of dress, or their marital status. Particularly vulnerable are single heads of households (whether divorced, separated, or widowed), who need their jobs badly; timid and insecure women who lack self-confidence and career-related education and experience; women who are eager to be accepted and liked and find it difficult to refuse advances; saleswomen pressured by clients for sexual favors in exchange for business; and women who work in informal, nontraditional, or migrant labor situations. Sexual and racial minorities as well as those with disabilities are also at greater risk for sexual harassment.

DAMAGE TO VICTIMS

The physical, psychological, mental, emotional, and financial damage suffered by victims of sexual harassment are enormous. The American Psychiatric Association (APA) has recognized that performance stress caused by

sexual harassment and its effects on all aspects of the victims' lives is a major contributor to post-traumatic stress disorder. Sexual harassment in the workplace also has a destructive effect on the entire company. As the victim's work performance declines because of the stress of the harassment, coworkers also become less productive because they try to manage around the resulting problems. Employers are affected because of the great cost of disrupted productivity.

Victims of sexual harassment experience a sequence of changes because of the sexual harassment. Initially, victims often feel that the incident is an isolated event that will not be repeated. When it happens again and again, victims feel confused and blame themselves for not recognizing what was happening. As the harassment continues, victims develop anxiety and their concentration is impaired. They feel targeted, scrutinized, and trapped. They may avoid work or school, take a leave of absence, change jobs, or be fired. At the same time, victims may become angry and consider filing a lawsuit. Many victims do nothing, however, because their disappointment and frustration are overwhelming.

Victims who remain in those environments are scared, nervous, and irritable, and may suffer crying spells; some have nervous breakdowns as feelings of isolation, helplessness, and vulnerability become overwhelming. The psychological and emotional distress can lead to physical consequences, and victims become unable to sleep, leading to increased susceptibility to illness; others experience weight gain or loss, heart palpitations, headaches and muscle fatigue, and increased worry and anxiety. Some turn to alcohol and substance abuse to numb the effects of the workplace stress.

Sexual harassment may also affect its victims economically. Victims may be denied training opportunities, promotions, or raises. In retaliation for making a complaint, they may be reassigned to a more difficult position or transferred away from home and family. Filing a complaint can also be divisive in the workplace, as some employees will side with the victim and others will not. Conditions on the job may become intolerable and cause victims to resign. Harassment can have lasting effects, as it can negatively affect the victims' work records or make it impossible to get a reference.

BIBLIOGRAPHY

Boland, Mary L. *Sexual Harassment in the Workplace.* Naperville: Sphinx, 2005. Print.

Gregory, Raymond F. *Unwelcome and Unlawful: Sexual*

Harassment in the American Workplace. Ithaca: Cornell UP, 2004. Print.

MacKinnon, Catharine A., and Reva B. Siegel, eds. *Directions in Sexual Harassment Law.* New Haven: Yale UP, 2012. Print.

Morrow, Michael. "Sexual Harassment and Sexual Bullying." *TeensHealth.* Nemours Foundation, Aug. 2011. Web. 26 June 2014.

National Institute for Occupational Safety and Health. "Women's Safety and Health Issues at Work." *Centers for Disease Control and Prevention.* Centers for Disease Control and Prevention, 19 Nov. 2013. Web. 26 June 2014.

Neville, Kathleen. *Internal Affairs: The Abuse of Power, Sexual Harassment, and Hypocrisy in the Workplace.* New York: McGraw, 2000. Print.

Petrocelli, William, and Barbara Kate Repa. *Sexual Harassment on the Job: What It Is and How to Stop It.* 4th ed. Berkeley: Nolo, 1998. Print.

"Sexual Harassment." *Stop Violence against Women.* Advocates for Human Rights, 2010. Web. 26 June 2014.

Marcia J. Weiss

SEE ALSO: Hate crimes: Psychological causes and effects; Post-traumatic stress disorder; Prejudice; Sexism; Stress: Behavioral and psychological responses; Work motivation; Workplace issues and mental health.

Sexual orientation

TYPE OF PSYCHOLOGY: Biological bases of human behavior; Cognition; Cross-cultural; Developmental; Family; Social

Sexual orientation is a complex, multidimensional, umbrella term referring to the identification of masculine and feminine gender, qualities associated with each gender, capacities for erotic stimulation, behaviors causing erotic stimulation, the biology of reproduction, and fundamental elements of individual personality and personal identity that relate to these; sexuality has procreative, recreational, and relational dimensions.

KEY CONCEPTS
- Bisexuality
- Celibacy
- Erogenous zones:
- Erotic
- Gender
- Gender identity
- Gender role
- Heterosexual
- Homophobia
- Homosexual:
- LGBT

HISTORICAL OVERVIEW

Sexuality is usually manifested and experienced as orientation toward and attraction to people of the same gender, the opposite gender, or both. Sexual orientation is also referred to as "sexual preference." The term "preference," however, can imply that sexual attraction and orientation are chosen and voluntary, that one can will oneself to find another person sexually appealing. In fact, most research suggests the opposite: People find themselves attracted to an individual or a particular gender without having thought about that attraction or having consciously willed it. The attraction and orientation are not chosen. People can wish not to be attracted in the ways that they are, and they may choose not to act on these feelings, but the attraction felt and experienced is outside voluntary control.

A female athlete may wish not to have the sexual feelings she does for her teammates. A male chemistry major may want himself not to find a female classmate as distracting as she is. A female attorney who is happily married may want the sexual feelings she experiences for her male client to cease. A celibate priest may desire the sexual feelings that he has toward some male and female members of his congregation to go away. As much as these individuals may want to will such feelings away, success in this endeavor is unlikely. Each, instead, must choose how to cope with the feelings, from acting on them directly, to carrying on in spite of them, to pretending that the feelings are not there.

The historical evidence suggests that the prevailing belief in most societies was that people had either a homosexual or a heterosexual orientation; regardless of what made people attracted to their own or to the opposite gender, sexual orientation was "either-or." In the twentieth century, most social scientists and sex researchers came to think about sexual orientation as lying on a continuum marked by degrees of likelihood of finding one's own or the opposite gender attractive. Sexologist Alfred C. Kinsey and his associates published their landmark works, *Sexual Behavior in the Human Male* in 1948 and *Sexual Behavior in the Human Female* in 1953, in which they used a continuum of sexual orientation to quantify a range of attraction, from those who found only members of the opposite gender attractive (whom they defined as "heterosexual") to those who found only members of the same gender attractive (whom they defined as "homosexual"). Between the two extremes were the majority of people, who find both genders attractive and arousing in varying degrees-and thus are defined as "bisexual."

In determining sexual orientation, researchers once focused on the gender of sex partners, which also was the criterion on which laypersons generally focused. If a male usually had female partners, they would consider him heterosexual; if a female usually had female partners, they would consider her homosexual. Yet sexual orientation, how one is attracted by and toward others, is more accurately considered to be primarily the subjective experience of how one feels inside, not the overt behavior that one demonstrates outside.

Research has shown that, in any given individual, there can be a large discrepancy between the gender of one's actual partners and the gender to which one is more attracted and drawn. Social and cultural circumstances often affect, even determine, whether one will behave the way one feels. People who are primarily attracted to opposite-gender persons may be influenced to have, and even pursue, same-gender partners by particular religious beliefs, certain restricted environments (such as prison), or the sense that this behavior is or is not permissible. Orientation is better understood in the minds and feelings of persons themselves: which gender attracts, how often, and how much. Personal histories that include procreating children, marriage, homosexual activities, and bisexual experimentation should not be used to identify sexual orientation.

Although many studies followed the early work of Kinsey, most experts believe that Kinsey and his colleagues produced the most valid observations about sexuality and sexual orientation. Conducting research in this field is difficult. Different studies use different survey tools, and not all are equally reliable. In addition, many people will not candidly or honestly discuss their sexual attitudes, attractions, or behaviors. Nevertheless, the best estimates that rely and build on the Kinsey group's earlier work suggest that about 10 percent of the population in Western countries is primarily gay or lesbian and that an additional 10 percent of the population is primarily bisexual. (There is less research available on

non-Western nations, and much of what is available is methodologically less reliable.) In the United States, 60 million people are likely to be homosexual or bisexual. Far more important than the numbers, however, is the reality that gay, lesbian, and bisexual orientations are neither unusual nor peculiar. This remains true even though heterosexuality is the more common pattern of most people, most of the time—a finding true for all societies ever studied. Yet a minority pattern of attraction cannot, simply on the basis of numbers, be considered abnormal.

Expert and lay opinions about how sexual orientation develops differ, often considerably. Yet expert, if not lay, opinions do converge about when it develops: at about age four or five, which is a year to two earlier than when experts believe an individual's personal traits and characteristics emerge intact as an identifiable personality. Because erotic behavior and erogenous stimuli do not usually become an important part of one's personal world until puberty begins (the developmental marker used to interpret when childhood ends and adolescence begins), many do not learn what their orientation is until late adolescence or even well into adulthood. People who eventually come to have nearly exclusive heterosexual fantasies, attractions, and sexual affiliations often have had earlier, adolescent homosexual experiences. Likewise, people who eventually come to discover that their orientation is strongly homosexual have often married, borne children, and had long periods of gratifying heterosexual dating experiences.

Most people eventually come to identify their orientation, at least implicitly, in terms of direction and strength. Direction refers to the direction of sexual orientation, toward one's own or one's opposite gender. Strength refers to the degree of exclusivity associated with the direction of one's orientation: attracted only by the same or opposite gender, sometimes attracted by each, always attracted to each.

Bidirectional orientation is the least researched and least understood of sexual orientations. As with homosexual and heterosexual behavior, bisexual encounters, even if gratifying, do not in themselves mean that someone is bisexually oriented, and therefore bisexual. All sexual orientation is internal, not behavioral.

Some people, while learning about their sexual selves and their accompanying orientation, engage in experimental bisexual behavior. Some, with limited access to the gender toward which they are more predominantly or exclusively oriented, become sexually active with the gender toward which they are not oriented but which is more available. Some are sexually active with both genders for money. Some are sexually stimulated and aroused regardless of gender. (William H. Masters and Virginia E. Johnson, perhaps the leading sex researchers and sex educators of all time, label this group "ambisexual.") Some indicate that they have a definite orientation toward sexual activity with both genders. Among this last group, there are those who report having long-term, one-gender relationships that followed long-term, other-gender relationships, and there are others who report having concurrent sexual relationships with partners of both genders.

Although descriptions of active bisexuality are readily available in the research, the sheer variety of patterns substantially challenges research-based understandings of how sexual orientation originates and develops. What is known is that people with bisexual orientations are neither poorer nor better psychologically adjusted than heterosexuals or homosexuals, and that bisexuality, while poorly understood, reflects a comfortable and fulfilling sexual life and identity for a significant percentage of the general population.

THEORIES OF SEXUAL ORIENTATION

No other area of sexuality has generated more interest, theory, or research than orientation and how it originates. No one theory stands alone as proven, and not-yet-explained data shake the foundations of even the most useful theories. Nevertheless, scientific inquiry has disproven many earlier theories. The most promising theories fall into several categories, some of which can overlap to a degree: genetic, hormonal, psychodynamic, parental, familial, behavioral, societal, and cultural.

The first significant study of genetic causality for sexual orientation was published in 1952. The research compared one group of male identical twins with one group of male fraternal twins. In both groups, one twin was known to be homosexually oriented. Reasonably assuming that both twins of a pair would be exposed to essentially the same environments, the study counted how many second twins, whose sexual orientations were unknown at the start of the study, were also gay. If the rate of homosexuality for twins was higher among the group of identical twins than in the group of fraternal twins, it would be evidence that genetic makeup, which is virtually the same between identical twins, the main cause of sexual orientation.

Twelve percent of fraternal twins who were homosexual had a homosexual twin. Because male fraternal twins are genetically as similar and dissimilar as any pair

of brothers, and the rate of homosexuality among the fraternal set was close to the rates that the Kinsey group found in the general population, the results were initially considered a breakthrough. The study also showed, however, that the twin of every known homosexual in the identical set was also homosexual. One hundred percent concordance rates are rare in studies of identical twins (even studies which might compare heights or weights between identical twins would not achieve 100 percent concordance) and are almost nonexistent in all other social groups on any variable ever studied. This particular study and its unique finding needed replication to be believed. Two later studies, published in 1968 and 1976, had quite different results, and the view that sexual orientation was principally a product of genetic conditions and variability was abandoned, though most researchers still believe genetics provides contributory influence.

Investigation into the role that hormonal factors play in sexual orientation divides between research on animals and research on humans. Studies clearly show that altering prenatal hormone exposure leads to male or female homosexual behavior in at least several animal species. Among humans, a number of studies have had findings that link prenatal exposure to specific sexual orientation outcomes. For example, females who were exposed to male hormones (androgens), especially testosterone, were more likely to develop lesbian orientations; males with Kleinfelter's syndrome, a chromosomal abnormality marked by a deficiency in androgens, are known to develop gay orientations at a greater frequency than the population average.

Other research on humans has shown that there are different hormone levels between adult homosexuals and heterosexuals. Some studies have found lower testosterone in homosexual males, some have found higher levels of estrogens (though present in both sexes, they are usually considered female hormones) in homosexual males, and other studies have found both. At least one study found higher blood testosterone in homosexual females than heterosexual females.

While this evidence seems illuminating on the surface, it is far from conclusive. First, although many studies show different hormone levels between heterosexual and homosexual persons, several studies have also found hormone levels to be the same in both groups. Second, administering sex hormones to adults does not affect their orientation in any way. Third, prenatal overexposure or underexposure to sex hormones is relatively rare. It would not account for the differences in orientation that are observed in the general adult population, nor is it beyond reason to view cases of abnormal hormonal prenatal environments as extraordinary and unrepresentative of how sexual orientation usually develops. Fourth, while animal studies often describe processes in particular species that are readily analogous to processes in humans, this does not seem to be the case with human sexuality in general or human sexual orientation in particular.

What seems clear is that there is no one-to-one link between sex hormones and sexual orientation. Prenatal hormones, which are known to influence brain development in many ways, may play an indirect role in predisposing individuals toward adapting certain adult sexual behavioral patterns of greater or lesser bisexuality.

Psychodynamic explanations focus on the nature of parent-child relationships and how parents encourage or discourage the growth of their children. Several studies showed homosexual males to have been reared in homes where mothers were dominant and overprotective and fathers were weak, passive, or emotionally uninvolved, a family constellation seen with less statistical frequency among heterosexual males. Other studies, however, showed strained, distant relationships between homosexual men and their fathers but could not find evidence of maternal dominance and overprotectiveness. One study even described the fathers of homosexual males as under protective, generous, good, and dominant, while the mothers were not found to be overly protective or bossy. Another study simply found no differences in family constellation and dynamics between psychologically well-adjusted heterosexual and homosexual males and females. Given the varied results, the research outcomes from psychodynamic, parental, and familial studies lack cohesive evidence that homosexuality or any orientation results from poor parent-child relationships or dysfunctional family environments.

Behavioral, societal, and cultural theories assume that orientation is primarily learned as people become culturally assimilated and psychologically conditioned (rewarded and punished) for specific sexual feelings, thoughts, and behaviors. Therefore, in an environment where homoerotic feelings were accepted and valued, people would be more likely to develop homosexual, and perhaps bisexual, orientations. In an environment where homophobic attitudes were considered the norm, homoerotic feelings would more likely be abandoned. While these theories have utility in explaining certain sociological phenomena such as atypical gender role behavior (for example, tomboys) and observed shifts toward lesbian sexuality among some female rape victims, they seem to have less utility in explaining how orientation develops in the majority of the population.

CURRENT RESEARCH

Although answers to the question of how orientation develops are complex, researchers Alan P. Bell, Martin S. Weinberg, and S. K. Hammersmith published the two-volume work *Sexual Preference: Its Development in Men and Women* (1981) in an attempt to reveal the causal chain of sexual orientation development in more than thirteen hundred adult homosexual, heterosexual, and bisexual men and women. They based their findings both on lengthy face-to-face interviews with every person in their study and on a sophisticated and reliable statistical technique called path analysis.

Bell, Weinberg, and Hammersmith's research represents the most extensive collection of data on a large number of people in existence, and most experts are taking at least some of their findings to be conclusive. These results show that sexual orientation is strongly established in most people by late adolescence and that sexual feelings rarely undergo directional changes in adulthood. Atypical gender role behavior in childhood, such as boys preferring to play with dolls and not having an interest in more competitive activities, was found to be more likely than not to proceed homosexual orientations in adolescence and adulthood. Adult homosexuals and bisexuals had, on average, the same amount of heterosexual experience as heterosexual adolescents, though their heterosexual experiences were less rewarding and enjoyable than either their own homosexual experiences or the heterosexual experiences of heterosexuals. The study found that girls choosing their fathers as role models does not cause these girls to become lesbian (as several theories had maintained) and that the parental combination of a domineering, powerful mother and a weak, inadequate father does not cause homosexuality in males (as was once believed).

Although their study was methodologically well planned and statistically sound, Bell, Weinberg, and Hammersmith could not find solid support for any of the prevailing theories about the causality of sexual orientation. Some theories explain some of the observed data, and some theories seem to enhance understanding of the origins of sexual orientation in some elements of the population, but no theory or combination of theories explains all the data.

If this research has moved medical science along to some degree, it also serves to remind everyone, professional and nonprofessional alike, that the very complexity of human experience and how humans develop their identity warrants caution if it is ever to be accurately understood. The evidence is not complete. It is known that some aspects of the theories of the origins of sexual orientation are true and that others are false.

Learning one's own sexual orientation is a complex process requiring self-observation, self-reflection, and self-recollection. People discover what they like and who they like; the content and orientation of their sexual fantasies; and which gender feels closer to their sexual identity as persons (rather than the gender role that they feel a societal obligation to play). It is their own experiences of what is, and is not, sexually gratifying that teaches people how they are oriented sexually.

BIBLIOGRAPHY

Berzon, Betty. (2004). *Permanent Partners: Building Gay and Lesbian Relationships That Last*. Rev. ed. New York: Plume. A practical, realistic guide for same-gender partners in primary relationships. Berzon addresses the main conflict and confusing areas of relationships typically experienced by gay and lesbian couples.

Byer, Curtis O., Louis W. Shainberg, and Grace Galliano. (2002). *Dimensions of Human Sexuality*. 6th ed. Revised by Sharon P. Shriver. Boston: McGraw-Hill,. An excellent, thorough, well-organized textbook on all areas of sexuality, with highlighted topics of special interest.

Corinna, Heather. (2007). S.E.X.: *The All-You-Need-To-Know Progressive Sexuality Guide To Get You Through High School and College*. New York: Marlowe. A candid discussion of sex and sexuality for teenagers and young adults. Topics include anatomy, sexual orientation and sexual identity, relationships, safer-sex practices, sexual abuse and rape, pregnancy and contraception, and sexually transmitted diseases, including HIV.

Dibble, Suzanne L., and Patricia A. Robertson. (2010). *Lesbian Health 101: A Clinician's Guide*. San Francisco: UCSF Nursing Press. The first comprehensive textbook on lesbian health for clinicians and students. Helpful to general readers as well. Also provides insight into women's health in general.

Fairchild, Betty, and Nancy Hayward. (1998). *Now That You Know: A Parent's Guide To Understanding Their Gay and Lesbian Children*. 3d ed. San Diego, CA. Harcourt Brace. A standard and compassionate reference for families with gay sons or lesbian daughters. Discusses the nature of homosexuality, counsels parents on how to respond supportively to gay and lesbian children, and informs parents on the pressing health and emotional issues that affect gays and lesbians.

Katz, Jonathan Ned. (2007). *The Invention of Heterosexuality*. Chicago: University of Chicago Press. Using the now, well known premise of homosexuality as socially constructed, Katz, in this classic work, explores heterosexuality as a social construct as well.

Masters, William H., Virginia E. Johnson, and Robert C. Kolodny. (1995). *Human Sexuality*. 5th ed. New York: HarperCollins College. A well-organized, highly readable textbook covering biological, psychological, social, cultural, ethical, and religious perspectives on human sexuality.

Strong, Bryan, et al. (2008). *Human Sexuality: Diversity in Contemporary America*. 6th ed. Boston: McGraw-Hill. Excellent coverage of human sexuality and the differences and similarities across ethnicities, cultures, genders, and sexual orientations.

Paul Moglia

SEE ALSO: Gender; Gender identity; Self concept; Sexuality.

Sexual predatory behaviors

TYPE OF PSYCHOLOGY: Addiction; Biological bases of human behavior; Clinical; Counseling; Developmental; Forensic; Neuropsychology; Psychopathology; Psychotherapy.

Sexuality is a complex human behavior which can become problematic when sexual drive manifests in predatory behavior. While there are a wide variety of sexual behaviors, when the consent of a partner no longer is recognized, predatory behavior with psychiatric and legal implications can develop.

KEY CONCEPTS
- Aggression
- Antisocial personality disorder
- Psychopathy
- Rape
- Stalking

INTRODUCTION

While human sexuality is an evolutionarily developed capacity to engage in erotic experiences and responses, throughout history and literature, a theme of a cat-and-mouse pursuit has been consistent. Also through history, there are multitudes of examples of instances where one group would exert dominance over another through demonstrations of sexual aggression, the "spoils of war." When sexual encounters move from a mutually gratifying exploration to one seeking to use sexuality as a means of control or conquest, the dynamic moves into the realm of sexual predatory behavior.

The term *predator* spans a large and controversial spectrum, from online communication where someone aggressively seeks a sexual partner; to a rejected suitor who does not terminate the pursuit ("stalking"); to a trusted adult in a child's life who manipulates the victim into succumbing to sexual overtures ("grooming"); to the more conventional perception, the blatantly violent and angry assailant who seeks out a target to rape.

Variants in sexual preference and excitement have been categorized in the *Diagnostic and Statistical Manual of Mental Disorders* (5th ed., DSM-5) as paraphilias. Some go so far as to distinguish between those whose paraphilias simply represent a twist in sexual excitement from those whose sexual proclivity leads to criminal behavior. Some assert that a "sex offender" is not necessarily a predator, something that requires seeking multiple victims through predatory means and then exploiting them sexually. Predators are likely to recidivate and resist treatment. A sex offender, by comparison, generally has only one victim, often a family member, tends to stop once caught and is amenable to intervention.

ARCHETYPE OF THE PREDATOR

Despite concerted theoretical efforts (and many popular television and movie portrayals), there is yet to be one accepted prime example of the sexual predator. The stereotype of the "dirty old man" lurking around playgrounds seeking to entice children or the rapist lying in wait behind a bush or in a dark alley awaiting a victim to come by have been debunked as mythical. Even conventional wisdom which presumes the ascendency of the Internet with its ease of access to potential victims has led to a proliferation of such predation has been largely discredited.

According to the US Department of Justice's Center for Sex Offender Management (CSOM), the subset of sex offenders present with the following commonly identified characteristics:

- Deviant sexual arousal, interest, or preferences
- Cognitive distortions

- Social, interpersonal, and intimacy deficits
- Victim empathy deficits
- Poor self-management skills
- Under-detected deviant sexual behaviors
- History of maltreatment

It is important to reiterate that not all of these issues are present in every sex offender. The presence of any of these variables, alone or in combination, does not create a sex offender or necessarily causes anyone to commit sex offenses. Some of these features or characteristics can also be found in samples of other criminals or within the general population. The one consistent characteristic is gender. Although there are some examples of female sexual predators, the majority are male. Despite this lack of typological certitude, there are multitudes of general audience sources which attempt to provide the "profile" of a rapist or stalker. One website listed thirteen "telltale" behaviors, including: bullying, insensitivity/focus on self, excessive anger, brooding, mood swings, and a jock/gorilla mentality.

MOLESTATION

When sexual aggression does not involve the application of overt violence, it often is categorized as molestation. Commonly, this is how child sexual abuse is labeled. Some claim that the lack of violence mediates this being identified as predatory behavior. However, as initiating the encounter usually involves extensive preparation and manipulation – grooming – to secure the youth's participation, the distinction is problematic. The primary or exclusive adult sexual interest in prepubescent children is pedophilia; pubescent individuals approximately 11-14 years old, hebephilia; and ephebophilia, which later adolescence, approximately 15-19 years old. It is argued that the mere presence of such attraction does not indicate a sexually predatory nature; an overt act is required. Further, despite perceptions that adult attraction to children as a uniquely modern phenomenon, conflicting notions of childhood have been an ongoing struggle between social and legal norms and were prevalent in Victorian society.

STALKING

Unwanted attention directed at an individual can rise to the level of stalking. It commonly, but not universally, involves a sexual component. Generally, stalkers are categorized as psychotic or nonpsychotic. Most are nonpsychotic and may exhibit mental illnesses such as major depression, adjustment disorder, or substance dependence, or any variety of personality disorders (e.g., antisocial, narcissistic, paranoid, borderline, or dependent). The nonpsychotic stalker's pursuit of victims involves several psychological factors, including projection of blame, anger, dependency, obsession, minimization, hostility, denial, and jealousy. Conversely, the stalker often has no angry feelings towards the victim, but simply a longing that cannot be fulfilled. One attempt to categorize stalking behavior theorized five distinct types. Despite only one specifically mentioning sexual intent or predatory behavior, either or both may be involved regardless of underlying motivation.

Mullen, Pathé and Purcell's five stalkers types:

Rejected – seek to avenge, reverse, or correct, or a rejection (e.g., divorce, separation, termination);

- Resentful – mostly seek to frighten and distress the victim because of a sense of being wronged by the victim;
- Intimacy seekers - seek to establish a loving relationship with their victim, believing fate or destiny is bringing them together;
- Incompetent suitors – present a fixation or sense of entitlement to an intimate relationship with those who have attracted their romantic interest;
- Predatory - spy on the victim in order to prepare and plan an attack – often sexual – on the victim.

RAPE
It is sexual assault generally involving sexual intercourse or sexual penetration of some form committed without a person's consent. It involves aggression on a spectrum ranging from coercion, abuse of authority, physical force, or against a person who is incapable of valid consent, such as one who is unconscious, incapacitated, or unable to legally consent. While commonly viewed as crime of aggression, it can also involve otherwise consensual sexual relationships which are deemed inappropriate by law, i.e., statutory rape. The definition has evolved as societal norms change. Historically, in many societies, rape was deemed a crime of theft of a man's property (a husband or father), meaning that by definition a wife could not be raped by her husband. However, marital rape is now more commonly considered as a form of domestic violence. Similarly, acquaintance (or date) rape is recognized as a non-consensual act despite the parties having, at least initially, shared a potential romantic/sexual interest in one another. Such assaults can involve overt violence, perhaps after an advance is rebuffed, or

opportunistically follow one person's intoxication and subsequent incapacitation. A more predatory practice involves bringing an incapacitating drug to the encounter, the obvious intent to initiate the sexually assault once the companion is unable to resist.

RELATIONSHIP TO PSYCHOPATHY
Robert Hare is well known for his work to categorize and help identify those who suffer from psychopathy; generally defined as a personality disorder characterized by enduring antisocial behavior, diminished empathy and remorse, and disinhibited or bold behavior. Hare's additional specific features strike a common theme with those associated with sexual predators. Interpersonal/emotional features include: glib and superficial; egocentric and grandiose; lack of remorse or guilt; and, lack of empathy. Social deviance factors include: impulsive; early behavior problems; need for excitement; and adult antisocial behavior. Some researchers assert that psychopaths have a preference for violent sexual behavior. There is evidence that psychopathic offenders are more likely to commit rape than other offenders, and rapists score higher on measures of psychopathy than do other offenders. Additionally, there is evidence that boldness can contribute to the prediction of positive attitudes toward sexually predatory tactics, both directly and through its interaction with disinhibition.

CONFINING SEXUALLY VIOLENT PREDATORS
The US Supreme Court's 1997 decision in *Kansas v. Hendricks* allowed individual states or the federal government to impose stringent oversight on sexually violent predators (SVP) after the completion of their original sentence if found to have a "mental abnormality" or personality disorder and deemed likely to commit additional sexual offenses. They may be forcibly committed to a mental facility after release from prison, or incur stricter reporting requirements than other sex offenders. In many states, the legal test for "mental abnormality" is much lower than for mental illness.

CONCEPTUAL CRITICISM
While forms of sexual violence have existed essentially since the dawn of humanity, some argue that the evolution of the term "sexual predator" has arisen more from a political agenda following a spate of horrific and highly publicized cases in the late 20th century. In response, throughout the U.S., laws were passed creating requirements for the registration of sex offenders after comple-

tion of incarceration, restrictions on the geographical location of housing for such people, and the continue civil commitment of SVPs. However, the efficacy of such interventions, indeed, the prevalence of sexual predatory behavior has been called into question. One analysis of the legislative debate leading to the federal version of Megan's Law (creating a federal database of sexual predators) revealed that much of the parliamentary debate focused on evocative anecdotes of particularly heinous crimes against children, failing to reveal how rare such crimes were or detailing how the proposed law would affect many more people than just those who committed such horrendous offenses. Furthermore, research by the Crimes Against Children Research Center found the publicity about online "predators" who prey on naive children using trickery and violence to be largely inaccurate. It was found that internet sex crimes involving adults and juveniles are more likely fit the definition of statutory rape rather than a more predatory model of sexual assault or pedophilic child molestation.

BIBLIOGRAPHY

Association for the Treatment of Sexual Abusers (ATSA). http://www.atsa.com/ The leading professional organization for this population, their website provides many resources for both the general public and professionals.

Mullen, P.E., Pathé, M., Purcell, R. (2008). *Stalkers and their Victims*, 2e. Cambridge University Press: Cambridge. An update to the book that produced the stalker typologies, it includes explorations of cyberstalking, stalking in the workplace, stalking of celebrities, female and juvenile stalkers.

Ramsland, K. & McGrain, P. N. (2009) *Inside the Minds of Sexual Predators*. Santa Barbara, CA: Praeger. Seeks to explore this intentional criminal behavior, describing the different types of sexual predators and explaining why they choose to commit their specific type of predatory acts.

RAINN (Rape, Abuse & Incest National Network). https://rainn.org/ This is the nation's largest anti-sexual violence organization, with many resources for those dealing with the aftermath of sexual assault.

Salter, A. (2004). *Predators: Pedophiles, Rapists, and Other Sex Offenders*. New York: Basic Books. "This is not a book with complete and comfortable answers. It will not finish with a checklist for identifying a sex offender.... But if I do my job right, reading this book will make it harder for sex offenders to get access to you or your children," Salter says by way of introduction. Despite some much

publicized media cases, Salter believes there are many misunderstandings about sexual predators.

Stephen P. Hampe

SEE ALSO: Abuse; Dominance; Pleasure; Psychosexual behavior; Sex; Sexuality.

Sexual variants and paraphilias

TYPE OF PSYCHOLOGY: Psychopathology

Sexual variations, or paraphilias, are unusual sexual activities in that they deviate from what is considered normal at a particular time in a particular society; paraphilias include behaviors such as exhibitionism, voyeurism, and sadomasochism. It is when they become the prime means of gratification, displacing direct sexual contact with a consenting adult partner, that paraphilias are technically present.

KEY CONCEPTS
- Exhibitionism
- Fetishism
- Frotteurism
- Sexual masochism
- Sexual sadism
- Transvestic fetishism
- Voyeurism
- Zoophilia

INTRODUCTION

Paraphilias are sexual behaviors that differ from the society's norms; a paraphilia is classified as a psychological disorder when the deviant fantasies, sexual urges, or behaviors cause the individual significant distress or impairment in social, occupational, or other important areas and persist for longer than six months, or when they cause harm to others. Psychologist John Money, who has studied sexual attitudes and behaviors extensively, claims to have identified about forty such behaviors.

TYPES OF PARAPHILIAS

Exhibitionism. Exhibitionism is commonly called "indecent exposure." The term refers to behavior in which an individual, usually a man, experiences recurrent, intense sexually arousing fantasies or urges about exposing his genitals to an involuntary observer, who is usually a female. The key point in exhibitionistic behavior is that it involves observers who are unwilling. After exposure, the exhibitionist often masturbates while fantasizing about the observer's reaction. Exhibitionists tend to be most aroused by shock and typically flee if the observer responds by laughing or attempts to approach the exhibitionist. Most people who exhibit themselves are adolescent or young adult men. They tend to be shy, unassertive people who feel inadequate and afraid of being rejected by another person. People who make obscene telephone calls have similar characteristics to the people who engage in exhibitionism. Typically, they are sexually aroused when their observers react in a shocked manner. Many masturbate during or immediately after placing an obscene call.

Voyeurism. Voyeurism is the derivation of sexual pleasure through the repetitive seeking of or intrusive fantasies of situations that involve looking, or "peeping," at unsuspecting people who are naked, undressing, or engaged in sexual intercourse. It may also involve secretly filming or photographing the target. Most individuals who act on these urges masturbate during the voyeuristic activity or immediately afterward in response to what they have seen. Further sexual contact with the unsuspecting stranger is rarely sought. Like exhibitionists, voyeurs are usually not physically dangerous. Most voyeurs are not attracted to nude beaches or other places where it is acceptable to look because they are most aroused when the risk of being discovered is high. Voyeurs tend to be men in their twenties and may have a high sex drive along with strong feelings of inadequacy.

Sadomasochism. Sadomasochistic behavior encompasses both sadism and masochism; it is often abbreviated S & M. The term "sadism" is derived from the marquis de Sade, a French writer and army officer who was horribly cruel to people for his own erotic purposes. Sexual sadism involves acts in which the psychological or physical suffering of the victim, including his or her humiliation, is deemed sexually exciting. In masochism, sexual excitement is produced in a person by his or her own suffering; the preferred means of achieving gratification include verbal humiliation and being bound or whipped. The dynamics of the two behaviors are similar. Sadomasochistic behaviors have the potential to be physically dangerous, but most people involved in these behaviors participate in mild or symbolic acts with a partner they can trust. Most people who engage in S & M activities are motivated by a desire for dominance or submission rather than pain. Interestingly, many nonhuman animals participate in pain-inflicting behavior before coitus.

Some researchers think that the activity heightens the biological components of sexual arousal, such as blood pressure and muscle tension. It has been suggested that any resistance between partners enhances sex, and S & M is a more extreme version of this behavior. It is also thought that S & M offers people the temporary opportunity to take on roles that are the opposite of the controlled, restrictive roles they play in everyday life. Both sexual sadism and sexual masochism are considered disorders when the fantasies, sexual urges, or behaviors cause significant distress or impairment in social, occupational, or other important areas.

Fetishism. Fetishism is a type of sexual behavior in which a person becomes sexually aroused by focusing on an inanimate object or a part of the human body. Many people are aroused by looking at undergarments, legs, or breasts, and it is often difficult to distinguish between normal activities and fetishistic ones. It is when a person becomes focused on the objects or body parts, called "fetishes," to the point of causing significant distress or impairment that a disorder is present. Fetishists are usually men. Common fetish objects include women's lingerie, high-heeled shoes, boots, stockings, leather, silk, and rubber goods. Common body parts involved in fetishism are hair, buttocks, breasts, and feet.

Pedophilia. The term "pedophilia" is from the Greek language and means "love of children." It is characterized by a preference for sexual activity with prepubescent children and is engaged in primarily by men. The activity varies in intensity and ranges from stroking the child's hair to holding the child while secretly masturbating, manipulating the child's genitals, encouraging the child to manipulate his or her own genitals, or, sometimes, engaging in sexual intercourse. Generally, a pedophile who sexually abuses a child is related to, or an acquaintance of, the child, rather than a stranger. Studies of imprisoned pedophiles have found that the men typically had poor relationships with their parents, drank heavily, showed poor sexual adjustment, and were themselves sexually abused as children. Pedophiles tend to be older than people convicted of other sex offenses. Not all pedophiles sexually abuse children, however. For a diagnosis of pedophilia, the individual should be at least sixteen years old and at least five years older than the target child or children.

Transvestic Disorder. "Transvestism" refers to dressing in clothing of the opposite sex to obtain sexual excitement. In the majority of cases, it is men who are attracted to transvestism. Several studies show that cross-dressing occurs primarily among married hetero-sexuals. The man usually achieves sexual satisfaction simply by putting on the clothing, but sometimes masturbation and intercourse are engaged in while the clothing is being worn. In some cases, gender dysphoria, persistent discomfort with gender role or identity, is present along with transvestic disorder.

Frotteurism. Frotteurism encompasses fairly common fantasies, sexual urges, or behaviors of a person, usually a male, obtaining sexual pleasure by pressing or rubbing against a fully clothed person, usually female, in a crowded public place. Often it involves the clothed penis rubbing against the woman's buttocks or legs and appears accidental.

Zoophilia and Necrophilia. Zoophilia involves sexual contact between humans and animals as the repeatedly preferred method of achieving sexual excitement. In this disorder, the animal is preferred despite other available sexual outlets. Necrophilia is a rare dysfunction in which a person obtains sexual gratification by looking at or having intercourse with a corpse.

DIAGNOSIS AND TREATMENTS

A problem in the definition and diagnosis of sexual variations is that it is difficult to draw the line between normal and abnormal behavior. Patterns of sexual behavior differ widely across history and within different cultures and communities. It is impossible to lay down the rules of normality; however, attempts are made to understand behavior that differs from the majority and to help people who find their own atypical behavior to be problematic or to be problematic in the eyes of the law.

Unlike most therapeutic techniques in use by psychologists, many of the treatments for paraphilias have historically been painful, and the degree of their effectiveness has been questionable. Supposedly, the methods were not aimed at punishing the individual, but perhaps society's lack of tolerance toward sexual deviations can be seen in the nature of the treatments. In general, attempts to treat the paraphilias have been hindered by the lack of information available about them and their causes.

Traditional counseling and psychotherapy alone have not been very effective in modifying the behavior of paraphiliacs. Some researchers believe that the behavior might be important for the mental stability of paraphiliacs. If they did not have the paraphilia, they might experience mental deterioration. Another hypothesis is that, although people are punished by society for being sexually deviant, they are also rewarded for it. For

the paraphilias that put the person at risk for arrest, the danger of arrest often becomes as arousing and rewarding as the sexual activity itself. Difficulties in treating paraphiliacs may also be related to the emotionally impoverished environments that many of them experienced throughout childhood and adolescence. Convicted sex offenders report more physical and sexual abuse as children than do the people convicted of nonsexual crimes. It is difficult to undo the years of learning involved.

Surgical castration for therapeutic purposes involves removal of the testicles. Surgical castration for sexual offenders in North America is very uncommon, but the procedure is sometimes used in northern European countries. The reason castration is used as a treatment for sex offenders is the inaccurate belief that testosterone is necessary for sexual behavior. The hormone testosterone is produced by the testicles. Unfortunately, reducing the amount of testosterone in the blood system does not always change sexual behavior. Furthermore, contrary to the myth that a sex offender has an abnormally high sex drive, many sex offenders have a low sex drive or are sexually dysfunctional.

In the same vein as surgical castration, other treatments use the administration of chemicals to decrease desire without the removal of genitalia. Estrogens have been fairly effective in reducing the sex drive, but they sometimes make the male appear feminine by increasing breast size and stimulating other female characteristics. There are also drugs that block the action of testosterone and other androgens but do not feminize the body; these drugs are called "antiandrogens." Used together with counseling, antiandrogens can benefit paraphiliacs and sex offenders, especially those who are highly motivated to overcome the problem. More research on the effects of chemicals on sexual behavior is needed; the extent of the possible side effects, for example, needs further study.

Selective serotonin reuptake inhibitors (SSRIs), a class of antidepressants, and some antianxiety medications have shown promise as medical treatments. SSRIs commonly have the side effect of lowering the patient's sex drive and may also reduce compulsions as they do for obsessive-compulsive disorder. Such treatments may be best suited for nonviolent paraphiliacs who have an accompanying mood disorder or other condition.

Aversion therapy is another technique that has been used to eliminate inappropriate sexual arousal. In aversion therapy, the behavior that is to be decreased or eliminated is paired with an aversive, or unpleasant, experience. Most approaches use pictures of the object or situation that is problematic. The pictures are then paired with something extremely unpleasant, such as an electric shock or a putrid smell, thereby reducing arousal to the problematic object or situation in the future. Aversion therapy has been found to be fairly effective but is under ethical questioning because of its drastic nature. For example, chemical aversion therapy involves the administration of a nausea- or vomit-inducing drug. Electrical aversion therapy involves the use of electric shock. An example of the use of electric shock would be to show a pedophile pictures of young children whom he finds sexually arousing and to give an electric shock immediately after showing the pictures, in an attempt to reverse the pedophile's tendency to be sexually aroused by children. Less drastic variants such as covert sensitization, which relies on an unpleasant thought of punishment as the negative reinforcer, or masturbatory satiation, which seeks to supplant the undesired paraphilic fantasy with an acceptable alternative during masturbation, have also been developed.

Often, cognitive behavioral therapies, including harm reduction, acceptance and commitment therapy (ACT), dialectical behavior therapy (DBT), and functional analytic psychotherapy (FAP), are used in conjunction with other treatments. These therapies seek to reduce, not eliminate, the problematic behavior or to help the patient identify underlying emotional conditions that trigger the thoughts or behaviors and cope with them in more acceptable ways. Other techniques have been developed to help clients learn more socially approved patterns of sexual interaction skills.

In general, the efficacy of the techniques mentioned is quite variable, depending in part on the paraphilic disorder involved and the individual's motivation. Unfortunately, most therapy is conducted while the paraphiliacs are imprisoned or in a residential treatment facility, providing a less than ideal setting, and reoffending is common among paraphiliacs who have committed criminal sexual offences.

DISTURBANCES OF COURTSHIP BEHAVIOR

Beliefs regularly change with respect to what sexual activities are considered normal, so most therapists prefer to avoid terms such as "perversion," instead using "paraphilia." Basically, "paraphilia" means "love of the unusual." Aspects of paraphilias are commonly found within the scope of normal behavior; it is when they become the prime means of gratification, replacing direct sexual contact with a consenting adult partner, that paraphilias are technically said to exist. People who show atypical sexual patterns might also have emotional problems, but it is thought that most people who participate in paraphilias also participate in normal sexual behavior with adult partners, without complete reliance on paraphilic behaviors to produce sexual excitement. Many people who are arrested for paraphilic behaviors do not resort to the paraphilia because they lack a socially acceptable sex partner. Instead, they have an unusual opportunity, a desire to experiment, or perhaps an underlying psychological problem.

According to the approach of Kurt Freund and his colleagues, some paraphilias are better understood as disturbances in the sequence of courtship behaviors. Freund has described courtship as a sequence of four steps: location and appraisal of a potential partner, interaction that does not involve touch, interaction that does involve touch, and genital contact. Most people engage in behavior that is appropriate for each of these steps, but some do not. The ones who do not can be seen as having exaggerations or distortions in one or more of the steps. For example, Freund says that voyeurism is a disorder in the first step of courtship. The voyeur does not use an acceptable means to locate a potential partner. An exhibitionist and an obscene phone caller would have a problem with the second step: They have interaction with people that occurs before the stage of touch, but the talking and the showing of exhibitionistic behaviors are not the normal courtship procedures. Frotteurism would be a disruption at the third step, because there is physical touching that is inappropriate. Finally, rape would be a deviation from the appropriate fourth step.

As a result of social and legal restrictions, reliable data on the frequency of paraphilic behaviors are limited. Most information about paraphilias comes from people who have been arrested or are in therapy. Because the majority of people who participate in paraphilias do not fall into these two categories, it is highly difficult to talk about the majority of paraphiliacs in the real world. It is known, however, that males are much more likely to engage in paraphilias than are females.

BIBLIOGRAPHY

Allgeier, E. R., and A. R. Allgeier. "Atypical Sexual Activity." *Sexual Interactions.* 5th ed. Boston: Houghton, 2000. Print.

Bradford, John M. W., and A. G. Ahmed, eds. *Sexual Deviation: Assessment and Treatment.* Philadelphia:

Elsevier, June 2014. Digital file.

Downes, David, and Paul Rock. *Understanding Deviance: A Guide to the Sociology of Crime and Rule-Breaking*. 6th ed. New York: Oxford UP, 2007. Print.

Laws, D. Richard, and William O'Donohue, eds. *Sexual Deviance: Theory, Assessment, and Treatment*. 2nd ed. New York: Guilford, 2008. Print.

Lehmiller, Justin J. *The Psychology of Human Sexuality*. Malden: Wiley, 2014. Print.

Stoller, Robert J. "Sexual Deviations." *Human Sexuality in Four Perspectives*. Ed. Frank A. Beach and Milton Diamond. Baltimore: Johns Hopkins UP, 1978. Print.

Ward, Tony, Devon Polaschek, and Anthony R. Beech. *Theories of Sexual Offending*. Hoboken: Wiley, 2006. Print.

Weinberg, Thomas S., and G. W. Levi Kamel, eds. *S and M: Studies in Sadomasochism*. Rev. ed. Buffalo: Prometheus, 1995. Print.

Wilson, Glenn, ed. *Variant Sexuality*. New York: Routledge, 2014. Digital file.

Deborah R. McDonald

SEE ALSO: Abnormality: Legal models; Abnormality: Psychological models; Adolescence: Sexuality; Homosexuality; Law and psychology; Rape and sexual assault; Sadism and masochism; Sex hormones and motivation; Sexual behavior patterns; Sexual dysfunction; Transvestism.

Shift work

TYPE OF PSYCHOLOGY: Biological bases of human behavior; Clinical; Counseling; Consulting; Health; Organizational; Social

Shift work constitutes any regular work schedules that occur outside of the traditional 9-to-5 day shifts, and is rapidly becoming more common. Shift work can result in impaired psychological functioning and increased risk for psychiatric and medical morbidities, and therefore is an important area of research. Other common consequences include disturbed sleep, reduced alertness during work, reduced work performance, reduced quality of life, and increased risk of accidents. These consequences may be addressed with some combination of alternative shift scheduling, behavioral interventions to improve daytime sleep, controlled light exposure, and medication use.

KEY CONCEPTS:
- Circadian rhythms
- Circadian misalignment
- Shift-work disorder
- Sleepiness

Shift work is an often overlooked area of study that has great relevance to psychological health and functioning. As the economy globalizes, the demand for a 24-hour workforce also grows, resulting in a more employees working outside the traditional 9-to-5 day shift. In fact, as many as 1 out of 4 workers in the United States begin their shift between 2 pm and 6:30am, with an estimated 38 million individuals engaging in regular shift work. More importantly, a notable proportion of shift workers are involved in safety-sensitive operations, such as traffic control, transportation, or management of power stations. As such, it is important to understand the consequences that shift work may have on psychological health and functioning. In fact, several historical events have pointed to the disastrous consequences associated with shift work related impairments. Examples include Exon Valdez, Chernobyl, and the American Airlines flight 1420 crash, all of which occurred during the night shift. Given the growing demand for shift work and the elevated vulnerability for impaired psychological functioning, increasing attention has been paid to shift work and its consequences.

THE BIOLOGY OF SHIFT WORK

Although many shift workers experience difficulties in work performance and health complication, not everyone reports such difficulties. The prevailing theory is that individuals who report difficulties experience a misalignment between their internal circadian rhythm and their work schedules. Specifically, the human sleep/wake system is partially governed by an internal biological clock that regulates a host of physiological and psychological functions that fluctuates across the 24-hour day. One example of an important function is alertness, which usually increases as the morning progresses, and decreases later in the day. This internal clock is generally calibrated based on exposure to natural sunlight (or manufactured bright light), and occurs relatively independent of sleep. This explains why individuals will often report a resurgence of energy in the morning, even after a night of sleep deprivation. Exposure to bright light also suppresses the production of melatonin, an endogenous hormone that promotes sleep.

Workers on the traditional day shift are generally operating on a schedule that is well aligned with their internal rhythms; going to bed at night and waking in the morning with the ebb and flow of alertness governed by their circadian rhythms. However, individuals working outside of the day shift are often attempting to remain vigilant and functional when their circadian rhythms are down-regulating alertness and up-regulating sleep-related processes. Similarly, these workers are also often attempting to sleep during the daytime, when their circadian rhythms are promoting wakefulness and its associated functions. Consequently, shift workers often report decreased amounts and poorer quality sleep relative to day workers. Moreover, the impairments from circadian misalignment are further compounded by a cumulated amount of sleep debt that is accrued over multiple days of poor and inadequate sleep.

CONSEQUENCES OF SHIFT WORK

Shift Work Disorder. A range of consequences may occur as a result of misalignment between one's work schedule and circadian rhythms. While some people are able to adjust appropriately, many workers experience decreased task performance, with some even developing medical and psychiatric morbidities. Most notably, some individuals experience impairments that meet criteria for Shift Work Disorder (SWD). According to the *International Classification of Sleep Disorders Criteria*, SWD is characterized by insomnia and/or excessive sleepiness resulting from shift work that has been on-going for at least 3 months. Because much of human physiology is also governed by a biological clock, shift workers may also experience dysregulated physiological functioning, including increased insulin resistance, malabsorption, gastrointestinal difficulties, electrolyte imbalance, obesity, increased inflammation, and cardiovascular illness.

Reduced Sleep Time. Shift workers commonly report an average of between one to three hours less sleep than day workers, mostly as a function of attempting sleep during times when their circadian rhythms are promoting wakefulness. It is also not uncommon for shift workers to curtail sleep due to family or social obligations. A myriad of research on sleep loss has pointed to immediate and notable impairments. It has been shown that as little as 3 hours of sleep loss can result in driving impairments comparable to that occurring at legal limits of alcohol intoxication. This level of impairment is a likely explanation for the 50% increase in risk for automotive accidents in shift workers according to researchers.

Similarly, neurocognitive performance also degrades with sleep loss, including decreased vigilance, reduced response times, increased errors, reduced capacity for error correction, and impaired learning/memory.

Insomnia. In addition to reduced sleep time, shift workers also reported poor quality sleep. This often manifests as difficulty falling or staying asleep. For some individuals with vulnerabilities to insomnia (e.g., family history, increased sleep reactivity to stress, etc.), shift work may be a precipitating factor for the onset of insomnia. In fact, in a 2004, large epidemiological study of the greater Detroit area, 18.5% of night workers reported clinically significant insomnia, which was more than twice the reported rate of insomnia in day workers. In addition to its immediate consequences, insomnia is also a significant risk factor for comorbid psychiatric illnesses such as depression and anxiety, as well as cardiovascular illness such as hypertension. In fact, recent evidence from 2014 suggests that individuals suffering from insomnia are at 45% increased risk for mortality from cardiovascular illness.

Sleepiness. Sleepiness is also commonly reported in shift work, and is a major contributing factor to occupational difficulties and decreased quality of life. As expected, shift workers both report and demonstrate increased sleepiness relative to day workers. A study comparing nurses working various shifts found that as high as 35% of nurses working the night-shift report accidentally falling asleep at work, compared to only 3% in nurses working the day or evening shift.

Impaired Information Processing. Sleepiness can also adversely impact work performance due to impaired information processing. In fact, research has demonstrated reduced brain activation following sleep deprivation, particularly in regions responsible for executive functioning. This may explain why several domains of attention are generally negatively impacted by sleep loss. Firstly, lapses in attention are more likely to occur during sleepiness, which is important because it detracts from one's ability to achieve and maintain work productivity, and increases risk for errors of omission. Furthermore, research has also indicated that sleepy individuals may experience hyper-reactivity to novel stimuli in the environment which may also result in increased distractibility. Finally, sleepiness has also been associated with impaired learning, as demonstrated by both decreased quantity of items recalled, and degradation in the quality of the memory recalled. Together, the consequences of reduced work performance from sleep loss and sleepiness in shift workers may trigger a cascade of events (poor performance review, job loss, etc.) that significantly impact quality of life and mental health.

Impaired affective (emotional) processing. In addition to impaired cognitive processing, sleepiness also impacts affective functioning. It has been established that sleep deprivation is related to decreased positive affect (feelings), such as cheerfulness or joviality, and increased negative affect (feelings), such as hostility. Moreover, imaging research has found that that sleep loss leads to reduced connectivity in the frontolimbic pathway, indicating that sleep deprived brains are less able to regulate emotions, particularly in those that are negatively valenced. This translates to an amplification of emotional experiences, suggesting that shift workers who are sleepy have increased reactivity to stressors compounded by impaired stress management.

Sleep-deprived shift workers may also experience distortions in affective processing that impact social functioning. Prior research showed that, compared with non-sleep-deprived individuals, sleep-deprived individuals have more difficulty recognizing happy and angry facial expressions of low to moderate intensity. This is important because facial expressions carry substantial weight in determining appropriate social interactions, and can have damaging consequences if misconstrued. For example, failure to repair ruptures in relationships with co-workers can lead to brewing discontentment and decreased workplace morale, as can failure to share or celebrate with a colleague's happiness. Additionally, sleep-deprived individuals may also be more distracted by negative stimuli that are task-irrelevant, suggesting that shift-workers may be more distracted by environmental or social stressors at work, even if it does not impact their task at hand.

Sleep-dependent changes in positive affect are also relevant to psychological functioning and health. In particular, sleep-deprived individuals may show increased risk taking behaviors. Prior research has demonstrated that sleep deprived individuals had increased sensitivity to reward and decreased aversion to punishment following sleep-loss. This may lead to impulsive decisions and high-risk behaviors that can result in long-term negative outcomes. In fact, some individuals may even experience hypomania or mania symptoms following sleep-deprivation.

Accidents. Sleep-loss and sleepiness in shift work is also associated with increased risk for accidents that result in property damage, injury, or even death. Most notable accidents are related to falling asleep behind the wheel. This is particularly relevant to night and early morning shift workers. Night shift workers with a misalignment between their endogenous circadian rhythms and their work schedules are likely commuting during the early morning hours, when their circadian alertness is at the lowest. Early morning-shift workers are also at increased risk for sleepy driving during their commute to work due to reduced sleep time.

Accidents do not have to be confined to falling asleep at the wheel. Studies in medical personnel working unconventional shifts have found increased rates of percutaneous injuries from sharp medical instruments increased diagnostic and medication errors as well as increased rates of patient death. Furthermore, reported sleep disturbances have been shown to significantly predict both increased risk of injury and accidental death at work.

Medical Morbidities. Due to that fact that most physiological systems have a circadian component, shift-workers are often at increased risk for medical morbidities due to dysregulated functioning of these systems. Hunger, food preference, and metabolism are important examples of biological systems that have a strong circadian component. Consequently, shift-work has been associated with poor eating habits, increased risk of duodenal ulcers, and increased cardiovascular morbidity and mortality. Similarly, shift work may also increase risk for cancer. For example, large prospective studies have noted a 36% to 60% increase risk for breast cancer. Though studies of the underlying mechanisms are still underway, it has been suggested that a mediating factor in the relationship between shift work and cancer risk may be a reduction of free radical scavenging related to melatonin suppression from exposure to nocturnal light. In turn, the reduction of free radical scavenging leads to a reduced tumor-inhibition.

INTERVENTIONS
Adjustments in shift scheduling. There are a number of ways in which the impairments from shift work can be addressed. One way is through adjustments to the type of shift work. While it is generally thought, and even advised, that permanent night-shift may improve outcomes due to its stability, there is little evidence to support this. In fact, both objective and subjective measurements of sleep indicated that night shift workers show greater reductions in sleep duration compared to evening and slower rotating shift workers. In terms of

rotating shifts, adjustments can be made to both direction (shifts that progress with earlier versus later start times) and speed (the rate and increment of each change in shift start time). Most individuals are likely to respond better to forward-rotating rather than backward-rotating shifts. This is because the majority of individuals possess an endogenous circadian rhythm that is slightly longer than 24 hours, which in the absence of bright light leads in a natural delay every 24 hours. This means that when light exposure is purposefully controlled, delaying circadian rhythms can be achieved with relative ease. Slower-rotating shifts, such as those with three of more weeks per shift schedule, have also been associated with increase sleep time in workers relative to rapid-rotating shifts (e.g., multiple rotations within a week), suggesting better work performance and health outcomes.

Improving sleep. Given that sleep disturbance and insomnia is common in shift work, improving sleep quantity and quality can also aid in reducing work and health impairments. It is often recommended for shift workers to increase sleep opportunities in ways that also allow for personal, social, and familial obligations to be met. This can sometimes be achieved using two sleep periods. The first period is considered an "anchor" sleep, which is scheduled to occur every day (even during off-days), and would typically last approximately four hours. Ideally, daily obligations should be scheduled outside of the anchor sleep. The second sleep period would last another three to four hours, and can be taken at irregular times depending on work and other responsibilities. In cases where the sleep difficulty is related to insomnia, seeking treatments such as Cognitive Behavioral Therapy for Insomnia can help individuals address issues with falling and staying asleep in the context of shift-work.

Studies have also shown that naps prior to the start of shift-work may be an effective countermeasure that improves alertness and performance during the shift, as this would allow for some dissipation of sleep pressure prior to work. Other studies have also found that naps in combination with caffeine use can also reduce workplace sleepiness and improve work performance.

Light. Interventions using deliberate and appropriate timing of bright light exposure (~10,000 lux at the cornea) have also gained empirical support. Because endogenous circadian rhythms are usually calibrated by natural sunlight, this can be harnessed via the use of artificial bright light. Exposure to bright light close to bedtime can induce a phase delay of the internal clock, whereas exposure to bright light approximately 2 hours before habitual

wake time, or closely after the habitual wake time, can induce a phase advance. When used appropriately, each hour of exposure to bright light should incur a 30 minute shift in the biological clock. Alternatively, the use of light blocking goggles can also be helpful, such as during instances when shift workers need to run errands during daylight shortly before their scheduled sleep time.

Melatonin and Medications. The use of exogenous melatonin can also be used to aid in sleep timing. When endogenous melatonin levels are low (typically during the day), administration of exogenous melatonin between doses of 1.0 and 10 mg can increase total sleep time. Use of exogenous melatonin paired with dim-light prior to scheduled sleep time can also aid in sleep promotion during the day.

Benzodiazepines have also been used to aid in daytime sleep, with research showing that individuals on simulated shift-work were able to improve daytime sleep by 30-60 minutes a day using benzodiazepines, though this did not appear to improve alertness during the night. On the other hand, alerting medications such as modafinil can also be used to improve various outcomes in shift work, including sleepiness while driving, psychomotor vigilance, as well as objectively defined sleepiness based on the Multiple Sleep Latency Test

BIBLIOGRAPHY

Kryger, M. H., Roth, G., Eloni, D. M., & Dement, W. D. F. *Principles and Practice of Sleep Medicine.* (2005). WB Saunders, Philadelphia. This text is widely considered one of the main references in sleep medicine, and covers a broad range of current topics in the science and practice of sleep medicine written by experts in the field. It is also regularly updated as the field of sleep medicine evolves.

Monk TH, Folkard S. *Making Shift Work Tolerable.* Boca Raton, Fla: CRC Press; 1992. Written by two of the most prolific scientists in the science of shift work, this text guides the reader through the diverse experiences of shift workers, and discusses problems arising from working non-traditional hours. Written in jargon-free language, this text is accessible to anyone who is interested or is working as a shift worker.

Wright KP. *Circadian Rhythm Sleep Disorder: Jet Lag Type (Jet Lag Disorder).* In: Winkelman JW, Henderson S, Kotogal T, et al, editors. Case book of sleep medicine—a learning companion to the International Classification of Sleep Disorders, 2nd ed. Westchester, Ill: American Academy of Sleep Medicine; 2008. This is a chapter in a case-based learning text that accompanies the *International Classification of Sleep Disorders,* and provides a clinical depiction of cases in sleep medicine, including diagnostic history, laboratory testing, and clinical interventions. This accompaniment is an excellent case-study approach that adds volume and nuance that is not captured in the diagnostic criteria.

Philip Cheng

SEE ALSO: Occupational health; Stress; Work; Work conditions; Work rest cycles.

Shock therapy

TYPE OF PSYCHOLOGY: Psychotherapy

Electroconvulsive therapy, or shock therapy, is the controlled application of an electric current to the brain to induce a seizure. This treatment is used primarily for severe and debilitating mental disorders, such as major depression. It is a controversial treatment that has both proponents and opponents.

KEY CONCEPTS
- Anterograde amnesia
- Brain hemispheres
- Depression
- Grand mal seizure
- Mania
- Neurotransmitters
- Psychotropic medication
- Retrograde amnesia
- Schizophrenia
- Somatic therapy

INTRODUCTION

Electroconvulsive therapy (ECT), also known as shock therapy, is a somatic, or physical, form of therapy that is used for some individuals who suffer from severe mental disorders. It involves the direct application of an electric current to the brain. Typically, this current lasts for up to one second at a rate of 140 to 170 volts. The purpose of this electrical charge is to induce a grand mal seizure that will usually last for thirty to sixty seconds. The seizure that is induced is similar to those experienced in some types of epilepsy. It is through this grand mal seizure that ECT has its beneficial effect in reducing the symptoms of the patient.

The use of electrical charges as a medical treatment has been reported for centuries. As early as 47 c.e., Scribonius Largus used an electric eel to treat headaches. During the sixteenth century, Ethiopians were reported to have used electric catfish to expel evil spirits from the bodies of the mentally ill. Direct electric charges for the treatment of nervous complaints were also reported during the eighteenth century in Europe.

The modern application of electric current for the treatment of individuals with mental disorders began in 1938. It was at this time that two Italians, Ugo Cerletti, a psychiatrist, and Lucio Bini, a neuropathologist, invented the first ECT machine for use on humans. Cerletti and Bini first used their newly developed ECT machine to induce convulsions for the treatment of schizophrenic patients, and they reported that the treatment was a success.

ECT was introduced into the United States in 1940, at which time it quickly became the major somatic treatment for all severely disturbed individuals, regardless of mental disorder. By the mid-1950's, its use began to decline rapidly for several reasons, including the introduction of psychotropic medications, increasing demands for civil rights for the mentally ill, and concerns about potential adverse effects of ECT. Subsequently, however, a growing body of research has indicated that ECT is an effective treatment for some severe mental disorders. This research has led to a gradual increase in the acceptance of its use, particularly in the treatment of severely depressed individuals.

When ECT was first used for the treatment of mental disorders, the patient would be strapped to a table and, without any medications or other medical safeguards, would be administered the electrical current and sent into a convulsion. During this convulsion, the patient would thrash around on the table, often being left with broken limbs and other physical complications. In its later use, prior to administration of the ECT, the patient is given a muscle relaxant, which completely immobilizes the body, and anesthesia, which makes the patient completely unconscious. The result of these safeguards has been a much safer treatment of the patient.

THEORIES OF EFFICACY

Although ECT has been demonstrated to be an effective treatment, it is not known how and why ECT works. The theoretical basis of the original use of ECT had to do with the observation that schizophrenia and epilepsy rarely occur together, suggesting that the two are mutually exclusive. Based on this observation, it was hypothesized that, if a seizure could be induced in a schizophrenic, the schizophrenic symptoms could be eliminated. Physicians had tried previously to induce such seizures by means of injections of insulin, camphor, and other chemicals, but these approaches proved to have more disadvantages relative to ECT.

Although this early theory of the mechanics of ECT has been refuted, there still is little knowledge of how and why ECT actually works. The only fact that has been firmly established is that it is the seizure that ECT induces that creates any positive changes in the patient's symptoms. There is no clear-cut explanation, however, of how the seizure creates the changes. Several theories have been developed to explain the process, most of which center on ECT's effect on neurotransmitters.

Neurotransmitters are chemicals that are used in the brain to transmit messages from one cell to another. One well-accepted theory holds that abnormalities in the level and utilization of certain neurotransmitters lead to the development of mental disorders such as depression, schizophrenia, and mania. Consequently, it is thought that ECT, through the creation of a seizure, somehow affects the level and utilization of some of these neurotransmitters, and that it is this process that reduces the patient's symptoms of mental disorder. While research to investigate how ECT works continues, it is important to remember that, as with all somatic treatments, ECT does not cure the disorder; it provides only temporary relief from the symptoms.

Despite its reported effectiveness, ECT remains a controversial treatment for mental disorders. Opponents point to potential adverse effects that ECT can cause, particularly the possibility of permanent brain damage resulting from the induced seizure. These opponents, who highlight the negative effects that ECT can have on a patient's memory, prefer the use of alternative treatment methods. The public media have served to exacerbate negative perceptions of ECT by depicting it as an inhumane treatment that is used only to control and punish malcontents, not to help the severely disturbed. There is perhaps no better example of the media's distorted depiction of ECT than that found in the film *One Flew Over the Cuckoo's Nest* (1975), in which ECT was used as a brutal method to control and manage the main character. As a result of these misunderstandings and distorted perceptions, ECT is often not used when it might be helpful.

USES

It has been estimated that each year 60,000 to 100,000 people in the United States receive electroconvulsive therapy. This form of treatment has been used to treat a variety of mental disorders, including severe major depression, schizophrenia, and mania. Several surveys have indicated that more than three-fourths of individuals who receive ECT have been diagnosed as suffering from severe major depression. The second-largest group of individuals receiving ECT consists of those who have been diagnosed as schizophrenic. While there is substantial evidence that ECT is effective in the treatment of severe major depression, the evidence supporting the use of ECT to treat other disorders is not as strong.

Generally speaking, ECT is not seen as a treatment of choice. It will most likely not be the first treatment given to someone suffering from a severe mental disorder. Instead, it is typically viewed as the treatment of last resort and is used

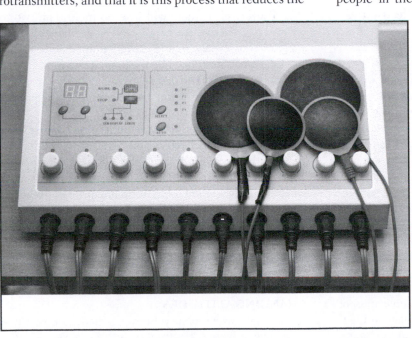

Photo: iStock

primarily to treat individuals who do not respond to any other treatments. For example, a typical course of treatment for an individual suffering from debilitating severe major depression would be talking therapy and one of the many antidepressant medications. For most people, it takes two to four weeks to respond to such medications. If the patient does not respond to the medication, another antidepressant medication may be tried. If, after several trials of medication, the patient still does not respond and continues to be severely depressed, ECT might be considered a viable option.

There are a few individuals for whom ECT might be considered the treatment of choice. These individuals include those who are in life-threatening situations, such as those who show symptoms of severe anorexia or strong suicidal tendencies, or those for whom medications would be damaging. ECT might be used to treat pregnant women, for example, since it presents fewer risks for a fetus than medication does, or individuals with heart disease, for whom medications can cause severe complications.

Because of the stigma attached to ECT as a result of its historical misuse and its characterization in the popular media, many physicians believe that ECT is not used as widely as it could and should be. Often, ECT is suggested as the treatment of choice, but because of its stigma, other approaches are tried first. The effect of this decision is to deprive the patient of an effective treatment and delay or prevent remission.

TECHNIQUES AND EFFECTS
When ECT is indicated for the treatment of a mental disorder, it usually involves five to ten applications of ECT administered at a rate of two or three per week. The number of ECT treatments given, however, will vary depending on the individual's medical history and the severity of the presenting symptoms. ECT is always administered by a physician; it cannot be ordered by a psychologist. When ECT is applied, many medical safeguards are used to prevent or minimize adverse effects. They include the use of a muscle relaxant, anesthesia, and oxygen. These medical procedures have made the use of ECT much safer than it was during the days when the patient would thrash about the table, breaking bones.

Additional refinements in the use of ECT have made it even safer. One such refinement is the application of unilateral, rather than bilateral, ECT. In unilateral ECT, the electric shock is sent through only one of the brain's two hemispheres. Usually, the shock is sent through the right hemisphere, which controls abstract thinking and creativity, rather than the left hemisphere, which controls language and rational thinking. While usually as effective as bilateral ECT, in which the shock goes through the entire brain, unilateral ECT has been shown to cause fewer adverse side effects.

Despite the refinements in ECT and the caution exercised in its use, there are several documented potential adverse side effects. Although most research indicates that these effects are temporary, some researchers suggest that ECT can cause permanent brain damage. The major adverse effects of ECT relate to how well the patient's brain functions after the treatment. The most common effect is extreme confusion and disorientation in the patient on awakening after an ECT treatment. Generally, this confusion will last for only a few minutes to a few hours.

Another serious concern about ECT's effects on the cognitive functioning of the patient has to do with the patient's memory. ECT can cause retrograde amnesia, the inability to remember things from the past, and anterograde amnesia, the inability to memorize new material. Both forms of amnesia are most noticeable in the first days and weeks after the ECT treatments have stopped. With the passage of time, the patient will slowly remember more from the past and will regain or strengthen the ability to remember new material. In most patients, this recovery of memory will take no more than two to six months. The patient may, however, permanently lose memories of events that occurred immediately before the ECT treatments or while the patient was hospitalized for the treatments. The degree of memory loss appears to be related to the number of ECT treatments the patient received.

Research investigating permanent brain damage from the use of ECT has been mixed. Some research has indicated that any application of ECT will cause brain damage and that more brain damage will occur as more treatments are applied. Long-term impairment in the patient's memory is one effect that has thus been identified as permanent. Other researchers, however, have reported that ECT does not cause permanent brain damage. In the meantime, ECT is used cautiously, and research continues into its potential adverse effects.

CHANGING ATTITUDES
Before the advent of psychotropic medications, there were few effective treatments for the severely mentally ill. Numerous treatment methods were attempted

to help relieve the symptoms of mental illness. Among these methods were bloodletting, the use of leeches, and immersion in water. Perhaps the most common approach was the permanent institutionalization of severely mentally ill individuals. This was done not only to control patients but also to protect others, since patients were viewed as a threat to others and themselves.

As a result of the ineffectiveness of these treatments and the growing concern about the institutionalization of the mentally ill, a number of new treatment approaches were developed and applied. Among these new approaches was electroconvulsive therapy. Electroconvulsive shock therapy was first used on schizophrenic patients, and the treatment met with some success. It was also tried on depressed and manic patients, with even greater success. As a result of these successes and the lack of other effective treatment approaches, ECT quickly came to be a commonly used treatment for individuals who suffered from a variety of mental disorders.

Many factors caused ECT to fall out of favor during the late 1950's. First, the earlier applications of ECT held significant dangers for the patient. The risk of death was approximately one in one thousand, and the risk of physical damage, such as broken bones, was even greater—in fact, such damage was noted in up to 40 percent of the patients. Concerns about complications continue today, and their focus is the impact of ECT on cognitive functioning.

Another factor that led to the decline in the use of ECT was the development and introduction of psychotropic shock therapy versus medications. These medications revolutionized the treatment of the mentally ill and led to thousands of patients being deinstitutionalized. In terms of both effectiveness and safety, it soon became evident that the use of these medications was substantially preferable to the use of ECT.

A third major influence on the decline of ECT's use was the growing civil rights movement for the mentally ill. Many community and religious leaders began to advocate the fair and humane treatment of the seriously mentally ill. These individuals saw ECT as an undesirable treatment method, used as an instrument for controlling and punishing individuals who could not defend themselves. This view of ECT as inhumane soon came to be widely held. ECT was perceived as a method to control, rather than help, patients—as a punishment rather than a therapy.

These and other factors led to the substantially decreased use of ECT. Subsequently, however, well-designed research has begun to define ECT as a relatively safe treatment method that may be the best therapy in certain situations. Additionally, refinements in the application of ECT have increased its effectiveness and reduced its complications. As a result of not only the ambiguity about its potential adverse effects but also the emotional issues related to its use, the controversy about ECT and its relative risks and benefits is likely to continue for many years.

BIBLIOGRAPHY

American Psychiatric Association. *Electroconvulsive Therapy: Report of the Task Force on Electroconvulsive Therapy of the American Psychiatric Association.* Washington, D.C.: Author, 1978. This report provides the results of a major task force charged with examining the clinical use of ECT. It thoroughly reviews the issues in a very readable format. Extensive recommendations for the use of ECT are provided.

Baldwin, Steve, and Melissa Oxlad. *Electroshock and Minors: A Fifty-Year Review.* Westport, Conn.: Greenwood Press, 2000. Reviews the history and development of guidelines and resolutions for the use of ECT on children from three years old through adolescence and cites case histories by decade from the 1940's to the 1990's.

Breggin, Peter R. *Electroshock: Its Brain-Disabling Effects.* New York: Springer, 1979. This book describes many adverse effects of ECT, but severe mental dysfunction in particular. Citing research from both animal and human research, this author makes a strong argument against the use of ECT, stating that it is no more effective than a placebo and considerably more dangerous.

Fink, Max. *Electroconvulsive Therapy: A Guide for Professionals and Their Patients.* New York: Oxford University Press, 2009. Written by a doctor who has had fifty years of clinical experience with electroconvulsive therapy. He claims that new therapies have made it a much safer treatment, and he discusses the ethical issues involved in its treatment.

Friedberg, John. *Shock Treatment Is Not Good for Your Brain.* San Francisco: Glide, 1976. Provides a strong condemnation of ECT. The author believes that mental illness is a myth and that the use of ECT is unnecessary as well as inhumane. This book, which is written in a personal, nontechnical manner, includes interviews with seven individuals who have received ECT and are opposed to its further use.

Shorter, Edward, and David Healy. *Shock Therapy: The History of Electroconvulsive Treatment in Mental Illness.* New Brunswick, N.J.: Rutgers University Press, 2007. The authors aim to shatter the myths attached to shock therapy and contend that it is a frontline lifesaving treatment for many who suffer from debilitating mental illness. In the process, they present a comprehensive history of shock therapy and the controversies it has generated in the medical community.

Mark E. Johnson

SEE ALSO: Abnormality: Biomedical models; Antidepressant medications; Depression; Drug therapies; Lobotomy; Mental illness: Historical concepts; Neuropsychology; Psychopharmacology; Psychosurgery; Schizophrenia: Theoretical explanations; Synaptic transmission.

Short-term memory

TYPE OF PSYCHOLOGY: Memory

Short-term (or working) memory refers to the mental process of temporarily retaining and manipulating information for the production of a wide range of cognitive tasks, including comprehension, problem solving, and learning.

KEY CONCEPT
- Anterograde amnesia
- Elaborative rehearsal
- Maintenance rehearsal
- Phonological loop
- Trace life
- Visuo-spatial sketchpad

INTRODUCTION

A woman needs to make a telephone call and a friend has just told her the number to call; she does not have pencil and paper to write down the number. Two options are immediately available to help her remember the number. She could repeat the number over and over until she makes the call (a technique known as maintenance rehearsal), or she could give the number some kind of meaning that would help her recall it (elaborative rehearsal). The mental process that allows a person to perform those operations is commonly called short-term, or working, memory.

William James, in 1890, used the term "primary memory" to describe the information under conscious awareness (immediate memory) and the term "secondary memory" to describe inactive information (indirect memory). This type of dualism evolved into the terms "short-term memory" and "long-term memory," a distinction that was based on the idea that each memory type was independent and was the result of different underlying mental processes.

In 1968, Richard Atkinson and Richard Shiffrin further developed this approach by proposing a stage model, or modal model, of memory that included the sensory register, the short-term store, and the long-term store. Subsequently, extensive research programs focused on the short-term store. These experimental findings resulted in the view, postulated by Alan Baddeley in 1986, that emphasizes the mental processes involved in the memory function rather than describing a static (inactive or passive) storage bin where information is saved. With this approach came the label "working memory" and the metaphor of a mental workbench performing a wide range of cognitive operations. As Henry Ellis and Reed Hunt explained in 1991, "Memory is determined by what is done to the information, not by where the information is stored." This is the view of an active, mental process characterized by specific functions and limitations.

CHARACTERISTICS

Three basic characteristics define short-term memory: trace life, storage capacity, and nature of the code. With respect to trace life (the amount of time information can be retained in working memory without further processing), Lloyd Peterson and Margaret Intons-Peterson demonstrated in 1959 that current, active information in the working memory bank is subject to rapid forgetting (in about twelve seconds) if the information does not receive further processing. They showed that if people are not allowed to rehearse or elaborate information they have just encountered, that information is lost. For example, they asked people to recall a series of letters, but immediately after they indicated the letters to be recalled, the people in the experiment were required to count backward by threes. The activity of counting backward interfered with remembering the letters. Similarly, if one is trying to recall a telephone number one has just heard but is interrupted on the way to the telephone to call it, the telephone number is usually lost.

In 1956, George Miller wrote a paper entitled "The Magic Number Seven, Plus or Minus Two" that made a strong and influential case regarding the storage capacity of short-term memory. His notion has been tested in a variety of settings, using a variety of information units. Whether people are asked to remember a list of letters, numbers, or words, or even a group of objects, most people remember about seven items. This finding has produced a wide range of applications. Telephone numbers, one may note, are composed of seven numbers.

Further study of the capacity of short-term memory revealed the ability to "chunk" information and, in so doing, remember more information than merely seven individual, independent bits of information. This process involves reorganizing single bits of information (with the assistance of information previously encoded in long-term storage) into larger units of information. For example, one could remember each individual letter of the word "chunk" and recall five letters, c-h-u-n-k (hence, five units). One might also form the letters into one unit and, instead, recall the word "chunk" (one unit). Chunking dramatically increases the amount of information that can be retained in short-term memory.

To account for the nature of the code (the form used to understand and store information), Baddeley designed a model of working memory that includes the phonological loop (a concept describing the coding of speech-based information in working memory) and the visuo-spatial sketchpad. A wide range of experimental evidence indicates that a phonetic (or acoustic or sound) code is used in short-term memory. For example, if a person is asked to retain a list of words or letters and the items sound alike, fewer items are recalled and more errors are found. On the other hand, if the items sound different, recall is better and fewer errors are found. Baddeley referred to this as the phonological similarity effect and explained that this effect occurs because the short-term memory store is based on a phonological code. Accordingly, items that sound similar will have similar codes.

In addition, related to the phonological code is the word-length effect. In essence, this refers to the finding that words with more syllables take more time to read and are less likely to be recalled from short-term memory than are monosyllabic words. On the other hand, if a word takes longer to read and to pronounce (either aloud or to oneself), the opportunity for a strong memory trace is greater.

The visuo-spatial sketchpad in Baddeley's model refers to the use of an imagery code in short-term memory.

For example, one might imagine one's kitchen and focus on the location of the sink. To do this, one most likely generates a mental image of the kitchen. Another example of the visuo-spatial sketchpad involves recognizing words or patterns when a person is reading. Still another example of this function is the process in which people engage when comparing two shapes. In a test in which people are asked to indicate whether geometric clusters are similar or different when they are presented in different orientations, experimental evidence indicates that most people engage in mental rotation to make their decisions about the figures. In other words, they imagine the particular geometric cluster turned in different directions and compare it to each of the other figures.

IMPORTANCE TO DAILY LIFE

The essential role of short-term memory is usually taken for granted until some event disrupts the memory process. In a hypothetical example of the consequences of not having a properly functioning short-term memory system, a man named Bill wakes up one morning without one. First, he gets out of bed (he can still walk, because he has the benefit of long-term memory) and trips over his cat. He finds himself on the floor but cannot remember how he got there. He walks to the bathroom to brush his teeth, but when he gets there he does not remember why he is there. He wanders into the kitchen to make coffee; he puts water into the coffeemaker and bends down to pet the cat. Then he rises and fills the coffeemaker with water again, because he does not remember the event that happened only a few seconds before.

The telephone rings, and Bill answers it. His friend Jane asks him to meet her in fifteen minutes; he agrees and hangs up. In the meantime, the water from the coffeemaker is spilling over the kitchen counter, and Bill has no idea why that is happening. The doorbell rings, and his next-door neighbor asks to borrow some milk. Being a good neighbor, Bill agrees to get some milk and goes into the kitchen. Once there, Bill realizes that he must turn off the coffeemaker. He steps in the spilled coffee, then goes into the bedroom to change his socks. Meanwhile, the neighbor whom Bill has forgotten leaves. Eventually Jane calls to ask why Bill did not meet her.

One's very existence and quality of life depend on the functioning of short-term memory. The preceding example may seem preposterous, yet there are a large number of cases of people who have impaired short-term memory. Several types of events can result in memory deficits and disorders, including head injuries, strokes, and disease-related dementia.

AMNESIA

The term "amnesia" refers to a class of disorders that involve various types of memory dysfunction. Some types of amnesia are associated with loss of long-term memory functioning. In these cases, a person may be able to learn new information but has difficulty recalling previous information. Other types of amnesia are associated with impaired short-term memory. These people have difficulty learning new information but can recall previously learned information. There are amnesiacs who have memory deficits relating to both short-term and long-term memory.

In general, when short-term memory is impaired, people are unable to process and retain new information effectively. The case of American neurosurgeon William Scoville's patient H. M., described in the 1950s, provides an interesting example of short-term memory impairment. H. M. suffered from a severe form of epilepsy that could not be controlled by medication. Scoville surgically removed portions of H. M.'s brain (the temporal lobes) in an attempt to remedy the epilepsy problem.

After the surgery, H. M. experienced striking short-term memory impairment, called anterograde amnesia. H. M.'s memory disorder was studied in depth, and many of the characteristics that define short-term memory functions were illuminated. H. M. was able to remember information from his past, but he was unable to remember new information. For example, H. M.'s mother reported that he could still mow the lawn, because he remembered how to do so, but he was unable to find the lawn mower when he left it parked somewhere.

H. M. was unable to remember or recognize anyone he met or any place he visited after the surgical procedure. He engaged in intense conversations with people but subsequently could recall neither the conversation nor the person with whom he had the conversation. Moreover, H. M. was taught procedures for accomplishing tasks, and his performance of a task revealed that he had learned the task; however, H. M. consistently claimed that he had never before performed the task. In other words, he did not remember the event of learning the task, but his performance revealed that he had retained some of the skills associated with the learning event.

Clearly, the short-term memory process, though often taken for granted, is an essential and integral part of mental functioning. This process also plays a major role in the study of psychology.

EARLY INTEREST IN MEMORY

With the first humans came the first speculations about mental processes. Inherent in studies of mental activities are studies of memory, since memory is necessary for learning. The role of memory was a central element of philosophies of the mind. This point is exhibited in historical accounts of the mind that referenced memory processes. These accounts reveal the underlying theories of mental processes postulated at the time of the philosophies.

For example, both Aristotle and Plato used the analogy of a wax tablet to describe the memory process. According to this perspective, experience was merely stamped into the brain. These views are consistent with the idea of memory being a static store or receptacle rather than a dynamic process. These static views assume a passive organism rather than an active, dynamic information processor.

This concept of memory continued through the ages, changing very little until the science of psychology arose in the late nineteenth century. As psychology evolved, so did the field of memory. This evolution is reflected in a change from the static, storage view of memory to the idea of memory as an active process. This change parallels the evolution of the image of humans as passive experience-storage units to seeing humans as active information processors; this evolution is often called the cognitive revolution. Whether the change is called evolution or revolution, it happened largely as a result of the foundation provided by innovative research such as that conducted by the German psychologist Hermann Ebbinghaus.

EBBINGHAUS'S CONTRIBUTIONS

In the early 1880s, Hermann Ebbinghaus moved the study of memory from the domain of philosophy to the domain of science when he embarked on an intensive investigation of the memory process. Ebbinghaus used himself as an experimental subject and spent two years memorizing nonsense syllables to see whether simple repetition would facilitate the recall process. Keeping copious notes in a strict scientific environment, he found that rote rehearsal improved the memory retrieval process.

Ebbinghaus's work was particularly important because it showed that mental processes could be simplified and studied using a rigorous, scientific method. In addition, he proved data that are fundamental for understanding memory processes, and that paved the way for the vast program of memory research that is flourishing today.

Studies associated with short-term or working memory focus on dynamic, immediate, cognitive activities. In general, these mental processes are involved in understanding the world; specifically, these investigations advance knowledge about learning, comprehension, problem solving, thought construction, and expression. Trends include mapping regions of the brain and discovering neurotransmitters (brain chemicals) that are affiliated with working memory activities. The working memory process provides a rich domain for investigations of mental activities. Many researchers believe that future investigations of the process will reveal the keys to discovering the essence of mental activity.

BIBLIOGRAPHY

Alloway, Tracy Packiam, and Ross Alloway. *Working Memory: The Connected Intelligence.* New York: Psychology, 2013. Print.

Baddeley, Alan D. *Working Memory.* New York: Oxford UP, 1987. Print.

Baddeley, Alan D., Michael W. Eysenck, and Michael C. Anderson. *Memory.* 2nd ed. Hove: Psychology, 2015. Print.

Deutsch, Diana, and J. Anthony Deutsch, eds. *Short-Term Memory.* New York: Academic, 1975. Print.

Ellis, Henry C., and R. Reed Hunt. *Fundamentals of Human Memory and Cognition.* 4th ed. Dubuque: Brown, 1989. Print.

Henry, Lucy. *The Development of Working Memory in Children.* Los Angeles: Sage, 2012. Print.

Johansen, Noah B. *New Research on Short-Term Memory.* New York: Nova Biomedical, 2008. Print.

Miyake, Akira, and Priti Shah, eds. *Models of Working Memory: Mechanisms of Active Maintenance and Executive Control.* New York: Cambridge UP, 1999. Print.

Neath, Ian. *Human Memory: An Introduction to Research, Data, and Theory.* 2nd ed. Belmont: Thomson, 2003. Print.

Solso, Robert L. *Cognitive Psychology.* 8th ed. Boston: Pearson, 2008. Print.

Wyer, Robert S., and Thomas K. Srull. *Memory and Cognition in Its Social Context.* Hillsdale: Erlbaum, 1989. Print.

Pennie S. Seibert

SEE ALSO: Alzheimer's disease; Cognitive maps; Ebbinghaus, Hermann; Encoding; Forgetting and forgetfulness; James, William; Kinesthetic memory; Long-term memory; Memory; Memory: Animal research; Memory: Empirical studies; Memory: Physiology; Memory: Sensory; Memory storage.

Shyness

TYPE OF PSYCHOLOGY: Personality; Psychopathology; Social psychology

Shyness is characterized by social interaction that is inhibited by anxiety and negative self-preoccupation and is often considered a form of social anxiety disorder. Its prevalence increased by 10 percent in the 1990s. Cognitive behavioral and pharmacological treatment strategies have proven to be effective.

KEY CONCEPTS

- Genetic environmental interaction
- Inhibition
- Isolation
- Loneliness
- Personality trait
- Physiological arousal
- Social functioning
- Social phobia

INTRODUCTION

Shyness is characterized by inhibited behavior and feelings of awkwardness and anxiety in social situations. It can include symptoms that are behavioral, physiological, cognitive, and emotional. It can adversely affect social or professional functioning. Among those who are predisposed toward the personality trait of shyness, it can become a part of their self-concept; it can also be induced by experiences of failure or rejection in social situations that lead to poor self-esteem

Research supports a genetic/environmental interaction explanation for shyness. The expression of shyness in children can be modified by parents and other environmental factors, although slight tendencies to act shyly in novel situations will remain. Cognitive behavioral strategies and pharmacological interventions that focus on decreasing social withdrawal and increasing social participation have proven effective.

POSSIBLE CAUSES

Jerome Kagan and colleagues' work supports shyness as being a function of both nature and nurture. Longitudinal studies that followed three- to four-year-olds into adulthood reported shyness to be one of the most persistently stable traits; studies that followed children into the eighth year reported that 75 percent of children maintained their earlier shy or sociable styles. In addition, parents and grandparents of inhibited compared with uninhibited children are more likely to report also being shy. The genetic predisposition involves easily aroused sympathetic nervous systems in fetuses and infants; later in life, social and performance situations stimulate these easily aroused nervous systems, resulting in social fear and anxiety and inhibited behavior.

In 25 percent of cases, those who are predisposed do not become shy, usually through environmental factors. Parents, for instance, may moderate the expression of shyness by helping predisposed children learn to not act shyly through balancing the levels of comfort versus

Photo: iStock

harshness that they extend to upset infants and by promoting social interaction. However, underlying tendencies to behave shyly in new circumstances among those who are so predisposed remain.

Shyness can be situationally induced and develop in adulthood among some who were not shy at younger ages as a result of social performance and achievement failures, feelings of unattractiveness, or other reasons that can lower self-esteem and create future evaluation apprehension and social fear.

DIAGNOSIS

Lynne Henderson and Philip Zimbardo report that the prevalence of shyness increased in the United States from about 40 percent to 50 percent during the 1990s. Shyness has been considered a variant of social phobia (the third most widespread mental health problem in the country), which has a prevalence of only 13 percent, suggesting that those who are shy are not seeking treatment. The manifestations for both shyness and social phobia are similar: discomfort concerning interpersonal interaction (including conversing with and meeting others), the establishment of intimacy, participation in small groups, situations of authority, and assertiveness.

In social situations, shy individuals report experiencing behavioral symptoms, such as inhibition, nervousness, and avoidance of feared situations and eye contact; physiological symptoms, such as an increase in heartbeat, muscle tension, perspiration, and feelings of faintness, dizziness, nausea, and stomach unsettledness; cognitive symptoms, such as negative thoughts and beliefs about the self, the situation, and others; and emotional symptoms, such as low self-esteem, excessive self-consciousness, sadness, dejection, loneliness, depression, and anxiety.

TREATMENT

Treatments for shyness are successful and similar to those for social phobia, according to Henderson and Zimbardo. They may include pharmacological treatments and cognitive behavioral therapy, which focuses on moving individuals from being socially withdrawn, anxious, and self-preoccupied with negative thoughts to being comfortable with social participation and interpersonal relationships. The strategies can include exposure to the feared situation simulated in treatment, in vivo, or using visualization in imaginal desensitization; flooding, or exposure to the feared situation in vivo or imaginally until anxiety is lowered (extinction); anxiety management; progressive muscle group relaxation and/ or controlled breathing; social treatment; communication, coping, and assertiveness skills training; and the replacement of negative thoughts and emotions with more positive ones. Paradoxical intention, where clients learn to control their fear responses, and writing up positive self-statements called affirmations have also been found to be effective. Individual, group, and home therapy are used.

IMPACT

Shyness appears to be a universal phenomenon, varying from a prevalence as low as 31 percent in Israel to a high of 57 percent in Japan. Shyness can result in a pattern of avoidance of people to the extent that self-imposed isolation and painful, heart-wrenching loneliness can result. Fewer opportunities for social-skills development due to technology and other social and economic factors, such as the replacement of interactional board and other games with solitary television and computer entertainment and social interaction with computer and telephone recording devices, may play a role in exacerbating the problem of shyness, according to Zimbardo and colleagues.

BIBLIOGRAPHY

Antony, Martin M., and Richard P. Swinson. *The Shyness and Social Anxiety Workbook: Proven, Step-by-Step Techniques for Overcoming Your Fear*. Oakland: New Harbinger, 2008. Print.

Butler, Gillian. *Overcoming Social Anxiety and Shyness: A Self-Help Guide Using Cognitive Behavioral Techniques*. New York: Basic, 2008. Print.

Gillet, Catherine. *The Shyness Solution*. Avon: Adams Media, 2013. Print.

Henderson, L., and Philip Zimbardo. "Shyness." *Encyclopedia of Mental Health*. Ed. Howard S. Friedman. San Diego: Academic, 1998. Print.

Jones, W. H., and B. N. Carpenter. "Shyness, Social Behavior, and Relationships." *Shyness: Perspectives on Research and Treatment*. Ed. W. H. Jones, J. M. Cheek, and S. R. Briggs. New York: Plenum, 1986. Print.

Kagan, J. "Temperament and the Reactions to Unfamiliarity." *Child Development* 68 (1997): 139–43. Print.

Kagan, J., D. Arcus, and N. Snidman. "The Idea of Temperament: Where Do We Go from Here?" *Nature, Nurture, and Psychology*. Ed. R. Plomin and G. E. McClearn. Washington: APA, 1994. Print.

Rubin, Kenneth H., and Robert J. Coplan. *The Development of Shyness and Social Withdrawal*. New York: Guilford, 2010. Print.

Schmidt, Louis A., and Jay Schulkin, eds. *Extreme Fear, Shyness, and Social Phobia*. New York: Oxford UP, 2003. Print.

Weeks, Justin W. *The Wiley Blackwell Handbook of Social Anxiety Disorder*. Malden: Wiley Blackwell, 2014. Print.

Debra L. Murphy

SEE ALSO: Anxiety disorders; Environmental factors and mental health; Fear; Genetics and mental health; Implosion; Introverts and extroverts; Phobias; Systematic desensitization; Zimbardo, Philip.

Sibling relationships

TYPE OF PSYCHOLOGY: Developmental psychology

Sibling relationships have been the object of increasingly detailed theoretical analysis and scientific investigation since the 1970s. Such relationships show both change and stability over the life span. They are characterized by both rivalries and helpfulness, with helpfulness predominating.

KEY CONCEPTS
- Attachment theory
- Bidirectional influences
- Blended family
- Family systems theory
- Secure attachment
- Social cognition

INTRODUCTION

Sibling relationships grow out of interactions among children within a family. Such interactions occur on many levels and involve behaviors as well as the emotions and cognitions that accompany them. Sibling relationships begin at the time the first child becomes aware that a brother or sister has been added to the family and often continue into old age, ceasing only on the death of a sibling. Because they often last from early childhood to old age, sibling relationships are frequently the longest-lasting relationships in an individual's life. Siblings' relationships differ from those among friends in that they are not voluntary, cannot be terminated at will, and—during childhood—are daily and intimate in nature.

Prior to the 1970s, research concerning children's development within families tended to stress parental influences on children's behavior. By the 1970s, however, developmental psychologists had discovered that they needed more elaborate theoretical explanations to account for the variety of child behavior seen in their studies. In 1968, Richard Bell reviewed the existing literature and concluded that parents influence children and children also influence parents. This has been called a pattern of bidirectional influences.

As developmental researchers came to accept the bidirectional influences view, other theorists soon broadened perspectives on family dynamics. Family systems theory was articulated by writers such as psychiatrist and family therapist Salvador Minuchin in his 1974 book *Families and Family Therapy*. In this view, the behaviors and roles of all members of a family are interdependent, each influencing the others. Relationships frequently became researchers' fundamental units of analysis, with all relationships seen as having the potential to influence one another and the entire family system. An ongoing rivalry between two brothers, for example, has the potential to erode the quality of their parents' relationship. In the 1980s and 1990s, systems-oriented researchers incorporated into their understanding of sibling relationships additional variables, including social class, culture, genetic factors, child temperament, and individuals' levels of social cognition(the ability to think and reason about interactions among people). Researchers also began to consider the relevance of ideas proposed by British psychiatrist John Bowlby in his three-volume work *Attachment and Loss* (1969–80). Bowlby's attachment theory, which suggested that humans are biologically predisposed to form early social relationships, reinforced the notion that relationships develop early and are important in the subsequent development of the individual. At an early age, infants can become emotionally attached to familiar persons, including siblings.

The history of scientific attempts to understand sibling relationships, then, has been characterized by increasing appreciation for the complexity of such relationships and the diversity of contexts in which siblings learn to relate to one another. This complexity has created numerous methodological challenges for researchers.

METHODOLOGICAL ISSUES

Disparities among families with regard to number of children and spacing between children complicate investigators' attempts to discover general principles that describe all sibling relationships. In addition, children's gender is a variable that could influence relationships between siblings, and gender mix, too, varies across families. Birth order—being an oldest or youngest child in the family, for example—also may influence children's interactions with brothers and sisters.

With so many variables operating and so much diversity possible across families, researchers have tended either to do relatively straightforward descriptive studies or to restrict their investigations to a subset of all possible family types. Early research attempted to assess the impact of global factors such as birth order, family size, or gender on variables such as personality or intelligence. As family systems theory began to influence research, however, investigators began studying relationships among siblings and the various forces to which these relationships respond. Studies carried out in the systems theory framework have generally limited their scope to a particular family type, such as two-child families with children under the age of five.

Even with such necessary limitations, however, investigators still have to consider several other methodological issues. They must decide whether they will get information through interviews, questionnaires, or direct observation of sibling interactions. If using an interview or questionnaire, they must decide whether to question parents, children, or both. If observations are to be done, should they be done in a laboratory or in participants' homes? Another consideration is the type of siblings who will be studied. It has been common practice to study full siblings who share the same mother and father. However, half siblings, stepsiblings, and adoptive siblings may also be of interest, and researchers must decide whether to include them in their studies as well.

Psychologist and researcher Victor Cicirelli, in his 1995 book *Sibling Relationships Across the Life Span*, argued that sibling relationships must be studied longitudinally. Because sibling relationships can last a lifetime, it is valuable to know how they both change and remain the same over the entire life span. Only by studying such relationships over the long term can researchers develop an integrated, coherent body of knowledge about siblings' lifelong relationships.

CHILDHOOD

As infants and children grow, they change. The same can be said of childhood sibling relationships, for both members of any particular sibling pair are changing as individuals as their relationship grows. Research on the development of sibling interactions during childhood has been limited, but based on available information, some general observations can be reported.

Infants often do become emotionally attached to a sibling, just as they do to their mothers, fathers, and other caregivers. When the sibling relationship is positive and supportive, a secure attachment is likely to develop. Secure attachments during infancy predict healthy patterns of exploration as children get older, as well as successful adjustment to school and social situations.

Older children, being cognitively and physically more advanced than their younger brothers or sisters, tend to be leaders in sibling interactions. Younger siblings often imitate older brothers or sisters. Older children frequently act as linguistic interpreters as younger siblings learn to talk. As both siblings grow, the younger child becomes increasingly capable of actively participating in mutual activities; simultaneously, the older child may show increasing interest in the relationship.

An older sibling attends school and begins relating to peers earlier than a younger brother or sister, who may seek the advice of the older child when starting school. From the preschool period to school age, sibling pairs tend to remain fairly stable with regard to the proportions of positive and negative behaviors they exhibit. As children get older, they typically experience less adult supervision, which may pose a risk for sibling pairs with a predominantly negative relationship.

An observational study of the development of early sibling relationships published in 1982 illustrates the influence of family systems thinking on research. Judy Dunn and Carol Kendrick observed the development of sibling relationships for the first fourteen months after families had a second child. Older siblings were one and a half to three and a half years old when the new baby arrived. Dunn and Kendrick visited families in their homes several times and found that a majority of firstborns became more demanding and more likely to engage in naughty behavior in the weeks immediately following the younger child's birth. Crying, clinging, and jealousy increased. Despite the negative reactions, however, most older siblings also reacted positively to the new child, cuddling the baby, helping take care of it, and showing concern when it cried. They also showed gains in taking care of their own needs independently. Siblings were especially likely to develop a close relationship with one another if, when speaking to the older child, mothers referred to the baby as an individual with interests, needs, and preferences. This finding is in keeping with family systems theorists' belief that relationships within a family are interdependent.

ADOLESCENCE

The course of sibling relationship development during adolescence is less well understood than is the case for younger children. There is some evidence that the intensity of sibling relationships—for both positive and negative elements—may peak during early adolescence. Thereafter, power tends to become increasingly equivalent, and there is less tendency and less need for the older sibling to nurture the younger one. Conflict tends to be greater for siblings who are closer in age. Generally, same-sex siblings remain closer during this stage of life than do brother-sister pairs. Middle-aged siblings report recalling a drop in sharing and understanding during adolescence, followed by a resurgence of those characteristics during adulthood.

ADULTHOOD

Little research on adult sibling relationships was done before the 1980s. That done thereafter tended to be largely descriptive or normative in nature. Cicirelli contends that this has occurred in part because researchers studying adulthood have worked in isolation from those studying childhood and adolescence.

Existing investigations suggest that affection characterizes most adult sibling relationships and that feelings of closeness may increase as siblings age. This may be particularly true for sisters. Relationships among adult siblings tend to be similar to friendships and often involve family celebrations or recreational activities. Elderly siblings often discuss family issues and reminisce.

Negative feelings between adult siblings are also reported, but overt hostility is rare. Affectionate feelings among siblings appear to be somewhat lessened in adults who spent part of their childhoods in a blended family (that is, a new family created by the remarriage of a parent). The few adult siblings—probably less than 11 percent—who have relatively little contact with one another have not been systematically studied.

RIVALRY AND HELPFULNESS

Both rivalry and helpfulness characterize sibling relationships across the entire life span. Joan Newman reviewed the literature on these features of siblings' interactions in 1994 and suggested that conflict between siblings may be inevitable, owing to maturational discrepancies in social cognition between children of differing ages who are involved in an intense, complex, daily relationship. In part, the complexity of such relationships derives from their having both egalitarian qualities and inherent inequities (such as when one sibling is old enough to drive and the other is not). Newman points out that cognitively immature youngsters could hardly be expected to negotiate such relationships without feelings of competition, jealousy, or frustration.

Questionnaire and interview studies of older children and adults reveal widespread memories of competition, arguing, and verbal aggression in childhood sibling relationships. Memories of physical aggression are rare. Observational studies suggest that, although children show negativity in interactions with siblings more often than with peers or parents, negativity is not the predominant mode of relating.

Observational studies by Gene Brody and colleagues in 1982 and 1984 showed that eight- to ten-year-olds who were playing with a younger sibling tended to adopt cooperative but unequal roles (such as teacher and pupil). As children got older, there was some tendency for girls to play with a younger sibling more so than boys, perhaps because girls engage in more nurturant play activities and boys engage in more competitive physical activities.

Different studies have reported different proportions of positivity and negativity in sibling relationships. In part, the inconsistencies may be due to the methods used. Newman points out that parents' reports may overemphasize rivalries while direct observations of children reveal relatively placid interactions. Children often report a mixture of feelings and attitudes. Further, because sibling relationships themselves often embody considerable variability, researchers can expect fluctuations in their findings.

BIBLIOGRAPHY

Bank, Stephen, and Michael Kahn. *The Sibling Bond.* New York: Basic Books, 2008. Print.

Brody, Gene H. "Sibling Relationship Quality: Its Causes and Consequences." *Annual Review of Psychology* 49 (1998): 1–24. Print.

Brody, Gene H., ed. *Sibling Relationships: Their Causes and Consequences.* Norwood: Ablex, 1996. Print.

Cicirelli, Victor G. *Sibling Relationships Across the Life Span.* New York: Plenum, 1995. Print.

Diderich, Monique. *Sibling Relationships in Step-Families: A Sociological Study.* Lewiston: Edwin Mellen, 2008. Print.

Dunn, Judy. *From One Child to Two.* New York: Fawcett Columbine, 1995. Print.

Dunn, Judy, and Carol Kendrick. *Siblings: Love, Envy, and Understanding.* Cambridge: Harvard UP, 1982. Print.

Feinberg, Mark E., Anna R. Solmeyer, and Susan M. McHale. "The Third Rail of Family Systems: Sibling Relationships, Mental and Behavioral Health, and Preventive Intervention in Childhood and Adolescence." *Clinical Child and Family Psychology Review* 15.1 (2012): 43–57. Print.

Kluger, Jeffrey. *The Sibling Effect: What the Bonds Among Brothers and Sisters Reveal About Us.* New York: Riverhead, 2011. Print.

Milevsky, Avidan. *Sibling Relationships in Childhood and Adolescence: Predictors and Outcomes.* New York: Columbia UP, 2011. Print.

Newman, Joan. "Conflict and Friendship in Sibling Relationships: A Review." *Child Study Journal* 24.2 (1994): 119–52. Print.

Faye B. Steuer

SEE ALSO: Affiliation and friendship; Attachment and bonding in infancy and childhood; Birth order and personality; Family life: Children's issues; Family systems theory; Stepfamilies.

Signal detection theory

TYPE OF PSYCHOLOGY: Sensation and perception

Signal detection theory is a mathematical model for understanding how sounds or other stimuli are detected in the presence of background noise. It replaces classical threshold theory in psychophysics and provides a method for separating a person's sensitivity to a stimulus from any bias or response criterion..

KEY CONCEPTS
- Bias
- Catch trial
- Correct rejection
- False alarm

- Hit
- Miss
- Noise
- Psychophysics
- Sensitivity
- Threshold

INTRODUCTION

Signal detection theory is not so much a "theory" in the traditional sense as it is a term used to describe certain types of measurement procedures. Developed by mathematicians and engineers at the University of Michigan, Harvard University, and the Massachusetts Institute of Technology in the 1950s, signal detection theory is based on a method of statistical hypothesis testing and on findings in electronic communication. It provides a method to measure two factors independently: a person's sensitivity to sound or other stimulation, and any bias (a consistent tendency to respond positively or negatively in a situation) or decision criterion the person might adopt that affects his or her performance during a sensitivity test.

A typical measurement procedure might involve detection of sound in a quiet room. In an acoustically insulated chamber, an individual puts on earphones and is told to pay attention to a small warning light that comes on periodically. The individual is instructed to report, for each occurrence of the warning light, whether a sound is heard through the earphones at that time. The sounds coming through the earphones vary in intensity, though not in frequency; they may initially be of very low amplitude, or they may be readily audible. Indeed, the warning light may come on with no sound at all; this is a "catch" trial—a situation designed to catch someone who simply pretends to hear a sound every time the light comes on. No matter what the sound, the individual being tested must respond with "Yes, I heard a sound" or "No, I heard nothing."

Much of the time the response is "yes" when a sound is present; this is called a hit, because it is a correct recognition of the stimulus. Often, when no sound is presented, the individual says "no," giving a correct rejection. Sometimes, however, the response is "yes" when no sound is present, which is a false alarm, and sometimes the individual says "no" when the sound is in fact present, which is a miss. Thus the experimenter collects data showing the number of hits, false alarms, misses, and correct rejections for each individual participant.

Individuals are told exactly what proportion of the trials will be catch trials (in a study measuring sensitivity to certain stimuli, a trial in which no stimulus is presented). This gives them some idea of what to expect. If the experiment were set up with 90 percent catch trials and participants in the study were given no knowledge of this, they might think, hearing so little, that something was wrong with the earphones. These same people would expect a session with 20 percent catch trials, for example, to sound very different. When there is a lower proportion of catch trials, individuals tend to respond "yes" more than when the proportion is higher; thus, they maximize hits and (since there are few catch trials) cannot make many false alarms. If there is a high proportion of catch trials, individuals tend to say "no" more, thus making fewer false alarms, but also making fewer hits. Thus, both hits and false alarms vary depending on the number of catch trials, even though the sound intensities are exactly the same in each of these conditions.

ROLE OF EDUCATED GUESSING

If one took part in a trial without putting on the earphones, one could only guess whether a sound is present. In guessing, however, one might guess "yes" more frequently if told there would be few, rather than many, catch trials. This educated guessing is what a normal participant does. When unsure as to the presence of a sound, people guess; the probability of guessing "yes" is given by the proportion of catch trials. The psychologist collecting these data determines the number of hits and false alarms for each individual and compares them with a "guessing line": the percentage of hits and false alarms for a participant who merely guesses. The degree of difference between these two modes of response is a pure measure of sensitivity; bias has been eliminated with the guessing baseline. Sensitivity is high when the individual hears most of the sounds presented and has to guess on few of them, and it is low when many of the responses are guesses.

DETERMINING BIAS AND EFFECT OF PERSONALITY

The experimenter also determines each person's bias, or decision criterion, in responding. The decision criterion, which changes whenever the number of catch trials changes, may also be influenced by other factors. For example, there is always some noise going on when a stimulus is received. Even in an acoustically quiet chamber, there are sounds from one's own heart, blood rushing through vessels, and breathing. These vary from moment to moment, and they influence perception of other sounds, particularly those that may seem very weak. Outside a quiet chamber, there are other noisy background sounds: hums of air conditioners, computers, street traffic, and so on.

In addition, people who participate in these measurement studies bring different decision criteria that are characteristic of their own personalities. For example, a participant may not respond with a "yes" unless absolutely certain that a sound is present, saying "no" otherwise and thus failing to make all the hits—but also making few false alarms. Another might respond with a "yes" whenever it seems as though a sound could conceivably be present and say "no" only when absolutely certain there is no sound. These two people might have the same sensitivity—that is, they could perceive the sounds equally well—but the number of sounds presented that they identify correctly would be different. They would therefore achieve equal measures of sensitivity but very different measures of bias. Signal detection theory, then, provides an ingenious method for the measurement of an individual's sensitivity to sounds or other stimuli independent of factors that impinge on that individual's decision.

PERCEPTUAL VIGILANCE
Signal detection methods are applied in studies in which a stimulus or event is to be detected. Used to separate sensation from motivational bias, these methods are most successful with simple stimuli.

One of the earliest and simplest of these studies involves perceptual vigilance. The basic task is to detect a few signals against a background pattern of noise similar to the signal. The best known of these displays is the Mackworth clock, which presents clockwise jumps of a black pointer across a white field. The signal jumps are twice as large as the repetitive background jumps, and they occur at irregular time intervals ranging, for example, from forty-five seconds to ten minutes. The noise occurs at a high rate and is constant, regular, and monotonous.

An observer sits in a small cubicle for half-hour periods, watching this moving pointer and responding only when the pointer makes a long jump. At the beginning, attention is high and the observer makes few errors. As time goes on, however, the observer tires, loses concentration, and begins missing signals. The jumps all begin to look alike; after an hour or so, one in every four or five long jumps may be missed. There are few, if any, false alarms.

This vigilance decrement occurs with listening tasks as well. In fact, it is a common observance in nearly all tests of attention and is applicable to many everyday situations: factory workers monitoring displays on shift, inspectors in industry examining merchandise for flaws, even students sitting in classrooms listening for important points in lectures. Although psychologists were aware of these declines before the theory of signal detection was formulated, their study changed with the method. They began to address new questions. What difference does the nature of the noise make? How might the observer shift the bias, or criterion of response, over time or different situations?

It is perhaps not surprising to find that sensitivity is higher when the signal is most different from the background noise. More interesting is the finding that if there are very few signals, there often is no measurable decline in sensitivity, even if the observers miss more signals over time. This occurs because they also make fewer false alarms over the same time; that is, they become more cautious in their responses—a shift in bias. One sees shifts of bias of this sort in many situations. For example, a physician may diagnose a disease on the basis of insufficient data in cases where failure to detect it would be disastrous and making a false alarm would be relatively insignificant. On the other hand, military personnel would not want to begin sending out retaliatory nuclear weapons against an enemy unless they are absolutely certain that the attack to which they are responding is actually occurring. A false alarm here would be unthinkable, so they exhibit extreme caution—a very high bias against a response.

USE IN HUMAN RESEARCH AND PSYCHOLOGY
Signal detection theory has been helpful in applied human research, perceptual studies, and studies of memory. Measures of sensitivity in memory parallel those in perception. Effects of variables such as aging, brain dysfunctions such as epilepsy, brain insults such as concussions, or periods of oxygen deprivation have been examined more recently for their effects on sensitivity. In a 1977 signal detection study of head-injured patients, Diane McCarthy found that patients recovering from concussions show, during the acute stages of head injury, sensitivity scores similar to an elderly population and considerably lower than normal control subjects. They also show some residual deficit six weeks later, even when the head injury is not severe. Interestingly,

this shows a period of reduced sensitivity to stimulation, not merely confusion.

Signal detection theory has provided a routine method in experimental psychology. It is applied in situations where a pure measure of sensitivity, unaffected by changing criteria, is desired. Additionally, it may be used when the target of interest is the criterion or bias itself—for example, in studies of personality factors in response decisions.

STUDY OF THRESHOLD

In the late nineteenth century, experimenters in psychophysics—the study of the relationship between the physical properties of stimuli and the ways in which they are perceived—questioned how accurately people's perceptions correspond to the physical stimulation they receive. They asked to what extent a person's reported perception actually reflects the physical changes happening in the real world.

One way of answering this was to try to discover how strong a stimulus needs to be before it is noticed or detected. There are sounds, for example, so soft that they cannot be heard, or can be heard only by a few individuals, and there are sounds so intense that all hearing individuals detect them. At what point in increasingly intense levels is a sound just barely detectable? Psychophysicists called this level the threshold, or limen. They assumed that this level of intensity was like the threshold of a door, in that one is either inside or outside, never in between. They assumed that all sounds less intense than the threshold—all stimulation that is subliminal, or below the limen—would never be detected and that all sounds more intense than the threshold would always be detected.

With this theory in hand, experimental psychologists began measuring thresholds. For example, they determined empirically how much sugar must go into a certain amount of distilled water at a given temperature before it can be tasted, how intensely a 440-hertz sound has to be played under certain acoustical conditions before it is heard, and how intense a spot of white light has to be in a darkened room for a dark-adapted subject to detect it in peripheral vision. However, while making measurements, they ran into difficulties.

Measured thresholds were always imprecise, as the only measurement taken was the occurrence of hits. They were unlike the threshold of a door, a line with no breadth. Sometimes an individual would report hearing a sound that was very weak, then report not hearing a sound that was quite a bit more intense. Most of the time, however, intense sounds were heard and weak ones were not, so that researchers calculated an average—an intensity of sound that a subject reported hearing 50 percent of the time. This they defined empirically as the threshold, assuming that their inability to measure a point perfectly was attributable simply to procedural error or imprecise measurement.

Increasingly, however, researchers began to recognize that threshold measures were contaminated, or confounded, by other factors, such as how important it seemed to a person not to let a sound go unnoticed or not to appear foolish by saying a sound was heard when there was no sound at all. Signal detection theory provided an alternative, a method for determining a person's sensitivity to a stimulus independent of any bias in response. These methods are now a standard part of experimental psychology, providing another way to determine how perceptions correspond to physical changes in the real world.

BIBLIOGRAPHY

Commons, Michael L., John A. Nevin, and Michael C. Davison, eds. *Signal Detection: Mechanisms, Models, and Applications*. Hillsdale: Erlbaum, 1991. Print.

Gescheider, George A. *Psychophysics: The Fundamentals*. 3rd ed. Hillsdale: Erlbaum, 1997. Print.

Gold, Joshua I., and Hauke R. Heekeren. "Neural Mechanisms for Perceptual Decision Making." *Neuroeconomics: Decision Making and the Brain*. Ed. Paul W. Glimcher and Ernst Fehr. 2nd ed. Waltham: Academic, 2014. 355–72. Print.

Levine, Michael W. *Fundamentals of Sensation and Perception*. 3rd ed. New York: Oxford UP, 2000. Print.

Ludel, Jacqueline. *Introduction to Sensory Processes*. San Francisco: Freeman, 1978. Print.

McNicol, Don. *A Primer of Signal Detection Theory*. Mahwah: Erlbaum, 2005. Print.

Pierce, W. David, and Carl D. Cheney. *Behavior Analysis and Learning*. 5th ed. New York: Psychology, 2013. Print.

Sunderland, Matthew, Tim Slade, and Gavin Andrews. "Developing a Short-Form Structured Diagnostic Interview for Common Mental Disorders Using Signal Detection Theory." *International Journal of Methods in Psychiatric Research* 21.4 (2012): 247–57. Print.

Szalma, James L., and Peter A. Hancock. "A Signal Improvement to Signal Detection Analysis: Fuzzy SDT on the ROCs." *Journal of Experimental Psychology* 39.6

(2013): 1741–62. Print.

Wickens, Thomas D. *Elementary Signal Detection Theory*. New York: Oxford UP, 2002. Print.

Bonnie S. Sherman

SEE ALSO: Attention; Decision making; Hearing; Pattern recognition; Sensation and perception.

Skinner, B. F.

BORN: March 20, 1904, in Susquehanna, Pennsylvania
DIED: August 18, 1990, in Cambridge, Massachusetts
IDENTITY: American behaviorist psychologist
TYPE OF PSYCHOLOGY: Learning

Skinner was the founder of radical behaviorism and one of the most influential psychologists of the twentieth century.

B. F. Skinner spent his boyhood in a middle-class family in a small town in Pennsylvania. He studied literature and received a B.A. from Hamilton College in New York. After an unsuccessful year as a writer, Skinner was inspired to enter graduate school in psychology by the works of Ivan Petrovich Pavlov and John B. Watson. At Harvard University, where he was influenced by William J. Crozier and Walter S. Hunter, Skinner proved to be a clever inventor, creating an apparatus used to study the behavior of white rats. He earned his Ph.D. in 1931 and remained at Harvard until his first faculty appointment, in 1936, at the University of Minnesota. In 1945, Skinner became professor and chair of the department of psychology at Indiana University. He returned to Harvard in 1948 for the duration of his career. He retired as professor emeritus in 1974, remaining professionally active until his death in 1990.

Skinner's science of behavior was controversial and often misunderstood. He maintained that the behavior of organisms, including people, is a function of three factors: genetic heritage, past experiences, and current circumstances. He advocated an understanding of behavior based on directly observable aspects of the environment, not because unobservable factors such as thinking and feeling did not exist but because they were not readily accessible for study and control. His techniques of behavior management through changing aspects of the environment, usually the consequences of behavior, have proven powerful and useful for many species and situations.

Between 1930 and 1990, Skinner published numerous articles and books. *The Behavior of Organisms* (1938) laid out the beginnings of his science of behavior. He wrote two books explaining his views to a broad audience: *About Behaviorism* (1974) and *Science and Human Behavior* (1953). His utopian novel, *Walden Two* (1948), described a fictional community guided by his principles of behavior. His most controversial book, *Beyond Freedom and Dignity* (1971), argued that a technology of behavior could help solve societal problems.

Skinner founded two areas of psychology: the experimental analysis of behavior, which investigates basic behavioral principles, and applied behavior analysis, which seeks solutions to specific problems. His work spawned dozens of scientific journals devoted to these issues. Skinner was widely recognized as the most influential psychologist in the twentieth century. He received numerous awards, including in 1990 the first-ever Citation for Outstanding Lifetime Contribution to Psychology from the American Psychological Association.

BIBLIOGRAPHY

Bjork, Daniel W. *B. F. Skinner: A Life*. Washington, D.C.: American Psychological Association, 2006. Comprehensive biography of Skinner's life and work by an eminent historian of psychology.

_____. "Burrhus Frederic Skinner: The Contingencies of a Life." *In Portraits of Pioneers in Psychology*. Vol. 3, edited by Gregory A. Kimble and Michael Wertheimer. Hillsdale, N.J.: Lawrence Erlbaum, 1998. Chapter-length summary of Skinner's life and work.

Demorest, Amy. *Psychology's Grand Theorists: How Personal Experiences Shaped Professional Ideas*. Mahwah, N.J.: Lawrence Erlbaum, 2005. Explores the lives and theories of Skinner, Sigmund Freud, and Carl R. Rogers.

O'Donohue, William, and Kyle E. Ferguson. *The Psychology of B. F. Skinner*. Thousand Oaks, Calif.: Sage Publications, 2001. An examination of behaviorism. Includes bibliographical references and an index.

Wiener, Daniel N. *B. F. Skinner: Benign Anarchist*. Needham Heights, Mass.: Allyn & Bacon, 1996. Biography of Skinner by a student and colleague. Contains a complete bibliography of his work.

Amy L. Odum

See Also: Behaviorism; Conditioning; Radical behaviorism:
B. F. Skinner; Skinner box.

Skinner box

Date: 1930s forward
Type of psychology: Learning; Psychological methodologies

The Skinner box (or operant chamber) is an apparatus invented by the psychologist B. F. Skinner in the 1930s. It is used in the experimental analysis of animal behavior, particularly in studies of Pavlovian (classical) and instrumental (operant) conditioning.

Key Concepts

- Controlled environment
- Cumulative recorder
- Free operant responding
- Laboratory apparatus
- Operant chamber
- Respondent-operant distinction
- Schedules of reinforcement
- Shaping

INTRODUCTION

The modern Skinner box consists of a chamber housed in a sound- and light-attenuating shell and connected to a computer through an interface. This arrangement ensures a uniform, controlled environment that minimizes extraneous and distracting stimuli during an experiment. For rats and mice, the chamber is usually equipped with one or more manipulanda (for example, a lever to be pressed or a chain to be pulled). Responses are detected electronically (through closure of a microswitch) and recorded by computer software. The rodent chamber typically has a device that dispenses food (for example, 20- or 45-milligram pellets) or a liquid (for example, water or sugar solutions) into a magazine tray located near the manipulanda, and is equipped with speakers (to present auditory stimuli) and lights. Presentations of these events are programmed using computer software. Operant chambers for rodents are manufactured with grid floors that can be set up for delivery of faradic stimulation (electric shock) for use in Pavlovian studies of fear conditioning and instrumental studies of punishment or escape and avoidance learning.

Operant chambers for pigeons generally have either a projector to display visual stimuli on a response key that is pecked by the pigeon or an LCD panel for displaying computer-generated images, and a hopper to present grain that can be accessed through an opening in the magazine tray. Head entries into the magazine tray to retrieve a reward can be detected automatically by interruption of a photobeam. Operant chambers may be modified for use with small primates.

The operant chamber is typically used for the study of changes in behavior as a result of its consequences.

HISTORY

The Skinner box was one of many inventions created by the radical behaviorist B. F. Skinner. While a graduate student in psychology at Harvard, Skinner began experiments to understand the variability of behavior and to investigate the conditions that affected the strength of behavior. He constructed an experimental chamber with a feeding device that registered a rat's contacts as it retrieved measured quantities of food. Later, Skinner equipped his box with a horizontal bar that, when pushed down by the rat, would cause a feeder to dispense a pellet into the magazine tray. In *The Behavior of Organisms* (1938), Skinner devotes three pages to a discussion of his use of the lever press response as an operant. The typical lever was a 1/8-inch brass rod, 6 centimeters (cm) long, mounted 8 to 10 cm above the floor and protruding 1 cm into the chamber. The rat had to exert about 10 grams of pressure to depress the lever and register a response on a cumulative recorder. Among the merits of the lever press response mentioned by Skinner were the ease and spontaneous frequency with which the response was made by rats. Another advantage he noted was that this operant required stimulus support and therefore could not occur in the absence of the actual lever.

Throughout the 1930s, Skinner used an operant chamber fitted with a lever for rats. Following his work on Project Pigeon in the early 1940s, Skinner constructed a modified operant chamber for pigeons and in subsequent work used pecking at a response key as the operant. The pigeon's superior vision and longer life contributed to his decision to switch organisms.

IMPACT ON RESEARCH

The Skinner box provided researchers in the 1930s with a laboratotry apparatus that had several highly desirable advantages over mazes and runways. Data collection was substantially less labor- and time-intensive. Larger numbers of animals could be studied, which increased the power of statistical analysis and the likelihood of detecting lawful properties of behavior by averaging across individuals. The cumulative recorder, another of Skinner's ingenious inventions, provided an immediate and continuous record of the rate of behavior (a measure of its strength) that could be mechanically averaged across subjects by the Summarizer, also developed by Skinner.

In addition to these practical benefits, there were significant theoretical impacts of the new apparatus. Arguably the most important was the distinction Skinner was prompted to make on the basis of his studies with the operant chamber between two kinds of responses, respondent (Pavlovian) and operant (instrumental). Whereas respondents were elicited by preceding stimuli, operants were controlled by their consequences (the reinforcement contingency).

Shaping by successive approximation was a technique developed by Skinner to train animals to perform complex actions. The operant chamber also allowed him to develop his theory of how schedules of reinforcement influenced behavior in lawful ways. It is no accident that slot machines use a variable ratio schedule of reinforcement.

Contemporary psychology reflects the impact of the modern operant chamber in many ways. Empirical challenges to classical temporal contiguity theory (for example, blocking and contingency) emerged from studies using changes in the rate of a free operant to assess learning. Postconditioning manipulations of a response-contingent outcome have illuminated the processes involved in instrumental learning. Behavior modification programs use the principles of operant conditioning.

Effects of Skinner's work with the operant chamber have extended beyond psychology to behavioral economics, behavioral pharmacology, and personalized instruction. Skinner did not raise his daughter Deborah in an operant chamber, contrary to urban legend, but he did build the baby tender, which was designed to provide a safe and comfortable environment for an infant. Skinner's *Walden Two* (1948) describes a fictional utopian community that raised its children using the principles of operant conditioning.

BIBLIOGRAPHY

Ferster, Charles B. "The Use of the Free Operant in the Analysis of Behavior." *Psychological Bulletin* 50.4 (1953): 263–74. Print.

Lattal, Kennon A. "JEAB at 50: Coevolution of Research and Technology." *Journal of the Experimental Analysis of Behavior* 89.1 (2008): 129–35. Print.

O'Donohue, William, and Kyle E. Ferguson. *The Psychology of B. F. Skinner*. Thousand Oaks: Sage, 2001. Print.

Rutherford, Alexandra. *Beyond the Box: B. F. Skinner's Technology of Behavior from Laboratory to Life, 1950s–1970s*. Toronto: U of Toronto P, 2009. Print.

Schachter, Daniel L., Daniel T. Gilbert, and Daniel M. Wegner. "B. F. Skinner: The Role of Reinforcement and Punishment." *Psychology*. 3rd ed. New York: Worth, 2014. 278–80. Print.

Vargas, Julie. "Biographical Information." *B. F. Skinner Foundation*. B. F. Skinner Foundation, n.d. Web. 25 June 2014.

Ruth M. Colwill

SEE ALSO: Aversion therapy; Behaviorism; Conditioning; Radical behaviorism: B. F. Skinner; Skinner, B. F.

Sleep

TYPE OF PSYCHOLOGY: Consciousness

The study of sleep stages and functions involves descriptions of the electrophysiological, cognitive, motor, and behavioral components of various sleep stages as well as the potential functions served by each. The sleep-wake cycle is one of several human circadian rhythms that regulate human attention, alertness, and performance.

KEY CONCEPTS
- Circadian rhythms
- Desynchronized electroencephalogram (EEG)
- Hypnagogic imagery
- Myoclonia
- Nonrapid eye movement (NREM) sleep
- Paradoxical sleep
- Rapid eye movement (REM) sleep
- Synchronized electroencephalogram (EEG)

INTRODUCTION

Sleep, one of the most mysterious of human circadian rhythms (human biological cycles that fluctuate on a daily basis), can be characterized as a naturally induced alteration in consciousness. Although the sleeper may appear to be unconscious, many complex cognitive, physiological, and behavioral processes occur during sleep. For example, parents may sleep through a nearby police siren yet easily awaken to their crying infant.

Efforts to understand sleep have focused on behavioral

and electrical changes that occur each night. During every moment of a person's life, the brain, the eyes, and the muscles are generating electrical potentials that can be recorded by a polygraph. Minute electrical signals are conveyed through tiny disk electrodes attached to the scalp and face, which are recorded by the polygraph as wave patterns that can be described in terms of frequency, amplitude, and synchronization. Frequency is measured by the number of cycles per second (cps), amplitude by the distance between the peaks and troughs of waves, and synchronization by the regular, repetitive nature of the waves.

MEASURING STAGES OF SLEEP

Use of the polygraph has resulted in the identification of four stages of nonrapid eye movement (NREM) sleep, as well as a special stage referred to as rapid eye movement (REM) sleep. Rapid eye movement sleep Each stage is described in terms of electrical changes in brain-wave patterns, speed and pattern of eye movements, and muscular activity in the body. Brain-wave activity is measured by the electroencephalogram (EEG), eye movement patterns by the electrooculogram (EOG), and muscle activity by the electromyogram (EMG).

Three EEG patterns can be described for NREM sleep. First, as a sleeper progresses from stages one through four, the waves increase in amplitude or voltage from approximately 50 to 100 microvolts in stage one to about 100 to 200 microvolts in stage four. Second, the frequency of the waves decreases gradually from 4 to 8 cps in stages one and two to 1 to 4 cps in stages three and four. Last, the waves become progressively more synchronized from stages one to four, so that by stage four, the waves assume a slow, regular pattern sometimes called S-sleep, for slow-wave sleep or synchronized sleep. Each of these patterns is reflected in the type of brain-wave activity present, with stages one and two consisting predominantly of theta waves and stages three and four of delta waves.

In addition to the changes in brain electrical activity, the EMG records a gradual diminution of muscular activity as the sleeper progresses through each stage of NREM sleep. By the onset of stage four, the EMG is relatively flat, revealing a deep state of muscular relaxation. In fact, virtually all physiological activity is at its lowest during stage four, including respiration, heart rate, blood pressure, and digestion. In this sense, stage four is considered to be the deepest stage of sleep.

COGNITIVE ACTIVITY CYCLES DURING SLEEP

The sleeper is not in an unconscious state but in a different level of consciousness. Cognitive activity is present in all stages of NREM sleep. Hypnagogic imagery, consisting of dreamlike images sometimes indistinguishable from REM dreams, is present in stage one. Subjects are easily awakened during this sleep stage, and regressions to a waking state are quite common. Often, these regressions occur because of myoclonias, which are brief jerking movements of the muscles. Since stage one is sometimes viewed as a transitional state between sleeping and waking, it should not be too surprising that sleep talking occurs primarily in this stage. Stage one sleep lasts for approximately fifteen minutes.

The sleeper is somewhat more difficult to arouse during stage two, and the cognitive activity present is more thoughtlike and fragmentary than in stage one. If the subject recalls any mental activity, then it is rather sparse. Stage two also lasts for approximately fifteen minutes.

It was once assumed that dreams occur only in REM sleep, but it is now common knowledge that dreams of a different variety occur in stages three and four. These dreams are not of the narrative or storylike variety found in REM sleep; rather, they resemble nonsequential thoughts, images, sensations, or emotions. As might be expected in the deepest sleep stage, it is quite difficult to awaken the sleeper who is in stage four. Paradoxically, a subject awakened in stage four will often claim not to be sleeping. Finally, sleepwalking, night terrors, and bedwetting, all of which are developmental disorders, occur predominantly in stage four. Stage three lasts approximately ten minutes, while the first episode of stage four usually lasts about fifty minutes.

Suddenly, about ninety minutes after falling asleep, the subject rapidly regresses back through the stages of NREM sleep to a special stage usually called stage one-REM sleep, or sometimes simply REM sleep. Three major changes occur in the electrical activity measured in this stage. First, the EEG pattern becomes highly desynchronized, resembling a combination of waking and stage one-NREM brain-wave activity. For this reason, REM sleep is sometimes called paradoxical sleep, because it is paradoxical that elements of a waking EEG should be present in a sleeping condition. Second, the EMG recordings become almost completely flat for most skeletal muscles, resembling paralysis. Finally, there is an onset of rapid eye movements, as measured by the EOG.

DSM-IV-TR CRITERIA FOR DYSSOMNIAS

BREATHING-RELATED SLEEP DISORDER (DSM CODE 780.57)

Sleep disruption, leading to excessive sleepiness or insomnia, judged to be due to sleep-related breathing condition

Disturbance not better accounted for by another mental disorder and not due to direct physiological effects of a substance or another general medical condition (other than a breathing-related disorder)

CIRCADIAN RHYTHM SLEEP DISORDER

Persistent or recurrent pattern of sleep disruption leading to excessive sleepiness or insomnia due to mismatch between sleep-wake schedule required by person's environment and circadian sleep-wake pattern

Sleep disturbance causes clinically significant distress or impairment in social, occupational, or other important areas of functioning

Disturbance does not occur exclusively during course of another sleep disorder or other mental disorder

Disturbance not due to direct physiological effects of a substance or general medical condition

Types:
- Delayed Sleep Phase Type: Persistent pattern of late sleep onset and late awakening times, with inability to fall asleep and awaken at desired earlier time (DSM code 327.31)
- Jet Lag Type: Sleepiness and alertness at inappropriate time of day relative to local time, occurring after repeated travel across more than one time zone (DSM code 327.35)
- Shift Work Type: Insomnia during major sleep period or excessive sleepiness during major awake period, associated with night shift work or frequently changing shift work (DSM code 327.36)
- Unspecified Type (DSM code 327.30)

PRIMARY HYPERSOMNIA (DSM CODE 307.44)

Predominant complaint is excessive sleepiness for at least one month (less if recurrent) as evidenced by either prolonged sleep episodes or daytime sleep episodes occurring almost daily

Excessive sleepiness causes clinically significant distress or impairment in social, occupational, or other important areas of functioning

Excessive sleepiness not better accounted for by Insomnia, not occurring exclusively during course of another sleep disorder, and not accounted for by inadequate amount of sleep

Disturbance does not occur exclusively during course of another mental disorder

Disturbance not due to direct physiological effects of a substance or general medical condition

Specify if Recurrent (periods of excessive sleepiness lasting at least three days occurring several times a year for at least two years)

PRIMARY INSOMNIA (DSM CODE 307.42)

Predominant complaint is difficulty initiating or maintaining sleep, or nonrestorative sleep, for at least one month

Sleep disturbance (or associated daytime fatigue) causes clinically significant distress or impairment in social, occupational, or other important areas of functioning

Sleep disturbance does not occur exclusively during the course of Narcolepsy, Breathing-Related Sleep Disorder, Circadian Rhythm Sleep Disorder, or a parasomnia

Disturbance does not occur exclusively during the course of another mental disorder (such as Major Depressive Disorder, Generalized Anxiety Disorder, or delirium)

Disturbance not due to direct physiological effects of a substance or general medical condition

NARCOLEPSY (DSM CODE 347.00)

Irresistible attacks of refreshing sleep occurring daily over at least three months

Presence of one or both of the following:
- cataplexy (brief episodes of sudden bilateral loss of muscle tone, most often in association with intense emotion)
- recurrent intrusions of elements of rapid eye movement (REM) sleep into the transition between sleep and wakefulness, as manifested by either hypnopompic or hypnagogic hallucinations or sleep paralysis at beginning or end of sleep episodes

Disturbance not due to direct physiological effects of a substance or another general medical condition

(conrinued)

Cognitive activity, in the form of narrative or story-like dreams, is rich and varied in REM sleep—hence the term "D-sleep," for dreaming or desynchronized sleep. It is interesting to note that the rapid eye movements correspond closely with dream content. For example, if a person dreams of something running from left to right, the direction of rapid eye movements will also be left to right.

Throughout the remainder of the night, a cycle of approximately ninety minutes will be established from one REM episode to the next. Altogether, the sleeper will experience four to five REM episodes in a typical eight-hour sleep period, with each one lasting for a longer interval than the previous one. The first REM episode may last only five to ten minutes, while the final one may be thirty to forty minutes or longer in duration. In contrast, S-sleep episodes decrease in length throughout the sleep period and will disappear completely after two to three episodes.

STUDY OF SLEEP DEPRIVATION

Although a description of sleep stages can be provided with relative ease, identifying a clear function for sleep is a more difficult proposition. Nevertheless, applications of sleep research are inextricably linked with the functions of sleep. For the typical layperson, the seemingly obvious function of sleep is to repair and restore the body after daily mental and physical exertion. This commonsense approach has been formalized by science as the repair and restoration theory. One of the most frequently used methods to assess this theory is to examine the mental and physical effects of sleep deprivation. If the primary function of sleep is to repair the body, then loss of sleep should disrupt cognitive, motor, and behavioral processes. Early laboratory research with animals seemed to support this position. If sleep deprivation in laboratory animals persisted for a sufficient time, usu-

NIGHTMARE DISORDER (DSM CODE 307.47)

Repeated awakenings from major sleep period or naps with detailed recall of extended and extremely frightening dreams, usually involving threats to survival, security, or self-esteem; awakenings generally occur during second half of sleep period

On awakening from frightening dreams, person rapidly becomes oriented and alert (in contrast to confusion and disorientation seen in Sleep Terror Disorder and some forms of epilepsy)

Dream experience, or sleep disturbance resulting from awakening, causes clinically significant distress or impairment in social, occupational, or other important areas of functioning

Nightmares not occurring exclusively during course of another mental disorder (such as a delirium, Post-traumatic Stress Disorder) and not due to direct physiological effects of a substance or general medical condition

SLEEP TERROR DISORDER (DSM CODE 307.46)

Recurrent episodes of abrupt awakening from sleep, usually occurring during first third of major sleep episode and beginning with panicky scream

Intense fear and signs of autonomic arousal, such as tachycardia, rapid breathing, and sweating, during each episode

Relative unresponsiveness to efforts of others to comfort person during episode

No detailed dream recalled; amnesia exists for episode

Episodes cause clinically significant distress or impairment in social, occupational, or other important areas of functioning

Disturbance not due to direct physiological effects of a substance or general medical condition

SLEEPWALKING DISORDER (DSM CODE 307.46)

Repeated episodes of rising from bed during sleep and walking about, usually occurring during first third of major sleep episode

While sleepwalking, person has a blank, staring face, is relatively unresponsive to communication efforts by others, and can be awakened only with great difficulty

Amnesia for episode on awakening (either from sleepwalking episode or the next morning)

Within several minutes after awakening from sleepwalking episode, no impairment of mental activity or behavior seen (although short period of confusion or disorientation possible)

Sleepwalking causes clinically significant distress or impairment in social, occupational, or other important areas of functioning

Disturbance not due to direct physiological effects of a substance or general medical condition

PARASOMNIA NOT OTHERWISE SPECIFIED (DSM CODE 307.47)

ally between three and twenty days, then death ensued. To maintain sleep deprivation in animals, however, it is necessary to keep them active. Perhaps the continuous activity, rather than the sleep deprivation, killed the animals.

If it were possible to allow animals to rest and relax, but not sleep, then would the sleep deprivation still prove fatal? This question was addressed by anecdotal accounts of human sleep deprivation during the Korean War. As a means of extracting confessions from American soldiers, Korean military intelligence operatives commonly subjected prisoners of war to sustained bouts of sleep deprivation. In the face of overwhelming exhaustion and clear signs of personality disintegration, American soldiers were often induced to sign confessions of their alleged war crimes. On the other hand, Randy Gardner, a seventeen-year-old high school student, experienced sleep deprivation for 264 hours to get his name in the *Guinness Book of World Records* with no apparent permanent effects and no profound temporary deficits. Why would people respond in such radically different ways to sleep deprivation? One hypothesis proposes that severe adverse effects arise as a function of stress and inability to rest and relax, rather than from the loss of sleep. Furthermore, laboratory investigations with volunteer subjects suggest that those individuals who exhibit severe reactions to sleep deprivation almost always have some predisposition to abnormal behavior. Sleep researchers would not deny that sleep serves to restore the body; however, rest and relaxation may serve the same restorative functions in the absence of sleep, which would suggest that repair and restoration is not the sole or even the primary function of sleep.

ADAPTIVE THEORY OF SLEEP

To redress the shortcomings of the repair and restoration theory, an alternative theory of a need to sleep has been proposed. The adaptive theory of sleep or evolutionary theory of sleep postulates that the need to sleep arose in the course of biological evolution as an adaptive mechanism to conserve energy during the evening hours, when it would be inefficient to search for food and other resources. Sleep, according to this view, serves a function similar to the hibernation observed in several species of mammals. These animals reduce their metabolic processes to barely detectable levels during winter to conserve energy when food resources are scarce. To do otherwise would threaten the survival of these animals. It is important to note that the adaptive theory still considers

sleep to be a real need; in essence, sleep is a remnant of the human evolutionary past when human forebears did not have the convenience of twenty-four-hour supermarkets to acquire their sustenance. Humans deprived of sleep will become just as irritable and ill-tempered as a groundhog prevented from hibernating.

Several predictions have been generated from the adaptive theory. First, the theory predicts that predators such as large cats and bears, which obtain most of their nutrients in one large meal per day, would sleep much more than grazing animals such as cattle and horses, who must eat frequently to survive. A second prediction of the theory is that predators such as wolves and mountain lions, which have few natural enemies, would sleep more than prey such as rabbits and guinea pigs, which are at risk if they fail to maintain constant vigilance. Finally, animals such as bats, which are well protected by the environment in which they live, would sleep for relatively long periods of time. These predictions are documented by scientific observations, which provide support for the adaptive or evolutionary theory of sleep.

CLINICAL APPLICATIONS

The functions of sleep are extremely important in clinical applications. If the repair and restoration theory lacks strong scientific support, then attempting to recover lost sleep time may serve no functional purpose. Indeed, most subjects expect to sleep for several hours longer than normal after staying awake for 24 hours, presumably because they believe that sleep is required for repair and restoration of the body. In practice, however, most subjects report only 4 to 6 total hours of poor-quality sleep following such deprivation. Even after 264 hours of sleep deprivation, Gardner slept for only 14 hours and 40 minutes the first evening, then resumed a normal nocturnal sleep pattern of 8 hours per evening.

Knowledge of sleep stages may be especially valuable in diagnosing and treating sleep disorders, since the frequency, patterns, and symptoms of these disorders may be associated with specific stages of sleep. For example, knowledge of the muscular paralysis that accompanies REM sleep has been instrumental in diagnosing the cause of male impotence. Partial or total erections are present in about 95 percent of REM periods in men. Therefore, men who complain of impotence yet demonstrate normal REM erections can be diagnosed as suffering from psychologically based impotence. These patients may benefit from psychotherapy or sexual counseling. In contrast, men who do not achieve REM erections are diagnosed as suffering from organically based impotence and require hormone therapy or surgical implantations.

Nocturnal enuresis, or bed-wetting, is a stage four developmental disorder present in about four to five million children annually in the United States. The exact cause of this disorder is undetermined, although the extreme muscular relaxation during stage four sleep likely contributes to its occurrence. To prevent nocturnal enuresis, the patient must learn to associate a full bladder with waking up. Typically, a special apparatus placed under the child sounds a loud buzzer when urine completes the circuit. Eventually, in the absence of the buzzer the child will learn to associate the feeling of a full bladder with waking up.

EMERGENCE OF RESEARCH

Since sleep is a universal human experience, it is probably safe to conclude that it has interested people since the dawn of humanity; however, scientific inquiry into sleep is a relatively recent phenomenon. Early interest in sleep arose during the late nineteenth century from a need to isolate the brain structure responsible for lethargy syndromes. Similarly, the electrophysiological study of sleep originated with a discovery in 1875 by the English physiologist Richard Caton that the brain continually produces low-voltage waves. This discovery was largely ignored until 1929, when a German psychiatrist, Hans Berger, found that he could record from large groups of neurons by attaching electrodes to the scalp and the forehead. Berger's discovery marked the beginning of modern electroencephalography. With the advent of EEG recordings, it was not long before A. L. Loomis, E. N. Harvey, and G. A. Hobart found, in 1937, that such recordings could be used to differentiate stages of sleep. In 1952, Nathaniel Kleitman at the University of Chicago gave Eugene Aserinsky, one of his new graduate students, the assignment of watching the eye movements of sleeping subjects. Aserinsky quickly noted the rapid, darting nature of eye movements during certain times of the night, which differed from the usual slow, rolling eye movements observed at other times. William Dement later coined the term "REM sleep"; sleep in which slow, rolling eye movements predominate later came to be known as NREM sleep (for nonrapid eye movement sleep). Finally, in 1957, Dement and Kleitman presented the current system of four NREM sleep stages and stage one-REM sleep.

IMPORTANCE TO PSYCHOLOGY OF CONSCIOUSNESS

As a naturally induced alteration in consciousness that can be studied objectively with electrophysiological recording equipment, sleep has assumed a prominent role in the psychology of consciousness. Electrophysiological recording techniques that were originally developed in sleep research are now widely used to study other aspects of consciousness, such as hemispheric asymmetries, meditation, sensory isolation, biofeedback, dreams, and drug effects on the brain and behavior. In addition, sleep is one of the few alterations in consciousness that plays a central role in several areas of psychological inquiry. For example, physiological psychologists are concerned with the neurobiological mechanisms underlying sleep, as well as the functions of sleep. From their perspective, sleep is simply one of many human behaviors and cognitive processes whose biological basis must be ascertained. Developmental psychologists are interested in age-related changes that occur in sleep and attempt to develop applications of those findings for concerned parents of young children. Finally, physicians and clinical psychologists are often presented with patients who suffer from physical and psychological stress as a function of sleep disorders. These professionals are interested in developing effective drug and psychological therapies that can be used to treat sleep-disordered patients. Sleep is a concern in many areas of psychology.

Because sleep is universal in humans, it will continue to play a major role in consciousness studies and throughout the discipline of psychology. Future research will likely focus on applications of sleep research to industrial settings that employ shift workers. The emphasis will be on reducing fatigue and improving performance among employees by gradually adjusting them to shift work and by changing employee work schedules infrequently. In addition, research will seek ways to improve diagnostic procedures and treatments for a variety of sleep disorders, including insomnia, hypersomnia, sleep apnea, narcolepsy, and enuresis. The focus will be on developing effective drug and psychological therapies. Finally, pure research will continue to examine the functions of sleep and to delineate more clearly the adverse effects of sleep, even those of a temporary nature.

BIBLIOGRAPHY

Coren, Stanley. *Sleep Thieves: An Eye-Opening Exploration into the Science and Mysteries of Sleep.* New York: Free Press, 1997. A wide-ranging exploration of sleep research. Coren is one of the major researchers in the relationship between sleep deficit and major industrial accidents, such as the 1989 Exxon Valdez oil spill, the 1986 Chernobyl nuclear plant disaster, and the 1986 Challenger space shuttle explosion.

Dement, William C. *The Promise of Sleep*. New York: Dell, 2000. Dement, founder of the sleep disorders clinic at Stanford University, provides a nontechnical, personal report of current findings in sleep research, drawing a connection between sleep and general health. Offers a guide to remedying sleep deficits and alleviating insomnia.

Empson, Jacob, and Michael B. Wang. *Sleep and Dreaming*. 3d ed. New York: St. Martin's Press, 2002. An overview of scientific sleep research and popular beliefs about sleep.

Hobson, J. Allan. *Dreaming: An Introduction to the Science of Sleep*. New York: Oxford University Press, 2005. Traces theories and physiological research into dreaming since the 1950's. Addresses dreaming disorders such as nightmares, night terrors, and sleepwalking.

_____. *Sleep*. Reprint. New York: W. H. Freeman, 1996. A broad and interdisciplinary view of sleep research, combining knowledge drawn from neurology, psychology, and animal behavior studies. The nontechnical language and lavish illustrations are two major advantages of this book. Highly recommended for high school and college students.

Jouvet, Michel. *The Paradox of Sleep: The Story of Dreaming*. Translated by Laurence Gary. Cambridge, Mass.: MIT Press, 2001. The scientist who discovered the relationship between REM sleep and dreaming discusses the stages of sleep, the meaning and evolutionary function of dreams, and many other topics.

Kryger, Meir H., Thomas Roth, and William C. Dement, eds. *Principles and Practice of Sleep Medicine*. 4th ed. Philadelphia: Elsevier Saunders, 2005. An examination of sleep and its disorders. Includes bibliography references and an index.

Rosen, Marvin. *Sleep and Dreaming*. Philadelphia: Chelsea House, 2006. Addresses topics such as the biology of sleep, sleep disorders, dreams, and the application of dreams in psychotherapy.

Schenck, Carlos H. *Sleep: A Groundbreaking Guide to the Mysteries, the Problems, and the Solutions*. New York: Avery, 2008. A sleep researcher looks at all aspects of sleep and discusses some unusual conditions that can develop related to sleep, such as sleepwalking, sleep terrors, and sleep-related eating disorders.

Richard P. Atkinson

SEE ALSO: Brain structure; Circadian rhythms; Consciousness; Consciousness: Altered states; Dreams; Insomnia; Narcolepsy; Reticular formation; Sleep apnea.